José Clemente Orozco
in the United States, 1927–1934

Dawn Ades

Alicia Azuela

Jacquelynn Baas

Karen Cordero Reiman

Rita Eder

Renato González Mello

Diane Miliotes

James Oles

Francisco Reyes Palma

Víctor Alejandro Sorell

José Clemente Orozco
in the United States, 1927–1934

Renato González Mello and

Diane Miliotes EDITORS

Hood Museum of Art | DARTMOUTH COLLEGE

in Association with W. W. Norton & Company | NEW YORK · LONDON

This exhibition was organized by the Hood Museum of Art, Dartmouth College, in collaboration with the Museo de Arte Carrillo Gil, Mexico City, and the Instituto Nacional de Bellas Artes, Mexico, and supported in part by grants from the National Endowment for the Arts, the US-Mexico Fund for Culture, and the Rockefeller Foundation. Its presentation at the Hood Museum of Art is generously supported by the George O. Southwick 1957 Memorial Fund, the William B. Jaffe and Evelyn A. Hall Fund, and the Philip Fowler 1927 Memorial Fund.

EXHIBITION SCHEDULE:

San Diego Museum of Art, San Diego, California
March 9–May 19, 2002

Hood Museum of Art, Dartmouth College, Hanover, New Hampshire
June 8–December 15, 2002

Museo de Arte Carrillo Gil, Mexico City
January 25–April 13, 2003

Designed by John Bernstein

Printed in Spain (D.L. TO: 141-2002)

LIBRARY OF CONGRESS CATALOGING IN PUBLICATION DATA

José Clemente Orozco in the United States, 1927–1934 / Dawn Ades…[et al.].

p.   cm.

Includes bibliographic references and index.

ISBN 0-393-04176-X

1. Orozco, José Clemente, 1883–1949—Exhibitions. 2. Mural painting and decoration, Mexican—United States—Exhibitions. 3. Mural painting and decoration—20th century—United States—Exhibitions. I. Ades, Dawn.

ND259.07 A4 2002

759.972—dc21   2001039692

Frontispiece/fig. 1: *José Clemente Orozco*, 1930, photograph by Edward Weston, gelatin silver print, © 1981 Center for Creative Photography, Arizona Board of Regents Collection.

Jacket/cover illustration/fig. 182: *Hispano-America* from *The Epic of American Civilization*, 1932–34, fresco, 120 x 119 in (305 x 302 cm), reserve reading room, Baker Library, Dartmouth College, Hanover, New Hampshire.

English translations of essays by Renato González Mello, Alicia Azuela, Francisco Reyes Palma, and "Anthology of Critical Reception" are by James Seale-Collazo. English translation of essay by Rita Eder is by Anna Deeny.

Reproductions of the work of José Clemente Orozco authorized by Alfredo, Clemente, and Lucrecia Orozco and by the Instituto Nacional de Bellas Artes y Literatura. Works of art by José Clemente Orozco: © licensed by Orozco Family through VAGA, New York, NY.

Reproductions of the work of Diego Rivera authorized by Banco de Mexico (© 2001 Banco de México Diego Rivera and Frida Kahlo Museums Trust. Av. Cinco de Mayo No. 2, Col. Centro, Del Cuauhtémoc 06059, México, D.F.) and by the Instituto Nacional de Bellas Artes y Literatura.

Reproductions of the work of David Alfaro Siqueiros © Estate of David Alfaro Siqueiros/Licensed by VAGA, New York, NY, and authorized by the Instituto Nacional de Bellas Artes y Literatura.

Unless otherwise noted, reproductions of work by Thomas Hart Benton © T. H. and R. P. Benton Testamentary Trusts/Licensed by VAGA, New York, NY.

All reproductions of *The Epic of American Civilization* © Trustees of Dartmouth College, Hanover, New Hampshire.

All paintings and drawings owned by the Hood Museum of Art and Dartmouth College were photographed by Jeffrey Nintzel.

Contents

Foreword

José Clemente Orozco is undoubtedly one of the greatest twentieth-century artists that Mexico has contributed to world culture. While his work and especially his achievements as a distinguished muralist have been thoroughly studied both in Mexico and abroad, the significance of this traveling exhibition is that it will offer the public an opportunity to deepen its understanding of Orozco's artistic production in the United States between 1927 and 1934.

During the seven years that Orozco lived and worked in the United States, he came into contact with an urban and mechanical world that was not entirely to his liking but that nevertheless managed to exert an undeniable influence on his work. In this regard, he recalled in his autobiography:

> One morning…something very serious was happening in New York. People were rushing about even more than usual and wherever a group gathered the discussion was hysterical. Fire trucks and Red Cross sirens shrieked madly on every side, and the extras [newspapers], great bundles of which were fetched on trucks, flew from hand to hand. Wall Street and the neighborhood were a raging sea of activity.
> […]
> The municipality found itself obliged to open soup kitchens, and in the outlying districts there were frightening lines of powerful men queued up, hatless, in old clothes that offered little protection through hours of sub-zero weather as they stood on the frozen snow.

The artist's recollections allow us to understand the remarkable thematic transition that took place in his work as Orozco momentarily set aside topics related to the Mexican Revolution and national rural life in favor of those linked to American urban modernity, workers, unemployment, and the economic depression that began in 1929. Yet he always approached these subjects with a critical view, skeptically questioning the achievements of Western civilization.

At the Consejo Nacional para la Cultura y las Artes (National Council for Culture and Arts), it is our ongoing commitment to encourage the study and appreciation of the most outstanding figures in the history of Mexican art and to provide public access to diverse visual and curatorial discourses that, in this case, broaden our horizon of knowledge regarding Orozco. Our gratitude goes to the generous private collectors whose loans have made possible this exceptional opportunity to reassess the contributions of the great muralist.

— SARI BERMÚDEZ | *President,*
Consejo Nacional para la Cultura y las Artes

Foreword

The Instituto Nacional de Bellas Artes (National Institute of Fine Arts), through the Museo de Arte Carrillo Gil, is proud to host this exhibition that, thanks to the initiative of the Hood Museum of Art at Dartmouth College in Hanover, New Hampshire, will show for the first time in Mexico the work created by José Clemente Orozco during his seven-year residency in the United States. *José Clemente Orozco in the United States, 1927–1934* offers audiences in Mexico and the United States the opportunity to better understand one of Mexico's most transcendent artists through an unprecedented survey and in-depth analysis, giving us access to works made at a crucial moment in the life of Orozco as well as the lives of Mexico and the United States as nations.

Considering the vast differences in cultural environments between both countries at this time—in the United States, the greatest economic crisis of the twentieth century; in Mexico, the postrevolutionary period and Vasconcelist spirit—Orozco's emigrant status and his contact with modern art influenced his themes, pictorial style, and working methods in a decisive way. Upon returning to Mexico to continue his work, having been invited to paint a mural at the Palacio de Bellas Artes, José Clemente Orozco was already placed among the Mexican artists who would contribute most to the international artistic landscape of the twentieth century.

This exhibition allows us to admire more than 110 works, including easel paintings, drawings, prints, and preparatory studies for murals, as well as mural reproductions from Pomona College, the New School for Social Research, and Dartmouth College; these pieces are all part of Orozco's legacy to humanity and comprise a little-known aspect of Mexico's cultural heritage.

José Clemente Orozco in the United States, 1927–1934 brings together works drawn from the most important collections in North America, private and public, as well as some very important contributions from the Instituto Cultural Cabañas, the Museo de Arte Carrillo Gil itself, and Mexican private collections. The exhibit is the result of the efforts and research of the most renowned Orozco specialists in the world. To all of them go our appreciation and gratitude on behalf of the Instituto Nacional de Bellas Artes.

—SAÚL JUÁREZ VEGA | *Director General, Instituto Nacional de Bellas Artes*

7

Lenders to the Exhibition

Allen Memorial Art Museum, Oberlin College, Oberlin, Ohio

Baltimore Museum of Art

Cleveland Museum of Art

Dartmouth College Library, Hanover, New Hampshire

Alfonso Dau

Detroit Institute of Arts

Hermes Trust Collection, courtesy of Francesco Pellizzi

Hood Museum of Art, Dartmouth College, Hanover, New Hampshire

Instituto Cultural Cabañas, Guadalajara, Mexico

Nikki R. Keddie

Robert L. and Sharon W. Lynch Collection

Rodney and Gussie Medeiros

David P. Mixer

Museo de Arte Carrillo Gil, Mexico City

Museum of Modern Art, New York

New School University Art Collection, New York

Orozco Farias Family Collection

Philadelphia Museum of Art

Pomona College, Claremont, California

Private collections

Rosemary Rieser

San Diego Museum of Art

San Francisco Museum of Modern Art

William H. and Shirley Wilson Family

Acknowledgments

As the scholarship gathered in this book suggests, the history of Mexican artists' contributions to the visual culture of the United States is at once broad, complex, and captivating. These men and women succeeded in creating a stylistically diverse, socially challenging body of work. Comprised of numerous frescoes in California, Michigan, New York, and (somewhat anomalously) New Hampshire, as well as countless easel paintings and works of graphic art, all done between the late 1920s and the mid-1940s, such works could not be ignored. Indeed, critics of the day noted this original contribution and wrote passionately about its values. Debates about this conspicuously hybrid imagery were staged on multiple levels, pitting ancients against moderns, aesthetics against ideology, and regional perspectives against international ideals. The interpretive quarrels surrounding this pictorial legacy remain urgent today, generations after these representations were first unveiled. The work that José Clemente Orozco created in the United States from 1927 to 1934 is absolutely crucial to these debates, and it continues to merit our intense scrutiny and appreciation. This catalog, like the memorable exhibition that it accompanies, may thus be said to fill an ongoing cultural need.

Orozco worked at Dartmouth only from 1932 to 1934, but *José Clemente Orozco in the United States, 1927–1934* has been a major preoccupation of the Hood Museum of Art for more than a decade. The importance of the project, then, demands to be seen in a wider context. Like other memorable exhibitions with significant publications organized by the museum—for example, *The Independent Group: Postwar Britain and the Aesthetics of Plenty* (1990); *The Age of the Marvelous* (1991); *Goddess and Polis: The Panathenaic Festival in Ancient Greece* (1992); *James Gillray: Prints by the Eighteenth-Century Master of Caricature* (1994); *Intimate Encounters: Love and Domesticity in Eighteenth-Century France*

(1997); *Winter's Promise: Willard Metcalf in Cornish, New Hampshire* (1999)—this project makes vivid the institution's commitment to ambitious research and engaging curatorship. Since talk about an important show of Orozco's work first took place in the late 1980s under the directorship of Jacquelynn Baas, hundreds of individuals throughout the world have assisted the institution in this highly specialized effort. These devoted friends, colleagues, and critics all will doubtless share in the satisfaction that the long-awaited realization of this project brings. It is a privilege for me therefore to acknowledge many of the key contributions that have gone into its success.

Because this project is fundamentally concerned with the phenomenon of transnational cultural exchange, it makes sense to begin by thanking colleagues in Mexico. The assistance of the artist's family has been invaluable and instructive. Orozco's children—Alfredo Orozco, Clemente Orozco, and Lucrecia Orozco Valladares—were as generous with their time as they were diligent in their roles as custodians of their father's memory. Each helped us by providing new knowledge and a sense of personal engagement that is admirable.

The Mexican Government has lent its support to the project, and I hasten to express our deep gratitude to the following individuals at the Consejo Nacional para la Cultura y las Artes/CONACULTA (National Council for Culture and Arts): Sari Bermúdez, president; Saúl Juárez Vega, general director, Instituto Nacional de Bellas Artes/INBA (National Institute of Fine Arts); Ignacio Toscano, former general director, INBA; Jaime Nualart, coordinator for international affairs, CONACULTA; María Teresa Márquez, communications director for international cultural affairs, CONACULTA; Lic. Luis Norberto Cacho, director for legal affairs, INBA; Carmen Bancalari, deputy director for international affairs, INBA; Gabriela López, national coordinator for visual arts, INBA; Walther Boelsterly, director, National Center for Conservation and Register of Artistic Patrimony, INBA; and at the Instituto Cultural Cabañas, Guadalajara, Gutierre Aceves Piña, Rubén Páez, and Elena Matute.

This project was developed in tandem with colleagues at the Museo de Arte Carrillo Gil in Mexico City, to which the exhibition will eventually travel. We are especially thankful for the professional support from Sylvia Pandolfi Elliman and Osvaldo Sánchez Crespo, former directors, Ana Elena Mallet, and the museum's new team, now under the direction of Patricia Sloane: Sylvia Navarrete, deputy director; Renato González Mello, research/guest curator; Caterina Toscano, communications coordinator; María Bostock, exhibitions coordinator; Ricardo Pineda, production; Esther Fernández, registrar; Mario Bocanegra, installation; Mauricio Guillén, designer; Pilar Gilardi, editorial coordinator; Grecia Vázquez, press coordinator; Ilda Luna, public relations; Ernesto Solís, webmaster; Consuelo Almada, educational services; Martín Sandoval, library; and Tomás Canchola, video.

Additionally, we would like to credit the following colleagues and institutions, also in Mexico, who lent their expertise in research for the exhibition: at the Instituto de Investigaciones Estéticas, UNAM, Dr. María Teresa Uriarte, director; Rita Eder; Carmen Block; Ernesto Peñaloza; Eumelia Hernández; and Minerva Zea; at *El Informador*, Guadalajara, Carlos Alvarez del Castillo and Rosanna González Gerini; and Ulises Canchola, Dafne Cruz, Alberto Dallal, Estela Duarte, Luis Martín Lozano, Patricia Martínez Gutiérrez, Xóchitl Medina, Pablo Piccato, and Armando Sáenz. Beatriz Berndt Léon Mariscal was the principal research assistant to guest curator Renato González Mello, and she has our deep gratitude.

I am very pleased that the San Diego Museum of Art, a museum with diverse collections serving a large binational region, will host this important exhibition on the U.S. West Coast. I should like to thank Don Bacigalupi, executive director, for his immediate enthusiasm for this project and for his commitment to Latin American art; he has made SDMA a natural partner for this successful collaboration.

I extend my gratitude to many other members of the SDMA staff who have worked diligently to launch this exhibition in San Diego: Betti-Sue Hertz, curator of contemporary art, for leading the SDMA team in all aspects of organizing the presentation, helping ensure its success; Claudia Leos, assistant curator of collections and exhibitions, and Rachel Evans, curatorial assistant, for their assistance on coordination and installation efforts; Heath Fox, director of administration, for his keen assistance with negotiations and logistical details; Julia Kindy, senior development officer, Susannah Stringam, senior marketing officer, and Chris Zook, public relations officer, for their support of the project and work to promote it throughout the West; Maxine Gaiber, director of education, for her efforts in adapting educational materials and programs to serve the San Diego audience; Gwen Gómez, community access coordinator, for her important work of Spanish translation of didactic and interpretive materials and community outreach; and lastly, Louis Goldich, chief registrar, and his staff for their skillful handling of shipping and loan requirements for these important works of art.

The Hood Museum of Art has benefited from significant grant support for the exhibition throughout all its many stages. The National Endowment for the Arts provided critical funds for the planning and implementation phases of the exhibition, and we have benefited from David Bancroft's assistance at the endowment. Similarly, the US/Mexico Fund for Culture gave its financial support to these same steps of organization and execution, and program officer Beatríz Nava Rivera was of great help throughout. The Rockefeller Foundation provided significant funding for the implementation stage, and its associate director, Tomás Ybarra Frausto,

10

took special interest in the project. Mr. Ybarra Frausto's sustaining guidance and conceptual rigor have been appreciated by everyone at Dartmouth, especially by me. At Dartmouth College, we are fortunate to have many campus partners who have subsidized programs associated with *José Clemente Orozco in the United States, 1927–1934*. I wish to credit the Hopkins Center and the Leslie Humanities Center for their efforts to enhance awareness of the monumental work by Orozco at Baker Library as well as associated works in our exhibition.

Lenders to the exhibition, to whom we obviously feel the keenest sense of gratitude, are recognized in a separate section of this catalog. We are particularly grateful, as well, to the following institutions and individuals who have assisted us with research, locating works and reproductions, and other tasks that have made both the exhibition and its catalog so visually compelling: Christie's — Ana Sokoloff and Jennifer Doyle — Sotheby's — Isabella Hutchinson, August Iribe, and Jennifer Josten — Galería Arvil, Mexico City — Armando Colina — Los Angeles County Museum of Art — Ilona Katzew — Mary-Anne Martin, Fine Art — Mary-Anne Martin and Rosita Chalem, New York City — Santa Barbara Museum of Art — Diana DuPont — Museum of Modern Art, New York — Kynaston McShine — Cleveland Museum of Art — William Robinson — and Whitney Museum of American Art — Max Anderson, as well as John Anton, Maria Balderrama, Cristina Cuevas-Wolf, Anna Indych, Antoinette May, and Naomi Sawelson Gorse. Jeffrey Nintzel helped with most of the photographic work in Hanover, New Hampshire, and beyond, including imaging for the computer guide. In addition, we have relied extensively upon the professional expertise of Thomas Branchick and Leslie Paisley of the Williamstown Art Conservation Center, with the assistance of Mikka Gee, for vital support with conservation problems. Colleagues at the New School for Social Research — Stefano Basilico and

Katherine Goncharov — and Pomona College — Steven Comba, Marjorie Harth, and Elizabeth Villa — provided outstanding factual data and advice.

Both the exhibition and the catalog owe a debt to leading scholars who have contributed mightily toward these components. The essays that follow reflect the quality work that ten experts have brought to this task. I thank these writers for their commitment and patience throughout the long process leading up to this public presentation of their ideas. Among this group, I want to signal, first and foremost, the outstanding contribution of Renato González Mello, the project's guest curator and coeditor of the catalog. The project would be entirely different without his energy and gracious manner. Timothy Rub, the former director of the Hood Museum of Art, shared with Mr. González the task of initiating the idea of a binational exhibition, and he negotiated the arrangements for this with members of the Mexican national museum administration. It gives me considerable satisfaction to congratulate Mr. Rub on his role in developing this undertaking. Mr. Rub invited consultants on several occasions to help shape the project, and their important role must also be recognized. In particular, I thank Dawn Ades, Jacquelynn Baas, Karen Cordero Reiman, Francisco Reyes Palma, and Víctor Alejandro Sorrell. Kelly Pask did remarkable work drafting the object entries and exhibition chronology. James Seale-Collazo and Anna Deeny translated essays from Spanish to English, all the while keeping the integrity of the authors' ideas at the fore. The catalog received the most rigorous critique from reviewers Thomas Gretton and Mari Carmen Ramirez. Their readings significantly improved the text. At W. W. Norton, we wish to thank James Mairs, vice-president and senior editor, and John Bernstein, designer, for this handsome book.

The dynamic content of *José Clemente Orozco in the United States, 1927–1934* owes a lot to the prevailing intellectual climate of Dartmouth College.

Thanks begin with the president of the institution, James Wright, to whom I am most grateful for his inspired vision of the museum's role in cultural life. Beyond the president's office, the project has received essential help from the provost's area. Barry Scherr, former provost Susan Prager, and Associate Provost Barbara Gerstner all deserve credit. In this regard, Margaret Dyer Chamberlain, who served as the acting director of the Hood Museum of Art from the end of 1999 until the beginning of 2001, made key decisions about this large undertaking as it neared completion. We should also thank the following individuals in a variety of administrative departments: Facilities Planning—Reed Bergwall, Shawn Donovan, and Jack Wilson—Hopkins Center—Lewis Crickard, Margaret Lawrence, and Elinor Marsh—Dartmouth Film Society—William Pence and Sydney Stowe—Libraries—Debra Agnoli, Patricia Carter, John Crane, Phil Cronenwett, Sarah Horton, Richard Lucier, Anne Ostendarp, Cynthia Pawlek, Barbara Reed, Cynthia Shirkey, and Miguel Valladares. The contributions of the General Counsel's Office, under the direction of Robert Donin, call out for singular applause. Mr. Donin and former Assistant Counsel Allegra Lubrano did more than one might expect to ensure the success of this ambitious undertaking.

The project benefited of course from many colleagues throughout the academic community at Dartmouth. We should like to acknowledge the following faculty members, each of whom has played a key role: Ada Cohen, Kathleen Corrigan, Jonathan Crewe, Christina Gomez, Paul Goldstein, Jim Jordan, Agnes Lugo-Ortiz, Marysa Navarro, Deborah Nichols, Israel Reyes, Adrian Randolph, Angela Rosenthal, Ivy Schweitzer, Silvia Spitta, Marsha Swislocki, and John Watanabe, as well as Dartmouth liaison to the Latino community Alex Hernandez Siegel. We are also grateful to Elizabeth Alexander, Barbara Krieger, Lucretia Martin, and Karen Miller for their fine support. Tilmann Steinberg, Hany Farid, and Otmar Foelsche provided key imaging and computer didactics to the exhibition. Joan Kelly provided text for the computer guide that was a model of clarity. The following Dartmouth students have made contributions: Alexandra Checka (2001), Colleen Corcoran (2001), William Danon (1995), Kerrin Egalka (2004), Heather Egger-Kofke (2002), Allison J. Evans (2002), Lauren Fog (2001), Jennifer Henry (1999), Raymar Rossoukh (1996), Jethro Rothe-Kushel (2003), Angela Scott (1998), Jacqueline Tran (1996), Athena Waligore (2001), and Tim Zeitler (2001). Jennifer Pelaez (2001) worked tirelessly on the project throughout her senior internship at the museum, and for this reason she deserves separate and sincere thanks.

At one point or another, practically every member of the Hood Museum of Art's staff has been involved in *José Clemente Orozco in the United States, 1927–1934*. I appreciate the spirit with which these colleagues have made these contributions. Their enthusiasm for this challenge has been impressive and the project stands as yet further proof of the extraordinary professional skills at the museum. Some staff members were deeply involved on a more or less continual basis, and I should like to express special thanks to those individuals. Kellen Haak, collections manager, and his registrarial staff—Rebecca Fawcett, Cynthia Gilliland, Deborah Haynes, and Kathleen O'Malley—arranged for all loans, object care, and shipping. Evelyn Marcus and Nick Nobili developed an impressive design for the museum's presentation of the exhibition and oversaw the installation in Hanover. Key administrative support came from Mary Ann Hankel, Mary McKenna, Nancy McLain, Sharon Reed, and Roberta Shin. Lesley Wellman, curator of education, worked diligently with her team—especially Kris Bergquist, Elisabeth Gordon, and Linda Ide—to solicit feedback from community groups in the Upper Valley of New Hampshire, and they shaped a strong focus for the show's educational

12

outreach. Curator of Academic Programming Katherine Hart created an ambitious suite of events for the campus and helped with details of the catalog production, as did the other curators Barbara MacAdam and T. Barton Thurber and curatorial assistant Amelia Kahl. Nils Nadeau put in long hours editing and improving the catalog and brought the lengthy manuscript to its final state. Juliette Bianco, exhibitions manager, was equally skillful in her coordination of the complex issues surrounding the production of the exhibition and this catalog, and she performed impressively under numerous deadlines and unrelenting pressure.

Finally, I wish to congratulate guest curator Renato González Mello, Timothy Rub, now director of the Cincinnati Art Museum, and Diane Miliotes, the project's in-house curator since Mr. Rub's departure from the Hood in 1999, for the fine work they have accomplished. In addition to enjoying their contributions to this catalog, we all may take inspiration from their curatorial dedication. Their teamwork has mirrored the epic ambition that characterized Orozco's own efforts in Hanover from 1932 to 1934. Thanks to them, the monumental impact of the artist's entire U.S. sojourn can now be appreciated and reevaluated by a broad public.

— DERRICK R. CARTWRIGHT | *Director*

Introduction

Timothy Rub

A little more than a decade ago, when I was working as associate director of the Hood Museum of Art at Dartmouth College, I attended a meeting that had been convened by several members of the faculty to discuss the Columbian Exposition held in Chicago in 1893. Organized to celebrate the 400th anniversary of Christopher Columbus's first voyage to the New World, it was perhaps the most impressive of the many world's fairs held in this country during the last decade of the nineteenth century and the first several decades of the twentieth. It was also a remarkable example of the triumphalist spirit that marked the end of westward expansion on this continent and the emergence of the United States as an economic and political power on the international stage.

I walked back to my office after that meeting through the reserve reading room of Baker Library, a large study hall that houses one of the finest works of art on the Dartmouth campus, José Clemente Orozco's mural *The Epic of American Civilization*. Covering nearly thirty-two hundred square feet, this monumental work took Orozco almost two years to complete and was the last major project he undertook before he returned to Mexico in 1934 after nearly seven years in this country. Looking at the mural, I was struck, as many observers have been, by the structure and principal themes of the narrative that Orozco used for his history of American civilization and how radically they differed from the ways in which his contemporaries, in both Mexico and the United States, approached the same subject.

The encounter significantly altered my perception of Orozco's work and encouraged me to look at the Dartmouth mural in a broader context. Coming at the end of an extended stay in this country and just before the period in which Orozco created what many consider his finest works—a remarkable series of murals in Mexico City and Guadalajara— *The Epic of American Civilization* is crucial to our understanding of his development as an intellectual and an artist. If this premise is accepted, then it may also be argued that the seven years that Orozco spent in this country in the late 1920s and early 1930s constituted one of the most important periods in his career.

"There was little to hold me in Mexico in 1927," Orozco recalled in *An Autobiography*, "and I resolved to go to New York, counting upon generous support from Genaro Estrada, Secretary of Foreign Relations, who found the money to defray my journey and stay of three months. It was December, and very cold in New York. I knew nobody, and I proposed to begin all over."[1] Discouraged by the hostile reception given to the murals he had recently completed in the National Preparatory School in Mexico City, he made this decision in equal measure out of a sense of frustration over his prospects for securing new mural commissions in his native country and out of the enormous confidence he had in his own talent and artistic vision. It also reflected an emerging trend, which at the time was only in its infancy: the development of a stronger and more complex artistic relationship between the two countries. This phenomenon was fueled in part by a growing interest in Mexican art, both historical and contemporary, in the United States as well as by the recognition on the part of many Mexican artists that this country represented a potentially rich source of patronage for their work. In this regard, Orozco was certainly optimistic about his prospects for success. Ultimately he did accomplish what he had set out to do, returning to his native country in the summer of 1934 with the promise of an important mural commission (at the soon-to-be-completed Palace of Fine Arts) and his reputation as one of Mexico's foremost living artists firmly established.

Aided by only a modest grant from the Mexican government and encouraged by the promise made by the American critic Anita Brenner of an exhibition of drawings from his series *Mexico in Revolution*,

Orozco found that his first months in New York did not meet his expectations. Although warmly welcomed by the expatriate Mexican community, he soon realized that it would be far more difficult than he had imagined to establish himself in an unfamiliar and highly competitive market. On the other hand, Orozco clearly found much in the city to inspire him. It served as the subject of the first paintings he produced in this country (e.g., *The Elevated* [1928], *Queensboro Bridge,* and *Eighth Avenue* [figs. 64, 53, and 54]) and, more significantly, provided him with a thorough introduction to European and American art.

By the middle of 1928 Orozco had also begun to move well beyond his immediate circle of acquaintances among the Mexican expatriate community, actively seeking to forge relationships that would prove instrumental in helping support his work and establish his reputation. That summer he was introduced by Anita Brenner to Alma Reed, a sometime journalist and woman of means with a deep interest in Mexican art and culture who was to become Orozco's dealer and agent, and, through her, to the members of the Greek poet Angelos Sikelianos's Delphic Circle, a group of artists, writers, and social activists dedicated to the cause of universal brotherhood, as well as to other influential figures who would help promote his work.

Gradually, Orozco's efforts met with increasing success. An October 1928 exhibition of twenty-two drawings from his *Mexico in Revolution* series at the Marie Sterner Gallery on East Fifty-seventh Street was followed by an exhibition of oil paintings, mural studies, and photographs (of his murals at the National Preparatory School) at the New Students' League in Philadelphia in February 1929; an exhibition of his paintings of New York subjects at Edith Halpert's Downtown Gallery the following month; a large exhibition of 113 paintings, drawings, lithographs, and mural studies at the Art Students League in New York in the second half of April;

the inaugural exhibition of Reed's new gallery, the Delphic Studios, a show devoted exclusively to Orozco's work, in October; and an exhibition of his drawings and lithographs at the Art Institute of Chicago in December. With this increased exposure came increased critical support, not only from writers, both Mexican and American, who had a special interest in promoting Mexican art and culture, but also from a number of critics—notably Lewis Mumford—who saw in the paintings of the Mexican muralists a vision that was deeply imbued with humanistic values and far more persuasive than the art of their North American contemporaries.

Orozco continued to exhibit his work regularly during the next several years, but after 1930 his time and attention were increasingly taken up with mural painting. Having come to the United States to secure just such an opportunity, Orozco welcomed the invitation he received in January of that year to create a mural in the refectory of the newly completed Frary Hall at Pomona College in Claremont, California. The following autumn he returned to New York and began work on a mural decoration for the New School for Social Research, a commission secured for him by Alma Reed. This project, completed in January 1931, was followed by the final and largest of the three murals produced by Orozco during his extended stay in the United States, *The Epic of American Civilization* in Baker Library at Dartmouth College.

Although the murals at Pomona College, the New School for Social Research, and Dartmouth College are perhaps the best known of the works Orozco created in the United States in the late 1920s and early 1930s, the artist worked in a broad range of media during this period, producing easel paintings, drawings, and prints. While always representing himself as a "mural painter" in an effort to secure the commissions for this type of work that he believed were his due, Orozco was nonetheless

15

sensitive to the new market in which he found himself and demonstrated a keen, if somewhat cynical, awareness of what American patrons expected of Mexican painters. It was, moreover, during the years that he spent in New York in the late 1920s that he was first able to study for an extended time the work of contemporary American and European artists. This was certainly part of his agenda in coming to the United States, and there is no doubt that the encounter, which was complex and not without its difficulties, proved enormously useful for Orozco.

When the artist arrived in New York in late 1927, it is clear that he was neither without a plan for what he hoped to accomplish while in this country nor alone. Indeed, as Orozco notes in *An Autobiography*, his visit was made under the official sponsorship of a department of the Mexican government. He could, moreover, count on the friendship and support of a sizable expatriate community of Mexican artists and writers, many of whom had gravitated to New York to take advantage of new opportunities there and the growing vogue for things Mexican. (Among his acquaintances were José Tablada, who wrote a weekly column for the Mexican newspaper *El Universal,* and Miguel de Covarrubias, the celebrated cartoonist.) Orozco was an astute observer of this phenomenon, and the efforts he made both to distance himself from its more purely commercial and folkloric manifestations and, at the same time, to turn it to his advantage provide important insights into the way in which Mexican culture was understood in this country. As he noted in a letter of July 1928 to his close friend Jean Charlot, "Decidedly, this 'Folklore' business is lucrative…for the 'sharpies' and there's still more to be gained from it, you'll see."[2]

Nevertheless, if Orozco hoped, perhaps emulating Diego Rivera's success, eventually to secure commissions for murals and thereby to gain recognition internationally and in his own country, he was also willing to make his way in the competitive New York market by other means. In this regard, the efforts of Anita Brenner, a journalist and champion of Mexican art, and Alma Reed were instrumental in helping him achieve this goal. Brenner was one of the first champions of Orozco's work and helped popularize his powerful drawings of the Mexican Revolution. She was soon supplanted, however, as the artist's principal supporter by Reed, without whose patronage and tireless promotion of his art Orozco could not have accomplished all that he did in the United States.

As noted above, implicit in all the work that Orozco, and indeed many of his expatriate contemporaries, produced during this period was the issue of his identity as a "Mexican" artist. He certainly realized that the success of his reception in artistic circles in this country was based in part on his use of Mexican subject matter, seen first in the drawings of the *Mexico in Revolution* series and somewhat later in his stark and deeply compelling paintings of Mexican peasants, villages, and the revolutionary hero Emiliano Zapata. In purely stylistic terms, these works, of which paintings such as *Mexican Hills* (1930 [fig. 30]) and *Mexican Pueblo* (1932 [fig. 257]) are characteristic, reflect his recent experience as a mural painter and his studied avoidance of any approach to Mexican subject matter that could be considered folkloric or picturesque. They are constructed of broad, simply defined, yet monumental forms. Likewise, the color scheme that Orozco used in these works is also relatively simple, limited in most instances to green and ocher. Still, within these self-imposed constraints he was able to create images that possess an austere beauty, a great dignity, and a sense of permanence. The meaning of the many paintings, drawings, and prints of Mexican subjects that Orozco produced in the United States during this period remains somewhat enigmatic. Beyond the obvious appeal these works held for the American market, it is clear that they reflect

Orozco's respect for the indigenous cultures of his native country and his involvement with the agenda for the development of a new, postrevolutionary art in Mexico developed by the Syndicate of Painters and Sculptors (of which he was a member) in the early 1920s. He had, moreover, a deep attachment to and respect for the art of the Mexican people. As Charlot perceptively observed in the foreword to *The Artist in New York,* a volume of correspondence that remains one of the best sources of material on Orozco's activities in the United States in the late 1920s, "Though he spoke slightingly of folk art, Orozco could not fail to commune, in village chapels, with the tragic mood of the many *bultos* and *santos*—statues carved out of a beam by the local carpenter, images daubed on zinc by house painters."[3] Finally, as Renato González Mello notes in his perceptive essay on the work that Orozco produced in the United States, the artist's choice of such subject matter may also have been strongly influenced by the agrarian utopianism of Angelos Sikelianos's Delphic Circle.

On the other hand, it is clear that from the very beginning of this, his second sojourn in the United States, Orozco actively sought to counter the perception that he was a painter only of Mexican themes, both by treating other subjects in his murals, easel paintings, and works on paper and by engaging in an active dialogue with the various stylistic manifestations of contemporary art as he encountered them in New York. Thus, while in 1928 and 1929 he continued to produce drawings for his *Mexico in Revolution* series and to create lithographs based on them (thus allowing for a wider distribution of these images and providing him with more income), at the same time Orozco also created a number of impressive paintings and drawings of the new and very different environment in which he found himself. Attracted by the city's architecture and the mechanical forms of its bridges and elevated railways, as he had been when he first

visited New York a decade before, Orozco created a number of simple yet starkly powerful images (e.g., *Queensboro Bridge* or *Eighth Avenue*) that, in their dark, almost monochrome palette and emphasis on the impersonality and loneliness of urban life, reflected not only his uncertain personal situation but also his belief that this was the type of painting that would find a clientele in New York. In both form and content, it reflected not only an awareness of the work of the artists of the Ashcan School, notably John Sloan and George Bellows, but also, and perhaps more directly, Orozco's awareness of and sympathy for the work produced by American Scene painters such as Thomas Hart Benton, whom he would have encountered through his association with the Art Students League.

How Orozco negotiated a relationship with contemporary American and European art while forging a singular and truly powerful artistic identity of his own as a Mexican artist, but one who was not willing to conform to any easy definitions of what constituted Mexican art, is one of the most fascinating questions that arise from a consideration of his work of the late 1920s and early 1930s. He confronted this issue time and again during his sojourn in the United States, and his varied approaches to it reveal a sophisticated and, on occasion, contradictory response to the challenge of creating an individual expression that was of his experience as a Mexican yet represented a broader engagement with contemporary culture. For example, in 1930, while Orozco continued to create his series of iconic scenes of Mexican life and the rural landscape (several of which were exhibited in the Metropolitan Museum of Art's landmark exhibition of that year, *Twenty Centuries of Mexican Art*), he was also producing a number of paintings and works on paper that reflected his acquaintance with several progressive pictorial styles and his interest in adapting them to his own needs. Thus *Cemetery* (1931 [fig. 272]), a superbly painted and truly hallucinatory image of

17

a graveyard, may be seen as belonging to the long tradition of "philosophical" images favored by Mexican painters as well as a response to the emergence of surrealism as a mode of artistic discourse in Europe and the United States. Similarly, *Elevated* (1929–30 [fig. 58]) and *The Dead* (1931 [fig. 51]) reveal Orozco's encounter with expressionism and geometric abstraction, both of which had a lasting influence on his later work, particularly the murals he painted at Dartmouth College and in Guadalajara. In this regard, Orozco made good use of his time in New York and of his exposure—for the first time and at a relatively advanced age—to contemporary American and European art. There is no doubt not only that it had a deep and lasting influence on his work but also that it was critical for his artistic development. As Charlot observed, "There is in his correspondence, once allowance is made for Orozco's tempestuous moods, the feeling of a belated adolescent awakening at meeting for the first time artists of the caliber of Seurat, Matisse, and Rouault. Though he was then in his mid-forties, Orozco can be said to have been in New York an innocent abroad."[4]

"Mural painting began under good auspices," Orozco recalled in his autobiography. "Even the errors it committed were useful. It broke with the routine into which painting had fallen. It disposed of many prejudices and served to reveal social problems from a new point of view.…The painters and sculptors of the coming time would be men of action, strong, sound, well trained; ready like a good laborer to work eight or ten hours a day. They found their way into shops, universities, barracks and schools, eager to learn and understand everything, and as soon as possible to do their part in creating a new world. They wore overalls and mounted the scaffoldings."[5] By virtue of his academic training, which had emphasized history painting and defined professional success in terms of public commissions, as well as through his involvement with the Syndicate of Painters and Sculptors in

Mexico City in the early 1920s, Orozco was committed to the enterprise of mural painting and, it would be fair to say, devoted all his energies to securing opportunities to undertake this type of work. Moreover, there is no doubt that the success of the efforts he made, with the assistance of such friends and supporters as Alma Reed and Eva Sikelianos, to exhibit his work in New York and other cities throughout the United States was instrumental in helping him gain three important mural commissions in this country: at Pomona College in Claremont, California; the New School for Social Research in New York; and Dartmouth College in Hanover, New Hampshire.

Orozco was invited to create a mural in the newly completed refectory in Frary Hall at Pomona College at the urging of a faculty member, José Pijoán. Accepting this commission with little expectation of any financial gain, but with the hope that it would serve to draw public attention to his talents as a muralist, Orozco chose to paint a large wall at the end of the dining hall with the theme of Prometheus, the figure in Greek mythology who stole fire from the gods to give to humankind and was punished with eternal torment for this deed of noble self-sacrifice. After completing this work in the spring of 1930, Orozco quickly returned to New York to begin work on a mural in the dining room of the New School for Social Research. Designed by the Austrian émigré Joseph Urban, the building and the embellishments planned for its interior were intended to showcase some of the most progressive aspects of contemporary art. Thus the award of a mural commission to Orozco (another went to Thomas Hart Benton) represented the realization of his efforts to paint a mural in New York and to be recognized as an artist of the same stature as other Mexicans of his generation, particularly Diego Rivera. Far more complex, both compositionally and in terms of its subject matter, than the mural at Pomona, Orozco's mural at the New School for Social

Research also represented his most direct engagement with contemporary politics and social issues.

In one, albeit fairly limited sense, the third and final mural produced by Orozco in this country, *The Epic of American Civilization* in Baker Library at Dartmouth College, represented a synthesis of these two approaches, blending as it does both the mythic and the contemporary. Painted over two years and completed in the spring of 1934, this was also the largest of the three murals that Orozco painted in this country and technically the most accomplished. If at Pomona College Orozco dealt with one moment (the chaining of Prometheus to the rock) in a single story, and if at the New School for Social Research he combined a number of disparate images (of different political leaders and political systems) into a composition that was not unified by a single narrative structure, at Dartmouth he sought to do both. Further, in *The Epic of American Civilization* Orozco brought together the two themes that had dominated his work over the five previous years: his continuing interest in Mexico and, in particular, its indigenous cultures, and his engagement with the art and culture of the contemporary world. Certainly the most ambitious work that he produced in the United States, this mural represents a masterful synthesis of Orozco's artistic development to date. In addition to bringing together a number of familiar themes, it placed them in the service of a concept—a narrative structure that pairs the foundation myth of Mexico, the story of Quetzalcoatl, with an extraordinary montage of images of the "modern" world that begins with the conquest of Mexico by Hernando Cortez in the early sixteenth century and ends with an apocalyptic scene—that marks Orozco's emergence as a history painter of remarkable vision and authority. In *The Epic of American Civilization,* one can also discern—indeed, in this regard, the mural almost serves as a summary statement—all that he had learned and all the influences he had assimilated as a painter during this

important period in his career. For example, if the composition of the first section of the mural (i.e., that which deals with the arrival and departure of Quetzalcoatl) represents a masterful recasting of the pictorial strategies Orozco had introduced in his murals for the National Preparatory School, then the approach he adopted in the second section, with its abrupt compositional transitions from panel to panel and its radical shifts in style from scene to scene, offers a virtual catalog (and, one might argue, a critique) of his encounter with contemporary art in the United States, from American Scene painting and social realism to precisionism and expressionism. Finally, and just as significantly for the mural commissions that Orozco was to undertake in Mexico in the second half of the 1930s, *The Epic of American Civilization* represents his coming to terms with his exceptional gifts as a caricaturist. He had begun his career making caricatures and gained a considerable reputation for his obvious talents in this field, but he was always troubled by this talent (Charlot recalled Orozco "considered it somewhat disreputable") and had taken pains to separate his work as a caricaturist from the more lofty enterprise of producing high art in the form of easel paintings and murals. It was during the two years he spent at Dartmouth—away from the pressures of New York and with sufficient time to consider his conceptual approach to the design and execution of this mural—that he finally was willing to harness this unique talent in the service of history painting. The results, as may be seen in such later panels as *Gods of the Modern World* (fig. 183) and *Modern Human Sacrifice* (fig. 185), are nothing short of remarkable and should be acknowledged as among the finest achievements of mural painting in the twentieth century.

In June 1934 Orozco returned to Mexico, his reputation firmly established. Over the next six years he went on to create what are now regarded, with good reason, as some of his greatest works:

19

the mural titled *Catharsis* in the Palace of Fine Arts in Mexico City and three murals in Guadalajara—at the university, the governor's palace, and in the chapel of the Hospicio Cabañas. Technically accomplished, they are remarkable not only for giving full expression to Orozco's formidable skills as a draftsman and colorist but also, and more importantly, for their complex vision, both mordant and deeply compassionate, of the tragic fate of humankind. Considered in relation to the work that he had completed at the National Preparatory School the year before he left for the United States, these murals represent the full flowering of his talent and suggest, perhaps as effectively as any of the works he created between 1927 and 1934, just how important the years that Orozco spent in the United States were for his artistic development.

Yet this period in his career is still not well known. Save for the murals at Pomona College, the New School for Social Research, and Dartmouth College—and, perhaps, his lithographs—his output of these years is insufficiently documented and remains largely unfamiliar to scholars and the general public. This publication and the exhibition it accompanies represent the beginning of an effort intended to fill in the historical record and to pose a number of questions that are crucial to our knowledge not only of the development of Orozco's work and thought in the late 1920s and 1930s but also of the next chapter in his career. They will also help us gain a richer understanding of Orozco's relationship to contemporary culture in both Mexico and the United States.

José Clemente Orozco in the
United States, 1927–1934

Orozco in the United States:
An Essay on the History of Ideas

Renato González Mello

For Chepa

f the principal ideologues of Mexican nationalism had one characteristic in common, it might
be this: Quite a few of them developed their
ideas from the encounter with the *non*-Mexican.
This is true of Fray Servando de Mier, the Dominican
friar whose heretical ideas concerning the Virgin
of Guadalupe forced him into a long exile in Europe,
where he wrote extensively about New Spain
(which he saw become independent during his lifetime).[1] It is also true of José Vasconcelos, secretary
of education under the revolutionary government of
Álvaro Obregón, who formulated his anti-U.S. nationalism during several prolonged periods of exile,
a nationalism that grew more radical as time passed
but that was always defined precisely by its opposition to Anglo-Saxon thought.[2] We can also say the
same for the Mexican painters, who emigrated
(nearly always voluntarily) during the first half of
the twentieth century and who returned from
Europe or the United States acutely aware of what,
in a Western and Eurocentric context, could be said
to be specifically "Mexican."

José Clemente Orozco's long stay in the
United States, from 1927 to 1934, was a determining
factor in his intellectual maturation, his solution to
problems of style, and his self-definition with respect
to Mexicanness. The essays in this catalog, and the
exhibition of which they are a part, seek to contribute to an understanding of these issues, although
they also seek, by placing themselves within the
fissures in the history of ideas, to address problems
wider in scope. What paths led to the popularity
of Mexican nationalism in the United States? What
differences and similarities existed, what comparisons and exchanges took place, between intellectuals
of both nations? How were these dialogues, debates,
disagreements, and exchanges articulated within the
political sphere on both banks of the Rio Grande?
How were they articulated within the painting,
the avant-gardes, the generations, the dreams, and
the imaginations of different groups and individuals,

of different artists and intellectuals? What, in turn,
did it mean to be a painter and a Mexican working
in the United States during the 1930s?

This essay tackles these questions in a general
manner. It focuses on the artist's biography and
on the history of ideas in North America in order to
address the following issues. First, it will analyze
how Orozco situated himself in relation to the nationalisms that circulated in the New York intellectual
circles he frequented. It will also analyze an inescap-
able problem in the study of Mexican mural
painting, its public context. What made the muralists'
painting "public," despite its frequent esotericism?
What was "public" in Mexico, and what was "public"
in the United States? This, then, is an essay on the
political situation of the Mexican muralists in the
United States, as it related to ideology in general and
to nationalisms in particular. While the easel paintings Orozco created in the United States are the
subject of a separate essay in this catalog, this essay
will specifically analyze those paintings whose
content relates to the problem of nationalism.

The Flaneur and the Academy Student

José Clemente Orozco was born in Zapotlán, in the
Mexican state of Jalisco, in 1883.[3] A few years later
his family emigrated to Mexico City, and he started
evening drawing classes at the Academy of San
Carlos. In those days a visual artist's training began
very early, much as it does in musical studies today.
In his youth Orozco passed through or flirted with
other callings: He studied to become an agronomist,
graduated from the National Preparatory School,
and worked as an architectural draftsman. At age
twenty-one, he had an accident involving gunpowder
that led to the amputation of his left hand, and
shortly thereafter, in 1906, he entered the academy,
this time to begin formally his study of painting.

His early history introduces us to one of the
most important problems he faced later as a painter,

his position on the continuum from "high to low."[4] In his autobiography, written in the early 1940s, he narrates an episode that may be imaginary and, therefore, of particular importance. He writes that as a child he would pass by the workshop of the popular engraver and cartoonist José Guadalupe Posada and watch him work, spellbound; he would enter the workshop to "snatch up a bit of the metal shavings that fell from the minium-coated metal plate....This was the push that first set my imagination in motion and impelled me to cover paper with my earliest little figures; this was my awakening to the existence of the art of painting."[5] Shortly thereafter, he says, he enrolled in night classes at the academy. Muralism's official chronicles tend to give undue importance to this dubious memory as a quasi-divine "revelation," an episode of hagiography.[6] The painter's text is, however, more subtle: He reveals a value system in which Posada's workshop had a relevance equal to that of the classrooms of the academy.

The Academy of San Carlos, an art school founded in the waning years of the viceroyalty, was in full bloom at the turn of the twentieth century. Although it felt the influences, the criticisms, and the onslaughts of the modern styles, it was still the state's principal instrument related to the arts.[7] Posada was well outside that circle of power. He was an illustrator for lowbrow, scandalous, or, at best, marginal newspapers. His cartoons were reassessed and revalorized by the muralists in the 1920s; during Orozco's childhood, however, Posada was not appreciated in intellectual circles, and his workshop was not one of the hegemonic centers of art.[8] Moreover, although Posada's calling was typically a private business, through his display window he was in public view as he worked. Orozco claims that this workshop was more "public" than the academy's state-sponsored classrooms, which were in turn part of a project, the eminently public project, of modernizing Mexican life.

The paradoxes do not end there. In his youth, already enrolled in painting classes at the academy, Orozco took up political cartooning. He did not draw for the high-volume commercial press but for small opposition newspapers not very different from those that printed Posada's work. Furthermore, although a student movement led the government in 1913 to support the creation of an impressionist school of painting on the outskirts of the city, Orozco resisted participating in it.[9] He set up a studio in the center of the city and began painting watercolors of scenes of prostitution. In his autobiography he says he read Balzac's and Maupassant's novels, skipping the descriptions of landscapes, "impatient to follow the principal characters in their adventures."[10] He was, by literary and artistic calling, a *flaneur* or a bohemian, not an excursionist.[11]

What Orozco painted during those years were watercolors depicting life in Mexico City's brothels, a series that he gave the general title *The House of Tears* (fig. 2). In these, as in some of his newspaper cartoons, he commented upon social life and the public discussion of private life. But his choice should also be seen from a political point of view. In his wanderings through Mexico City's slums, he searched for scenes with social and ethical content, as the poet José Juan Tablada saw in 1914: "Here

Fig. 2 · **The Pimp's Share**, 1913–15, watercolor, Museo de Arte Carrillo Gil, Mexico City/INBA 17210.

23

is supreme harmony of Beauty and Good, given substance in a work of art!"[12]

Orozco's most important activity in this first stage of his career was his political cartooning. In the cartoons he was fiercely critical of the regime of Francisco I. Madero. In 1910 Madero ran for the presidency in opposition to Porfirio Díaz, who had been in power for more than thirty years. After the elections Madero declared that electoral victory had been stolen from him and called for a revolution, which was ultimately successful. He was the winning candidate in the elections that followed the uprising. His political program was strictly liberal, as that term had been used in Mexico during the nineteenth century to refer to the ideology that advocated democracy, separation of church and state, and, in sum, the construction of a "civil society" as the basis of the state's legitimacy.[13] As a consequence, his government allowed the opposition press a freedom hitherto unknown in Mexico.

Orozco participated in the newspapers that were read by the groups unhappy with the new regime. In his autobiography, he states: "Every day the assistant editors met with the editor and heatedly discussed political affairs, and the discussion gave off enough light to supply pertinent articles and cartoons. The scapegoats were, naturally, political figures of the first rank....I might equally have gone to work for a government paper instead of the opposition, and in that case the scapegoats would have been on the other side. No artist has, or ever has had, political convictions of any sort. Those who profess to have them are not artists."[14]

The preceding lines reveal a deep "political conviction," one very much in tune with the reactionary publications on which he worked: *El Ahuizote, Multicolor, Ojo Parado* (fig. 3). This conviction refers not to the adequacy of any political party's program but to Orozco's belief that politics was a world of pure will to power, a realm completely free of convictions, absolutely subordinated to the militants'

loyalty. The "scapegoats" might have been different, but they would always be there. Public opinion was a hierarchy of victims and executioners.

Madero's regime ended in 1913, when a coup d'etat led by General Victoriano Huerta established a military dictatorship. This coup was followed by a new armed insurrection, this time headed by Venustiano Carranza and called "constitutionalist" because of its goal of restoring the constitution. When constitutionalism triumphed in 1914, the different factions that backed it began fighting among themselves. In 1914 troops led by Pancho Villa and Emiliano Zapata, enemies of Carranza, occupied Mexico City. Orozco, with another painter, Gerardo Murillo (known as Doctor Atl), joined Carranza and his supporters and fled with them to the city of Orizaba. There he helped publish a newspaper, *La Vanguardia,* for which he drew cartoons. His cartoons were of course anti-Huerta, but they were also anti-Villa and anti-Zapata.

This first stage of Orozco's artistic career is therefore defined by its ambiguity. Although he was a student at the academy, he made his living drawing cartoons that later embarrassed him for two reasons: the marginality of the newspapers in which they appeared and their ferocity in attacking President Madero, considered the Apostle of

Fig. 3 · "Los neo-serviles" ("The Neo-Serviles"), from **El ahuizote** (September 20, 1911).

LOS NEO-SERVILES

....¿Me seguiréis...?
...¡Hasta la ignominia, señor!

24

Democracy by the revolutionary governments. In 1916 Orozco mounted an exhibition of his watercolors and social cartoons. The symbolist topics of his work were well received by critics, but he was not satisfied.[15] He then decided to emigrate to the United States for the first time, and he remained there until late 1919, first in San Francisco and then in New York. We know that during that period Orozco painted movie posters; that in going through customs in Laredo, Texas, many of his paintings were destroyed because they seemed "pornographic" to the customs officials; and that he spent some time in New York in the company of David Alfaro Siqueiros and Juan Olaguibel.[16] This essay later takes up the most important aspects of that first visit.

The Paradoxes of Muralism

The artistic production for which Orozco is best known, his revolution-themed murals, drawings, and oil paintings, began slowly during the 1920s. Before the revolution, there had been projects in Mexico aimed at decorating official buildings. Orozco says in his autobiography that in 1910, led by Doctor Atl, he and other fellow students at the National School of Fine Arts were preparing to paint murals at the National Preparatory School. This would perhaps have placed their paintbrushes at the service of Porfirio Díaz's ancient régime. The revolution caused those plans to be postponed, and so this could hardly be considered a precursor of muralism.[17] During the 1920s, when the Sonoran general Álvaro Obregón consolidated a new revolutionary government, the secretary of public education, José Vasconcelos, began a vast project of cultural promotion: publishing classic works at accessible prices, editing literary journals, and commissioning mural painting.[18] This last category underwrote Orozco's new period, although he also contributed illustrations to some of the classics published by SEP (Secretaría de Educación Pública, or the Secretariat for Public Education).[19]

For many years muralism has been considered the clearest expression of revolutionary ideology. Recent studies have demonstrated that Vasconcelos and the muralists carried out a project of spiritual renovation, inspired by Schopenhauer and Bergson, which the Mexican intellectual elites had been trying to accomplish since the turn of the century regardless of the "revolutionary" or "reactionary" orientations of different governments.[20] The "generations" of Mexican intellectuals who lived through the end of the Porfirian regime and the rise of the new state saw themselves as knights in a struggle between civilization and barbarism; this imagery was fed by a civil war whose violence they imagined from Mexico City but only occasionally witnessed. Service to the postrevolutionary state was affirmed as patriotic, civilizing action. Within this framework, modernization was the medicine that would prevent any further eruptions in a country they viewed with apprehension. The revolution was seen as a violent outburst whose energy could be constructively channeled. Mexican revolutionary painting was, in this sense, a rhetoric at the service of this civilizing modernization. One of those intellectuals, Pedro Henríquez Ureña, said of a mural by Diego Rivera: "Perhaps the best symbol of contemporary Mexico is Diego Rivera's vigorous fresco in which, as the armed revolutionary stops his mount for a rest, the rural teacher appears surrounded by adults and children as poorly dressed as she, but animated by a shared vision of the future [fig. 4]."[21]

However, this "public art" not only served revolutionary propaganda but also had its own complexities and secrets. Most of the murals by Orozco, Rivera, Roberto Montenegro, and Xavier Guerrero, especially during the 1920s and 1930s, had some esoteric content: Rosicrucian in Rivera's case; alternately Freemason or theosophist in Orozco's. In some cases, this allegorical character is very clear, and there is even evidence of the iconographic program. For example, Orozco's 1925 mural at the House of Tiles

25

in Mexico City, titled *Omniscience*, is strictly Masonic and leaves no space for revolutionary ideology (fig. 5). The iconographic program is precise:

—Back wall—

Two large figures:

Spirit and its form: matter.

The two parts of the whole: the masculine principle, creative, aggressive and eternal. The feminine principle, gracious, soft, always waiting. He gives—she receives.

Central figure—is at once wisdom and grace.

Figures related to the first two:

Destiny

The superior force, unknown (the head cannot be seen), which is the divine origin of Man, God of the Gods: These figures also have human form; Man creates and destroys Gods at his whim and fancy!

Upper part: secondary decoration

The gift

Powerful hands deliver to other hands the fire of grace.[22]

The "omniscience" to which the title refers is the final goal of Masonic initiation. To attain it, one must be prepared; the neophyte must renounce his lack of harmony, promoting the absolute dominion of the masculine, rational principle in his personality. Through this means, man ascends to a new divine vital principle; he becomes "a sharer in Omniscience, and co-operator with Deity."[23] The rough-hewn stone and the finely worked stone are classic symbols of the Masonic tradition.

However, in other frescoes by Rivera and Orozco, the division between propaganda and esoteric emblem is unclear. The peasants in their sandals, wide-brimmed hats, and coarse cotton trousers can of course be seen with the transparency Henríquez Ureña attributed to them, but an esoteric reading of nearly all the frescoes is also possible, in which the Mexican peasants and landscapes are

Fig. 4 · Diego Rivera, **Rural Schoolteacher**, 1923–24, fresco, Secretariat for Public Education, Mexico City, photograph by Bob Schalkwijk.

part of a secret vocabulary. Explaining his frescoes at the National School of Agriculture in Chapingo, Rivera said he had "achieved, if that is the word, 'an iconography'...."[24] That fresco's main panel confirms this statement. It refers, as was de rigueur, to the modernization of rural Mexico, but even the most cursory perusal reveals the symbols of the four elements, the opposition between the feminine principle (the earth) and the masculine principle (fire, wind), and the masculine's necessary domination and control over the feminine, over what flows (such as channeled water)[25] (fig. 6).

There are, then, two misconceptions concerning Mexican muralism that I wish to emphasize. It has long been a matter of consensus that the work of the muralists sprang from the Mexican Revolution, but this was a complex process, and it is not possible to simplify its relationship to painting. Most specialists agree that the revolution was "Tocquevillean": a social change, above all, a change of state that, far from wiping clean the ancient régime, undertook with renewed vigor the goals of economic, political, and social modernization that were already in effect during the Porfiriato.[26] In this context, mural painting cannot be considered the expression of a revolutionary program, except insofar as one can demonstrate that there *was* such a program, which contemporary historians deny.

Moreover, mural painting was as "public" as the state that emerged from the revolution. This new régime was of course republican and legalistic, but it was also crisscrossed by individual or group interests, each with its respective secret languages. This is why mural painting reveals the existence of esoteric codes; *this is why it was public.*

Imaginary Americans and Professional Mexicans

In 1923 and 1924 Orozco painted his first murals at the National Preparatory School in Mexico City. The old Colegio San Ildefonso building that housed the school was an important symbol for Mexican elites. In it, the Porfirian youth and many of the revolution's functionaries and intellectuals had been educated, Vasconcelos and Orozco himself, to name just two. Orozco's first murals, on the building's ground floor, were strictly esoteric. They refer to the cyclical death of the sun, to the initiate's struggle with the forces of nature, and to his rebirth at the culmination of the initiation rite.[27] But Orozco changed. He decorated the preparatory school's second floor with gigantic caricatures of political figures of the period and even went so far as a caricature of God the Father. This challenge, together with different political circumstances, led to the cancellation of his contract and his scandalous expulsion by a group of students in mid-1924.[28] This repression plunged Orozco into a deep crisis. He devoted himself more ferociously than ever to drawing caricatures for *El Machete,* an organ of the Union of Revolutionary Painters, Sculptors, and Engravers in Mexico, which was closely affiliated with the Mexican Communist party's political positions. He renewed his participation in other marginal opposition periodicals with fewer pretensions to social redemption, very similar to those he had illustrated during the previous decade.[29]

27

Fig. 5 · **Omniscience**, 1925, fresco, House of Tiles, Mexico City, photograph by Bob Schalkwijk.

Fig. 6 · Diego Rivera, **The Liberated Earth with Natural Forces Controlled by Man**, 1926–27, fresco, Autonomous University of Chapingo, Mexico (formerly National School of Agriculture), photograph by Bob Schalkwijk.

Fig. 7 · **The White House**, 1925–28, oil on canvas, Museo de Arte Carrillo Gil, Mexico City/INBA 17236.

Fig. 8 · **The Rape**, 1926–28, ink over graphite on paper, Philadelphia Museum of Art; purchased with the Lola Downing Peck Fund from Carl and Laura Zigrosser Collection 1976; 1976-97-32.

During the time he was away from the preparatory school, Orozco began visiting the young journalist Anita Brenner to show her his cartoons. Soon Brenner became his promoter and went so far as to plan the publication of an album of them.[30] But the painter was not proud of his political drawings and became indignant when the magazine *Mexican Folkways* identified him with one he had recently published ("If I don't sign those lousy things it is because I don't want to be identified with them and I think that my wishes should be respected").[31] It was then that he began to paint oils with revolutionary themes, such as *The White House* (1925–28, [fig. 7]). In 1926 he executed "a painting to be included in the forthcoming book *Idols behind Altars,* a scene from the revolution."[32] It was not the first painting in the series; in December 1925 he had also sent a photograph of *El muerto.*[33] That same year Orozco was able to return to the National Preparatory School to finish his murals. He destroyed his first frescoes on the ground floor and replaced them with others whose esoteric content was hidden among the rural landscapes and scenes of revolution. He stopped drawing cartoons.

Anita Brenner had memories of the revolution. Fearing the Anglophobe revolutionary troops, her family had fled to the United States. "Train of wounded, bugles in the night, sound of wheels carrying men to be executed—sighs of soldier's wives & groans of gangrened....Fat general eating

hardboiled egg with his knife...barrels of blood-soaked cotton, dung heaps of it....Young bull torn apart by howling men tugging each at a leg of the roaring, bawling beast."[34]

In her conversations with Orozco, he told her about "when he and Atl, during the Revolution, took Orizaba. They pillaged churches and established newspapers in them."[35] These conversations must have included the episodes the painter recounted in his autobiography: pillaged churches, their furnishings turned into fuel for ovens, executed Zapatistas, hamlets under assault, trains full of wounded. "People got used to killing, to the most pitiless egotism, to the glutting of the sensibilities, to the naked bestiality."[36]

Fig. 9 · **Wounded**, 1926–28, ink on paper, Museo de Arte Carrillo Gil, Mexico City/INBA 16993.

In September 1926 Brenner noted with some concern that Orozco was going through a crisis: "He says he is all disoriented, and doesn't know what is what in painting."[37] She seized the opportunity. "I shall have him make me a group of revolutionary drawings. The pretext: a client. He wouldn't sell to me."[38] The supposed collector was "a fictitious American."[39] The strategy was successful. A couple of weeks later Orozco had completed two drawings, and she demanded that he "make enough for an exhibition" (figs. 8, 9, 10, and 11).[40] Each meeting with her "dealer" expanded the collection of the supposed north-of-the-border collector. The crisis abated. From the first Brenner could see the success of her request: "He achieved the fusion of the grandeur of his frescoes and the intimate conciseness of his drawings."[41] It was a matter, finally, of achieving a synthesis of the extremes touched upon in Orozco's painting: initiation and laughter, tragedy and farce, painting and caricature.

They titled the series that resulted from this splendid intrigue *The Horrors of the Revolution,* to establish a parallel with Goya's *Disasters of War.*

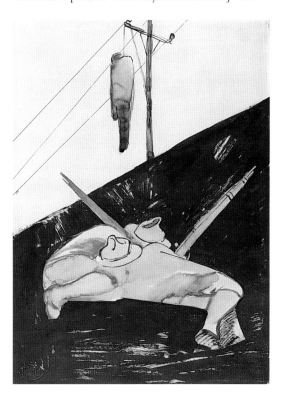

During Orozco's time in New York, the drawings were also frequently exhibited under the title *Mexico in Revolution.* Brenner had proposed a new context that would transcend the categories of "high and low," since Orozco was trying to place himself precisely at the upper end of that problematic scale. If he didn't like being seen as a cartoonist, his new drawings permitted him to mix the stylistic devices of his cartoons with those of his academic training in order to take a position in relation to a new problematic: the classicist draftsman's reason in the face of the disorder of things; the intellectualism of his compositions in the face of twisted and macabre humor.

Anita Brenner had been born in Mexico,[42] the daughter of Latvian Jews, and educated in Texas. She returned to Mexico in the 1920s, and during the period when Orozco was seeing her, she had begun to collect material for a book on "Mexican art in all its epochs," which was to culminate in the famous *Idols behind Altars* (1929),[43] the first consistent apologia for postrevolutionary Mexican painting.[44] In that book, she traced a framework for the history of Mexican art in terms of two opposing tendencies: the construction of the temple and the destruction of language. She imagined the succession of Mexican societies as organized around the temple;

Fig. 10 · **The Requiem**, 1926–28, ink on paper, Museo de Arte Carrillo Gil, Mexico City/INBA 16991.

Fig. 11 · **The Hanged Man**, 1926–28, ink on paper, Museo de Arte Carrillo Gil, Mexico City/INBA 16977.

29

thus, for the Mexicans, "the activities of the people were governed by consideration of the thing which was always biggest before their eyes. The temple was the complete and accurate symbol of the nation, and of its history and method of life."[45] She thought that this organic quality had been maintained throughout the viceroyalty, independence, and the nineteenth century; that mural painting would occupy the spiritual place of the temple; and that the painters ought to be seen as prophets. Awed by his work at the preparatory school, she described Orozco in biblical language: "It is not clear which of his permanent fulminations turned laughter into the stones that mobbed him, or if these really were the cause. One can never tell about mobs, and perhaps the noble Saint Francis or the Indian Christ, beardless in a long robe, burdening his great cross, started violent contradictions muttering in the beholders."[46]

Despite this, Brenner saw an opposing tendency in Mexican intellectual history, ironic and intellectualist, although mystical.

> Pre-Hispanic Mexican divinity, like pre-Hispanic art, was an abstract thing. The gods which Christian images supplanted were not beings, but complexes, dynamic, disintegrating, constantly reassembling groups of geometric forms and philosophic symbols and emotional associations. Each god had multiple forms and many symbols and attributes, many "masks." There were traditional moulds, but none rigid or constant, and rarely was one identified only with a certain deity. Worship was a longing, not to acquire the god's character and mode of life (which was never defined) but rather an identification with some attribute or function of divinity.[47]

Brenner believed that after the conquest this intellectualized universe had survived in popular memory as an image of chaos.

Idols behind Altars was an ideological success. It counterposed the construction of the temple to the purely rationalist operation with symbols of divine attributes; Brenner postulated a messianism that had yet to find full flower and, consequently, was in a permanent state of expectation, invention, and interpretation. These counterpositions included, on the one hand, law and hermeneutics, Talmud and cabala and the periodization of history around the metaphor of the temple, and on the other, the daring operations to combine divine names.[48] It also counterposed priestly religion to popular traditions made up of proverbs and jokes.[49] Brenner appears to have seen esoteric mysticism and public messianism as frankly revolutionary phenomena.[50]

Her theory of language, perfectly acceptable in an intellectual environment steeped in esotericism, Bergsonism, and Neoplatonism, allows one to see Orozco's drawings as the apocalyptic hallucinations they surely were in their time. In their lack of reason, in the rebellion against all things, it was possible to forestall expectation and glimpse the end. In their caustic humor, one might well find an echo of the intellectualism that Brenner attributed to the ancient Mexicans and that survived in popular culture only as a marijuana smoker's hallucination; on the other hand, behind the image of the suffering, persecuted people, the brilliant promoter saw the artist as prophet, as a rebuilder of the temple. Clearly, Orozco's painting also had its chiliasm.

Given this intellectual context, it is not surprising that Brenner should have imagined an American as a possible buyer for these drawings. Although her "fictitious American" had yet to materialize, toward the end of 1925 Brenner left a significant notation in her diary: "Diego wants English lessons."[51] Two years later she made plans with Alfonso Pruneda, chancellor of the university, for an exhibition of Mexican art to be presented in New York.[52] She signed a contract with Orozco to be his official representative and planned with him an

30

exhibition of drawings in the metropolis,[53] to which she moved to arrange both projects. Without receiving any sort of confirmation, Orozco left for New York in December 1927. He broke off his friendship with Brenner upon realizing that she had not yet prepared anything.[54] Although, in the following years, he did all he could to prevent the publication of *Idols behind Altars*,[55] his promoter had in fact done a thorough job. The drawings were well received by the North American public. In May 1928 he wrote to his wife that his drawings "have travelled hand to hand all over New York, and they seem never to run out, because they sell and I replace them with new ones. They multiply like rabbits!"[56] The drawings won him an exhibition in 1928 at the Marie Sterner gallery that consisted entirely of the "revolutionary" drawings.[57]

Orozco had had his own motives for jumping ahead of Brenner's plans. The Mexican writer José Juan Tablada, in New York since the previous decade, had been laying the groundwork for a sort of Mexican invasion. Horrified by films about bandits and by the lack of any Mexican presence in the metropolitan cultural centers, he was an active promoter of the careers that the cartoonists Luis Hidalgo and, especially, Miguel Covarrubias had begun in that city. He also organized several Mexican exhibitions and took on the task of publishing articles on Mexican art, one of which was devoted to Orozco. Tablada reported regularly on these activities to Mexico's Secretariat of Foreign Relations, from which he received a stipend during the 1920s. He also regularly wrote a column in *El Universal*: *"Nueva York de día y de noche"* ("New York by Day and by Night"). One of his columns, in June 1927, seems to me to be of fundamental importance. Tablada realized that interest in Russian art was waning and, more important, that a deep-rooted North American tradition sought to incorporate foreign cultural traditions, in view of the fact that North American culture was at times perceived to

be in its infancy. "On the one hand are we, a people rich in manifestations of beauty, in pure aesthetic products, but without a market to consume them, without the culture or wealth in our own midst to absorb those products....On the other hand is this nation, overflowing with riches to satisfy its smallest whims and capable of absorbing and purchasing our artistic products in every possible form, from the greatest architectural project to the most trivial object of art....Never has the law of supply and demand offered us a more propitious occasion to affirm our spiritual capacity...."[58]

Orozco exchanged correspondence with Tablada and surely had the latter's ideas very much in mind in thinking that he might be able to establish himself in New York. The first thing he did upon arriving was become a professional Mexican. Now, let us delve into the intellectual context within which his heterodox Mexicanism was received.

The Slum and the Continental Panorama

When Orozco arrived in the United States in 1927, he brought with him the memory of his first visit to that country between 1917 and 1919. He had stayed in San Francisco. There he had established, with Fernando Galván, a movie poster business that he describes in his autobiography with a cynicism similar to that reserved for his political cartoons (it was not, after all, an altogether different technique): "Galván sallied out in search of 'orders' and got a good one: to do hand-painted announcements of pictures for a couple of movie houses; but no such 'painting by hand' was actually called for, only a simple deception: the colored lithographs that they gave us as models could be pasted onto cardboard and given three or four brush strokes of oil paint."[59]

The trick was, in effect, very simple; moreover, the only noticeable difference between theirs and many other movie posters was that Orozco and

31

Galván did not produce mass quantities. The painter knew about manipulating images, which he had learned during his cartooning period. Siqueiros remembered that Orozco later worked in a factory that made little plaster angels, painting them with an airbrush.[60] There is some evidence that he attended drawing classes at the California School of Fine Arts at this time.[61] As was his custom then, he tried to cover all the steps between the high and the low, and that could also be said of his choice of work.

His many-hued activities gave him time to wander about the city. He had departed Mexico because of his disagreements with art critics, but also "wanting to see the United States" as if he were the spectator of a continental panorama. In his wanderings through Mexico City's poor neighborhoods, Orozco's universe was the city, and his limit was the impressionists' open-air schools. Orozco passed through both the high and the low; although he always looked from above, he was part of that urban life. His memory of San Francisco was different; he went to "the bohemian headquarters of San Francisco, with their cabarets, their dance halls, their Italian restaurants, and their saloons in the style of the Forty-niners…the studios of sculptors and painters there, passed the joyous, noisy, money-laden crowd which filled this world…revelry [*parranda*] and madness were everywhere, and everywhere the Kaiser, with horns to match his mustache, was being thrust into the flames 'to Make the World Safe for Democracy.'"[62]

The difference is evident: In the United States, Orozco acquired a global consciousness, but unlike other travelers, he did not become "citizen of the world" but remained a spectator.[63] In Orozco's memoirs, there is an insurmountable difference between his memory and the scene, which he imagines as gigantic. Perhaps this was why he remembered a song that was popular during his stay and whose title bespoke that distance, "Over There."

It is not known exactly when Orozco moved to New York and wandered through it in the company of David Alfaro Siqueiros and Juan Olaguibel.[64] They had heated discussions. "I have forgotten what my own stand was, but I do, as I say, remember that I differed with them, and they with each other. Without conflict there would be no films, no bull fights, no journalism, no politics, no free struggle, nothing."[65] The world here was conceived as a spectacle ("bullfights…wrestling…politics"), violent and disjointed, satirical. Orozco remembered with pleasure the Coney Island sideshows, where "great and marvelous things happen": fat or bearded women, children in incubators, tattooed sailors. Orozco conceived the artistic world too as a gigantic farce, a flea circus in which the skinny fleas lynched the fat ones. Museums were big tops that rented clown acts to the highest bidder.

Fig. 12 · **Vaudeville in Harlem**, 1928, lithograph, San Francisco Museum of Modern Art; 35.3071.

Fig. 13 · **Coney Island Side-Show**, 1928, oil on canvas, private collection, courtesy Galería Arvil, Mexico City.

32

The painter applauded or jeered; one may suspect that occasionally he went further than this, but he did not climb up onstage except to do what was his: painting. In everything else, he observed from a sort of cage. The audience might cry with the characters, or scream with them, but it had no right to take part in the action, regardless of the type of show it was. If satire tired the audience, one could fall back on all sorts of cheap tricks. In his autobiography, Orozco tells the story of the Great Depression and its cure: the war, recovery through the arms industry. "Nations had recourse to the practice of the third-rate tenor who, whenever he sang a false note, would immediately shout 'Viva, Mexico!' and pull the tricolor from his pocket."[66]

At the beginning of his second stay in New York, Orozco followed a similar path: He visited museums and neighborhoods, perhaps slums. His description of the city leads one to suspect a literary pattern, the patchwork of cultures with which John Dos Passos sewed his *Manhattan Transfer*. Orozco went in search of the small theaters (as in Mexico) and even made a lithograph (*Vaudeville in Harlem,* 1928 [fig. 12]) and an oil painting (*Coney Island Side-Show,* 1928 [fig. 13]) after them. He refers with sly enthusiasm to the same Yiddish theater that inspired Bertolt Brecht's aristocratically tempered interest.[67]

But unlike what happened with his early work in Mexico, which was nourished by popular culture, variety theater, and the impertinent humor of the poor, Orozco's experience in New York did not find a "floating world" to feed his iconography. On his first visit, the customs officials in Laredo had destroyed many of the watercolors he was carrying. "I was given to understand that it was against the law to bring immoral drawings into the United States."[68] On his second trip, he tried to draw cartoons for the *New York Times,* also without success. If one is to believe the rosy memory of Alma Reed, the editor thought them "too good" but was concerned that

En New York

one of the painter's sample drawings was a rather fierce satire of an "art committee."[69]

One can imagine some of the reasons for the editor's reluctance, and Orozco's own, by looking at a caricature entitled *In New York,* published in the Mexican magazine *L'ABC* in 1925, that is attributed to Orozco (fig. 14). A man, presumably a Mexican, has woken up and is beginning to dress. A naked African American woman is seated on the bed behind him, the sheets in disarray around her. The man says, in almost untranslatable Spanish: "And now, sweetie, it's important that you wear no makeup and as little clothing as possible so those yankees can't accuse me of 'white slavery.'"[70] It is a caricature that derides American social structure, but it is unlikely that Orozco ever showed anything of this sort to an American publisher. Here Orozco deplores the fact that the man could be indicted in this situation, something he views as extraordinary. Prostitution was legal in Mexico during the Porfirian regime, and even when banned by revolutionary governments, soliciting remained socially acceptable and not a felony. The caricature also shows a detached view of American racial categories under the dubious assumption that Mexicans do not have such a preposterous and exclusionary system. The caricature mocks a social structure that stresses racial separation and, even more, a moral system that was, for a male Mexican viewer, exoticist and irrational. There seems to be no critical self-reflection

Fig. 14 · Attributed to José Clemente Orozco, "En New York" ("In New York"), from **L'ABC** (November 22, 1925), 8.

33

in the caricature, but rather a presentation that implies plain common sense, indicated by the conflation of racial and gender constructions. But this naiveté was two-sided, so to speak. Orozco well knew that such satire would have been unacceptable to American publishers, no matter where they stood on the political spectrum. It is unlikely that he ever tried to publish such a caricature after the shock of his experience with U.S. Customs in 1917. He probably made some attempt to publish other caricatures, but a similar cultural gap prevented him from succeeding. In 1935 he was still afraid to mail a certain lithograph to the United States "because it represents a nude, and that may be against the law."[71]

Communication between the high and the low was not unknown in North American culture in those years, and other Mexicans, including Miguel Covarrubias, who was fairly successful in following that path, understood this. Orozco, on the other hand, never adapted to the rules that governed such traffic in the northern country. On the one hand, the definition of pornography, the space of the intimate that may legally be exhibited publicly, was stricter in the United States than in Mexico. His symbolist watercolors or his cartoons were not, in this sense, an appropriate means of breaking into the North American scene. I shall venture another explanation: In the North American metropolis, social differences passed through rigorous racial classification.[72] Orozco came from a country where the dominant discourse made (and makes) racial mixture the ultimate goal of evolution.[73] He was able to perceive the poor on the subway (*The Subway*, 1928 [fig. 15]) and even to imagine social violence (*The Strike*, 1926–28 [fig. 16]); through a lack of perception or, more likely, a conscious decision, he made no reference in these works to the racial differences that in the United States are intertwined with class differences and sometimes prevail over them. Nor did he choose to refer to this important subject in his Mexican works, unless it was allegorically, to refer to *mestizaje*

(*Cortez and Malinche* [fig. 17]) or in aggressively racist works, such as his 1935 *Turistas y aztecas*. The only two exceptions to this rule are *Vaudeville in Harlem*, which celebrates the vitality of this North American genre, and *The Hanged Men* (1933 [fig. 80]), explored in detail in the essay addressing Orozco's portable work.

But beyond this, his sly and distant observation of the scene would not yield success in a medium

Fig. 15 · **The Subway**, 1928, oil on canvas, 16 ⅛ x 22 ⅛ in (41 x 56.2 cm), Museum of Modern Art, New York, gift of Abby Aldrich Rockefeller, 1935, photograph © 2001 The Museum of Modern Art, New York.

Fig. 16 · **The Strike**, 1926–28, ink on paper, The Hermes Trust Collection, courtesy of Francesco Pellizzi.

34

that sought political commitment. The morbid humor that Anita Brenner saw in his work was tolerable insofar as the scenes were Mexican. In the few works, already mentioned, in which Orozco explored iconography similar to that of North American realism, his results were not too different, for example, from those of Reginald Marsh: show business, the theater, and the street. But perhaps the most lasting intellectual result of those first attempts may not have been the paintings so much as the global consciousness, the image of a *world in general,* of a tension between that world scene and the "American scene." As we shall see, this tension was fundamental to his later development.

Those Marvelous Skyscrapers

Having opted not to follow the flaneur's downward path, Orozco tried another avant-garde method. In January 1929, a year after his arrival in New York, Orozco published, in *Creative Art,* his only manifesto, "New World, New Races and New Art."[74] In this text, he rejected both the slavish copying of European ruins and museums and the equally slavish "pillaging" and copying of aboriginal American cultures. He advocated the creation of a new art: "Already, the architecture of Manhattan is a new value…is the first step. Painting and sculpture must certainly follow as inevitable second steps."[75] He then supported the promotion of "pure," "strong," and "disinterested" mural painting for the benefit of the people: "If *new* races have appeared upon the lands of the *New World* such races have the unavoidable duty to produce a *New Art* in a new spiritual and physical medium."[76] Orozco maintained that "any other road is plain cowardice,"[77] and that the only path toward progress was "the architecture of Manhattan," expression of the spirit of the "New World," whose expansion was "inevitable." Although Orozco carefully avoided making reference to "America," a term that in English leads to disagreeable confusion for Latin Americans, he clearly made Manhattan into a continental symbol and opposed it, as such, to the "Old World": "something that has nothing to do with Egyptian pyramids, with the Paris Opera, with the Giralda of Seville, or with Saint Sofia."[78] Moreover, his evolutionism was so stark that he even contrasted New York's architecture with the old art of the Continent: "…any more than it has to do with the maya palaces of Chichen Itza, or the 'pueblos' of Arizona."[79]

This aesthetic "Monroeism" may have several sources. For some time North American literature had equated Manhattan's buildings with the civilizing energy of ancient civilizations.[80] There was also a Mexican antecedent in Manuel Maples Arce's

Fig. 17 · **Cortez and Malinche**, 1926, fresco, National Preparatory School, Mexico City, photograph by Bob Schalkwijk.

35

first stridentist manifesto of 1921. This text had been distantly inspired by Filippo Tommaso Marinetti's *Futurist Manifesto,* although Maples Arce's work reflected the changes of the previous decade: It refused to subscribe to or propose a particular current, declared the death of isms, and included among its subscribers all sorts of intellectuals from every modernist tendency in Europe and America (most of whom had never heard of Maples Arce and his manifesto). Maples Arce's modernity was unified, transparent, and without contradictions: It encompassed Pierre Reverdy, Diego Rivera, George Bellows, and Piet Mondrian, to name a few. Like Marinetti's text, it exalted technology in a country with vast, largely undeveloped rural areas. "Let us cosmopolitanize ourselves. It is no longer possible to rest on conventional chapters of national art. News travels by telegraph; there are dromedary clouds above the skyscrapers, those marvelous skyscrapers so reviled throughout the world, and through their muscular tissues the electric elevator rumbles."[81]

For reasons explored in the essay on the artist's portable work, Orozco's urban landscapes are far from this faith in modernity; for now, it is worth noting that he tried both paths at the beginning of his stay in New York. Both are related to three fundamental problems in twentieth-century art: the secret correspondences between the high and the low, avant-garde utopias, and the affirmation of national identity. This last problem was no longer central in Europe since the academies' fall from grace; on the American continent, things were different. The Mexican muralists—Rivera, Orozco, and Siqueiros—had received academic training. This did not make them neoclassicists in the eighteenth-century sense of the word (although sometimes they approached this), but it infused their work with Aristotelian and Neoplatonic categories. Nor could the Ashcan School, the precisionists, or the different forms of "realist" painting that were

dominant in the United States during the 1920s and 1930s be considered "academic." In New York the European avant-garde experiments were well known; there were artists who had worked in Europe, like Stuart Davis; there were even expatriates like Marcel Duchamp. But in the United States, as in Mexico, public opinion fed into a nationalist project that, across the Atlantic, held at best a subordinate role: the formation of nationalist schools.[82]

Orozco had tried to situate himself in this nationalist context using the tools and discourse of his Mexican training; he was only partly successful. The group of intellectuals with whom he associated from 1928 on permitted him to follow new paths and gave his New York landscapes a critical temper diametrically opposed to his quasi-futurist 1929 manifesto. All these changes, doubts, and corrections were visible in his painting. However, as this was taking place, Orozco continued for several more years to paint and draw the revolutionary scenes he was already producing upon his arrival, making them less violent, less critical, even more consistent with the nationalism that was expected of them. He created, beginning in 1928, numerous revolution-themed lithographs, almost always copies or reworkings of his drawings, paintings, and murals of the same theme. "I assure you," he wrote his wife, "that if the drawings I made, the 'horrors,' had been engravings instead, I would have sold many already."[83] In late 1929 he wrote his wife about a millionaire client: "She is a very naive and friendly person and she made me promise that in the future I would only paint happy things."[84] For his next exhibition, he spoke of his paintings in these terms: "They are pretty and full of color. There are no more dead bodies or black. Everything very bright and happy."[85] On another occasion, he confessed to Jean Charlot: "[T]here are a number of awful new little folkloric pictures that I dashed off quickly at the last minute."[86]

36

The Delphic Circle [87]

In 1928 Anita Brenner introduced Orozco to Alma Reed (fig. 18), who was to become his agent and companion in the years to come.[88] Reed was Eva Sikelianos's secretary and lived with her in her Fifth Avenue apartment. There Mrs. Sikelianos had a salon she called the Ashram, which was equal parts esoteric society and literary circle. She was the daughter of Courtlandt Palmer, who in the previous century had run an open debate society called the Nineteenth Century Club, where people with opposing points of view, primarily religious, met to discuss their differences. Palmer had tried to export the project to Europe, with foreseeable results: For the intellectual traditions of nineteenth-century Europe, it was an experiment that made no sense. His enthusiasm had earned him Oscar Wilde's scorn: "I do not think very much of Mr. Courtlandt Palmer's ideas: but his style is wonderful!"[89] As a result of this incident, which revealed deep conflicts, Eva Palmer always had a visceral distrust of the turn-of-the-century aestheticism in which she grew up.[90] A devoted theater lover since her adolescence,

this daughter of a patrician family met with little success in her own land. At her Connecticut secondary school, the principal ended the rehearsals of a Swinburnean chorus on the ground that it was "too exciting for both you and the other girls."[91] Her evocation of the United States' cultural independence with respect to Europe, declared by Emerson in the nineteenth century, stood in clear contradiction to her activities.[92]

Eva Palmer Sikelianos was married to the Greek poet Angelos Sikelianos, a nationalist whose ideology made him comparable to the Mexican poet Carlos Pellicer. A reader of Bergson, Nietzsche, de Maistre, and Schuré, as well as Claudel and d'Annunzio, Sikelianos was inspired by ancient sculptures to compose Parnassian poems.[93] Peasant festivals, ancient mythology, and the spirit of Christianity were combined in lyric poetry that was at times interwoven with esotericism.

> In the beatific pink light of the dawn, here
> I am, going up with hands upheld
> The divine serenity of the sea calls to me, to fly
> to the celestial ether
> But the sudden breaths of the earth which boil
> in my breast make me hesitate
> Oh Zeus, heavy is the ocean, and my loose hair
> like a rock makes me sink
> Run, zephyrs, Oh Kymozoe, oh Glauke: come,
> take my arms from my shoulders
> I did not expect, so suddenly, to find myself
> surrendered to the embrace of the sun.[94]

Between the wars Sikelianos was frankly conservative without being radical. During World War II he joined the resistance and distanced himself from d'Annunzio,[95] as well as from other fascist-leaning intellectuals.

Sikelianos had a sophisticated plan for universal salvation: the Delphic movement. According to its statement of purpose,[96] the Delphic movement hoped to mobilize the elites to remedy the world's chaos,

Fig. 18 · Alma Reed in New York, 1928, photograph courtesy Antoinette May.

37

thus restoring "order, rhythm and authority."[97] This regenerative movement would be a "single, world-wide" spiritual beacon,[98] composed of spontaneous, disinterested groups that would place themselves "on a higher level than the current oppositions in international relations or class relations."[99] These groups, moved by the moral force of the elites, would centralize efforts. The University of Delphi would be created in response to this need for spiritual centralization, taking advantage of the ecumenical spirit that characterized that ancient Greek sanctuary. Delphi was charged with maintaining the elites as a "moral corps" that would block the return to savagery. Delphi was the appropriate site because it brought together spiritual currents from both East and West. It would educate the Greek people and break down national and religious barriers. The Delphic *ónfalos* would place itself thenceforth among all the "initiates" and among all peoples disposed to the dominion of spirituality and goodwill. The resulting principle of human unity would aid the strengthening of superior individuals as well as the development of just laws and institutions for the masses. A "super-Hellenic" policy would bring about "the institution of games to educate the race, the abolition of the death penalty, the equality of political rights between the sexes," and "great social reforms."[100]

The University of Delphi would strive to resolve the problems of class struggle at once; it would foster reconciliation among elites, whose distance from the masses was the true cause of wars; and it would promote greater interest in Eastern culture among Westerners. An analogous movement would need to take place in the East. There would be a conservatory, where a newly invented musical instrument would be taught, bringing together musical notation systems from both hemispheres. A school of sociology would energize the elites of the world to rethink the meaning of hierarchy among their peoples.

Sociology would dominate the economic sciences, which would seek a worldwide equilibrium between industry and agriculture that was indispensable in light of the latter's moral importance.

The resulting Delphic "organism" would be hierarchically divided. A central organ would be in charge of restoring and maintaining the dominion of the "universally active principle" that, according to "all the great initiates," constituted the "highest synthetic form" of humanity. Next in order would be the University of Delphi. Finally, an economic organization would promote the fundamental powers of individuals. To encourage this "world-wide spiritual and collegiate league," and in commemoration of the Amphictyonic League, festivals would be held in Delphi.

The sources of the Delphic project are clear. On one hand, one could point to any number of conservative projects, particularly in Auguste Comte's "religion of humanity."[101] Likewise, the project has esoteric characteristics. We know from Orozco's own writings that upon entering Sikelianos's Ashram he underwent an initiation ritual presided

Fig. 19 · Eva Sikelianos at the First Delphic Festival, 1927, photograph from the archives of Vivette Tsarlamba-Kaklamani, courtesy John P. Anton.

over by a patriarch of the Greek Orthodox Church.[102] Sikelianos was an avid reader of Edward Schuré, especially his occultist works, such as *The Great Initiates.*[103] Nikos Kazantzakis wrote in his diary that in his conversations with Sikelianos there was a "supreme desire: to create a religion."[104]

Eva Sikelianos was, to a great extent, the organizer and patron of the Delphic festivals held in Delphi, Greece (fig. 19). It was she who produced, in 1927, *Prometheus Bound,* and three years later *The Supplicants.* In each she organized a chorus whose music was arranged in the Byzantine style.[105] The Delphic festival also included a Greek regional craft fair and gymnastics exercises held by the Greek Army.

The Initiates

Eva Sikelianos was in New York between 1927 or 1928 and 1929, attempting to raise funds for a second Delphic festival.[106] Orozco was presented at her salon, the Delphic Circle, underwent an esoteric initiation, set up a small informal exhibit at the Ashram with a small studio in which to work, and established important relationships with the intellectuals who gathered there.[107] I have presented a fairly extensive summary of the Sikelianoses' ideas because they go a long way toward explaining why Orozco felt so at ease in the Delphic Circle. In Mexico too there had been promoters of peasant culture (Anita Brenner, Frances Flynn Payne, Frances Toor) and intellectuals with St.-Simonian dreams of redemption (Vasconcelos, Doctor Atl, Pellicer, Lombardo Toledano). Furthermore, the Delphic Circle was an esoteric society, with which Orozco also had some experience. Above all, despite its Greek origin, Mrs. Sikelianos's salon was a place where the most diverse nationalisms met: There were Lebanese, Greek, Hindu, North American, Dutch, and Mexican intellectuals, each one with a national and universal idea! It was precisely the

milieu the painter needed in order to locate himself in the context of North American public opinion, whose nationalism had not been easy for him to comprehend at first. Orozco had had difficulty interpreting the North American social consensus around race; the Delphic Circle's nationalisms offered him a new way to approach the problem, counterposing national liberation to universal history, the needs of the majorities to the dreams of the elites.

The most important intermediary in this relationship was Alma Reed. On the one hand, her well-known trip to the Yucatán as a *New York Times* correspondent had resulted in a love relationship with Governor Felipe Carrillo Puerto, whose socialist experiment is beyond the scope of this essay.[108] It is worth noting, however, that Reed made her trip in the company of the Carnegie Institute's archaeological expedition to the Yucatán.[109] So Reed was familiar with these discussions and with the political rhetoric of Mexican radicalism. Between her experience in Yucatán in the early 1920s and 1928, when she met Orozco, she had translated several of Sikelianos's poems into English, attended the 1927 Delphic festival, and become involved in other archaeological enterprises. Thus she could hardly have been in a better position to interpret the diverse aspirations that converged at the Ashram, as well as Orozco's own. I shall quote her recollection of the first Delphic festival: "Standing upon the prometheic rock where Aeschylus's drama had been staged, Sikelianos told how, a few hours earlier, in Arachova, he had walked upon the hallowed ground where the first, and decisive, battle to free the Greek people from the bitter yoke of centuries had been fought. 'But for the people to be truly free,' he warned, 'it is not enough to only be rid of the national yoke. It is also necessary to throw off the spiritual yokes which, for centuries, shallow in comparison to their pure spiritual heritage, have been imposed on us.'"[110]

39

The Ashram was full of similarly paradoxical purposes: on the one hand, national liberation; on the other, spiritual regeneration; nationalism and aestheticism. Orozco perceived these conditions perfectly. In his autobiography, he remembers the nationalism of the different people who frequented the Sikelianoses' salon, particularly Sarojini Naidu, an Indian nationalist and "a collaborator with Gandhi who had been educated at Oxford and spoke perfect English." These three soothsayers became interested in comparing the peasants of Greece, Mexico, and India. "Mme. Naidu in particular felt for the unfortunate Mexican peons in their struggle against injustice, and believed that their plight was similar to that of millions and millions of untouchables in her own land."[111] In the 1960s Alma Reed remembered with great emotion the admiration of the Greek poet Kostes Palamas, one of Sikelianos's closest friends, for the language of the Greek people: "In the 20s, during the years I lived in Greece, I met Palamas and witnessed the deep admiration he had, not only for the Athenian intelligentsia, but for the ordinary citizens from all over the country."[112] Orozco, often hostile to attempts to elevate popular arts, recognized the similarity between the Greek crafts that decorated the Ashram and the work of Mexican artisans. For Eva Sikelianos, this was a crucial matter. Angelos Sikelianos was related by marriage to Isadora Duncan, with whom Eva shared a taste for Greek tunics. For Mr. and Mrs. Sikelianos, it became a matter of principle that Eva should wear a tunic she herself had woven, and this caused something of a journalistic flurry in the early years of the century (fig. 20). Eva insisted that all the costumes for the Delphic festivals be tunics woven by artisans. She and her husband believed that the renaissance of these and other crafts could boost the Greek economy.[113] In this, they agreed with Naidu, who had brought from India the experience of homespun cloth as a form of resistance to Britain's monopolistic colonialism.[114] In a broad attempt to revive this

Fig. 20 · Eva Sikelianos with self-designed mask and costume for the production of **Prometheus Bound**, First Delphic Festival, 1927, from the **Mentor**, vol. 15, no. 4 (May 1927), 23, photograph Wide World.

Delphic spirit, Orozco participated in May 1929 in a tableau vivant in charro attire during a benefit function before New York's high society at Madison Square Garden.[115] To make the comparison complete, Orozco moved his studio to the Sikelianos apartment and established there a small Mexican *rinconcito*: He decorated a piece of furniture (fig. 21) and painted a couple of *pulqueria* paintings: *The Temptress* and *Have Another* (fig. 22; later version).[116] Privately, he complained to Jean Charlot: "The same as in Mexico! The same damn thing: encouragement of Greek folk arts (the serapes are exactly alike!!), dances with Greek flageolets."[117] However, the Delphic Circle's populism had an impact on him: His Mexican scenes became progressively less violent (figs. 23, 24, and 25). "Among the objects of Greek folk art with which Mme. Sikelianos's house was profusely decorated was homespun [cloth], and the resemblance of this to certain modern serapes…was remarkable. *The setting was consequently a happy one for my sketches from the Revolution.…*"[118] In September 1925, after seeing several of Georges Rouault's works, Orozco asked Charlot: "Tell me something: Was Rouault acquainted with things

Fig. 21 · The Mexican corner (**rinconcito mexicano**) at the Ashram, with furniture hand-painted by Orozco, from Alma Reed, **Orozco** (Mexico City: Fonda de Cultura Económica, 1955), fig. 54.

Mexican, such as, for example, the saints of the churches, the scourged Christ of Holy Week, illustrated pennysheets, or pulque-shop painting?"[119]

Had it been only for this nationalism, Orozco's participation in the Delphic Circle would surely have been brief. His break with Anita Brenner, after all, had been partly the result of the nationalism he feared in *Idols behind Altars*. His censure of Diego Rivera's exotic nationalism is well known: the nationalism of jicaras, pyramids, wide sombreros, and flower vendors. But Mrs. Sikelianos's circle also had an aestheticist, frankly esoterical side that allowed Orozco to situate himself as ambiguously as Masonic iconography had allowed him to do in Mexico. On the one hand, there was Sikelianos's warning about the need to undertake a personal renewal at the same time as national liberation: to put an end to political atavisms, but also to the spiritual ones. Paintings such as *The Martyr* (1930, fig. 26) show the depth of Orozco's commitment to whatever was esoteric and theosophic in Sikelianos's work: The initiate appears kneeling, with his arms forming a cross. He looks upward, whence a new light illuminates him. Behind him there runs a path that passes between two pyramids: Egypt, the imaginary homeland of all hermetic knowledge. The painting is reminiscent of *The Dedication*, the Sikelianos poem that Reed translated into English and that describes the reincarnations of an initiation. The poem's initiation was Blakean; it did not spurn communion for the sake of its Orphic mysteries. The initiate's path would exclude neither the greater world nor the smaller one, and his aspiration would be, in the end, to erase that difference: "No heed he gives to that which is near or to that which is far, for now the whole earth lies beneath his every step."[120]

This is also the case of Sarojini Naidu, whose father, she boasted, was an alchemist.[121] Her erotic poetry is notable, far from any hermetic fantasy of rationalist purification:

O Love! Were you a basil-wreath to twine
  among my tresses,
A jewelled clasp of shining gold to bind around
  my sleeve.[122]

Fig. 22 · **Have Another**, 1930, oil on canvas, Cleveland Museum of Art; 1943.539.

It is now worth considering separately three authors whose writings and drawings directly influenced Orozco's work. The first is Kahlil Gibran. Orozco enjoyed his poetry, especially his aphorisms and Neoplatonic parables. *The Prophet,* which was read aloud at the Ashram, was illustrated by Gibran himself.[123] Although Orozco mistrusted his "Between Centuries" symbolism, some of Gibran's writings inspired Orozco's murals at the University of Guadalajara.[124]

Leonard Charles Van Noppen, a frequent member of the Delphic Circle, was the author of a sonnet that Orozco and Reed took the trouble to translate into Spanish: "Come Ye Living."

Come Ye Living, fight against the dead!
Rise up, make war, for they have sold the future
  to their dark prison
Slay, slay the despot Yesterday! Arise, the day
  is here!"[125]

41

The poem, Reed says, inspired Orozco's fresco at Pomona College, and the painter wanted it read during the mural's inauguration. It had the tone of a mythological text but was also a diatribe against the kaiser and had been included in a volume of anti-German poems. The imagery had an apocalyptic overtone, as did all the sonnets in *The Challenge.*

Perhaps none of the members of the Delphic Circle had a stronger impact on Orozco than Emily Hamblen. As Jacqueline Barnitz has already noted, it was Hamblen who introduced Orozco to Nietzsche's thinking.[126] On the occasion of an exhibition of works by Orozco at the Ashram, Hamblen delivered a lecture in which she compared the painter with William Blake. She equated the two artists' work with her perception that "the wind-swept spirit of man…as excessive development of the rational faculty has changed his conditions of living and the accustomed relation to his fellow man, apparently even to his gods—that troubled spirit has found little registration in art."[127] Orozco was one of the initiates who had transcended this limitation. Hamblen, like Sikelianos and Gibran, believed that culture was the work of privileged men: Nietzsche, Blake, Whitman. Fascinated by irrationalism, she devoted numerous pages to Blake, which became visible in Orozco's work. If Pomona's *Prometheus* leads one to suspect a reading of *The Marriage of Heaven and Earth,* it is beyond doubt that many of the figures at Dartmouth College are sometimes literal appropriations of the emblems Blake drew for the Book of Job, about which Hamblen wrote an extensive commentary.[128] In her detailed study *On the Minor Prophecies of William Blake,* Hamblen noted that the origins of Blakean poetry lay in the separation between emotional and rational faculties, between masculine and feminine, between body and soul. Blake had come face-to-face with an emblematic tradition that saw the body as an image of the macrocosm, as the codex of a world artificially divided into reason and emotion. The text in which

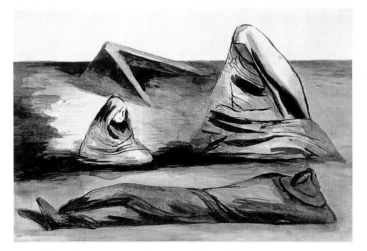

Fig. 23 · **Ruined House**, 1926–28, ink on paper, Albertina, Vienna.

Fig. 24 · **Tears**, 1926–28, ink and graphite on paper, collection of Alfonso Dau, photograph courtesy Sotheby's.

Fig. 25 · **La cucaracha 3**, 1926–28, ink and graphite on paper, Museo de Arte Carrillo Gil, Mexico City/INBA 17018.

Blake had explained this division in greatest detail was, according to Hamblen, *The Marriage of Heaven and Earth*. Although this work was, to a large extent, an inversion and a satire of Swedenborg's revelations, Hamblen proposed that it was a legitimation of prophecy and revelation as ways of knowing.[129]

For Orozco, knowledge of William Blake was decisive. For a long time he had believed in the project of rationalistic purification of the arts. With Hamblen's ideas, Orozco appropriated an openly irrationalist body of thought. Reflection upon Blake flooded his work and pushed him many years later toward the boundaries of Enlightenment thought, proposing a radical, demonic irrationalism, an anarchism that privileged personal rebellion and, cyclically, elevation and communion with the world. His murals in Mexico City and Guadalajara between 1934 and 1939 were filled with furious and blazing angels (fig. 165).

Beyond esoteric mysteries, Blake's influence on Orozco is very complex. The world scene between the wars was apocalyptic. Orozco might have found Blake attractive because of his narrative of global destruction and regeneration. More important, though, is Blake's awareness of the authoritarian viewpoint brought about by the Enlightenment. The image of Urizen, a ruler measuring the world with dividers, a detached spectator above every worldly desire, led Orozco to reflect upon his own viewpoint. It is no coincidence that Orozco developed a mediation on the "scene" within the world scene, acquiring a new awareness of sight as an instrument of power and, thus, as a revolutionary instrument. A new consciousness of the ambiguities of both the viewer's and the painter's individual viewpoints substantially modified his first impressions as a foreign immigrant wandering New York City streets and museums. His painting gained a new political relevance, becoming a realm for the negotiation of the issues implied by such expressions as "New York Scene," "American Scene," or, one might add, "World Scene." His panorama was transformed into a discourse on the construction and weaknesses of the Western perspective, nurturing an iconography that subverted authoritarian chiliasm and hierarchical allegory for a spiraling subtext underlying new scenes of devastated cities and flaming ghosts.

Nation and Progress

For Emily Hamblen, Walt Whitman was the third prophet of a new world, one in which man would recover his capacity for communion with what is truly human in his own nature.[130] If her reading of Nietzsche had been somewhat conservative, and her reading of Blake was full of hermeneutic fantasies and untenable anachronisms, her image of Whitman the "initiate" was rigorously nationalistic: "That some people awaits its bard? Walt Whitman believed this. He believed that he, himself, was the bard and America the nation. Not geographic America alone, but that America which stands

43

for the yet-to-be-animated spirit of the West which is to oppose, complement, justify and transcend the spirit of the East."[131]

There was also reflection in the Ashram concerning North American nationalism. In this regard, Hamblen's thinking was conventional: She saw Whitman as a mystical romantic and therefore as an initiate and prophet of a limitless "America" ("Not geographic America alone"). The "American" spirit would be nourished by desire and by the landscape, by nature and by the democratic civic spirit. In 1932, when Orozco was commissioned to paint his mural at Dartmouth College, the head of the college's art department was Artemas Packard. We know of his ideas through a book published in 1942 by the Delphic Society.[132] Packard saw an internal contradiction in the romanticism of United States culture: "We seem to be determined to turn every child in the land into a little lord or lady and, as far as possible, to convince them [sic] that they are endowed with a streak of genius which excuses them from the kinds of self-discipline and social responsibility which their dunderheaded elders have to accept in order that civilized society may exist."[133] It is not surprising that Dartmouth College should have been full of critiques of the most important traditions of North American public life: town life, elementary and higher education, rituals of war. Lewis Mumford perceived this in his lucid notes on the murals.[134] These frescoes do not hide the contradictions to which Packard pointed, but in the final analysis Packard shared the nationalism of Eva Sikelianos and Emily Hamblen. For this educator, the idea of "art for art's sake," of pure art, "has been characteristically propagated by the intellectually exclusive and socially anti-democratic elements in our society."[135] Packard reproached the European avant-gardes for their excessive intellectualism, their aristocratic baroqueness. True aesthetic ideas, in his view, would more closely conform to the laws of nature.[136] But it would be wrong to

constitute a science of art in order to find these laws. Packard united common sense and intuition, borrowing this last category from Benedetto Croce. In spite of his demand for conformity to natural forces, he declared that true aesthetic knowledge did not produce abstract concepts.[137]

When John Dos Passos visited Mexico in 1927, he did not overlook the contradictions among the muralists; he also perceived the limits of the Mexican Revolution, whose promises to redistribute land were frequently rhetorical.[138] However, he envied the Mexican painters because, unlike his own countrymen, they had succeeded in jettisoning their admiration for European modern art.[139] Dos Passos, like many other Americans, thought this was a radical move, one justified by the landscape: "Your first morning in the City of Mexico. The sunlight and the bright thin air, the Indian women sitting like stone idols behind their piles of fruit or their bunches of flowers, the sculpture on old red colonial buildings and the painting on the pulque shops, all tie you up into such a knot of vivid sights that you start sprouting eyes in the nape of your neck."[140]

To the Mexicans' dismay, North American intellectuals had set their sights on Mexico in search of the exotic, but they were also in search of the "American," in its most latent and disturbing sense.[141] It must be understood that their search for nature, for "the chirps of the Mexican muleteer and the bells of the mule,"[142] as Whitman put it, was a search for their own origins. Thus Stuart Chase's fascination with communal labor in Tepoztlán, which made him evoke the Jeffersonian spirit of the first citizens of the United States.[143] This search for origins was also the source of the North American intellectuals' interest in Mexico's artists and their peculiar reconstruction of Diego Rivera as the representative par excellence of Indian Mexico. What they sought in the muralists was the civic virtue, the public ethic they did not see in modern European aesthetes. Thus Artemas Packard mused:

Fig. 27 · **Anglo-America** from **The Epic of American Civilization**, 1932–34, fresco, Baker Library, Dartmouth College, Hanover, New Hampshire.

Fig. 28 · **Hispano-America** from **The Epic of American Civilization**, 1932–34, fresco, Baker Library, Dartmouth College, Hanover, New Hampshire.

If, in the past, the growth of democracy seemed to impede the growth of Art, the way in which "Art-interests" themselves have operated to impede the growth of democracy is one of the most interesting phenomena in the American social scene. There is no more striking illustration of what the sociologists call the "cultural lag" than the remarkable persistence (and even active cultivation) in modern America of the charming notion that aesthetic appreciation is a special manifestation of "aristocratic" instincts. Unquestionably this is one of the things that has worked most powerfully to isolate the fine Arts from their normal relation to the practical Arts and to confirm them in their tendency to concentrate on trivial and meaningless interests as remote as possible from the interests of the average man.[144]

The above led Packard to an illuminating conclusion: The community, the public, had the right to censure

"public" art if it did not contain desirable civic virtues.[145] This is very important in that it allows us to understand the persistent public opposition to the Mexican's frescoes as the outcome of this populist discourse.[146] It should be said on Packard's behalf that contrary to his theory of aesthetic lynching, he refused to compromise with members of the Dartmouth College community when some protested against Orozco's frescoes.[147]

The idea of an "American civilization," with all the ambiguities implicit in the concept of "America," is a founding myth in the United States.[148] I don't believe Orozco was ignorant of this mentality, especially considering his manifesto "New World, New Races and New Art." The pamphlet that was published for the inauguration of his mural at Dartmouth College, *The Epic of American Civilization,* had a note by the painter on its first page: "But the important point regarding the frescoes of the Baker Library is…the fact that it is

45

an AMERICAN idea developed into American forms, American feeling, and, as a consequence, into American Style."[149] More than six decades later Orozco's murals and his ideas, as well as their reception, contain elements that can and should concern us. The narration of this epic of "civilization" supposed that "America" was torn between two extremes, represented by the panels of *Anglo-America* and *Hispano-America* (figs. 27 and 28). In the latter, Orozco painted Emiliano Zapata in an allegory in which the southern guerrilla opposed "imperialist oppression," according to the murals' inauguration pamphlet. This allegorical figure, representing all "Latin America," would possess attributes "desirable in themselves and complementary to the attributes represented in the Anglo-American panel," to wit: "attributes of cooperation, deliberation, reasonableness, discipline."[150] This contraposition already had a long history among Latin American intellectuals; it originated in José Enrique Rodó's essay *Ariel.* Rodó's book has been criticized precisely for what concerns us here: its justification of Latin American elites faced with the double menace of North American culture and their own countries' masses.[151] It was, then, a contraposition that placed "culture" on the side of "Latin America" and named "civilization" as an attribute of the "imperial" masters; religion and faith on the Latin side, pragmatism on the Anglo-Saxon, as in Rubén Darío's poem: "And, since you have everything, one thing you lack. God!"[152] Alfred Barr himself, in his introduction to the exhibition catalog *Twenty Centuries of Mexican Art,* wrote in 1940: "The more thoughtful of us will not see the exhibition without provocative reflections about the nature and value of our two civilizations, for Mexican culture, as expressed in its art, seems in general to be more varied, more creative, and far more deeply rooted among the people, than ours. The Mexicans, of course, have one great advantage over us. They have an incomparably richer artistic past—two pasts in fact: a European

and a native, both of which survive in modified form today."[153]

This is thus a discourse in which both sides are potential victims. In his murals and texts, Orozco used two contradictory ideological traditions: Arielism and Monroeism. He located himself in the interstices of the discourse of "America" and turned that discourse into a space of negotiation. The imaginary American had taken shape, finally, as a metaphysical category that could be located somewhere between the provincial U.S. schoolmistress, the guerilla hero, the enlightened Latin American, and the Whitmanian prophet. There is an entire diplomatic history behind this intellectual one.

Nationalism and Universalism

But the Mexican muralists did not entirely fulfill the expectations placed on their "public" art. They did not always portray natural man and his democratic virtues; much more often, they set about tracing vast projects of world dominion and aristocratic elevation. Let us take two examples. In 1931 Orozco decorated the dining hall of the New School for Social Research. His portrait of Lenin, in harmony with that liberal university's tradition, has been much noted. But close scrutiny will permit the viewer to discover the decorations' "iconographic program," which is an illustration of Sikelianos's dreams of regeneration. In the *Table of Universal Brotherhood* (fig. 29), for example, portraits of several members of the Ashram can be detected.[154] This meeting of initiates from different races and nationalities was placed between two long walls that represent the social struggles of East and West. In the latter case, Orozco portrayed Sarojini Naidu next to Mahatma Gandhi. As if this were not enough, at the other end, on the wall where the entryway is located, a working family is about to sit down to eat. The fire burns in their hearth, food and books are on their table, and through their window a structure may be seen amid the landscape. Sikelianos had warned, in his *Plan général,* against excessively centralized projects and wanted the Delphic movement to contribute to "reintegrating…the people itself to the tradition of the earth and to its own traditions, inculcating anew the profound dogma…that the Earth itself is more than the people because she is the mother of all her descendants."[155] Outside the dining hall there is another panel that presents man in his three aspects of creator, maker, and designer, a long-standing theme in Orozco's work.[156] It is reminiscent, as is the Pomona College mural, of Sikelianos's ideas about the universal education to be offered at the University of Delphi. In sum, the New School mural presents a tension between city and country, between the return to the earth and a new world elite. The two extremes of this polarization were of interest to the Delphic Circle's diverse nationalisms, but Orozco emphasized world government, leaving to a secondary panel the reencounter with the earth, which was of great importance to the Whitmanian nationalism of the "Delphians," as well as for the Ashram's other nationalisms.

In this regard, Diego Rivera was more radical. His frescoes at the Detroit Institute of Arts (fig. 215), and the ones that were destroyed at New York's Rockefeller Center (fig. 251), seem to illustrate the "technocratic" utopia advocated by Stuart Chase, whose book on Mexico Rivera had illustrated.[157] Technocracy proposed centralized economic planning by experts, intensive use of technology to shorten working days, the blurring of class differences, and the substitution for money of some rational unit of measure; in place of dollars, there would be energy certificates denominated in joules.[158] The Detroit murals are scenes of the Ford assembly plant at River Rouge, a place where, according to Terry Smith, Taylorism, scientifically designed industrial production, became North American democracy's "other." In the long "struggle between the city and the plan," the plan triumphed at River Rouge.[159] Rivera's frescoes do not portray any substantive criticisms of this form of industrial planning. In his Rockefeller Center fresco, Rivera went even further, portraying a Soviet worker, taken from the five-year plan propaganda, controlling a world whose future could be seen, perfectly planned.

Orozco did not share this vision of Soviet planning, but his adherence to the Delphic movement must be seen in the context of his times. The period between the wars teemed with world salvation projects like Sikelianos's, some more conservative, others more nationalistic. These twentieth-century utopias were fueled by the economic crisis of 1929 that seemed a call for limits on the excesses of the market, competition, and industrialization. It is

Fig. 29 · **Table of Universal Brotherhood**, 1930–31, fresco, New School for Social Research, New York City, photograph courtesy Dartmouth College Library.

47

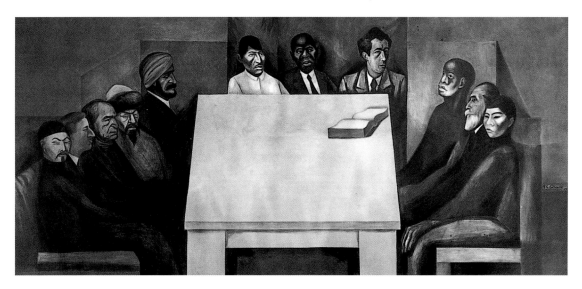

worth making a comparison here. In the last decade there was ceaseless talk of the fall of communism and the establishment of a new world order; in the 1930s, public rhetoric insisted just as obsessively on the imminence of an apocalyptic class war and the end of capitalism, even of history itself. This incipient global consciousness was liberalism's limit in two of its most important terrains, nationalism and individualism. Orozco's work in the United States was, to a large extent, a negotiation of contradictory ideas, dissonant thoughts, and incommensurable scales.

It is in his few references to the race problem that we can see the importance of this negotiation. After his timid attempt to follow Covarrubias's path with *Vaudeville in Harlem*, Orozco was even more cautious. At the New School, he represented two "Negroes" at the *Table of Universal Brotherhood*.[160] One of them is dressed in a tunic; the other presides over the meeting and wears a coat and tie. From this opposition, some commentators have conjectured that the first is an African and the second an

American. Although the idea is plausible, the portrayal's ambiguity should also be considered, for in these two figures, it opposes other categories as well: peasant and urban, traditional and modern, national and universal. With his Mexican background, Orozco understood that Depression-era intellectual rhetoric demanded a politicization of the race problem and that Covarrubias-style modernist aestheticism would not be well received.[161] But he took care to place his reflection in a specific context; recourse to a "universal" scope allowed him to escape from the complex North American racial discussion and allude to an equality that, being similar in appearance to the U.S. "melting pot," could not be discussed only in those national terms of reference. The mural was certainly a provocation, but it is significant that in spite of this (and Lenin's picture), it fared better than Rivera's mural at Rockefeller Center.[162]

At Dartmouth College, Orozco also addressed the race problem, although more carefully. One of

Fig. 30 · **Mexican Hills**, 1930, oil on canvas, Museo de Arte Carrillo Gil, Mexico City/INBA 17253.

the panels of the section titled *Modern Industrial Man* (fig. 190) portrays a worker who, from his facial features, could be of African descent, although this characterization is not entirely clear (especially if the standard for representing "Negroes" was Covarrubias's drawings). At this school, famous for its Christianization of North American Indians, Orozco painted an epic of the pre-Columbian civilizations of Mexico and Central America. His only reference to North American Indians is on the lateral panels that represent totems, cautiously referred to by the pamphlet published for the murals' inauguration as "decorative"[163] (figs. 175 and 176). The "American epic" is resolved with a rhetorical displacement, a common operation within North American culture, especially in its relations with Latin America and Mexico. The United States' past always appears as a recent past. If even Alfred Barr agreed that Mexican culture was much older, it was then possible to dream through a different history. In the monograph on Orozco published by Delphic Studios in 1932, Alma Reed wrote: "Americans may be the children of all races, but we belong to this soil and its destiny involves our own. The modern Mexican occupies an identical relation to the same soil. This elemental bond, perhaps, has given the artists of Mexico a sense of being at home in our country, and to the artists from the United States, the beneficent feeling of coming at last into a long-withheld heritage when they journey to the ancient cities of the Maya and the Aztec."[164] If, as Croce says, "all history is present history," Orozco's murals at Dartmouth College speak of North America's cultural history as much as or even more than Mexico's. They refer to the difficult problems of racial integration, national identity, imperialism, and utopia, but they place them in a context that, on the one hand, softens their national political content but, on the other, makes radical positions possible within a global context.

"…And an Intimate Reactionary Sadness"

In his celebrated poem "El Edén subvertido," Ramón López Velarde imagined his youthful memories betrayed, his homeland devastated by the revolution, in ruins, all its hinges rusty while he walked through the doorways.[165] Something similar happened to Orozco. Far from Mexico, he idealized the Mexican landscapes of his memory (figs. 30, 31, 257, and 258). After 1930, his Mexican-themed works became fewer in number and somewhat changed. He returned to a subject that had nourished his cartooning during the 1910s. At that time he had represented Emiliano Zapata as a diabolical outlaw. In 1930, having finished his Pomona College mural, he painted a series of pictures for the exhibition *Mexican Arts* at the New York Metropolitan Museum of Art.[166] These paintings, such as *Wounded Soldier,* reiterate the monumentality of *Prometheus* and its sculptural quality (figs. 32 and 33).[167] The most famous painting of this series depicts Zapata. A small oil study for this painting belongs to the Carrillo Gil collection;[168] the full-scale painting shown at the Metropolitan Museum is now at the Art Institute of Chicago (figs. 34 and 35).[169]

The study for the painting is fairly close, in spirit, to Orozco's early caricatures of the peasant

Fig. 31 · **Mexican House**, 1929, oil on canvas, Allen Memorial Art Museum, Oberlin College, Oberlin, Ohio, gift of Mrs. Malcolm McBride, 1943, photograph by John Seyfried.

49

leader. The hero enters a dwelling. His appearance is greeted by a chorus of lamentations, and his gestures have the ferocity that the nineteenth-century elites attributed to pre-Hispanic idols. I can only refer here to one of the most recurrent paranoid fantasies of the powerful classes: the restoration of the idols, human sacrifices, and presumed barbarity of the ancient civilizations. Orozco himself devotes a chapter of his autobiography to ridiculing Mexican indigenism ("Great Teocalli would still be standing, though thoroughly disinfected to keep the blood of sacrifices from going bad, and to enable us to turn it into blood pudding…").[170] In his first article on Orozco, in 1913, the poet José Juan Tablada had included an invocation: "May never a breath of human passion come…to remind me that I am …a miserable citizen of the motherland that Carrancistas and Zapatistas murder."[171] The study Orozco painted in 1930 shows that his point of view had changed little, but the final version of the painting does register a difference. The peasant hero's face appears sweetened, serene and with a tidy mustache. The surrounding figures are barely sketched in the study; in the final version, however, they appear carefully modeled. The painter's intent in presenting this much less aggressive version at the Metropolitan was surely to create a contemporary icon, at once a hero, initiate, and revolutionary. The terror associated with his entry is that of tragic heroes. Tablada himself perceived it thus, in his review of the exhibit.

And what we say is pictorially demonstrated by several works of Orozco and Rivera on the same subject: Zapata conceived by Rivera as an individual hero, as a person and painted on a panel at the aforementioned Secretariat as if …singing a sentimental tenor's *aria* (fig. 36).

The same Zapata, conceived by Orozco, in the Metropolitan's admirable painting, as what he really is, more than a man, humanly imperfect,

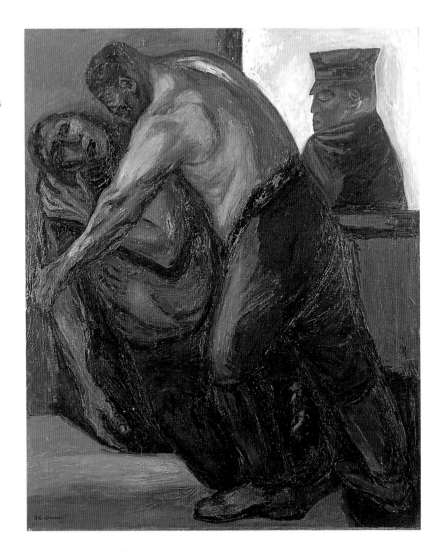

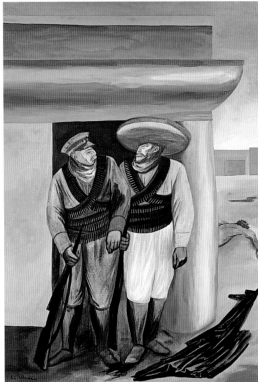

Fig. 32 · **Wounded Soldier**, 1930, oil on canvas, Cleveland Museum of Art; 1954.864.

Fig. 33 · **Mexican Soldiers**, 1930, gouache on paper, collection of Rodney and Gussie Medeiros, photograph by Don Pierce.

an incontrastable and redemptive social force: The land belongs to the tiller....

Such an idea takes on a terrible grandeur in Orozco's canvas, and seems to deepen and expand the Metropolitan Museum's hall toward the tragic regions of the human drama of the heroic epic, of Aeschylean terror....[172]

The different versions of Zapata had repercussions in his Dartmouth College mural. Again, Orozco is ripening a subject in his easel paintings; he later brings it, amplified, into his mural painting. In the Baker Library panel, Zapata's effigy is universalized and becomes an allegory for Latin America (fig. 182; see fig. 27). It is possible that in this risky operation, Orozco may have had in mind the words of Anita Brenner:

Central and South Americans uncomfortable under dictatorships and other archaic unfortunate institutions when they ponder the Mexican oil laws or prepare to emulate Zapata, nearly always nail somewhere in their dwellings a photograph of one of his frescoes. Too, many an American schoolteacher has been shocked and subsequently mellowed, departing

to Kansas, Texas, California or New Jersey with a new and disturbing vision....That people who think last in terms of painting, and people whose most common language is plastic, may be brought thus to share a single affection by a man of genius is an achievement significant to all America. Art critics at least acknowledge the continental distinction.[173]

This is quite a paradox. Emiliano Zapata was defeated precisely because he did not articulate his strictly regional demands, for which he was the spokesperson within the national discourse.[174]

The oil painting *Zapatistas,* from 1931, now part of the collection of the Museum of Modern Art, New York (fig. 37). This is a very confident work. It is Mexican as well as "revolutionary," although it is also one of the many "revolutionary" works whose

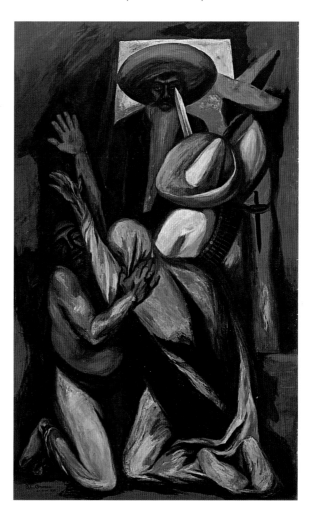

Fig. 34 · Study for **Zapata**, 1930, oil on canvas, Museo de Arte Carrillo Gil, Mexico City/INBA 17265.

Fig. 35 · **Zapata**, 1930, oil on canvas, 70 ¼ x 48 ¼ in (178.4 x 122.6 cm), gift of the Joseph Winterbotham Collection, 1941.35, photograph © 2001, The Art Institute of Chicago, all rights reserved.

51

critical thrust ends up appearing tenuous. In 1935, after returning to Mexico, Orozco made a lithograph of almost the same subject (fig. 38). It is a merciless caricature of the agrarian caudillo and his hosts, who no longer appear as a parade but as a mass. Orozco used near-Lombrosian conventions in his satire. All the lithographs he made in 1935, as well as his mural at the Palace of Fine Arts, Mexico City (1934 [fig. 252]), bear witness to his uneasiness upon reencountering "the subverted Eden." Now, under the presidency of Lázaro Cárdenas (1934–40), mass society and its organizations were flourishing. These lithographs' powerful critical thrust is somehow an expiation of the concessions the artist had made to the North American public. Orozco felt, like López Velarde, "an intimate reactionary sadness."

Question and Desire

A comparison is in order here. George Grosz arrived in the United States, to stay permanently, a few years after Orozco. The unrestrained criticism he had practiced during the Weimar Republic was sweetened beyond recognition. Grosz had dreamed of the United States as utopia, as the "New World," since childhood. "His enthusiasm, however, soon evaporated. The merciless and brilliant chronicler of the Berlin street life of the twenties was struck dumb by the city he so often visualized but which, rising up before his eyes, seemed to forbid all further comment."[175] The idea of the "world in general" was identified by him with one of the nationalist discourses at play, the North American.

At the opposite extreme, Federico García Lorca was in New York between 1929 and 1930. Alma Reed affirms that he, Orozco, and Gabriel García Maroto met a few times and that the Andalusian poet theorized about the integration of the arts.[176] His book *Poeta en Nueva York* leaves little room for reflection on nationalisms. The city, certainly, appeared to him with all its peculiarities: its racial

diversity, the haughtiness of its monuments to prosperity, the loneliness it engendered. He also found himself obliged to think in universal terms, as if he were speaking of a "global metropolis." Images of sea and travel are recurrent in this collection; "Africa" invades New York; the landscape is lonely and apocalyptic: "Canyons of masonry imprisoned an empty sky." But his was an atypical landscape, nothing topical, "stripped and pure sky, identical to itself," which confronted the poet with his loneliness, with love punished: "the lone world, by the lone sky." Orozco's trajectory through New York is a morass of uncertainties, many of them

Fig. 36 · Diego Rivera, **Zapata**, 1923–24, fresco, Secretariat for Public Education, Mexico City, photograph by Bob Schalkwijk.

52

having to do with nationality; the Granadian poet's was generally far from that inquisitive animus: "No, no. I do not ask, I desire." Orozco did ask.[177]

Living in Error

The differences between North American and Mexican art patronage are worth exploring in relation to Orozco. In Mexico during the 1920s, there were no stable commercial art galleries.[178] Orozco had found buyers such as Genaro Estrada, as well as something very unusual: a patron willing to pay for a mural, in the person of Francisco Sergio Iturbe. The lack of an established market made it practically impossible to make a living by selling his artwork. The need to support a family made him turn, from time to time, to political cartooning.[179]

For Mexican artists in those years, a twentieth-century Mexican proverb aptly described their situation: "He who lives beyond the government's budget lives in error." The only secure source of income for an artist was public-sector employment, as a muralist, a teacher, or both.[180] Orozco also drew for the editorial department of the Secretariat of Public Education.[181] However, this was not a trouble-free option. Orozco had begun his murals at the National Preparatory School in 1923 and in 1924 had been forced to abandon them as the result of complicated political circumstances associated with José Vasconcelos's resignation as secretary of public education.[182] This situation had caused him to be laid off from work at the secretariat and at the academy. Anita Brenner's "fictitious American" surely appeared more promising.

53

Fig. 37 · **Zapatistas**, 1931, oil on canvas, 45 x 55 in (114.3 x 139.7 cm), Museum of Modern Art, New York, given anonymously, 1937, photograph © 2001 Museum of Modern Art, New York.

For their emigrations to the United States, Orozco and Rivera received different state support. On the one hand, cultural exchange between the two nations was promoted by Dwight Morrow, the U.S. ambassador who restored normal bilateral relations after the revolution.[183] Morrow had paid in 1930 for a mural by Rivera in Cuernavaca, which he donated to that city as a token of friendship. He also intervened in some of the commissions that the muralists received in the United States.[184] Besides this, Orozco received a small subsidy from the Secretariat of Foreign Relations to establish himself in New York.[185]

In the United States, Orozco's patronage changed substantially. In the first place, it is worth recalling that Orozco was awarded three mural commissions, one of them substantial, each from a North American university: Pomona College, the New School for Social Research, and Dartmouth College. While these institutions were liberal to varying degrees, as a rule they tolerated Orozco's frescoes much better than Mexican state institutions did. Before and after traveling to the United States, Orozco was forced to interrupt his frescoes at the preparatory school, the Supreme Court of Justice, and the Hospital of Jesus the Nazarene in Mexico City. Diego Rivera was not so lucky, since his North American commissions came more often from large corporations: the San Francisco Stock Exchange;

the Detroit Institute of Arts, under the watchful eyes of the Ford family; and Rockefeller Center. This last site's fresco was destroyed under circumstances that have yet to be fully examined, but in which Nelson Rockefeller's discretion played a decisive role.[186] The Mexican muralists received no direct commissions from any level of the U.S. government to paint mural decorations.

Unlike Mexico, there was an art market in the United States, and there were also, more so than in Mexico, occasional buyers for Orozco's painting. Among his collectors, Orozco could count Juliana Force, later the first director of the Whitney Museum, who bought a group of his drawings shortly after the painter's arrival (figs. 39, 40, and 41).[187] Other buyers can be found in the list of works included in

Fig. 38 · **Zapatistas**, 1935, lithograph, Museo de Arte Carrillo Gil, Mexico City/INBA 17202.

Fig. 39 · **Aristocratic Dance**, 1926–28, ink on paper, Museo de Arte Carrillo Gil, Mexico City/INBA 16973.

Fig. 40 · **Battlefield, no.1**, 1926–28, ink and graphite on paper, Museo de Arte Carrillo Gil, Mexico City/INBA 17021.

this catalog (fig. 42). Orozco tried, unsuccessfully, to exhibit with Kraushaar, but the latter "was horrified" by his work;[188] he also made an attempt to exhibit at the New Art Circle.[189] Orozco held his first formal exhibition at the Marie Sterner gallery in 1928;[190] this was followed by others at the Downtown Gallery in 1929,[191] the Art Students League of New York in 1929,[192] and the New Students' League in Philadelphia.[193]

The exhibition at the Marie Steiner gallery was well received. This led Eva Sikelianos, who was about to return to Europe, to take Orozco's "revolutionary" drawings with her in order to promote an exhibition in Paris.[194] The exhibition was inaugurated at the Fermé la Nuit Gallery in February 1929[195] and received glowing praise from Gaston Poulain.[196] Soon, however, Orozco began to have reason for a change of heart. In March 1929 he received a letter from Francisco Sergio Iturbe:

> You recommended to me a woman who came from Europe. I went to see her immediately since she came on your behalf. The second time I saw her, she disappointed me, proposing that I give her $25,000, not for your work, but for her; don't trust women.
>
> P.S. Two days ago, just before it closed, I saw your work on the Revolution displayed in a tea house in Paris. A little later and I would have

missed it; no one told me about it; it must be the work of that ill-willed Greek woman.[197]

Shortly thereafter, Orozco wrote his wife that Alberto J. Pani, then of the Mexican embassy in Paris, had tried to block his exhibit.[198] In April, *El Universal*'s tireless Ortega, scandalmonger extraordinaire, reproduced a diatribe in *Paris-Midi.* "All is ruins and mourning. Tragic memories. Memories of revolution.... An escapee from the Mexican revolution, José Clemente Orozco has lived there—in Mexico—through abominable days." Ortega concluded: "This is what José Clemente Orozco's adventure has come to, the great painter who now causes in Europe the greatest harm to his country."[199] Orozco wrote to *El Universal* categorically denying that he had carried out any anti-Mexican activity whatsoever.[200] This episode distanced him from Eva Sikelianos, although not from her friends or her ideas. It is not clear if once Eva Sikelianos left for an extended stay in Europe, the meetings at the Ashram continued, but it seems unlikely. A year later, in February 1930, Orozco wrote to his wife, "As for the festivals in Greece, I know nothing about them, nor am I interested."[201]

The success of his first exhibitions, and the end of the Delphic Circle meetings, led Alma Reed, already the painter's representative, to set up her own gallery. Delphic Studios opened in July and was

Fig. 41 · **The Reactionary**, 1926–28, ink on paper, Museo de Arte Carrillo Gil, Mexico City/INBA 16980.

Fig. 42 · **Dynamited Train**, 1926–28, ink over graphite on paper, Philadelphia Museum of Art; purchased with the Lola Downing Peck Fund from Carl and Laura Zigrosser Collection, 1976; 1976-97-31.

formally inaugurated in October 1929.[202] It had a permanent display of Orozco's work, although at its inauguration there was an exhibition by Thomas Hart Benton as well. There was also a "little Greek room" with icons and Persian rugs.[203] It was, notwithstanding Mrs. Sikelianos's absence, a characteristically Delphic center.

Delphic Studios survived the Depression. It was, for Orozco, an effective showcase for his work. Alma Reed's representation allowed him to obtain or consolidate three commissions to paint frescoes in the United States, in addition to others he turned down.[204] It is worth mentioning that Delphic Studios also mounted exhibitions of other Mexican artists' work[205] and eventually published some books, among them an important catalog of Orozco's work.[206] Despite these considerable successes, the relationship was not without its problems. The painter's wife, Margarita Valladares, remembered many years later: "At first there was some confusion between them because Mrs. Reed expected Orozco to produce works of the same type as he had produced in Mexico, that is, revolutionary scenes, Mexican landscapes, etc., but he felt the need to renew himself with the stimuli that surrounded him.... The exhibitions in that gallery confused critics. The scenes of executions, hangings, blood and violence were out of place next to the less stormy New York scenes."[207]

Although the painter is likely to have complained in these terms to his wife, this testimony must be taken with a grain of salt. In her biography of Orozco, which primarily focuses on his New York years, Reed gives no indication of any such fondness for the exotic and even takes the painter's side in his argument with Diego Rivera.[208] Delphic Studios, with its Eastern paraphernalia, must surely have led visitors to expect exhibitions full of exoticism, but we have already seen how the Delphic Circle was precisely an effort to unite cosmopolitanism and nationalism. It was, as we have seen,

Orozco himself who hastened to consolidate his "Mexican" image.

Other conflicts are seen through his correspondence. In his letters, Orozco constantly complains of the loans his promoter had to take in order to keep up the gallery and that its opening had led him to break with the Weyhe Gallery, which was selling his prints.[209] In the middle of the Depression the painter reflected: "[Y]ou will understand that without the famous gallery, it would have been impossible for me to have the success I have had, and if the present is rather bad, the future, the near future, appears quite bright."[210] Orozco returned to Mexico in 1934. By then the Galería de Arte Mexicano, for years the primary gallery in Mexico, virtually the only one, had been established.[211] He held exhibitions and doubtless sold artwork. I have no data to suggest that state sponsorship was more lucrative than sales, but I can say that as far as public opinion was concerned, it had a determined effect. Orozco continued to receive commissions to paint murals, practically all of them from government institutions.[212] In 1940 he returned briefly to New York to paint the six movable panels of *Dive Bomber and Tank* (fig. 233) in the highly politicized context of the *Twenty Centuries of Mexican Art* exhibition at the Museum of Modern Art. This exhibition was sponsored by Nelson Rockefeller as part of a vast project of rapprochement between the two countries that was very similar to the one begun by Ambassador Morrow.[213] In 1943 the artist was named a founding member of the Colegio Nacional.[214] That academy's members were responsible for delivering lectures each year, but Orozco preferred to present a yearly exhibition at its facilities. From then on the annual exhibition at the Colegio Nacional continued to mark the stages of his career, except in 1947, when the recently founded National Institute for the Fine Arts organized a retrospective exhibition—also "national"—in his honor.[215] In a country whose regime was consolidating itself almost permanently, everything began to be seen as "national," and Orozco had an important place in that discourse.

Nonetheless, we may be sure that he learned quite a bit from his New York experience. After his return to Mexico, he was better able to negotiate between the different state discourses and the universalism of his own work. He painted his most important frescoes between 1936 and 1939 in Guadalajara, and for this he began a fruitful dialogue concerning the situation of the state of Jalisco in the nationalist consciousness of his time. To a great extent, his Mexican work after returning from New York is a constant debate between the national, the regional, and the universal.

Biography

Whoever wishes to write Orozco's biography will face a difficult task. Except for a couple of letters to his daughter, Lucrecia, he is nonexistent as a character.[216] Practically none of his texts reveals his inner life, his feelings, his intimate sadnesses or joys. His autobiography is the first art history text that deals with his work and its historical context, but it has very little to say about him personally. Within this category, Alma Reed's book *Orozco* is a mediocre hagiography. I know of no text that achieves any depth in this regard, which, in truth, is not central to his painting. This is why Octavio Paz considers him rather limited: "Limited because in his painting I find many things missing: the sun, the sea, the tree and its fruits, smiles, caresses, an embrace."[217]

Orozco's *An Autobiography* is a narrative that follows many of the conventions of picaresque literature; its protagonist is defined by an extreme individualism and recounts his adventures with such raw cynicism that he seems almost ingenuous. Orozco wanders through the high and the low like Lazarillo de Tormes, sees tyrants and canonized

saints up close though he has also passed through slums and practiced the most improbable trades.

Orozco traveled to New York to "break the piñata," as we say in Mexico. The first few months of his stay were anything but pleasant. Phillip Russel visited him in 1928 and found him deeply depressed. He lived very uncomfortably in a poorly lit basement. "Lack of facility in English, the absence of friends and the dense middle-class neighborhood had got on his nerves....He was given to long silences and to questions he was apt to say just yes or no. He had a way of baring his teeth like an old wolf when he was bored or annoyed."[218] Shortly after his arrival in New York, he considered becoming a commercial artist, "that is, drawing or painting advertisements...it would be very sad to come to that, but it would have been worse to die of hunger."[219] It is not clear that the options Brenner and Tablada had offered him had been closed, but he hastened to distance himself from both of them.[220] Reed's recollections suggest he was in a state of intense nostalgia, as much for his country as for his family,[221] alternating with moments of excitement. His letters to his wife confirm the unpredictability of his moods: Sometimes he reviews his "successes," other times he complains of tiredness, of lack of money, or even of having to write and paint "with only one hand!"[222]

Orozco did not like the self-portrait he painted shortly after arriving in New York ("very bad and Rembrandtesque") and even refused to admit having painted it (fig. 43).[223] This oil painting employs intense chiaroscuro and an earthy palette. Presented neatly dressed and in a three-quarter pose, the painter wears a grim expression. Orozco did not use a white preparatory ground for the painting and restricted the use of light tones. He painted the portrait in a moment of loneliness and introspection. His "successes" led him down other paths, all of them incompatible with any form of introspection, and even Reed was surprised that the oil painting

57

Drama (fig. 44) contained personal content. In her opinion, this was the result of a rejection by the writer Julia Peterkin, whose portrait he also painted (fig. 63).[224] Of his trip to Europe, in 1932, we have his own description in his autobiography: agile, charming, and superficial. Perhaps Orozco went with the hope of making the grand tour, but he soon realized it was no longer possible. "When the tourists arrive in the spring the inhabitants of picturesque places arrange their fraudulent stage settings in the very streets, don the garb of a century ago and expose the stores of furniture and other objects described in novels."[225] A Mexican who hated North American tourists could hardly fail to notice scenery and costumes.

It was his only trip to Europe. He tells, in his autobiography, an anecdote about "some very famous Chinese artists" who, after traveling throughout Europe, declared that Raphael's cartoons were the greatest works of art they had ever seen. "So on arriving I went directly to the Victoria and Albert Museum of Industrial Arts, and I saw for myself that the Chinese artists were right."[226] The apparent haste and frivolity with which he narrates his trip bear witness to a new awareness or, rather, a choice. Orozco would not try to directly involve himself in the European scene (later projects to paint in the USSR and in Rome failed).[227] Henceforth he would situate himself on the American continent and what he saw as its epic history, in order to reflect upon the world scene. In his autobiography, the description of his frescoes at Dartmouth College directly follows the narration of his European trip. The text ends suddenly a few pages later with his return to Mexico.[228] The Dartmouth College murals inaugurated a new world consciousness in his work. At the New School for Social Research and in many other works, he had referred to the idea of the world in general; however, something had been missing: point of view, defined in the Baker Library frescoes as "American." It is not surprising that, during a

brief return in 1936, he received a warm ovation from the members of the Congress of American Artists.[229]

A decade later, reflecting on Orozco's work and World War II, the historian Edmundo O'Gorman mused regarding the 1944 painting *Victory* (fig. 45):

> But now the great war in the West has become, as it could not help but do, the explicit subject of his artistic intuition and his concern as a man of America; and faced with the bold paintings in which Orozco reveals to us his peculiar way of sensing and portraying the great catastrophe, whose suggestions had gathered for some time like a distant rumor, barely attracting our attention, are now deep and articulate voices, so pregnant with prophetic and enlightened meaning that they cannot be ignored. Because if Orozco is the voice of America that cries out, then what is America?[230]

The opposition between the national and the universal had changed radically. Despite his disagreements with nearly all his patrons and agents, Orozco had had a productive exchange with each of them. Faced with his work, we may recall Anita

Fig. 43 · **Self-Portrait**, 1928, oil on canvas, Museo de Arte Carrillo Gil, Mexico City/INBA 50255.

Fig. 44 · **Drama**, 1930, oil on canvas, private collection, courtesy Galería Arvil, Mexico City.

Brenner's ironic consciousness, the Sikelianoses' universalism, Van Noppen's apocalyptic poems, Emily Hamblen's Blakean fascination, and, no less than all those intellectual relationships, the painter's persistent misogyny. Thanks to the changes he had experienced, the discussions in which he had participated, all those signs of vitality that the history of art so often subsumes under the dubious and passive category of "influences," the relationship between the national and the universal was no longer merely a problem of identity. Orozco had understood that identities are historical constructions (he had seen several in the process of formation). Together with the problem of being, there was now a more modest one, of perspective. One does not belong to an identity: One looks out from it.

Orozco returned to Mexico in 1934, temporarily, Reed thought. In 1935 she assured A. Washington Pezet of the American Artists Group that Orozco would be in Mexico only "temporarily for the painting of the fresco in the National Theatre and to visit

his mother."[231] Pious as these reasons might have sounded, Orozco did not attempt to return to the United States for many years.[232] In 1940 he stayed briefly in New York, and from there he wrote to his wife that Delphic Studios had just closed and that everyone was calling Alma Reed a "crook." He reported that he had run into her on the street and found her "pitiful" and that he refused to answer her calls. In spite of this, it seems he continued to see her because he even assured his wife that she smelled bad, "something like a dead dog." He referred sardonically to her as "Deepest to you."[233] Shortly thereafter, Orozco told Inés Amor that Reed had made unauthorized impressions of his lithographs.[234] We know this from his private correspondence, published many years later.

Nostalgia is the dominant note in his subsequent trips to New York. In 1940, during his brief stay to paint *Dive Bomber and Tank,* he wrote to his wife: "[S]ometimes I forget that I am here under different conditions, and I walk through the streets

59

suffering just as when I had only a quarter for lunch."[235] On this same trip he met the historian Justino Fernández, who said of him: "I remember how much he used to like the vigorous masses of the New York skyscrapers, particularly at nightfall, when their contrasting profiles make the urban landscape dramatic."[236]

Orozco made one last attempt to establish himself in New York between September 1945 and March 1946,[237] in the company of the Mexican ballerina Gloria Campobello.[238] His letters show profound displeasure. The Mexican fad and the variety of North American realisms were on the verge of falling from public favor. "I'm tired of my own clownings and those of the School of Paris. At a dinner I met Dalí and his wife Gala. It's better not to speak of one's neighbor. He's doing the same thing I am. I'm guilty of the same sins as he...

In this New York it is hard to work, everything turns into dinners, cocktails, dances, meetings, running around, shows, interminable lectures, atomic bomb, gas light, et cetera, et cetera, you know."[239]

We know of few paintings from this last trip to Manhattan. Most are dance hall scenes that are reminiscent of Covarrubias's *Negro Drawings* and the Antibes drawings of Picasso (whose work interested Orozco during the 1940s). The most important document we have from those months is his 1946 self-portrait in the collection of the Museo Carrillo Gil (fig. 46). Significantly, it is one of the few paintings the painter dated, and it also indicates the place where it was painted, "NY." His style here is far from the blurry monumental figures of recent years. The painter appears clearly delineated against a background of sharp geometric light and shadow. He also appears to be a man younger than his

Fig. 45 · **Victory**, 1944, oil on canvas, Museo de Arte Carrillo Gil, Mexico City/INBA 17291.

Fig. 46 · **Self-Portrait**, 1946, oil on canvas, Museo de Arte Carrillo Gil, Mexico City/INBA 17300.

sixty-three years, in sharp contrast with his appearance in photographs from this period. Nor does he
have the fierceness of some of his other self-portraits;
it is, like the one from 1928, a formal jacket and tie
self-portrait. It is also a lucid autobiographical
reflection and one of his few truly personal paintings. In early 1930s New York he had become
acquainted with the purest and least symmetrical
styles, as well as geometries and chiaroscuros; he
had admired the city scenery, which in this painting
is now indecipherable through the window. He had
constructed a place for himself. Fifteen years later,
the New York panorama had changed enough that
this place now appeared anachronistic, so that
Orozco could no longer attempt to reconstruct it,
but only to evoke it.

Public Painting and Private Painting: Easel Paintings, Drawings, Graphic Arts, and Mural Studies

Renato González Mello

The Mexican muralists are known as such because they affirmed the ethical, political, and aesthetic superiority of mural painting over *pintura de caballete* ("easel painting"). The painters proposed this rigid distinction in their 1923 *Manifesto del Sindicato de Obreros Técnicos Pintores y Escultores:*

> We *repudiate* so-called easel painting and all the art of ultra-intellectual circles because it is aristocratic, and we glorify the expression of *Monumental Art* because it is a public possession. We proclaim that any aesthetic expression alien or opposite to the popular sensitivity is bourgeois and should disappear, since it contributes to the perversion of our race's taste.... We *proclaim* that since this social movement is one of transition between a decrepit order and a new one…the creators of beauty must put forth their utmost efforts to make their production of ideological value to the people, and the ideal goal of art, which now is an expression of individualistic masturbation, should be one of beauty for all, of education and of battle.[1]

The muralists never tired of declaring that their true production was public and mural. Siqueiros called his easel paintings artistic gymnastics (*gimnasia plástica*), and Orozco, shortly after his arrival in the United States, said: "The highest, the most logical, the purest and strongest form of painting is the mural. In this form alone, it is one with the other arts—with all the others. It is, too, the most disinterested form, for it cannot be made a matter of private gain; it cannot be hidden away for the benefit of a certain few."[2]

In this text, Orozco summarized the Mexican artists' expectations regarding mural painting. Not only did he claim citizenship for the muralist, but painting itself would regain, in its mural form, citizenship in the republic of the arts. In mural painting, there is a desire for totality. Orozco

repeated: "It is for the people. It is for ALL."[3] Easel painting could not aspire to this totality. But the muralists did not end this often rejected practice. From muralism's manifestos, one might infer that smaller formats hampered integration among the arts or between the arts and the people; one might also infer that easel painting was a freer, more personal, even avant-garde practice, supposedly devoid of the rhetorical obligations that public painting entailed.[4] It was this perspective on things that led Octavio Paz, in his praise of some pumpkins Siqueiros had painted, to observe: "They are compositions from which two flaws of nearly all his work are absent: gesturing and eloquence. They are forms, simply *forms,* which emit a highly concentrated emotion."[5]

The problem, however, is more complicated than that. The division between mural painting and easel painting is based on an ideological division between the public and the private. The Mexican Revolution had substantially modified the boundaries between these two spheres, shrinking the sphere of private property and expanding the boundaries of public property. If this change was at times only rhetorical, this is precisely why the eminently political discussion of the nature of property and the scope of public power took on renewed importance. For this reason, the defense of mural painting as public property placed the foundations of the artistic discussion on this very division between public and private, which was seen as theoretically irreducible. But this rhetorical structure brought with it many areas of ambiguity, where the frontier of the "public" was not clearly defined. Murals, for example, often drew upon an esoteric code that restricted their public character.[6] In fact, not all the practices different from mural painting were thought to oppose it. Siqueiros and, beginning in the 1930s, the members of the Taller de Gráfica Popular gave graphic production at least as much importance as mural painting.[7] Yet despite these undefined and often debated areas, the muralists were taken as such to the end of their lives and maintained the radical difference between one practice and the other as though it were a matter of parallel worlds between which communication was impossible. This strict theoretical difference allowed for critical reflection on the two supposedly opposed practices. In his manifesto, Orozco referred to mural painting as "the purest…form of painting…the most disinterested form." This is a complete and deliberate inversion of terms: Easel painting was presented as impure ("an expression of individualistic masturbation," "a matter of private gain"), whereas mural painting on public buildings, at once admonitory and political, was presented as pure.[8] This theoretical difference also generated an intense debate on the techniques, genres, particularities, and correspondences between mural painting and its alternatives, including the possibility that each of these practices could solve problems that originated in its opposite.

The muralists, especially the famous Siqueiros, Rivera, and Orozco, had been educated in a school of fine arts that retained many of the practices of the nineteenth-century academies.[9] But fresco painting, which was used for mural decoration, was not part of that education, and in the muralists' testimonies there is no mention of any academic work with techniques of engraving or lithography.[10] Their reinvention of these techniques, together with the compositional demands of large-format historical painting, caused them to question and then to transform the themes and modalities they employed in smaller formats.

This essay will address the easel painting, drawings, and prints that Orozco completed while in the United States and will consider the extraordinarily intricate links between mural and easel painting. At the outset it is necessary to define the meanings that two additional problems, which will be mentioned repeatedly in the following pages, had for Orozco. The first is the problem posed by the notion of style and the history of styles. The second is the close conceptual relationship between mural painting and architecture.

For Orozco, style was evidence of the individual and irreducible: It was opposed to any premeditation and could not be taught; it did not reveal affinities among painters and could not even be used to compare them. To understand this mentality, a bit of history is necessary. Recalling his years at the academy in his autobiography, Orozco refers to the abandonment of traditional drawing methods. Since the eighteenth century, students at the Academy of San Carlos had been forced to follow a tortuous path in learning to draw. They began by copying their professors' engravings or drawings and later used as models the plaster copies that the school had acquired since its founding. Then they were allowed to copy from life with human models. Finally, they were able to initiate their own compositions. In each of these steps, they were obliged to go from the simple to the complex: First, they copied such details as hands or feet, and only later, entire figures. With some variations, including the use of photography as a "witness" against which to gauge what they drew, this pedagogical mode lasted from the academy's founding until Alfredo Ramos Martínez took charge in 1913.[11]

In 1903 the Pillet system had been instituted at the academy. It taught drawing by beginning with plane geometric figures, then moving on to prisms illuminated by a lamp from different angles. The objects were copied from life, although the drawing of human figures continued to begin with plaster copies and photographs. Also in 1903 the Catalan professor Antonio Fabres began a new teaching method that favored drawing from live models in different positions and from different perspectives.[12] Fabrés gave more importance to live-model drawing than to the arduous traditional path to drawing human anatomy. According to several accounts, after his departure the students in his workshop "substantially" modified his teaching technique: "Our models no longer stayed in the same position day after day. Drawing was still conscientious, but it was done rapidly, to train hand and eye. Our new exercises consisted in little by little reducing the time spent in copying from life until we could make the swiftest rough drafts, in less than a minute, and later we began to draw and paint from a model in motion. There were no longer any photographs with which to compare our efforts, and the necessary simplification of the instantaneous sketch *brought out the personal style in each student.*"[13]

In his pioneering article on Orozco, José Juan Tablada confirms the procedure: "He would tell me that he had drawn a great deal from life at the School of Fine Arts, but now, avoiding 'academicism,' he only studied models in motion, taking impressions, observations, storing them away to paint them later."[14] Doctor Atl, who was not formally a professor at the academy, but certainly was an important example for its students,[15] boasted that he would draw from memory.[16] We know that, in his first years in New York, Orozco drew several sketches of "Park Avenue types" in a notebook.[17] In 1931 Orozco suggested to Jorge Juan Crespo de la Serna, his assistant at Pomona, that he "go out to the street with pencil and paper and draw from life and also from memory. Pretend that you are a student at the Academy, under the watchful eye of an academic teacher. And you will see that the result will be anything but academic."[18] It was supposed that speed, economy of resources, and lack of reflection would prevent the student from modifying whatever his personality might dictate. The drawing was only partly the result of its author's observation of a model. Memory and character were to prevail over skill, over style, and over the conventional manner of representation that was taught in the academies. "Draw only taking the natural as a guide, and without attempting 'style,' but sincerely, just as you *feel* things."[19] The purpose of this ritual was to avoid the deformation imposed by educational systems and their academic prints or plaster figures, which were frequently still copied during Orozco's time. Reason was to be suspended so that it would yield to character.

Siqueiros had had a similar education.[20] Diego Rivera, on the other hand, had received a more orthodox training.[21] Perhaps because of this, in the 1940s he remembered his travels through Europe as though narrating an episode of contagion: "He went off to Spain, where the clash between Mexican tradition, the example of older painting, and modern Spanish environment and production, working upon his timidity, which had been taught out of respect for Europe, disoriented him, making him produce detestable paintings, far inferior to those done by him in Mexico prior to leaving for Europe...."[22] This was a point of view different from Orozco's, for whom the academic "Mexican tradition" could be considered "detestable" as well. But despite their differences, both painters conceived style to be something antithetical to their training, the opposite of the academy and what it represented.

This is not the place to analyze the manner and degree to which humanist art theory survived in that

Fig. 47 · **Lying in Wait**, 1913–15, watercolor on paper, Museo de Arte Carrillo Gil, Mexico City/INBA 17212.

institution.[23] It is significant, however, that it was still referred to by its eighteenth-century name, the Academia de San Carlos, the San Carlos Academy. When Orozco was a student there, it had been renamed in terms whose administrative modernity was consistent with other, far deeper changes, Escuela Nacional de Bellas Artes, the National School of Fine Arts.[24] Orozco and Siqueiros participated, between 1911 and 1913, in a long student protest to transform the teaching methods for drawing. In 1913, when Alfredo Ramos Martínez began an "open-air school" for nonconforming students that he named Barbizon, Orozco did not join the resulting project for stylistic renewal: "Out in the open air, the Barbizonians were painting very pretty land-scapes, with the requisite violets for the shadows and Nile green for the skies, but I preferred black and the colors exiled from impressionist palettes. Instead of red and yellow twilight, I painted the pestilent shadows of closed rooms, and instead of the Indian male, drunken ladies and gentlemen"[25] (fig. 47).

Again, it is important to pay attention to the terms of the opposition. Orozco presents the matter as a strictly individual decision, a struggle of "me" against "them." And true style, in this binary opposition, could only belong to "me." But years later, when he found himself in a "syndicate" that promoted "public" art, his point of view would necessarily find itself in crisis, as happened to him in New York. This was especially true since mural painting had, for the muralists, special conditions. Not only should it express some form of ethical, political, and social commitment, but its composition should be program-matic.[26] Above all, mural painting had to be consis-tent with architecture. Its structure and forms should not conflict with those of the buildings. It was, to use the precise term, "decoration." In the 1940s Manuel Rodríguez Lozano complained bitterly of those who had abandoned this dogma, which for him was still entirely valid:

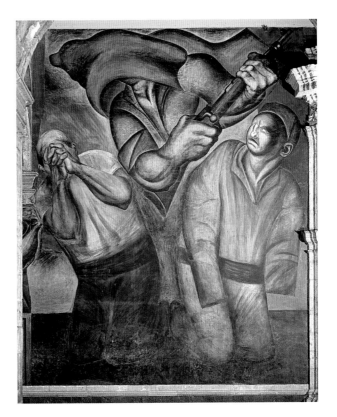

Mexico's modern muralists have made a funda-mental mistake, trying to pull up the radish by its leaves. Like tenors, they want to move to center stage and stand out over everything. Forgetting architecture, forgetting that buildings are constructed on a human scale, they decorate them with figures measuring four meters or more and annihilate the arch's grandeur, the building's majesty. They do not take into account the construction material, its tone or color, and they invade walls with garish colors. They forget that the first law for decorating a building is to submit to its architectural laws, the tone of its construction, so that the decoration may be, in this case, a complement to the architecture.[27]

Fig. 48 · **Revolutionary Trinity**
(second version), 1926, fresco,
National Preparatory School, Mexico
City, photograph by Bob Schalkwijk.

65

Yet that is exactly what was thought and practiced in the 1920s. In his murals at the National Preparatory School in Mexico City, Orozco had shown great respect for the old colonial building. Even in those panels that referred to some form of destruction, his figures hunched over to fit into arches and the imposts of the vaults as though to buttress them; their hands linked over the keystones of arches (fig. 48). This care can still be seen in *Prometheus* at Pomona College (fig. 110).

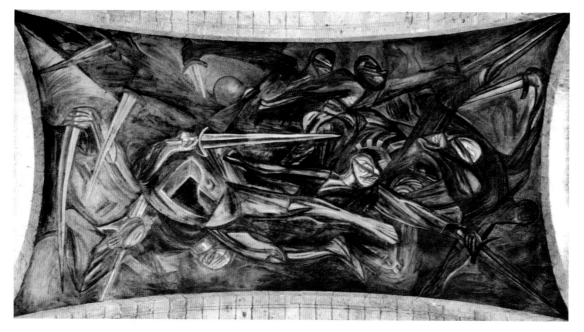

Fig. 49 · **Scenes from the War**, 1937–39, fresco, Hospicio Cabañas, Guadalajara, photograph by Rubén Páez Kano.

Fig. 50 · Courtyard view of Orozco's frescoes, 1923–26, National Preparatory School, Mexico City, photograph by Bob Schalkwijk.

Although the hero's body is somewhat disjointed, his thick legs and torso seem to support the Gothic arch in which they are inscribed. At the New School for Social Research, Orozco painted a composition based on Dynamic Symmetry, a mathematical ratio similar to the golden section that, when finished, superseded the building's proportions and disrupted and divided the continuous panel of the wall (the Preparatory School also had long panels, but Orozco did nothing like this). In 1947, reflecting on his mural painting, he affirmed that murals could be painted in two ways:

a) conserving the architecture
b) destroying the architecture

In contemporary Mexican murals, both can be found. It is not that one is good, and the other bad....[28] (fig. 49)

Such a statement would have been unthinkable twenty years earlier, when the only "good" painting was that which conserved the architecture.

Siqueiros appears, in this respect, close to Orozco in his premises (if not in his outcomes). In *Cómo se pinta un mural* ("How to Paint a Mural," 1951), he prescribed for budding muralists the obligation to "consider geometrically" the architectural structure, removing, if necessary, "coats and layers" accumulated throughout the centuries so that the new decoration could interact with the structure.[29]

But Siqueiros also considered the interaction between the architectural space and its occupants. In his numerous writings on the subject, he maintained that the observation of mural painting was a dynamic act; in fact, it was the spectator's movement that created the space of both painting and architecture.[30] What Orozco and Siqueiros had in common was a vision of architecture that overlooked decoration and typologies, instead placing the buildings' artistic and symbolic value solely in their structural elements. The muralists' compositions, even their

palettes, should interact with the buildings' skeleton and materials. In a 1928 article, Jean Charlot had this in mind when describing the painter's palette at the National Preparatory School, "with the dense earth reds below, the medium grays of the mezzanine and the atmospheric pinks and blues of the top floors"³¹ (fig. 50). The "dense earth reds below" corresponded to the *tezontle*.³² "The medium grays of the mezzanine" were meant to prevent the dissolution of the three-story building's solidness: There had to be a gradual succession of shades, not an abrupt contrast that would impose a new order on the existing structure. Finally, the last floor had no additional weight or structure upon it. A spectator who viewed the whole from the facing balcony, across the patio from where the frescoes were, would have seen the sky above the "atmospheric pinks and blues" used to reinforce this ascending feeling. With similar purposes in mind, Diego Rivera decorated the mezzanine of the Secretariat for Public Education with grisaille.³³

The importance of architectural analysis in the muralists' work was more than simply pragmatic. At times Rivera participated in the design or remodeling of the buildings he decorated, as in the National Stadium and the secretariat; he was even allowed to design a couple himself. Though Orozco lacked such pretensions, his urban landscapes are a critical reflection on architecture. That these landscapes seldom appeared in his murals, and almost never with such polemical character, is a consequence of the conceptual division between "mural" and "easel."

Lessons in Art History

The foregoing was a partial, schematic vision of the terms in which the muralists discussed their art. Here we shall look at how Orozco, using those premises, tried to interpret the North American and international painting he saw in New York and how his own artistic practice led him to reformulate them.

The first things that must be considered are his visits to museums. During his earlier stay in the United States he had surely walked through several, but what he saw and reflected upon in 1928 is minutely recorded in his letters to Jean Charlot. It is clear that he moved through the halls of the Metropolitan Museum of Art with the spirit of an artisan who goes to study the secrets of his colleagues, especially their use of color. His sympathies and differences are extremely significant: "Renoir impressed me very much, I liked him exceptionally well";³⁴ "the Goya who turns the impasto of color into craft";³⁵ "I went every morning for a week to study Cézanne";³⁶ Seurat: "One feels guilty and sinful in the presence of his light-filled picture";³⁷ Velázquez: "If to paint is to put colors on a surface, only his equals can do it with the same mastery and perfection";³⁸ Titian: "a great man, the living, enduring past";³⁹ Villon: "small, clear, very simple pictures."⁴⁰ Despite having backgrounds similar to Orozco, two artists inspired great disdain in him: "What idiot said that Toulouse-Lautrec was a painter—or even a magazine illustrator? Constantin Guys annoys me."⁴¹ His admiration for Villon, Seurat, Cézanne, Velázquez, his contempt for Monet and Degas ("Monet with his market of cheap flowers"),⁴² his enthusiasm for Renoir, which gradually waned ("The second or third time one sees Renoir, he disappoints. Why?"),⁴³ all brought him to a sudden revelation: "A man standing painted by Cézanne. And another painted by Manet. The former is planted on the ground as solidly as a rock. The latter is falling...."⁴⁴ At the same time, Orozco showed a growing admiration for Picasso (December: "I tried desperately to be enthusiastic but couldn't"; January: "[H]e disconcerts, disquiets, wounds, impassions, repels, and then attracts vigorously"; March: "[He] is like a glass of fresh, pure water").⁴⁵ But after indulging himself in these comparisons, he noticed the narrative underlying the museum's installation, a discourse with which he was not sympathetic:

67

"In the Metropolitan Museum, there are rooms and rooms, but the curious thing is this: among the American paintings you suddenly find a Cézanne, then more Americans, then another Cézanne, and then a Pissarro and then Claude Monet, and in other exhibitions they are mixed in with Picasso and Dufy and other French artists. I don't know why they do this, because only a blind man can confuse the one with the other."[46] He boldly dismissed this underlying narrative, which he thought of as opposing artistic practice. Thus he would end up embalming and burying the impressionists: "They are all right in the *history* of art, but I don't know what they have to do with *Art*."[47] He became acquainted with an official art history in which schisms and differences appeared very muted.[48] Orozco's practice was to go to the museum and paint in his studio. The boundary between the public and the private had changed. This was an artistic transformation at once so radical and so subtle that he became aware of its importance only when he returned to Mexico and considered the sites of his earlier activity: the street and the classrooms of the academy.[49] In the latter, of course, different ideas concerning the historical legitimacy of the arts were taught.[50] What was not taught was the idea of art history as an autonomous whole, a coherent progression in spite of its gaps, one that could be read by artists in museum halls as a succession of styles. The painter himself would be surprised by the news: "And I don't know what the devil I'm doing in art *Criticism,* damn it!"[51]

It is thus quite natural that he should have expressed interest in Franz Roh's book *Realismo mágico*.[52] This German critic was a contemporary of Gustav Hartlaub, the writer who had coined the concept of new objectivity to refer to certain Weimar-era German painters, particularly those who were the most socially critical. Roh reacted against the supposed exteriority of this characterization and proposed the concept of magical realism to reassert the dominion of art over reality.[53] The distinctive

Fig. 51 · **The Dead**, 1931, oil on canvas, Museo de Arte Carrillo Gil, Mexico City/INBA 17268.

element in his book was that he refused to erase the past and insisted on seeing the succession of styles in a historical dimension of different rhythms.[54] Determined to find a time beyond ruptures and manifestos, Roh thus conceived of an evolution that began with impressionism, went through expressionism, and arrived at postexpressionism.

The key was in "expressionism." Roh seems to have understood this term in its original sense, referring generally to modernist painting after impressionism.[55] It encompassed works that are now called expressionist, together with cubist, futurist, and fauvist pieces. Expressionism had been a demonic "irrationalism."[56] In it, objects moved about disjointedly, constantly threatening to jump out at the viewer, proclaiming a hard-line subjectivism. Postexpressionism effectively sought a "new objectivity." After the storm, "the polished rock emerged,"[57] and men, purified, had reconciled themselves with reality. "From this point of view, those concepts of discipline, purity, cosmic equilibrium, devotion and pacification are rediscovered that, consciously or unconsciously, had found their way into the new paintings."[58] Demonic irrationalism had been replaced by a "magical *rationalism*"[59] in which, as in the Renaissance, paintings constituted a parallel reality that nonetheless served to dominate the world: "magical because of its reverence toward that 'rational' ordering of the world, as though it were miraculous, and upon which it founds and builds, or vigorously rejects any anarchist attempt against that ordering. (This includes, of course, the zealotry of the left and the right, in those artists who dabble in politics.)"[60] Roh saw this as a foundational rupture.[61]

Orozco studied Roh's text conscientiously. On one page of his notebooks, he transcribed the table that appears at the end of *Realismo mágico* and compares the characteristics of expressionism and postexpressionism (fig. 275).[62] This reading led Orozco to take sides. Surely the most significant of all his New York paintings, *The Dead* (1931 [fig. 51]) shows a debacle of skyscrapers twisted, cut in pieces, and laid out by a powerful and irrational force. For intuitive contemplation to replace rationalist observation, and for a communion with things to be achieved, a considerable dose of violence has been necessary. Using Roh's terms, as Orozco did, this would be a deliberately expressionist painting. "[E]xpressionism must have been felt as something crashing in from outer space. Now, not only the fluid parts of the world, but the world itself, the vast continent and the earth's firmest foundations shook."[63] *The Dead* has a precise iconographic

source. Roh devoted an extensive reflection to Paul Citroën's *Metropolis* (1923 [fig. 52]):

> Whoever can penetrate, without prejudices, the intense magic of that piling up of the global metropolis will have difficulty extracting himself from the nearly unending effect it produces. Just as an aesthetic once was born of Laocoon, so should there be derived from here the aesthetic of a new time, an aesthetic that would oppose, firstly, absolute objectivity to formal objectivity and, secondly, the division into pieces of organic composition. For this piling up, now abrupt, now soft, of pieces rigorously related amongst themselves by the object, by space, by placement, but all of them completely finished, independent and closed unto themselves, can develop a sense that we shall never find in an organicist composition.[64]

Fig. 52 · Paul Citroën, **Metropolis**, 1923, collage, Prentenkabinet der Universiteit Leiden, © 2002 Artists Rights Society (ARS), New York/Beeldrecht, Amsterdam.

69

Fig. 53 · **Queensboro Bridge, New York**, 1928, oil on canvas, Museo de Arte Carrillo Gil, Mexico City/INBA 17241.

Fig. 54 · **Eighth Avenue**, 1928, private collection, courtesy Sotheby's.

70

Orozco's painting is the complete opposite. Roh thought that this "new Laocoon" was the symptom of an age that rejected all rhetoric, all baroque artifice. *The Dead* revisits the expressionist topic of the "world city,"[65] stressing its apocalyptic and, therefore, baroque implications.

Roh proposed an alternative to the usual narration of modern art criticism that had troubled Orozco in his visit to the museum. Magical realism is built upon the Bergsonian notion of becoming, a conception of time in history that avoids the linearity of positivism and historicism.[66] Although it is improbable that Orozco would have delved deeply into Bergson's intuitionism (as some Mexican intellectuals did during the revolution),[67] the theosophic notion of a space of *n* dimensions, which was also opposed to linear time, and the knowledge of Nietzsche that he received from Emily Hamblen[68] provided him with a frame of reference with which to understand the scope of Roh's theoretical postu-

lates. The latter's notion of realism (a magical art to dominate reality) was closely related to esoteric thought. But as his notes' comparative table shows, Orozco was most interested in the possibility of understanding the formal characteristics of modern art in a system of oppositions that went beyond each painter, like Picasso, or each movement, like impressionism. In sum, what he was interested in was the possibility of a holistic, universalizing, though not teleological, interpretation. And this effort yielded him a new frame of reference for thinking about "style" as a problem located between the extremes of individual expression and a world history that took place over an extraordinarily long evolutionary time frame. This allowed his painting to be transformed; *The Dead* gives evidence of that transformation.

But the foregoing is too narrow an interpretation for such a complex painting. It is not merely that Orozco should have chosen, in this case, Roh's

71

Fig. 55 · **New York Factory, Williamsburg**, 1928, oil on canvas, private collection, courtesy Galería Arvil, Mexico City.

Fig. 56 · **Fourteenth Street, Manhattan**, 1928–29, oil on canvas, private collection, photograph by Bob Schalkwijk.

Architecture and Democracy

In his manifesto "New World, New Races and New Art" (1929), Orozco writes: "Already, the architecture of Manhattan is a new value…[it] is the first step. Painting and sculpture must certainly follow as inevitable second steps."[69] Orozco made that architecture the object of his landscapes since his arrival. In 1928 he painted *Queensboro Bridge, New York*; *Eighth Avenue*; *New York Factory, Williamsburg*; and *Fourteenth Street* (figs. 53, 54, 55, and 56). One might speculate that these paintings led to the writing of the manifesto, but text and painting are difficult to compare. Although the bridge in *Queensboro Bridge* can be seen as a civilizing artifact, it appears in the painting as a compositional element. There is no human activity, as if painting the building were a matter of archaeological precision. The on-ramp and the bridge's foundations oppose the vertical structure that holds up the tensors. The structure as a whole opposes the dense wintry atmosphere, true in all of these paintings. On one hand, it is evident that Orozco was trying to turn "the impasto of color into craft," as he had said of Goya. But in *Queensboro Bridge* there is the purpose of imposing the composition on the craft. The chimney rationalizes space: It gives the space a center while opposing it to the bridge. The density of the atmosphere is no more than a secondary device. In this regard, it is very significant that Orozco wrote to Jean Charlot of a painting that had been returned to him: "They ruined my poor picture because they decided to put it in an old frame that was smaller and they didn't hesitate to cut it! You can cut an impressionist picture in any way you choose, but you will ruin one based on composition if you cut it."[70]

"New World, New Races and New Art" makes an analogy between painting and architecture, and *Queensboro Bridge* does too, although more problematically. Were it not for the chimney, it would be a self-sufficient structure and a self-sufficient composition. But the composition must deal with the opposition between the bridge framework and the chimney, an element whose symbolic freight is considerable; it is a conventional emblem of evolution. As often happens in Orozco's work, this symbolic reference is not given free rein. The superimposition of the on-ramp and the foundations and the line of boundary stones at the bridge's entrance all refer to a possible rationality. But the contraposition of a barely visible underground structure with light, airy structures and an underworld with elegant surface-level technology; the impossibility

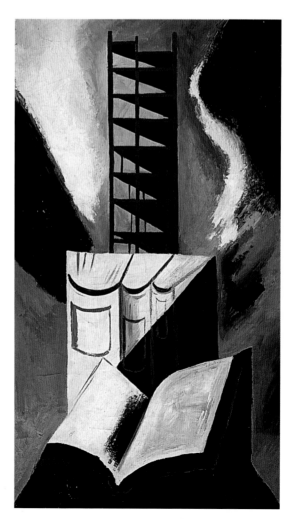

Fig. 57 · **The World's Highest Structure**, 1928–30, oil on canvas, Orozco Farias Family Collection, photograph by Rubén Orozco.

72

"expressionistic" categories. This painting's pictorial, compositional, and allegorical devices were the result of a deep ideological transformation.

of seeing the painting as an evolutionary succession; and the evidence of formal and symbolic contradictions within it make any smooth, shallowly evolutionist interpretation practically impossible. What the painting denies, in effect, is the possibility of a first impression.

While Orozco struggled with this problem in his landscapes, an important debate on architectural theory was taking place. Orozco's membership in the Delphic Circle placed him close to a disagreement that would lead him to new forms of urban landscape.

Claude Bragdon, a regular attendee to the Delphic Circle,[71] published a booklet entitled *Architecture and Democracy* in 1918. In it, he praised one of Louis Sullivan's landmark structures, the Prudential Building.

> One feels that here democracy has at last found utterance in beauty; the American spirit speaks, the spirit of the Long Denied. The rude, rectangular bulk is uncompromisingly practical and utilitarian; these rows on rows of windows, regularly spaced and all of the same size, suggest the equality and monotony of obscure, laborious lives; the upspringing shafts of the vertical piers stand for the hopes and aspirations, and the unobtrusive delicate ornament which covers the whole with a garment of fresh beauty is like the very texture of their dreams. The building is able to speak thus powerfully to the imagination because its creator is a poet and prophet of democracy. In his own chosen language he declares, as Whitman did in verse, his faith in the people of "these states"— "A Nation announcing itself."[72]

Lewis Mumford, who knew some of the Delphic Circle members and was also an important patron and critic for Orozco, differed from Bragdon. In *The Brown Decades* (1931), he criticized him explicitly:

More than anything, the mischief lay in the notion that on the foundation of practical needs the skyscraper could or should be translated into a "proud and soaring thing." This was giving the skyscraper a spiritual function to perform: whereas, in actuality, height in skyscrapers meant either a desire for centralized administration, a desire to increase ground rents, a desire for advertisements, or all three of these together—and none of these functions determines a "proud and soaring thing." It was but a step from Sullivan's conception to the grandiose and inefficient tower buildings that mark the last two decades of American skyscraper development.[73]

This was a profound disagreement. "Organic Architecture," wrote Bragdon, "is the product of some obscure inner necessity for self-expression which is sub-conscious."[74] Bragdon took this postulate even farther. For him, the symbolism was religious in nature. Art, insofar as it was symbolic, could be equated with the church's sacraments: In both cases, there was a form that referred to, and was somehow a vehicle for, a substance.[75] Mumford's ideas, on the other hand, were secular. He saw in the arts an expression of the "spirit of the times." For him, American virtues had been strengthened during World War I but had languished since its end. The same thing had happened at the end of the Civil War. "War does not bring the martial virtues into the subsequent peace: it merely prepares a richer soil for the civilian's vices."[76] There were of course exceptions: bridge-building engineers, realist painters, heroes of an epoch whose contributions had lain in the shadows for a long time. Those "brown decades" after the Civil War had been dominated, on the one hand, by the pomp and excess of the belle époque and, on the other, by the absence and negation of desire. This had been voiced by the painters, from Whistler

73

through the precisionists. "It is not Puritanism; it is not even a denial or an unconsciousness of sex; but it is a refusal to accept the earth and the sweat, the heavy tactile sense of flesh and muscle, that one finds in Rubens and Renoir. The result, so far as painting goes, is a certain tidiness of line, a certain orderliness of arrangement—the sort of tidiness and orderliness one might find in a bachelor's apartment."[77] And if George Bellows had rebelled against that frigidity with his paintings of exuberant flesh, Mumford awaited an architecture that might express the civil virtues of the United States in opposition to the ambiguous skyscrapers.

But there was more in Bragdon's theory than a celebration of height. Step-back skyscrapers, peculiar to the New York skyline, were the result of a code that banned the erection of buildings similar to single-bodied columns. Beyond a certain height, their floor areas gradually had to become smaller. This code was instituted to protect the skyline, but it also made some compare the new buildings with ziggurats, and Manhattan with a second Babylon. Bragdon said that such a building was like "a feudal baron surrounded by his vassals."[78] Mumford's critique of the American skyscraper was contrary to such hierarchical representations. From his point of view, modern architecture's excess of verticality gave buildings the pedantic appearance of classic columns, sometimes even with "base, shaft and capital." He saw in that trend a mannered style that was at odds with reality. "For one thing, the steel cage is not in itself a vertical system of construction: it is rather a system of articulated cubes. A brick wall will stand after a fire though the connecting beams have been gutted away: without its horizontal ties a steel wall must come down."[79] Bragdon analyzed buildings' structure and decoration to establish a rigorously codified symbolic value for them based largely on theosophic ideas. Mumford did not deny architecture's potential symbolic value, but he refused to interpret it with any "language" that could be codified

in a manual. Instead he pointed to the contradictions between the structure and function of buildings, over and above imaginary hierarchies. In his search for positive "American" values that architecture might express, he looked to the work and ingenuity embodied in any building—that is, to its history. He made an epic of the construction of the Brooklyn Bridge but did not take on the openly imperialistic interpretations of American architecture.

It is hard to determine how familiar Orozco was with this debate. Bragdon regularly attended Delphic Circle meetings, and Orozco knew him as the translator into English of Uspenskii's *Tertium Organum.*[80] Among Orozco's friends and acquaintances in the United States, Mumford held an important place.[81] It is clear that the Dartmouth College frescoes have much to do with Mumford's ideas, especially the section entitled *Modern Industrial Man,* in which one of the panels depicts the construction of a bridge, and another the structure, beams, and joists of a large, though not very tall, building (figs. 188–192). There is also a painting that directly shows Orozco's disenchantment with the "civilizing" meaning of Manhattan skyscrapers, *World's Highest Structure* (fig. 57). It is important, first of all, that the title should refer to "structure." Whatever his knowledge of debates concerning architecture, his loss of innocence with respect to it stemmed from a growing skepticism about the coherence between buildings' structural elements and their symbolic value. Since this belief represented something of a dogma for the muralists, a careful study of the problem is in order.

The urban landscapes Orozco painted after 1928 are very different from *Queensboro Bridge.* Though they are also large structures, they now occupy most of the pictorial surface. For example, in *Elevated* (1929–30 [fig. 58]), the construction twists and climbs over the surface; the spatial composition is not clear, nor does it take an aerial perspective; as in *Queensboro Bridge* there is an evident disproportion

Fig. 58 · **Elevated**, 1929–30, oil on canvas, Museo de Arte Carrillo Gil, Mexico City/INBA 17238.

between the stairs and the monumentality of the structure, which is thus called into question; the train station is crowned not by an elegant frame with tensors but by bristles with sharp points. The pictorial composition does not originate with the architecture but imposes itself upon it. This also happens in *The Dead,* in which the buildings no longer dictate a compositional autarchy but are instead pulled by forces presumably external to their own proportions.

Franz Roh's categories shed a good deal of light on the meaning of this transformation. At first glance, it might appear that Orozco was opting for a tormented, disproportioned art, as Roh defined "expressionism." However, a closer study leads to a different interpretation. Roh thought of painting as an *ars regia* with which to dominate the world. For this, he argued, paintings ought to be autonomous, transparent, rational spaces. Orozco also thought in these terms and was more than acquainted with their esoteric origins,[82] but his works are far from Roh's conclusions. Orozco had been moved, as had Roh, by Cézanne's apples and the construction of his space; however, this led him not to defend the rights of the object but to strike the table with his hand. It did not occur to him to "vigorously reject any anarchic threat" to the cosmic order.[83] Roh saw in postexpressionism something of the "engineering spirit."[84] Orozco may have seen himself as an engineer, but he specialized in demolition. In sum, in Roh's postexpressionism, there was a validation of the object as the origin of reason that Orozco wound up rejecting. Although he shared the notion of magic, precisely because of this he depicted the domination of things by overwhelming external forces.

Beneath this agreement-disagreement, there is yet another, deeper reason. Orozco rejected the notion of the work of art as a portable amulet and preferred the enchantments of an art whose social impact was thought to be vast. "The great abstract system of expressionism had tended more or less

toward mural painting in order to fill, with free rhythm, broad surfaces that might act effectively from a distance upon the viewer. But with post-expressionism, easel painting blossoms again, the framed painting, the easily transportable work of art...."[85] For a Mexican intellectual of the 1920s and 1930s, this choice was unthinkable, because it was inconceivable that a mural should act "from a distance" on the viewer. The nearness of things and symbols could be threatening or ridiculous, but it was an article of faith regarding the objects and

Fig. 59 · **Portrait of Eva Sikelianos**, 1928, oil on canvas, Museo de Arte Carrillo Gil, Mexico City/INBA 17244.

symbols of power and the state. Once more, the discussion revolved around the boundaries between the public and the private.

Although Roh was visibly important and allowed Orozco to take a position on matters that were new to him, the transformation in his painting is also related to his practice of painting itself. More precisely, it is related to knowledge of theories concerning a practice that he thought to be craftlike and traditional.

Civilized Women and Lamidito Portraits

In October 1928 Orozco began a portrait of Eva Sikelianos (fig. 59). "Something new, with a complicated palette and treated as a wall. The model is very interesting, she is a lady of 55, golden hair and Greek costume. A very cultivated person."[86] Eva Sikelianos was in fact precisely that; Orozco complained that there were few like her in New York, especially in the summer, when those who had the means escaped the city. "The worst thing is that the 'civilized' people go to the country, to Europe, to Mexico, anywhere. By civilized I mean the cultured people and those who have money and spend it on art."[87] To paint Sikelianos's portrait, Orozco moved his studio to his patron's apartment. Before starting, he offered a toast to Greece, its poets and artists, "among whom he courteously included Angelos Sikelianos." He approved the idea that his model should wear the self-woven Greek tunic that was her pride as well as a necklace concerning which a mysterious legend of bad luck was circulating.[88] Orozco and Reed agreed that the wealthy Eva Sikelianos, with her long locks of hair, her tunic, and her necklace, was "like an embodiment of the integral beauty which was Greece."[89] It was, then, a ritual among "civilized people."

The characters portrayed in a caricature, *The Committee on Art* (1932 [fig. 60]), were also "civilized" and "people with money who spend on

art"; such characters also appear in the painting *Successful People* (1931 [fig. 61]). Without realizing that her words could be perfectly applicable to the Delphic Circle, Alma Reed described the painting: "[I]t was a corrosive commentary not only on the spiritual sterility of the 'idle rich' but on the female domination of the American scene as well....The supercilious matron is in haughty and aggressive command."[90] Although it is clear that Orozco did not apply the same standard of judgment equally,

Fig. 60 · **The Committee on Art**, 1932, black wash, Baltimore Museum of Art, gift of Blanche Adler; BMA 1933.61.2.

Fig. 61 · **Successful People**, 1931, oil on canvas, private collection, courtesy Mary-Anne Martin/Fine Art, New York, photograph courtesy Sotheby's.

77

I find the differences interesting. The portrait of Eva Sikelianos glorifies a personality. By the profusion of associated signs and cabalistic rituals, it is properly the portrait of an initiate. Although its classicism might refer to universal norms, the portrait exalts its model's individuality. Orozco's devices for satirizing the other "civilized people" were different. The members of the "art committee" were not wearing such attractive clothing, and the painter condemned them to the anthropological uniformity of racial type. At the same time, Reed's comments make one think that the satire hinged on gender: In this multitude of rich people, the problem is that the women are giving the orders. But it is also women (Eva Sikelianos, Alma Reed, her niece Patricia [fig. 62], Julia Peterkin [fig. 63]) who appear in Orozco's New York portraits—all of them "civilized."

Besides having a "very cultured" model, the Sikelianos portrait was "something new, with a complicated palette, and treated like a wall," according to Orozco. At first glance, the palette does not seem complicated, at least not in any sense that might refer to a theory of color. It is a spectrum of pigments composed mainly of earth tones that is similar to that of the 1928 *Self-Portrait* (fig. 43). The complication lies in the use of glaze and varnish

to create volume (as in the black brushstrokes of the tunic) and flesh tones. Orozco also plays with color blending of different densities. At the academy, Orozco had been in Germán Gedovius's chiaroscuro workshop. Siqueiros remembered Gedovius's class for the thick blending of paint, sometimes applied directly from the tube, and the importance given to textures.[91] Now, although the Sikelianos portrait makes a display of chiaroscuro, its varied blending is discreet. The painter referred to this style of painting as *lamidito,* according to the recollection of one of his Dartmouth assistants: "*Lamido* is what a dog does when he licks his wounds. 'Lamidito,' applied to painting, means that the artist goes over the same area over and over again, like an artisan, not like an artist painting with *bravura....* Lamidito is something like a school exercise."[92]

In effect, no one who saw this painting could doubt that Orozco was an artist trained in an academy. In the *Portrait of Eva Sikelianos,* Orozco imposed a geometric order: The model's arm is bent in front of her to serve, visually, as a "base." Orozco

Fig. 62 · **Patricia**, 1930, oil on canvas, location unknown, from Alma Reed, **Orozco** (Mexico City: Fondo de Cultura Económica, 1955), fig. 117.

Fig. 63 · **Portrait of Julia Peterkin**, 1929, oil on canvas, Museo de Arte Carrillo Gil, Mexico City/INBA 17248.

was also referring to this when he spoke of treating it "like a wall": the attachment to an imaginary constructive order. Here, Orozco drew from Cennino Cennini's *Libro dell'arte*.[93] With regard to fresco painting, Cennini concentrated on painting faces and volumes; he advised delineating figures and applying shades with verdaccio, applying the colors only later on. However, he warned against the temptation of beginning with darker shades and superimposing lighter ones, as in oil painting. "Others prefer to first apply the flesh tones, later earth green and lastly the white, and it is done. But it is a technique of those who know little of this art," he wrote, and repeated: "Do not forget that, if you wish your work to appear fresh, your brush must not leave its area in applying the different types of flesh tones, and in the end must fuse them kindly."[94]

But Orozco always had trouble with this way of conceiving and practicing fresco painting. In many of his murals, there are strong contrasts between light and dark that go beyond human figure modeling. In his work in Guadalajara (1935–39), he managed to make a white pigment sufficiently dense for him to apply—in violation of Cennini's prescriptions (and those of almost any ancient or modern treatise writer)—the brighter coats over the darker ones. Before reaching that extreme, he painted at least a few panels, such as the one that opens the set at the New School for Social Research, whose dense shadows, to the left, are broken by the luminosity of the figures, even by a rainbow![95] This is why it is significant that he said of his *Portrait of Eva Sikelianos* that it was treated "like a wall." The darkness of that work would have made

Fig. 64 · **The Elevated**, 1928, oil on canvas, collection of Rosemary Rieser, photograph by Jeffrey Nintzel.

it impractical, given the materials available at the time, for fresco painting. A similar chromatic and technical oxymoron is related to the opposite of mural painting: Not only is it an easel painting, not only is its palette dark, but it is also a portrait in which the character appears with the attributes that have given her public fame. We have found, then, a new boundary between public and private, now related to a theory of color that nonetheless was conceived as a "craft."

In comparison, the portrait of Julia Peterkin (1929 [fig. 63]) shows a very different theory of color. The opposition of blue and orange suggests something that is borne out in his notebooks, Michel Eugène Chevreul's theory of simultaneous contrasts.[96] The juxtaposition of primary colors opposite one another on the chromatic circle, according to Chevreul, made each one's complement appear. This was a common device in European modern painting. Orozco had seen enough works by Matisse and Villon to perceive its importance and, even more, to interpret the meaning it was given. Orozco summarized Chevreul's theory in his notebooks and immediately added: "*Contrast* (inequality) creates proportion, creates *drama*, creates *movement*. Art is order."[97]

In later works, particularly in the different *Elevated* paintings (figs. 64 and 58), Orozco subverted the structure's geometric order and imposed upon it a chromatic order. It is no longer the beams and

pillars that give order, but the oranges, greens, and indigo blues. In spite of the disproportionate shapes, *Elevated* (1929–30 [fig. 58]) is a painting that refers to an ideal order to be found not in lines but in contrasts. In this work, among very few others, Orozco abandoned "composition" in the academic sense, not only the adjustment of shapes to a system of proportions but the fitting of the narrative within a rational space. "Contrast…creates drama," but this drama would no longer be the looting of a church, the execution of a guerrilla, or the burial of a revolutionary. The "movement" of the painting, its order, would be set by the relationship between colors.

This radical change in Orozco's easel painting became visible, although more slowly, in his murals. The careful flesh tone work in *Prometheus* makes it, still, a *lamidito* mural (fig. 110); at the New School, Orozco leaned toward the geometric order of Dynamic Symmetry (figs. 134 and 135). Only after his trip to Europe, during the time he was painting

Fig. 65 · West wing of **The Epic of American Civilization**, 1932–34, fresco, Baker Library, Dartmouth College, Hanover, New Hampshire, 2001.

Fig. 66 · **Modern Migration of the Spirit** from **The Epic of American Civilization**, 1932–34, fresco, Baker Library, Dartmouth College, Hanover, New Hampshire.

the Dartmouth College frescoes, did he decide to use color as a compositional device, in the multicolored flags, the yellowish torso of Christ, the chromatic spectrum of the gods of the Mesoamerican pantheon: the cobalt blues, the cadmium yellows (figs. 65 and 66). The change was not merely from an effeminate, *lamidito* brush to a virile one, full of bravura, as his assistant Carlos Sánchez believed; it also went from earth tones, varnishes, and academic nuances to the pure and intellectualized primary colors of avant-garde painting. Not surprisingly, it was Lewis Mumford who, in his article on the Baker Library murals, acknowledged the compositional value of the colors: "The long hall where the Orozco frescoes stand is broken by a projection of the wall on each side of the loan desk and by the alcove opposite. At the east end a series of columns breaks and frames the panels beyond. The highest pitch of yellow and orange is reserved for these distant panels; but the painting begins on a somber note, resonant and grave like the notes of a bass violin."[98] The change in style depends upon another, more important change: one of paradigm. Pre-Chevreul theories of color were based on the Newtonian idea of the continuousness of the white-light spectrum, whereas Chevreul's was based on contrasts and had considerable influence on the practice of the arts. In this regard, Georges Roque notes: "Thus, one has seen, the nature of the work itself undergoes a deep transformation, even if time is required for all the consequences of this transformation to be seen anew. Beginning with the law of contrast—and indeed, this point is perhaps the most important contribution of science to art—the picture is no longer regarded so much as a surface of illusionistic inscription, but as a field of forces and of tensions, an autonomous field whose constituent elements—chiefly colors in this case—form an organic whole in their interaction."[99]

The critique of architecture and the theory of color intertwined to constitute a new way of approaching walls by *attacking* them, in effect, by subverting their structural values to give rise to a new order. Color imposes a narrative succession; its contrasts constitute the episodes and interact with the symbolic formations of allegory. Above all, this theory of color brought Orozco to establish a new formal and symbolic relation between mural painting and architecture. Chromatic contrasts reorganize architectural space. At the same time, the relationship between the paint and the walls is no longer one of subordination. The building's structure bore, in the colonial Mexican buildings, a historic freight that the muralists took on as part of the nationalist discourse. On the walls of Dartmouth College, the relationship between painting and architecture became dialogical. Painting speaks to the building's symbolic and institutional value, something that goes beyond the solidarity between its composition and the architraves, doors, walls, and imposts. At this deep level of symbolic representations the relationship has become critical.

"90 Percent Architecture"

When he arrived in New York, Orozco had had ample experience in press illustration, as a cartoonist. However, he had rarely practiced the graphic techniques favored by educated artists: lithography, engraving, and etching. In 1928, seeing how successful his revolutionary-themed drawings had been in the United States, he decided to have them reproduced (figs. 67, 68, and 69). His first lithographs were printed in George C. Miller's printshop. Miller was a leader in the use of modern methods: He used zinc plates, rather than stones, for artistic lithography; he also encouraged artists to obtain counterproofs using an intermediate roller—that is, an offset procedure. Because of this, in Orozco's "public" art there may nonetheless be said to be a private procedure; the painter declared himself satisfied with a technique that allowed him to take

81

Fig. 67 · **The Flag**, 1928, lithograph, Philadelphia Museum of Art; purchased with the Lola Downing Peck Fund from Carl and Laura Zigrosser Collection, 1976; 1976-97-36.

Fig. 68 · **The Requiem**, 1928, lithograph, Philadelphia Museum of Art; gift of Henry P. McIlhenny, 1943; 1943-82-1.

Fig. 69 · **Ruined House**, 1929, lithograph, Philadelphia Museum of Art, purchased with the Lola Downing Peck Fund from Carl and Laura Zigrosser Collection, 1976; 1976-97-53.

82

the plates home to draw in the privacy of his own studio. "I'm delighted with the new procedure. A most entertaining toy; it will last me a good while."[100] Orozco was used to industrial illustration, in which the cartoonist or illustrator is part of a team. This new "most entertaining toy" would allow him to work apart from that organization.

After copying five of his own drawings, Orozco sent to Mexico for photographs of his murals at the National Preparatory School in the hope of interesting some architect: "I sent telegrams asking for photos with architecture, that is, in which there is 90 percent architecture and only 10 percent painting, because an architect can't be interested in doodlings except as part of the building."[101] He then made several lithographs based on the photographs, in which he emphasized the architectural aspects, and displayed them together with the preparatory drawings for his murals at the school (figs. 70 and 71). He met with resounding success: Frank Lloyd Wright proposed that they work together on future projects. But precisely in this moment of triumph, Orozco declined to participate, claiming his need for independence.[102] He was not seeking independence merely from the architect. The exhibition of drawings, photographs, and lithographs established a way of relating to architecture in which he himself was no longer confident. Part of that image of his own work was the very meticulous lithographic reproduction of some fragments of the murals, including architectural elements, as in *Grief* (fig. 71) or *Franciscan.* Orozco used the lithographic crayon to imitate the texture of the many successive, transparent brushstrokes of fresco paint. As we have seen, that academic manner of painting had also begun to find itself in crisis.

When Delphic Studios opened in 1929, Orozco broke with the Weyhe Gallery, which had an exclusive contract to sell his successful lithographs.[103] Perhaps for this reason, he temporarily had to change printers, to a different one who, as Jean Charlot said,

made poorer-quality prints.[104] His new prints no longer attempted to copy his earlier works (except for *Revolution,* which reproduces the oil painting of the same title); there is a less subtle use of shades of gray, and the drawings are less painterly and more linear.

Besides their superficial Mexicanness (*Mexican Landscape* [fig. 73], *Mexican Pueblo* [fig. 72], *The Maguey* [fig. 75], and so on), these new prints give added importance to composition. In some cases, such as *The Maguey* and *Mexican Pueblo,* Orozco used the golden section. In others, such as *Leaving* and *Mexican Landscape,* this interest in mathematical order is less important than the narrative, which is, as in his earlier drawings, tragic. *Mexican Peasants Working* (fig. 74) is an exception. In it, neither terrain features nor vegetation have the symbolic character Orozco usually associated with them; see, for example, *Mexican Landscape,* in which some capriciously strewn rocks oppose the ruined (or unfinished) order of some walls, or *The Maguey,* in which this Dionysian plant functions as a symbol of virility although, as in symbolist painting, its closeness to the feminine has mutilated it. *Mexican Peasants Working* lacks that contraposition of masculine and feminine, nature and culture. The Indian bearers are equated with vegetation

Fig. 70 · Detail of **Revolutionary Trinity** (second version), 1926, fresco, National Preparatory School, Mexico City, photograph by Bob Schalkwijk.

Fig. 71 · **Grief**, 1930, lithograph, Hood Museum of Art, Dartmouth College, Hanover, New Hampshire; PR.985.40.2.

83

and are, themselves, "nature." In *Mexican Pueblo,* a procession of women is led toward the abyss by a mysterious dwarf, with an architectural caprice in the background. In *Mexican Peasants Working,* there is no caprice, no reference to death. In *Mexican Pueblo,* the spiderweb of geometric composition is evident; not so in *Mexican Peasants Working.* In *Mexican Landscape,* Orozco reduces the characters' anatomy and physiognomy to a few essential lines that identify them with the structure or with the rock; all of them have as much solidity as the mountains in the background. In *Mexican Peasants Working,* the figures are also simplified, but they lack this weight. In *Leaving,* Orozco made discreet use of the reamer to give a few luminous touches; in *Mexican Pueblo* and *Mexican Landscape,* he preferred to counterpose the crayon strokes to very intense blacks. In *Mexican Peasants Working,* he used the lithographic crayon as though it were a piece of charcoal. This may not be Orozco's best print, all in all, but it is surely one of his most ironic.

In 1929 Orozco illustrated the English translation of Mariano Azuela's *Los de abajo* (*The Underdogs* [figs. 76, 77, and 78]), the novel that set the standard for Mexican literature on the revolution.[105] Enrique Munguía, who was in charge of the printing for Brentano's, chose the painter. "I preferred Orozco over Rivera to do the illustrations....I don't know why, Rivera gives me the impression of being an insensitive sketcher, bold, to be sure, but simplified to the point of affectation. Orozco, on the other hand, hasn't managed to tame himself. He is skittish. His artistic world is still in chaos. He comes close to drowning in a tropical cascade of virgin colors, when suddenly he decides to get lymphatic."[106]

The Underdogs is, then, a work that moves away from the diplomatic and ideological interests that are explained in this catalog's biographical essay. The illustrations repeat the topics of the *Mexico in Revolution* drawing series, although their technique is different. On the one hand, their compositions are not as closed as those of the drawings. On the other, they use no ink wash, and Orozco drew them as if scratching with ink on paper.[107] From his experience as a cartoonist, Orozco knew well the possibilities of industrial illustration. The reproductions of his drawings would not be faithful to shades or hues. As in *Mexican Peasants Working,* there is a disquieting equation with nature: the ragged arms of the fighters in *The Battle* (fig. 79), so similar to the dead trees in the background; the corpses of the dead, whose lines are almost lost in those of the ground; the dead tree in another of the drawings, which serves as a tomb and as a symbol of death at the

Fig. 72 · **Mexican Pueblo**, 1930, lithograph, San Francisco Museum of Modern Art, 35.1651.

Fig. 73 · **Mexican Landscape**, 1930, lithograph, San Francisco Museum of Modern Art; 35.1644.

same time. These drawings anticipate Orozco's works in the 1940s, after his stay in Guadalajara.[108] They are, so to speak, the diametric opposite of *lamidito,* of academic composition and imprint. For the moment this somewhat anomalous drawing manner was to take him to one of his most notable works of this period.

The Hanged Men (fig. 80) is a work whose critical violence is unmitigated by irony; it is an accusation. It was printed to be included in a portfolio by the Contemporary Print Group in 1933[109] and is characterized by its economy of media. The lithographic crayon and the reamer with which Orozco drew the flames present two opposing forces: one of them organic, the other unidirectional and overpowering; one of them complex, the other simple and brutal. But in the figurative protocol of *The Hanged Men,* very similar to the one in *Mexican Peasants Working,* we can acknowledge history's critical distance. As in other works, the figures are ragged, loose, even truncated. Dead branches are equated with suffering bodies: both lifeless, both mutilated (the lynching victims have been castrated), and both "nature."[110] It is as if the perfect order of the machine of life were convulsed by the flames. Far from "purifying" them, the fire allows the figures communion and reintegration with the natural world. Fire was a symbol Orozco derived from William Blake's work. *Books* (fig. 81) is a genuinely Blakean work, with its squares, dividers, and those pages that burn as the only way to become true knowledge. In *The Hanged Men,* fire bears an opposite value. In an intellectual milieu that sought to follow in Emerson's and Whitman's footsteps to communion with that "America" whose stress was on nature; in this country, which fancied Mexican peasants as the timeless inhabitants of a pristine Eden; in a context in which realist painters rescued parochial traditions, the dream of a wild, agricultural country that grew like the grass, nothing could be more disturbing than to portray oneness with

nature as an act of violence. The portfolio had a significant title, often attributed to the print by Orozco: *The American Scene.*[111]

The Hanged Men thus engages a public problem particular to the United States, in that country's terms and under its conditions. During the thirties, numerous antilynching propaganda works associated racism's victims with nature.[112] What is of interest here is that for this eminently public work, Orozco should have used the repertoire of industrial graphics—that is, the devices he shared with José Guadalupe Posada,[113] the scratchboard and the dismembering of figures as a figurative tool. These devices also appear in *The Dead,* although with narrative intent in the structures of the buildings that are undone, dismembered, unsewn, and

85

Fig. 74 · **Mexican Peasants Working**, 1929, lithograph, Hood Museum of Art, Dartmouth College, Hanover, New Hampshire; PR.930.15.1.

Fig. 75 · **The Maguey**, 1929, lithograph, Philadelphia Museum of Art; purchased with the Lola Downing Peck Fund from the Carl and Laura Zigrosser Collection, 1976; 1976-97-42.

collapsed. There is, in that use of line, another (elastic) limit between public and private, and this limit does not coincide with the boundary that political discourse imposes on the two spheres.

In Paris in 1932 he drew two more stones in the Atelier Desjobert, of which he printed only one, *Unemployed* (fig. 82).[114] This print's technical resources (the reamer, tusche, and lithographic crayon) are not the same as those used in *The Hanged Men*. This is a lithograph that looks like one, and it does not attempt to re-create the appearance of painting, drawing, or industrial illustration.

The Mural Studies

The French historian Philippe Aries affirms that the categories of public and private do not always coincide with the definitions of political history, which situate the former in the sphere of the state and the latter in the individual, the family, and intimacy.[115] The muralists proposed a public art that would be public property, but many things in it are not public, whereas in their easel paintings, supposedly

destined for private consumption, many public things do reside. Ultimately, not all the technical devices or theories of art or history that we have discussed were properly public or private, unless we propose a less rigid definition than that put forth by traditional political history. Style, which Orozco supposed to be strictly private, became a hinge between the two spheres, between what mattered to him and what mattered to the public at large. In undertaking mural painting, however, the Mexican painters built a fortress of restrictions that had to do precisely with the public character of that painting; with its belonging to the state or to corporations, with the admonitory and juridical discourse; with its aspiration to the same monumentality that the buildings it decorated possessed. These were not always consistent conditions. Mural painting was to be pedagogical but esoteric, sober but epic, monumental but avant-garde. Easel paintings did not always have these restrictions, although we have seen that there were others, perhaps more severe: They were to be autonomous and rationally constructed; they were to show things and originate

Fig. 76 · **Bandit and Girl**, illustration for **The Underdogs**, 1929, ink on paper, private collection, photograph courtesy Sotheby's.

Fig. 77 · **Soldiers' Wives**, illustration for **The Underdogs**, 1929, ink on paper, San Francisco Museum of Modern Art; 35.2999.

Fig. 78 · **The Hanged Man**, illustration for **The Underdogs**, 1929, ink on paper, Robert L. and Sharon W. Lynch Collection, photograph by Douglas M. Parker Studio.

Fig. 79 · **The Battle**, illustration for **The Underdogs**, 1929, ink on paper, location unknown, from Mariano Azuela, **Los de abajo** (Mexico City: Fondo de Cultura Económica, 1983), 15.

Fig. 80 · **Hanged Men**, about 1933, lithograph, Philadelphia Museum of Art, purchased with the Lola Downing Peck Fund from Carl and Laura Zigrosser Collection, 1976; 75-36-10.

in them. At times conditions similar to those of mural paintings were imposed upon them (as in the *Portrait of Eva Sikelianos* [fig. 59]).

This relationship is most evident in the preparatory drawings for the murals. The idea that these were drawings and studies intended only for personal study, for the painter's dialogue with himself, must be discarded from the first. This may be so in some cases, but during his stay in New York Orozco exhibited his drawings for the murals at the Preparatory School; surely, he foresaw that the studies he made in the United States would eventually be exhibited (as in fact happened).[116] The preparatory drawings may also be seen as arguments about the larger work, more so than the easel paintings, but not as strictly utilitarian subproducts.

The vast majority of known studies for *Prometheus* are life studies, especially of torsos and hands (fig. 124). In them Orozco used the "ragged" style that we have already seen in his graphic work and that can be seen in some parts of the mural: in the masses at Prometheus's back and, above all, in the lateral panels, which portray other episodes

Fig. 81 · **Books**, 1929–30, gouache on paper, location unknown, from Alma Reed, **Orozco** (Mexico City: Fondo de Cultura Económica, 1955), fig. 97.

Fig. 82 · **Unemployed**, 1932, lithograph, San Francisco Museum of Modern Art, Albert M. Bender Collection, gift of Albert M. Bender; 35.3001.

87

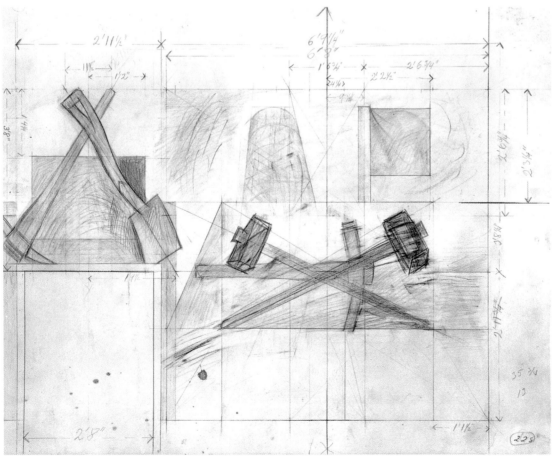

Fig. 83 · Study for central panel of the mural **Prometheus**, Pomona College, 1930, graphite on paper, Pomona College, Claremont, California, P2000.2.1 © Pomona College and Clemente Orozco, 2000.

Fig. 84 · Study for west wall of the mural at the New School for Social Research, New York, 1930–31, graphite on paper, Hood Museum of Art, Dartmouth College, Hanover, New Hampshire; D.988.52.206.

88

from Hesiod. The hero's figure is, however, different; its anatomy has been carefully modeled, using a complex set of transparencies. This does not mean that the hero's body has classical proportions. At first glance, it does seem to follow this pattern, but a more careful observation reveals somewhat disjoined and excessive legs, barely finished hands, and a schematic face. The studies for the mural show Orozco subordinating Prometheus's figure to the lines of the architecture: He made the figure's center of gravity, the loins, coincide with the intersection of the principal compositional lines (fig. 83). The difference between this figure and the lateral panels is so important that one restorer of the murals thought that the lateral panels were someone else's work, perhaps that of Jorge Juan Crespo de la Serna.[117] However, we have already seen Orozco himself shift from loose strokes to small-brush *lamidito*.

Since mural painting was "public," it imposed an obligation for a rational, at times even mathematically coherent, composition that would allow the viewer to glimpse the perfection that was attributed to the world of "pure forms." Shortly before starting his murals at the Preparatory School, Orozco had written: "The only emotion it must generate and transmit must be that which is derived from the purely plastic, geometric, coldly geometric phenomenon, organized by a scientific technique."[118] In his autobiography, he refers to the use of Dynamic Symmetry in the New School for Social Research murals. This was a system of proportions studied by Jay Hambidge, whose widow attended Delphic Circle meetings. Orozco's explanation is extremely interesting.

According to the author of *Symmetry* there are two sorts of art: the dynamic and the static. To the first belong the arts of Greece and Egypt in their mature periods. To the second he relegated all other art without exception. The forms created by Greeks and Egyptians are dynamic

because they structurally comprise in themselves the principle of action, of movement, and for this reason can grow, develop, and multiply like the human body and all living beings. When this development is normal it produces rhythm and harmony, which are precisely what we mean by beauty. In this lies the supremacy of Greek and Egyptian art over all others.[119]

In Dynamic Symmetry, unlike in life drawing, the artist's personal style does not appear; the body's proportions are subjected to an ideal mathematical logic. Although he did not always use this particular compositional system, Orozco did employ some systematic composition in all of his murals. This is why his preparatory drawings are, in many cases, life drawings such as he recommended to Crespo de la Serna, but there are also, in many of them, studies of the dimensions of walls and even copies from anatomy handbooks.

Fig. 85 · Composition study for **Migration**, 1932–34, ink on paper, Hood Museum of Art, Dartmouth College, Hanover, New Hampshire; w.988.52.14.

89

However, we only have a few almost definitive studies for the New School for Social Research mural. In them, one can see the careful mathematical arrangement of the composition in accordance with Dynamic Symmetry (the drawings are full of numbers and crosses [fig. 84]). We know of no anatomical studies for this mural, nor have we found any studies that might show a fundamentally different composition from that of the mural itself. This is highly significant. In other murals, it is common for the first preparatory drawing to be very different from the final version. The most frequent reason for change was usually to be found in some human figure, whose study and resolution forced the painter to transform the whole composition. At the New School, on the contrary, attention to the composition as a whole seems to have prevailed, subordinating the individual figures.

It is in the Dartmouth College studies that we can see the painting method Orozco was to use in the years to come, particularly in his murals at the Palace of Fine Arts and in Guadalajara. For each panel at Dartmouth, we find, first, a study with thick brushstrokes in ink (fig. 85); later, a very schematic compositional drawing (fig. 93), followed immediately by an individual work on each figure (figs. 86 and 87); then, the final preparatory drawings, to be transferred to the painting surface (figs. 95, 88, and 89). Often there are two final composition studies, one for the upper and one for the lower portions. If, in the process, Orozco tried to resolve a particular figure, the entire composition could change. For example, in the initial version of the panel *Modern Migration of the Spirit,* Christ appears naked in the study, his back to the viewer, in the process of chopping down the cross (fig. 90). A later study, fairly rudimentary, presents another idea. A very geometricized body appears, facing the viewer: a rectangle crowned by an oval. On the same sheet of paper, Orozco superimposed the outlines of a human figure (fig. 91). In successive versions, all fairly schematic, he drew variations on the same

Fig. 86 · Figure study for **Migration**, 1932–34, graphite on cream paper, Hood Museum of Art, Dartmouth College, Hanover, New Hampshire; D.988.52.16

Fig. 87 · Study of head for **Migration**, 1932–34, ink on paper, Hood Museum of Art, Dartmouth College, Hanover, New Hampshire; W.988.52.12

Fig. 88 · Transfer drawing of head with open jaw for **The Departure of Quetzalcoatl**, 1932–34, graphite on tracing paper, Hood Museum of Art, Dartmouth College, Hanover, New Hampshire; D.988.52.77.

Fig. 89 · Transfer drawing of head for **Modern Migration of the Spirit**, 1932–34, graphite on tracing paper, Hood Museum of Art, Dartmouth College, Hanover, New Hampshire; D.988.52.199.

theme. In each, the figure faces the viewer and has one hand raised, although the cross changes position (figs. 92, 93, and 94). With the overall problem solved, Orozco made anatomical studies for each detail of the main figure, which appears in great detail in the final drawings (fig. 95).

Gods of the Modern World followed a similar procedure. The first study has a very few schematic traces of the final composition (fig. 96). There are numerous anatomical studies, especially of the child's skeleton, for which Orozco consulted George Arthur Piersol's manual of anatomy (figs. 97 and 98).[120] He did similar muscular and skeletal studies of figures with other panels (fig. 99). The final studies for *Modern Migration of the Spirit* are practically écorchés (anatomical renderings of the body with the skin removed in order to reveal the musculature [fig. 94]).

For *Gods of the Modern World*, as with many other panels, another type of study has been preserved: a gouache (fig. 100). In it, the compositional lines are less important than the equilibrium between light and shadow. For other panels, such as *The Coming of Quetzalcoatl, Ancient Human*

Sacrifice, and *The Departure of Quetzalcoatl* (figs. 101, 102, and 103), there are also small tempera studies, in which Orozco studied the balance of colors. It is possible that in some cases, such as an oil painting of *The Departure of Quetzalcoatl* that is preserved at Dartmouth, these may not be preparatory drawings but later reworkings. Orozco copied fragments of his murals in different media: in his lithographs and, for example, in the version of *The Trench* that is in the collection of New York's Museum of Modern Art, which reproduces a mural at the Preparatory School in Mexico City. But the abundance of studies of color, light, and shadow for the Dartmouth murals corroborates something I stated earlier in reference to the painter's technique: In this set of frescoes, color contrast is at least as important to composition as geometry and chiaroscuro.

In summary, in the studies for Orozco's murals, which were, in the final analysis, large-format historical painting, we can see two opposing tendencies. On the one hand, he paid attention to structure — that is, anatomy and overall composition — in whose design he included considerations of color. On the

91

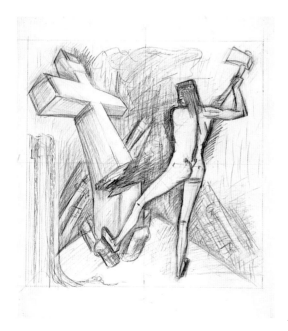

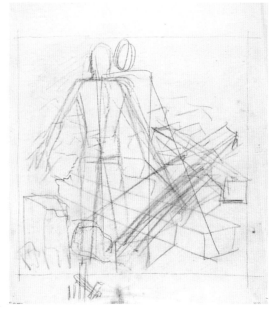

Fig. 90 · Composition study of Christ chopping the cross for **Modern Migration of the Spirit**, 1932–34, graphite on tracing paper, Hood Museum of Art, Dartmouth College, Hanover, New Hampshire; D.988.52.207.

Fig. 91 · Composition study for **Modern Migration of the Spirit**, 1932–34, graphite on tracing paper, Hood Museum of Art, Dartmouth College, Hanover, New Hampshire; D.988.52.196.

Fig. 92 · Composition study for **Modern Migration of the Spirit**, 1932–34, graphite on tracing paper, Hood Museum of Art, Dartmouth College, Hanover, New Hampshire; 988.52.211.

Fig. 93 · Composition study for **Modern Migration of the Spirit**, 1932–34, graphite on tracing paper, Hood Museum of Art, Dartmouth College, Hanover, New Hampshire; D.988.52.208.

Fig. 94 · Composition study for **Modern Migration of the Spirit**, 1932–34, graphite on tracing paper, Hood Museum of Art, Dartmouth College, Hanover, New Hampshire; D.988.52.200.

Fig. 95 · Composition study for **Modern Migration of the Spirit**, 1932–34, graphite on tracing paper, Hood Museum of Art, Dartmouth College, Hanover, New Hampshire; D.988.52.197.

other, he drew from life: the human figure regardless of its ideal proportions or its place in the composition. For example, the side panels of the section *Modern Industrial Man* at Dartmouth represent two groups of workers (figs. 189 and 191). The origin of this representation is to be found in a drawing at the Cabañas Cultural Institute, Guadalajara (fig. 104). This drawing, or an earlier one, may have been made during Orozco's trip to Europe, since it has a clear affinity with the lithograph *Unemployed* (also called *Workers* [fig. 82]), which he had printed in Paris. It is a street scene, such as he advised Crespo de la Serna to create, and this — not the general composition, not the epic, not chromatic contrast — is the origin of the panel.

So the mural studies are, above all, a negotiating tool: between the painter's personal style and the obligations imposed by space and narration; between these obligations and the decorum demanded by the hierarchy of characters; between composition and figuration. The separation between public and private, which is constitutive of mural painting, not only refers to the works' status as state property or as goods bought and sold on a market but also includes their use of figurative and compositional devices. The boundary is more complex than it first appeared.

Conclusions

The Mexican muralists reactivated a set of problems related to the theory of painting. The opposition between public mural painting and private easel painting necessitated numerous reflections

Fig. 96 · Composition study for **Gods of the Modern World**, 1932–34, crayon and graphite on paper, 18 ½ x 25 ⅛ in (46.9 x 63.6 cm), Museum of Modern Art, New York, gift of Clemente Orozco Valladares, photograph ©2001 Museum of Modern Art, New York.

93

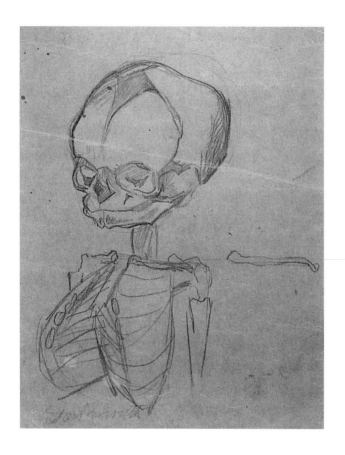

Fig. 97 · Study of fetal skeleton for
Gods of the Modern World,
1932–34, graphite on paper, Hood
Museum of Art, Dartmouth College,
Hanover, New Hampshire;
D.988.52.173.

Fig. 98 · Anatomical studies for
Gods of the Modern World,
1932–34, graphite on tracing paper,
Hood Museum of Art, Dartmouth
College, Hanover, New Hampshire;
D.988.52.167.

Fig. 99 · Anatomical studies,
1932–34, graphite on tracing paper,
Hood Museum of Art, Dartmouth
College, Hanover, New Hampshire;
D.988.52.250.

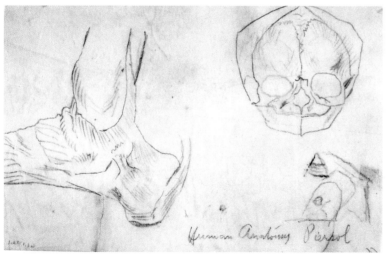

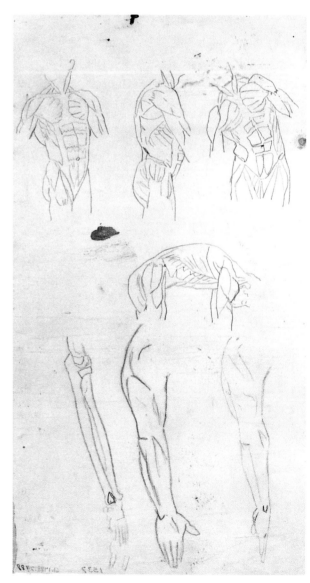

94

and experiences to adjust this schematization, and the practice of painting itself, to realities and theories that were not always related to the separation between the individual and the state, or between the market and society. The argument that style was strictly the product of individual intuition forced them, in order to render their pedagogical and political project plausible, to construct something reminiscent of humanistic art theory and its obsession with *decorum,* with the composition, in painting history, of a story that conforms either to the facts or to a higher, ideal truth.[121] The Mexican historian Justino Fernández attributes to Orozco the achievement of something that can only be called a restoration: "One must stand for the rights of an art of issues and purposes…and, therefore, struggle against the idealistic, decadent aestheticism of the late nineteenth and early twentieth centuries, whose artistic goal was a superficial beauty, or rather, a certain type of beauty, from which concept our own time has moved on to the super-valorization of tactile or intellectual qualities."[122]

It seems that things were more complicated. It is true that mural painting imposed conditions, at times constrictions, and that these had to do with the veracity of events portrayed, the coherence of the narration, the ideas expressed, and the hierarchy of characters represented. The great number of preparatory attempts for some compositions, such as *Modern Migration of the Spirit* and the panel *Hispano-America*; Orozco's assertions about the "very cultivated person" Eva Sikelianos and her portrait "treated as a wall"; the long negotiation between different national and symbolic discourses:[123] All these feed into the idea of a moderate conservatism, often attributed (sometimes with good reason) to mural painting.[124]

But there were other areas of reflection and practice. The theory of architecture offered a new space for thinking on both the public character and the utility of mural painting; it was, moreover, the

natural place to think through the problem of decoration. This permitted Orozco to conceive of the problems of structure in pictorial terms and to transpose onto canvas, with some violence, the symbolic imperatives that were attributed to public buildings. In the long run, this production of monuments and cataclysms brought him to question seriously the subordination of decoration to architectural structure. For this, it was important to know theories of color that differed considerably from a supposedly traditional practice of mixing pigments, varnishes, and turpentine. The outcome of this personal revolution was the integration of figurative devices, contrasting colors, and symbols, transcending an initial opposition between personal "style" and conservative, academic, architecture-respecting, sober, and public painting of history. Orozco did not erase the opposition between mural and easel; what he did was make that theoretical artifact productive.

Magical realism's importance for this process of critical reflection and artistic production must not be underestimated. Drawing from Bergson, Roh had proposed an evolutionary process in which the subject of his history, painting, underwent cycles

95

Fig. 101 · Study of warriors' heads for **Ancient Human Sacrifice**, 1932–34, tempera on paper, Instituto Cultural Cabañas, Guadalajara/INBA 13797, photograph by Rubén Orozco.

Fig. 102 · Composition study for left half of **The Departure of Quetzalcoatl**, 1932–34, gouache on paper, Hood Museum of Art, Dartmouth College, Hanover, New Hampshire; w.988.52.80.

of order and fragmentation in an endless process of becoming. Orozco came from a world in which two intellectual currents were in conflict: on the one hand, Spencerian evolutionism, in which he was undoubtedly trained as a student at the National Preparatory School, and, on the other, a milieu soaked in Bergsonism, of which the speculations of José Vasconcelos are only the most important example among many.[125] As happened with many Mexican intellectuals, Orozco's writings and art are located between these two poles: between the organicist dream of "New World, New Races and New Art" and the hallucinatory vigil of *The Dead.*

Finally, it should be noted that experimenting with old and new graphic production techniques led him to modify his drawing and eventually his painting. In all these changes, the notion of an absolutely public art worked to drive a theory and a practice in which, in the end, Orozco moved the boundaries between public and private, but in areas that did not strictly belong to the political sphere: in his way of conceiving the composition of history painting, as well as his way of dragging the pencil, which for him had an irreducible and personal value. The division is, then, more complex than it seems; it is not just between public, admonitory mural painting, conservative and even subordinated to the needs of the state, on the one hand, and personal, formalist, and free easel painting, on the other. The very sources of his thought and practice force us to see this opposition as a difficult and central process, in which the public and the private are historically reconstructed in the production of each painting, lithograph, drawing, or mural.

Fig. 103 · Composition study for right half of **The Departure of Quetzalcoatl**, 1932–34, gouache on paper, Hood Museum of Art, Dartmouth College, Hanover, New Hampshire; w.988.52.82.

Fig. 104 · Study of workers for **Modern Industrial Man**, 1932–34, graphite on paper, Instituto Cultural Cabañas, Guadalajara/INBA 15138, photograph by Rubén Orozco.

97

Prometheus Unraveled: Readings of and from the Body: Orozco's Pomona College Mural (1930)

Karen Cordero Reiman

The subject is not pleasant: it makes one think,
the first duty of any college whatever.

— HAROLD DAVIS[1]

Prometheus Encountered

When one walks into Frary Hall, a staid and somewhat austere neo-Gothic dining hall at Pomona College, the mural that fills the arch on the far wall, José Clemente Orozco's *Prometheus,* transforms one's sense of place and one's complacence. The wooden paneling and detailing contrast with the white plaster, recalling an oversize Protestant church; the clearly defined linear organization, reiterated by the tables, evokes an ethos of order and restraint. In contrast, the huge nude figure of Prometheus that dominates the mural, spanning the height of the arch and seeming to push at the very point of its vertical union—as if to defy the structural stability of the edifice and all it symbolizes—constitutes a disturbing and enigmatic presence. This figure introduces a cultural and philosophical other into the everyday experience of the college students who encounter it during their mealtimes, questioning their own bodily integrity and the physical and epistemological limitations of their humanity, things that the very activity the building is destined for, eating, reaffirms (figs. 105, 106, and 107).

One doesn't see all of the mural at first. In fact, of the four panels of which the monumental work is composed, only the main panel is visible until one comes very close to the piece. Even this panel is cut off by the ogival arch within which it is recessed, in such a way that Prometheus's Atlantean gesture is hidden at the point of maximum drama, making it unclear, initially, whether he is holding up or pushing off some superhuman weight or defending himself and the human mass that surrounds him from the flames that dart from above and seem to

melt his upper extremities. This enigmatic quality suggests a work that does not reveal its meaning easily or immediately, as contemporary perceptual habits tend to demand; instead, it requires that its spectator come close, under its overhang, and twist his or her body upward, straining to encompass the mural in its integral conception, only to discover that this is never possible, or rather, possible only as a function of movement, memory, and historical imagination. One could even say that *Prometheus* has various configurations or perceptual possibilities, which surely influence the construction of its meanings: the immediate view as seen from the door; the closer and more familiar experience of the members of the university who commune with it daily during their repast, accumulating the multi-layered reflections of repeated observation; and the perspective of the viewer who deliberately approaches the mural in its own right, entering its intimate space, enfolding him or herself within its panels and trying to capture and articulate the relationship between them.

Fig. 105 · Frary Hall during dining hours, Pomona College, Claremont, California, 1993, photograph by P. Channing.

98

From this latter vantage point, it becomes clear that the dramatic central panel forms part of a broader whole, completed by two long, thin panels on the side walls of the niche and one panel above. After the complexity and tension of the initial image, the ceiling panel seems extraordinarily simple and serene, mostly filled by a saturated, flatly applied cobalt blue background that is punctuated by a central geometric composition of interlocking blocklike forms in tones of sepia and umber, not quite symmetrical in their individual proportions and in the body they constitute. From the sides of this mass surge red forms that tend toward the shapes of irregular triangles, cut short in this aspiration by their flamelike terminations. From this centralized, virtually abstract image, one moves to the sides, to find two daring panels that combine abstract and figurative modes of rendering. To the right, or east, is a stylized rocky landscape in tones of sepia, green, and gray, suddenly flattened in the center by an abstract square. Around the edges of the square, the tail of a lengthy serpent entwines itself, linking two dark, elongated male centaurs, profiled against the darkening sky, with the more robust earthy-toned female centaur below, which is battling the snake coiled around her body and trying desperately to recover a small child centaur that seems to have fallen from her arms. To the left, or

west, we find a scene composed of more fragmented, semiabstract elements. In the lower register, geometric areas colored with gestural brushstrokes suggest fragments of earth, sea, and air and are traversed on the left by a branch and on the right by a dark, bayonetlike form that together mark linear axes from the lower corners to the center of the panel, where they nearly converge to form a triangle. Here, from a flame arising from the sea, emerges in turn the head of a cow with upraised, ethereal human arms; the flame appears to be the body of this composite creature, which has been interpreted as the mythical Io. Above and to the left, a thick branch, which might also be seen as an arm, marks a diagonal from the cow's head to the upper left corner, while

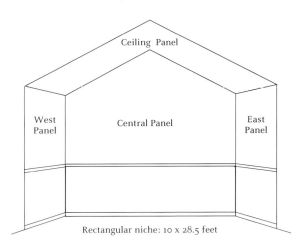

Rectangular niche: 10 x 28.5 feet

Fig. 106 · General view of Frary Hall, Pomona College, Claremont, California, photograph by R.C. Frampton.

Fig. 107 · Diagram of **Prometheus**, 1930, fresco, Frary Hall, Pomona College, Claremont, California, created by Barbara Krieger.

Fig. 108 · Oblique view of **Prometheus**, 1930, fresco, Frary Hall, Pomona College, Claremont, California, photograph by Nathan Zakheim.

99

to the right, an area of craggy rock takes shape out of an airy mass of white-gray paint. In the opening articulated between this rocky outcropping and the branch or arm come forth the upward-turned, masklike visages of a bearded man and a woman, commonly identified as Zeus and Hera.

From no single vantage point can the viewer encompass the whole composition, and in fact most analyses have centered on the primary and most easily perceivable panel (fig. 108). The narrow niche forces one to emulate the upturned position of Zeus's and Hera's faces, experiencing the varied emotions and sensations evoked by the diverse panels and attempting to puzzle out the relationship of the complex representations that surround one.

But whatever the viewpoint one adopts before *Prometheus,* an awareness of the primacy of corporeal experience and the limits of its representation is inevitable. The absence of recognizable mimetic forms in some instances makes one only more conscious of one's own volumetric and kinesthetic existence. The force and vitality of the images reside in the dialogue they establish, indeed compel, between human bodies themselves and between those bodies and the architectural and pictorial forms and spaces they inhabit and consume. The expressive terms of this dialogue, as articulated by Orozco's artistic construction, provide not a coherent narration but a vital poetic experience of form, matter, and symbol and the disintegration

or questioning of their boundaries. It is this aspect, of which we are made more aware by the art of the past thirty years and by poststructuralist theory and practice, that will constitute the central perspective of this essay.

Prometheus Recounted

Throughout his life, [Jackson] Pollock repeatedly referred to Orozco as "the real man" and consistently remarked that Prometheus, *Orozco's mural at Pomona College in California, was "the greatest painting in North America."*

— L. KENT WOLGAMOTT [2]

The 1930 *Prometheus,* the first of three murals that Orozco painted in the United States, has been touched upon in all major general studies of Orozco and has been the subject of detailed interpretation by several authors. The testimony of Jorge Juan Crespo de la Serna, Orozco's close friend and assistant at Pomona, in a 1952 essay,[3] the narrative of Alma Reed in her impassioned 1955 biography of the artist,[4] and the correspondence related to the mural's production published by Luis Cardoza y Aragón in his 1959 monographic study[5] provide invaluable primary sources. David W. Scott's penetrating analysis and contextualization of the mural in a 1957 article emphasize its importance as a transitional work that summarizes and culminates the

Fig. 109 · Ceiling panel of **Prometheus**, 1930, fresco, 7 x 28.5 feet (2.1 x 8.7 m), Frary Hall, Pomona College, Claremont, California, photograph by Schenk and Schenk Photography.

developments in Orozco's earlier murals in Mexico and introduces thematic and stylistic innovations that determine the future development of his work and his mural production in particular, both in the United States and Mexico.[6] Drawing on the early writings of Cardoza y Aragón and on the testimony of Crespo de la Serna, Scott emphasizes the totemic quality of the Promethean hero for the artist's production and points out the link between the personal and intellectual biography of the artist in determining its selection and interpretation. Moreover, he carefully locates the work in the context of Orozco's stylistic and thematic development and in the art historical context in which he was trained, noting the mural's combination of a Renaissance monumentality and idealized treatment of space and anatomy with symbolism's expressive subversion of classical subjects. His rigorous research and astute interpretative ability laid the foundation for all more recent studies of the subject and unequivocally established its pivotal quality: "As Orozco the myth-maker became able to create his own symbols directly, with an immediacy of expression which freed him from dependence on ready-made signs and on direct allusions to the Greeks, the Indians, or the Mexican Revolution, he painted new worlds peopled by new men, driven by the unseen forces of life."[7]

Jacqueline Barnitz's study of Orozco's involvement with the Delphic Studios during his extended sojourn in New York in the late 1920s and early 1930s traces Orozco's knowledge of Greek culture and documents the influence of this particular philosophical and literary context on his conceptualization of the Prometheus myth at Pomona.[8] She notes that his early classical education was enriched by the contemporary resignification of the Titan by the members of the salon established by Eva Sikelianos and Alma Reed as a metaphor for the existential dilemma of modern man and by his contact with Emily Hamblen, the translator of Nietszche into

Fig. 110 · Central panel of **Prometheus**, 1930, fresco, 20 x 28.5 feet (6 x 8.7 m), Frary Hall, Pomona College, Claremont, California, photograph by Jeffrey Nintzel.

English, from whom he learned of the philosopher's interpretation of Prometheus in *The Birth of Tragedy,* as a rebel, a self-made god, and a free man.

The study of occult symbolism in Orozco's work by Fausto Ramírez sheds new light on the ways in which the presence of these convictions in the Mexican intellectual milieu of the early twentieth century was confirmed and reaffirmed by the contacts the artist established in the United States, providing the groundwork for new interpretive directions in the reading of Orozco's work that have been followed up in recent years by Renato González Mello.[9]

Laurance P. Hurlburt, in his 1989 book *Mexican Muralists in the United States,* provides an in-depth study of the *Prometheus* mural and its process of creation, taking Scott's research as a basis and synthesizing many of the other published sources on the subject as well as primary source material drawn from the archives on the mural at Pomona's Montgomery Art Gallery, the college libraries, and oral and written testimonies.[10]

In addition, the analysis and interpretation of the *Prometheus* mural in the context of broader studies of Orozco and Mexican muralism by Justino Fernández, MacKinley Helm, and Antonio Rodríguez, among others, enrich the interpretive

101

panorama, basically concurring with regard to the place of the mural in Orozco's development while varying in the nuances of their interpretations of the work's meaning on the basis of formal analysis and references to different readings of the Prometheus myth in literary sources.[11]

Formally and conceptually, scholarship on the Pomona mural has clearly established and understood it as a transitional work in relation to Orozco's earlier murals in Mexico and his later ones in both the United States and Mexico. While many conceptual and formal continuities with his previous production can be found, the grandiosity of the iconographic scheme and its multiple levels of signification set it apart from the murals in the National Preparatory School, with their more culturally and historically specific iconography, and foresee the conceptual complexity and philosophical nature of later compositions, such as those of Dartmouth and Guadalajara. Moreover, the formal treatment both of the composition as a whole and of the anatomy of the figures represented constitutes a definitive departure from the academic conceptions that underlie his earlier compositions. In *Prometheus,* Orozco integrates into a new expressionist posture the diverse attitudes toward the body evident in his previous work and incorporates ideas assimilated through his close and direct examination of European art of the late nineteenth and early twentieth centuries during his stay in New York from 1927 to 1929. As González Mello has concluded:

> This is a moment of rupture, as important for Orozco's work as the painting of the *Demoiselles d' Avignon* was for Picasso. It is in this mural that we can see the undermining, for the first time, of his academic formation. Previously he had employed nonacademic forms such as caricature, even in his frescoes. In some panels, such as *The Trinity* in the Preparatory School, he had painted quite grandiloquent figures, but without challenging

the particular unity and coherence of each one of them. If *Prometheus* is important it is because it threatens one of the most deep-set academic prejudices: that which posits the essential rationality of human anatomy. This mural is not an avant-garde painting, but something even more radical: a painting which subverts Mexican academicism in one of its strongest bastions, that of the use of life drawing as the basis of figure painting. And it does this not from outside, through the proposal of a completely different system, but from within, by taking Rodin's monumentalism to its ultimate consequences, to an extreme which disarms its fundamental logic.[12]

What is now necessary, on the basis of this historiographical consensus, is a closer visual analysis of the mural and the corresponding drawings, in order to understand more clearly and specifically the creative process and aesthetic proposition of Orozco's mural at Pomona in terms of his innovations in visual language. It is particularly important to take into account the four parts of the mural as an integral

Fig. 111 · West panel of **Prometheus,** 1930, fresco, 15.3 x 7 feet (4.6 x 2.1 m), Frary Hall, Pomona College, Claremont, California, photograph by Jeffrey Nintzel.

Fig. 112 · East panel of **Prometheus,** 1930, fresco, 15.3 x 7 feet (4.6 x 2.1 m), Frary Hall, Pomona College, Claremont, California, photograph by Jeffrey Nintzel.

conception. Most studies of the mural have focused on the main, central panel. The upper and two side panels are generally treated summarily, if at all, and indeed, several authors consider the themes of these sections of minor importance and their style inferior (figs. 109, 111, and 112). Hurlburt has argued, citing Nathan Zakheim's restoration reports, that the two side panels are most likely attributable in large part to Crespo de la Serna rather than to Orozco himself.[13] I do not concur with this pejorative judgment or with their reattribution. Rather, they seem to me to be areas in which Orozco experiments with more radical avant-garde stylistic and compositional strategies, combining abstraction and figuration in ways that anticipate later works in his oeuvre. They serve a transitional stylistic function in relation to the completely abstract forms of the upper panel and, if anything, reveal more clearly than the immediately visible main panel the sophistication of the mural's conception. The work as a whole encompasses a discourse on figuration and abstraction, on what can be represented and what only symbolized. I believe that Orozco's interpretation and resignification of the Prometheus myth, as well as the vision of man that he consolidates in this work, can be better understood if we analyze the mural's four sections as part of an integral proposal in which their formal differences, as well as their conceptual relationship, play a key role.

The story of the commission of the Pomona mural is well documented in the existing studies,[14] so I shall not dwell on the details here but instead develop some of their implications. The motor driving the commission was the Catalan art historian José Pijoán, then employed as an art history professor at Pomona College, who, in dialogue with Sumner Spaulding, the architect of the recently completed refectory, Frary Hall, suggested that a mural would serve as a fitting decoration for the arch above the fireplace on the north wall of the austere salon and fulfill the function of "warming" the space

visually while providing perspectival closure. Originally the college had experimented with a tapestry, clearly suggesting its desire to build upon the certain monastic, medieval quality associated with much American university architecture, which refers to the historical origins of the concept of the university itself. This artifice was ultimately rejected, however, and replaced by the proposal of a mural, which was not only more economical but more readily adaptable to the specific exigencies of Spaulding's architecture and more explicit in its fulfillment of a didactic and inspirational purpose akin to that of the altarpiece that would have occupied the equivalent position in the religious edifices evoked by the construction.

Pijoán's suggestion that the work be done by a Mexican reveals, on one hand, the prestige and publicity that Mexican muralism had enjoyed over the previous decade in the U.S. press and, on the other, the particular importance of Hispanic heritage in southern California. Pijoán originally thought of Diego Rivera, whose work was already well known in the United States, but Crespo de la Serna, then teaching at the Chouinard Art School in Los Angeles, suggested that Orozco would be better for the job and introduced Pijoán to his work. The architecture itself establishes certain resonances with Mexican visual culture. The exterior of Frary Hall evokes the edifices of Franciscan missions and their dependence on Spanish Romanesque models, though the interior takes up the Gothic ogival arch; and its subdued and streamlined rendering, as well as its wood paneling and rafters, gives an Anglo-Saxon tone to the neomedieval construction. The projected didactic decoration of a space that recalled a religious temple yet fulfilled a secular and more universal function corresponded closely to the projects in which Orozco had participated in Mexico during the preceding decade, as part of José Vasconcelos's plan to resignify colonial and neocolonial edifices through their incorporation, occupation, and decoration in

103

connection with the program of the Ministry of Education.

The possible subjects for the mural proposed by Pijoán, which ranged from a Last Supper with an Indian Christ to the founders of North American universities accompanied by ten great figures of North and South American history, suggest his particular interest in the reconceptualization of historical, mythological, and religious subjects in provocative modern terms, which would invite reflection on cultural heroism and innovation in a universal and transcultural context. In light of research by Fausto Ramírez, Renato González Mello, and Marina Vázquez on the importance of Freemasonry for the conceptualization of the art of this period and muralism in particular, it is clear that the interpretation of historical and mythological figures as members of an underlying symbolic genealogy of Masonic masters coincided felicitously with the general conception proposed by Pijoán.[15] Existing correspondence and documentation, as well as a portrait Orozco painted at the time picturing Pijoán surrounded by flames, suggest that the artist and the art historian shared a close identification with Prometheus and agreed in their conception of the artist and intellectual as tormented, visionary martyrs, a theme that is clearly one possible reading of the Pomona mural.[16] The final selection of the subject of Prometheus lent itself both to the theme of cultural heroism and to the possibility of integrating multiple levels of signification and interpretation in the conception and reception of the mural.

Various literary and philosophical treatments of the Prometheus story have been cited as probable sources, to support various specific interpretations of the mural. Among them are the classical Greek texts. Hesiod in the *Theogony* and *Works and Days* narrates Prometheus's theft of fire from the gods as a gift to man in the context of a broader historical-mythological narration about the Titans, a race of giants, and their conflicts with the Olympian gods.[17]

These texts highlight the hostile and rebellious character of the Titans and Prometheus's ingenious perspicacity, which serves as a foil for the passionate ego of Zeus. As Carl Kerényi has noted in his detailed study of the Prometheus myth, the Titans were earlier gods and thus in an intermediate position between the Olympian gods and man; their name is associated with non-Greek peoples, or otherness, and Hesiod's narrative serves to explain and justify the established hierarchy.[18] Aeschylus, in *Prometheus Bound,* the only survivor of his four plays dealing with this hero, focuses specifically on Prometheus's character and plight, emphasizing that his suffering is the inevitable consequence of his putting himself in the place of man and of his consciousness of injustice, which at once liberates him and binds him to his fate. Like the animals, he experiences bodily suffering, but unlike them, he refuses to submit to "the order of things."[19]

Orozco was surely familiar with Greek culture and mythology through the classical models present

Fig. 113 · Group of actors, Second Delphic Festival, 1930, including Eva Sikelianos (seated center), photograph from the archives of Thanos Burlos/Vivette Tsarlamba-Kaklamani, courtesy John P. Anton.

in his academic training and through the renewed importance accorded to classical culture by the generation of the Ateneo de la Juventud and to mythological imagery by the generation of such modernist artists as Julio Ruelas. These latter two facets of the cultural avant-garde revived metaphysical concerns in late-nineteenth- and early-twentieth-century Mexico.[20] In fact, Orozco is probably responsible for the introductory vignette for *Prometheus Bound* in the 1921 edition of Aeschylus's tragedies published by the National University of Mexico as part of Vasconcelos's educational and artistic program, in which the translation and distribution of classical texts played a key role.[21] Orozco's involvement with the Delphic Circle in New York in the latter 1920s coincided with the rehearsals of *Prometheus Bound* for its presentation in Delphi in 1930 as part of the group's messianic quest to revive ancient Greek cultural heritage in the modern state, and he designed the poster for these efforts (fig. 113). Moreover, he was present for their discussions of the contemporary implications of the drama with respect to man's anguished battle for spiritual freedom, and he surely knew Alma Reed's 1927 translation of a text by Giuseppe Consoli Fiego that deals with Prometheus's final liberation and expiation by means of the elements: air, water, and fire.[22]

Among the later symbolic interpretations of the myth, that of Fausto Ramírez emphasizes the importance of the association of Prometheus with the visual arts, on the basis of the version of the myth in Ovid's *Metamorphosis,* in which he models his body in clay and animates it with the divine fire, thus becoming the first sculptor and the maker of man, a master artisan who challenges the notion of divine privilege.[23] Justino Fernández cites Boccaccio's interpretation of the Titan as the provider of knowledge and technology, symbolized by fire, to the unenlightened human race.[24] The personal assimilation of these symbols by Orozco has been convincingly argued by Scott; Orozco's sense of himself as

an isolated, misunderstood artist led him to identify with the anguished, superhuman figure, while the fact that he had lost a hand and damaged his eyesight and hearing in an explosion as an adolescent surely gave specific personal, corporeal meanings to the fiery metaphor.[25]

Of the modern poetic interpretations of the myth that can be related to Orozco's work, that of MacKinley Helm mentions Shelley's *Prometheus Unbound,* a lyrical drama that constitutes an imaginative reconstruction of the lost final tragedy of Aeschylus, conceived as a prophetic vision of the future of humankind.[26] Orozco's contact in the Delphic Studios with Emily Hamblen, who translated Nietzsche and established certain similarities between his perspectives and the artist's work, suggests that he knew the German philosopher's writings on Prometheus, which highlight Goethe's vision of the Titan as a self-named god, an individual who frees himself through the act of creation, offering salvation to humankind through knowledge and will. For Nietzsche, Prometheus represents an active masculine principle, in justified revolt against oppressive or usurped power, who symbolizes the necessity of sacrilege and consequent suffering.[27]

While many or all of these sources and interpretations may have been present in the process of conceptualization of the mural and can help illuminate the interpretive choices made by Orozco, the dependency of many studies of the Pomona *Prometheus* on literary sources and their relative lack of attention to its visual content and possible visual models are surprising in light of its artistic force and innovation. The potent literary substrate of the Prometheus theme cannot be denied and surely contributed to its acceptance as an appropriate subject for a liberal arts college as well as to its continuing pertinence. However, the approach that Orozco took was anything but literary. The narrative references evoked by the topic were suppressed or relegated in favor of a symbolic synthesis that erases the logical time and space of narration and involves us in a complex, innovative visual logic.

Prometheus Dismembered

In every painting, as in any other work of art, there is always an IDEA, never a STORY. The idea is the point of departure, the first cause of the plastic construction, and it is always present all the time as energy creating matter. The stories and other literary associations exist only in the mind of the spectator, the painting acting as the stimulus.

— JOSÉ CLEMENTE OROZCO[28]

At Pomona, Orozco did not paint any of the stories or literary versions of the Prometheus myth. His conception of the subject comes closest perhaps to that of Shelley, who saw Prometheus as a prophet, and certainly to that of Nietszche, drawn from Goethe, for whom the Titan was a symbol, a posture, a surge of masculine energy, larger than life, that challenges the gods. The ambiguity of the mural's apparent narrative crux, coinciding with the ogival arch, in fact leads me to question the fixed identity of the protagonist and the subject matter. In revisiting the literary sources mentioned above, as well as various visual representations of Prometheus, I think it possible that Orozco, like Shelley, was in part imagining the final lost chapter of Aeschylus's Promethean cycle: the liberation and expiation of Prometheus through the action of the elements, rather than the legend of his theft of fire or his torment. The theme explored in the panels seems to be that of the passage from animalistic instinct to specifically human (and godlike) consciousness and liberation, but in relation to a nonrepresentational, nonanthropomorphic conception of divinity, as if it were the perfection of form, which cannot be represented in bodily terms. Moreover, this representation of the protagonist, if we search for its visual

antecedents, seems to conflate the identities of various heroic rebels, particularly Christ and Satan. What we have here, then, is a poetic visual and spatial construction, not a narrative, a fact that resonates with the association with Shelley and Goethe but, more important, with the postulates of late-nineteenth- and early-twentieth-century avant-garde art, assumed and integrated by Orozco during the process of his early work and, more intensively, during the years in New York that directly preceded his realization of the Pomona mural.

The modernity of Orozco's working method and artistic proposition lies in the nonnarrative, nonmimetic structure of *Prometheus,* in the visual, sensorial, and spatial metaphors presented in the work. The use of literary and philosophical antecedents and the vital experiences that gave them personal significance for Orozco is not translated literally into the work; rather, it forms the basis for a visual and material construction that reconfigures and synthesizes, in symbolic terms, underlying myths and archetypes of Western culture, as well as personal and contemporary social experiences, by its evocation of corporeal sensations through formal language. In interpreting the Pomona mural, one can appreciate Orozco's capacity for the integration of these elements into a new visual and conceptual configuration that takes on independent life as a forceful visual statement.

In itself, the decision to focus on the Prometheus theme through a symbolic presentation of a Nietzschean vision, embodied in the physical presence and semivertical posture of the central

Fig. 114 · Attributed to José Clemente Orozco, illustration for Aeschylus's **Prometheus Bound,** from Aeschylus, **Tragedies** (National University of Mexico, 1921), 9, courtesy José Luis Barrios Lara, Mexico City, photograph by Agustín Estrada.

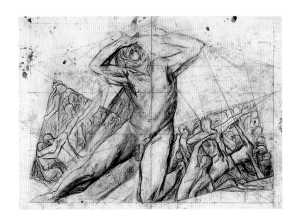

figure of the panel, clearly separates Orozco's representation from more literal, narrative versions of the subject (fig. 114). The Prometheus chained to a rock, his hands immobilized and his crouched body silhouetted against the ominous dark crags, that Orozco re-creates in his ink illustration for the 1921 edition of Aeschylus's tragedies is absent here.[29] Moreover, the elements, including rock (or earth), fire, water, and air, are present as symbols rather than as scenery. Considering the stagelike format of the niche where the mural is located and recalling Orozco's experience of the rehearsals of *Prometheus Bound* in the Delphic Studios, one might imagine the mural as a contemporary dramatization of the classic manuscript, in which it is reinterpreted in terms of the ways it sheds light on modern

dilemmas and with recourse to contemporary aesthetic paradigms, fragmenting time and space in the manner of Brecht or Beckett or indeed André Gide in *Prometheus Misbound.*

In visual terms, perhaps the closest paradigm for the compositional structure of the Pomona *Prometheus* is the work of Paul Cézanne, whose painting Orozco had studied carefully in New York and admired for the firmness of its construction.[30] This may seem surprising, since the mural does not "look" like Cézanne on a superficial level, but we must be aware in this context of Orozco as a mature artist, one whose manner of assimilation of the work of the artists he admired was not direct or simple but instead integrated conceptually into his own already firmly established artistic convictions. If we look carefully, however, we can see how the equal visual weight accorded to abstract and figurative elements in *Prometheus* draws on Cézanne, as does the way in which Orozco materializes space in response to structural and symbolic rather than mimetic necessities. (See, for example, the volumetric areas of blue, echoing the color of the upper panel, that assert themselves in the lower register of the main panel of *Prometheus*, suggesting, without representing, the presence of sky or water; a similar

Fig. 115 · Study for central panel, 1930, graphite on paper, Pomona College, Claremont, California; P2000.2.1 © Pomona College and Clemente Orozco, 2000. For larger reproduction, see fig. 83.

Fig. 116 · Study of leaning figure (central panel), 1930, charcoal on paper, Pomona College, Claremont, California; P2000.2.15 © Pomona College and Clemente Orozco, 2000.

Fig. 117 · Study of torso from back (central panel), 1930, charcoal on paper, Pomona College, Claremont, California; P2000.2.11 © Pomona College and Clemente Orozco, 2000.

Fig. 118 · Study of back of torso with left arm raised over head (central panel), 1930, charcoal on paper, Pomona College, Claremont, California; P2000.2.14 © Pomona College and Clemente Orozco, 2000.

107

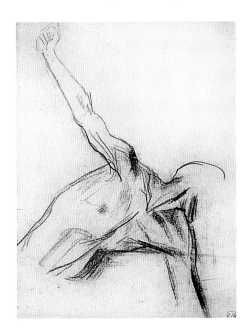

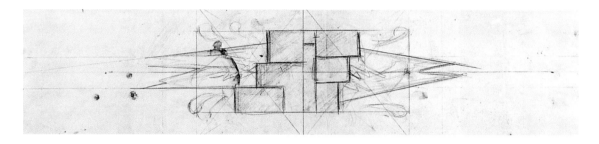

treatment is given to the flames that descend, in a configuration alluding to a star or to angel's wings, from above, as well as to the flames in some other areas of the mural.) Moreover, the forceful linear structure of each of the panels, which subordinates illusionistic logic to the principles of Dynamic Symmetry[31] and foregrounds the role of the body as a structural, linear element in the composition, recalls Cézanne's bathers and the ways in which the figures in those works respond to a symbolic and structural, rather than a narrative, conception. The extant drawings for *Prometheus*[32] make this amply clear, with their careful tracing of a linear matrix that

focuses the visual energy of the viewer on the central point of each panel and, in the case of the north wall panels, directs our vision up toward the crux of the arch and, implicitly, toward the abstract Godhead on the ceiling panel (figs. 115 and 83).

The use of the body as a structural element also echoes Auguste Rodin, another artist greatly admired by Orozco and his generation,[33] particularly for the way he reuses certain figures, changing only their positions and orientations in order to transform their compositional functions.[34] The clearest examples of this in *Prometheus* are the three male figures in the central panel, whose arms, outstretched to form a cross (though in two cases the left arm is bent at the elbow), create a formal echo that relates the two sides of the axial image yet assume very different expressive nuances: one a Dantesque lover absorbed in an amorous reverie, another seeming to usher the masses toward some central goal, and a third, knife in hand, threatening an invisible victim. These figures are emphasized and clearly delineated in the preparatory drawing for the central panel as well as in the anatomical studies for the mural, along with the Prometheus figure and another figure at his lower right, whose posture seems to be an inversion and reversal, on a less monumental scale, of the twisted position of the Titan (figs. 116, 117, and 118). Another source of historical inspiration for the conflated structural and expressive use of the figure here is surely El Greco, though Orozco has radicalized his strategies in light of the fragmented treatment of time and space and the unabashed primacy of linear structure in twentieth-century painting.

Fig. 119 · Study for ceiling panel, 1930, graphite on paper, Pomona College, Claremont, California; P2000.2.2 © Pomona College and Clemente Orozco, 2000, photograph by Schenk and Schenk Photography.

Fig. 120 · Study for west panel (Zeus, Hera, and Io), 1930, graphite on paper, Pomona College, Claremont, California; P2000.2.3 © Pomona College and Clemente Orozco, 2000.

108

The abstract Godhead in the ceiling panel is a key element in unraveling the conceptual development of the mural. In correspondence with David Scott, Crespo de la Serna noted that Orozco had originally painted a large head of Zeus in this position but eliminated it "because he wanted a more abstract symbol, a symbol with no relation to time or space."[35] This testimony, corroborated by the superimposition of forms in the preparatory sketch for this section, suggests a significant reconceptualization of the mural program, particularly since the head of Zeus reappears in the upper register of the lateral left panel; it would seem that originally Orozco's intent was a more literal narration of the myth, with Zeus as the source of fire. In replacing the Olympian god with an abstract divine principle, expressed through the rational vehicle of geometry, Orozco's mural adopts a closer correspondence to Masonic precepts of hierarchy and stresses an evolutionary transformation in the concept of divinity and man's relationship to it. The Olympian god is relegated to an intermediate position, his hegemony contested both by Prometheus and by Orozco. He is presented in a natural setting dominated by the forces of the elements and animalistic instinct in anthropomorphic form, and he is victimized by his human passions and foibles, manifested in the hybrid figure of Io, which occupies a central position in the left panel, and in his anguished entrapment between two females (Io and Hera).[36]

Here, too, the preparatory sketch for the panel gives an important clue to Orozco's conceptual evolution of the project (fig. 119). Originally the rectangle in the lower right corner was occupied by a skyscraper, recalling the artist's New York paintings of the late 1920s and the fact that in a 1929 article in *Creative Art,* "New World, New Races and New Art," he posited the skyscraper as a paradigm for a new configuration of the visual arts, which he predicted would find its culminating expression in muralism:

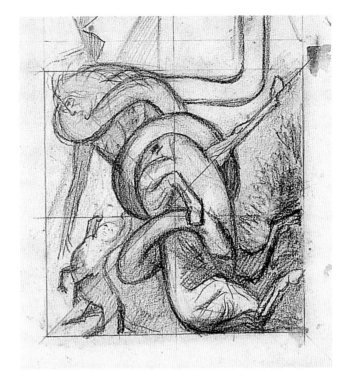

Fig. 121 · Study of centaur and baby (east panel), 1930, graphite on paper, Pomona College, Claremont, California; P2000.2.5 © Pomona College and Clemente Orozco, 2000.

Already the architecture of Manhattan is a new value, something that has nothing to do with Egyptian pyramids, with the Paris Opera, with the Giralda of Seville, or with Santa Sophia, any more than it has to do with the Maya palaces of Chichén Itzá or with the "pueblos" of Arizona.

…The architecture of Manhattan is the first step. Painting and sculpture must certainly follow as inevitable second steps.

The highest, the most logical, the purest and strongest form of painting is the mural. In this form alone, is it one with the other arts—with all the others.[37]

The replacement of this paradigmatic artifact, alluding directly to technology's role in the establishment of a new aesthetic order, with an abstract (and indeed almost abstract expressionist) form traversed by a bayonetlike gesture—perhaps allusive of a thunderbolt—confirms Orozco's movement toward a more symbolic visual rhetoric rather than a literal, mimetic vocabulary (figs. 120 and 121). Moreover, in substituting for the skyscraper a multivalent symbol, Orozco suggests the failure of Zeus and the old order to achieve the ideal of divine perfection expressed by the rational, symbolic geometry of the Godhead in the ceiling panel, while presenting a model for a new, nonobjective expressionist aesthetic that prefigures the developments of the postwar period (and surely explains the admiration expressed for the mural by U.S. artists of the next generation, such as Jackson Pollock).

The presence of a perfect square—perhaps a rock transformed into a divine symbol by the art of technology—in the center of the east panel suggests once again the hidden, rational intentionality that propitiates the decadence and destruction of the old instinctual order of the centaurs, where animalistic passions reign. The serpent, a symbol of knowledge and cunning[38] as well as masculine prowess, echoes the form of this abstract element as it slithers away from the two defeated, emaciated male centaurs to battle the still-robust female. The greater vitality of the female actors in both side panels perhaps alludes to the patriarchal mythology of their dominant, irrational component. Indeed, the complex, intertwined, curving forms articulated by the female centaur and the section of the snake that battles her are balanced by the rational, geometric, linear structure that orders the upper register of the scene, where a new regime is taking hold.

The visual antecedents of Orozco's aesthetic proposal in these panels can be traced, in part, to Byzantine and Trecento art and their specific derivation in Giotto, which has often been mentioned in the literature and criticism regarding this mural. In particular, the use of the intense and saturated flat blue surface, and its coloristic echo in other sections of the mural, marks a deliberate recuperation of a representational mode of the fourteenth century, in which, as Julia Kristeva has astutely noted, the pigment is at once a signifier of the quotidian perceptual experience of the sky, an allusion to the celestial abode, and a recognition of

painting as a signifying practice, marking a transitional moment in the conscious separation of the perceiving subject from the represented object.[39] The use of geometric forms to refer to the divine principle was already part of Orozco's visual vocabulary in his 1921 illustrations for *The Divine Comedy*, which appeared in the same series published by the National University as Aeschylus's *Tragedies* (fig. 122); in several of the capitular vignettes, the celestial ambit is evoked by a conglomerate of cubic and prismatic shapes.[40] Orozco's aesthetic reflections, a result of the broader visual education offered by New York's museums, allowed him to synthesize these preexisting affinities and intuitions into a more complex and conscious aesthetic program.

The treatment of the human body and, in particular, the posture of Prometheus are other important keys to the complex symbolic iconography of the Pomona mural. The traditional iconography of the

Fig. 122 · Attributed to José Clemente Orozco, illustration for Canto XVI of Dante's **Divine Comedy** (National University of Mexico, 1921), 457, photograph by Agustín Estrada.

CANTO DECIMOSEXTO

H nobleza de la sangre! Aunque seas muy poca cosa, nunca me admiraré de que hagas vanagloriarse de ti a la gente aquí abajo, donde nuestros afectos languidecen; pues yo mismo, allá donde el apetito no se tuerce, quiero decir, en el cielo, me vanaglorié de poseerte. A la verdad, eres como un manto que se acorta en breve, de modo que si cada día no se le añade algún pedazo, el tiempo

hero, which highlights an earthbound figure who suffers corporeal martyrdom, underlining his humanity and carnality, is replaced here by a vigorous giant who tends toward verticality. His hands, freed from bondage, reach for the sky, for the fire associated with immaterial godliness and spiritual illumination, stressing the existential dilemma of human consciousness and intellectual desire, more akin to a mystical conception of divinity. Prometheus reaches for the fire and at the same time is consumed by it, his paradoxical predicament mirrored in the dualistic representation of the human race on either side of his body, at once liberated and enslaved by its consciousness.

The representation of giants, as Frida Gorbach has shown, was linked in the late-nineteenth-century Mexican culture in which Orozco was raised not only with the Christian iconography of such figures as St. Christopher but with the representation of human anomalies for scientific study. In the Hall of Teratology (the scientific study of biological abnormalities) inaugurated in 1895 in the National Museum of Mexico, the exhibition began with a portrait of the giant Martín Salmerón, presented here as a freak of nature to be explained and analyzed, while at the same time the visual image testified to and confirmed the impossibility of reducing such a phenomenon to rational objectivity.[41] Orozco seems to have approached his subject in a manner similar to the author of this portrait of a real giant, beginning with the academic conventions of human anatomy and proportions and then exaggerating them, extending them in order to achieve a visual distortion that would speak of the Titan's strangeness, his otherness, his intermediate status between humanness and godliness (fig. 123).

The model for the figure of Prometheus was John Goheen, an oversize student of the college who, along with Crespo de la Serna, posed for the life drawings on which the bodies in the mural were based.[42] But the rendering of the figure of

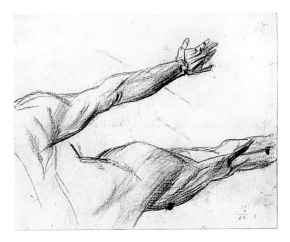

Fig. 123 · Study of right forearm and detail (central panel), 1930, charcoal on paper, Pomona College, Claremont, California; P2000.2.9 © Pomona College and Clemente Orozco, 2000.

Prometheus in the mural does not follow the academic procedure that aimed to record the anatomical logic of the human figure or derive from it ideal proportions. While, at first glance, it may seem Michelangelesque in its monumentality, upon closer study, the shading and coloristic treatment of the muscles seem to decompose their volumes, and the drawing, particularly the connection of the legs to the torso, seems awkward, disjointed, and illogical, as if to suggest an estrangement of the protagonist from his own body, his conversion into something more than a body.

In Orozco's National Preparatory School murals of the 1920s, two strategies are deployed regarding the body: first, that of caricature, the distortion of the

Fig. 124 · Two studies of an arm (central panel), 1930, charcoal on paper, Pomona College, Claremont, California; P2000.2.6 © Pomona College and Clemente Orozco, 2000.

Fig. 125 · Study of raised left arm with outline of head (central panel), 1930, charcoal on paper, Pomona College, Claremont, California; P2000.2.13 © Pomona College and Clemente Orozco, 2000.

111

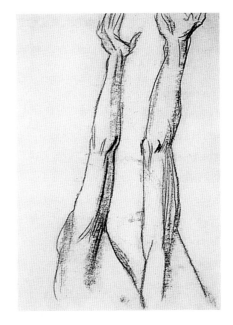
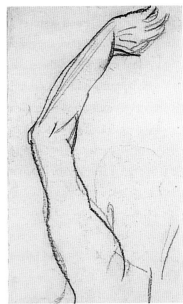

body with clear moral implications (a version of the monstrous, though filtered through irony and humor), and second, a more architectonic mode—solid and volumetric in the avant-garde classic sense—that is continued in *Omniscience* (fig. 5), painted for Francisco Iturbe in the House of Tiles. In the Pomona *Prometheus*, this paradigm is broken, separating clearly the pictorial rhetoric of Orozco's murals from that of their architectural setting. The human body—or human consciousness, represented by Prometheus's body—becomes a site of existential conflict, disintegrating and disjointed.

Prometheus's arms, flexed at the elbows, are overcome by the fiery mass that descends from above, enveloping and merging with his hands, while another rush of flames seems to shoot up from below. Many of the drawings for the mural also focus on arms and hands, which become key expressive elements in the composition (figs. 124 and 125). They reach up in longing, aspiring to become one with the fire that descends, and in the case of many of the figures in the crowd on the left, the tips of their fingers are truncated (as are those of Io in the west panel) to express their boundless desire. On the right, however, a mass of anonymous heads predominates; the arms and hands represented are more academic in their rendering and forceful in their musculature and gestures, but each points in a different direction, suggesting the isolation of individual wills within the crowd.

Elaborating on Scott's comments on the artist's personal identification with the mural's protagonist, one can imagine that Orozco's insistent concern with the visual registry of hands, and their primacy as expressive features in the mural, may reflect—as Sally Stein has argued for Dorothea Lange's repeated representation of awkwardly positioned feet—his own heightened consciousness of these members as a result of his physical maiming.[43] At the same time, the sense of estrangement from the body, projected by the figure of Prometheus,

may well reflect the artist's own experience of alienation from the body as an integral organism, a reaction experienced, as Ruth Behar has shown, by many who suffer long-term or permanent bodily injury.[44] The communication of this content, however, in the rendering of anatomy transforms this corporeal experience into a metaphor for the human condition, for the desire to be more than a body, more than a mortal entity, and the desire or even the conviction that the spirit is capable of transcendence.

Prometheus's posture, however, makes it unclear whether he is recoiling from or submitting to the fire, putting into doubt the consequence of this human desire. In an earlier sketch, now lost, but published in the Claremont Colleges' *Student Life* in 1930[45] (fig. 126), the figure is more clearly oppressed by the celestial flames, but in the final version he tends more toward verticality, and his movement and the outcome of his incipient fusion with the celestial fire are more ambiguous. The fact that the expressive weight of the images lies

Fig. 126 · Sketch for **Prometheus**, 1930, graphite on paper, from **Student Life** (April 17, 1930), 2, Pomona College Archives, Special Collections, Honnold/Mudd Library, The Claremont Colleges.

Fig. 127 · Photograph of 1917 exhibition of Alberto Fuster's **The Triptych of the Rebels**, showing original disposition of the panels, from **Revista de revistas**, vol. 8, no. 400 (December 30, 1917), 14, courtesy Biblioteca de Arte Mexicano/Ricardo Pérez Escamilla, photograph by Agustín Estrada.

primordially in the figures and that the central image is devoid of particularizing narrative elements permits its association and metaphorical identification with other monumental, heroic figures, in acts of transcendental rebellion or defiance.

Among those identities that can be related to this Prometheus are those of Christ, whose sacrifice for humankind has often been associated symbolically with that of the Greek hero, and of Lucifer or Satan, the fallen angel, who represents the other pole of the possible outcome of Prometheus's quest. Both in fact are present, along with Prometheus, in the *Triptych of the Rebels* (about 1910) by the Mexican academic painter Alberto Fuster (fig. 127), a work that Orozco singles out for praise in his autobiography and may well have observed in progress.[46] The triptych is surely an important conceptual antecedent for the central figure of the Pomona mural, the quintessential rebel; in its original configuration, Christ occupies the central position, Satan the left, and Prometheus the right.[47] A 1917 review by the critic Alfonso Toro highlights its outstanding expressive force and technique, noting: "The rebels are: *Lucifer, Jesus Christ,* and *Prometheus,* in whom we find synthesized the battle of humankind

against the unknown, against the omnipotent forces of nature."[48] All three are academic studies of heroic male nudes, and the representation of Prometheus, following the traditional narrative convention, shows an anguished figure chained to a cliff, his muscular tension and facial grimace transmitting extreme pain, as an eagle devours his viscera before the viewer in a graphically explicit manner. This Prometheus, however, has much less to do with Orozco's representation than the other two rebels: Christ, whose crucified body decisively parts the central panel into two, and Lucifer, who, in a posture of awkward contrapposto comparable to that of the Pomona hero, strains upward to escape from his dark prison (figs. 128, 129, and 130).

This is not a case of direct formal quotation but rather of the integration and resignification of an image that had engraved itself on Orozco's memory, in consonance with the Masonic propensity for conceptually conflating heroic figures. Antonio

Fig. 128 · Alberto Fuster, **Jesus Christ** panel from **The Triptych of the Rebels**, about 1910, oil on canvas, Museo Salvador Ferrando, Tlacotalpán, Veracruz/INBA, photograph by Agustín Estrada.

Fig. 129 · Alberto Fuster, **Prometheus** panel from **The Triptych of the Rebels**, about 1910, oil on canvas, Casa de la Cultura de Tlacotalpán, Veracruz/INBA, photograph by Agustín Estrada.

Fig. 130 · Alberto Fuster, **Lucifer** panel from **The Triptych of the Rebels**, about 1910, oil on canvas, Casa de la Cultura de Tlacotalpán, Veracruz/INBA, photograph by Agustín Estrada.

113

Fig. 131 · Felipe Santiago Gutiérrez, **The Fall of the Rebel Angels**, 1850, oil on canvas, Patrimonio Cultural e Histórico de la Universidad Autónoma del Estado de México, Toluca, photograph by Arturo Piera, courtesy Museo Nacional de Arte/INBA.

114

Rodríguez too has noted a similar association with Lucifer: "Orozco's *Prometheus* appears more a rebel angel who, instead of bringing fire to man, brings down upon them the divine curse."[49] Indeed, in *The Fall of the Rebel Angels* (1850) by Felipe Santiago Gutiérrez (fig. 131), another Mexican academic painting probably well known to Orozco, the position of the legs and torso of one of the fallen angels, again a careful anatomical study of a male nude, is virtually identical to that of the Pomona Prometheus, but in reverse. The shape formed by the descending flames behind Orozco's figure recalls, without representing, the angel's wings, while at the same time evoking a divine fire that punishes and purifies, consumes and gives life.[50]

The conceptual relationship between the myth of Prometheus and that of the Fall is also emphasized by Nietzsche, whose importance to Orozco has already been mentioned. He sees the "active sin" of Prometheus as an expression of the dignity of sacrilege, assumed as a masculine, Aryan, upward-striving value, which he contrasts with the Semitic interpretation of sin as a passive, feminine attribute,[51] and he relates this duality to the simultaneously Apollonian and Dionysian nature of the Prometheus myth:

In the heroic impulse towards the universal, in the attempt to step outside the spell of individuation and to become the *single* essence of the world, the individual suffers within himself the original contradiction hidden in things, that is, he commits sacrilege and suffers....Whoever understands the innermost core of the Prometheus story—namely, the necessity of sacrilege as it is imposed on the Titanically striving individual—must also immediately sense how un-Apollonian this pessimistic conception is, for Apollo wants to bring individual beings to rest precisely by drawing boundaries between them, boundaries which his demands for self-knowledge and moderation impress upon us again and again as the most sacred laws of the world....The sudden surge of the Dionysian tide lifts the small individual mountains of waves on its back, as the brother of Prometheus, the Titan Atlas, did the earth. This Titanic impulse, to become as it were the Atlas of all individuals and to carry them even higher and further on a broad back is the common element shared by the Promethean and the Dionysian principles....So the essential duality of the Aeschylean Prometheus, his simultaneously Dionysian and Apollonian nature, might be expressed in conceptual terms as follows: "All that exists is just and unjust and equally justified in both."[52]

The symbolic character of the representation invites the viewer to associate the image as well with other iconographic themes suggested by the composition—for example, the Last Judgment, which is clearly evoked by the powerful central figure of Prometheus, who seems to divide the surrounding crowd into two distinct groups. Prometheus's body, becoming more than itself, more than a human body, divides the composition abruptly to form a kind of Dantesque inferno, in which the diverse corporeal responses of humankind reflect the disorientation provoked by the decisive

moment. The fiery context of the background and the general color scheme reinforce the apocalyptic, infernolike atmosphere of the central panel of the mural, giving an expressive importance to fire— a vehicle of punishment, martyrdom, and purification—rather than to the sea and rock that appear in the adjacent panels and constitute the scenario of more traditional representations of the Prometheus myth. The boon stolen from the gods for humankind by Prometheus is presented here as a symbol of the dangerous potential adumbrated by his audacity: Man, in pushing beyond his limits, abdicates the security of the gods' protection and of salvation and may become a demigod, but he also assumes the consequences of ambition, consciousness, and reason. The social and political atmosphere of the year 1930, encompassing the threat of fascism and the 1929 stock market crash, the consequences of which Orozco had observed firsthand in New York,[53] surely influenced the apocalyptic perspective from which he addressed his chosen topic and the ways in which he represented the crowd, the social mass, which was to become an important theme in his future work.

The sketchy, Daumier-like brushwork used to register the mass, drawing out their gestures and marking their social identity, contrasts with the carnality of Prometheus and the male figures in the foreground. As in the case of the Titan, they are treated as expressive symbols, manifesting different attitudes toward the symbolic holocaust that are clearly associated with characteristics of race and gender, coinciding with Nietzsche's paradigm. On the left side, primarily female figures and some with clearly indigenous features raise their hands and visages, eyes closed, in longing and blind acceptance of the divine will expressed by the fire. In the foreground, a couple recalling Dante's Paolo and Francesca are absorbed in each other, but the more forceful gesture and articulated anatomy of the male, who extends one arm toward the fiery heavens, suggests a greater degree of consciousness and will, even in his submission. On the right, a predominantly masculine and Caucasian mass assumes attitudes of anguish and despair, expressed through their tortured, masklike faces and bowed heads.[54] In their responses, the dualistic symbolic implications of fire are played out, converging only in the figure of Prometheus, set apart by the consciousness that constitutes his inferno and his liberation.

The divine principle, present as a potentiality in the side panels, is articulated here in a new problematic relationship with man's existential dilemma, which has been transformed through the primacy of consciousness over instinct, embodied in the figure of the Titan. Our physical empathy and intellectual engagement with the painting and its diverse modes of representation permit a multivalent symbolic reception of Orozco's philosophical and aesthetic proposition and its implications, which is expressed in terms of a new formal and iconographic strategy. Body and spirit are convened in a new configuration that pushes beyond the traditional definitions of Renaissance representation and narration to propose new modes of creation and reception.

Prometheus Re-membered

As part of the "Artes de Mexico" celebration, Montgomery gallery is exhibiting 17 of the preparatory sketches for Prometheus, *on loan from the Orozco family in Guadalajara. The real value of such an exhibit, of course, is that one can view* Prometheus *in his full, pre-emasculated glory.*

…He's not just that eunuch titan you see at first glance, he's an idealist. Contemplate revolution, contemplate new orders, and remember our Hispanic roots.

— CHAD FRICK[55]

The translation of physical and emotional empathy onto a symbolic and philosophical plane has not always been confirmed, however, in the quotidian reception of the Pomona *Prometheus* by its most frequent audience, the students who dine in Frary Hall. At the time of its creation, the disgruntlement of faculty members, authorities, and members of the Claremont community, unsympathetic to modern aesthetic proposals, was carefully documented and, predictably, gradually waned in the face of the critical, commercial, and historical recognition of Orozco.[56] Anxiety aroused not by Prometheus's distorted anatomy, strident colors, or flamboyant nudity but by his apparent lack of masculine genitalia has been the source, however, as university documents show, of a continuous history of ridicule, vandalism, and student pranks that reveals, surely, the typical sophomoric obsessions of many college students, but also, perhaps, new perspectives on the mural's corporeal discourse and its implications.

While the preparatory sketch for the main panel includes Prometheus's genitalia, existing documentation suggests he was originally finished without it, in the hope of warding off prudish critics, but perhaps also—we might suspect—to emphasize more radically his separation from instinctual force, in contrast with the Renaissance antecedents in which sexual prowess was equated with human completeness and integrity. The testimony of a member of the college administration at the time of the mural's painting confirms that Prometheus's tiny sexual organ was painted on al secco as an afterthought and thus not completely integrated into the surface through the fresco process, leading to its rapid deterioration.[57] Given the particular concerns and anxieties of the collegiate audience at Pomona, this aspect, understood literally rather than metaphorically, has assumed over the years a disproportionate importance in the reception of the piece, accentuated perhaps by the fact that the diagonal axes of the image converge precisely at the point where the penis should be. Reactions have included the taping on of a surrogate penis made of Christmas tree bulbs and a breadstick,[58] the surreptitious painting on of a well-endowed member with acrylics,[59] satirical articles and caricatures in the college newspaper,[60] and, of course, the corresponding indignant reactions of faculty, students, and administrators concerned with the mural's preservation and correct aesthetic appreciation (fig. 132).[61]

Curiously, however, this aspect of Prometheus's anatomy, as well as the public reaction it incited, has received no attention in formal historiographical accounts. The students' repeated demands and frustrated attempts to "complete" Prometheus are perhaps finally a confirmation of the implications of Orozco's challenge in this mural to academic anatomy and canonical humanistic precepts and his proposition of a new spiritual and rational, rather than visceral, order, as well as a confirmation of the difficulties it implies. The focus on art as a multivalent conceptual language, not as narration, invites, as more recent twentieth-century art has shown, a more active and engaged participation of the public in the construction and appropriation of its meanings, which must be understood as part of a social process rather than dogma. In the end, this carnavalesque battle between students and authorities (or the Titans and the gods, one might say) belongs too to the history of *Prometheus* and its legacy, confirming the vitality and continued pertinence of Orozco's mural to the life of the college community that shares its abode.

Fig. 132 · Caricature accompanying article "Prometheus Unbound, Myth Revealed," from **Student Life** (November 7, 1972), Pomona College Archives, Special Collections, Honnold/Mudd Library, The Claremont Colleges.

117

The Murals at the New School for Social Research (1930–31)

Diane Miliotes

Hailed at their completion as the "first true frescoes in New York," José Clemente Orozco's mural cycle in the dining room of the New School for Social Research was also the city's first example of modern Mexican mural art.[1] It was certainly unforeseeable that it would one day become New York's only surviving permanent example from the influential Mexican public art movement, the inspiration for several waves of U.S. muralism before and after World War II. Each of the big three Mexican muralists (Orozco, Diego Rivera, and David Alfaro Siqueiros) was drawn to this country's most important artistic center during the 1920s and 1930s, yet surprisingly little remains there of the public work that made these artists famous. Although their presence in the city was much heralded and debated at the time, almost all their murals in New York, whether portable or site-specific and permanent, have been destroyed or scattered. Incredibly, besides the New School cycle, New York's only other surviving mural by any of these artists is Orozco's *Dive Bomber and Tank,* a constellation of six portable panels commissioned by the Museum of Modern Art in 1940 (fig. 233).[2]

That Orozco's murals at the New School should survive at all seems like poetic justice given their buffeting over the years by critical, institutional, and environmental forces. Addressing the theme of universal brotherhood and the political possibilities for the future, they are among Orozco's most politically topical murals, and they are among the first U.S. wall paintings to represent Vladimir Lenin and Joseph Stalin, fully two years before Rivera's aborted attempt to include a portrait of Lenin in his mural at Rockefeller Center. Critical response to the murals was mixed, although more for aesthetic than thematic reasons.[3] Portions of the murals were temporarily censored during the 1950s at the hands of New School administrators.[4] Moreover, of the several Orozco murals in the United States, they have suffered the most from physical deterioration and

neglect over the years, although their recent restoration now allows visitors to gain a fuller sense of the artist's original conception.[5]

The murals have perplexed scholars largely because their aesthetic peculiarities and political content do not seem to fit easily into the prevailing vision of Orozco as a bravura painter and nonpartisan, humanist artist, especially in relation to the evident political commitments of his two famous compatriots, Rivera and Siqueiros. Because of this, much of the scholarship on the murals has had the

Fig. 133 · Orozco in front of the **Table of Universal Brotherhood** at the New School for Social Research, about 1930s, photograph courtesy Dartmouth College Library, photograph by Paul Hansen.

effect of downplaying their significance within Orozco's oeuvre and even of dismissing the work, by portraying it variously as an unsuccessful aesthetic experiment with Jay Hambidge's compositional system of Dynamic Symmetry; as work unduly influenced by one of its primary patrons, the artist's dealer Alma Reed, and the Delphic Circle, a utopian intellectual group dedicated to international peace and brotherhood with which she was associated; or as a political aberration in the context of more circumspect, ambiguous, or overtly critical works by the artist.[6]

The conflicting responses of the contemporary critics and some recent scholars signal many of the aesthetic, thematic, and contextual complexities that need to be underscored in order to ascertain the cultural significance of these murals. Salient among these complexities are aesthetic experimentation, provocative or esoteric subject matter, and the multiple intellectual contexts of the Delphic Circle and the New School, all traversed by Orozco's own ambitions within the New York art world, where he had been trying to carve out a place for himself since arriving in the United States in December 1927. The New School murals represented his first major public gambit in this arena, and a high-profile one at that: a commission for an institution associated with liberal education and modernism and one of the first opportunities to arise in the United States to adapt public mural art to a modern, international style architectural structure. Clearly sensitive to the commission's importance and placement, Orozco wrote to his wife, Margarita Valladares: "This work is going to bring good things, being right here in New York and in such a magnificent place, one that couldn't be better, already you can imagine how everyone flocks to see it daily."[7] Orozco's high expectations for the mural's success contrasted sharply with the initial reviews, dealing him, according to his biographer Reed, "the worst blow of his entire New York experience."[8]

In these murals Orozco chose to elaborate certain Delphic ideas in pictorial form within the very specific institutional and architectural context of the New School. The New School as an institution not only shared certain liberal ideals with the Delphic group but also offered Orozco the unprecedented artistic challenge of practicing modern Mexican mural art within a truly contemporary architectural setting and, in doing so, provided an opportunity to launch himself as a public painter within the New York art world. It is the complex intersection of Orozco's artistic ambitions and challenges, the institutional mission of the New School, and his interest in the Delphic project that is the focus of this essay.

A View of the Murals

The New School mural cycle was painted in the fifth-floor lounge and dining room (now a hallway and a conference room, respectively) of the New School building on West Twelfth Street, Manhattan, constructed in 1930 and designed by the Austrian architect Joseph Urban (figs. 134, 135, and 136).[9] The murals are oriented along cardinal points, with north, south, east, and west panels in the interior of the room, as well as the exterior lounge panel at the north. The three north-south panels are allegorical in theme; the lateral east-west panels are political-historical.

The lounge panel *Science, Labor, and Art,* framed between the two entrances to the room, introduces the cycle as a whole, as well as its prevailing red ocher palette, some of its basic themes and iconography, and the mixture of formal languages deployed (fig. 137). Monumental, classically proportioned figures of a scientist and an artist ply the tools of their trades, deep in thought and reaching for divine inspiration. Their intellectual creativity is resolved and brought to constructive fulfillment in the silhouetted figure of labor,

119

wielding traditional work tools.[10] A stagelike setting frames and reveals their activities, with cubistic or expressionistic splintering on the left and the sharply flattened folds of a curtain pulled aside at the right, already signaling the tension and play between abstraction and figuration that are evident throughout the cycle. In this regard, the prominent triangles, as pure form and as useful tools for both artist and scientist, imply both the productive employment of supposedly rational and timeless techniques and Orozco's use of the geometrically based compositional system Dynamic Symmetry. This allegory of learning, creativity, and complementary effort, a particularly appropriate theme for an educational institution, suggests the possible construction of a renewed future society when considered in relation to the other two allegorical panels (*Homecoming of the Worker of the New Day* and *Table of Universal Brotherhood*).

As one of the overarching themes of the murals, the path toward such a goal is not presented as unproblematic. On the contrary, tensions and contradictions traverse its organization and formal means. This is immediately apparent upon one's entering the main room, as there is no indication of a narrative sequence to follow. The viewer encounters a room of modest size, thirty by thirty-two feet, with murals covering the available space on all four walls, divided nearly symmetrically by four doors and two windows, and bare of architectural details apart from the black slate wainscoting that extends about one-third of the way up the walls under each panel. The same warm ocher palette dominates, against which grays, blacks, and creams stand out; the ocher is also regularly punctuated by green and blue accents of sky, plant, shawl, or abstract elements that create rhythmic coloristic links between the four panels.

The arrangement of the panels into allegorical and political-historical scenes, although conceptually consistent, disrupts the possibility of any linear,

sequential, or progressive narrative reading. This nonnarrative organization does not allow for an immediate apprehension of the murals as a whole but only for an initially fragmentary or partial experience. One could even say that such an organization requires a great degree of activity and inquisitiveness on the part of the viewer in order to bring together and untangle the correspondences, contrasts, and disjunctures within the mural program.

Because of the current configuration of the room, it is difficult to occupy its center, presumably

Figs. 134 and 135 · General views of the murals at the New School for Social Research, 1990s (current configuration as a conference room), photographs courtesy New School University Art Collection.

the ideal location from which seated diners would have viewed the murals. However, upon entering the room, the visitor is immediately drawn to the primary allegorical panel, *Table of Universal Brotherhood,* which faces the entrance and is framed by windows on the south wall (fig. 138). Eleven male representatives of various races and ethnic groups are seated around a vast expanse of table; the figures include portraits of several members of the Delphic Circle or associates of Orozco, from left to right: a Mandarin Chinese; Lloyd Goodrich, American art critic; Leonard Charles Noppen, Dutch American poet; a Tartar; a Sikh; a Mexican peon; an African American; Rubin, a Jewish artist from Palestine; an African; the French philosopher Paul Richard; a Cantonese "coolie."[11] Placed against an abstract architectural backdrop, the faces of these individuals are for the most part carefully rendered while their bodies and dress suggest a common humanity in their generalization, with the exception of the trio of "despised races," an indigenous Mexican peasant, a black man, and a Jew, which heads the table.[12] The group's mysterious inactivity and lack of interaction seem to contradict the panel's fraternal theme, leading one commentator to describe the scene as a gathering of "eleven unhappy beings…looking as if they were sorry that any such notion as universal brotherhood had ever been hatched."[13]

In contrast with the public face of this ambiguous utopia, the allegorical panel on the facing north wall, *Homecoming of the Worker of the New Day,* represents an idealized vision of the private domestic comforts and affections that reward productive labor in a future society (figs. 139 and 140). Its table, both mirroring and contrasting the facing panel, is laden with the fruits of the earth and knowledge, yet as Jacquelynn Baas has observed, the family's searching expressions sound a note of underlying anxiety.

On the east and west walls, entitled *Struggle in the Orient* (fig. 141) and *Struggle in the Occident* (fig. 142) respectively, the mural's thematic focus

and formal challenges shift. Rather than the centralized and self-contained allegorical panels, the political-historical scenes are divided into several panels spread across long, rectangular walls, inviting comparison within and across these wall treatments. Each emblematic panel represents political trends or alternatives, usually embodied by various national liberation struggles and their leaders on the "periphery" of the modern world, particularly Mexico, the Soviet Union, and India.[14] The mirroring effect of the themes on the east and west walls suggests a commonality, even universality, to human oppression and the corresponding desire for liberation.

From left to right on the west wall, socialism is represented by Felipe Carrillo Puerto, the slain governor of Mexico's Yucatán State, who had been Reed's fiancé at the time of his death in 1924. His heroic portrait, placed high on the wall, flanks the ancient pyramid at Chichén Itzá, symbol of the

Fig. 136 · Diagram of the murals at the New School for Social Research, New York, 1930–31, fresco, created by Barbara Krieger.

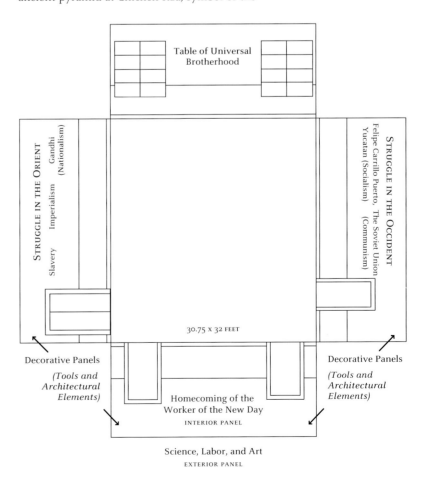

Table of Universal Brotherhood

STRUGGLE IN THE ORIENT
Gandhi (Nationalism)
Imperialism
Slavery

STRUGGLE IN THE OCCIDENT
Felipe Carrillo Puerto, Yucatan (Socialism)
The Soviet Union (Communism)

30.75 X 32 FEET

Decorative Panels
(Tools and Architectural Elements)

Decorative Panels
(Tools and Architectural Elements)

Homecoming of the Worker of the New Day
INTERIOR PANEL

Science, Labor, and Art
EXTERIOR PANEL

121

state's Mayan heritage. Carrillo Puerto's social, political, and cultural reforms in land distribution, electoral, education, and family welfare issues are also referred to in the banners of the "Leagues of Resistance" and the meeting of a "feminist league."[15] Organized into a rectangular block yet loosely rendered, the gathered leagues, the people, are treated almost as a mass, quite distinct from the photo-based portrait of their leader.[16] Linked by a setting (or rising?) sun, the right-hand panel again poses a hierarchical relationship between elite leaders and the people. Here communism is represented by the Russian experiment, including a poster portrait of Lenin. Both he and the Red Army battalion beneath him are drained of color, which the New School director Alvin Johnson described as part of a "color language" Orozco employed to designate orders that belong to the past. To the right, the potential for violence is organized into a new, highly regimented social order, comprised of a synchronized line of workers marching toward the symbol of new labor, a factory rendered in precisionist perfection in the adjoining panel. Though the workers are often interpreted as portraying ethnic groups of the republics, Anreus argues that they more likely represent

"an international family of communism." Stalin is distinguished from the workers in dress yet portrayed as a leader who is now part of their corps.[17]

The left-hand panel of the east wall breaks the pattern of portraying national liberation projects by depicting the rebellion of African and Asian slaves alongside manacled white-collar workers. In this most dramatic and expressively rendered panel within the cycle, they appear to become fully carnal as they break out of the abstract frame representing their bondage. At the right, a slave begins to rise against imperialism, symbolized by a cohesive bloc

Fig. 137 · **Science, Labor, and Art**, from the murals at the New School for Social Research, New York, 1930–31, fresco, 6.5 x 14.5 feet (2 x 4.4 m), photograph courtesy New School University Art Collection.

122

Fig. 138 · **Table of Universal Brotherhood**, from the murals at the New School for Social Research, New York, 1930–31, fresco, 6.5 x 14.5 feet (2 x 4.4 m), photograph courtesy New School University Art Collection.

of British and Indian colonial forces and gas-masked soldiers. They in turn confront a serene image of Mahatma Gandhi, representing nationalism, flanked by a woman dressed in a simple sari. Some commentators identify her as the poet and Indian nationalist activist Sarojini Naidu, a member of the Delphic Circle (fig. 143).[18] Gandhi floats in a blank, monochromatic space, virtually without context except for the stylized rendering of a mechanized tank that casts a threatening shadow over him.[19] This unmediated juxtaposition of figurative and abstract elements is reiterated in the above-door and corner decorative panels on the east, north, and west walls, which present allegories of manual and technological labor, featuring complements of traditional tools, factory buildings, and abstracted architectural structures.

Commission and Conditions

The New School commission brought to fruition Orozco's long-standing search for a mural wall in New York, the city that he considered the most important artistic, intellectual, and political forum for his work in the United States. The journalist Alma Reed, who later became Orozco's agent, began to aid him in this search soon after they met in August 1928, eight months after his arrival in New

Fig. 139 · **Homecoming of the Worker of the New Day** and adjacent decorative panels, from the murals at the New School for Social Research, New York, 1930–31, fresco, 6.5 x 32 feet (2 x 9.8 m), photograph courtesy New School University Art Collection.

123

Fig. 140 · Detail of **Homecoming of the Worker of the New Day**, from the murals at the New School for Social Research, New York, 1930–31, fresco, photograph by Peter Juley and Sons, courtesy Dartmouth College Library.

Fig. 141 · **Struggle in the Orient** and adjacent decorative panel, from the murals at the New School for Social Research, New York, 1930–31, fresco, 6.5 x 30.7 feet (2 x 9.6 m), photograph courtesy New School University Art Collection.

Fig. 142 · **Struggle in the Occident** and adjacent decorative panel, from the murals at the New School for Social Research, New York, 1930–31, fresco, 6.5 x 30.7 feet (2 x 9.6 m), photograph courtesy New School University Art Collection.

York.[20] Reed had become deeply interested in the muralists and in Mexico when she was on extended assignment in that country during the 1920s, and she sought out Orozco upon hearing that he had come to live in New York. Through Reed, Orozco immediately gained entry into the Delphic Circle or Ashram, Eva Sikelianos's literary and intellectual salon, the ideas of which were to have an important impact on the concept behind the New School murals. The Delphic Circle provided Orozco with critical connections that he had not yet known in New York: a sympathetic and stimulating intellectual and political community, his first sustained access to American patronage, and an informal venue in which to display his works.

During the fall of 1928, Reed became Orozco's unofficial dealer and devoted herself to arranging exhibitions and promoting his work. Apart from seeking a market for Orozco's art and, they hoped, some financial stability, these efforts had the ultimate goal of obtaining mural commissions in New York and elsewhere in the United States that would establish the artist's international reputation as a public painter.[21] Reed and Orozco attributed such importance to a public display of his fresco-painting talents that a year later, with several successful exhibitions to Orozco's credit but no commissions, they had begun to consider extreme measures. The October 1929 inauguration of Reed's Delphic Studios, an eclectic contemporary art gallery and permanent showcase for Orozco's small-format work, provided a pretext, the opportunity for Orozco to paint a fresco on the wall of a small terrace of the East Fifty-seventh Street building that housed the gallery. The fresco would be visible from the street and thus might serve as an advertisement for the gallery as well as the artist. This "desperate" plan was never executed and soon became moot when, in January, a colleague approached Orozco about the possibility of painting a fresco at Pomona College, his first official U.S. commission.[22]

Ultimately, Reed's persistence paid off in securing a genuine and high-profile commission in New York. While Orozco was in California painting at Pomona College during the spring of 1930, Reed continued to run Delphic Studios and scout for New York mural opportunities, despite the diminished prospects following the stock market crash. At an Architectural League exhibition, Reed noticed Joseph Urban's designs for a building to house the New School for Social Research, a progressive institution for adult education and an emerging center for modern art. Discovering that this project was going forward despite the virtual halt in new building construction caused by the crash, Reed approached Lewis Mumford, then a lecturer at the New School,

for an introduction to the school's director, Alvin
Johnson. Believing that Orozco's work complemented the New School's mission, Reed proposed
that Orozco execute a mural in the new building.[23]
Urban and Johnson had in fact been considering
mural decoration for two rooms on the third and
fifth floors.[24] Already an admirer of Mexican
muralism, Johnson responded with enthusiasm and
surprise to Reed's proposal: "Alma Reed, agent of
José Clemente Orozco, called on me with the astonishing proposal that Orozco would contribute a
mural painting gratis as a tribute to the ideals of the
New School.…[W]hat could have been my feeling
when Orozco, the greatest mural painter of our
time, proposed to contribute a mural…? All I could
say was, 'God bless you. Paint me the picture. Paint
as you must. I assure you freedom.'"[25]

However, the financial terms and negotiation
of the commission appear to have been somewhat
more complicated than merely a donated mural.
Cost of materials and some other future compensation, perhaps by a New School patron pleased with
the resulting mural, were also discussed, although
Reed and Johnson give opposing accounts regarding
who proffered these terms. In any case, it may have
been difficult for Reed to propose any substantial
upfront compensation for the project in such a
precarious economic climate. Orozco's letters to his
wife from this time also record Reed's report of an
offer, made by Urban, to pay the artist five hundred
dollars for materials and possibly some other
compensation, as well as the cost of his trip back to
New York from California.[26] The payment for materials appears to have been covered, as was the train
trip, according to an exchange of letters between
Reed and Johnson dating from spring 1931. This
exchange probably marked a last attempt by Reed
to obtain any additional satisfaction and seems
to confirm that no substantial compensation was
ever paid.[27] In this regard, the U.S. ambassador to
Mexico, Dwight W. Morrow, and his wife, Elizabeth

Cutter Morrow, supporters of the New School and
key U.S. promoters of Mexican culture, had been
approached as possible benefactors, although their
aid appears not to have materialized.[28] As with his
Pomona College commission, Orozco again found
himself in the unfortunate situation of completing
a mural without compensation for his labor, in painful contrast with the sums commanded by his rival
Diego Rivera. Orozco and Reed sought to justify
this in terms of the New School mural's great potential for critical exposure, further underscoring the
lengths to which the artist was willing to go in
order to gain another foothold in the New York art
market and some share of the public spotlight.

In the end, Johnson's promise of artistic
freedom was perhaps the most significant term of

the commission, set within broad parameters by the director. "A mural painting, I thought, should express a great idea. It could not today be a religious idea, but it could be a social, humanistic idea. I asked each painter [Orozco and Thomas Hart Benton] what he considered the most powerful living monument of our time. Benton fixed on the gigantic technological urge that was remaking the economic center of the world. Orozco fixed on the revolutionary movement stirring all around the periphery of the technological center" (fig. 229).[29] In asking them "to work within the framework of contemporary life…[and] to paint a subject…of such importance that no history written a hundred years from now could fail to devote a chapter to it,"[30] Johnson sought to "lift painting out of the modern rut of inconsequence and give it the rightful place it has held in every vital civilization—that of expressing ideals and prophecies."[31] These sentiments regarding the reinvigoration of the mural as a relevant artistic form within modern society of course accorded with one of the founding principles of Mexican muralism as well as with Orozco's own views.[32] Johnson's image of mural art as an active, not merely decorative, medium, at once didactic,

historically rooted, and visionary, would certainly play out in Orozco's ambitious and panoramic mural concept.

Orozco's preparations for the New School commission seem to have begun in earnest in late September 1930 on the train journey to New York from California. Since Johnson had requested that the New School mural be finished by January 1 for the building's inauguration, Orozco planned to return to New York with time to spare before the building construction had progressed to a state of readiness for the commission.[33] According to his traveling companion Reed, this eastward journey marked an important period of conceptualization for the mural:

> On the train, Orozco spent some hours each day…on the preliminary sketches for the New School murals. A few days before our departure Dr. Johnson had sent him the blueprints of Urban's building plans, with the specifications for the dining room. As we crossed the continent, the theme of the proposed murals was the main topic of our conversation.

Orozco was especially concerned with the relation of his fresco project to the aims and the curriculum of the New School. With the rare intuitive penetration that guided all his aesthetic decisions, he realized that history-shaping trends —political, social, and economic—constituted the logical theme. He listened with sympathetic interest to my explanations of Dr. Johnson's enlightened program for adult education and commented approvingly on the veteran educator's efforts for world peace and his long fight against racial segregation. The painter said he desired to interpret not only the scope and implications of the studies pursued at the New School, but to suggest Dr. Johnson's wide range of humanitarian interests and his expressed personal objectives of social justice and brotherhood.[34]

Fig. 143 · Detail of **Struggle in the Orient**, from the murals at the New School for Social Research, New York, 1930–31, fresco, photograph courtesy Dartmouth College Library.

Fig. 144 · Orozco and his assistant Lois Wilcox on the scaffold, 1930–31, photograph courtesy New School University Art Collection.

127

Many of these concerns were ultimately problematized in the New School murals, but Reed completed this narration by suggesting her own influence on their conception: By the end of the journey, Orozco had also decided to commemorate Felipe Carrillo Puerto, the slain socialist leader from the Yucatán, perhaps as a kind of gift or concession to Reed.[35]

Throughout the fall Orozco worked on preparatory drawings for the murals with the expectation that the New School walls would be ready to paint by November 1 and that the project would take only five to six weeks to complete.[36] Orozco shared his studies with Johnson during this time, and just a few days before the date scheduled to commence painting, Orozco reported to Margarita that Johnson had approved all of his plans for the murals.[37] While stressing the worthiness of the project, Orozco's letters to his wife also convey his eagerness to finish the mural quickly, given the meager financial support. However, this desire for quick completion

turned into increased time pressure when the walls of the dining room were not ready to receive Orozco's attention until November 11.[38] In addition to the monetary and time pressures, the physical circumstances Orozco encountered were less than ideal. Because of the delay in construction, the artist was obliged to begin painting despite his concerns that the building's walls had not had sufficient time to settle and that no tests regarding the effects of the heating system had been done. Construction of the building also continued unabated, adding to Orozco's "nervous strain."[39] Despite these difficulties, Orozco completed the murals in mid-January 1931 after forty-six and a half days of work, working with a single assistant, Lois Wilcox; they were inaugurated along with Benton's murals on January 19 (fig. 144).[40]

Like the terms of his commission, Orozco's work environment makes clear that the artist was in no position to set conditions and was working under certain pressures not of his own making. In contrast with these circumstances, Orozco's letters of these weeks to Margarita project an image of the mural's smooth progress, as well as their innovation and inevitable success.[41] That he expressed similar confidence in their quality and significance to Crespo de la Serna, his assistant at Pomona, suggests the project's high stakes for the artist: "It seems that it is turning out well and moreover is something completely different from what I have done up until now. This truly is not the son of Pomona."[42] This sense of the New School murals as a turning point in his own artistic development was partly marred by the initial negative reviews. This had the unexpected result of generating a lively public debate in the press about the murals' merits, which ultimately drew twenty thousand visitors to view them in the first ten weeks after their completion.[43]

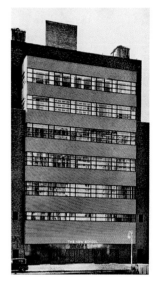

Fig. 145 · Facade, New School for Social Research, New York, designed by Joseph Urban, completed 1930, from **Architectural Record**, vol. 69, no. 2 (February 1931), 138, reprinted with permission from **Architectural Record** ©1931.

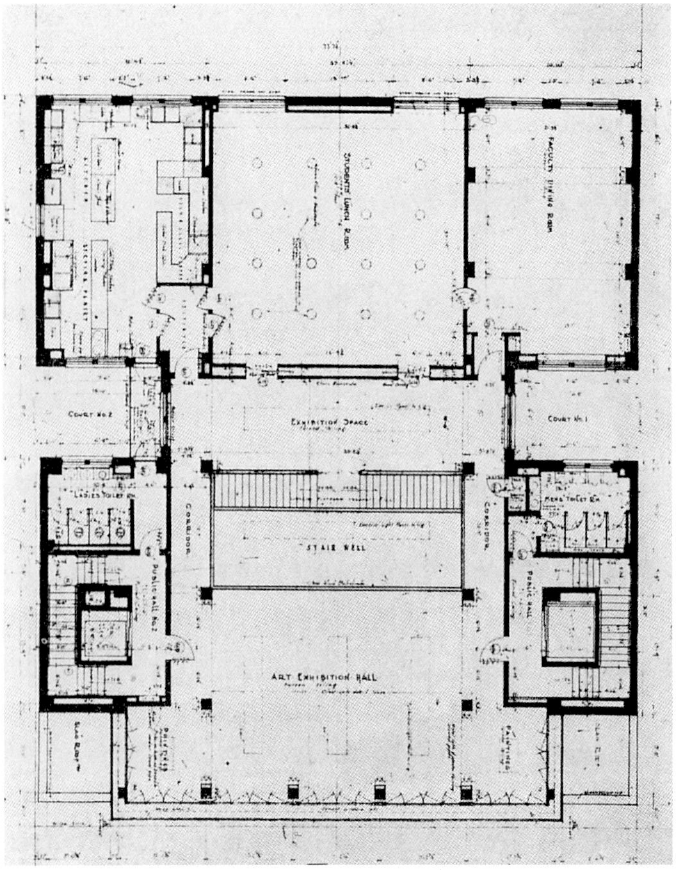

Fig. 146 · Floor plan, fifth floor, New School for Social Research, New York, from **Architectural Record**, vol. 69, no. 2 (February 1931), 150 top, reprinted with permission from **Architectural Record** ©1931.

The New School: Institution and Edifice

Orozco's murals at the New School held a privileged position within Urban's new international style building and thus within the educational institution's emerging project to shape itself into a center for modern culture (fig. 145). The building's fifth floor had been given a special role "as the center of the social and artistic life of the institution"[44] and was planned in conjunction with the library on the floor below (fig. 146). The floor revolves around a central lounge area, where the initial panel of Orozco's cycle was located, and the grand double stairway leading down to the library; surrounding this core were the art exhibition hall at the front of the building and, on the other side, the main dining room, smaller faculty dining room, and service rooms. From the lounge area, students, faculty, and visitors using the fifth floor would be invited to explore various activities designed to promote social discourse, learning, and cultural enrichment: They could relax in the lounge area, view changing exhibitions, socialize in the dining room, or descend Urban's elegant stairway to the library (fig. 147).[45] The Orozco murals were thus positioned as a permanent contribution to life within the institution's new social and artistic core and a centerpiece within its primary social spaces, the lounge and main dining room.

Urban's building and the murals' place in it were in many ways the results of recent changes in the New School's mission that brought modern art and culture into its center and associated the institution closely with modernism. Founded in 1918 by dissident Columbia University professors and intellectuals associated with the *New Republic,* the New School was designed as an alternative to dominant university structures and culture. Its aim was to foster the "reconstruction" of modern society through dual programs in social research and advanced adult education. Its founders hoped to

Fig. 147 · Double staircase leading from the library to the fifth floor, 1931, from **Architectural Record**, vol. 69, no. 2 (February 1931), 144, reprinted with permission from **Architectural Record** ©1931.

advance society along what they considered more rational and egalitarian lines and help create informed and active citizens prepared to participate in this transformation. The school's ethos was humanist, progressive, and cosmopolitan, with commitments to open critical inquiry and academic freedom. Its faculty and students were not associated with any one political or social philosophy, although the school's democratic humanism refused to countenance views seen as regressive (such as antidemocratic or racist philosophies).[46]

Alvin Johnson, a midwestern "equalitarian democrat" and an economist and classicist by training, was one of the school's original trustees, becoming director in 1923 when the school was located on West Twenty-third Street in Manhattan's Chelsea neighborhood.[47] During his first years as director, he oversaw the broadening of the school's curriculum beyond social science courses to include psychology, arts, and cultural offerings, which were seen as part of the larger endeavor of social research and integral to understanding social transforma-

129

tions. Johnson and other administrators determined to attract to the school's open and liberal environment faculty members who represented modern perspectives in these fields, such as Leo Stein (art), Doris Humphrey (dance), Aaron Copland (music), Waldo Frank (literature), and Lewis Mumford (architecture). These critics, writers, and practitioners "introduced their students to 'modern' cultural developments even as the New School acted as patron and forum for their work. In this manner, the New School came to represent 'modernism,' broadly defined as artistic creativity, social research, and democratic reform."[48]

The association of the New School with modernism had important implications for the future of the school, the planning of the new building, and the choice of muralists. When the school, which had outgrown its old quarters, lost its lease in 1928, Johnson and the board of trustees began to search for a site near a major transit hub in order to plan a purpose-built structure. They envisioned a building that would fully accommodate the offerings of the broadened curriculum, including specialized arts spaces, as well as the growing student body that the school attracted from around the city. Johnson personally took charge of the project, locating a site on West Twelfth Street in Greenwich Village and arranging shoestring financing even in the aftermath of the 1929 stock market crash.[49]

Johnson saw the project as an opportunity not only to fulfill the functional needs of the school but also to provide a visual symbol of the institution, one that would enhance the school's modern identity and attract important patronage. In keeping with his commitment to advanced arts of the time, he determined that "the building should be in a modern style, because I did not want a conventional building which perpetuated all the architectural anachronisms against which any honest adult educator would be in revolt." Moreover, he envisioned

the New School building as a modern cultural center that would both embody and foster what he saw as the potential transformative role of modern culture in society. For these reasons, he was drawn to a modern "functional" style of architecture not yet well known in the United States and later commonly referred to as the international style. In its purest form, such architecture grew out of the functional requirements of the building, creating a unity between these underlying structures and simplified exterior form.[50]

Johnson identified two contemporary architects, Joseph Urban and Frank Lloyd Wright, who he thought could create an "architecturally distinctive" building expressive of New School goals.[51] Pessimistic about the possibilities of attracting either architect, Johnson was thus delighted when a New School patron offered to introduce him to Urban, who enthusiastically accepted the commission for only a modest fee.[52]

An extraordinarily versatile architect, illustrator, and interior and stage designer, Urban was recognized by the time of his death in 1933 as one of the most influential designers in America. Born and trained in Vienna, he circulated in advanced art circles from the beginning of his career, executing early architectural projects in Central European art nouveau styles current at the turn of the century. His success and wide-ranging talent soon led him to stage, exhibition, and interior design work. After his move to the United States in 1911, it was in those areas that he became best known, designing for such diverse concerns as the *Ziegfeld Follies,* the Metropolitan Opera, and the Metropolitan Museum of Art. After 1925 he set about reestablishing himself in architecture, and this seems to have been a factor in his willingness to take the financially precarious New School commission.[53]

Urban regarded the New School building as "a special project and his masterpiece."[54] His building was one of the first in New York to incorporate

130

international style principles and was recognized by numerous contemporary commentators as one of the city's most advanced expressions of architectural design.[55] The desire of New School authorities to construct a building coherent with the school's ethos—"modernist," "cosmopolitan," "straightforward, rational and unafraid," "understanding of the spirit of the past; but [living] in the present"[56]—was not lost on these commentators. They hailed Urban's ability to humanize and invigorate architectural form and interior space through his use of light, color, and simple elegant line reminiscent of a streamlined art moderne style. For example, wrap-around strip windows on the main facade were designed to allow maximum outdoor light into classrooms and formed an integral decorative element of the cantilevered center portion of the facade, which was further articulated by strips of cream and black brick, giving the building a bold yet balanced profile in relation to its black brick core. Although wall colors in the present building have been altered, the original interior featured specially designed color schemes for each room, including those on the fifth floor. Large blocks of rich color, ninety different shades in all, were used throughout the building, not merely as decorative ornament but as spatial or plastic elements, an approach toward coloristic wall treatments that had resonances with Orozco's understanding of the function of his murals. Urban developed color schemes with the room's function and lighting in mind and often employed color to create emotional impact or to help focus attention on a particular location. These color treatments were clearly visible from the street.[57]

The new building's intended function as both an educational institution and a modern art center was also expressed in the arrangement of the interior spaces, particularly in the integration of artistic spaces into the entire learning environment of the building, a feature much noted at the time.[58]

This was especially apparent on the fifth floor, where Orozco's introductory panel, lit from both sides by recessed courtyard windows (now blocked off), would have been the central focus of the lounge area and clearly in view as one ascended the stairs or walked between the exhibition hall and the lounge. The walls of the lounge and exhibition hall were painted gray with white ceilings and columns, neutral colors that would have further emphasized Orozco's panel as a focus for the room.[59] The main dining room itself, where the rest of Orozco's cycle appeared, represented the major space dedicated to social discourse and interactions on the fifth floor.

It is within these architectural and institutional frameworks that Orozco proceeded to conceptualize his mural program. In a letter to his wife, he offers this description of the room and his working conditions: "The room is going to be truly extraordinary as interior decoration, the wainscoting and the floor are going to be of a single material, slate, the same kind that is used for blackboards in schools, only used here in large blocks, and the walls are straight with semispherical recesses for the lamps. Everything has been on my recommendation and they consult me about all of the details."[60]

This statement is interesting for several reasons. Orozco's description gives us a contemporary image of the room in which the slate floor and wainscoting, as opposed to the current contrasting wall and floor arrangement, would form a single, dark gray color block, potentially setting off the rich, ocher-hued palette of the frescoes and enhancing their floating effect along the upper portion of the walls. Although Orozco expressed admiration for such details of the room, especially the use of slate, some of these features presented him with compositional and organizational challenges as well as provided points of critique for commentators. The height of the wainscoting confined the frescoes to the upper three-fifths of the walls, creating two long lateral walls and three panels of similar size in a parallel arrangement in

131

the lounge and on the north and south interior walls. The above-door and corner spaces created panels that proved difficult to develop on the scale of the others, which Orozco solved by using symbolic treatments rather than risk relegating any major theme or personality to these areas. Some commentators, expecting a grand room with floor to ceiling murals, bemoaned the high placement of the frescoes on the walls and questioned Orozco's compositional solutions.[61] They failed to note that the use of the high wainscoting, which extended just above the heads of seated diners, was a practical necessity determined by the function of the high-use room and was designed to protect the walls from splattered food or the impact of furniture (fig. 148). The height of the murals also provided seated diners with unobstructed views of the paintings.[62]

Orozco's statement above also sheds further light on the kind of collaboration that characterized the New School project. Urban clearly viewed the overall conception of the dining room as a collaboration with Orozco, echoing Johnson's promise of artistic freedom: "[Urban] not only welcomed the proposals of the artists but agreed that the artist should have a determining voice in the development of the whole room in which his mural was to appear."[63] A revealing example of this was the lighting scheme for the room: "Mr. Orozco's desire was for general illumination which gave equal importance to all objects in the room without emphasis on the murals. He wished by this method not to exhibit the paintings as decorations but to keep them as much as possible a part of the life of the room."[64]

Even more telling than Urban's attention to Orozco's lighting request is what this statement suggests about how the artist understood the paintings to function in a modern architectural space and in this room in particular. He proposed their holistic, integrated relationship to the space and its activities rather than their construal as supplemen-

tary ornament merely applied to surfaces, concepts very much in tune with Urban's ideas about the plastic use of color in the building.

There seems to have been considerable convergence of opinion among artist, sponsor, and architect in these and related matters. Johnson and Urban agreed that the muralists selected should represent the progressive spirit of the school, much as Urban's architectural forms did. Their paintings should not be "subtle decorations on the wall, like the murals of Puvis de Chavannes, concessions to the architects who wished to enclose the occupier entirely in the measured space, but paintings that enticed the mind abroad, like windows looking out on real life."[65] Moreover, Urban "recognized that in modern architecture, which aims at the maximum of open air effects, the mural painting that refuses to 'stay on the wall' has a rightful place,"[66] concepts that partake of advanced European thinking about the relationship between modern art and architecture, such as those associated with the Dutch de Stijl movement. This projective action of the mural allowed by the modern architectural frame dovetails with Orozco's concern to make the works an integrated part of the activities of the room.

These perspectives on the place of mural painting took exactly the opposite position from that of most of the critics of Orozco's murals. These supporters of genteel mural painting associated with the "pallid graduates of the American Academy

Fig. 148 · Seated diners, about 1950s (seating does not reflect original room configuration), New School for Social Research, New York, photograph courtesy New School University Art Collection.

132

at Rome"—just the sort deliberately rejected by Urban and Johnson—had difficulty grasping the organization of Orozco's murals and were disturbed by what they saw as fragmentation and lack of an expected narrative sequence.[67] E. A. Jewell suggested that the room would have been better served by "a loosely flowing, continuous arabesque or a rhythmically ordered mosaic," a recommendation that Orozco regarded as in total contradiction with the New School's modern architectural frame.[68] As we shall later see, Orozco's refusal of a sequentially readable narrative seems to be very much part of his concept for the functioning of the murals within the room.

In fact, his wish "not to exhibit the paintings as decorations but to keep them as much as possible a part of the life of the room" signals a departure in various ways from his previous attitude toward the interaction between architecture and mural art. Orozco, as an artist and former architectural draftsman, had always shown great respect for and sensitivity to the architectural settings of his murals, carefully planning his designs to complement the rhythm and format of the historic or revivalist structures in which he was commissioned to paint.[69] In some cases, he exploited unusual architectural spaces, such as the stairwell paintings at the National Preparatory School in Mexico City, or made powerful compositional use of a distinctive architectural feature, like the neo-Gothic arch for the main panel of *Prometheus* at Pomona College (fig. 108). However, at the New School, he was confronted with at least two challenges distinct from his previous mural projects. He would have to discover ways to adapt his mural art to the functional international style architecture, as many have noted, and attempt to create a compositional and thematic program appropriate to the modern architectural framework. In addition, for the first time, Orozco was presented with a room configuration that held the possibility of surrounding the viewers—in this case, diners—

with a mural program and thus offered an opportunity to elaborate more complex spatial and thematic relationships among individual panels.[70] In contrast, his previous mural commissions in Mexico City and Orizaba, Veracruz, all demanded to be viewed frontally or, in the case of the long walls at the National Preparatory School, as a sequence of scenes arranged along the long, arcaded colonial corridors. Even in Frary Hall at Pomona College, also a dining hall, the niche that holds the murals has a primarily frontal orientation, and full viewing of all panels requires a visitor to enter a space separate from the main activity of the room. The New School thus marked Orozco's first attempt to grapple with new issues related to the modern architectural frame of his murals and to their holistic organization within an all-encompassing space, problems that he encountered again to varying degrees at Dartmouth, in Guadalajara in the Hospicio Cabañas cycle, and in other later works. To help him confront these challenges at the New School, Orozco called upon "ancient" solutions to modern problems gleaned from his Delphic community in New York.

Delphic Solutions

"You are always going to feel very much at home here, Almita," the artist said with his happiest smile as we entered the dining room [of the New School]. "You will be among your friends; it is just another Ashram."[71]

The relationship of the Delphic Circle or Ashram with the New School murals, and with various aspects of Orozco's work and career as a whole, is by now widely recognized, although there is still debate about its meaning and depth of importance.[72] In the case of the New School murals, Orozco's contact with the salon had a profound impact on the primary compositional strategy he chose, Dynamic Symmetry, as well as the murals' themes

133

and content. One could also see Orozco's deploy-
ment of "Delphic solutions" as a confirmation of a
sense of artistic and intellectual belonging.

The Ashram itself was the apartment near
Manhattan's Washington Square that Alma Reed
shared with Eva Sikelianos, American dancer and
actress and wife of the Greek tragic poet Angelos
Sikelianos, founder of the Delphic movement.[73]
Upon hearing Orozco's desire to see a truly egalitarian worldwide body replace the current League
of Nations, Mrs. Sikelianos described to him the
concept of the movement:

> [She] explained to Orozco that the concrete,
> operative realization of his concept of brother-
> hood was the life-long dream of her poet-
> philosopher husband. She related how for
> twenty years she had worked with him in an
> effort to restore world harmony in the spirit
> of the ancient Amphictyonic League, which for
> several centuries had functioned at Delphi
> [Greece] as the first League of Nations. The
> Delphic movement hoped to succeed, she
> said—where other efforts to unite humanity,
> directed by militarists and politicians, had
> failed—by bringing together the intellectuals,
> the great ones, the true elite of the earth in
> order that they might pool their genius for the
> advancement of mankind.[74]

Angelos Sikelianos laid out the principles and aims
of the Delphic movement in detail in *Plan général
du mouvement delphique, Université de Delphes*
(1929).[75] The plan called for a movement of human
unity and brotherhood in the spiritual realm,
operating beyond politics and national interest, not
limited by race, class, nation, religion, or sex. In
order to effect this, it suggested reactivating ancient
spiritual centers associated with eternal human
truths and values in the hope of applying this
wisdom to the problems of the contemporary world.
Key among these spiritual sites would be Delphi as

the ancient "center of the earth" and a point of synthesis between east and west. A University of Delphi
would be founded there for the education of elites
from every corner of the globe, who would be
trained as devoted servants of the masses and seek
to reestablish a relationship of genuine trust with
them. Delphi would also be the site of annual festivals designed to bring into the present the spirit of
ancient Delphi through educational games, displays
of arts, culture, and local traditions and products as
well as serve as a forum for addressing world issues.
However, the plan proposed to resist centralization
by fostering local industry and creativity, at the
same time that it sought to identify commonalities
among all peoples and to foster a synthesis of
human knowledge for the general good.

The Delphic Circle was an attempt to embody
the principles of this utopian project on a small
scale and to provide a mechanism to raise awareness and funding for the Delphic movement and
festivals, of which Eva Sikelianos was the principal
organizer. Reed had been drawn to the movement
after meeting the Sikelianoses in Greece, where she
had translated some of the poet's writings into
English. Acting as Mrs. Sikelianos's secretary, Reed
traveled back to New York with the older woman
in 1928. The Sikelianos apartment, decorated in
modern Greek style with handmade textiles and
other handicrafts, became the movement's New York
base and the scene for intellectual and esoteric
gatherings that attracted an international group of
artists, intellectuals, social and religious thinkers,
politicians, and activists as well as socially
concerned society matrons. The gatherings had an
intellectual or cultural focus, featuring performances by Mrs. Sikelianos, dancing and reciting
Aeschylus's *Prometheus Bound* in the original; readings by Sarojini Naidu, the Dutch poet Leonard
Charles Van Noppen, or the Lebanese writer Kahlil
Gibran; and lectures by the Nietzsche and Blake
scholar Emily Hamblen or the French philosopher

134

Dr. Paul Richard, among others. Orozco's works were also informally exhibited, and he was baptized into the group in an esoteric ceremony under the name of Panselinos, the Byzantine painter.[76]

Although Orozco at times expressed bemused detachment from these proceedings,[77] Reed's biography and his descriptions in his own autobiography indicate that he seems to have genuinely admired the aspirations of the Delphic movement and sympathized with the commitments of Reed, Eva Sikelianos, and others to worldwide peace, pacifism, and nationalist and liberation causes in Greece, India, and elsewhere, which recalled for him Mexican revolutionary struggles. In many ways, these concerns paralleled the liberal commitments and values of Johnson and the New School, to which the artist would also respond in the New School commission. Moreover, as Renato González Mello has noted, the ideas and the example of the Delphic Circle played a key role in shaping Orozco's broadened international perspective upon human struggle, as expressed in his mural art after his arrival in the United States. In addressing complex international audiences and expectations in the United States quite different from the Mexican context for his murals, Orozco initially turned to such "universal" themes as Prometheus, a choice also influenced by his experience in the Delphic

Circle. In the New School murals, however, Orozco marked out for the first time in his public work an *international* terrain of representation in both allegorical and historical terms (for example, *Table of Universal Brotherhood* and the personages and movements depicted on the east and west walls), a shift in focus that was to have a lasting impact on the political scope of the rest of his mural oeuvre. In this regard, his identification with Delphic concepts enabled him to take a broad international perspective in addressing human struggle and political conflict and in doing so to address new audiences. This released him from enmeshment in purely Mexican national concerns and at the same time allowed him to sidestep directly addressing issues in the U.S. national panorama that he found difficult to apprehend or engage.[78] It thereby also provided a way to begin repositioning himself in the larger art world as an artist capable of encompassing a world panorama, not just a Mexican one.

In organizing this new vision, Orozco drew upon a compositional system, Dynamic Symmetry, that also had resonance within the Delphic Circle. Dynamic Symmetry was a theory developed by the Canadian geometrician Jay Hambidge, whose widow, Mary Hambidge, Orozco met at the Delphic Circle. Dynamic Symmetry was widely used as a compositional system in Europe and the United

Fig. 149 · Study for **Homecoming of the Worker of the New Day**, 1930–31, graphite on paper, New School University Art Collection, New York, WP 1133.

135

States during the 1920s, and Mrs. Hambidge was so impressed with Orozco's grasp of the theory that she proposed collaborating with him to complete her husband's investigations. In his autobiography, Orozco described the theory and his interest in it with regard to the New School murals:

> This painting [the New School murals] is of a special nature in being based upon the geometric-aesthetic principles of the investigator Jay Hambidge. Apart from purely personal motives of expression, I wanted to discover how convincing and useful those principles were and what their possibility was.
>
> [Hambidge's] central idea was to discover the relations between art and the structure of natural forms in man and plants, and then, on a basis of historical data and direct measurements of temples, vases, statues, and jewels, to formulate an exact and scientific statement of the construction of objects of Hellenic art. He had begun his work in 1900, and afterwards he was supported by Yale University in investigations in Greece and in museums throughout Europe. He published a treatise, *Dynamic Symmetry*; an analysis of Greek temples; …a study of vases; and finally a review with the title *The Diagonal*.[79]

Hambidge's system is based on a theory of proportions of areas, rather than lines. It uses squares and their diagonals to derive root rectangles, especially golden section rectangles, which have consistent relationships defined by the Pythagorean theorem between the long and short sides. From these relationships, an infinite series of commensurate and proportional forms can be elaborated. According to Hambidge, these forms have a living and dynamic quality because they are based on organic principles of growth and movement found in nature and humans. These same proportions were supposedly used in ancient Greek and Egyptian art, thus rendering them dynamic, as opposed to all other artistic traditions based on mirror or crystalline symmetry, which Hambidge thus designated static.[80] For Orozco and other artists, Dynamic Symmetry not only held out the possibility of dynamizing and activating compositions but also represented a path to the "secret to beauty" through an ancient, seemingly timeless, rational system based in the natural world and now rediscovered and brought into

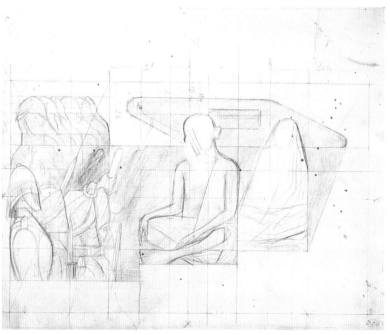

Fig. 150 · Study for **Struggle in the Occident** (Lenin), 1930–31, graphite on paper, Instituto Cultural Cabañas, Guadalajara/INBA 14858, photograph by Rubén Orozco.

Fig. 151 · Study for **Struggle in the Orient** (Gandhi), 1930–31, graphite on paper, Instituto Cultural Cabañas, Guadalajara/INBA 14657, photograph by Rubén Orozco.

contemporary relevance,[81] aspirations reminiscent of the Delphic project itself.

As Laurance Hurlburt has shown, Orozco's application of these principles can be seen in many panels but is perhaps easiest to apprehend in the Yucatán panel, where it forms the foundation for the overall composition as well as particular triangular and rectangular elements, such as the banners and pyramid or the blocked group at the bottom. Its use is also evident in the extant preparatory studies for the murals, all except one being final or near-final composition drawings (figs. 149, 150, 151, 152, 153, 154, and 84). Here the elaboration of diagonal axes and triangular and rectangular forms to structure composition and align individual elements is distinct from studies for earlier murals, which rely on a simple grid system. In addition, there is an unusual study that appears to show the entire west wall blocked out as rectangular geometric patterns, although intriguing similarities to other panels, especially those on the east wall, suggest that it may have been used on both walls in an attempt to create some compositional consistency (fig. 155). No life, figure, or transfer drawings survive, if they ever existed, so it is difficult to ascertain Orozco's creative process in the application of Dynamic Symmetry from the final composition studies alone.[82] There is evidence that Orozco modeled the portrait of Carrillo Puerto on a photograph in Reed's possession. In contrast, he painted Lloyd Goodrich's portrait onto the wall directly from life when Alvin Johnson failed to appear for the sitting.[83] This suggests that such details were completed at a final stage, once the overall compositional frame-

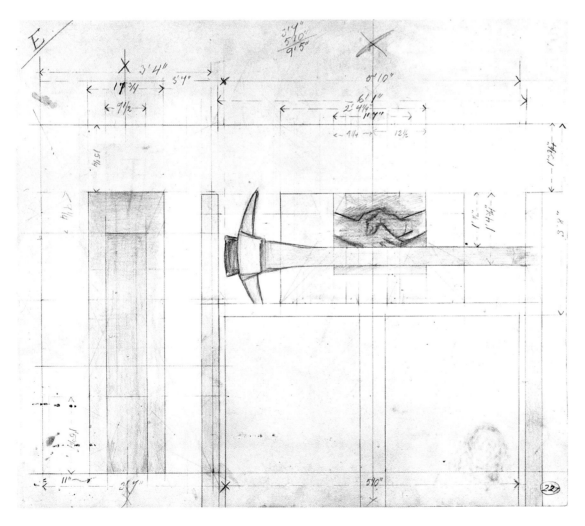

Fig. 152 · Study for east wall, 1930–31, graphite on paper, Hood Museum of Art, Dartmouth College, Hanover, New Hampshire; D.988.52.244.

137

work had already been established, conforming to Orozco's working process for the Dartmouth College murals as well.

Although Orozco later modified his use of Dynamic Symmetry, saying that after the New School, he "abandoned [its] overrigorous and scientific methods, but...kept what was fundamental and inevitable in it and with this...shaped new ways of working,"[84] the reasons for its use in the New School commission are clear from a Delphic Studios press release: "The frescoes are intended to be 'structural' paintings and a logical consequence of the architectural organization of the construction itself. They are intended to be public paintings, designed to serve the intellectual community represented by the school and will therefore be executed in a modern spirit that harmonizes with its progressive and advanced ideals."[85]

In keeping with his responsiveness to the architectural frame of his murals, Orozco turned to what he saw as a rational, "progressive," and "universal"

geometrical compositional system that would help him to create a mural appropriate to a modern architectural structure and to New School ideals. In the absence of the usual architectural clues that aid in organizing a mural program, such as arches, molding, and other detail work, he chose to use principles of Dynamic Symmetry to create an underlying framework for the dining room's rectangular panels of varied dimensions.[86] In doing so, Orozco also made a connection between modern architecture and rational systems that reveals a great deal about his attitude toward modern technology. In "New World, New Races and New Art" (1929), Orozco had already praised the architecture of Manhattan, meaning its skyscrapers, as a "new value" that constituted a "first step" toward creating an "art of the New World."[87] This confidence in technology is still largely evident in his New School murals, the first of his public paintings to address this issue thematically, and appears most consistently in the decorative panels, which feature a factory with

Fig. 153 · Study for north wall, 1930–31, graphite on paper, Instituto Cultural Cabañas, Guadalajara/INBA 12983, photograph by Rubén Orozco.

Fig. 154 · Study of tools, 1930–31, graphite on paper, Instituto Cultural Cabañas, Guadalajara/INBA 13026, photograph by Rubén Orozco.

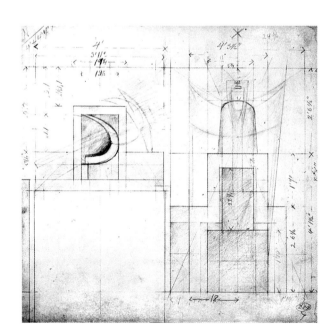

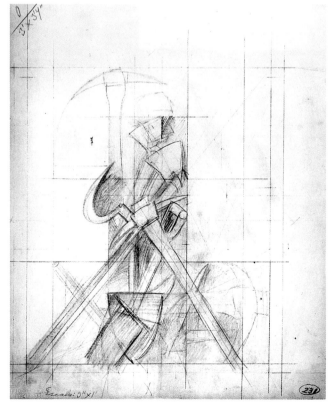

smokestack and abstracted skyscraper forms as symbols of productive labor. Yet there is already some hint of the more critical stance Orozco later assumed toward modern technology, especially its destructive potential, in the east wall panels, where Gandhi is confronted by soldiers in gas masks and the shadow of an abstracted tank looms over him.

Orozco's efforts to "dynamize" his paintings appear to be of a piece with his concern to make the murals "part of the life of the room." However, the question of whether application of Hambidge's theory actually worked to energize the compositions is open to debate. Many commentators have found them stiff and lifeless, exactly the opposite of the stated intention. Even though it is now difficult to re-create the original viewing situation, because the current furnishings do not allow visitors to circulate or be seated in the center of the room, large unadorned blocks of color do seem to float on the wall's surface or serve to project monumental figures forward. Some further clue to their effect, real or desired, can be gleaned from Reed's account of the inauguration of the murals: "As the reception guests assembled, the dynamic forms on the dining room wall seemed to be living beings mingling with the crowd. When I mentioned this to Orozco he explained that the illusion was a calculated effect. He had kept in mind, he said, that ordinarily the murals would be seen when the room was filled with seated luncheon or dinner guests. The suggestion of life which, for me at least, conveyed a reality that probed beyond appearance to spiritual essence, enhanced the startling, dramatic impact of the painted walls."[88] Orozco's desired effect of intermingling, even convergence, of pictorial representation and viewer gives us a hint of what he may have envisioned the room to be as a functioning environment and his expectations for an active, inquiring viewer.[89] As we shall see, it may also suggest the possibility of layered meanings within the artist's claim to Reed that the room was "just another Ashram."

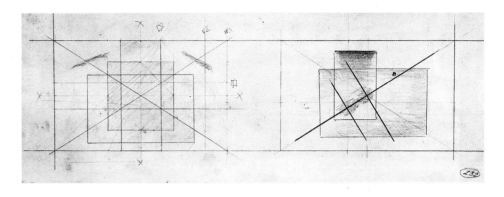

In Search of an Activated Space

In addition to the oft-noted representation in the murals of members of the Ashram and some of their admired spiritual and political leaders, such as Gandhi, González Mello has observed the Delphic conception behind the cycle's iconographic program: the gathering of men, presumably elites, of all nationalities and races in peace and deliberation in *Table of Universal Brotherhood*; the balancing of these elites with the return to the earth and local tradition represented by the domestic scene in the facing north panel *Homecoming of the Worker of the New Day*; and the nationalist struggles, represented in the east and west panels by Mexico, Russia, and India, important to Sikelianos's concept of uniting Eastern and Western knowledge and traditions at Delphi. However, the murals are not simply an adaptation of the Delphic program. They suggest the broad goal of societal renovation shared by the Delphic Circle and the New School, albeit through different means. Moreover, in the integration of specific political-historical leaders and projects, Orozco goes far beyond what Sikelianos's specifically nonpolitical program had envisioned to accommodate Johnson's concerns to explore contemporary social and political solutions.[90]

Perhaps the implications of Orozco's attempt to interrelate these projects can be taken even further with the function of the room and the organization of the panels in mind. The three allegorical panels clearly lean toward Delphic concerns, especially in

Fig. 155 · Study of geometric patterns, 1930–31, graphite on paper, Hood Museum of Art, Dartmouth College, Hanover, New Hampshire; D.988.52.261.

139

the mirroring interior panels, in the attempt to balance the ideals of intellectuals and workers, urban and rural, public and private. As mentioned previously, this relative consistency is disrupted by the arrangement of lateral historical panels, which does not suggest or force a single sequential reading. Rather, viewers in the original dining room configuration, seated at the center of the space, would have found themselves surrounded, even confronted, by the various historical alternatives presented on the east and west lateral walls, none of which seems overtly privileged over the others; in fact, they allow themselves to be read in a variety of ways. These emblematic panels, each self-contained yet also placed in careful relation to one another along each wall and across the intervening space of the room, create a complex cross weaving and dialogue among them. This, I believe, was part of Orozco's "calculated effect" and a spur to viewer engagement in which he or she is consistently decentered by the organization of the program as well as by its proposals of future liberation emanating from outside the European and U.S. metropoles. Each panel addresses the viewer through distinctive formal means that underscore their contrasting philosophies: the agitated forms of violent rebellion (slaves), the contained figure of individual resistance (India), and the regimentation and hierarchies of the newly organized social orders achieved through mass revolution (Mexico and Russia). Despite these distinctions, which suggest a reading of the panels as historical options from which to choose, the panels' arrangement also implies their reading as complements or equivalents that all serve a common goal of national liberation and the attainment of human peace and harmony. The west panels, for example, could be read as a complementary pair of "martyred" leaders and the organized social orders they helped found, as opposed to the eastern panels, which form a pair in their departure from a clearly hierarchical leader-mass configuration. The east wall itself presents the contrast, as well as the evolution, of violent rebellion to pacifist resistance. At the same time, the panel arrangement equates, as well as sets in confrontation, the Mexican and Indian national liberation struggles, whose similarities of culture and oppression Orozco is known to have observed, at the same time that he acknowledged their vastly different means for achieving their goals.[91]

Ultimately, the debative atmosphere and environment created by the lateral panels resolve thematically and visually in the allegory of *Table of Universal Brotherhood.* In keeping with Delphic ideals, this table of elites, representing an array of nationalities and races, is a meeting of equals and significantly has no single clear leader, but is headed by a trio of "despised races." Nor does this fraternity—for the gathering is curiously and frustratingly male, especially in light of the vital role of women in the Delphic movement and the life of the New School—yet engage in discussion or negotiation. They appear to wait expectantly around the massive cream-colored table, "a high altar"[92] whose wide and open surface emphasizes the breadth of the fraternal circle and the commonality of those gathered. At the same time, this empty expanse and the blank open book that lies upon it suggest a gulf and divide that have yet to be bridged in constructing an ideal future world. It is a tabula rasa, waiting to be inscribed and created. In contrast with the energy of some of the historical panels, the static quality of this gathering and its obtuse silence in relation to its stated fraternal theme return the overarching question of the murals back to the viewer. The demand that he or she puzzle this through is further suggested by the table dramatically tilted into the room, which gives a clue to what would set this gathering into motion within the logic of Orozco's painted dining room. In a room actually filled with tables and seated diners, and as the social heart of the building devoted to discussion and civil discourse, it is irresistible to read this pitched *Table of Universal Brotherhood* as an open invitation to gather and to join in vital and constructive debate. Indeed, the mural's invitation is extended to another group of elites, both the faculty of the New School and their students, who were part of the school's program for "educating the educated" and the "intellectually adult."[93]

In this context, Orozco's concern to dynamize his compositions and make them "part of the life of the room," his attention to architectural and institutional contexts, and his varied yet evenhanded treatment of various political-historical alternatives and their complex, nonnarrative arrangement seemed to have the larger purpose of actively fostering debate regarding the future path of humankind, made even more urgent by Depression era crises. If the cycle lacks some of the irony and critical edge that became more pronounced in his later murals, this fact appears moderated by the urgency and seriousness of the issues, to which Orozco nevertheless resists offering any specific solutions. In the end, his claim to have created "just another Ashram" did not exist purely in the imaginary space of representation. These murals also sought to invoke and extend the ideals and practice of the Delphic Circle as a place of international gathering and exchange, so important to Orozco's experience in New York. At the same time, this invitation to the table presumes the necessity to come to grips with the chaos, multiple perspectives, and dissonances of the contemporary world. The prospective viewer in the New School dining room, a New World elite trained within the confines of the building itself, is asked to begin to respond to the challenges of the future by actively engaging within this real space of discourse and construction, the intellectual community of the New School and its ultramodern edifice.

The Epic of American Civilization:
The Mural at Dartmouth College (1932–34)

Jacquelynn Baas

*The Picture speaks to me of truths impossible
for me to put into words and of which I did not
ever know before.*

— MAX BECKMANN

Interpreting Orozco's Epic [1]

The Reverend Eleazar Wheelock founded Dartmouth
College in 1769 in Hanover, in what was then the
royal province of New Hampshire. Dartmouth was
chartered by the king for "the education and instruction of Youth of the Indian Tribes in this Land
…and also of English Youth and any others." Its pred-
ecessor was Moor's Charity School, which Wheelock
had established in Lebanon, Connecticut, in 1754,
ostensibly for the purpose of educating the local
Indians, an idea more popular among both schools'
English supporters than among the purported recip-
ients. The nation's ninth-oldest college, Dartmouth

was named in honor of its benefactor, the second
earl of Dartmouth, to whom, in 1768, Wheelock sent
"a small specimen of the produce and manufacture
of the American wilderness": a pipe, tobacco pouch,
knife case, and several other articles.[2]

Dartmouth's remote location in the New
England wilderness fostered an active commitment
on the part of its faculty and administration to
providing students with examples of the "natural
and moral world," as museum and library collections
were thought of in the eighteenth century. This
commitment to providing accessible cultural
resources continued into the twentieth century. One
of its most notable manifestations is *The Epic of
American Civilization,* the mural that José Clemente
Orozco was commissioned to paint in the large
basement-level reserve reading room of Baker Library
in the spring of 1932. Built in 1928 and lovingly
maintained and expanded since then, Baker Library
is both the physical center of the campus and the
intellectual center of college life. The reserve reading
room still retains its original function and is thus
not only a public space but a place where more than
three generations of Dartmouth students have spent
a great deal of time (figs. 158, 159, and 160).

The Epic of American Civilization is a pivotal
work in the career of one of the most significant

Figs. 156 and 157 · Views of west
wing (top) and east wing (bottom),
reserve reading room, Baker Library,
Dartmouth College, Hanover,
New Hampshire, 1930s, photographs
courtesy Dartmouth College Library.

artists of the twentieth century. José Clemente Orozco was fifty years old when he left Dartmouth in the winter of 1934. Although even greater artistic achievements lay ahead, *The Epic of American Civilization* remains one of the most developed summaries of Orozco's philosophy. It is also, in the opinion of many critics, the greatest mural cycle in the United States. Yet, outside Dartmouth, published studies of the mural have been few, and none, with the exception of Lewis Mumford's perceptive 1934 article in the *New Republic,* has focused exclusively on this masterpiece.[3] In this first section and in those that follow, I shall attempt to provide an account of its development and bring a number of issues to bear upon its interpretation.

A key to understanding Orozco's work in general and *The Epic of American Civilization* in particular is an awareness of the relation between the artist's passionate idealism and his pessimism. Spain's greatest filmmaker, the late Luis Buñuel, declared that "man is never free, yet he fights for what he can never be, and that is tragic."[4] Orozco's sense of the human condition was based on a similar conviction of tragic impasse. Two years before embarking on the Dartmouth mural, Orozco painted a mural at Pomona College titled *Prometheus,* a theme that was strongly influenced by Aeschylus's *Prometheus Bound,* which Eva Sikelianos had produced in 1927.[5] When the chorus of that play asks the tormented Titan the nature of his transgressions against the tyrant-god Zeus, Prometheus gives two. Conveying fire to mortals, by which they shall "master many arts," is not the first he cites. First place is given to the planting of "blind hope" in the heart of man, taking from him the "expectancy of death." Prometheus, unlike man, unlike even Zeus, has the gift of foresight. But all his news is bad news. If his defiance of tyranny brought the wrath of Zeus upon him, his certain knowledge of impending disaster is the only weapon he has; it is his key to freedom.[6]

Orozco knew death. As Michael Brenson has pointed out, "Death…is the ultimate wall, and death is perhaps the ultimate subject of Orozco's art."[7] It is more omnipresent even than the violence, corpses, and cadavers that litter his works—the same, after all, could be said of many artists of his generation (and others). With Orozco, death is always there, no matter what the subject. Its presence can be as mild as the anxious expressions worn by the ostensibly happy family at the New School (fig. 139) or as threatening as the beckoning black rectangles that are the leitmotif of his art, from his 1926 fresco *The Gravedigger* at the Preparatory School (fig. 161),

Figs. 158–160 · View of west wing (left), general view (center), and view of east wing (right), reserve reading room, Baker Library, Dartmouth College, Hanover, New Hampshire, about 1980, photographs by Jochen Littkemann.

Fig. 161 · **The Gravedigger**, 1926, fresco, National Preparatory School, Mexico City, photograph by Bob Schalkwijk.

Fig. 162 · **War**, 1926–28, ink on cardboard, Museo de Arte Carrillo Gil, Mexico City/INBA 16983.

to the omnipresent gaping black doorways in his drawings and prints, such as *War* (fig. 162), to the great *Metaphysical Landscape* (fig. 278), painted one year before his own death.

Orozco's knowledge was shaped by the experience of ten years of civil war that gripped Mexico during the second decade of the twentieth century, at the outset of his career. He tells us what the revolution meant to him in his autobiography, the tone of which shifts into ironic gear whenever the subject threatens to engage his emotions: "To me the Revolution was the gayest and most diverting of carnivals, that is, of what I take carnivals to be, for I have never seen one."[8] His drawings tell another story, as does his friend Jean Charlot: "Not until 1926 did Orozco put down in a black-and-white set of drawings the cruel images that had festered in his heart for over a decade. Even so, the artist shied away from the fact that what once had been flesh, bone, and blood—mostly blood—now was art. When I suggested Goya's war etchings as a prototype for the series, Orozco reproved me, in the soft subdued voice he used when in anger: 'I am not Goya. Goya is only a painter.'"[9] This indirect, ironic response was typical of the artist's verbal, in contrast with visual, communication. For Orozco, art was not just painting; it was how he communicated the things he knew. Through his art, he shared his trauma and his anger, which he insisted over and over, in many forms, are our trauma and should

be our anger. We may or may not want to know, much less believe, but he will say it anyway. This was his role.

Orozco was twenty-seven when the revolution began and thirty-four when he left Mexico for San Francisco in 1917. Some measure of the brutality he witnessed during those years is conveyed in the fifth chapter of his autobiography:

> The world was torn apart around us. Troop convoys passed on their way to slaughter. Trains were blown up. In the portals of churches wretched Zapatist peasants, who had fallen prisoners to the Carrancistas, were summarily shot down. People grew used to killing, to the most pitiless egotism, to the glutting of the sensibilities, to naked bestiality.... In the world of politics it was the same, war without quarter, struggle for power and wealth...underneath it all, subterranean intrigues went on among the friends of today and the enemies of tomorrow, resolved, when the time came, upon mutual extermination.[10]

Because he was haunted by the savage treachery of this period, Orozco's humanist idealism took a resolutely apolitical form. He saw the dogmas of political and religious salvation, like concepts of race and nationality, as idols corrupting understanding, preventing the emancipation of the human spirit. Only by throwing off the shackles of the

Fig. 163 · **Christ Destroying His Cross**, 1923, fresco, National Preparatory School, Mexico City, Archivo Fotográfico IIE-UNAM.

144

creeds and prejudices that have enslaved humankind to authoritarian purposes can a "New World," a genuine harmony of individual expression and social purpose, come into being.[11]

The American continent, where migrating peoples have mingled for centuries, figured in Orozco's imagination as the symbolic stage for his ultimate triumph of the human spirit. The walls of the reserve reading room in Baker Library at Dartmouth College, a school whose own history encompassed "Indian Tribes…English Youth and any others," struck him as a perfect location for his vision, the key elements of which he had distilled well before coming to Dartmouth. In 1929 he had been given the opportunity to express his views in the January issue of *Creative Art*: "The Art of the New World cannot take root in the old traditions of the Old World nor in the aboriginal traditions represented by the remains of our ancient Indian peoples. Although the art of all races and of all times has a common value — human, universal — each new cycle must work for itself, must create, must yield its own production — its individual share to the common good."[12]

Orozco's title for his Dartmouth mural, *The Epic of American Civilization*, may have been influenced by his New York colleague Thomas Hart Benton's ambitious painting series of 1923–30, *The American Historical Epic*. (Orozco's patron Alma Reed showed Benton's work at her Delphic Studios gallery, and in 1931 Benton had recommended Orozco to the Dartmouth art faculty.[13] Inspired by Spencer's *History of the United States*, Benton's series eventually comprised eighteen paintings, although he had planned to do seventy-five.[14] He included racial and economic conflict in his

Fig. 164 · General view of frescoes, 1937–39, Hospicio Cabañas, Guadalajara, photograph by Bob Schalkwijk.

Fig. 165 · **Man of Fire**, 1937–39, fresco, Hospicio Cabañas, Guadalajara, photograph by Bob Schalkwijk.

145

visual history, which he organized into "chapters." But his perspective was different from Orozco's: Benton's series was, in the end, an anti-epic. He wished "to present a people's history in contrast to the conventional histories which generally spotlighted great men, political and military events, and successions of ideas."[15]

Traditionally an epic is a long narrative poem on a heroic theme. Early epics, such as the *Iliad* and the *Odyssey,* are written versions of national oral legends. The conventions of the modern literary epic include a hero who founds a new civilization (a "city of destiny," like Virgil's Rome) in a mythic time that is continuous with known history. This hero performs notable deeds, often including a descent into the underworld. The style of the epic is appropriate to its exalted theme and is characterized by extended similes in which apparently different subjects are extensively compared. This format, which would have been familiar to Orozco through his affiliation with Eva Sikelianos's and Alma Reed's Delphic Circle, was well suited to his mural aesthetic, which found its inspiration in heroic, dualistic themes of conflict, self-sacrifice, and regeneration.

The Dartmouth hero, Quetzalcoatl, is allied thematically with other tragic heroes adopted by the artist during this middle period of his career: the Christ destroying his cross, who made a first, brief appearance at the Preparatory School in 1923 (fig. 163) and reappears in the Dartmouth cycle; Pomona College's *Prometheus* of 1930[16] (fig. 110); and the magnificent *Man of Fire* from 1939 in the dome of the Hospicio Cabañas in Guadalajara (figs. 164 and 165). The fate of the Man of Fire, who rises to heaven in flames, is an alternative to that of Dartmouth's Quetzalcoatl, who departs on a raft of serpents. In another version of the myth,[17] Quetzalcoatl immolates himself, ascending in flames to heaven, where he becomes the Morning Star. Whatever their nominal identities, Orozco's mythic heroes were united by a common mission of self-sacrifice for the sake of the enlightenment and liberation of humankind. For Orozco, whose aesthetic was imprinted by the experience of the Mexican Revolution, this liberation is a painful and tragic process whose outcome is far from secure.

Orozco took advantage of the division of Baker Library's reserve reading room into east and west wings to portray America's "two cultural currents," the indigenous and the European. A sequential listing of the twenty-six panels of *The Epic of American*

Fig. 166 · Diagram of **The Epic of American Civilization**, 1932–34, fresco, reserve reading room, Baker Library, Dartmouth College, Hanover, New Hampshire, created by Barbara Krieger.

146

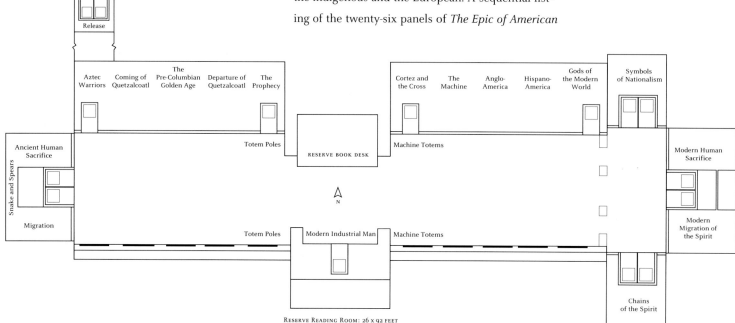

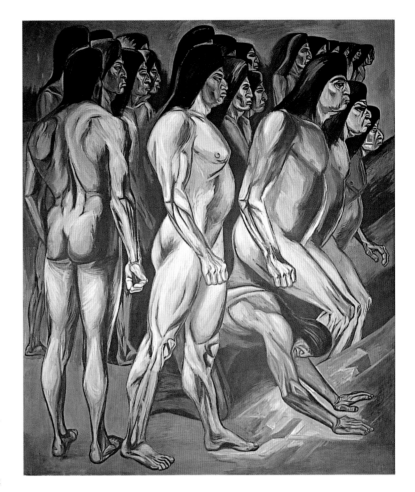

Civilization (fig. 166) from left to right is useful for the discussion that follows, but it should be kept in mind that their arrangement is not strictly chronological, either internally (in keeping with a historical order of events) or externally (the order in which they were painted). On the left-hand panel of the western end wall of the reserve reading room is *Migration* (fig. 167). To its right, over the doorway in the center of the western end wall, is a small panel, *Snake and Spears* (fig. 168). Balancing *Migration,* on the right side of the western wall, is *Ancient Human Sacrifice* (fig. 169). Turning the corner to the long north wall of the west wing, *Aztec Warriors* (fig. 170) decorates the small panel over the door that leads to the hallway connecting Baker Library with the art history building, Carpenter Hall. (Orozco painted *Release* [fig. 193] over a door in this hallway.) The north wall features three large compositions: *The Coming of Quetzalcoatl* (fig. 171), *The Pre-Columbian Golden Age* (fig. 172), and *The Departure of Quetzalcoatl* (fig. 173). The departing Quetzalcoatl points to another small overdoor panel at the end of the wall: *The Prophecy* (fig. 174), which was in fact the first panel Orozco painted in the reserve room.

The last two compositions of the west wing, together called *Totem Poles* (figs. 175 and 176), were painted on the tall, narrow wing walls that flank the entrance to the central reserve desk portion of the room. Their opposites are the *Machine Totems* (figs. 177 and 178), painted on the wing walls at the west end of the east wing. The long north wall of the east wing features five compositions: *Cortez and the Cross* (fig. 179), *The Machine* (fig. 180), *Anglo-America* (figs. 181 and 27), *Hispano-America* (figs. 182 and 28), and *Gods of the Modern World* (fig. 183).

The eastern end of the east wing is contained within an alcovelike space. On the north wall of this alcove is another small overdoor panel, *Symbols of Nationalism* (fig. 184). Two large compositions flank the doorway of the east wing, corresponding to those of the west wall at the far end of the room: *Modern Human Sacrifice* (fig. 185), showing a victim of modern warfare, and *Modern Migration of the Spirit* (figs. 186 and 66), with its battered but triumphant Christ. Another small overdoor panel, *Chains of the Spirit* (fig. 187), completes this section. Finally, across from the reserve desk, on the south wall at the center of the room, is a depiction of contemporary American life in five compositions on three panels collectively titled *Modern Industrial Man* (figs. 188, 189, 190, 191, and 192).

Fig. 167 · **Migration** from
The Epic of American Civilization,
1932–34, fresco, 120 x 105 in
(305 x 267 cm).

Fig. 168 · **Snake and Spears** from
The Epic of American Civilization,
1932–34, fresco, 24 x 93 in
(61 x 236 cm).

147

Orozco thus presents the mythic history of the Americas up to the arrival of Cortez in the west wing of Baker Library's reserve reading room, while the European-influenced, "modern" phase is presented in the east wing, along with a mythic vision of the future in the form of *Modern Migration of the Spirit*. Both parts of the mural cycle contain a prophetic figure—Quetzalcoatl in the west wing, Christ in the east wing—linked by Cortez, the historical antihero.

Commission and Response

The idea of bringing José Clemente Orozco to Dartmouth to execute a mural seems to have occurred to members of the art faculty at Dartmouth around the time their new building, Carpenter Hall, was completed in 1929. The following year the department's chairman, Artemas Packard, supported by a young member of the art faculty, Churchill P. Lathrop (who had brought Orozco's work to Packard's attention), began a campaign to realize their vision of obtaining for the college the services of one of the two important Mexican muralists then working

in the United States, Diego Rivera and Orozco. According to Lathrop, Orozco was the preferred choice from the beginning.[18] They organized several exhibitions of Orozco's prints and drawings in the galleries of Carpenter Hall in order to make his work better known in northern New England. The persistence of Orozco's New York dealer, Alma Reed, was an important factor in Orozco's favor and may have helped to offset a tendency among potential supporters of a mural for Carpenter Hall to

Fig. 169 · **Ancient Human Sacrifice** from **The Epic of American Civilization**, 1932–34, fresco, 120 x 105 in (305 x 267 cm).

Fig. 170 · **Aztec Warriors** from **The Epic of American Civilization**, 1932–34, fresco, 74 x 56 in (188 x 142 cm).

Fig. 171 · **Coming of Quetzalcoatl** from **The Epic of American Civilization**, 1932–34, fresco, 120 x 205 in (305 x 521 cm).

148

favor the better-known Rivera. Chief among these supporters was the Rockefeller family; Nelson Rockefeller, Dartmouth class of 1930, had been a student of Lathrop's.

On February 20, 1931, Reed wrote to Packard that Orozco wanted to "go on with the type of work that he did in Pomona College and which he calls the New World epic painting   taking great traditional themes, such as the Prometheus, and giving them a meaning for today." On May 22, Packard responded, stating that members of the art department had been thinking of this project and how it might be accomplished, and that "some of us are predisposed in favor of Señor Orozco." Moreover, he wrote, the exhibition of Orozco's lithographs that Reed had sent to be shown at the Carpenter Hall galleries the previous year had done "a good deal to prepare the way for him. We have been thinking for a long time of the advantage of having some good murals in our Art Building and have been slowly encouraging the idea among those who might be interested in helping the project. These questions present themselves repeatedly: 1. How much would it cost? 2. What choice would we have as to subject and design— i.e., how would we know we were getting what we wanted? & 3. How would we choose the right man to do them?" Three days later Reed answered that the cost "would depend entirely upon the surface to be covered and the condition of that surface." As for subject matter, "Orozco feels that a subject may be selected in either of two ways. First, there is the entirely personal, original conception of the artist, influenced by the functional aspects—the use and geometry of the wall to be decorated. The second source, which he feels, strongly, offers appropriate subjects for the decoration of a college or university, is the great, eternal and universal material of Greek mythology, given a modern and original application to the problems and psychology of our own age."

Reed went on to argue why Orozco should be Dartmouth's choice, proposing the mythological

Fig. 172 · **The Pre-Columbian Golden Age** from **The Epic of American Civilization**, 1932–34, fresco, 120 x 175 in (305 x 445 cm).

149

Fig. 173 · **The Departure of Quetzalcoatl** from **The Epic of American Civilization**, 1932–34, fresco, 120 x 205 in (305 x 521 cm).

Fig. 174 · **The Prophecy** from **The Epic of American Civilization**, 1932–34, fresco, 74 x 56 in (188 x 142 cm).

subject of Daedalus. Reed's description of Orozco's themes provides a valuable perspective, not only on his earlier *Prometheus* mural at Pomona College but on ideas he was to develop at Dartmouth:

> At Pomona College, California…he has depicted in a panel, 26 feet high by 35 feet in breadth, Prometheus, as the symbol of the creative artist, whose face and hands are burned for every new gift brought to humanity—mankind, perhaps, remaining indifferent. The emphasis of this interpretation of Aeschylus is on personal heroism—the struggle—the pursuit of highest values regardless of reward or gratitude. For the decoration of an art building, a great theme suggests itself—the myth of Daidalos in its original Greek connotation—"Daidala," in the most ancient usage, meaning "works of art." Orozco has a splendid interpretation and modern application of this myth based upon man's striving to escape from the mechanistic—the urge towards pure creation—the release of the creative faculties. He also has several other subjects which he would be pleased to submit as soon as he knows the available wall space and the number of panels desired.

These two motifs—selfless rebellion against tyranny for the sake of human values and the freedom to create—were linked. For Orozco, the highest human ideal was "the release of the creative faculties." Prometheus's gift of fire was the dual gift of creation and liberation from dependence on a tyrannical god. Although the final mural would, to say

the least, encompass "several other subjects," this would remain its theme.

Chairman Packard did not make much headway with raising funds for an art department mural.[19] By November 1931 Reed was again pressing him about Orozco's interest in the Dartmouth mural project: "I am wondering if there is any development on the matter of the murals for Dartmouth. Do you not think it would be advisable for Sr. Orozco to submit his drawings for the project, based, of course, on the architectural setting for the murals? He would be pleased to come to Dartmouth at any time, on his own responsibility, in order to take measurements."

Orozco's offer to come at his own expense to assess the scope of the project was a turning point. Members of the art department responded with a creative idea for funding a mural by José Clemente

Fig. 175 and 176 · **Totem Poles** from **The Epic of American Civilization**, 1932–34, fresco, each 120 x 30 in (305 x 76 cm).

Fig. 177 and 178 · **Machine Images** from **The Epic of American Civilization**, 1932–34, fresco, each 120 x 30 in (305 x 76 cm).

North wall overview, pre-Cortesian section, continuous scan by Hany Farid.

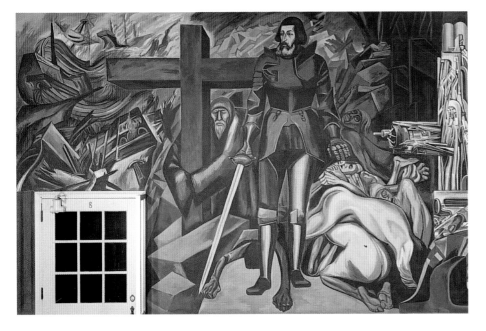

Fig. 179 · **Cortez and the Cross** from **The Epic of American Civilization**, 1932–34, fresco, 120 x 182 in (305 x 462 cm).

Fig. 180 · **The Machine** from **The Epic of American Civilization**, 1932–34, fresco, 120 x 118 in (305 x 300 cm).

Fig. 181 · **Anglo-America** from **The Epic of American Civilization**, 1932–34, fresco, 120 x 103 in (305 x 262 cm).

Fig. 182 · **Hispano-America** from **The Epic of American Civilization**, 1932–34, fresco, 120 x 119 in (305 x 302 cm).

151

North wall overview, post-Cortesian section, continuous scan by Hany Farid.

Orozco for Dartmouth. Churchill Lathrop recalled: "Early in 1932, we had a brilliant revelation, an idea that might move the stalled project off dead center. The department had a small lecture budget;[20] so, why not invite Orozco to give a lecture-demonstration on fresco painting? Such an unusual lecture, by a scholarly artist, would attract considerable student and community attention, and it would produce a few square feet of fresco: a small sample mural. Work-in-progress on even a small mural would have educational value. Also, the presence of Orozco would give the community the chance to observe his skill and judge his character."[21]

Finally, on the weekend of March 18–20, 1932, Orozco visited Dartmouth. During discussions of the project, he and members of the art department became excited at the possibility of his executing a mural in a much more favorable location than

Fig. 183 · **Gods of the Modern World** from **The Epic of American Civilization**, 1932–34, fresco, 120 x 119 in (305 x 302 cm).

Fig. 184 · **Symbols of Nationalism** from **The Epic of American Civilization**, 1932–34, fresco, over door area: 55 x 96 in (140 x 244 cm).

Fig. 185 · **Modern Human Sacrifice** from **The Epic of American Civilization**, 1932–34, fresco, 120 x 130 in (305 x 330 cm).

Fig. 186 · **Modern Migration of the Spirit** from **The Epic of American Civilization**, 1932–34, fresco, 120 x 126 in (305 x 320 cm).

Fig. 187 · **Chains of the Spirit** from **The Epic of American Civilization**, 1932–34, fresco, over door area: 55 x 96 in (140 x 244 cm).

153

Carpenter Hall. They set their sights on the large reserve reading room on the ground floor of Baker Library, with which Carpenter is linked by a pedestrian passageway. On April 6, Packard wrote President Ernest M. Hopkins:

> I have completed arrangements with José Clemente Orozco to come to Dartmouth under the auspices of the Department of Art during the first week of May "to give instruction in the technique of fresco painting." For purposes of demonstration he will use the brick walls of the passageway connecting Carpenter Hall and Baker Library. It is specifically understood that the total cost of this undertaking is not to exceed $500. Aside from its immediate value to students in Art courses, Mr. Orozco has graciously consented to do this as a means of helping us arouse interest in our larger scheme of obtaining a series of mural paintings for Carpenter Hall. In order to spare him any professional embarrassment I have agreed not to announce publicly the fact that the painting he does at this time will be in the nature of a free will offering and is not to be paid for at the rates expected of a man of his standing.

Whether or not Hopkins was aware of it, Packard was being disingenuous on the point of just where he hoped the "larger scheme" for a series of mural paintings would emerge. The library reading room was already in his mind. This is evident from a much-edited draft of a letter Packard intended for President Hopkins, written three weeks later

but apparently never sent; at least, no copy of a final letter exists in the Dartmouth archives. Dated April 26, 1932, the draft reads:

> Mr. Goodrich [Nathaniel L. Goodrich, then librarian of the college] has become very much interested in the possibility of getting Orozco to do something on the walls of the nearby basement corridor of the library. I have told him the Department of Art would be perfectly willing to relinquish any prior claim for Carpenter Hall if the way seemed clear to keep Orozco on working after he finishes the small piece which

Fig. 188 · Left-hand panel, **Modern Industrial Man** from **The Epic of American Civilization**, 1932–34, fresco, 114 x 59 in (290 x 150 cm).

Fig. 189 · Left-hand panel, **Modern Industrial Man** from **The Epic of American Civilization**, 1932–34, fresco, 114 x 60 in (290 x 152 cm).

Fig. 190 · Central panel, **Modern Industrial Man** from **The Epic of American Civilization**, 1932–34, fresco, 40 x 214 in (102 x 544 cm).

he has agreed to do for us—since the library walls in question (which Orozco has not seen) are infinitely preferable from every point of view to the walls in the passageway between Carpenter and Baker for his particular type of painting.

Knowing that Mr. Orozco has been saving what he conceives to be the most important idea of his career (what he calls an "Epic of America") until just the right wall for it was offered him, I have begged him to bring a set of sketches with him when he comes next week showing how he might develop this theme for the spaces in the library, if those walls were made avail‑able. Since such large spaces are not easily to be found, I am pretty sure that he will become so eager to do his masterpiece there that the question of immediate remuneration will bother him as little as in the case of the comparatively small job in the passageway…. In short, we stand a good chance of getting a great deal more than we originally bargained for and I am extremely anxious to make no mistake at this crucial point in the proceedings.

The message was received, for on April 28 President Hopkins wrote a memorandum to the college treasurer, Halsey Edgerton: "You doubtless have heard that we are bringing the latest sensation in mural painters, or at least one of the two latest sensations, to Hanover in the person of Orozco. I have offered to utilize $500 of the Rockefeller tutorial money to pay for his presence here, partly because he may be that useful to the Department of Art and partly because of Mrs. Rockefeller's enthusiasm about these two Mexicans."

An argument for commissioning wall decorations for the college would not have been easy to make during the Depression, when members of the faculty were sustaining reductions in their salaries. President Hopkins's diplomatic skills (as well as

his wit) are evident in his justification of this expenditure to the conservative college treasurer:

Fortunately, Orozco, who is a flaming red communist, is favorably disposed toward us as an institution, which he considers eleemosynary. He makes the distinction that the faculty are not eleemosynary and ought to be annihilated because they profiteer on the students' need for education. This is a particularly interesting point of view at the present moment. He like‑wise is said to have told Mrs. Bliss, while he was doing a mural in her house, that he hoped she would be assassinated.[22]

All of this detail is written because of the fact that I have agreed with Mr. Goodrich that I should be glad to have the walls of the reserve desk room downstairs in the Library covered with some kind of color, be it good, bad, or indifferent. Presumably Orozco's is good, even though I can't make anything out of it.

Fig. 191 · Right-hand panel, **Modern Industrial Man** from **The Epic of American Civilization**, 1932–34, fresco, 114 x 59 in (290 x 150 cm).

Fig 192 · Right-hand panel, **Modern Industrial Man** from **The Epic of American Civilization**, 1932–34, fresco, 114 x 60 in (290 x 152 cm).

155

Likewise, if we were reckoned as capitalists, I suppose we would have to pay $25,000 to $50,000 for having it done.[23] If he is willing to do it for $500, why well and good.

This is really a letter of warning. Please do not oppose him at any point. I'd hate to lose a good treasurer and you represent all that he abhors.

The next day Packard cabled Reed that chances looked extremely good for the "larger project if we can turn interest in that direction the moment Orozco arrives." Indeed, Packard organized a barrage of campus publicity for the artist's second visit to the college on May 2, 1932. The college newspaper, the *Dartmouth,* carried a series of articles. Under a headline J.C. OROZCO TO EXHIBIT ART OF PAINTING FRESCO, the *Dartmouth* of Monday, May 2, cited the initial Daedalus plan, noting that "the location where Orozco will work has not yet been definitely decided…. Announcement of the location and scope of his work will be made later in the week, at which time his sketches will be available for publication."

The fresco that Orozco painted upon that occasion (figs. 193, 194, 195, and 196) has been titled variously *Release, Man Released from the Mechanistic,* and, more descriptively, *Man Released from the Mechanistic to the Creative Life.* It was originally proposed as a focal point of a mural cycle in the corridor connecting Carpenter Hall and the library[24] on the theme of the Greek mechanical genius Daedalus. According to Orozco, the subject of this small panel was intended to be "post-war" in theme. In a press release dated May 25, 1932, he was quoted as stating that *Man Released from the Mechanistic* "represents man emerging from a heap of destructive machinery symbolizing slavery, automatism, and the converting of a human being into a robot, without brain, heart, or free will, under the control of another machine. Man is now shown in command of his own hands and he is at last free to shape his own destiny." That Orozco seriously

Fig. 193 · **Man Released from the Mechanistic to the Creative Life**, 1932, fresco, 89 x 89 ½ in (226 x 227 cm), Baker Library, Dartmouth College, Hanover, New Hampshire.

Fig. 194 · Orozco on scaffold with **Man Released from the Mechanistic to the Creative Life**, May 1932, photograph courtesy Dartmouth College Library.

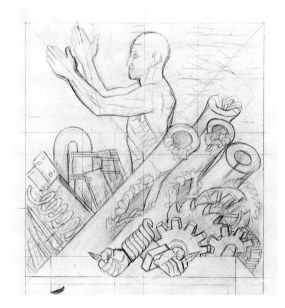

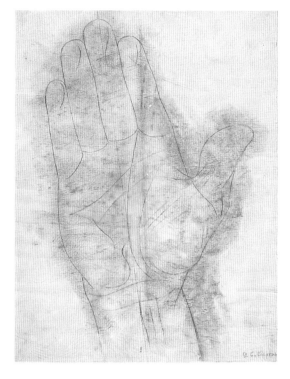

Fig. 195 · Study for **Man Released from the Mechanistic to the Creative Life**, 1932, graphite on paper, Hood Museum of Art, Dartmouth College, Hanover, New Hampshire; D.988.52.262.

Fig. 196 · Study of a hand (back) for **Man Released from the Mechanistic to the Creative Life**, 1932, graphite and red chalk on tracing paper mounted to laid paper, Hood Museum of Art, Dartmouth College, Hanover, New Hampshire; D.992.20.1.

Fig. 197 · **Daedalus: Project for Fresco mural,** 1932, reproduction of a drawing from Alma Reed, **José Clemente Orozco** (New York: Delphic Studios, 1932), n.p.

157

the sun in this drawing resembles Orozco's own visage, suggesting an identification on the part of the artist with his self-sacrificing Man of Fire god-heroes.[27] The myth of Daedalus, on which Alma Reed was so keen, would have taken him down another path. He had been content to please her when the theme suited him, as at Pomona College, and when she was the de facto patron, as at the New School. But in considering the larger space in the Dartmouth library reserve room, Orozco abandoned the Greek mythological subject that Reed had been promoting. In a letter of May 22, 1932, she confessed to Packard:

I felt very foolish on the train when I glanced over Orozco's note-book and realized how completely he had organized the Quetzalcoatl project. He had written me nothing about this and I had no chance to talk it over with him while at Dartmouth, so it all came as a surprise …now I realize how silly my suggestion of placing Daedalus on the other large panel must have seemed to you. As Orozco pointed out, there is enough material in the Quetzalcoatl

considered a larger mural cycle built around the theme of Daedalus is indicated by a drawing in one of his notebooks that gives the plan of this corridor with extensive notations regarding the painting space available along both walls[25] and by a drawing with the caption "Daedalus: Project for Fresco Mural, 1932," which was reproduced on the last page of Alma Reed's 1932 picture book *José Clemente Orozco* (fig. 197).[26] The flaming head of

myth, as he already conceives of it, to fill every wall in the college.... Orozco is very insistent upon the present and future aspects of the theme which lifts it entirely out of the historic and archaeological class.

In his own prospectus for the Dartmouth mural (handwritten on Hanover Inn letterhead), Orozco outlined his theme:

> The American continental races are now becoming aware of their own personality, as it emerges from two cultural currents—the indigenous and the European. The great American myth of Quetzalcoatl is a living one embracing both elements and pointing clearly, by its prophetic nature, to the responsibility shared equally by the two Americas of creating here an authentic New World civilization. I feel that this subject has a special significance for an institution such as Dartmouth College which has its origin in a continental rather than in a local outlook—the foundation of Dartmouth, I understand, predating the foundation of the United States.[28]

A more schematic version of Orozco's intentions at this early moment in the project is preserved in Packard's handwritten notes from his May 1932 discussions with Orozco:

> The Epic of Civilization on the American Continent developed in terms of the American myth of Quezacoatl [sic] (the symbol of the Power of Good in the Universe).
>
> (It is to be understood that there is no literary or other record of the exact implications of this ancient myth of Quezacoatl and that this interpretation grows out of the inspired idealism and creative imagination of Orozco. There is no paralele [sic] to it in existence. It is in every sense an *original* work not a work derived or imitated from any other man.)

There follow two more pages of notes in which Packard recorded his preliminary discussions with Orozco about the development of the cycle. These reveal that the two long north walls of the reserve room were originally planned to "represent the constructive, affirmative, *positive* aspects of the myth." Specifically, the north wall in the west wing was to depict "the Plumed Serpent (Quezacoatl) representing *Heaven & Earth.*" Here Quetzalcoatl "comes among the Toltecs and teaches them the arts. This brings about a long period of Prosperity, Peace, Fraternity and great accomplishments: Architecture, creation of American agriculture—maize, squash, fruits etc.—various handicrafts." The north wall of the east wing would have depicted the "New Culture of the American continent according to the prophecy of Q.: New Culture / New Religion / New Art / New Architecture (Spanish-Ren.-N.Y.) / The Machine as a factor human happiness. The Dream of an Ideal Culture of the Future growing out of all this."

In contrast, the four panels of the west and east walls were intended to represent "the barbaric aspects of human nature (both European and American) operating against the constructive civilizing forces of human nature." On the two west panels would have been shown the "destruction of the Toltec Empire & Coming of the Aztecs: *Xochitl* discovers alcohol (pulque from the maguey plant) and presents it to the King Tecpaucoltziu. (This represents the destructive vices and superstitions—opposite of the influence of Quezacoatl) and brings about the resumption of human sacrifices." The two east panels were to have depicted the "destruction of the Indian civilizations (from Alaska to Patagonia) by the White Man. *Conquest* (Cortez) Destruction of all the indigenous civilizations—introduction of modern weapons of destruction."

With her letter of May 22, Alma Reed enclosed an outline that was more developed. It indicates that the two long, north, "positive" walls would each have been divided into three sections. In the west

158

wing (which was executed essentially as planned), Orozco intended to present Quetzalcoatl appearing among the Toltecs, "The Golden Age," and "The Prophecy." Two small overdoor panels on this wall were to show "The Migrations from the North" and the "European Invasion." The east wing would have continued with "The Return of Quetzalcoatl," "The Future Golden Age," and "Our Time," while two overdoor panels here would have represented "Agriculture" and "Science and Industry."

This second outline contained minor alterations in Orozco's original scheme for the four panels of the west and east "barbaric" walls. The theme of drunkenness had disappeared and, in addition to "The Aztec Invasions," the west walls were to show "Huitzilopichtli, God of War." The east walls would have depicted "Spaniards—Cortez, and War between Europeans and Indians." General informa-tion was also provided about the content of four narrow vertical panels opposite the west and east walls, subjects that seemed to be less resolved: "Decorative panels; Natural products of Continent. Figures." Finally, subjects were proposed for the section at the center of the south wall, opposite the reserve reading desk: "'The Mayflower' / The Norseman / Immigrants, to America."

Packard made several weekend visits to New York to discuss details of the commission, and on June 9, 1932, a contract was signed by J.C. Orozco, Artemas Packard, and Dartmouth's treasurer, Halsey Edgerton. Here it is agreed that Orozco would complete a mural project comprising 2,090 square feet (this figure apparently did not include the section across from the reserve desk) and give "such instruction in the technique of fresco paint-ing as he cares to at his convenience." The project was to be completed within eighteen months, and the artist was to be paid a total of $5,200: $4,000 in compensation and $1,200 for travel, room, and board.[29] Upon the execution of the agreement $250 was paid, while $1,250 was to be paid on the completion of the "panel on which Orozco is now working." (Orozco had begun the right-hand west wing overdoor panel [fig. 174] in early June; the $1,250 paid on its completion later that month financed a three-month trip to Europe.) Beginning in the fall, increments of $200 were to be paid on the first of each month, with the balance payable upon completion of the project.

Ultimately, Orozco was paid considerably more. By November 1933 it was clear that he would not complete the project by January 1. President Hopkins's respect and concern for the artist are revealed in a memorandum he sent to the college bursar on November 23:

> In the development of [Orozco's] murals…he has taken on much added space over anything that was originally contemplated.… With the additional work to be done, however, and with the decreasing span of time, it has seemed to me perfectly apparent that the last panels would have to be a slap-dash effort, largely without the merit of the careful work done on others.… On the other hand, I should be very unwilling to have him quixotically continuing his work and meanwhile being in financial distress because of added contribution.
>
> Consequently, I took up with the Trustees at their last meeting the general principles involved and received their favorable assent to going on with Orozco up to July first…pay-ments to cease, however, at such point before July first as his work may be completed. There was also a $500 appropriation for materials. In short, at the expiration of the present arrange-ment, will you please continue payments to Orozco so long as he may be here at the rate of $2500 for six months, and will you make avail-able to him $500 for expenses in connection with materials, etc. for his painting.

159

Orozco finished the mural on February 13, 1934. Three days later President Hopkins instructed the bursar: "May I ask for such slight irregularity as may be necessary in your practices to make Mr. Orozco's final payment at the present time and to have it figured on the basis to April 9. He is completing his work almost immediately and technically we are not obligated beyond the present month, but I should like to include the extra month's allowance for the sake of covering every possible question and making it the more comfortable for him to get his family back to Mexico."

In total, then, Dartmouth College paid José Clemente Orozco approximately $7,000 for painting *The Epic of American Civilization,* in addition to $500 for *Man Released from the Mechanistic.* Accounting records further show that the college incurred $2,177.05 in expenses in connection with the project, for a total cost of approximately $10,000.[30] This was the figure used by Hopkins in subsequent correspondence, although at the artist's request, the cost of the mural was treated in a confidential manner.[31]

On June 18 and 19, 1932, a little more than a week after the contract had been signed, the commission was heralded in a two-part article in the *Dartmouth* by Leo Katz, who, Alma Reed tells us in her biography of Orozco, was an "internationally known artist, author, and lecturer" chosen by her to assist the muralist in the early phases of the project (fig. 198).[32] Despite its positive tenor, Katz's article hints at potential problems with the public perception of the Dartmouth commission.

> I have been at many institutions where the desire to be progressive has been quite obviously on the program. Almost invariably, alas, I found a stubborn and paradoxical attempt to deal with new problems along conventional lines.... Of all this I haven't found a trace in Dartmouth. I don't hesitate to admit that I am utterly amazed at the courage and broadmindedness with which this institution has acted in this particular case. One has to come from a hot-house center like New York, where lately an unhealthy ballyhoo about "national art," "American art for America," and similar battle cries have saturated the atmosphere of the art world, ...in order to appreciate the fact that there exists a place far removed from the centers of "Art" where silently out of a sincere desire to fight in the front trenches of life and to catch up with the...changes that are so essentially characteristic of our time a plan was conceived and made possible which is so much nearer to the truly creative nature of the very heart of our burning problems of art and culture.[33]

That Dartmouth was not quite such an ivory tower as Katz implied is indicated by a letter of June 29, 1932, from Hopkins to Packard. Hopkins instructs Packard to cease his independent fundraising for the project, citing the problematic public perception that the college was raising money for "extravagant"

Fig. 198 · Orozco and Leo Katz on scaffold with **The Departure of Quetzalcoatl**, June 1932, photograph courtesy Dartmouth College Library.

purposes. "Likewise," Hopkins wrote, "the always present reservations in a small group of our local people has been present so that I am trying to give due attention to the policy of an ounce of prevention …in anticipating troubles which may arise."[34]

Katz's article was intended to ease acceptance of a project that, by its very nature, was bound to be controversial.[35] In her biography of the artist, Alma Reed relays an account by Katz of his time at Dartmouth as Orozco's assistant that provides a more personal point of view:

> On Sundays Orozco used the day mostly to concentrate on the work of the coming week, while I usually dictated to a secretary some article in defense of the painter for the College bulletins and magazines. Already during the first months appeared numerous protests from alumni and other interested people against having this "beautiful New England College" ruined by what they called "brutal Mexican stuff." They had to be reminded that Dartmouth was founded for the Indians. I really admired the College president because he refused to listen to all that unfriendly, sometimes even threatening outpouring of narrow-minded prejudice. Professor Packard, the head of the Art Department, was a steady, enthusiastic admirer and never seemed to doubt the importance of the undertaking.[36]

Critics of the project tended to fall into three camps. First there were those, alluded to in the letter of June 29, 1932, to Packard from President Hopkins, who regarded the project as an extravagance, not appropriate for a sober New England college like Dartmouth, particularly during hard times. Second, the fact that the college had hired a Mexican artist was the focus of a chauvinistic brand of protest that was particularly ironic in light of Orozco's criticism in the mural itself of just such destructive nationalistic impulses. These critics had been mentioned in

the spring of 1932 by Katz in the *Dartmouth*, with his reference to the "unhealthy ballyhoo" in New York about "'American Art for America.'" The situation did not improve. One year later, in June 1933, a group of American artists organized themselves into a National Commission to Advance American Art and drew up a "regret list," with Dartmouth at its head. The national press picked up the story, and Dartmouth gained notoriety in the *New York Times* and other eastern papers for "employing a Mexican painter to depict 'The Epic of Culture in the New World.'"[32] When artists like John Sloan and Rockwell Kent rose to Dartmouth's defense, however, the ultimate result was, within the art world at least, more positive than negative.[38]

The third source of criticism was a predictable defensive reaction to Orozco's strong imagery and unflinching social commentary. These took the form of letters to the president and comments in the media. An unusually polite protest was sent to Hopkins from a group signing its letter simply "Boston Mothers": "When our sons go to college a great many temptations come into their lives to drag down rather than build up character.... Therefore, why not do as much as possible to uplift.... Hanover has such beautiful scenery, that pictures of her hills in winter and summer, her campus, her winding rivers, etc., would have made an ideal subject for mural paintings. something beautiful to remember rather than hideous subjects. We would be everlastingly grateful to you if the pictures could be destroyed."[39]

Other comments were less decorous: "The walls of Dartmouth now contain as savage an attack on American civilization as ever issued from the councils of red revolution. Orozco has shouted forth in paint the Communist Manifesto. He has laid on the indictment without mercy, subtlety or humor. What he says seems bitter and surprisingly naive. We will do well to accept his challenge…clear out such corruption."[40]

161

President Hopkins's responses to such suggestions were unfailingly kind but firm in support of the principles of a liberal education:

There are those who do not like to change their pre-conceived ideas in regard to what music or poetry or paintings should be, and to them, of course, all modern work of this sort is anathema. There are 100% Americans who have objected to the fact that we employed a Mexican to do this work, but I have never believed that art could be made either racial or national. There are those who object to the fundamental ideas suggested, but my conception of a college is a place where such ideas should be considered. There are those who object to some of the panels…who do not consider them quite "nice," but certainly if that be a criterion of judgment many of the great works of the medieval masters would have to be removed from the Louvre and other galleries restricted to the greatest in art.[41]

The numerous suggestions from alumni and others that the frescoes be destroyed were undoubtedly influenced by the commissioning and destruction of Diego Rivera's mural at Rockefeller Center in 1933–34. Against the wishes of his patron Nelson Rockefeller, Dartmouth Class of 1930, Rivera painted the head of Lenin in a fresco commissioned as the centerpiece of the new RCA Building. When Rivera was dismissed on May 9, 1933, and the unfinished panel finally destroyed on February 9, 1934, the resulting publicity had inevitable repercussions at Dartmouth.[42]

It should be kept in mind that the protests that greeted Orozco's public murals in the United States were no stronger, and in fact were considerably

Fig. 199 · Work in progress on the west and north walls of **The Epic of American Civilization** (Orozco on scaffold with **Ancient Human Sacrifice** and two observers), fall 1932, photograph courtesy Dartmouth College Library.

162

less violent, than the reactions that had greeted his work in Mexico less than a decade earlier.[43] Also, in comparison with the financial problems associated with the commissions for Pomona College in Claremont, California, and the New School in New York City,[44] the Dartmouth situation must have seemed close to ideal. In his autobiography, Orozco had this to say about Dartmouth: "The Administration and the 2500 students of the College were enthusiastic in their support of the Fine Arts project, so I set to work. I had complete freedom to express my ideas; no suggestion or criticism of any sort was ever made."[45]

The marked shift in focus from plan to finished project that characterized the Dartmouth mural had already surfaced in Orozco's previous major mural commission, the Preparatory School murals in Mexico City. Jean Charlot, his colleague there, pointed out that only one of the many themes proposed in Orozco's first program ever corresponded with a completed panel.[46] Moreover, of the panels he painted in the first campaign in 1923–24, most were destroyed or altered and repainted by the artist in 1926. There too the mood went darker. Charlot described the shift as "from a constructive to a destructive assertion, from optimism to pessimism."[47] Orozco was quite capable of developing a program to please a client, but the final result was another matter. Where he stuck with the program, as at the New School, the result was wooden and unconvincing. Where he left the path for parts unknown, as at Dartmouth, the results were astonishing.[48]

Orozco signed and dated his last Dartmouth panel (fig. 177) on February 13, 1934. Three days later there was a dinner for him, his wife, Margarita, and others involved with the project. The student leader for this celebration, Carl B. Hess, read the following statement from President Hopkins, who could not be present: "I want to bespeak the satisfaction that I have had officially and personally in

the presence among us of Mr. Orozco as a guest; I want to testify in regard to the sweetness of character and the loftiness of motive which have inspired his work; and I wish to make a record of the high value I attach to the personal influence he has exerted while among us and the abiding worth of the pictorial art which he leaves with us."[49]

After another three days, Orozco, Margarita, and their three children returned first to New York and then to Mexico. The artist's final statement about his accomplishment was published in the *Dartmouth* on February 17: "Each panel has been a new experience, it has presented new problems. I have experimented with color, and organization of material. I am just beginning to realize what I have done and what all this has done to me." It is an unusually candid and vulnerable statement, this admission that, for Orozco, mural art was a process, not a program.

Fig. 200 · Orozco with **The Departure of Quetzalcoatl**, June 1932, photograph courtesy Dartmouth College Library.

The West Wing: The Coming and Departure of Quetzalcoatl

The murals in the west wing of the reserve reading room in Dartmouth's Baker Library form a coherent cycle around a mythic moment in the ancient history of the Americas, a vision of cultural fulfillment that was extinguished by jealousy, superstition, and aggression (fig. 199). Associations with the name Quetzalcoatl range from that of a religious icon—the plumed serpent whose earliest-known images date to the second or third century and

163

whose dualistic symbolism encompassed heaven and earth—to that of legendary leader Ce Acatl Topiltzin Quetzalcoatl, whom the Aztecs, who saw themselves as the cultural heirs of the Toltecs, promoted as a Toltec culture hero who thus would have lived sometime in the ninth to twelfth century. Written versions of oral accounts of the Toltec priest-ruler Topiltzin Quetzalcoatl are preserved in about a dozen variants in Spanish, French, Italian, and Nahuatl (the language of the Aztecs). Of the last, only five fragments survive, all dating to the mid-sixteenth century and recorded by Friar Bernardino de Sahagún in codices now in Madrid and Florence. Perhaps not surprisingly, given his own religious calling, Sahagún's interpretations, along with those of the other influential historian of the Aztecs, Fray Diego Durán, emphasized the Christ-like attributes of Topiltzin Quetzalcoatl, particularly his self-sacrifice for the sake of his people.[50]

Whatever Orozco's intermediate sources,[51] he seems to have based his visual account of Quetzalcoatl primarily on Fragments C and D of the Sahagún codices. The first portrays Quetzalcoatl as savior and bringer of light, while the second describes the fall of the Toltec empire along with an account of Quetzalcoatl's departure on a raft of serpents. As he himself emphasized,[52] however, Orozco did not simply turn this material into a narrative. Rather, he adapted its archetypal features—the bringer of civilization who is cast out by his own people and prophesies his return after a period of destruction—to his own sense of the frustrated hopes of human history. Our interpretation, then, must be guided by the artist's visual cues rather than by any particular version of Quetzalcoatl's protean identity, either as a legendary figure or as a pre-Cortesian god.

Orozco began his work in the reserve room with one of the smaller panels, *The Prophecy* (called *Europe* at an early stage), over the door at the east end of the long west wing wall, nearest the central

Fig. 201 · Study for the **Pre-Columbian Golden Age**, 1932–34, gouache on paper, Orozco Farias Family Collection.

delivery desk (fig. 174). This would seem an odd place for the artist to begin, but at this point the contract had not yet been signed and the commission was apparently not fully secure. In an unpublished account written by Carlos Sánchez, an artist from Guatemala who had graduated from Dartmouth in 1923 and became Orozco's assistant, we learn why the color appears to have been applied in smaller, more delicate strokes in this panel than elsewhere:

> Still being on trial, he had to paint another tentative panel in the Baker Library basement next to the space in the middle of the hall, where they dispensed books and received returned books from the students…. If I remember correctly, it represented riding medieval knights in armor. These were painted not in Orozco's fast strokes, but in what he himself of others would derogatorily call "estilo lamidito." Mexicans use a lot of diminutives. *Lamido* is what a dog does when he licks his wounds. "Lamidito," applied to painting, means that the artist goes over the same area over and over again, like an artisan, not like an artist painting with "bravura," because his demon impels him to express himself…. Lamidito is something like a school exercise. The work suffers because of this.[53]

The delicate fresco technique of *The Prophecy* does resemble that of the earlier *Release* (fig. 193) more than that of its neighboring *Departure of Quetzalcoatl* (fig. 173), the panel to the immediate left of the little overdoor panel he had just finished. With the contract presumably in hand, Orozco painted the top portion of *Departure* in a markedly freer style. He left for Europe before completing this composition (fig. 200).[54]

After his return, Orozco painted at the opposite end of the long north wall the complementary overdoor panel to *The Prophecy,* the panel showing *Aztec Warriors* (fig. 170), where stonelike faces emerge from eagle and jaguar costumes emblematic of the warrior class. Aztec warriors engaged in a continuous "sacred war." The primary purpose of this systematized aggression was to supply sacrificial victims whose hearts and blood would feed the sun and thus ensure the wellbeing of the universe. In the foreground of this composition is a monumental sculptured head of a feathered snake: Quetzalcoatl as the plumed serpent, icon of Aztec power. Similarly, the complementary panel depicting the European invasion shows armor-masked soldiers bearing the Christian cross in the form of a huge piked weapon (fig. 174). This image declares the militant nature of the god into which European culture transformed Christ and his teachings. Thus, on either side of the scenes that depict the appearance of the legendary Quetzalcoatl, his golden age, and his departure, we are offered complementary glimpses of the organized brutality of a humanity alienated from what Orozco called the "Power of Good in the Universe."

Between these two bracketing images, we are addressed by *The Coming of Quetzalcoatl* (fig. 171).[55] According to various accounts, this Toltec priest-ruler created fire, fostered the cultivation of corn and the art of carving stone, developed the science of astronomy, and discouraged the practice of human sacrifice. Quetzalcoatl's appearance in the

Dartmouth mural accords with descriptions of him as clear-eyed, white-bearded, white-robed, and powerful.[56] In Orozco's painting, the humanity of Quetzalcoatl's piercing eyes and powerful hands breaks the spell of the earlier gods arrayed behind him. According to Artemas Packard's artist-approved description, they represent "the figures of the older gods who symbolize the forces which influence the destinies of men. From left to right they are specifically the God of Greed [Xipe Totec], dressed in the skins of his victims; the God of Magic [Tezcatlipoca], with feet of smoking mirrors; the God of Rain and Storm [Tlaloc]; the God of Death [Mictlantecuhtli]; the God of War [Huitzilopochtli], with feet of feathers; and the God of Fire [Huehueteotl], whose home was in the cone of the volcano Orizaba."[57] In contrast, Quetzalcoatl "is represented as arousing

Fig. 202 · Composition study for left half of **The Departure of Quetzalcoatl**, 1932–34, gouache on paper, Hood Museum of Art, Dartmouth College, Hanover, New Hampshire; w.988.52.81.

165

men from their intellectual and spiritual torpor to learn the arts of civilization. To the right of the sleeping figures is a group of people conversing together on the porch of a Toltec house, a symbol of the beginnings of co-operation and understanding without which no society can exist."[58] To the right, in a panel called *Agriculturist, Sculptor, and Astronomer,* are depicted personifications of "the outstanding accomplishments" of the Toltecs (figs. 172 and 201).

This legendary golden age of Quetzalcoatl, which takes up over half of the long west wing wall, is depicted as a peaceful time of cooperation, creativity, and understanding. Orozco's expressive emphasis across the length of this wall is on the classically balanced powers of eyes and hands, signifying knowing and doing, the true sources of human culture. Bringing the light of knowledge and peace, Quetzalcoatl awakens the human race from isolation and ignorance to cooperation and creativity.

But the complementary human tendency toward superstition, greed for power, and aggression compels the beneficent hero-god to depart on a raft of serpents. In *The Departure of Quetzalcoatl*

(figs. 173 and 202), the enemies of Quetzalcoatl are depicted as "evil priests and magicians who sought by a series of treacheries and enchantments to counteract his beneficent influence and to regain control for the powers of darkness over the minds and hearts of men. Witchcraft and human sacrifice were re-established and in their wake followed war, disease, and the destruction of Tollan, the great Toltec city."[59]

This last major panel of the west wing shows a "disappointed messiah, who, renounced by his people, departs into the East…on a boat made of serpents, prophesying that he would return in five hundred years with other white gods who would destroy the civilization of those who failed to follow his precepts and set up a new civilization in its stead" (figs. 203 and 204).[60]

Historically, this prophecy was fulfilled by the coming of Cortez, the Spanish conquistador who was identified by the Aztecs with the returning Quetzalcoatl. Because of the magnificence of Teotihuacán, the ancient site north of Mexico City that was excavated by Manuel Gamio during the Mexican Revolution, this city was believed during Orozco's time to be the legendary Toltec capital Tollan. The result of Gamio's extensive work, *La población del valle de Teotihuacán,* was published

166

Fig. 203 · Study of Quetzalcoatl for **The Departure of Quetzalcoatl**, 1932–34, crayon on tracing paper, 32 ¼ x 24 ⅛ in (81.7 x 61.1 cm), Museum of Modern Art, New York, gift of Clemente Orozco Valladares, photograph ©2001 Museum of Modern Art, New York.

Fig. 204 · **Self-Portrait**, 1932–34, gouache on paper, Jacques and Natasha Gelman Collection of Twentieth-Century Art, The Vergel Foundation, New York.

by José Vasconcelos's Secretaría de Educación Pública in three massive volumes in 1922. Gamio's volumes were in the collection of Baker Library when Orozco was working there (they had entered the collection on October 21, 1930), and the artist no doubt consulted them in the course of planning his compositions. (In his autobiography Orozco relates that Baker Library had "a collection of books in Spanish which by itself is greater than many very important libraries in Spanish America."[61])

The two pyramids above which Quetzalcoatl rises in the Dartmouth mural are the Pyramid of the Sun and the Pyramid of the Moon at Teotihuacán (fig. 205). Despite his scorn for "Mexicanist" painters who imitated the style of pre-Cortesian frescoes in their own work, Orozco had a great deal of respect for the artistic accomplishments of the ancients in the realm of both art and architecture. For example, in a letter dated April 25, 1928, he wrote to George Biddle: "[B]y [no] means fail to see the ruins of San Juan Teotihuacán, better than Egypt, one hour by railroad from the City of Mexico or by automobile. You will never forget the piramids [*sic*], frescoes, subways, museum and small towns nearby."[62] The sculptor carving at the center of Orozco's *Agriculturist, Sculptor, and Astronomer* (fig. 172) is creating decorative architectural motifs similar to those found at Teotihuacán, illustrated in Gamio as "Fragments of frescoes in the 'Temple of Agriculture'" (fig. 206). Appropriately, Orozco's sculptor is working directly next to a grower of corn.

These motifs also show some resemblance to the carved stone architectural elements excavated in the mid-1920s at the Toltec-Mayan site of Chichén Itzá, Yucatán. Moreover, the temple-topped pyramid that serves as a backdrop for the treacherous priests in *The Departure* (fig. 173) resembles the edifice at this site known as El Castillo (fig. 207). Orozco's friend and correspondent Jean Charlot worked every January through May from 1926 through 1929 at Chichén Itzá, serving as staff artist for excavations sponsored by the Carnegie Institution. The two-volume publication of this excavation, *The Temple of the Warriors at Chichén Itzá, Yucatán,* appeared in May 1931 and entered the collection of Dartmouth's Baker Library the following month.[63]

Alma Reed too had close personal links with Chichén Itzá, and in her biography of Orozco she asserts her role in the planning of these panels: "I supplied assorted data on the culture of the ancient Maya—much of which Orozco used. I was familiar with the subject as a result of my archaeological studies in Yucatan where I reported the Carnegie excavations at Chichen-Itzá for the *New York Times*. It is possible that I communicated some of my own ardent admiration for the mother race of the American continent, especially for its great culture hero, Kukulcan, the Maya embodiment of Quetzalcoatl, to whom many admirers likened Felipe Carrillo Puerto."[64]

Fig. 205 · "Pyramid of the Sun at Teotihuacán," from Manuel Gamio, **La población del valle de Teotihuacán** (Mexico City: Talleres Gráficos, Secretaria de Educación Pública, 1922), vol. 1, opposite p. 130.

Fig. 206 · Watercolor renditions of "Fragments of frescoes in the 'Temple of Agriculture,'" from Manuel Gamio, **La población del valle de Teotihuacán** (Mexico City: Talleres Gráficos, Secretaria de Educación Pública, 1922), vol. 1, opposite p. 138.

Fig. 207 · "View of Chichén Itzá," with "El Castillo" at top center, from Earl H. Morris et al., **The Temple of the Warriors at Chichén Itzá, Yucatán** (Washington, D.C.: Carnegie Institution, 1931), vol. 2, plate 25, used with permission of the Carnegie Institution.

167

In *An Autobiography*, Orozco provides a more specific account of Alma Reed's associations with the Yucatán and its governor, the assassinated Felipe Carrillo Puerto: "Alma Reed had been in Mexico to write some articles for the *New York Times*. In Yucatán she had met the Governor, Felipe Carrillo Puerto, and falling in love they planned to marry. While she was on her way home to prepare for the wedding, Carrillo Puerto was assassinated in the outbreak of the de la Huerta revolt."[65] Orozco had paid overt homage to Carrillo Puerto in a panel he painted at the New School for Social Research in 1931, before coming to Dartmouth. Behind the New School depiction of Carrillo Puerto (fig. 141) looms a clear representation of El Castillo. Chichén Itzá was developed by the Toltecs as they moved eastward into the Yucatán Peninsula, and some versions of the Quetzalcoatl myth have the Toltec priest-ruler moving through the Yucatán before departing by sea. Although, in her biography, Reed tended to overemphasize her own importance in the development of Orozco's projects, the site from which Quetzalcoatl angrily departs on his raft of serpents in the Dartmouth mural may well have been meant to evoke Chichén Itzá. The association of the Yucatán with the assassination of Carrillo Puerto thus lends an added edge of betrayal to this scene of treachery.

These three narrative panels of the west wing—*The Coming of Quetzalcoatl, The Pre-Columbian Golden Age,* and *The Departure of Quetzalcoatl*—show a clear influence of the art of William Blake, which Orozco would have been quite aware of at this time through the research and writing of his fellow Delphic Circle member Emily Hamblen.[66] Like Orozco, Blake endorsed a revolutionary response to the need for change, and he was similarly obsessed with concepts of struggle between forces of good and evil, light and darkness. Blake's *America: A Prophecy* and *Europe: A Prophecy,* in which he integrated the American War of Independ-

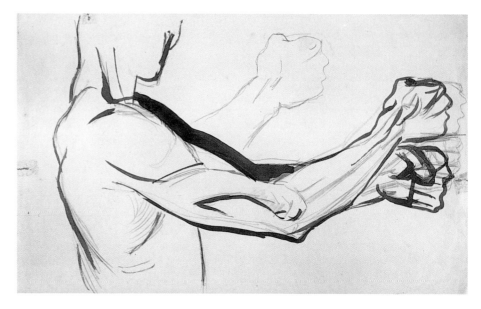

ence and the French Revolution into his grand mythology, no doubt influenced Orozco's own conception of his epic of the Americas. Even clearer is the visual evidence of Blake's stylistic influence on the rhetorical poses and gestures of Orozco's figures[67] and on the poetically graphic delineation of musculature in the central figure of *The Golden Age* (figs. 172 and 208).

According to Orozco's first plan for the mural, the long walls of each of the wings of the reserve

Fig. 208 · Study for **The Pre-Columbian Golden Age**, 1932–34, ink on paper, Hood Museum of Art, Dartmouth College, Hanover, New Hampshire; D.988.52.64.

Fig. 209 · Orozco on scaffold with **Ancient Human Sacrifice**, fall 1932, photograph courtesy Dartmouth College Library.

168

reading room were to represent "the constructive, affirmative, *positive* aspects of the myth," while the far end walls of each wing would have presented "the barbaric aspects of human nature operating against the constructive civilizing forces of human nature." In the west wing, this thematic organization resulted in the presentation of Aztec culture, which succeeded that of the Toltecs, to the left of the Toltec period shown on the long north wall. Thus, reading from left to right, in the "first" panel of the room we see the migration of the Aztecs into central Mexico (fig. 167); in the right panel we see the resumption of the ancient practice of human sacrifice that, according to some versions of the legend, had been eliminated under Quetzalcoatl (fig. 169); and, above the doorway, we observe a symbolic statement of the ferocity of Aztec society in the form of a rattle-snake flanked by spears (fig. 168). Although awkward chronologically, this organization has the advantage of permitting an easy narrative transition from Quetzalcoatl's departure and prophecy to the *Cortez* of the east wing.

In *Migration,* the Aztecs[68] are shown marching in lock step phalanxes toward their destiny: the conquest and absorption of indigenous cultures into a single, totalitarian society. We are alerted to the significance of the migration panel by the contrast drawn between its grimly militaristic figures (the fallen marcher dramatizes the price extracted) and the harmoniously varied culture suggested in the panels devoted to Quetzalcoatl's epiphany. (It is also interesting to compare these figures with the marching Zapatistas in Orozco's painting from the previous year [fig. 37].)

Ancient Human Sacrifice takes up the right-hand side of the west wall (figs. 209, 210, and 211). Orozco's emphasis is not on the Aztecs' sun worship (Quetzalcoatl is the only light bringer here), but on their dark, chthonic obsession with war and human sacrifice. The image that presides over this ritual was described by Orozco as Huitzilopochtli, god of

Fig. 210 · Composition study for **Ancient Human Sacrifice**, 1932–34, graphite on cream paper, Hood Museum of Art, Dartmouth College, Hanover, New Hampshire; D.988.52.33.

Fig. 211 · Study of victim for **Ancient Human Sacrifice**, 1932–34, charcoal on paper, Hood Museum of Art, Dartmouth College, Hanover, New Hampshire; D.988.52.31.

169

war and patron god of the Aztecs. Visually, however, this image is more closely identified with the head of the goddess Coyolxauhqui, who was decapitated by Huitzilopochtli.[69] The priest who carries out the ritual is masked, as are the victim and other participants, emphasizing the blind impersonality of this sacrifice of human life to a dead god.

These two panels introduce the theme of bondage to an abstract, mechanistic destructiveness, a theme that the panels of the east wing restate in even more monstrous terms. The two narrow vertical panels on either side of the east doorway of the west wing serve as parenthetical statements of this theme. Here totem poles representing caricatures of Northwest Coast bird images symbolize the fetishism of native religion in North America (figs. 175 and 176). These two panels, along with the little *Snake and Spears* over the west doorway (fig. 168), were painted at the end of the project, just before the last two panels, the *Machine Totems* (figs. 177 and 178), in the east wing.[70] They introduce into the cycle a reference to the native inhabitants of North America and may have been meant to accord with a frequently used justification for the appropriateness of this particular mural cycle for Dartmouth, the earliest years of which were linked with the goal of educating Indians.[71] Whatever the rationale, no part of the mural better clarifies the artist's uncompromising humanism, which condemns primitive religion as absurd fetishism. Far from idealizing tribal societies, Orozco here implies that they too contribute to the authoritarian legacy of humankind.

As the mural developed, the horrors of the modern world loomed larger than the artist's original vision of an "authentic new world civilization," which Orozco in the end relegated to the section of the south wall facing the reserve desk.[72] This shift to a darker vision may have been influenced by the artist's only visit to Europe during the summer of 1932, when he had barely begun the frescoes

of the west wing.[73] In Europe, he encountered the despair left by World War I and the rising dictatorship that augured another world war. In his autobiography, Orozco recalls accounts published in European newspapers of war scandals, "documented beyond dispute, of the shameful politicians and the dealers in cannon fodder. Exposures of how Germany and the Allies had exchanged critical materials during the progress of the First World War and so prolonged that war in the interests of big speculators."[74] He returned to Dartmouth with a darker view of the likelihood of an imminent answer to the problems of humankind and with a sharpened sense of a perennial pattern of dehumanization. This experience influenced the final form of Orozco's *Epic,* wrenching its poetic conventions into an antithesis. His epic hero, Quetzalcoatl, is finally, tragically confined to the realm of mythic promise, while the founding of the historic city would simply begin another cycle of human misery, with Cortez as its militarized antihero.

Fig. 212 · Composition study for **Cortez and the Cross**, 1932–34, tempera on paper, Instituto Cultural Cabañas, Guadalajara/INBA 14560, photograph by Rubén Orozco.

170

The East Wing: Cortez and the Modern Era

The scenes of the east wing of the reserve reading room shift our attention from indigenous American history and myth to their counterparts after the European conquest. The subject originally proposed by Orozco for the long, "positive" north wall was "The New Culture of the American Continent." Soon after starting the mural, perhaps as soon as the completion of the top part of his *Departure* panel in June 1932, certainly not long after his return from Europe that fall, Orozco conceived the visual logic of beginning his east wing walls with the fulfillment of Quetzalcoatl's prophecy in the form of the coming of Cortez. The first panel of the east wing depicts "Cortez's Ships Destroyed by Himself," followed by "Hernan Cortez, symbolizing the conquest of the continent under the aegis of the Cross and the end of the old civilization" (figs. 179 and 212).[75] His godlike status reinforced by the large cross behind him, Cortez is portrayed with a curiously self-absorbed tenderness amid the carnage. This stylistic dissonance parodies the conventions of Spanish Renaissance portraiture contemporary with Cortez, whose El Greco-like serenity conveys an unwavering faith in the righteousness of his cause.[76] The face of Cortez is so eerily out of key with the expressionist context of human suffering that it becomes another kind of mask, while the prominent cross that gives Cortez his authority provides a visual link between this panel and the final panel of the east wing, in which Christ destroys his cross.

The Cortez panel presents a complicated image that benefits from comparison with earlier and later versions by Orozco of the same subject. The extensive frescoes that he executed in 1923–24 and 1926 in the main courtyard of the National Preparatory School in Mexico City contain a number of compositions that found later expression in the mural at Dartmouth.[77] The depiction of a nude Cortez with his Indian consort, Malinche, over the stairway leading

Fig. 213 · **Conqueror-Builder and Indian Worker**, 1926, fresco, National Preparatory School, Mexico City.

Fig. 214 · **Cortez and Victory**, 1937–39, fresco, Hospicio Cabañas, Guadalajara, photograph by Bob Schalkwijk.

171

from the courtyard to the first floor (fig. 17), presents a paternalistic figure who holds down the prone body of a young native man with his right foot while reaching with his left hand to restrain Malinche from offering assistance. At the same time, however, their right hands are grasped in a gesture of equality. Nearby depictions of primitive, almost stupefied "Ancient Races," a "Conqueror-Builder" who plans grand projects for an Indian worker (fig. 213), and a Franciscan who wraps an emaciated Indian in a smothering embrace further confirm Orozco's ambiguous view of a conquest that brought both good and evil.

Orozco's great 1936–39 fresco cycle at the Hospicio Cabañas in Guadalajara has as its over-arching theme Mexico before and after the Spanish Conquest. In this sense, it is a further development of the Dartmouth cycle. The *Man of Fire* in the dome has already been mentioned. In vaults on either side of the dome are flanking portrayals of a Franciscan holding a cross like a sword over the bent back of an Indian and a Cortez whose armor has become a machine with a gaping hole where his heart should be (fig. 214), a pointed parallel with the sacrificial victim of an Aztec goddess shown nearby. As at Dartmouth, the Guadalajara Cortez holds a sword in his right hand, while dismembered Indians are piled at his feet and flames rise in the background.

In these three cycles, which span a little more than a dozen years, we see Orozco moving by degrees, not from a brighter to a darker depiction of Cortez and the changes that the coming of European civilization brought to the American continent, but rather to a more forceful expression of the savagery that characterized both indigenous and European cultures at the time of the conquest. Cortez is finally neither hero nor villain. He is a mindless, heartless expression of the mechanistic society that spawned him, no more or less admirable than the brutal society that he destroyed.

In the second panel of the east wing, the gray steel of Cortez's armor becomes a monstrous, chaotic presence: Toward the center of this wall, we are confronted with Orozco's expressionistic representation of *The Machine* (fig. 180). Its gray and jagged mass appears to feed on the piled human bodies at Cortez's feet like some demonic incarnation of antihuman materialism. The message, surely, is that the impersonal chaos of the modern era permits no more concern for human life than did the murderous rituals of the Aztecs. *The Machine,* which symbolizes the mass regimentation of modern society for inhuman goals, is the controlling theme of this wing. Its presence is starkly emphasized in the two vertical panels on either side of the doorway (figs. 177 and 178). Here we see fantasies of machines possessed by their own life, modern equivalents of the totem idols depicted in the west wing (figs. 175 and 176).

The 1920s and early 1930s in America were characterized by an increasing consciousness of the drawbacks as well as the potential advantages of the machine age. World War I had contributed to a growing awareness that modern life was bringing unforeseen horrors as well as increasing productivity. Machine guns, tanks, long-distance artillery,

Fig. 215 · Diego Rivera, **Detroit Industry**, north wall, 1932–33, fresco, Detroit Institute of Arts, gift of Edsel B. Ford, photograph © 1991 Detroit Institute of Arts.

and aerial bombardments not only killed but maimed in unthought-of ways, while modern medicine produced living corpses. In *An Autobiography,* Orozco wrote of an exhibition of photographs he had seen in Europe during the first summer of his Dartmouth project: "photographs showing soldiers who lived on with their faces partly or completely shot away.... Philanthropists could boast of having supplied them with masks which gave them a human appearance. Others had lost not only their faces but arms and legs, and miraculously went on living, transformed into beings which beggared the most lurid artistic imagination."[78]

But the machine appealed to the artistic imagination in positive ways as well. In May 1927, the year that Orozco arrived in New York from Mexico, Jane Heap of the *Little Review* organized a Machine-Age Exposition designed to convince artists that they should "affiliate with the creative artist in the other arts and with the constructive men of [our] epoch: engineers, scientists, etc."[79] In the spring of 1930 Orozco's friend Lewis Mumford lectured at the New School for Social Research on "Creative Expression and the Machine," and in 1930–31 he wrote *Technics and Civilization,* published in 1934 with, as its frontispiece, Orozco's "Cortez and the Machine" from the Dartmouth mural. It is likely that the artist shared with the critic an attitude toward the machine described in *Technics and Civilization*: "No matter how completely technics relies upon the objective procedures of the sciences, it does not form an independent system, like the universe: it exists as an element in human culture and it promises well or ill as the social groups that exploit it promise well or ill. The machine itself makes no demands and holds out no promises: it is the human spirit that makes demands and keeps promises."[80]

It seems apparent that Orozco was inspired, or at least energized, by Diego Rivera's contemporary depiction of the machine in his *Detroit Industry* fresco cycle, painted between July 1932 and March

Fig. 216 · Study of gears and girders for **The Machine**, 1932–34, graphite on tracing paper, Hood Museum of Art, Dartmouth College, Hanover, New Hampshire; D.988.52.119.

1933 (fig. 215).[81] Rivera devoted considerable time to the study of machinery at the Ford Motor Company's River Rouge plant, which was his subject. Orozco, working in rural New England, relied on other sources. In the Dartmouth archives, there is a copy of a letter of July 7, 1933, from Dartmouth's reference librarian to the director of the Century of Progress Exposition in Chicago, requesting photographs that the artist could use as models:

> The specific items requested are:
> Electrical—motors, Dynamos, Turbines, etc.
> Steam Shovel
> Locomotives
> Lathes
> Linotype
> Rotary Press

> …we feel in considering the permanence
> of the frescoes, that we should make available
> to the artist pictures of the machine as it
> has been perfected at the time when his work
> is being executed.[82]

Orozco made at least one study for this panel that appears to have been done from photographs (fig. 216). But the final panel resembles Rivera's work more than any of the "specific items" called

173

Fig. 217 · Composition study for **Anglo-America**, 1932–34, graphite on paper, Hood Museum of Art, Dartmouth College, Hanover, New Hampshire; D.988.52.174

Fig. 218 · Composition study for **Anglo-America**, 1932–34, graphite on paper, Hood Museum of Art, Dartmouth College, Hanover, New Hampshire; D.988.52.131.

Fig. 219 · **Destruction of the Old Order**, 1926, fresco, National Preparatory School, Mexico City, photograph by Bob Schalkwijk.

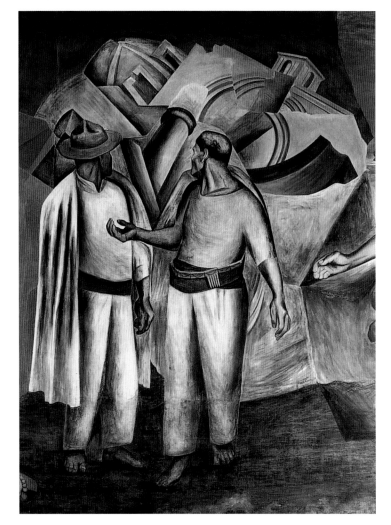

for by the librarian on Orozco's behalf. The theme seems to have elicited from both artists visual and cultural associations between machines and primitive gods.

One cultural manifestation of machine civilization is the cold, repressive world of the schoolhouse and town meeting depicted in the panel entitled *Anglo-America* (fig. 181).[83] Alma Reed tells us that Orozco "regarded the growing tendency toward standardization as the most dangerous ailment of modern society. He...lost no opportunity to deride our national mania for over-organization. Many of his devastating caricatures pilloried the 'committee,' which he viewed as a symbol of futility and one of the most harmful of American institutions."[84] Here Orozco fuses critiques of American Puritanism and of organization-man anonymity, blending them into the life-denying gray that extends across the entire wall.

This vision of repression is complemented by the violent scenario of *Hispano-America,* exploding in revolution and all but destroyed by imperialistic exploitation (fig. 182). *Anglo-* and *Hispano-America* are among the few finished compositions upon which Orozco has been quoted at length. After the completion of his project, the artist was interviewed by the *Dartmouth,* and these two panels provided the pretext for an analysis of the cultures of the two Americas:

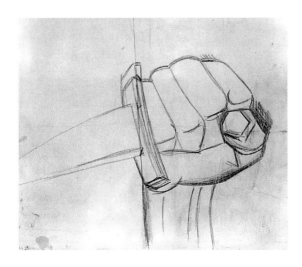

It is the rebel spirit that the United States needs, the spirit of the Latin American, who will try to preserve his individuality and honor and self-respected at any cost.... The picture of the town meeting illustrates part of the American political idealism which supposes that talking about public problems will keep order and peace and save the world. That is only half of the question, however, for discussion only ends in compromise. But the Latin American mind cannot be understood by the North Americans.... They have the capacity to put up with a situation just so long. Then they get mad. So, you see, the unrest and instability of the southern republics, which Americans cannot comprehend, is perhaps the good thing. The weakness may be a sort of strength.[85]

According to Orozco's autobiography, he found New Englanders to be "country folk, hostile and formal in their dealings with outlanders and new arrivals, but most cordial on closer acquaintance, and

Fig. 220 · Study of head for **Hispano-America**, 1932–34, graphite on cream paper, Hood Museum of Art, Dartmouth College, Hanover, New Hampshire; D.988.52.154.

Fig. 221 · Study for **Hispano-America**, 1932–34, graphite on paper, Hood Museum of Art, Dartmouth College, Hanover, New Hampshire; D.988.52.174.

175

anxious to be neighborly, to understand one, and to help out with the greatest good will, disinterest, and courtesy."[86] In other words, cold and unappealing, exactly how he depicted his grim schoolmarm, her robotlike charges, and the zombielike participants in a New England town meeting (figs. 217 and 218). On the other hand, he lavished much love on the gorgeous painting of wheat at the bottom left of this composition, which corresponds to the equally beautifully painted corn in the *Golden Age* panel of the west wing (fig. 172). It is likely that in *Anglo-America,* Orozco was attempting to evoke a thematic parallel with the *Golden Age* of Quetzalcoatl: The earlier panel's themes of agriculture, cooperation, and education all have counterparts here, and the dominant blue and gold coloration of *Anglo-America* reinforces the visual connection.

The more vivid comparison is with its neighboring *Hispano-America,* a more fully developed version of Orozco's 1926 composition *Destruction of the Old Order,* on the ground floor of the Preparatory School in Mexico City (fig. 219). There Orozco enjoyed the leeway allowed him by his subject to experiment with the cubist compositional device of multiple points of view. He continued experimenting with cubism in his depiction of *The Machine* at Dartmouth. In *Hispano-America,* he extended cubism's multiple viewpoint to the human figure of the foreign general about to stab the rebel in the back. For Orozco, however, cubism was an expressive, not an analytical, style; its purpose was to foreground emotional content (figs. 220 and 221).

In 1940, when Orozco was asked if a preliminary sketch for the fresco *Dive Bomber and Tank* (fig. 233) was the head of an aviator, he replied, "'Yes perhaps,'—he turned the sketch upside down—'or, it might be a bomb. A picture must be capable of being looked at from any direction.... I plan to paint this fresco so that the individual panels can be turned upside down or rearranged in any order, changing but not disturbing the basic composition.'"

The interviewer then asked whether Orozco's choice of a dive bomber as his subject had any political motivation. The artist answered: "'Of course not. I simply paint the life that is going on at present—what we are and what the world is at this moment. That is what modern art is, the actual feeling of life around us or the mood of whatever is just happening. As for political significance, that can be found in any painting if the observer wishes to see it there.'"[87]

In *Hispano-America,* Orozco's political commentary is anything but passive. It is not difficult to see caricatures of Woodrow Wilson and Winston Churchill in the figures to the left and General Pershing in the figure to the right of the rebel, who

Fig. 222 · **Pancho Villa**, 1931, oil on canvas, Museo de Arte Carrillo Gil, Mexico City/INBA 17271.

resembles Pancho Villa, the Mexican "bandit" who in 1916 extended his rebellion across the border into the United States.[88] The real bandits in *Hispano-America* are the top-hatted, mask-wearing capitalists behind the general, whose crotch is in suggestive proximity to the prominent buttocks of the foreground figure with his nose buried in Mexican gold. U.S. investment in Mexico at the time of the revolution was extensive, three times that of other foreigners, twice that of Mexicans. Americans controlled 75 percent of Mexican mines and almost 60 percent of Mexican oil.[89] In his painting *Pancho Villa* of 1931 (fig. 222), Orozco depicts the rebel leader as a Cortez-like figure: heroic in his stance and attire, destructive in his impact. In the Dartmouth fresco, there is greater emphasis on the rebel's heroic integrity, which contrasts sharply with the murderous, greedy figures surrounding him.

The *Dartmouth Alumni Magazine* of November 1933 gave the title of this panel as "Hispano-America — The Rebel and His International Enemies."[90] Orozco's rebel is a hero standing alone against foreign capitalistic greed and imperialism. The artist summarized his message when he proposed the subject to Artemas Packard:

> The best representation of Hispanic-American idealism, not as an abstract idea but as an accomplished fact, would be, I think, the figure of a rebel. Hispanic-America, in its century of independent life, has been the victim of the most cruel and unjust aggressions. It has been invaded, enslaved, dispossessed, exploited, deceived by enemies posing as friends. But the foreign aggressor or the local exploiter or dictator always meets with the resistance of the people and their leaders, who rise in armed protest to oppose the brutal force. In every case there is the rebel — sometimes a most humble and illiterate man, sometimes a student in the university, sometimes a real bandit, sometimes

a saint. He may be poor or rich, but he is always an idealist who sacrifices everything in life to struggle for a fundamental human or social cause.... If there is any need for expressing in just one sentence the highest ideal of the Hispanic-American rebel, it would be as follows: "Justice whatever the cost."[91]

"Justice whatever the cost" is the quintessential motivation of the Orozco hero.

The wrecked buildings in the background of *Hispano-America* encompass modern as well as colonial architecture, belying Orozco's assurance to Packard that "after the destruction of an armed revolution remains a triumphant ideal with a chance of realization."[92] John Hutton was closer to the mark when he asserted: "For Orozco, revolutions occur as the negation of an unacceptable present, not the harbingers of a better future."[93] Leonard Folgarait points out that the word "revolution" "means coming back to the same point in a circular pattern, over and over again."[94] This was certainly Orozco's sense of its meaning: the event and its cause, inextricably linked.

Fig. 223 · Composition study for **Gods of the Modern World**, 1932–34, graphite on tracing paper, Hood Museum of Art, Dartmouth College, Hanover, New Hampshire; D.988.52.155.

At the end of this long north wall is the unforgettable *Gods of the Modern World* (figs. 183 and 223), perhaps the best known of all the images of the Dartmouth mural. In it, academicians, supposedly the guardians of the accumulated knowledge of humankind, are depicted as living corpses presiding over the stillbirth of useless knowledge while behind them the world goes up in flames. Several of Orozco's "gods" wear European academic garb. In retrospect, he seems to have been remarkably penetrating in his perception of the failure of the European academic establishment to question the rising fascism that led to World War II.

Orozco had not yet reached this point in the execution of his program when he wrote his manuscript for the *Dartmouth Alumni Magazine* of November 1933. There this subject is described as "The End of Superstition—Triumph of Freedom."[95] A shift from historical to mythic time on the north wall of the east wing—from *Hispano-America* to "The Triumph of Freedom"—may have seemed too abrupt a transition. Or perhaps the last panel of this wall may have appeared too unimportant a position for such a culminating theme. Whatever the reason, he shifted his "Triumph of Freedom" to the right-hand side of the east wall, where, in the form of *The Modern Migration of the Spirit,* it parallels *Migration* on the corresponding west wall (figs. 186 and 167). For the end of the north wall, he devised the brilliant and startling vision of the gods of the modern world, who, according to Orozco's visual argument, fulfill the same deterministic function as the ancient gods

arrayed behind Quetzalcoatl at the opposite end of the room (fig. 171). The north wall of the east wing is itself balanced by the world in conflagration behind these dead gods of academia and the flames emerging from Cortez's burning ships.

The strength of this criticism of higher education's abdication of social responsibility derives in large measure from Orozco's powerful conjugation of birth and death imagery. The use of skeletons as symbols to effect pointed social satire is of course characteristically Mexican. One thinks first of Posada, who, Orozco tells us in his autobiography, was an early hero.[96] Orozco himself first used skeleton imagery in his 1925 caricatures for the Mexican journal *L'ABC.* The ineffectuality of academics was an even earlier theme. The August 10, 1912, issue of the opposition journal *El ahuizote,* for which Orozco produced caricatures during the early years of the revolution, contains a satiric depiction entitled *Doctors of Learning* (fig. 224), in which the "doctors" are depicted as blind buffoons. Although President Hopkins's account of Orozco's opinion of the Dartmouth faculty—that they "ought to be annihilated because they profiteer on the students' need for education"—may have been exaggerated for effect, Orozco expressed a similar view on another occasion. Alma Reed tells us that *Gods of the Modern World* "is a plastic variation on the theme of an informal talk the artist had given a short time before at the Art Department of Yale University when, to the amazement of the instructors, he told some two hundred students that they were all painting with the 'dead hand of the Academy.'"[97] Such overt criticism in the arms of academia may seem unusual, but this prickly stance was typical of Orozco, who eight years later offered a similarly scathing indictment of corrupt justice on the walls of the Supreme Court of Mexico.

A valuable eyewitness account of the creation of *Gods of the Modern World* is provided by Gobin Stair, a member of the Dartmouth class of 1933,

Fig. 224 · **Doctors of Learning,** from **El ahuizote,** August 10, 1912.

who served as Orozco's helper during the final phases of the mural. Stair recalled the creation of this particular panel as a "difficult time," adding: "I guess there was some reluctance or perhaps lack of enthusiasm around for what this section might 'say.' I was not involved in that higher-level concern but I was involved in the material, and he conveyed to me that I was to do some research. So I got him medical books with illustrations of skeletons, but also he wanted some baby skeletons and that was difficult. Luckily I found a bell jar with the skeleton of a fetus, and that, as you can see, is just what he wanted."[98] In fact, the message of *Gods of the Modern World* could not be clearer: What the modern world needs is not another generation of "educated" academics, dead to the burning issues of contemporary life, but more independent thinkers and doers. Fortunately, Orozco's perspective accorded well with the educational philosophy of President Hopkins, who defended this panel to a disgruntled Dartmouth widow and grandmother of a potential student: "I was exceedingly glad to have this panel interpolated among the others, because I felt that if, on the walls of an educational institution, we were to indict modern society in its other important phases the College ought certainly to recognize its own limitations and be willing to have indictment made of these."[99]

The panels of the east end of the east wing are in a kind of alcove where, at the time they were painted, the light must have been dimmer than in the rest of the reserve reading room. Perhaps partly for this reason, Orozco here markedly brightened his colors and reverted to a caricatural style, the swift impact of which he was a past master. To the right of *Gods of the Modern World* is his outraged portrayal of *Modern Human Sacrifice* (figs. 185 and 225), corresponding to *Ancient Human Sacrifice* on the far west wall opposite (fig. 169). The body of an unknown soldier, his skeletal hands still testifying to his final agony, is buried beneath the trappings

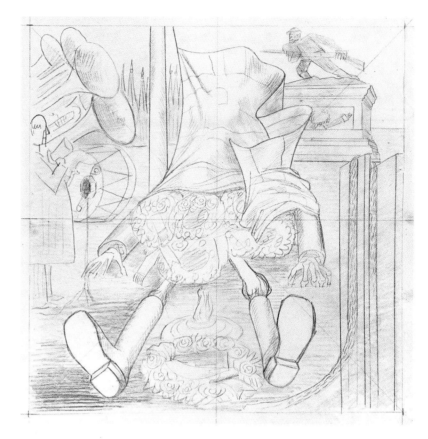

of patriotism: colorful flags, wreaths, monuments, speeches, brass bands, and the "eternal flame" that marks the grave of the decorously anonymous victim of modern nationalism. The overdoor panel to the left, showing a junk pile of totemistic animal symbols of warfare and empire from three historical eras, suggests the continuity between primitive and modern chauvinism (fig. 184).

The repeated cycles of brutality that take us from ancient through modern times finally come to an end in *Modern Migration of the Spirit* (figs. 186; 90–95). In this climax to the mural, the human spirit is dramatized as a Christ figure that rejects his sacrificial destiny by chopping down his cross and destroying the causes of his agony: militarism (represented by tanks and armaments), religion (the cross, a Buddha image, a minaret), and the authoritarian perversion of culture (a fallen Ionic column and the fragment of an Aphrodite). He appears to be flayed, like the sacrificial victims of the god of greed depicted in the west wing. This

Fig. 225 · Composition study for **Modern Human Sacrifice**, 1932–34, graphite on tracing paper, Hood Museum of Art, Dartmouth College, Hanover, New Hampshire; D.988.52.177.

179

theme of malevolent greed connects him as well with the rebel, whose enemies are motivated by lust for gold. Bearing the wounds of his oppression, his spiritual purification symbolized by the flamelike colors of his body and his torn flesh, this reincarnation of Quetzalcoatl has returned to cast off the chains that are symbolically associated with death in the overdoor panel to the right (fig. 187).

Modern Migration of the Spirit may seem an unduly anarchistic vision. But as with the death imagery of *Gods of the Modern World,* Orozco's vision is here characteristically Mexican, as Anita Brenner explained in *Idols behind Altars:* "In Mexican mood the messiah is always accompanied by disaster: an earthquake, a conquest, a revolution, the sacrifice of a ruler; death and pain. Therefore all the prophecies which promise restoration are complemented by announcements of catastrophe. New life, the fires rekindled by the ancient Mexicans after the end of each fifty-two-year cycle, was made after the darkening of these fires, destruction of possessions, with the sense of impending obliteration."[100] According to ancient Mesoamerican traditions, our age, the age of the "Fifth Sun," the age of Quetzalcoatl, will come to an end with earthquakes and fire. *Modern Migration of the Spirit* is the ultimate fulfillment of Quetzalcoatl's prophecy of return.

Orozco draws here on Eastern tradition as well, for iconographically his triumphant Christ is based on the Byzantine image of the Christ Anastasis, the crucified Christ who rises up, breaks down the doors of hell, and raises humankind to join him in his resurrection.[101] In a typical image of Christ Anastasis, the defeat of death is symbolized by the broken gates of his kingdom and the scattered keys, bolts, and nails that imprisoned the inhabitants of the underworld. In these images, Christ assumes the active stance that we see in the Christ of *Migration of the Spirit.* In several versions (e.g., fig. 226), the broken doors form a cross under Christ's feet, much like the cross in the Dartmouth panel. Orozco surely

Fig. 226 · **The Anastasis**, Skevophylakion Lectionary, eleventh century, fol. 1 (verso), from Anna Kartsonis, **Anastasis: The Making of an Image**, fig. 80, copyright © 1986 by Princeton University Press, reprinted by permission of Princeton University Press.

Fig. 227 · Composition study for **Chains of the Spirit**, 1932–34, graphite on tracing paper, Hood Museum of Art, Dartmouth College, Hanover, New Hampshire; D.988.52.188.

would have known images such as these. In *An Autobiography,* he writes of being rebaptized by his Delphic Circle friends, "with the name of Panselenos [*sic*]…a famous Greek painter of Byzantine times whose murals are to be found in Mistra…. As I returned to Manhattan on the ferry boat, across the enchanted bay of New York, my imagination was full of the elongated, rigid, austere images of the Apostles and the Virgin at the feet of the gigantic Pantocrat."[102] As always with Orozco, it is impossible

to draw simple conclusions from such comparisons. At most, we might consider the genesis of this image together with the overdoor panel to its right (fig. 187) and observe that Orozco utilizes religious symbolism to multiply associations, not to specify meaning. In a preliminary drawing for the overdoor panel (fig. 227), for example, a bishop's miter appears with the keys to these chains of the spirit. Orozco apparently rejected this symbol as too specifically anticlerical. (Nevertheless, if we examine the final composition closely, we notice that the vultures are wearing clerical collars.)

In these final two panels of the east wing, Orozco portrays the human spirit in the form of a triumphant resurrected Christ. But while the Christian tradition was an important source of imagery for the artist, he transformed its assumption of cosmic order into a blazing dreamworld of torment, outrage, and prophetic exclamation. For Orozco, order can be generated only from within, as a moral statement, not from without, as a confirmation of traditional dogma.

Coda: Modern Industrial Man

The panels across from the reserve desk, at the center of the south wall of the reading room (figs. 188–192), have traditionally been titled *Modern Industrial Man.* However, their rich, subdued coloration and utopian import are perhaps better conveyed by an earlier title, *The Dream of an Ideal Culture of the Future.*

These last five panels serve as a coda, balancing the lost utopia of Quetzalcoatl with a Depression-era vision of human possibility. The machine has been diverted from the exercise of power for its own sake to the service of humankind, while industrial man himself is shown planning and working cooperatively. This vision of the future recalls Quetzalcoatl's mythical golden age, projected (somewhat unconvincingly to our twenty-first-century eyes) from an age of stone to an age of steel. Its focal point—the central panel, which is over bookshelves—depicts the worker in a humanistic industrial society at last free to put down his tools and nourish his spirit. Appropriate to the location, he is reading a book.

In Orozco's original plan, the subjects for these panels had been described as "The Mayflower, The Norseman, Immigrants to America." By 1933 a revised plan for the mural ambitiously listed the subjects for the panels across from the reserve desk as:

EXPLORERS: Norsemen, Spanish, French, Dutch, English

SETTLERS: The Mayflower, the Pilgrims, the Indians

ELEAZAR WHEELOCK AND SAMSON OCCOM: symbol of the origin of Dartmouth College, of "Quetzalcoatl" in New England

WINNING OF THE WEST: Covered wagons, dead Indians

MODERN MIGRATIONS: Symbol of 19th & 20th century Immigration to America[103]

Fig. 228 · Study of Eleazar Wheelock with Indians, 1932–34, graphite on cream paper, Hood Museum of Art, Dartmouth College, Hanover, New Hampshire; D.988.52.265.

181

It is hard to believe that Orozco was ever serious about executing this ill-conceived plan. But there does exist a drawing for the central panel that shows Eleazar Wheelock teaching the Indians (fig. 228). The Indians, barrel, and book recall lines from Orozco's *An Autobiography* that convey his cynical view of Wheelock's "missionary" project:

> Dartmouth College in Hanover, New Hampshire, is one of the oldest of educational institutions in the American Union. Several years before the War of Independence it was founded by a missionary who wished to educate the Indians of the neighborhood. Eleazar Wheelock came along with a grammar, a Bible, a drum, and more than five thousand quarts of whiskey ["five thousand gallons of rum" in the traditional Dartmouth drinking song to which Orozco here alludes]. To the sound of his drum, the Indians assembled, drank his whiskey, and learned the idiom of the New Testament. Today there are no more Indians left to be educated after this admirable plan.[104]

As Orozco worked out the iconography of the east wing, these walls at the center of the room must have emerged as the only logical place for the "Future Golden Age," which had been displaced from the north wall by the expanding theme of "Our Time." The concept at this time of a golden age of the future was not unique to Orozco; it was a characteristic post–World War I, machine age metaphorical device for visualizing a bearable future. According to Orozco's fellow Delphic Circle member Claude Bragdon, "The Machine Age represents a period of power—if only for destruction. When power attains a certain maximum, it not infrequently changes to beauty—after the stalk, the flower; after the Iron Age, the Golden. But this Golden Age can come only as the result of some fresh outpouring of spiritual life, some change in the universal consciousness."[105] Orozco's *Modern*

Migration of the Spirit proposes just such a "change in the universal consciousness."

Seeking both conceptual and stylistic inspiration for his vision of an ideal modern culture, Orozco turned to the work of a colleague, the American muralist Thomas Hart Benton, with whom Orozco had worked at the New School and who had recommended Orozco to the Dartmouth faculty.[106] The deep diagonals into space, vertically stacked workers, cranes, motifs of transportation and industry, and general theme of construction in *Modern Industrial Man* echo the similarly dramatic elements of Benton's *City Building* (fig. 229) from his *America Today* mural, executed at the New School in 1930, at the same time Orozco was creating his own mural two floors above.[107]

On the other hand, the steel I beams that hang threateningly above the conferring workers in the left-hand section, and that have been transformed into dynamic structures in two other panels, were a favorite motif of Orozco's. He distorted them

Fig. 229 · Thomas Hart Benton, **City Building** from **America Today**, 1930, distemper and egg tempera on gessoed linen with oil glaze, 92 x 117 in (233.6 x 297 cm), Collection, AXA Financial, Inc. through its subsidiary The Equitable Life Assurance Society of the U.S. © AXA Financial, Inc.

expressively in his 1926 Preparatory School composition *The Conqueror-Builder and the Indian-Worker*
(fig. 213), and they appear as well in a number
of his New York paintings from the late 1920s and
early 1930s, where, with typical Orozcian dualism,
they convey both the energy and the oppressiveness
of American life (fig. 230).

The international style architecture depicted in
these panels is intended to signify a harmony of
function and beauty that is no longer dependent on
cultural ornament. Orozco studied architecture and
worked as an architectural draftsman early in his
career. The international style in architecture was
first celebrated as such at the Museum of Modern
Art in a 1932 exhibition that he may well have
attended. In the American skyscraper, Orozco saw a
totally new cultural expression that could serve as
a model for the art of the future: "Already, the architecture of Manhattan is a new value, something that
has nothing to do with Egyptian pyramids, with
the Paris Opera, with the Giralda of Seville, or with
Saint Sofia, any more than it has to do with the
Maya palaces of Chichen-Itzá or with the 'pueblos'
of Arizona.… The architecture of Manhattan is the
first step. Painting and sculpture must certainly
follow as inevitable second steps."[108]

The model for the central, reading figure in
Orozco's *Modern Industrial Man* was no doubt a
Dartmouth student (fig. 231). The final version
(fig. 232), however, not only is obviously a worker
but also appears to be of mixed race, a mestizo of
both European and Indian ancestry. Orozco offers
here a similar ideal to that of the dark-eyed young
man of the *Release* panel that he had painted in an
adjacent corridor eighteen months earlier (fig. 193).
The young man in *Release* rises from the confusion of postwar machinery to reach for the light.
The worker in *Modern Industrial Man* rests from his
labor of creating the future to nourish his spirit.
Alma Reed relayed Orozco's sense of the future of
his own country, the future of the rebel, who was

his model of change: "We have had enough of
revolution. We want time now to work and to rest.
The people are learning to think."[109]

Fig. 230 · **Winter**, 1932, oil on canvas,
Museo de Arte Carrillo Gil, Mexico
City/INBA 17275.

Conclusion

In *An Autobiography*, Orozco describes *The Epic
of American Civilization*: "The murals consist of
fourteen pictures of approximately ten by thirteen
feet in dimension, and ten smaller ones. In the first
of them the theme is that of 'Quetzalcoatl' but the
final paintings bear no very clear relation to this."[110]
His countryman Octavio Paz put it another way:
"[T]he work of art is always unfaithful to its creator."[111]
The Neoplatonist dualism of Orozco's conception
of painting—the marked separation and energizing
relationship between "idea" and "plastic construction"—was reflected in his preference for meanings
that are themselves generated through the opposition of such dualistic contrasts as "the barbaric
aspects of human nature" and the "power of good in

183

the universe." Moreover, despite the fact that *The Epic of American Civilization* by definition takes a chronological approach to its subject, no particular progress is implied. Both these factors contribute to the difficulties that Orozco had in creating, and viewers have in interpreting, this work.

In search of a conceptual framework that will allow us to bring the content of Orozco's *Epic* into focus, it is useful to compare his own description of his first Dartmouth panel, *Release* (fig. 193)—"man is now shown in command of his own hands and he is at last free to shape his own destiny"—with "state three" of Mexican Minister of Culture José Vasconcelos's analysis of the progress of civilization. The statement was published in 1923, the year Vasconcelos gave Orozco the Preparatory School commission, and Orozco surely knew it:

> A quick synthetic survey shows men organized at first into tribes whose collective law is strength.... From the first emerges the martial type dominated by material interests and unfit for a superior life.... A second period follows…in which internal organization and international relations are based on convenience and planning.... In this second period …intelligence affirms its superiority over the irreflectiveness of brute strength…yet this state is still not supreme. Higher than the fatalities of logic and all material and moral interest, there lingers in our consciousness the desire to act freely, at one with our sympathies. When this urge will become reality…the third state of society will have been reached, to wit the aesthetic period.[112]

An argument could be made that Orozco, consciously or unconsciously, organized his fresco cycle in the reserve reading room around a similar tripartite vision of human progress toward the ideal of an aesthetic society. The first, martial stage of civilization is represented both by the Aztecs, who are shown on the west wall marching into the Valley of Mexico and engaging in human sacrifice, and by the conquistador Cortez and the imperialistic comic opera of *Modern Human Sacrifice* on the east wall. The second, intelligent, cooperative stage appears in the west wing, with *The Coming of Quetzalcoatl*, and in the east wing, where the arrival of European civilization produces the orderly regimentation of *Anglo-America.*

Orozco and Vasconcelos shared with the European post–World War I avant-garde a utopian vision of a final stage of "aesthetic" freedom that would allow humankind to "act freely, at one with our sympathies." In Orozco's *Epic*, this vision is represented by two mythic moments that "linger in our consciousness": the legendary golden age of Quetzalcoatl, at the center of the north wall of the east wing, and the potential golden age of the future, depicted across from the reserve desk. For Orozco, as for his counterparts in Europe, such as El Lissitsky and László Moholy-Nagy, the advent of this era of creative freedom would require nothing less than a "destruction of the old order" (to quote the title of his composition at the Preparatory School). This is the role of the revolutionary Christ

Fig. 231 · Figure study for **Modern Industrial Man**, central panel, 1932–34, graphite on tracing paper, Hood Museum of Art, Dartmouth College, Hanover, New Hampshire; D.988.52.228.

184

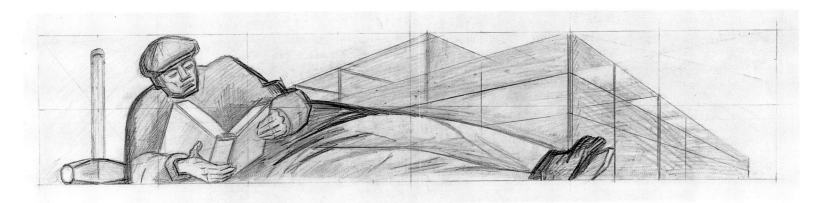

who breaks free of the bonds of history in the final panel of the east wing, a subject that in an early plan for the mural carried the title *The End of Superstition — Triumph of Freedom.*

Analogies such as these are fragmentary at best, and it is essential to stress once again that no matter how one chooses to analyze Orozco's work, his symbolism is always dynamic and multivalent. Rarely can his images be reduced to the kind of direct equations that are so available in the work of the other muralists or indeed in Alma Reed's point in support of the theme of Daedalus: that "'Daidala,' in the most ancient usage, mean[s] 'works of art.'" Orozco would have had little interest in such literary niceties. For him, art was not a language. It was "knowledge at the service of emotion." "Painting," he emphasized, "assails the mind. It persuades the heart."[113] *The Epic of American Civilization* "assails" us with a vision of history that is fiercely humanistic, individualistic, and, above all, unrelentingly critical.

From the perspective granted us by time, what is most striking about *The Epic of American Civilization* is Orozco's refusal to settle for easy solutions. He does not idealize any moment of the historical past or the historical process itself, nor does he pit the indigenous American civilizations against those of Europe. Moreover, despite the anarchist overtones of his vision of triumph, Orozco shows no trust in any specific political solution. His visual epic of the Americas is fueled by sheer indignation at the continuing degradation of the human spirit, in

patterns that are hauntingly similar in ancient and modern societies. "Only because of the hopeless," wrote Walter Benjamin, "is hope given to us." Orozco's work at Dartmouth embodies this paradox of an idealism inspired by pessimism. We may not want to see his message, or believe it, but to paint it was his Promethean role.

Fig. 232 · Study for **Modern Industrial Man**, central panel, 1932–34, graphite on paper, Hood Museum of Art, Dartmouth College, Hanover, New Hampshire; D.988.52.237.

185

Orozco at War: Context and Fragment in *Dive Bomber and Tank* (1940)

James Oles

"**A** tropical fire smolders behind the smartly tailored, urbane walls of the Museum of Modern Art, New York," runs the lead sentence of one exhibition review discussing the opening of *Twenty Centuries of Mexican Art* on May 14, 1940.[1] One could hardly conceive of a more transparent expression of the contemporary positioning of Latin American culture (as primitive, chaotic, natural) in counterpoint to that of the United States (as modern, controlled, urban). But if the writer meant merely to highlight the tonal or thematic difference of Mexican art, there were actual fires burning at the time in Europe and Asia, and José Clemente Orozco was about to bring them to the attention of the New York public. Just as he had explored the dismal consequences of urban life and the Depression during his earlier residence in the same city, Orozco now turned to subject matter that resonated directly with current anxieties. In *Dive Bomber and Tank,* a portable mural created expressly for the museum, Orozco rejected the timeless and picturesque imagery that had come to typify "Mexico" and "Mexican art" and instead selected a subject that would deny his audience any sense of escape.

In early May 1940 Orozco, commissioned by MoMA to paint a fresco for its upcoming exhibition, arrived in the United States for the fourth time. Jere Abbott, the museum's executive vice-president, had discussed the commission with Orozco the previous January, and the invitation was later confirmed by phone call from New York.[2] Orozco had completed three important mural programs in Guadalajara in the late 1930s, further confirming his prestige as an artist, and had recently begun a new mural cycle for the Gabino Ortiz Library in Jiquilpán, Michoacán, the birthplace of President Lázaro Cárdenas. He was partly persuaded to interrupt this project by the generous honorarium offered by MoMA; like most Mexican artists of his time, Orozco relied on U.S. collectors and institutions for a good percentage of his income. The MoMA commission must have

been particularly welcome, for his letters home indicate the weakness of the art market, in part because of the war.[3]

Orozco arrived in New York to find that the portable panels he had ordered were not yet ready; in fact, their construction was delayed while the staff hurriedly installed the enormous show in time for the opening.[4] He thus spent more than a month working on mural sketches and easel paintings in his hotel and complaining about the cold. In early June, when the panels were finally prepared and set up in the lobby, Orozco returned to the museum and, wearing coveralls to protect his shirt and tie, began to work in full view of the public (see photograph on p. 307). While he painted, he "made a

point of answering questions and explaining the problems of mural painting."[5] That he used no full-scale cartoon certainly contributed to the virtuosity of his "performance," which took only ten days. As in his previous three mural projects in the United States, Orozco did not work alone; his assistant in this case was the young painter Lewis Rubenstein, who later recalled that he was recommended for the job, "probably because more than any other American artist I was doing murals in true fresco."[6]

The completed version of *Dive Bomber and Tank* weighs almost one and one half tons and measures nine feet high by eighteen feet wide, divided into six separate panels, each nine feet by three feet. This horizontal format resembles nothing so much

as a monumental folding screen, placed flat against the wall. In the August 1940 issue of the MoMA *Bulletin,* which featured this project, Orozco presented six possible configurations of the panels, in groups of three, four, or six (see pp. 310–311).[7] This ability to deconstruct and reconstruct a large-scale painting seems unique for the time, but the original reason may have been mainly practical. In a letter of May 25, 1940, Orozco noted that the museum hoped "to send [the mural] I'm going to paint later to other museums. They'll ruin it, since fresco is a delicate thing and shouldn't be moved.... [There will be] six separate parts so it can be moved, packed and shipped."[8] Efficiency alone may not explain Orozco's proposed permutations, discussed later in

Fig. 233. **Dive Bomber and Tank**, 1940, fresco, 9 x 18 feet (275 x 550 cm), on six panels 9 x 3 feet (275 x 91.4 cm), Museum of Modern Art, New York, commissioned through the Abby Aldrich Rockefeller Fund, digital file © 2001 Museum of Modern Art, New York.

this essay, but the mural is most logically understood, and has always been exhibited, in what might be called its standard presentation (fig. 233).

Orozco had selected his subject—"*un aeroplano de bombardeo*"—as he traveled north by train to New York, and the MoMA's director, Alfred Barr, enthusiastically approved it after the artist's arrival.[9] While painting, Orozco changed his mind several times about the imagery and left the title to the museum's staff, according to an article in the *New Yorker*:

> Orozco…keeps making so many changes that the Museum people are not quite sure what to call it. His first sketch showed a more or less jumbled airplane embellished with a projectile, a couple of human legs, and a round object which might have been either an aviator's head or a bomb. The Museum's director, Mr. Alfred Barr, took a look at it and advised his publicity department to call it "The Dive Bomber." In subsequent drafts, Orozco inserted a rather large tank, and Mr. Barr directed that the title be expanded to "Dive Bomber and Tank." When we saw the half-finished fresco last week, Orozco had reduced the tank to a brief expanse of caterpillar tread and had added several enormous mask-like faces…. Mr. Barr was still standing pat on the second title.[10]

Indeed, Orozco generally ceded the selection of titles for his murals to art historians, since he believed textual descriptions overly limited the interpretation of his images. Yet despite its straightforward name, *Dive Bomber and Tank* is hardly illustrative of any particular event or instruments of war. The mural shows a fragmented heap of loosely abstracted machine and human forms, painted for the most part in a reduced palette of grays, blues, and rusty browns and arranged in a roughly symmetrical and triangular composition. Tank treads, chains, a bomblike projectile, and other, more obscure pieces of

metal twist and turn along a horizontal axis, while the tail section of the fallen airplane looms in the center, highlighted by an intense red triangle. Three human legs, three monumental heads, and curious snakelike forms also appear in the midst of the wreckage. Although Orozco never fully explained these details, he did concede that his general theme was "the subjugation of man by the machines of modern warfare."[11]

Despite its importance, *Dive Bomber and Tank* long remained in storage, in part because of its unwieldy size, in part because Orozco's *Zapatistas* (1931 [fig. 37]) served as a more explicitly "Mexican" example of the artist's oeuvre within MoMA's permanent installation, and perhaps in part because its particularly aggressive condemnation of the machine remained a "smoldering" presence within the "urbane walls" of the institution. Although included in two important temporary exhibitions in the early 1990s and placed on permanent view in 1998, the mural has only recently received scholarly attention. Its complexity, however, merits even closer analysis.[12]

This essay first explores the circumstances surrounding the creation and presentation of the mural at the Museum of Modern Art, where Orozco found it necessary to negotiate territory that had been "claimed" by Diego Rivera at the beginning of the 1930s. Critical as he was of mass entertainment, Orozco was deeply cynical about his role as a performer, painting before a live audience. His specific subject matter also resonates with the increasing march of war through Europe in the spring of 1940 and with diplomatic and economic undercurrents that shaped U.S.-Mexican relations at the time. The artist was particularly conscious of the institutional and political context that framed *Twenty Centuries of Mexican Art*. The mural, however, was not determined simply by the forces behind its commission and creation, for in both form and subject, it is deeply related to Orozco's previous work as an artist, particularly to his extended critique of the machine and modern war. In *Dive Bomber and Tank,* Orozco revisited the image of the junk heap that he first developed in the early 1920s as a symbol of the destructive forces of modernity. He purposely used a style marked by the fragmentation of forms and space, partly derived from cubism, as a rhetorical device that rejected both the fully abstract and the overtly didactic. In this final mural painted for a U.S. patron, Orozco was able to avoid the caricature and propaganda that inflected most contemporary images of World War II and instead created a machine age allegory that remains one of the most compelling and complex images of war done in the twentieth century.

Painting and Performance

In 1940 Orozco situated himself at the Museum of Modern Art as both muralist and antagonist. He agreed to "perform" as a leading Mexican artist, painting live for the public, but he also chose to reject the stereotyped Mexican imagery that had been featured in U.S. exhibitions and publications since the 1920s. To understand this dual position further it might first be helpful to examine Diego Rivera's earlier performance for the same institution.

Dive Bomber and Tank was not the first portable mural commissioned by the museum, as Orozco and his patrons well knew. In July 1930, through the intercession of Frances Flynn Paine, an art promoter supported by the Rockefeller family, Rivera was offered a one-man exhibition at MoMA, the second retrospective at that relatively new institution (the work of Matisse had been featured earlier in 1931). The show ran from December 23, 1931, to January 27, 1932, and was a critical and public success, testifying to the young institution's ability to pull in a mass audience.[13] That Rivera received such early attention was not surprising:

Alfred Barr had befriended Rivera in Moscow in 1927, and Abby Aldrich Rockefeller—in part because of her family's extensive financial interests in Latin America—had systematically begun to promote Mexican art both as a private collector and as a leading patron in the public sphere.[14] More important, Rivera was perhaps the most famous artist of the time from anywhere in the Americas. His command of a broad range of styles was compelling, and his nationalist vision agreed with many critics in the United States at the start of the Depression.[15]

Since Mexican art in general was most widely recognized for the murals of the 1920s, it was only natural that Rivera's frescoes be featured, and given the impossibility of bringing those murals to New York, new ones would have to be commissioned. Rivera painted eight works on site. He recycled imagery from his already famous programs in the Ministry of Public Education in Mexico City and the Palace of Cortez in Cuernavaca for the first four portable panels, at least three of which were ready by the time of the opening. A fifth panel, *The Uprising (Soldiers and Workers),* refers to Mexico but is not based on a previous mural. The three remaining panels—*Pneumatic Drilling, Electric Welding,* and *Frozen Assets*—took industrial labor and the Depression as their themes and were presented to the public at a second "opening" held in January.[16]

Of this later "triptych," *Frozen Assets* (fig. 234), an unambiguous critique of capitalism, raised the most controversy in the press, but all the panels were widely reviewed and illustrated, further boosting public attendance. These appear to have been the first portable panels in the history of Mexican muralism, but by the time Orozco arrived in New

Fig. 234 · Diego Rivera, **Frozen Assets**, 1931, fresco, Museo Dolores Olmedo Patiño, Mexico City.

189

York in 1940, Rivera had successfully employed the same technical strategies for several additional cycles, establishing even stronger precedents for *Dive Bomber and Tank*.[17] Orozco, who had long been in a sort of self-inflicted competition with Rivera, may have seen his 1940 mural as a response to the latter's panels of 1931–32.[18] His presentation of an international rather than nationalist subject recalls Rivera's three "industrial" panels, and he may have hoped to achieve similar critical attention by selecting a theme as topical and controversial as that of *Frozen Assets*. But Orozco went farther: His more politically ambiguous subject matter and his proposed rearrangement of the panels in different compositions situated his work as a more experimental alternative to the stereotyped image of Mexican muralism as didactic illustration. The greater overall scale of Orozco's mural may also provide evidence of his intent to place it more within the sphere of public art than Rivera's "frescoed easel paintings" (although ultimately it remained as much a "private" work of art as any of the others at MoMA).

Painting portable frescoes in a museum may have been innovative, but Orozco's *Dive Bomber and Tank* and Rivera's earlier panels upheld the tradition of large-scale salon paintings, in which size reflected thematic importance (such as David's *Coronation of Napoleon*) and in which monumentality meant attention in the crowded rooms of the salon (Courbet's *A Burial at Ornans*). More directly, perhaps, these portable murals recall the "one-picture, paid-admission, special exhibition" of Frederick Church's *Heart of the Andes* and *Niagara* in mid-nineteenth-century New York. As "serious art and popular entertainment," Church's paintings too had packed in the crowds.[19] At MoMA the heavy drapes and tropical plants that had accompanied *Heart of the Andes* were replaced by metal buckets, drop-cloths, and glasses filled with paint and by the artists themselves. Although Orozco ultimately took a more critical stance vis-à-vis his role as an artist

commissioned by the Museum of Modern Art, he and Rivera both were forced to work in a context in which art had become a theatrical spectacle (what later was called the blockbuster exhibition) with the artist as the featured celebrity.

Indeed, in 1931 and 1940 the Mexican artists were as much on display as their works. In both cases, the museum's publications commemorated this by including photographs of the artists in action, precursors of Hans Namuth's portrayals of Jackson Pollock. Of course, bringing muralists to the museum met several purely functional goals. Despite the expense of housing the artists, by having smaller murals done in New York, the curators solved the problem of shipping heavy and fragile works up from Mexico. Portable murals were also, as Rivera himself noted, appropriate in "a land where the buildings do not stand long."[20] Their creation also served as a professional workshop, allowing would-be muralists the chance to learn by example. In 1931 several U.S. artists were just beginning to consider a local mural renaissance; in 1940, although beleaguered, the Works Projects Administration and the Treasury Department's Section of Fine Arts continued to commission murals across the country, and many artists believed— wrongly, as it turned out—that these programs would survive the decade.

The performances of Rivera and Orozco, however, must also be seen as publicity stunts, carefully engineered to drum up public interest in ongoing exhibitions. If the monumentality of the originals was immobile, at least the technique and "feel" of fresco painting, which never translate well in reproduction, could be made visible to the audience. More important, bringing famous artists to the museum was a demonstration of the same authority and power that had generated those popular yet tragic anthropological displays of living human specimens at nineteenth-century world's fairs.[21] Nothing indicates that Rivera, the consummate entertainer, objected in any way to this popularizing of his work as a muralist, whether in New York or in Mexico.[22] The tremendous success of his MoMA retrospective in fact helped cement his preeminence among Mexican artists and virtually guaranteed subsequent commissions. But as the following anecdote reveals, Orozco himself was more skeptical of his participation in an exhibition that relied upon the spectacle of the other.

In her memoirs, the Mexico City art dealer Inés Amor recalled Orozco's contentious opinion of his live presentation at MoMA. At the time of the opening of *Twenty Centuries,* Amor was present at a dinner at Hillcrest, the Rockefeller estate in North Terrytown, New York, and was seated at the table of honor along with Abby Aldrich Rockefeller, Orozco, and Paine.[23] Paine turned to Orozco and asked:

Tell me, what are you doing in New York, *maestro?*
I'm working as a clown, Orozco answered.
As a clown?
Yes ma'am, in a circus.

I began to send him signals by kicking his legs under the table, trying to make him see that Rockefeller had paid for his trip. He couldn't have cared less and continued to explain to Mrs. Paine that the Museum of Modern Art was a huge circus and he the attraction, painting *Dive Bomber.*[24]

Amor might also have reminded Orozco that *Dive Bomber and Tank* had been commissioned through a fund in Abby Aldrich Rockefeller's name and that Mrs. Rockefeller had been a major sponsor of his mural cycle for Dartmouth College as well.

Orozco's impolitic dinner conversation bears closer analysis. On one level, he was making trouble in his own way, as Rivera had done by inserting a portrait of Lenin in his RCA mural of 1933. His comment pretends to assert a certain independence

from his patron and to distance himself from the mass appeal of *Twenty Centuries of Mexican Art.* He may even have been aware of Barr's own opinion of the institution: "This is not a traditional museum. This is a continual opening night; this is a three-ring circus."[25] But Orozco's critical view of exhibitions of Mexican art as spectacles, which he believed were biased toward rural stereotypes and the work of Rivera in particular, was hardly new. In 1928 Orozco had voiced his displeasure at a Rockefeller-funded exhibit of Mexican art curated by Paine for the Art Center in New York. As he wrote to his close friend Jean Charlot, "I can tell you that the only purpose of the show is to sell trinkets of 'Mexican folk art' (?), a commercial enterprise, for which our pictures have merely served as advertising posters."[26] Also, in a letter to his wife, Orozco referred to both Rivera's 1931 retrospective and the MoMA show as *mitotes,* a word that in Mexico originally referred to Aztec performances but that had come to mean any sort of exaggerated event or celebration, always with a sense of the theatrical.

But a circus is also a form of mass entertainment that combines death-defying feats, comedic performances, and often the presentation of the other as freak or curiosity. Here we should recall that Orozco was a muralist with only one hand. Orozco had already been drawn to similar arenas of popular entertainment, as his bordello-themed *House of Tears* watercolors of the early 1910s and his images of New York vaudeville shows of the late 1920s attest, not to show respect for mass culture but, on the contrary, to expose the shallowness of contemporary urban life and, by extension, the weakness of contemporary political structures and leaders. Orozco's "heroes" are not those who enjoy popular appeal but those whose prophecies are rejected or misunderstood. In his U.S. murals alone, we find a Prometheus shunned by his beneficiaries, a philosopher king (Quetzalcoatl) cast out by skeptics, and a Christ who destroys the burdens of

191

martyrdom placed upon him by institutional Catholicism.

For Orozco, the very success of the Museum of Modern Art in bringing in large numbers of spectators testified to its failure as an arena of critical intellectual potential. He might justify his personal compromise as a participant through a sarcastic self-definition that placed him in the role of entertainer, but he would create a mural that, in its frank and angered condemnation of mechanized warfare, would show that he was hardly clowning around.

War-Oil-Art

Twenty Centuries of Mexican Art was not only the public arena for Orozco's individual performance but also a spectacular event that was largely determined by more serious and dangerous spectacles then occurring in Europe and Asia. While, in general terms, one can see *Dive Bomber and Tank* as a response to Rivera's previous experience at MoMA and to Orozco's promotion as a public performer, it is also a work whose iconography explicitly counters the vision of Mexican art that audiences had come to expect. Instead Orozco's mural comments directly on the broader political and economic subtexts that had brought Mexican art to MoMA in the first place.

From the late 1920s through the 1930s, critics, dealers, collectors, and even tourists had ensured that the cultural renaissance that followed the Mexican Revolution was widely disseminated in the United States. Gradually a certain canon of artists and images was formed in the minds of the U.S. public, at least of those who paid attention to the culture of their neighbor to the south.[27] This canon, with subtle and arguably inconsequential modifications, was to endure for much of the twentieth century. Simply put, it consisted primarily of works by the leading muralists—Rivera, Orozco, and David Alfaro Siqueiros—and others whose iconography

was clearly and undoubtedly "local," like José Guadalupe Posada, Rufino Tamayo, Miguel Covarrubias, and, a bit later, Frida Kahlo. Most important of all, Mexican art had to look "Mexican." Although scenes of the revolution were widely seen and admired, colorful images drawn from traditional rural folkways dominated exhibitions and publications. The modern art was also frequently discussed and displayed together with both pre-Columbian and folk images that served to emphasize timeless continuities and racial difference. This discourse, visual and written, differentiated Mexican art from that of Europe or the United States and appealed to U.S. critics hoping to locate a more ancient, authentic, and communal culture on this continent.[28]

Mexican art was therefore hardly new to audiences in the United States when, in the summer of 1940, the Museum of Modern Art had three boxcars of ancient, colonial, modern, and folk art sent up from Mexico, enough to fill the entire building and transform the garden court into a Mexican marketplace.[29] Such a spectacle might have been more appropriate to the ongoing New York World's Fair (where a smaller display of modern Mexican painting was on view in the Mexican Pavilion), and it is likely that the organizers of *Twenty Centuries* understood the benefits of drawing on overlapping audiences. Indeed, because an exhibit on this scale had rarely been seen in any museum context, this was surely among the earliest of the megaprojects that were increasingly to shape curatorial practice in later decades. The financial and intellectual contribution of the Mexican government and leading Mexican scholars, as well as the publicity and attendance, was unprecedented; the show was less an example of colonialist appropriation than of Good Neighborly collaboration, although economic motivations ran equally deep.

By 1939, when MoMA decided to present a survey of Mexican art from its pre-Columbian beginnings to the present, the institution's permanent

Fig. 235 · David Alfaro Siqueiros, **Echo of a Scream**, 1937, enamel on wood, 48 x 36 in (121.9 x 91.4 cm), Museum of Modern Art, New York, gift of Edward M.M. Warburg, photograph © 2000 Museum of Modern Art, New York.

collection already included more works from Mexico than from any other Latin American country. Of course this was partly due to the undeniable importance of artistic events south of the border and to Mexico's close geographic and cultural ties to the United States, but it was also determined by the specific cultural and economic agendas of the Rockefellers, major patrons of the museum and, through Standard Oil, key players in an ongoing struggle over the ownership of Mexican oil reserves that had been building since the revolution. In this context, the decision to highlight Mexico in a major exhibition, one that might also serve to strengthen ties with a nation that would be an important ally should the war involve the United States, is hardly surprising.[30] But it was not just diplomacy that led MoMA to reorient its interests toward Latin America in the early 1940s. The outbreak of war had meant the cancellation of several projects that required European participation.

Not surprisingly, numerous writers framed *Twenty Centuries* in terms of events in Europe, even if the curatorial selection emphasized objects

temporally and culturally removed from that war. The museum's foreword to the exhibition catalog barely alluded to the conflict when it noted that Mexican art "preserves that gayety, serenity, and sense of human dignity which the world needs."[31] But if the museum and the Mexican government saw art as providing a convenient and practical escape from current events, almost every reviewer connected the tragedies of Mexican history to those already perpetrated by the Nazis. According to one critic, "The story of the Spanish conquest of Mexico is one of the most familiar chapters of world history, familiar because of its bloody thoroughness so akin to the fate of Poland and Holland today."[32]

Jean Charlot was even more insightful. As if writing in direct response to the catalog's foreword, he wondered aloud whether the exhibition should not have been more didactic: "Considering the world today, so cruelly different from the optimistic world of yesteryear, the art of Mexico at its most severe scores a prophetic point; it would have been a more responsible performance if the present show had courage enough to underscore it."[33] Along with just one other painting then on display—Siqueiros's *Echo of a Scream* (1937; fig. 235)—Orozco's *Dive Bomber and Tank* provided direct evidence of that "cruelly different" world of 1940. Indeed, these two works foreground the relevance of international events, even universal concerns, in sharp contrast with the localized "exotic" content of almost every other object included in *Twenty Centuries,* from the pre-Columbian and baroque sculptures to the paintings by Abraham Angel and Kahlo, not to mention the abundance of folk art.[34]

Of course Orozco had a distinct advantage: His mural was newly commissioned rather than selected, and it was completed at a crucial historical moment. Alfred Barr later recalled that the mural "was painted two months after Dunkirk. His mind, like ours, was full of the shock of the mechanical warfare that had just crushed western Europe."[35]

193

Orozco was relatively oblique in discussing the specific connection between his mural and the invasion of France, and scant evidence of his ideas permeates contemporary reviews, most based on an official press preview held on June 18, before the artist had actually begun painting. Emily Genauer, in the *New York World-Telegram,* reported that Orozco "said his purpose…was not to glorify war but to depict, because it's a thrilling phenomenon, the dynamic power which a bombing plane epitomizes."[36] (One wonders whether he slipped in this futurist blurb just to confuse his listeners at a particularly tragic moment.) The *New Yorker* simply noted that the artist was "in general trying to convey the idea of mechanized destruction typical of our times."[37] Orozco, however, was so vague that the reporter from the *New York Times,* "after saying 'My paper has to present something concrete to its public,' left in despair and wrote nothing."[38] Perhaps revealing a nervousness that the reporters would misinterpret Orozco's message, MoMA publicist Sarah Newmeyer reminded them that "Orozco is no propagandist. He is in no sense glorifying war, and in no sense knocking war."[39]

Newmeyer's comment seems disingenuous, given Orozco's clear condemnation of mechanized warfare and its ability to wreak total destruction — whoever the protagonist, whoever the victim. But perhaps this official MoMA disclaimer reflects the tense atmosphere of the late spring of 1940. The Nazi-Soviet Pact of August 1939 demobilized Communist opposition to Hitler until the German invasion of the Soviet Union in 1941. In both the United States and Mexico, this strategic move had allowed the curious convergence of isolationists and antifascists, both of whom may have opposed war in general but who now were unwilling or unable to take sides. Although the fall of Paris on June 14 was a signal that the "neutrality" of the United States (and Mexico) could not last much longer, the lines were still not fully clear. Indeed, the Mexican

government of Lázaro Cárdenas (and, after December 1, 1940, of his successor, Manuel Ávila Camacho) tread carefully, at once avoiding a confrontation with the local pro-Axis opposition of the right and negotiating "hemispheric unity" with the United States. In fact, despite diplomatic opposition to fascism, Mexico was to remain neutral until May 1942, five months after Pearl Harbor, when the Nazis sank two Mexican tankers and it quickly joined the Allies.[40] Orozco's mural for MoMA was thus painted in a politically murky moment, while debates between interventionists and isolationists still raged in both countries, and this may explain his refusal to "glorify" or "knock" either the Allies or the Axis explicitly. Yet the fact remains that the subject of Orozco's mural necessitates an antifascist reading. By June 1940 the Allies had had few opportunities to use their own dive bombers; it was the frightening shriek and deadly accuracy of the German Stukas that had created such havoc, first in Spain and now in France.

Although Orozco's subject relates to the terrifying bombing raids that had devastated civilian populations in the late 1930s, it is revealing that it was the recent German blitzkrieg that informed contemporary discussions of the artist's violent and loosely expressionist style, so unlike Rivera's careful, minute brushstrokes. Orozco's method had long been described in such bellicose terms as "smash" and "attack," but this time the allusions went even deeper. Just as the critics of *Twenty Centuries of Mexican Art* had viewed Mexican history through the lens of the European conflict, so was Orozco's rapid performance related to the invasion of France. MoMA's publicity department informed reporters: "He's blitzing right along on this thing."[41] The newspaper *PM* used a more unfortunate pun in the title of its review: "Orozco Blitzpaints Modern Museum Mural."[42] Even Orozco's support, a divisible assembly of parts liberated from architecture, underwent violence against its integrity, just like the political boundaries then being broken apart and reconfigured by new powers. In substance, then, as well as in subject, the MoMA mural reacted to the war in Europe.

Orozco's mural can also be linked to a second major issue, one that then dominated U.S.-Mexican relations and that concerned the principal patrons of MoMA in particular: Mexican petroleum. Indeed, *Time* magazine had already underscored the connection between art and oil as early as 1937: "Like Mexican oil, Mexican art is a commodity in which U.S. citizens take considerable interest. Those who want to get oil out of Mexico are having a tougher & tougher time. Those who want to see or buy Mexican art are having it easier & easier."[43]

The Mexican government, after years of negotiations with the foreign-owned oil companies, had finally nationalized the industry in March 1938. Following expropriation, and largely because of an ensuing boycott of Mexican oil by the United States, the Cárdenas administration, though hardly sympathetic to the fascists, found itself forced for economic reasons to trade oil to Japan, Germany, and Italy in return for much-needed raw materials and machine parts.[44] Although at first under pressure from domestic oil companies to maintain a hard line with Mexico, the Roosevelt administration finally pushed through a compromise (ostensibly more beneficial to Mexico than to the United States). The boycott was lifted in May 1940, just as Orozco began work, and a more detailed agreement was signed in November 1941. Hemispheric unity and regional market concerns had triumphed over the relatively more narrow interests of Standard Oil and others.[45]

In 1939, before this crisis was resolved, Nelson Rockefeller had arranged for a private conference with Cárdenas in Jiquilpan, to discuss the issues.[46] Although Rockefeller argued that he was simply there as a "layman" attempting to smooth out differences, it was hard to deny that his personal and family interests in Standard Oil were shaping the negotiations, specifically his proposal to grant Mexico minority ownership in what would remain foreign-owned companies. Not surprisingly, Cárdenas rejected that plan, but during the same meeting in Jiquilpan, Rockefeller, in his position as president of MoMA, had diverted attention (and attempted to facilitate the business dealings) by discussing the possibility of hosting an exhibition of Mexican art in New York.[47] If it was indeed hard to get oil out of Mexico, it was certainly easier to get the art. Cárdenas pledged to support the show, which he certainly saw as a public relations coup, given that articles criticizing Mexico on numerous fronts were then common in the U.S. press.

For both Rockefeller and Cárdenas, putting Mexican art in MoMA would serve as a diplomatic screen for ongoing political and economic traumas involving oil. Thus the general absence of antifascist or antiwar imagery in *Twenty Centuries of Mexican Art* not only reinforced a vision of Mexico as timeless and alluring but avoided the very controversies that had shaken relations between the two countries. At least on a conceptual level, oil and art would not mix. Just a year or so earlier, in fact, the "revolutionary" Cárdenas administration had ordered the destruction of Juan O'Gorman's *Religious Myths* and *Pagan Myths* (1937–38), part of a surrealist mural cycle for the Mexican airport at Balbuena. *Pagan Myths* was censored after the German ambassador complained about the artist's caricatures of Hitler and Mussolini at a time when Mexico relied on oil exports to the Axis.[48]

Orozco's 1940 mural was neither quaint nor timeless; it brutally violated viewer expectations about the "Mexican" content of Mexican art. Rejecting the use of Mexican art as a stage curtain to conceal backstage political and economic dramas, *Dive Bomber and Tank* comments directly on the European events that shaped *Twenty Centuries of Mexican Art*. In addition, it foregrounds two

195

instruments of technology that required that petroleum dear to the Rockefellers, coveted by the fascists, and needed by the (future) Allies, whether or not the artist ever intended the connection. The mural refers less to the human side of conflict than to the tragic consequences inherent in machines that, operated by friend or foe, depended on Mexican oil. In the context of an exhibition shaped institutionally and critically by the European war (despite efforts to present a diversion from those events), Orozco's decision to choose "the subjugation of man by the machines of modern warfare" as the overt theme for his MoMA commission made even more sense.

Orozco's Blitz

Mexico's leading cultural critic Carlos Monsivais once noted that "to the immense majority of Mexicans, including the significant minority with sympathy for the Germans, World War II seemed a spectacle, something immensely entertaining and distant, which gave the country, without warning, economic and social opportunities."[49] Those opportunities included a boom in the export of raw materials, increased industrialization, and the institution of the bracero program for migrant workers. But for the leading muralists, fully cognizant of the threat of fascism, the war represented more than just a time of increased trade and exchange across the border. Rivera, Siqueiros, and Orozco, in their own ways, all had exposed the international dangers of fascism long before the various Nazi invasions of the late 1930s. Rivera's *Hitler* and *Mussolini* panels, part of his *Portrait of America* cycle at New York's New Workers School (1933), were among the earliest important visual assaults on the leaders of European fascism done anywhere in the Americas. Siqueiros modified his *Portrait of the Bourgeoisie* (Mexican Electricians' Union, Mexico City [1939–40]) in the wake of the Nazi-Soviet Pact. The final version rejects explicit portraiture. Instead evil is

embodied by the parrot-headed demagogue dependent upon a standardized military and a brutal capitalist machine, threatened by a single proletarian soldier of monumental proportions.

Orozco avoided such clear-cut propaganda. He is on record as declaring that *Dive Bomber and Tank* had "no political significance," although it is impossible to take him at his word given that the mural's imagery is explicitly related to the war.[50] He actually made no specific mention of the tragic events of 1939–40 in either his 1942 *An Autobiography* or in "Orozco 'Explains,'" the cryptic essay included in the issue of the MoMA *Bulletin* devoted to *Dive Bomber and Tank*. The war that most affected him had taken place over twenty years before, although he recalled with absolute irony that "the Revolution was for me the most happy and fun of carnivals, or rather, as they say carnivals are, for I've never seen one."[51] By the mid-1930s, however, Orozco had indeed begun to explore the freaks and clowns of a more recent sideshow—namely, the rise of totalitarianism in Europe. These works further help inform the innovative strategies of *Dive Bomber and Tank*.

One might begin by noting that the themes of struggle and opposition, symbolized in *Dive Bomber*

Fig. 236 · **The Carnival of Ideologies**, 1936–37, fresco, Government Palace, Guadalajara, photograph by Bob Schalkwijk.

and Tank by the compression of tank and airplane, are basic to Orozco's work in general. According to Luis Cardoza y Aragón, "The desolate bitterness of Orozco, absent of hope, born from the *collision* between longing and reality, is but one of the most pronounced aspects of his psychology."[52] Octavio Paz interpreted the collapse of bomber and tank less as a historical "scene" than as an iconic device drawn from deeper currents: "Orozco's icon is not a god or an idea but a reality at once present here and now and eternal, universal, and concrete, a reality in perpetual struggle against itself. The icon is doubly threatened, by abstraction and by expression, by universality and by singularity."[53] Indeed, although in a poetic tone that says everything and nothing at the same time, this passage by Paz particularly recalls the fundamental oppositions that are present in *Dive Bomber and Tank* in form and image. In this way the mural resonates with El Lissitsky's famous constructivist poster *Beat the Whites with the Red Wedge* (1919)—perhaps *the* iconic representation of attack in the history of formal abstraction, revolutionary in both literal and figurative ways— although it lacks the poster's unambiguous and didactic intent.

Yet as the art historian Antonio Rodríguez later noted, "although organized differently, the forms of this mural appear with frequency in the previous work of Orozco."[54] The emphasis on the broken parts of the two machines relates specifically to the junk heaps of his mural cycles of the 1930s, in which piles of turbines and gears, pipes and chains, almost always painted a steely gray, symbolize catastrophes from the conquest to the machine age.[55] At Dartmouth, for example, Cortez is juxtaposed with such wreckage to signal the catastrophic, if unavoidable, impact of European warfare on the Americas; in *Catharsis* (Palace of Fine Arts, 1934 [fig. 252]), machine parts are part of a chaotic landscape of economic and social decadence, purified by fire. Other, less direct parallels also emerge: The "projectile"

that appears to the left of the MoMA mural recalls the knives that pierce bodies and magueys in several works of the 1930s, and even the use of destroyed vehicles as a metonym for war had appeared in *Dynamited Train* (1926–28 [fig. 42]), where Orozco painted the wreckage of a prebomber, pretank revolution.

More specifically, Orozco had referred to the events in Europe at least twice before, in his Guadalajara murals. In his cycle in the Government Palace (1936–37), the west wall, most frequently referred to as *The Carnival of Ideologies,* depicts a dense crowd of costumed figures, buffoons with facial features that allude to Mussolini, Roosevelt, Zapata, and Stalin (fig. 236). "Sickles, crosses, swastikas, Phrygian caps, fasces are all mixed together in the great show of symbols, slogans and ideologies. It would seem that they are all one to the painter, that the whole war of ideas is nothing but a farce."[56] In its reliance on caricature, this panel relates closely to Orozco's political cartoons of the 1910s and 1920s, as well as to the second-floor cycle at the National Preparatory School. His "triptych" of panels on the theme of militarism, from the west side of the south nave in the Hospicio Cabañas (1938–39), is much more abstract, almost precisionist. *The Dictators, Despotism,* and *The Militarized Mass* each include realistic strands of barbed wire in the lower section that protect lines of marching geometric figures, recalling the parade fields of Nuremberg. Unlike those in *The Carnival of Ideologies,* the principal figures in *The Dictators* are not identified by symbols or personal traits yet are equally carnivalesque; they have become anonymous, pseudoprimitive monsters, directing the mass formations of an undifferentiated, almost inhuman horde (fig. 237).[57]

In *Dive Bomber and Tank,* however, Orozco further "abstracted" his interpretation of events in

Fig. 237 · **The Dictators**, 1937–39, fresco, Hospicio Cabañas, Guadalajara, photograph by Bob Schalkwijk.

197

Europe and Asia, not only in formal terms but in relation to specific political ideologies. In this cataclysmic traffic accident, devoid of caricature or overt symbolism, war has been distilled to the basic concepts of death and destruction. This might be expected, since by 1940 the speeches and rallies of the late 1930s had given rise to horrifying and particular tragedies. It is clear that in the context of May 1940, Orozco must have known *Dive Bomber and Tank* would be understood as a critique of the blitzkrieg, yet the mural includes no explicit formal clues to direct this reading. Just whose dive bombers or tanks are these? One can read them as representing opposing forces (air versus land, Axis versus Allied), but their lack of explicit national or squadron markers and their equally ruined status seems to imply that all sides are equally guilty when machinery is used for destructive ends. Any desire for closure or clarity is frustrated, however, because the mural rejects the simplicity of propaganda and the didactic thrust of so much war art. Not only is the viewer denied the capacity to distinguish between "good" and "evil," but the composition overall stresses the inability to act: Faces are concealed, mouths and eyes pierced, machine parts bent and inoperative. This may be an antifascist mural, but it is not useful as propaganda.

The fact that Orozco's machines no longer work distinguishes his MoMA mural from other machine age metaphors of the period, from the wholly benevolent depictions of TVA dams that crop up in New Deal murals to the functional machines frequently depicted by Rivera. In *Man at the Crossroads* (1933 [fig. 251]), Rivera's fresco for the RCA Building in New York, television was presented in ambivalent terms, as a recent invention that could promote capitalism or Marxism, depending on who controlled the transmission. Rivera, however, used key illustrative clues, like the screens showing warfare and a May Day rally in the upper corners of the original RCA project, to indicate which path the

spectator and the corporation were to take.[58] Similarly, Rivera's depiction of the Ford automobile plant at River Rouge (*Detroit Industry* [1932–33], Detroit Institute of Arts [fig. 215]) shows the factory itself as neither good nor evil; it is those who run it that determine its impact upon the working class. Orozco himself echoed this dual usage of technology when he mentioned the printing press in his 1940 essay: "A few lines from a linotype in action may start a World War or may mean the birth of a new era." Unlike these other machines, however, Orozco's dive bomber and tank are shown as wholly inoperative because they are fundamentally different. They have no constructive capacity; there is no "good" service to which they can be directed. Moreover, as nonfunctional machines, they are of less use to propagandists.

In *Dive Bomber and Tank,* Orozco refused to articulate a political position strictly tied to Manichaean binaries (left versus right, democracy versus fascism). At a time when the terms "antiwar" and "antifascism" were frequently linked, Orozco eliminates the latter, divorcing the concept of war from any partisan specificity. This may be a result of the Nazi-Soviet Pact, which forced hard-liners to drop the antifascist line, but given Orozco's ideological independence, I think it is more likely that such ambiguity was meant to disarm the mural, figuratively and literally, of any propagandistic function beyond an admittedly important but generalized condemnation of war. The work features neither victims nor victors. Even at the end of World War II Orozco portrayed such trumpeted values as *Victory* (fig. 45) and *Liberty* (about 1945; Jacques and Natasha Gelman Collection [fig. 238]) as bloated prostitutes, ignorant of winners and losers.

Hardly ambivalent in its condemnation of war in general, *Dive Bomber and Tank* remains an ambiguous painting

Fig. 238 · **Liberty,** 1945, ink and charcoal on paper, Jacques and Natasha Gelman Collection of Twentieth-Century Mexican Art, The Vergel Foundation, New York.

vis-à-vis the alliances that had already been formed or that would soon be cemented, and in this way it more closely recalls the artist's earlier fresco panel *The Trench* (1926, National Preparatory School) than his Guadalajara panels of the 1930s (fig. 239). In both works, strong diagonals send the viewer in every direction, up and down, left and right, as if a formal reference to political confusion itself. In *The Trench*, possible interpretations are equally elusive: Just who are these "revolutionaries"? Do they represent rivals or partners in combat? Are they alive or dead? It is the overall tragedy of the revolution itself, rather than any declaration of allegiance, that is placed in the foreground. Orozco had reworked the subject of this 1926 panel in a large easel painting, entitled *Barricade* (1931), which entered the MoMA collection in 1937, and he may have seen *Dive Bomber and Tank* as a counterpoint to this earlier work. If exhibited side by side in the museum, they would form a diptych revealing his trajectory as a painter, a career thus far framed by two cataclysms, by two events with neither winners nor losers, by two tragic carnivals.

In keeping with his denial of any propagandistic function, there are also no heroes in Orozco's MoMA mural. Perhaps in reference to the original Fall, a snakelike form enters and exits through the "fallen" wreckage, providing the only indication of continued life.[59] But man himself is practically absent, except for his lethal creations. The caricaturesque leaders and mass formations of marching soldiers that dominate the Guadalajara panels are here reduced to an anonymous human figure or two (civilians? pilots?), inverted and half buried in the ruins of the machines. In fact, it is Orozco's avoidance of living human forms, and of historical specificity, that most distinguishes *Dive Bomber and Tank* from the two other major paintings about the bombing of civilians then hanging in MoMA. Both Pablo Picasso's *Guernica* (1937) and Siqueiros's *Echo of a Scream* foreground pained and howling

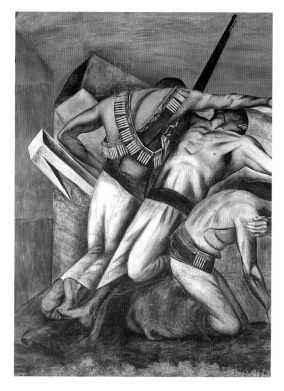

Fig. 239 · **The Trench**, 1926, fresco, National Preparatory School, Mexico City, photograph by Bob Schalkwijk.

faces to force the viewer to sympathize with the victims of fascism. Siqueiros, using propaganda photographs of a child abandoned in a bombed train station in Shanghai, relied on the concept of montage to expand the scream to catastrophic proportions; the painting is a "call to action" informed by an actual event. Although Orozco's mural resembles *Echo of a Scream* in its similar emphasis on the twisted wreckage of a world in which apocalyptic bombardments had become common, it completely rejects the strident humanism fundamental to Siqueiros and Picasso.

The ambiguity of the MoMA mural, as well as Orozco's continuing "response" to the work of his archrival Rivera, is also clear if we examine more closely the three large human faces, crushed by the machine parts and surrounded by heavy chains and spikes that penetrate mouths, noses, and eyes. To some extent these chains simply seem to stand for hair, just as they form the tail of the *Mechanical Horse* in the Hospicio Cabañas (fig. 256). Renato González Mello has also pointed out that as obstructions that seal eyes and mouths shut, they may

199

relate to the artist's own "explanation" of the mural, in which he objects: "The public refuses TO SEE painting. They want TO HEAR painting."[60] But they also refer to torture, to loss of control, to voices silenced and ears deaf to current events (hear no evil, speak no evil, see no evil?). Critics have variously described the faces as "human heads" or as reminiscent of Greek or pre-Columbian masks, but in coloration and scale they most resemble fragments of classical sculptures. Seen as such, these heads not only reinforce the theme of destruction in the mural as a whole but also bear comparison to details in Rivera's RCA mural (fig. 251).

A monumental sculpture of Jupiter, partly destroyed by a bolt of lightning, and a "crumbling statue of Caesar" flank the far sides of Rivera's *Man at the Crossroads*. According to Bertram Wolfe, these two sculptures represent "science destroying the gods" and "the liquidation of tyranny," respectively.[61] The fallen head of Caesar serves as a seat for three workers, as they look past Trotsky and Marx to the controversial portrait of Lenin. The thick lips and blank eyes of this head are particularly similar in formal terms to the heads in *Dive Bomber and Tank*, but Orozco's play a different role. Rivera used the broken sculptures as part of an explicitly revolutionary reading of history in which the victory of the proletariat is predicated on the destruction of the past (of religion and empire). In Orozco's mural, however, the heads lack any specific identity and seem more part of a general mass of detritus symbolic of the loss of a classical "order," like the sculpture of Venus in the background of his *Modern Migration of the Spirit* (fig. 186) or the fallen Ionic columns crushed by a tank and battleship in Siqueiros's *Portrait of the Bourgeoisie*. As in these two other examples, *Dive Bomber and Tank* alludes directly to the destruction of Western civilization by mechanized warfare. In "Orozco 'Explains,'" in fact, he included his very subject—"dive bombing, tanking or battleshipping"—in a list of threats to the physical

integrity of the walls on which frescoes are painted. War, as much as "poor planning" or "moisture," destroys art. But the sealed mouths of the monumental heads refer to censorship as well. One wonders whether Orozco, also painting (in a way) for the Rockefellers, restored and referred to something that they (in a way) had once destroyed.

Poems and Machines

Compelled by MoMA to describe *Dive Bomber and Tank* for the benefit of the public, Orozco responded with a caustic essay in which he elaborated upon a theme of much of his career: Art cannot be explained in words, and those who need it explained are fools.[62] In his text, he avoided any explicit discussion of his subject and instead insisted: "A painting is a *Poem* and nothing else. A poem made of relationships between forms.... This word *forms* includes color, tone, proportion, line, et cetera."[63] Although this reference to poetry simply reminds us that it is through their juxtaposition that the elements of a composition derive meaning, and though it might seem just a purposeful avoidance of the mural's obvious political overtones, it serves as an important guide to further unlocking Orozco's complex message.

More than a decade later the collector and art historian MacKinley Helm recalled this exact quote by Orozco, astutely observing that the muralist had "involved himself in an art-for-art's-sake conclusion that he would have been the first to repudiate if some other writer had set it down in a book." Helm then went on to suggest that "Orozco, aware of the Museum of Modern Art's partiality for formalist painting, was determined to have a try at formal abstraction," and he concluded that the effort had largely failed.[64] In a response from the left, Antonio Rodríguez later objected that *Dive Bomber and Tank* could hardly be considered abstract "when it expresses concrete shapes with such clarity," and he came out in favor of the work.[65] In 1940 Orozco was pushing the expected limits of Mexican art in general and muralism in particular. Informing his subsequent critics, however, is an even deeper anxiety: Could any didactic painting survive the "triumphs" of abstract expressionism?

Although neither Helm nor Rodríguez helps much in an analysis of the mural, which is neither a "formal abstraction" nor a painting marked by "such clarity" as to prevent complex and conflictive readings, there seems little question that Orozco hoped *Dive Bomber and Tank* would be read within the context of formal experimentation. The work in its standard presentation, though hardly a simple illustrative blueprint of machine forms, is not that difficult to decipher. But because continuous forms (such as the tail section of the plane and the tank treads to the right and left) are clearly interrupted by the mural's physical divisions, the alternate arrangements proposed by the artist are more abstract and turn the mural into a sort of machine for plastic manipulations. Orozco used this metaphor in "Orozco 'Explains,'" in which he describes art in general as a "machine-motor [that] sets in motion" the viewer's senses, emotions, and intellect. He continues: "Each part of a machine may be by itself a machine to function independently from the whole. The order of the inter-relations between its parts may be altered, but those relationships may stay the same in any order, and unexpected or expected possibilities may appear." Orozco must have wanted to provide a clear justification for the alternate arrangements, one of the most original and radical aspects of the mural. While the panels might theoretically function as "independent" works, the artist never indicated that they would or should be exhibited as such, but only that they could be reduced or reconfigured, "changing but not disturbing the original composition."[66]

Such manipulations of the pictorial surface, transforming the mural into a puzzle with more than one "solution," do generate new possibilities of interpretation. Orozco's argument seems fundamentally flawed, however, since by its very nature, and in general terms, a machine (or a poem, for that matter) cannot be rearranged into new configurations without a loss of function or meaning (the motor of an automobile does not work in the back seat). Similarly, changing the elements or subverting the order of a Renaissance painting (redistributing attributes, flipping foreground and background), would of course lead to a destruction of meaning, to chaos. Engineering, grammar, iconology: These all have set rules. But this painting is different, since order was never the point. It is crucial here to recall that the mural's title, which foregrounds the war machines, was supplied by Alfred Barr, not Orozco. What if the subject of *Dive Bomber and Tank* is not really, or not only, a dive bomber and tank?

Although the painted machines in the 1940 mural have crashed, the painting as machine continues to function since of course as an image it "works" upon our senses and intellect. But it also works because there is a level of signification in the mural that is attached not to objects (the war machines) but to fragments, and by their very nature, fragments (or chaos) retain meaning despite their arrangement. A MoMA press release written before Orozco began work records the following exchange, in which journalist and artist discuss just such a fragment: "When asked if a certain preliminary sketch was the head of an aviator, he said: 'Yes, perhaps,'—he turned the sketch upside down—'or it might be a bomb. A picture must be capable of being looked at from any direction.'"[67] Again, one might suspect that Orozco was playing with his audience, reworking that old joke about curators hanging abstract art upside down, but in the alternative arrangements of *Dive Bomber and Tank,* separate parts are indeed meant to be seen from different directions (some panels are even rotated 180 degrees). Orozco seems to be implying that the forms in his mural are actually "floating" signifiers, capable of

201

being read "from any direction." MacKinley Helm saw this as a formalist game, as an appeal to the aesthetic sensibilities of MoMA. It is, I would argue, precisely the contrary.

Throughout his career Orozco was deeply critical of the elusiveness of abstraction. In "Orozco 'Explains,'" he complains that just as operagoers demand booklets with descriptions of the action, so museumgoers insist on words as well. Tying art to theatrics, he notes: "To the amazement of the public the curtain goes up and nothing is on the stage but a few lines and cubes. The Abstract. The public protests and demands explanations, and explanations are given away freely and generously."[68] This critique recalls one of Orozco's more revealing cartoons, in which he ridiculed the interpretation of nonrepresentational painting (fig. 240). In "Cubist Painting and Critics" (1920), transparent caricatures of the Mexican artists Roberto Montenegro and Doctor Atl view a work on exhibition.[69] Montenegro, reading from a guidebook, cites a description of the painting that merits Atl's enthusiastic approval, only to correct himself: The catalog entry was for a different work. On hearing the second version, Atl approves with equal glee. Two decades before *Dive Bomber and Tank,* Orozco had lampooned the blind acceptance of words that describe pictures, but he also seemed to criticize cubism (and abstraction in general) as meaning both everything and nothing. In the early 1920s this position fully dovetailed with the postrevolutionary strategy of bringing art to the masses; cubism, as an "intellectual" form of representation, would be of little use in the public art about to be commissioned by the Ministry of Education.[70]

If cubism as a formalist movement seemed a dead end for Orozco (and others) in 1920, there was a particular type of cubism that had a certain utility. In two earlier works, *Destruction of the Old Order* (1926; National Preparatory School [fig. 219]) and *The Dead* (1931 [fig. 51]), Orozco used pseudocubist

PINTURA CUBISTA Y CRITICOS

-¿Y eso qué representa?
=Número 37 "Un desnudo bajando una escalera horizontal"
¡¡Colosal, soberbio!!

-!Ah, no, me equivoqué!
Es número 38 "Ojo de microbio tomando cerveza con el ideal cómico"
-¡¡Formidable!! ¡¡Tremendo!!

Fig. 240 · "Cubist Painting and Critics," 1920, from **El heraldo** (July 14, 1920), Archivo Fotográfico IIE-UNAM, photograph by Ernesto Peñaloza.

Fig. 241 · Diego Rivera, **Pan-American Unity** (detail), 1940, fresco, City College of San Francisco, California. © City College of San Francisco.

compositions, based more on observation than on intellectual understanding, as visual metaphors for ruins. In the fresco panel, "cubism" (or, perhaps more specifically, a Cézannesque assemblage of blocks) is actually the "old order" seen from the vantage point of postrevolutionary realism (the two armed campesinos). The stability of the human figures is in stark contrast with the fragmentation of the background, just as, theoretically at least, the stability of the postrevolutionary regimes had

corrected the social, cultural, and political weaknesses of the Porfiriato. In the 1931 painting of the New York skyline, a similar type of visual cubism is appropriated to represent the instability of the modern metropolis.

If, in the early 1910s, cubism had been seen as an engine for construction of a new visual space, by the end of the decade it was increasingly interpreted as a parallel to the destruction of real spaces (and real people) during World War I. This, as well as the need for a new didactic art, explains the representational strategies of the Mexican muralists, a position brilliantly summarized in Orozco's *Destruction of the Old Order.* On one level, then, *Dive Bomber and Tank* may be read as a continuation of this purposeful misuse of cubism, which is seen as a failed utopian strategy and thus perfectly appropriate to represent society's failure to avoid the chaos of militarism. But the mural must also be viewed as part of the artist's attempt to move beyond the first phase of muralism, to distance himself — visually, professionally, and politically — from the so-called social realism of his rivals Rivera and Siqueiros. In 1940 Orozco rejected the neo-Renaissance solidity of Rivera and the montage principles used by Siqueiros (as in his neatly contemporary mural for the Electricians' Union), both of which implied the noble and constructive possibilities of art. Rather, Orozco's chief competition was closer at hand: He had chosen the same basic subject as *Guernica,* an even more monumental work that was then on loan to MoMA. By doing so, he invited a direct comparison (which critics then and later frequently made) to perhaps the most famous political painting of the time.

Although *Guernica* draws from theories of collage construction and synthetic cubism, its ultimate effect is one of horrifying fragmentation, used to communicate the terrors of saturation bombings and the general angst of war. Like Picasso, Orozco reduced his palette to chilling and lifeless tones.

The mural also takes similar recourse to collage ("a painting is a poem," a juxtaposition of forms) precisely and ironically to "construct" an image of "destruction." But Orozco went beyond Picasso, adding the possibility of *physical* fragmentation of the mural as object to the *visual* fragmentation of the mural as image. He thus further underscored his basic theme — namely, the devastating capabilities of technology and modern warfare.[71] More than war machines, his subject is chaotic fragmentation itself. In the final analysis, this is why his machine age allegory can be broken up and the parts reduced, rearranged, flipped. In any of the proposed compositions, the metaphoric subject (chaotic fragmentation, machine age destruction) not only remains legible but is further underscored. In fact, by refusing ever to "use" Orozco's mural as a "machine" to generate new compositions, the museum has negated the most innovative aspect of the entire project.[72]

Fig. 242 · Ralston Crawford, **Bomber**, 1944, oil on canvas, collection of Neelon Crawford, photograph courtesy Hirschl & Adler Galleries.

Conclusion

As a major public statement about what was to be the most horrifying conflict imaginable, *Dive Bomber and Tank* had few equals in the United States, where almost no murals addressed the war, in part because the attack on Pearl Harbor was roughly coterminous with the demise of the New Deal art projects that, in any event, had rarely encouraged artists to wrestle with contemporary political problems. The minuscule Nazi brownshirt who appears as part of an attack on anti-Semitism in the upper left corner of Ben Shahn's *Jersey Homesteads* mural of 1937, commissioned by the Resettlement Administration, is a notable but minor exception.[73] Curiously, Rivera's own 1940 fresco *Pan-American Unity,* painted for the Golden Gate International Exposition in San Francisco, alludes to World War II in just one relatively small panel (fig. 241). Caricatures of Stalin, Hitler, and Mussolini, stills from the films *Confessions of a Nazi Spy* and *The Great Dictator,* bombers, parachutists, and gas masks all compete for attention in a dense, almost surrealist montage, leaving the viewer bouncing from parody to politics, and back again. Here, as in earlier murals, Rivera, like Orozco, used the bomber as a symbol of war and chaos but, in keeping with his dialectic view of history and society, placed it in opposition to more positive images of technology.[74]

Of the thousands of prints and paintings by U.S. artists that dealt with the war, the closest parallel to Orozco's mural may be the precisionist Ralston Crawford's paintings of twisted wreckage, such as *Bomber* (1944), which shows a destroyed building and fragmented plane (fig. 242). Crawford's emphasis on the abstraction of tragedy, rather than heroes, victims, or villains, was also idiosyncratic for its time and revealed his own loss in confidence in the machine age.[75] But the most famous, and most obscene, visual response to the war was created by the leading muralist in the United States, Thomas Hart Benton. His *Year of Peril* (1942), a series of eight easel-size images that, despite their size, were so widely circulated, both on posters and in at least one newsreel, that they were more "public" than any single mural could have ever been.[76] As in *Dive Bomber and Tank,* planes, chains, and fragmented body parts play a crucial role in Benton's series, evidence of a shared visual language of warfare

despite obvious formal differences. In *Indifference,* two bombers, one in flames, have crashed on a beach (fig. 243). For shock value, the decapitated head of a member of the crew lies in the foreground, as bloody and gruesome as the legs in Orozco's mural are understated and obscured. The raised tail section of one bomber, and the fire burning behind, also echo Orozco's composition, but the star painted on one wing clearly identifies the planes as "our own," unambiguously arousing the viewers' ire.

In *Exterminate!* (fig. 244), the most infamous work of Benton's series, bombers and tanks appear in the background as U.S. soldiers attack beefed-up caricatures of Hirohito (or perhaps Tojo) and Hitler, who wields a swastika-tipped scepter not unlike those carried in Orozco's *The Carnival of Ideologies.* Chains fall from the opened chest of the Japanese leader, directly recalling one critic's reading of the chains in *Dive Bomber and Tank* as "the spilling entrails of a disemboweled society."[77] But the purposes of these two "public" statements could not be more different. Benton, still the regionalist, incited Americans to action at the beginning of the war through crystal-clear images that practically define the contested term "propaganda." Not even Orozco's caricatures of dictators in Guadalajara approach Benton's overt attack. Because Orozco was a Mexican artist, his distance from the war, but not from war in general, allowed him to create the more lasting image.

Fig. 243 · Thomas Hart Benton, **Indifference**, 1942, from the **Year of Peril** series, oil on canvas, State Historical Society of Missouri, Columbia, Missouri.

Fig. 244 · Thomas Hart Benton, **Exterminate!**, 1942, from the **Year of Peril** series, oil on canvas, State Historical Society of Missouri, Columbia, Missouri.

In 1955 Alma Reed looked back and remembered that in 1940 Orozco had justified his depiction of a bomber with a rhetorical question: "Will there be anything else in our world as important as this instrument of annihilation for the next half-century?"[78] Reed's memory may have been tinged by her efforts to prove Orozco's prescience, but the comment rings true, as events at the close of the millennium have shown. Nonetheless, after the conclusion of *Twenty Centuries of Mexican Art, Dive Bomber and Tank* was removed from public view; according to Reed, it did not appear again until the museum's twenty-fifth anniversary exhibition in 1955.[79] By then, many things had changed.

As numerous critics, most particularly Serge Guilbaut, have discussed, a lot of other paintings, marginalized in the wake of abstract expressionism, were put into storage after the war.[80] After the bombs that destroyed Hiroshima and Nagasaki, visual allusions to bombardment continued but were now devoid of references to the machine, formally (if not ritually) purified. The clearest examples

appear in the paintings of Adolph Gottlieb, but Rufino Tamayo also depicted cosmic allegories in the late 1940s that Octavio Paz insightfully interpreted as "testimony of the powers that would destroy us as much as an affirmation of our will to survive."[81] Orozco's last mural in the United States has also survived, in storage or not, as a spectacular marker of the transition from realism to abstraction, from defeats to triumphs, that would define art and artists, and create and destroy canons, in the subsequent decades. Perhaps because Orozco knew the costs of war from his vantage point as a witness of the Mexican Revolution, his images of military conflict, from *The Trench* to *Dive Bomber and Tank*, highlight those costs without ever revealing a clear and present enemy, without his ever abandoning his belief that the task of the artist was to challenge rather than to explain. Orozco's distance from partisan allegiances also allowed him to create an image for the U.S. public that rejected the racism, historical specificity, and exaggerated fears and hopes that propaganda all too frequently carried in its wake. This distance is fundamental to the continuing importance of *Dive Bomber and Tank*. Long after Hitler and Hirohito, Marx and Stalin have passed to the pages of history, the threat of technology and the force of the bomber remain.

The first draft of this essay was completed in the summer of 1998. Since then, several generous colleagues, especially Serge Guilbaut, Cuauhtémoc Medina, Renato González Mello, Anne Higonnet, and Patricia Berman, as well as two anonymous readers, were crucial in helping me elaborate and clarify my ideas. A conversation with Andrea Fraser provided further critical insights. Jeanne Hablanian, of the Wellesley College Art Library, kindly assisted with long-distance research, and the staff of the Museum of Modern Art Library generously provided access to documentary materials.

The Making and Reception of the Imaginary
of Artistic and Revolutionary Mexico

Alicia Azuela

This essay seeks to contribute to the yet unfinished effort to measure and interpret Mexican art's impact on the United States during the 1930s. Beginning with an analysis of Mexican artists' reception within U.S. artistic circles during the difficult years of the Great Depression, it proceeds to review the social, political, and artistic factors that determined the scope and course of development of Mexican art in America. Both aspects are essential to evaluating such a complex and still-controversial moment in both countries' histories.

Of Witnesses and Chroniclers

In the early 1920s there arrived in Mexico a significant number of foreign cultural creators and promoters, drawn by the political and social changes that the 1910 revolution had brought to that country. Many of these intellectuals came from the United States. Some were fleeing the witch-hunt that Woodrow Wilson had unleashed against the U.S. political left in 1919 for its opposition to U.S. intervention in World War I.[1] Others were simply curious about the restructuring processes under way in Mexico during the period of relative social peace under President Álvaro Obregón.

This group of foreigners carried out an important part of their work as writers, addressing a wide gamut of subjects, including politics, economics, culture, and education. They also wrote novels, short stories, and travelogues, as well as a good number of articles dealing simultaneously with political and artistic issues, insofar as revolutionary triumphs were associated with a renaissance in the arts. Initially, these writers sought to go beyond "oil and mining affairs" (which U.S. private enterprise, with its extensive investments in Mexico, was bent on making the central issue), with the goal of "explaining to Americans the origins and causes of a matter so disquieting and incomprehensible for them as

the Mexican Revolution; the revolutionary governments' achievements of the past five years, and the principal challenges they face."[2]

Within the heterogeneous and heterodox range of these visitors' "radical" thought, there coexisted elements of anarchism, anarchosyndicalism, socialism, and liberal reformism. One essential element of empathy with the Mexican cause came from U.S. populism,[3] which influenced historians like Frank Tannenbaum and Carleton Beals, who were interested in Mexico as "a social movement, a political and intellectual tradition and as a topic of sociohistorical analysis by U.S. academics and intellectuals."[4] This system of thought was grounded in an understanding of rural affairs and a challenge to modernity and its technocratic capitalist corollary as it was indiscriminately applied in Mexico. Within this context, it is easy to understand the foreigners' openness toward and admiration of the Mexican artistic renaissance, since several of them had previously been interested in artistic expressions that were democratic, communitarian, and popular in their form, subjects, accessibility, and origins. This position came primarily from Walt Whitman's perception of culture as "a hopeful positive political and social force."[5]

Even a single author's texts reveal drastic changes over time. This stemmed not only from the accelerated and unforeseen historical circumstances but also from the progressive enrichment over time of what began as almost nonexistent sources of information and the improved analytic perspective allowed by the passage of time and the development of the necessary methodological tools.

Throughout 1920 the dominant form was the pragmatic essay, which analyzed and recapitulated the writers' experiences in Mexico. By the 1930s, with the growing professionalization of the social sciences, methodological resources that enhanced the scientific quality of analyses of the Mexican case were being brought to bear.[6]

The U.S. public welcomed Mexican artists and intellectuals to the north between 1928 and 1934, but the writings of the preceding decade had had greater academic impact; readers tempered their initial judgments with the opinions of their better-educated compatriots, who had arrived in the early 1920s.

Both Mauricio Tenorio and John Briton[7] are recognized as among the most important and representative authors of the "radical" ideological spectrum that took up the case of Mexico during the 1920s, along with Frank Tannenbaum, whose thinking was grounded in anarchosyndicalist populism; the populist socialist Carleton Beals; Anita Brenner, who blended both perspectives with a measure of esoteric doctrines; and the liberal reformer Ernest Gruening.[8] Although they published their most important work in the late 1920s and early 1930s, all four strove, in their journalistic writings, to present a positive image of Mexico.

Radical artists and intellectuals in both countries were influenced by the Mexican anthropologist Manuel Gamio, whose thought built cross-border bridges on matters as important as the artistic and historical perception of Mexico.[9] For writers in both countries, Mexico's pre-Hispanic artistic legacy became the most important material evidence of the nation's cultural greatness. In the popular arts, they saw the oldest and most vital manifestation of resistance to four hundred years of political and cultural oppression and the only space in which creativity was kept alive as a part of racial identity. Like the North American majority, with a "Poinsettian"[10] spirit they blamed colonialism for originating and propagating Mexico's most serious ancestral problems: despotism, feudalism, latifundismo, corruption, the disproportionate power of the Catholic Church, and the oppression of the indigenous peoples and their subjection to racial, cultural, and social discrimination.[11] Thus it was believed that, save for folk arts, Mexican colonial art was foreign to the nation's sensibilities. The postindependence phase was criticized for its alleged failure to produce the minimum of justice and liberty that would allow the country to be pacified. These authors, echoing modernist antiacademicism, ignored virtually the entire artistic production of the nineteenth century. The Porfirio Díaz regime was seen as a mere extension of the already endemic authoritarian characteristics inherited from the colonial era, despite the facts that the Porfirian intellectual leaders waved the flag of order and progress in the name of modernity and that the artists, in their efforts toward internationalism and currency, produced an elitist and Francophile culture. The U.S. authors under discussion all explained the armed struggle that began in 1910 as the result of a great social explosion, itself a product of four hundred years of poverty, corruption, and exploitation of the people. As an anarchist Tannenbaum saw the internecine strife as the price to be paid for peace, whereas Beals's pacifism led him to condemn all kinds of violence, and Brenner's esoteric historical viewpoint, as we shall see, regarded the revolution as part of the uninterrupted cycle of struggle between opposites.

Most U.S. texts on Mexico, beneath their particular emphases, referred to a collective effort toward "spiritual reconstruction" and fed the Mexican nationalist interpretive current that saw the social and artistic revolution as a single phenomenon. Consequently, they considered artistic production the result of a search for collective identity and of the community's demand for the right to education and culture.

Fine arts were, then, the center of attention for contemporary scholars, and hardly any of them respected the boundaries of time in constructing the eternal Mexican artist, who, in Gamio's words, "unearths and reveals the philosophy of the collective soul," and that artist's rich legacy.[12] With regard to popular art, the international elite's standards

207

were derived from pre-Boasian,[13] avant-garde anthropological models, which were based on the supposedly unconscious, anonymous, collective, and utilitarian nature of popular art. Thus, for example, Gerardo Murillo (Doctor Atl) and Katherine Anne Porter highlighted the artisans' primitiveness and innocence, their connectedness to earth and nature, and their consequent ability to decant, in their art, the essence of Mexico's popular soul, one in which "nearly all the birds and all the peoples sing."[14] Atl furthermore repeated the most ultraconservative, primitivist argument that this creative and warlike people "with a profound melancholy, or in the case of the religious poetry, with a subtle mysticism poses an innate and profound esthetic sense at the same time they have within them the dynamic energy which impels them to vengeance and to battle. Both possess that ardor without which art is impossible."[15] Many of the articles that were written in the United States on this subject applied both these facets—bloodthirstiness and artistic talent—to Mexicans in general.

Most of the foreigners interested in the matter recognized in "the spiritual conversion and the artistic and cultural blossoming, the most important revolutionary triumphs."[16] Next to the popular arts, and among the many artistic, literary, architectural, and sculptural manifestations, it was Mexico's mural that received the most attention. Carleton Beals shared with his colleagues the conviction that this movement drew its grandeur from the painters' desire to root themselves in the traditions of popular and pre-Hispanic indigenous art and that it was nourished by the same unbridled energy that had moved the revolutionary whirlwind. For Beals, the work of Rivera and Orozco, whom he saw as the greatest of Mexico's muralists, reflected both characteristics. Orozco's work, like the revolution itself, "is explosive, terrifying, grotesquely powerful." Rivera's perspective upon and empathy with popular causes was communist, "but his interpretation is

fundamentally quite native, neo-Aztec. He is planting his feet in the tracks of the pyramid builders."[17] North American writers followed the path of Mexican artists and intellectuals who found in creative energy and the indigenous heritage not merely the strength and originality of an artistic renaissance but also a hope for the rest of the continent to build a common, self-generated culture, one that could illuminate new possibilities for all humanity.

Among interpretations of the 1910 armed struggle that paired artistic renaissance and social revolution, Anita Brenner's *Idols behind Altars* was the most typical text in the field of art history, and it had the greatest impact (fig. 245). I believe this is because it represents the most complete and subtle synthesis of the ethical and aesthetic reasoning of that time, consisting of a series of premises derived from the archetypal elements with which revolutionary and artistic Mexico was identified, both within and outside its borders. This image was created by national and international educated elites together

Fig. 245 · **Anita Brenner**, 1920s, photograph by Tina Modotti, reproduced by permission of the Anita Brenner Estate.

with the artists in Mexico. Brenner's book had an international impact, having been published originally in English and then translated the following year into German. Furthermore, the extraordinary photographs by Edward Weston, Tina Modotti, and José María Lupercio gave shape to the stereotypical icons they represented: the Pyramid of the Sun in Teotihuacán, symbol of past pre-Hispanic grandeur and proof of the immortal genius of the race that had placed it there; the skulls of Guadalupe Posada, which manifested the Mexican's melancholy and black humor; the votive offerings and paintings of miracles, which came from the artistic vein in the soul of the nation; and the revolutionary murals, creations of the socially committed spirit and vocation of the artists of Mexico present and past.

Brenner, influenced by Jean Charlot and the Mexican artists themselves, absorbed and gave shape to the basic modern components of the artistic renaissance: its nationalist-inspired origin and its transcendentalist vision of human destiny grounded in the new religion of art. From these principles, she immersed herself in their disciplinary, ideological, and artistic sources: anthropology, nationalism, and the artistic avant-garde. She used a Boasian cultural relativism theory to select her objects of study, she interpreted historical processes from a cosmogony of human destiny, and she filtered both elements through the screen of indigenist Mexican nationalism with roots in the artistic avant-garde movements. With Manuel Gamio's help, Brenner defined the methodological principles and research questions around which the book was structured, and like him, she used a double framework for analyzing cultural development in general. Her first level of interpretation was evolutionist and progressive, in the scientific tradition of proceeding from "hard facts" that was similar to the premises of other writings of the time. Her second interpretive level was synchronic and circular. She used it to address artistic, religious, and traditional manifestations

"as part of a cyclical process of growth and disintegration."[18] In *Idols behind Altars,* this second way of conceiving time and space became fundamentally transcendentalist and brought her to interpret the artistic renaissance from the perspective of nationalism and avant-garde esotericism, two of the principal ethical and aesthetic elements constituting this artistic manifestation. She also used the image of the artist, who was expected to be an initiate, a spiritual guide, and a political leader of his people; in the artistic creator, she saw the sign and moving force of this transmutation within the circular process of sacrifice, death, and transfiguration. These interpretations of art and its creators had been elaborated by Friedrich Nietzsche during the second half of the nineteenth century and became important components of modern aesthetic thought. They were assimilated and shared and then served to bond artists and intellectuals of this period.[19]

Anita Brenner defined modern art by the same principles she used to typify Mexican art of all time: She stressed that Mexican art was closer to its indigenous ancestors than its European counterparts were to theirs because it had returned to its indigenous spiritual and artistic values, and she pointed out that art is public and serves a social function. Brenner foregrounded muralism because it "returned to art the social meaning and function which it had had in its greatest epochs."[20]

Idols behind Altars was an unprecedented success. Within a year of its publication in 1929, it received 129 reviews, including the major print media in New York, Chicago, San Francisco, Boston, Dallas, and Philadelphia.[21] The enthusiasm sparked by *Idols* was attributed by many of its critics to its wealth of information, its reader-friendly style, and especially the novelty of its subject, since this was the first time that the Mexican artistic renaissance, which many critics considered the most important movement of the time, was analyzed in English in its own psychological and historical context.[22]

209

Intellectuals of the stature of Waldo Frank and Ernest Gruening lauded Brenner for having succeeded in "the difficult feat of capturing the Mexican spirit, and of rendering an understandable version of the unique psychology of our neighbors,"[23] as well as for powerfully conveying the image of artistic Mexico that politicians, artists, intellectuals, and promoters of tourism alike were battling to rescue from the shadow of barbaric Mexico.

Following the success of her book, Brenner received an invitation from the New York Art Center to curate an exhibition of Mexican art cosponsored by the Mexican government and the Rockefeller General Education Board.[24] The exhibition opened on January 19, 1929. The exhibition catalog and the press stated that this even was further proof of the Good Neighbor policy brought to Mexico by the U.S. ambassador Dwight Morrow.[25] This was the second of numerous cultural events initiated by Ambassador Morrow. Their goal was to promote the fledgling Good Neighbor policy that his government had devised for Latin America and that at Morrow's initiative was being applied for the first time to Mexico.[26] Cultural diplomacy, in an informal manner, joined the important economic and political measures that the ambassador designed for Mexico. These were related to the debt that Mexico had with, among others, the S. P. Morgan Company, a bank to which the ambassador had ties. It was also related to the conflicts of American oil companies, which were constantly threatened by the application of Article 27 of the Mexican constitution, which affected their agricultural, mining, and oil properties there, and to any other issues that threatened U.S. interests in Mexico. This was the case with the Cristero War and the presidential succession after the assassination of General Álvaro Obregón. Morrow, using his political skills, protected the interests of his country while remaining mindful of Mexican sentiments, which were inflamed by his intervention in Mexican national affairs.

Morrow had President Plutarco Elías Calles's full support for his programs of cultural promotion. Since the beginning of the Calles presidency, culture had become a tool for effecting political legitimacy in the context of Mexico's international relationships. The fruits of Mexico's artistic renaissance were used to counteract the image of a "barbaric" Mexico conveyed through such serious conflicts as the Cristero War. In these efforts, Morrow and Calles recruited two important groups: U.S. private investors who had strong economic interests in Mexico and intellectuals from both countries who, as we have seen, had already established strong links with one another. Morrow invited U.S. private industry to support his cultural programs, with the goal of easing the tremendous tension between the oil sector and the Mexican government in the former's struggle to be exempted from compliance with Article 27. The Rockefellers, owners of Standard Oil, especially benefited from Morrow's diplomatic intercession, and it was they who provided the ambassador with the spaces and subsidies needed to promote his diplomatic cultural project. The New York Art Center, dedicated to the promotion, exhibition, and marketing of Mexican art, was created with the support of the Rockefeller General Educational Board. Jean Charlot, Carlos Mérida, and Diego Rivera, among many other Mexican painters, had their work exhibited in this space. Morrow also promoted the establishment of the Mexican Art Association in the hope of promoting "friendship between the people of Mexico and the United States of America by encouraging cultural relations and interchange of Fine and Applied Arts."[27] Among the association members were the Rockefellers, the Morgans, and Morrow's wife, Elizabeth Cutter Morrow, who, besides having a prominent place within the world of art patronage, had strong economic interests in Mexico.

Morrow and Calles knew how to take advantage of efforts made by artists and intellectuals of both countries to unite their nations through culture. Morrow and Calles's persistent struggle to erase through culture the barbaric image of Mexico projected outside the country by the revolution was crucial to ensuring the support of artists and intellectuals in Mexico. However, state support for cultural exchanges did not lessen the growing cultural harassment of political opposition groups in Mexico, including foreign artists and intellectuals, after the imposition of an official candidate for the presidency, and it was linked to the deep economic crisis, which led the government to slash cultural spending. These factors together produced an exodus of Mexican artists and intellectuals to the United States.

The Presentation of Revolutionary and Artistic Mexico

The first activities devoted to Mexican artists during the 1920s took place within the conservative, rationalist, consumer, and local cultural environment that prevailed in the United States during this decade, one that tended to favor a regionalist aesthetic within the fine arts.[28] This artistic tendency promoted a thematic and stylistic nationalism associated with rural and urban environments, akin to the optimistic, dynamic, and creative spirit that supposedly characterized the American people, and independent of the European avant-garde. Its main representatives, Thomas Hart Benton, John Steuart Curry, and Grant Wood, had a contradictory relationship with the Mexican muralists. On the one hand, for them, as for the rest of the American painters, Mexican muralism was the most appreciated and transcendent ethical and aesthetic model for public art. On the other hand, Mexican painters became a threat; they were serious labor and artistic competition. As we shall see, this situation was intensified by the consequences of the crash of 1929 for the world art market.

The public in the cities that hosted the Mexican art exhibits was far from indifferent to U.S. cultural diplomacy with Mexico. The association of the U.S. government and private industry with Mexican authorities in sponsoring art evoked the severest criticism. As suggested by Mr. Salsbury in *Art Digest*, it was hard to believe that American institutions would ally themselves with the supposedly Bolshevik regime of General Calles, discredited as it was for its persecution of the church and its policy of atheist education "for people who cannot read."[29] Nor was it comprehensible that Mexican artists should be commissioned to paint murals when, for example, Rivera himself had caricatured the Fords, Rockefellers, and even Ambassador Morrow, now his patrons, in the murals at the Secretariat for Public Education.

The new group of patrons for Mexican art had indirectly fomented this hostility with the great number of anti-Mexican articles that routinely appeared in newspapers like the *San Francisco Chronicle*. In order to wage their battle against the revolutionary government that attacked or threatened their economic interests in Mexico, these patrons relied upon such newspapers because they belonged to William Randolph Hearst and Edward Donhey, the most powerful landowners in Mexico and men who also felt their interests threatened by the application of Article 27.[30]

Ironically, in answering these criticisms, U.S. sponsors of Mexican culture often had recourse to the writings of leftist artists and intellectuals in both countries, which also sought to transform the negative image of revolutionary Mexico. As already pointed out, the collaborative work of U.S. and Mexican artists and intellectuals was crucial to the reception of Mexican art in the United States. They constructed and disseminated the image of an artistic and revolutionary Mexico in their many writings published on the subject in the United States. This construction was crucial to the very

211

perception that critics and the general audiences had of the Mexican art that was to be exhibited in their museums. This happened with *Idols behind Altars,* which inspired numerous museum guides that attempted to present artistic Mexico just as Brenner and her colleagues had done. Thus, in crossing geographic and ideological borders, the imaginary and the imagery that an educated elite had constructed around Mexico's social revolution and artistic renaissance traveled to several of the United States' most important libraries and museums with the sponsorship of the private philanthropic organizations that had economic interests in Mexico.

This was the case with the traveling exhibition that was shown in New York's Metropolitan Museum of Art on October 13, 1930, on the initiative of Ambassador Morrow and with a subsidy from the American Federation of Arts, through the cooperation of the Carnegie Corporation of New York, the owner of a consortium of mines in

Mexico, as well as the backing of the Mexican government (fig. 246).[31] Although Brenner was merely a consultant on this project, the description of the exhibition and the texts in the catalog evoke a staging of *Idols behind Altars.* The description stated that the five hundred pieces of fine and decorative arts assembled were an attempt to show the artistic aspects of the origin and development of Mexican civilization from the time of the Spanish Conquest to the present. It also explained that the pieces were selected to make known Mexico's true cultural and racial essence and to show the origin and development of its civilization, which was, it was claimed, the product of a double process of economic and political subjection resulting from the Spanish Conquest together with the people's *unconscious defense* of their own customs and traditions and an equally *unconscious* appropriation of the European culture imposed by the conquerors.[32]

Fig. 246 · Installation view of the **Mexican Arts** exhibition at the Metropolitan Museum of Art, New York, October 13–November 9, 1930, photograph courtesy Metropolitan Museum of Art.

For this reason, the museum authorities claimed to have placed on exhibit only those pieces that were products of the indigenous world and of indigenous appropriations of European culture.[33] They also announced that the catalog had been prepared with the express intention of presenting this artistic historical transformation. Thus the exhibition rooms were divided into two great sections. In the first section, "the unconscious manifestations of national characteristics" could be observed, covered the period from colonial times through the Porfirio Díaz regime. The second portrayed the new, self-conscious Mexican identity produced by the armed struggle of 1910, and the whole exhibition culminated with the Mexican Revolution/artistic renaissance dyad, which the public would particularly appreciate because of its popular art.[34]

The exhibition sparked different reactions; one of the most representative was the one expressed by a reviewer in *Arts* magazine,[35] who professed great disappointment since the objects on display, although interesting as examples of an approach to life totally different from the Americans' own, were not masterpieces. The review recognized a general French influence in the modern works, which nonetheless did not exclude their "genuine indigenous quality."[36] It found, however, that many of them were too "heavy-handed and purposely limited in scope to afford permanent satisfaction, yet they do embody a strong and fierce and emotionally true vision of life, and its predominating soberness ought to prove a welcome relief from our own cultivated cheerfulness."[37] This reviewer preferred the crafts possessed of the joy and vitality of "unspoiled minds"[38] over the contemporary art, which was characterized as of good quality but not terribly important. The craft pieces were better received because of their putative primitivism, vitality, and spontaneity.[39]

The reviewer's aesthetic criteria were representative of the stances of many of the art critics who wrote for the specialized press. For this sector, Mexican art, especially contemporary art, because of its links to the French avant-garde, did not seem particularly original. Nor was it of very good quality, whether because of the coarseness of its forms, the somberness or stridency of its colors, or the sordid and aggressive nature of its content. These formal characteristics were necessarily associated with the supposedly resentful, violent, and melancholy Mexican personality.

The United States of America in the Gaze of the Mexican Muralists

U.S. intellectuals who addressed artistic and revolutionary Mexico also influenced the reception of Mexican muralism by U.S. audiences. These intellectuals were able to identify with U.S. spectators, who followed the development of the muralists' work and paid attention to their many ethical and aesthetic proposals. In general, the Mexican muralists tried to represent issues of national and local relevance in the United States; this led some of the most important contemporary U.S. thinkers to take an interest in the Mexicans' work. The case of the reaction of the *New Republic*'s writers to Orozco's controversial murals in Baker Library at Dartmouth College illustrates this phenomenon.

This was one of the most influential groups of intellectuals at the time and included John Dewey, Lewis Mumford, Robert Lynd, Sidney Hook, and Reinhold Niebuhr. These men saw in this mural their common purpose of achieving a "coherent synthesis of self and society, culture and technology, thought and action."[40] One of the most solid and favorable reviews of Orozco was in fact written by Mumford, who elaborated on several of his analytic criteria from his now-classic article "Orozco in New England"[41] in his also classic book *Art and Technics*.[42] Mumford saw in Orozco's frescoes the fundamental qualities of great art: the use of mythic representa-

213

tions with strong symbolic content, referring to human as well as universal situations; the basis of ethical as well as aesthetic demands in the artist's commitment to transmitting his own lived experience, finding in it the deepest scope and meanings. In these frescoes, Orozco crystallizes the effort that any great artist makes to transmit what he may deem important "through a common language of symbols and forms, with a little bit of concentration, some intensity, something of that passionate delight that led [him] to its greatest climax through the very act of expression."[43]

Mumford acknowledged that the painter had the capacity to interpret with an unsurpassed mastery, in a contemporary formal language, the problems of modern man: "Those superb ideological leaps that put Orozco's symbols on a much higher level than any other contemporary mural painter: to the triumphant militarism of the early period of exploitation he ties the triumphant mechanism of the later period: the two are graphically connected—as they were in history—by the prostrate figures of Cortez's captives, who are represented as being fed into the maw of the machine." This language included the historical-philosophical allegory of the American continent's processes and characteristics, based on pre-Hispanic origin myths, and the symbolic allusion to the most serious conflicts throughout the hemisphere: the north with its mechanistic automatism, consuming material and intellectual goods, rationalist and Puritan; the south with its corrupt caudillo militarism, its fanaticism and ignorance. For Mumford, these frescoes' most important benefit, for the students of Dartmouth College, was the possibility of gaining an awareness of historical complexity and of the courage required to face the task of reconstruction "after the holocaust of contemporary civilization."[44]

Mumford's article was a defense against Harvey Watt's scathing criticism in *Art Digest*.[45] Watts

condemned the fact that a Mexican painter should have been permitted to "satirize English speaking traditions, spiritual, educational and academic" at the same time that the United States' most blue-blooded college allowed the "extremely tiresome traditions of an alien and somewhat abhorred civilization of the Toltec-Aztec cults"[46] to penetrate its student body.

The Mexican model of state-subsidized public art had enormous repercussions in the United States in both theory and practice, especially as the devastating effects of the stock market crash of 1929 began to be felt. The Depression naturally affected the market for art. Gallery closings were a daily occurrence, and finally even the Mexican Art Center ceased its exhibitions. The Federal Arts Project, intended to make work for artists, had not yet been established. The few contracts for mural painting were given mostly to foreign painters, among whom Orozco and Rivera held a privileged place.

U.S. painters reacted against this injustice. As in other areas of art, their responses had important ideological undertones. The American Artists' Professional League was formed precisely to fight for "The greater national recognition, protection and support of the achievements of American Artists in all fields."[47] It opposed "the frequent use of political and social wire-pulling by inferior foreign workers to the disadvantage of American work by foreign artists which are false, misleading, slighting, and misguiding to the American public."[48]

The National Commission for the Advancement of American Art criticized, in the same tone, the commissioning of Orozco to paint frescoes at the New School for Social Research and Dartmouth College.[49] Likewise, the Rockefeller Center scandal was attributed to Rivera's incapacity, as a Mexican, to understand the U.S. sensibility.[50]

The presence of the Mexican artists was, then, a delicate issue on the U.S. artistic scene. Their work and the constant scandals it provoked pointed to

214

conflicts as serious in the North American art world as the censorship of what little public art was being commissioned at the time and the preference for hiring foreigners in the face of the growing impoverishment of U.S. artists during the Great Depression. It also spurred widespread interest in public art as a tool for artists to engage with their communities and as a source of income for this hard-hit sector of the population.[51]

The scandal surrounding the destruction of Diego Rivera's mural at Rockefeller Center served as a catalyst for local problems; this was generally the role played by Mexican art. Despite international condemnation of the Rockefellers for whitewashing the mural, the issue nationally was the hiring of a foreign painter and beyond that the very meaning of public art. The censoring of the mural was nothing more than the culmination of a series of tensions between artists and their patrons over the scope of freedom of expression in the context of private or state sponsorship of works of art.

The Rockefeller consortium was itself forced to exhibit, at the MoMA in April 1932, the mural projects of sixty local artists. The painters demanded that, contrary to what happened at Rockefeller Center, contracts for public art be awarded after public bidding, so that considerations of quality, not favoritism and previous contacts, should govern the selection process.

The leftist artists who made up this opposition group had founded, to that end, the Society of Independent Artists. Among its members were John Sloan, Thomas Craven, and Ben Shahn. Without disregarding the Mexican muralists' important contributions to contemporary art, they demanded equal opportunity for U.S. and foreign artists. At the same time, they severely criticized the censorship of Rivera's work, as well as the exclusion, for ideological reasons, of members of their own group by the Rockefeller's selection committee, as had happened

to Ben Shahn for his famous painting *The Passion of Sacco and Vanzetti,* an homage to the two anarchists unjustly sentenced to death by the U.S. government.

The reception of Mexican art in the United States determined its impact and the recognition of its achievements in the field. The complex elements that made up the images of Mexico and Mexicans through their artistic expression were largely products of differences and antagonisms within U.S. public opinion. They also resulted from the series of political, economic, cultural, and artistic factions that circumscribed Mexicans' presence north of the border, such as the use of art as a diplomatic tool by powerful groups in both countries; the effects of the Great Depression on the North American economy, institutions, and worldviews; and a growing interest among the citizenry, and its political and economic elites, in public art. However, this long-term process of opinion making began and ended with the antagonistic stances of left- and right-wing sectors regarding Mexican art. These sectors produced a large body of writing and events favoring the Mexican presence in the United States just as readily as they rejected and demonized Mexican art with social content and with all the public artistic production that was then being carried out in the United States itself. This brief overview of the political, economic, and ideological environment that surrounded the introduction of Mexican art to the United States, together with the other essays that make up this catalog, will surely contribute to the deep and objective rethinking of this period in North American art, over and above the political beliefs of those who study it.

Mural Devices

Francisco Reyes Palma

In *Simulacra and Simulation,* Jean Baudrillard calls one of Jorge Luis Borges's texts "the most beautiful allegory of simulation." He is referring to the story of the ancient Chinese map makers who made such a meticulous map that it had to be spread over all China. As the empire declined, the colossal map also began to disintegrate, until it turned to dust and became part of the geography that had been its inspiration. Contemporary civilization parodies this allegory; its new map of globalism must cover the entire world if, at some point, it is to fulfill the destiny laid out in Borges's tale.[1]

In fact, the term "globalization" encapsulates the most recent metaphor in the West's social imaginary, a spectral double interchangeable with the terms "modernity" and "universality" but bereft of any humanistic remainder: pure cynical reason exposed. In this metaphor of the sphere, the West represents perfection as the absolute synthesis of form: the aestheticized image of the hoary imperial desire for conquest, in which the loss of physical borders and mental boundaries serves the best workings of capital and its logic of ever-widening accumulation. In spite of its brazen arrogance, this spatial metaphor, for tactical reasons, must hide its center and generate an extensive and homogeneous notion of surface, aided by the emergence of electronic hyperspace.

Globalism is presented as the defender of democracy and multiculturalism, although it is unable to conceal entirely exclusions rooted in hegemonic poles and well-worn traditions. It is shielded by the sacred principle of liberty and manifest in the action of the market as some sort of superorganic entity whose regulatory power endows it with a sense of divine right. It likewise has a temporal register, marking a stage of progress within the triumph of the capitalist paradigm, whose ideals are introduced with no opposition whatsoever everywhere on the planet even as they lead to generalized depredation and misery.

If modernism and nationalism went side by side up to the end of the twentieth century, in its waning years they split, and nationalism began to be viewed with suspicion. With the dismantling of these great totalizing paradigms came the crumbling of essentialized identities based on monolithic identification with the nation-state. Nevertheless, in precursors like Orozco, we can already see a skeptical attitude toward the great narratives of history and nation that developed in his time.

Perhaps taking account of the ascendant social imaginary will help us recognize more clearly the one that is displaced, although something always escapes this displacement, remaining in residual form or containing latencies and potential breaks, on even minimal fissures, pointing toward future possibilities. This suggests a series of questions: What were the innovations of muralism as a pictorial modality in its time? Was it a response to the demands of a historical epoch? Does it have a future as an expressive medium?

Indeed, the nation-state has been a substantial part of modernity. Within the paradigmatic imagi-

Fig. 247 · Courtyard view of Orozco's frescoes, 1923–26, National Preparatory School, Mexico City, photograph by Bob Schalkwijk.

nary of the nation-state, murals were a fundamental connecting mechanism for ordering experience and structuring subjectivity within the social sphere, making possible an encounter with the illusion of the state, the sensation of national belonging, of unity in diversity. If we accept the premise that peripheral countries have brought to modernity a divergent creativity based on a different construction of traditions, we may say that Mexican artists, beginning in the 1920s, set in motion an unprecedented and highly effective mechanism of time and memory control, mural painting.

Modernity in Dispute

Nonetheless, there remains the question of whether Mexican muralism should be considered something new. By mid-century the cold war had diminished the significance of monumental painting to a technical procedure derived from preceding centuries; meanwhile, the portable canvas remained identified with modernity and its vanguard. Thus did these stereotypes harden. Art criticism, firmly ensconced within the orthodoxy of the avant-garde model, could do no more than consider the use of murals historicist backsliding, as if easel painting were not itself technically a remnant of the past.

In any case, the dual aesthetic and political vanguard character of the Mexican movement, by connecting with a classicist will to high art, introduced a disruptive element into the more purist notion of avant-garde. There was also another point of friction, the open, communicative meaning of the painted wall as opposed to the self-referential character of intrapictorial dialogue in easel painting. Moreover, we must not forget the extensive production of canvases that followed the mural's affirmative example in Mexico.

These antagonisms having waned, Mexican muralism is now considered an academic curiosity, worthy of interest but removed from its claim to

represent modernity. Time and again, scholars go over the political and allegorical enunciations of the painted surfaces with content-focused zeal, ignoring their pragmatic innovations. I think the emphasis in understanding artistic objects may also be placed on the analysis of their operative logics, especially if they serve as a cultural technology, as significant devices within the hierarchical order of the imaginary.[2]

Space

Michel Foucault has drawn attention to the history of spaces as a history of power; in this sense, the mural, far from being an ornament attached to a structure, is a powerful machine that touches and disquiets society. In Orozco's terms, it would be an idea machine. We could refer to the invention of the wall as a contemporary, public, and political form of producing meanings, whose double inscription as a fictional space of pictorial representation and as a physical space situated within architecture brings us face-to-face with a web of multiple, heterogeneous inflections that serves a new type of commemorative and devotional function. Even the use of allegory presents elements different from those in ancient mural practice (fig. 247).

If the critics of the 1920s defined the first murals as decorative, this innocuous term concealed effective technologies of power aimed at reconstructing the country. Thus the mural device, understood as a vision and meaning machine, unfolded as part of the government's cultural activities in unison with artists' private initiatives and acted as a part of the materiality of physical spaces, as well as a mental realm, modeling consciousnesses and sensibilities.

Initially, during the phase of postrevolutionary reconstruction, painted buildings took the place of the church in being identified with prejudice and backwardness. Art sacralized the realm of secularized power and constituted a silent pulpit as eloquent as any from earlier periods. Of course the social grounding of muralism did not occur without spurts of rejection, violent at times, by the users of the first painted buildings. In order to discredit this pictorial modality, certain groups of young students coined the term *monotes* ("big, ugly mugs") to describe mural art and introduced direct action, a form of censure based on physically attacking the image, a sort of iconoclastic assassination taken from the experience of the Red Battalions of the Mexican Revolution, halfway between anarchism and what became fascist forms of action. In a parallel manner, government authorities applied selective censorship, the patron's privilege.

Given the economic situation after the revolution, the need for urban structures prevented the demolition of the ancien régime's symbolic edifices; however, it was enough to change a building's sign, assigning it a different character. By superimposing a mural on the architecture, spaces were resignified and new meanings implanted upon the specific history of the place. In this way, the function of colonial administrative centers, ancient palaces, or former churches was inverted, as they were transformed, for example, into schools or libraries at the service of the literacy and educational crusade. Above all, these buildings became insignia, representing the improvements the revolution had wrought.

Without a doubt, those most malleable and most subject to the murals' effects were students, although parents and teachers were also under their influence. While in general we think of science as the opposite of religion, in the Mexican case, art and pedagogy were the devices used to substitute for religious values. What better than those realms to maintain the rituals of the church and promote the development of secular heroes? In one way or another, the revolution's painters returned to the motif of exemplary lives now marked by the civil

more than the sacred. In this sense, the new muralism was a response not so much to the adoption of an ancestral technique as to the reinvention of its intellectual potential.

With a largely illiterate population, the introduction of writing was a strategic necessity for the inculcation of the modernist imaginary, within which the written word has the power of legislative truth, of a biblical mandate. The mural, however, is text and something more: It incorporates the sacral weight of the building together with the secular signification that has been added to it, and it erects itself as an institution. By institutionalizing the gaze, this pictorial expression became part of the homogenizing discourse that tended to erase historical fractures, social divergences, and even ethnic and class distinctions. This application, by creating new relationships within a space of collectivized desire, produced a sequence of phenomena that mobilized social energy.

The mural device constituted domination's most subtle face; in its search for a legitimizing consensus, it made the act of representation inherent in shared social practices, both individual and communal. Thus it brought to bear primary mechanisms of equalization and harmony and the capacity to interrelate contradictory elements, from which the certainty of temporal continuity can be derived. This was a novel use of the gaze, capable of creating a system of reiterating signs that resonated in the imaginary as a whole: Mexico as historical lineage incarnate.

In its first phase, the mural required a minor economic investment; artists' wages were comparable to those of skilled construction workers, although this aspect may have been somewhat exaggerated, since art professionals working within educational institutions received permanent, if meager, salaries. The fact is that building a new structure was vastly more expensive than merely adding mural paintings to one already built or renovated. Later, when the construction industry had been reactivated, it became difficult to conceive of a government-sponsored architectural project of any importance without a contribution from the muralists.

Just one example was the construction of the Abelardo Rodríguez Market in a working-class district of Mexico City, where a series of murals by a group of young artists, painted between 1934 and 1936, includes depictions of war, fascism, labor issues, and health education, themes that directly impact on the viewer (fig. 248). These are revolutionary social messages in which symbolic volumetric and chromatic abstractions coexist with didactic schema; they are pictorial narratives that employ principles related to cinematic montage or comic book sequencing with its characteristic balloons.

If the early colonial era (1521–60) substituted paintings on walls for printed words, like Bibles for the poor, the twentieth-century mural brought together elements that are now more identified with the mass media of the press, comic books, and film, a flexible system of strata in time and space, super-imposed through images and other ways of rearticulating events and concepts.

In the beginning the presence of murals in institutional spaces forced them open to any potential spectator, which, at least in appearance, ameliorated the hermeticism of public buildings under the Porfirio Díaz dictatorship. By reaffirming the open and visitable character of these places, more people were able to move through them. If the mural was there, anyone could have access to the space that held it; the sense of right of way was created and took over from the idea of the private, or more intimate, contemplation that is associated with easel painting.

From Center to Origin and Other Temporal Coordinates

Two principles of cohesion stand out within the regime of meaning that characterized Mexico's second, postrevolutionary modernity (which followed the initial modernizing project of the Díaz oligarchy): isomorphism, in the sense of self-identity and

Fig. 248 · Ramón Alva Guadarrama, **Field Work**, 1934–36, encaustic, Abelardo Rodríguez Market, Mexico City, photograph by Bob Schalkwijk.

transhistorical forms of identification with Mexico, and the paternalistic power of the center—in this case, Mexico City. Loyalty to the center was primary, for from it issued the capacity for decision making and the power to enforce it, a sure base from which to guard against centrifugal forces and the danger of violence as a disintegrating force. As the population center, Mexico City was the greatest beneficiary of the natural resources from all the other states, the seat of symbolic power, and the political and economic decision-making hub for the rest of the nation. The expansion of murals onto more and more buildings allowed this centrality of power to spread out like a subtle fabric. Soon the painters' activity reached all the states of the republic, and it is still expanding throughout the territory.

Among the ways that the Western mentality has imposed its domination upon the world is its demand that all societies follow a path toward progress, a linearity that does not discount the possibility of return and that establishes a point of origin that grounds and lineages and values that may prove timeless. From this perspective, it seems useless to deny the links between the mural movement and the Mexican Revolution, not because we may claim for the latter the coherence and sense of justice that is usually attributed to it but because it was a response to a situation of chaos, violence, and fear. These were epochal signs so intense as to mark a radical change at the core of the social imaginary and to establish a founding order, even at the expense of historical accuracy.

The revolution served as a threshold, a temporal rupture that marked the beginning of a new era regardless of how many vices and ideals it carried over from the earlier period. This is why so many histories resort to omission or to forgetfulness in order to maintain the revolution's prestige. A notorious case would be José Vasconcelos, the first promoter of the mural device, who deployed an effective cultural strategy based on activating the

guiding principle of the Díaz dictatorship's educational apparatus; in other words, he tried to give the country's educational system a centralized national direction, which his immediate revolutionary predecessors had dismantled.

The project's originality, which Vasconcelos carried out first as rector of the National University and then as minister of public education, lay in putting to work a missionary model, an enterprise of internal colonization aimed at erasing vernacular languages and ethnic diversity. In this way the redemptive, civilizing mystique of the philosopher turned statesman became the showpiece for a provisional project of mass culture, which highlighted popular manifestations insofar as they achieved a desirable level of high culture, "the leap to the classical" of a Mexico made up of educated, middle-class

Fig. 249 · Diego Rivera, **Ribbon Dance**, 1923–24, fresco, Secretariat for Public Education, Mexico City, photograph by Bob Schalkwijk.

mestizos, whom Vasconcelos considered the "cosmic race," the product of the mixing of two races.

Meanwhile, the Indian peoples, with their diverse cultural manifestations rooted in rural traditions, were condemned to extinction. Vasconcelos's proposal was an inversion of the genocidal solution perpetrated by the European empires and their postcolonial successors, but it remained, in the end, a stratagem for deferred cultural death that, with foresight, selected certain elements of the other's aesthetic to support its own cultural project with regard to origin and originality.

In several senses, the mural crystallized the revolutionary rupture of 1910 while its embers were still burning. Painters depicted the violent trauma with beautiful or powerful forms, symbolically stanching the wounds of the immediate past. Later they reformulated the more distant history of great national struggles, and although some facts were challenged, the mural device ultimately reaffirmed the idea of a historic continuum, the utopian belief in being the same throughout the centuries or—what amounts to the identical thing—reifying the transforming principle as unbroken persistence. The spectacle of memory redefined its own representation from a new end point, the revolution, which was at the same time a creative beginning, a horizon renewed by repetition, by the eternal ideological promise of the coming of the kingdom of justice and social equality.

Time of Return

As a collective subject and element of symbolic synthesis, the Indian was made the repository of the Mexican project's originality, a pastoral Arcadia to dissolve the brutal ruptures of history, a point of repetition constantly called upon to dissolve the contradictions within the Mexican historical process. Perhaps the most extreme example of this is the emblematic Indian of the vast Mexica empire,

referred to in English as Aztec, who fell before the Spanish onslaught only after waging the most heroic resistance. Unity around a center is the image that the postrevolutionary governments wished to project, as they erased any reference to the Mexicas' imperial and militaristic vocation. It is no coincidence that the nineteenth-century republican spirit selected for the national flag the image of the imperial eagle, the founding sign of the Mexica center of the universe, the navel city of México-Tenochtitlán, later to be the birthplace of the mural.

In monumental paintings and other postrevolutionary artistic manifestations, the ethnic and rural communities that had been the most violently disrupted by the revolutionary process took on a leading role. The Indian, in particular, became the identifying element of national poetics, the assimilated, binding agent; with this, the tendency to see indigenous peoples as a drag on the nation's development began to be reversed. To a large extent, the exoticist and primitivist propensities of the avant-garde contributed the key element in this process of identification at the same time that they fertilized the artists' expressive repertoire. Only Orozco, with his staunch sense of Hispanicity, abjured the process.

The Indian contributed a foundational element in an apologetics for the advancement of the hegemonic revolutionary faction; the idea of the Indian was a notion integrated with that other imaginary of modernity derived from the romantic spirit, the *people.* In this way a country divided for centuries attempted to exorcise what it considered the twin forces that had cursed it since the beginning: the lack of cohesion and the racial backwardness that blocked the path to progress.

Even before the revolution, the figure of the Indian had been the most affected by these uses, but soon it came to embody the self-image of the nation, its gestures captured in pictorial schemata decanted from avant-garde geometries and the

221

exoticisms. In the end Diego Rivera set forth a synthesis of "Indian" and "popular" that constituted the paradigm for the national. Where there had once been prejudice and contempt, now he projected a vision rich in primary affect, overflowing chromaticism, plastic rhythms of the timeless life of labor, brown bodies, and festive pleasures, a gaze inspired by the other's capacity to resist impositions, synonymous with ancient powers of resistance and the current revolutionary spirit (fig. 249).

If Rivera contributed greatly to dissolving chromatic racialism's codes of epidermic valuation, his synthesis of the Indian in no way ruled out fusion with a new technological order that he saw as capable of liberating humanity from the brutal burden of labor. Rivera took the images of the Indian, the peasant, and the worker to the limit with his representation of the Indian worker, harbinger of hybridization given shape in his mural *Pesadilla de guerra y sueño de paz* (Nightmare of War and Dream of Peace, 1952). Thus his initial paradises, conceived without contradiction, offered both an origin and a future to his anticipations of a socialist Eden of labor, an orientation opposed to Vasconcelos's liberal humanism but congruent with it in its requirement to efface ethnic particularities, making the Indian the mother subject of the worker. This path was far from another notion of progress and another modality of the state, communism.

Perhaps it was Rivera who most emphasized the value of traditions, who was most identified with the popular imaginary, with mechanist utopias, and who most vehemently chastised the destroyers of the originary paradise. In this artist's dialectic, the return served its function as indirect referent; it seems that the elements of synthesis could be found only at the extremes of history, in the remotest past or a distant future. All other events were arranged according to a system of absolute contrasts: old and new orders, tyrannical and revolutionary; positive or negative social classes. These binaries

served as generalizing mechanisms within Rivera's forms of expression, a system shared by other artists of his generation and later ones as well.

Orozco, on the other hand, used the Indian and the peasant as historical characters marked off by specific places and times (see, for example, his panel entitled *Ancient Migration*, Baker Library, Dartmouth College [fig. 186]). Meanwhile he placed the mestizo as the synthesis of ethnic contradiction, as the only possible horizon (as in the *Hispano-America* panel [fig. 182]). Likewise, from the archaeological viewpoint, this painter incorporated mythic figures of knowledge into his work, allegorized as rungs on the ladder of humanistic improvement: the return of the feathered serpent, the advent of a civilizing Quetzalcoatl, a metaphor of the artist's own life, of creative sacrifice in an act of human redemption.

Nonetheless, among the subjects to be represented, the symbolic key most highly developed by Orozco was that of the anonymous, politicized mass, shouting mouths presented among the modern irrational forces of the great modern city. This image was characteristic of his work as printmaker and could come only from a sensibility framed by a Jacobin persuasion.[3]

The Myth of Modernity

In mural painting, the figure of the Indian, often interchangeable with that of the peasant, was scarcely rivaled by that of the industrial worker. Each of these presences played its own integrative role, exalting the legendary, historic Indian, who emerged as an epic, totalizing source of Mexicanness while his concrete existence waned. Through iconographic reiteration of the revolutionary moment, the mural froze the disruptive potential of the image of the armed peasant, while it made the industrial worker into the icon of an aspiration. Even if the icons of the peasant and the Indian had an increas-

222

ingly sketchy survival, power by then had new resources for symbolic subjection.

Each muralist established his own economy of the gaze and created his own system of dominant figures, of continuities and relationships; however, these artists contributed to the official sphere such central concepts as the trilogy of the worker, the peasant, and the soldier (fig. 48). This was an indivisible unity representative of progress, understood under the rubric of "the people," a foreshadowing of a later corporate organization, with its estatelike forms of control, an idealized image of the mechanisms of hegemony that were organizing the new Mexican society.

As time went by, the mural device came to be a point of reencounters, a mirrored form of the state, a meaning-making artifact for organizing representation, for naturalizing artifice and then disguising it so as to avoid confrontation. However, as mechanisms of seduction and control were brought into play, the device of monumental painting not only consolidated the postrevolutionary government but also inaugurated its counterpart, a communist opposition party that developed almost synchronically, although both were surely brothers in their shared longing for the figure of the state.

Encouraged by both the nascent communist party and the party of the new bourgeoisie that emerged from the revolutionary process,[4] the artistic sector reaffirmed its dual role as aesthetic and political avant-garde, which, as part of the processes of modernization, took on a privileged sociopolitical position unimaginable for the more autonomous avant-gardes. The artists played a strategic role during the period of postrevolutionary reconstruction and took on a wide variety of pedagogical and disseminatory functions within the cultural apparatus that were later taken up by more specialized cadres.

Muralism incorporated elements of rationality and irrationality, bound together like strands of a rope, and it was not long before many of the mythic strategies of power seeped into this art. As the sacred character of art reinforced the aura of the secular so necessary to the functioning of a modern state, some artists shared the attributes of the cultural hero. Their characterization as selfless beings worthy of collective worship was more than mere rhetoric.

If any regime of visibility produces meaning, it creates at the same time its own opacity, its quota of silence and disfiguration. In the long run, those who benefited least from the iconic glorification of the Indian were the surviving indigenous ethnic groups themselves. Small nations were subjected to the principle of forced unity, to the loss of their own names and diversified cultural heritages in favor of the new model subject of development, the industrial worker. This image in turn was reduced to its pure productive connotation, the image of an abstract producer, separated from any referent that might give an account of the varied spectrum of communal, ethnic, or peasant cultural life.

The revolutionary intellectuals, who erected the mural as an instrument of struggle against officialization and coercive structures, deployed the measure of resistance that was indispensable for giving its dynamism to the power mechanisms of the state. For the first time in Mexico, mural painters and printmakers wound up constituting a publicly acknowledged social and political, not just cultural, force that saturated public spaces with frescoes, leaflets, and posters. This hierarchy went well beyond the pure realm of artistic production and was retained by the artists into mid-century.[5]

Border Crossings

Beginning in the second half of the 1920s, the modern muralist project was promoted as a strategy for condensing the national; in the following decade it overflowed north and south of Mexico's official

223

borders, situating itself within the problematic of cultural hegemony on a continental scale. It eventually opened the gateways to a cultural legitimacy that offered a universalist alternative of a different artistic model based on stability amid the changing of the autonomist avant-gardes, a model that distanced itself from the inconstancies of fashion, the market, and the pettiness of private appropriation.

Thanks to massive photographic reproduction, early muralism made an impact in the international press, particularly in the United States, where it served as the cultural opposite of what the U.S. press called revolutionary barbarism. The mural did not function in isolation; a series of exhibitions featuring paintings and prints by professional artists, along with displays of supposedly spontaneous children's painting and sculpture and objects of so-called folk art, played a role in international negotiations. This was a sort of diplomacy without portfolio, which

was joined by the enthusiastic commentary of some U.S. intellectuals and art critics and which laid the groundwork for a cultural prestige that, during the 1930s, encouraged the exodus of a significant number of Mexican artists to the powerful country north of the border. This period marked the transition from the Mexican Renaissance to the Mexican invasion of the United States.

The more conservative sectors of U.S. public opinion viewed the mural project as an intrusion, with more than a hint of some unified communist conspiracy. This interpretation overlooked the background of competition between the painters' particular mythologies and their ideological antagonisms, especially the conspiracy of silence of the Stalinists, led by Siqueiros, against the Trotskyite Rivera. Rivera was able to defend himself against their attacks, thanks to his accumulated prestige and his ability to create a successful pictorial formula

Fig. 250 · David Alfaro Siqueiros, **Tropical America** (rooftop view with Roberto Berdecio in foreground), 1932, fresco applied with air gun on cement, overlooking Olvera Street, Los Angeles, California, photograph courtesy Library, Getty Research Institute, Los Angeles (960094).

for the representatives of large-scale capital, especially Ford and Rockefeller, as patrons of art. Orozco, on the other hand, kept his distance from these ideological controversies, although he was obsessed with his professional rivalry with Rivera, who was the target of his private whisperings.[6]

The iconographic programs, writings, debates, and public declarations of these muralists, each in his own way, attempted to bridge the divide between technological civilization and culture, between the north and the south of the continent. Above all, they tried to map out a zone free of disagreements through the transcendent character of the mural and the shared disposition toward realist art. In a way, the mural project attempted to subdue its adversaries by presenting itself as the only continuation of the great art of the past and by acting as an ethics of aesthetic reception, removed from formalist self-containment but not from the hermeticism of allegory.

In the United States, the extermination of the original inhabitants of the American continent, together with the mechanisms of integration that blurred the differences between immigrants, forestalled any possibility of basing projects on old or new cultural traditions. Because of this, such commonplaces as "cultural vacuum" and "decadence" were applied without hesitation to the United States' mechanical civilization and were echoed throughout much of the country's own intellectual and artistic milieu. To some extent, the mural's aura and the growing interest in the great Mesoamerican tradition contributed to turning attention toward an experience that originated not in Europe but to the south. Nevertheless, the muralists working in the United States never lost their European perspective and considered the United States a necessary intermediating zone because of its art market, its strong network of museums, and the possibilities for international projection.

Although other Mexican muralists worked in the United States during the first half of the twentieth

century, only three remained in the cross-border memory, the not-always harmonious secular trinity of Diego Rivera, David Alfaro Siqueiros, and José Clemente Orozco. During their stay in the United States the three focused on the industrial world and thus modified their archaeological, primitivist, or exotic visions. Although Mexican muralism had previously been a nationalist endeavor, it was now to adopt a continental perspective, seeking universality and moving counter to the European experience, which had been seen as the only valid one until then.

Orozco was the forerunner of this opening of patronage in the United States and of the Mexican artistic presence in that country during its most significant phase, 1930–40. This was a critical period, between the Great Depression and the beginning of World War II; it produced two paradigmatic works in the history of art, Rivera's *Detroit Industry* in the Detroit Institute of the Arts (fig. 215) and Orozco's *The Epic of American Civilization* at Dartmouth College in New Hampshire.

Upon moving to the United States, the mural device changed its logic and did a thematic about-face. In reframing discourses of identity and origin myths as founding propositions for the entire region, the Mexican project attempted to place itself at the center of the struggle for cultural legitimation of the continent. It was to secure a beachhead on the international art scene and in time shattered the Eurocentric blindness, rooted in the Enlightenment, that promoted a vision of America as a degraded continent.

However, in traveling beyond their original borders, the artists south of the Rio Grande left behind their experience of almost exclusive state sponsorship and were forced to seek private, even corporate, patronage, adapting to a different sort of pragmatics. This transplanted muralism maintained, in some cases, its policy of minimizing costs and maximizing artistic surplus value; at Pomona

College, Orozco received only symbolic payments in exchange for transmitting his knowledge of muralism through the very process of creation. Another example is the series of portable panels in which Rivera laid out his mural technique for his 1930–31 exhibition at New York's Museum of Modern Art.

Likewise, the dialogue with U.S. architects was intense, and the problem of introducing murals into modern functionalist structures involved substantial conceptual changes. Orozco's frescoes at the New School for Social Research (1930–31), for example, had the effect of producing a virtual spatiality, creating monumental effects in a space so restricted that even easel paintings would feel cramped there. At the same time, Siqueiros's experience in open-air urban environments opened avenues of techno- logical innovation, as with *Tropical America* (1932), a cement fresco mural painted with an air gun on Olvera Street, Los Angeles, California (fig. 250).

Rivera at the time believed that industrial progress was a necessary precondition for prole- tarian revolution; Orozco, on the other hand, denied this and established a vision that subordinated the machine to art. Siqueiros, the technician, sought to foster an imminent social revolution and promoted mechanical and experimental renewal in expressive media.

Even the ways of addressing the past changed substantially upon contact with the United States. The migrant Orozco put forward a social history of the world, a living history laden with oppositions, whose approach to the past expressed to the industrialized world his underlying desire for an America integrated through art (Dartmouth College, 1932–34). Working within the higher code of art, Orozco issued an ironic negation of history and technological progress.

Orozco's statements erase the schism between art and machine through a conceptual apparatus for imagining possible futures. For him, Mexico and,

by extension, so-called Latin America embodied the cultural face of the artistic, whereas the United States glided down the path of scientific and techni- cal development, a geographic rift resolved only in the dream of continental complementarity, the contemporary creative tradition joined with indus- trial innovation. In this sense in particular, Orozco remained attached to the myth of progress as his source for cultural continuity; this was the Mexican artists' and promoters' founding charter for entering the international cultural arena.

Siqueiros was less concerned with representing machines than he was with employing them directly as an artist. Rivera produced an elegy to the machine age in Detroit and a 1933 mural dedicated to the promises of technological progress and social revolu- tion at the RCA Building at Rockefeller Center (fig. 251). The latter mural met with Rockefeller's censure for its inclusion of a portrait of Lenin, and it is no coincidence that Rivera then began a cycle of murals that presented U.S. history in detail from the perspective of class struggle (New Workers School, 1933).

Hounded by the memory of great historical conflicts and nurtured by the conviction of constant change as a battering ram to progress and moder- nity, the new Mexican realism placed its hopes on the transformative potential of education, the vitality of social forces, and art's capacity to conflate with the nation. It did not fear associating with public powers or accepting public sponsorship. But what made up this key argument for realism, so vehemently defended by the muralists?

Without ignoring its attachment to figuration and referentiality, social realism did not expect to exhaust itself in narrative. On the contrary, far from academic naturalism, it strove to affect the concrete world by having an impact on the viewer's concep- tions and emotions. It was designed as action upon the real, not its phantom; a transformation of social structures, not hollow iconism. It was a realism in

226

search of a critical power for the image, with the ability to lift the artist out of his self-absorption and give society a renewing impetus.

Regarding the antagonism between realists and abstractionists fostered by polarized confrontations, Mexican social realists could draw upon abstract modes. They derived them, however, not from a search for form in and of itself but from social experience, with symbolic collective subjects, personalized in such notions as the people, the masses, class, and proletariat. This realism sought to dynamize the real by taking up caricature as a way of allegorizing the negative forces of history, in the same manner that the European new objectivity employed distortion. Without a doubt, it was Orozco who most used this strategy as a modern pictorial source.

Many indicators lead us to see muralism as dramaturgy, as an art ahead of its time rather than of the past, as modernist history asserts; it is an art waiting for a new society, where it will reach its fullest expression. In any case, the identification of the mural with state art alluded to a future social structure, as yet uncreated, in which the mural

would be one of its foundations. Perhaps this makes muralism one of the most ambitious artistic utopias of the twentieth century, a kind of being in one time in order to speed the coming of another; this is a possible explanation for many of the criticisms that were leveled at the Mexican project, particularly those of anachronism and lack of destination.

We might recapitulate by saying that a para-Western nation like Mexico, where a diversity of cultural frameworks intersected, consolidated its creative identity and established its difference from the perspective of the excluded other, finally taking on the character of an alternative West and giving birth to an artistic offering with its own distinctive seal. Over time, and without meaning to, not only the other (Mexico) but the other's other (the Indian) allowed for the emergence of new hegemonic cultural poles, although the nation that was their source would be excluded from them. The emergence in the United States in the 1970s of a new mural upsurge among Chicanos and their demand for a consolidated identity are clear proof that this type of device was not exhausted but could even

Fig. 251 · Diego Rivera,
Man at the Crossroads, 1933
(May 1933 state), fresco,
RCA Building, Rockefeller Center,
New York (unfinished, destroyed
February 1934), photograph by
Lucienne Bloch, courtesy Old Stage
Studios, Gualala, California.

227

travel from one artistic imaginary to another: from modernity to postmodernity. Of course, there would be clear changes in the mural's function and content corresponding to different social situations.

Without a doubt, the Chicano community is the least closely linked to Orozco among the Mexican artists, despite his having been the one who spent the most time in the United States and who was the most integrated into its cultural scene. The name of José Clemente Orozco has inspired more reverence than stylistic followers. This situation is comparable to his fate in Mexico, at least until very recently, when neoexpressionists and postconceptualists have found in his work a deep, rich source for reflection.

Somehow, Orozco remains the most enigmatic of the muralists; situated in modernity or in postmodernity, he slips away, jumbling his own image. So we go from the character dressed like an office worker to his transfiguration into a damned artist; from the family man to the irate painter; from the emblematic icon of the left-wing radicalism of the 1936 American Artists Congress to the later creator of anti-Semitic sarcasms.

His painting remains even more elusive. We feel the contrast between the early Orozco, who developed a whorehouse aesthetic to expressive limits far beyond academies and avant-gardes, and the later one, melding with the man enveloped in flames, the alter ego of the artist sacrificed on art's altar. After his brothel scenes and most incisive caricatures, Orozco deploys his painting without concessions, leaving bright colors and pleasing forms behind. His brushstrokes preserve what is essential in a form and constitute a kind of pure painting of the real in all its coarseness.

As the pigment crystallizes and solidifies the wall's surface, it produces a pictorial modality that can endure the passing of centuries; its significance, however, is not limited to resisting decay but resides in the permanence of the concept, in the consolidation of the idea. At least this was how Orozco saw it.

His focus as a muralist always took precedence over avant-garde succession, witnessing the death of the previous tendency, the series of displacements that inexorably lead to the affirmation of another modality of progress, the artistic. Nonetheless, in gaining fame and recognition at the same time as the autonomous avant-garde, Orozco coincided temporally with it, although he followed a different trajectory.

From this painter's mural program, we can gain an understanding of artistic modernity as a universe torn away from theological explanation in order to be joined to life, a current form of critical materialism, reoriented through the emotional intensity of the religion of art. The fact is that Orozco's mural philosophy is foreign to the illusion of development and becomes progress without time, a cyclical return or, if one prefers, real permanence in the absolute imaginary of art.

If Rivera looked to the pre-Hispanic past and heavy industry to construct the collectivities of the future, and Siqueiros went the way of the new state's machinist utopia and its mechanical art, Orozco, for his part, disenchanted with social utopias, held out a ray of hope in the purifying power of art.

Even within his disappointment in the illusion of modernity, we must recognize that Orozco shared his colleagues' desire to endow their time with a great art, in tune with modernist thought but using a different code, with other poetics and other politics. Orozco projected his work in a dimension of time beyond death, a dimension unattainable except by gods, the dream of so many artists of modernity. He sought to transcend, although it might require a great physical strain. The Mexican muralists kept alive a great Western tradition, that of art with great aspirations, which took on the quality of an event amid the rhythm of everyday life. In contrast with domestic painting, the mural was the modern and commemorative form of the polis, associated with politics in its broadest sense, a constructive element of the state and its collective imaginaries.

In the last third of the twentieth century, as almost all the great ideological paradigms crumbled, the desire to deterritorialize imaginaries erases borders and mixes times and cultural universes, resulting in the mixing of individuals and collectivities, a true bricolage of the homogenizing spirit. No image brings us so near those apocalyptic landscapes of fusion and deterioration as do the trash heaps of history piled with obsolete emblems that Orozco depicts in his murals. This is a nihilism that some identify with the disenchanted mood we now call postmodernity, in spite of the fact that Orozco shared the previous imaginary, that of modernity, which partook of its own mixture of visual arts traditions.

Still, it may be asked whether the mural, founded on paradigmatic conceptions of art as a higher expression and of the state and large corporations as the modern entities that foster its existence, will not end up as part of this landscape of ruins figured by Orozco and whether the new contributions, from other collectivities and other sensibilities, will be able to overcome the totalitarian principle of the monument, by means of a public art founded on a more habitable and plural economy of the gaze.

Works Consulted

Anderson, Benedict. *Comunidades imaginadas.* Mexico City: FCE, 1993.

Baczko, Bronislaw. *Los imaginarios sociales.* Buenos Aires: Nueva Visión, 1991.

Castoriadis, Cornelius. *La institución imaginaria de la sociedad.* Barcelona: Tusquets, vol. 1, 1983; vol. 2, 1989.

Deleuse, Gilles. "Qué es un dispositivo." *Michel Foucault filósofo.* Barcelona: Gedisa, 1990.

Deleuse, Gilles, and Félix Guattari. *El anti-Edipo: Capitalismo y esquizofrenia.* Mexico City: Paidós, 1996.

Foucault, Michel. "Lenguaje y literatura," *De lenguaje y literatura.* Barcelona: Paidós, 1996.

———. "El juego de Michel Foucault," *El discurso del poder.* Mexico City: Folio Ediciones, 1983.

———. "El sujeto y el poder." *Revista Mexicana de Sociología,* vol. 2, no. 3 (July–September 1988), IIS-UNAM.

———. "Prólogo," in Jeremy Bentham, *El panóptico.* Mexico City: Premia, 1995.

García Canal, María Inés. "La noción de dispositivo en Michel Foucault," unpublished manuscript.

Against the Laocoon:
Orozco and History Painting

Rita Eder

The current notion of Mexican muralism as an ensemble of images of great visual and symbolic complexity, a laboratory in which meanings are constructed, owes much to certain iconological studies that have emerged over the last twenty years.[1] What may justly be called a new vision of this cultural movement has placed in doubt ideological interpretations that read the murals transparently, seeing them as the representation of historical and political themes bound to the social process of the Mexican Revolution of 1910. These interpretations have been useful to foreground muralism as an effective means to promote radical ideals while functioning as a state art that justifies its own participation in the construction of a new national identity. "In the last thirty years," wrote Octavio Paz in 1986, "the history of muralism has been reduced to the lineal development of one idea, one aesthetics and one objective." The poet gives responsibility for this simplification to critics and historians of supposed Marxist orientations on the one hand and to official ideology on the other.[2]

Against Politics: Humanism in the
Web of the Avant-garde

In the mid-twentieth century, certain critics sought to differentiate José Clemente Orozco from Diego Rivera and David Alfaro Siqueiros.[3] To Luis Cardoza y Aragón, "Orozco transformed his thoughts into emotion, and his emotion moves us and makes us think. Rivera and Siqueiros preached so that their ideas would become ideology. They proposed a system, while Orozco brought the parable of the destruction of the cross to all realms, to all ideologies."[4] The painter from Jalisco earned a growing reputation as the foremost modern artist of humanistic and universal ideals, one who was conscious of the necessary separation between art and ideology, between the properly artistic and the literary or narrative. The importance of the formal analysis of

Orozco's work gained much ground, as did the notion of his work as inexplicable: "Few artists were more sibylline in content and in form...few were more enigmatic. He was concerned with preserving enigmas, enigmas for which he certainly did not have all the keys."[5] The meanings of his complex iconography began to dissolve under the notion of his painting as pure emotion and mystery that in the wake of romanticism only the artist was able to produce. These qualities coincided with the European post-avant-gardism of the 1940s that Clement Greenberg characterized as the academic trap into which French artists had fallen while trying to emphasize expression and emotion at the expense of "coherence of style": "In the face of current events painting feels, apparently, that it must be more than itself: it must be epic poetry, it must be theater, it must be rhetoric, it must be an atomic bomb, it must be the Rights of Man."[6] With this observation, Greenberg points to the modern idea of history painting and the reasons why muralism would be dismissed by the avant-garde. Kirk Varnedoe refers specifically to this question in his text on abstract expressionism included in the catalog of the controversial exhibit *Primitivism and Modern Art*:

> Rivera, Orozco, Siqueiros et al., had been much admired for their revivification of the myths and forms of ancient civilization of their land, and for their use of this heritage as a focus of national unity and social renewal in the 1930s. However, disaffection with this kind of populist archaizing followed a general disenchantment with the Marxism that fostered it (a political shift made more decisive by reaction to the Hitler-Stalin pact of 1939). By 1940, when the Museum of Modern Art celebrated the melding of the archaic and the modern in the exhibition *Twenty Centuries of Mexican Art*, the heyday of the muralists had already passed. Their

rhetorically simplified naturalism, even in its most expressionistic moments, came to seem inadequate to the search of the more cosmic universals of the 1940s.[7]

The cold war and the different uses of culture are clear in Varnedoe's discourse and his compressed opinion of the muralists. Orozco in the 1940s, at the crossroads of the conflict between realism and modernism and its ideological connotations, was claimed by Mexican critics and artists to represent the possibility of a universal humanism, an art without politics, a conviction the artist revealed in his 1942 *An Autobiography:* "No artist has ever had political convictions of any sort. And those who profess to have them are not artists."[8]

How do we interpret such statements when faced with his works that contain ostensible references to the history and politics of his country and that reflect the contemporary climate of war in Europe? His interpretation of the diverse Mexican pasts and the symbolic complexity with which he engaged them suggest that Orozco did indeed address the questions proper to the philosopher and the historian.

The Tasks of History Painting in Muralism and the Western Canon

This essay intends to consider José Clemente Orozco's approach to history. His work in this regard is abundant and occupied him particularly throughout the 1930s. During this time he completed various mural cycles with historical themes, including *The Epic of American Civilization* in Dartmouth College's Baker Library, which he painted between 1932 and 1934 (figs. 156 and following). In 1938 he began what many consider his culminating work, the cycle *The Spanish Conquest of Mexico* at the Hospicio Cabañas in Guadalajara (figs. 164 and 165).

But how do we define history painting, particularly in Mexico during the first half of the twentieth century? Furthermore, how do we envision this problem from the perspective of postmodernity, which questions the notion of history as a grand narrative and opposes pure or Manichaean visions, preferring the complex to the accessible, the ambiguous to the clear?[9]

Part of history painting's role in nineteenth- and early-twentieth-century Mexico was the introduction of a new relationship with the indigenous past, one that is tied, however, to academic classicism. If pre-Columbian antiquity indeed had a totally different aesthetic conceptualization from classicism, the question for muralism became how to approach this antiquity's formal principles within contemporary artistic conceptions. Could muralists distance themselves from Manuel Gamio and his anthropological approach to pre-Hispanic art[10] as well as understand this other sensibility and its will to form? A tension develops in muralism when it confronts the indigenous past that resides in the contradictions between the cultural recognition of the indigenous past and its representation.

Another role for history painting in muralism is the symbolic representation of the new nation that emerges from the revolution. On the one hand, Rivera invented a narrative that corresponds to a utopia of the unified nation and moves toward a linear and progressive vision of history. This vision is characterized by descriptive voracity and a humanism in which each individual retains his physical integrity as an expression of a harmonious vision of the world. On the other hand, Orozco emphasizes the violence of revolution and war and points to the perversity of ideology. Here the narrative works against continuity through rupture and fragmentation. Orozco's sense of composition and symbolic content stages conflicts in the midst of the constrained rhetoric of the unified nation of Mexican liberalism. A product of pragmatism, the

231

unified nation was the main aspiration of political life in Mexico from the middle of the nineteenth century up until the idea of government that followed the armed conflict of 1910.

A third issue of history painting in muralism concerns the question of how to imagine the future and fulfill the social project of the revolution to realize utopia. Here the differences among the most prominent figures in muralism multiply. While his colleagues had a vision of the future, Orozco considered the future a theme of great complexity. His future is presented not as a social utopia but as a renewal of values based upon a great mythological or historical hero. His interpretations are possibly related to the concept of the eternal return contained in Nietzsche's *Zarathustra,* a text, as we shall see below, with which Orozco was familiar.

So how do specific characteristics of this genre in Mexico tie in with the established tradition of history painting as defined by the Western canon? From the times of Alberti, says Rensselaer W. Lee in his classic study *Ut Pictura Poesis: The Humanistic Theory of Painting,*[11] the only painter who deserved the title was one who dedicated himself to historical themes. By history, one here understands the modern or ancient fable, sacred or profane, that liberal studies was able to supply. The Bible and the literary texts of antiquity provided the principal sources of this genre. The history painter was required to be conversant with the works of poets and historians and to pursue relationships with cultured men in order to achieve invention, the academy's most highly regarded attribute.

The painter, like the poet, should study human nature extensively, and knowledge of literature could provide him or her with examples of human actions and the range and intensity of emotions. The French Academy inherited this humanism and, during the seventeenth century, maintained the preeminence of the history painter above those dedicated to still life, landscape, or genre painting.

The artist, like the historian, says André Felibien, should depict great events or, like the poets, themes that please and things capable of adorning, behind the veil of fable, the virtues of great men.

The humanistic theory of painting prevailed for more than two centuries, until the foundation of aesthetics as a discipline and the emergence of archaeology broadened the understanding of antiquity. In the last thirty years of the eighteenth century, Gotthold Ephraim Lessing came to oppose history painters. Influenced by J. J. Winekelmann, he thought the genre inferior because of its emphasis upon expression; a great painter must subordinate everything to the beauty of the body. Another problem for Lessing was history painting's constant use of allegory, whose obscurity and indecipherability he thought made it incapable of interpreting life.[12]

Allegory, History, and Style

Clement Greenberg had Lessing in mind when he defended formalism and abstract art through his repudiation of a humanistic theory of painting. This theory was identified in modern terms with any attempt at figuration or content at the expense of coherence of style. In 1940 Greenberg wrote a short essay, "Towards a Newer Laocoon," inspired by the title of Lessing's work *Laocoon: An Essay on the Limits of Painting and Poetry.*[13] Lessing had spoken of confusion in the field of the arts and of the necessity to focus the field so that the literary would not consume the visual. In his defense of abstract art, Greenberg explored the avant-garde and placed it in opposition to ideas. Given that they were infecting art with the ideological struggles within society, the avant-garde, he thought, needed to escape from ideas. Ideas, for the North American critic, are equivalent to theme. To avoid ideas demanded a greater focus upon form and the affirmation of the arts as independent vocations, disciplines, and

232

respectable fields in and of themselves, rather than as mere vehicles of communication. This was the "revolt against the dominance of literature,"[14] with theme being the most oppressive aspect of painting.

Lessing's old debate and the confusion pertaining to allegory within the visual arts reappeared in the twentieth century in an attitude that represented a fundamental aspect of the avant-garde: its condemnation of realism and the invention of an autonomous visual language free of any text. Orozco, at the other extreme, demonstrated an affinity for certain components of history painting. First of all, he recognized the necessity of allegory in his definition of the distinct technical and visual elements of muralism: "Regarding theme, I can say that it is a group of symbols that convey through their meaning an allegory of Mexican nationality and at the same time represent contemporary man."[15] Secondly, as far as the relationship between idea and theme is concerned, Orozco repeatedly distinguished one from the other, particularly in the text that he prepared for the Dartmouth murals: "In every painting, as in any other work of art, there is always an IDEA, never a STORY. The idea is the point of departure, the first cause of the plastic construction, and it is present all the time as energy creating matter."[16]

Although allegory and the painting of ideas form part of *ut pictura poesis,* in Orozco they acquire a very modern feeling. In *The Origins of the German Tragic Drama,*[17] written in 1925 but not widely available until 1955, Walter Benjamin discusses the notion of allegory, pointing out the difference between allegory and symbol, and develops a detailed argument about its relationships with history. In allegory, history is presented as a primordial and petrified landscape that, since its conception, has been filled with suffering and destined to fail. Its most distinctive iconography is the ruin and the destruction of classical architectural elements.[18] Benjamin's reflections stem from the opposition between classicism and the baroque. The qualities

of the first—harmony and clarity—do not allow for the full development of the idea of allegory that is present in the baroque as a light that momentarily illuminates the darkness. Benjamin unearths the etymological roots that define allegory as "mysterious instruction," a cave or a secret place of invention, a place of the hidden and spectral, the subterranean space buried among ruins and catacombs. The baroque allegory reveals our intuition about the problematic nature of art; its basic character is ambiguity as opposed to the clarity associated with classicism. The importance of this approach to allegory is that it reveals its persistence in the twentieth century as a key concept in the aesthetic debate on the tragic and the hermetic in modern expression. George Steiner points out the connection between the German expressionists and the authors of the German baroque and adds: "Benjamin closes with hints towards a recursive theory of culture: eras of decline resemble each other not only in their vices but also in their strange climate of rhetorical and aesthetic vehemence (the ambience of the *Ursprung* is sometimes that of Spengler). Thus a study of the baroque is no mere antiquarian, archival hobby: it mirrors, it anticipates and helps grasp the dark present."[19] This passage sheds light on some of Orozco's works in which allegory and history are related in the sense that Benjamin proposes.

The consideration of history in Orozco presents complexities in the intertwining of his use of allegory with the problem of style. In this regard, his early interest in dismantling academic classicism and the presence of the baroque in his work deserve further clarification. Justino Fernández addresses this issue when he says that the Prometheus painted by Orozco at Pomona College has elements in common with the style of El Greco, Michelangelo, or Tintoretto.[20] He also defines Orozco's art as simultaneously classical and baroque.[21]

If, in stylistic terms, it is true that the presence of classical composition in Orozco would seem to

structure and block the energy and dynamics of
bodies and forms, then the presence of the baroque
is characterized by an erasure of the limits of
figures and surfaces and by an understanding of the
world as an ever-changing portrait.[22] In this sense,
Orozco's paintings only begin to appear baroque in
the 1930s. Even the Palace of Fine Arts mural
Catharsis, dominated by movement and a welter
of bodies and weapons used to express a particular
human condition, conforms to this definition
(fig. 252). In his *Principles of Art History,* Heinrich
Wölfflin observes that the linear (classicism) and
the pictorial (baroque) correspond to different
perspectives of the world. In the former, we expect
the classical to reveal the solid figure, the permanent form, measurable and finite—the thing itself.
In the latter, it is changing appearances, open form,
and the union of parts that are subordinated to a
dominant theme.[23] In this regard, the historic and
mythological themes in Orozco are constructed
around the omnipresent hero who unifies and gives
meaning to all the parts; for example, Hidalgo in
the government building in Guadalajara (fig. 253)
or Juárez in the murals of the Chapultepec Castle,
Mexico City.

If the opposition between classicism and the
baroque was a fundamental theme of art history and
German cultural criticism in the first three decades
of the twentieth century, this interest has reemerged
in the guise of postmodernity. Omar Calabrese[24]
ponders the aesthetic taste predominant in our time,
one that is seemingly confused, fragmented, and
indecipherable. He proposes the term "neobaroque"
to describe different cultural phenomena in recent
times: The sciences speak of catastrophes, fractals,
and the theories of chaos; in the social sphere, there
is reference to the loss of integrity, globalism, and
mutability. In film and television series, Calabrese
also finds an arguably baroque response to a
changing and uncertain world. Similarly, the decade
of the 1930s, when Orozco deploys certain elements

of the baroque in his painting, is a moment of great
economic and political crisis. This style, emerging
toward the end of the sixteenth century, becomes a
resource that allows him, through allegory, to provide
an assessment of his time.

However, his work goes beyond the baroque
and is grounded in a pathos and exaggeration
of form that link it to expressionism. Octavio Paz
has defined Orozco's work in stylistic terms as
a transgressor of expressionism, but all the same,
according to the poet and critic, his aesthetic is
rooted in this artistic movement, which he defines
in a broad sense and which includes Grünewald,
Goya, El Greco, and Michelangelo. Paz also notes

Fig. 252 · **Catharsis**, 1934, fresco,
Palace of Fine Arts, Mexico City,
photograph by Bob Schalkwijk.

that Orozco might not have been a follower of the modern expressionists, but they certainly influenced his formal vocabulary.[25]

A look at the graphic work of Max Beckmann indeed reveals a kinship with Orozco in formal and expressive intentions. Perhaps it is not a matter of establishing who influenced whom but of detecting these affinities in the traces and treatment of certain themes that interested both artists: the circus, politics as parody, the reinterpretation of certain Christian themes, and, most of all, feminine sexuality as a forceful response to classical values. "Harmony" and "virtue" are replaced by a nudity that makes itself vulnerable in its deformity. At the same time, this

deformity generates monstrosity and introduces the sexualization of power in the link between the prostitute and domination, between the phallic side of woman and the image of militarization as a feminized man. The affinities with expressionism are not restricted to Beckmann. Of the two phases of this long-standing German artistic movement— on the one hand, the time just before World War I, when expressionism was tied to the avant-garde and the Paris school; on the other, expressionism as a political movement and phenomenon of war that produced, between 1914 and 1919, enormous quantities of engravings, posters, drawings, and paintings on the theme of the war industry and its victims—

it is the second to which Orozco shows strong affinities.[26] Here war scenes proliferated: dynamic landscapes reeking of gunpowder and death, the injured and the mutilated, anguished and distorted faces, the critical and grotesque portraits of the bourgeoisie and the military. Even if none of his texts acknowledges his interest in German art of the twenties and thirties, it is evident in his interest in the films of Fritz Lang and his familiarity with the painters and engravers associated with expressionism.[27] Beckmann and Otto Dix held exhibits in New York at the time Orozco was living there, and it is certainly possible that he was aware of these artists. It is this climate of war and destruction, the suffering body and cynical gestures, that would have impressed him.

Dartmouth: Between Hermeticism and the End of History

Muralism, like history painting, is complicated by its double language, one that is at once a public utterance and a kind of secret code, as much symbolic as formal. As noted earlier, recent scholarship has found this secret code to relate to theosophy and Masonic and Rosicrucian esotericism. Such studies have introduced to the reading of muralism a rich iconological alternative. Even earlier, a 1938 text by the poet and writer José Gorostiza referred to the "arid hermeticism" of mural painting; he complained of excessive realism at the same time as he condemned its secret codes.[28] Gorostiza's text provides an important early clue to observations, shared by his group of intellectuals, that the muralists were in fact aware of and used hermetic symbols in their works.

An esoteric interpretation of Orozco's art from an art historical perspective was undertaken for the first time in the early 1980s by Fausto Ramírez in his already classic work *Artistas e iniciados en la obra mural de Orozco.*[29] Ramírez convincingly

demonstrates the possibility that theosophic thought was deeply rooted in the cultural milieu of Mexico during the first decades of the twentieth century. He introduces the uneasiness within the double reading of Orozco's images that offers insight into the unity of such an enormously complex and apparently fragmented body of work, particularly the murals at Dartmouth and the Hospicio Cabañas.

To take up this thread in recent scholarship, for his analysis of the murals at Dartmouth College Renato González Mello was guided by a text[30] in

Fig. 253 · **Hidalgo**, 1937, fresco, Government Palace, Guadalajara, photograph by Bob Schalkwijk.

which Orozco affirms the primacy of the idea in all pictorial work. He proposes that there is an attempt to undermine the process of narration through means of the idea and that this is equivalent to allegory and to esoteric allegory in particular. He takes into account the axial relationships between the panels, viewing locations, and the position of the panels according to cardinal points. The names of the murals begin to acquire other meanings: Migrations and sacrifices are associated with rites or stages of an initiate in a secret ceremony. Sacrifices, as in the pre-Hispanic world depicted in *Ancient Human Sacrifice* (fig. 169), as well as such images as the birthing skeleton in *Gods of the Modern World* (fig. 183), are tied to the idea of anatomical exploration as a rite of passage, as an initiation.

The panel depicting Christ destroying his cross at the far left of this section, titled *Modern Migration of the Spirit* (fig. 254), is the key image in this regard. Christ confronts the spectator with ax in hand, with the open and enormous eyes of the enlightened initiate, already in possession of a sense of order. Christ gazes toward the other end of the room where men again embark on the path toward spiritual elevation (*Migration* [fig. 167]), related to the idea of the eternal return discussed by Nietzsche. This is well illustrated in the first half of the cycle in the myth of Quetzalcoatl, the civilizer who would return to reconstruct a new golden age.[31]

As this suggests, there are several ways of connecting Orozco's work with hermetic interpretations. One is the Masonic and Rosicrucian example mentioned above; another is through Benjamin's baroque allegory; a third is through Nietzschean concepts. The idea of the hermetic as a historical phenomenon held sway in many realms of interwar culture. In the case of Benjamin, says Steiner, there is a plea "for the rights of the esoteric. It is not only his material, the neglected plays and emblem collections of the German seventeenth century, that is esoteric; it is his critical task."[32] It is worth reflecting

Fig. 254 · **Modern Migration of the Spirit** from **The Epic of American Civilization**, 1932–34, fresco, reserve reading room, Baker Library, Dartmouth College, Hanover, New Hampshire.

237

further upon *Modern Migration of the Spirit* with this in mind. Behind the central figure of the martyred Christ with ax in hand is chaos, a pyramidal composition from which jut the mouths of cannons and rifles that fall crushed as if an earthquake had disrupted an original order. Upon the mountain appear a classical column split in two, a sculpture of Buddha, and a headless classical nude, the three figures echoing the fallen cross in the foreground. We seem to behold a different way of conceiving Christian themes, a transformation of the religious into secular history understood as the world's current agony. Another element is the ruin: The cross, classical order, and harmony appear as an accumulation of fragments. If the ruin is, as Benjamin points out with regard to baroque allegory, the form in which history enters the stage, it is a history that breaks with the idea of classical order as eternal life and, instead, assumes its decay.

The hermetic and the representation of chaos disrupting classical order may also relate to Orozco's familiarity with Nietzsche's fundamental theses from *The Birth of Tragedy* through the gatherings of the Delphic Circle, of which he was a member between 1928 and 1931. His *Prometheus* mural at Pomona College (fig. 110), based on Aeschylus's tragedy, is the first example of this influence insofar as the mythic character's body contains a synthesis of diverse emotions; the Dionysian chaos seems to overwhelm Apollonian classical order.

In this regard, the Dartmouth mural together with *Prometheus* at Pomona College reveal a turning point in Orozco's classicism. Perhaps one point of departure here was his discovery of El Greco at New York's Metropolitan Museum of Art; Orozco began to embrace a gradual anticlassicism that can also be connected to his interest in Nietzsche and his attitude toward ancient Greece, a topic widely discussed in the Delphic Circle. It was here that the artist met Emily Hamblen, English translator of the German philosopher and author of *Friedrich Nietzsche, and His New Gospel*. According to Gianni Vattimo, Nietzsche's initial impact "was more 'literary' or more generically cultural (in the sense of critique of culture, of reflection upon ideologies) than properly philosophical."[33] The title of Hamblen's 1911 book already indicates her spiritualist vision of Nietzsche as a prophet of modernity. Her work is dedicated to presenting a Nietzsche whose nihilism is misunderstood and to defending the symbolic and poetic form of his philosophy in *Zarathustra*.[34] *Zarathustra* is the philosopher's masterwork, in which he creates the world anew; the possibility of man's progress is located in his capacity to transform his consciousness. For Hamblen, *Zarathustra* is an allegory, and its fundamental theme is the eternal return. This is the search for the meaning of religious and metaphysical life, the pursuit of truth in culture, the deconstruction of history and of the horrible things that lie in caves. In this search, the spirit descends more deeply into itself and follows the tragic history of its own development. But the search ends in a single contin-

uous and indissoluble principle: the creative will that saves, redeems, and explains life.[35] What may have interested Orozco in this gospel is its critical vision of culture, religion, history, and all the values that redeem themselves in the creative principle. The eternal return is the capacity of man to question all values so that he may remake himself.

In *The Birth of Tragedy*, the other important Nietzsche text for the Delphic Circle, the philosopher, according to Vattimo,[36] questions the image of the Greek dominated by the idea of harmony, beauty, and equilibrium, which is identified with the classical and with one moment alone in Greek culture, fifth-century Athens. Christianity played a fundamental role in this image, which fixed antiquity within classical features already considered decadent and no longer vital. Here the Apollonian impulse, identified with the classical, tends to produce defined images, harmonious and stable forms; the Dionysian impulse embodies sensitivity toward the chaos of existence and the drive to submerge oneself in this chaos. For Nietzsche, the Apollonian and the Dionysian establish a power relationship within the individual. Human culture is the fruit of the dialectical game between these two artistic impulses that culminates in the Attic tragedy that emerges from the satyr's Dionysian chorus.[37] Thus the vitality of Greek culture falls outside the field of the arts and survives in popular wisdom, the tragic myths, and the diffusion of orgiastic myths.

Orozco's great doubt concerning both indigenous civilizations and modernity is related to the image received through his academic training of the Greeks as capable of producing beautiful works because they themselves were beautiful, harmonious, and serene. As a result, his images became progressively more expressionist and fragmented to the point of focusing upon a single corporeal element, the head without a body, the body without a face, or the body as a large mouth. He incorporates automatons and monsters, and one wonders if he did not intend to demolish the edifice of Apollonian culture stone by stone in order to highlight the other principle within it—that is, the Dionysian.

Not only did the tension between the Apollonian and the Dionysian problematize a visual language capable of speaking eloquently about the state of the world in the interwar period, but to a great extent, related to the notion of the past, in particular the pre-Hispanic past and its impressive monuments and sculptures. But how to approach this world from its own aesthetic perspective? Edmundo O'Gorman offers an interpretation in "El arte o de la monstruosidad,"[38] published in 1940. In this essay the Mexican historian addresses the spiritual relationship between contemporary Western sensibilities and the artistic world of the ancient Mexicans. The problem, according to O'Gorman, is how we react when faced with a world that is historically foreign. "When in the first third of the sixteenth century Europeans were able to contemplate the monumental statues of the ancient Mexicans, they could only be impressed by their ugliness. As men of the Renaissance, they were incapable of approaching this mythic world populated by stone monsters."[39] The concept of the monstrous provides the fundamental key to ancient Mexican art and art in general—that is, its conception as something outside the natural order. O'Gorman's dialogue is with classical Greece, with the Apollonian that corresponds to an ordered and rational vision of nature in which any interference means confronting the ominous and the alien. The motivation for these reflections is O'Gorman's encounter with the figure of Coatlicue, of which he says, "what first delights the mind with the impetus of the inevitable is its ominous monstrosity." This category, according to O'Gorman, can lead to a theory of art that questions Greek antiquity. In it "a gigantic fraud is uncovered because they represent the supreme and best-hidden disguise of the ordered and rational spirit so characteristic of the Hellenic mentality. It is the disguise

of masked reason whose very nature is irrational."[40] If the principal theme of Greek sculpture is the myth, the Greek classical world is artificial because it recognizes, as a fundamental law, the horror when faced with deformation or monstrosity. O'Gorman's article is historical testimony that attempts to ground an aesthetic approach to pre-Hispanic art. He finds a resource in the deconstruction of the classical through what it conceals, which could be defined as the Dionysian. The article is further evidence of the diffusion of ideas found in *The Birth of Tragedy*.

The importance for understanding Orozco's work of the Apollonian and Dionysian and particularly of their relationship to the ruin is suggested in his autobiography. He noted the strong impression made by his visit to Pompeii and the Villa of Mysteries during a 1932 summer trip to Europe in the early stages of the Dartmouth commission: "I learned much, much, of the art of painting. The streets of the dead city and the bodies still imprisoned in lava. The frescoes and the mosaics in the houses and the shops."[41] Orozco's descriptions of Pompeii convey history as ruins, the past, petrified by a natural disaster, unfolding before the eyes of the artist like a dramatic scene. The painter admired the groups of murals there for their relationship to the architecture and perceived Pompeii's influence in the understanding of antiquity as a ruin, a remnant of the ancient world. On the other hand, the Villa of Mysteries suggested to him the Dionysian rites and initiations that have contributed a truly complete picture of classical antiquity. Here Dionysian energy finds order in images that contain a secret code, divining arts and rites of passage. The murals presided over by a female figure, harmonious of body and ominous of face, recall the definition of tragedy in which the Dionysian is the opening of one body into another that is finally resolved in Apollonian images. This sort of rupture of one narrative sequence in favor of another recalls the sometimes chaotic mixing of themes and scenes in the Dartmouth murals.

239

This conflict and resolution of opposing forces and the appearance of catastrophe carry through Orozco's work in his fidelity to the image of history as a landscape of ruins, one particularly victimized by technology and the malignant power of the machine. In a previous article, I identified the relationship between the ideas of Lewis Mumford, promoter of Orozco at Dartmouth, and the artist's murals.[42] This relationship evolved from what I considered Orozco's profound interest in the mechanical and technological eras. This is evident in the way he approaches popular explanations for the conquest of Mexico, a disparate collection of myths that embraces both the theme of the prophecy and return of Quetzalcoatl, as well as the characteristics of the war technology used by the Spaniards. Orozco's attraction to mechanical forms suggested his paradoxical relationship to the menacing beauty of the machine. These factors also overlapped with the views of Lewis Mumford, the author of *Technics and Civilization,* who, in the inaugural ceremony at Baker Library, affirmed that the Dartmouth murals were an embodiment of the first fifteen chapters of his book.

In addressing both the pre-Hispanic past and the modern world, Orozco's Dartmouth murals are

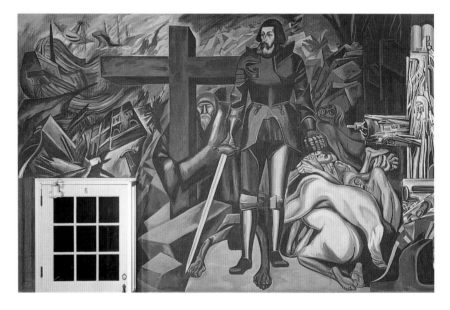

disconcerting because they do not display a clear progression of actions; rather, they present distinct scenes that coexist uncomfortably because of different historical eras and styles. Their modernity dwells in the visual paradoxes produced by the atmosphere of pre-Hispanic antiquity, wrapped in the silence of its mythic cities, in the rhythm of the elements and the cultivation of the earth and the arts ruled over by Quetzalcoatl and an ensemble of deities whose magical air is accentuated by their colored masks and the provocative tufts of feathers swaying in the wind (figs. 167–173). The panels

Fig. 255 · **Cortez and the Cross** from **The Epic of American Civilization**, 1932–34, fresco, reserve reading room, Baker Library, Dartmouth College, Hanover, New Hampshire.

Fig. 256 · **Mechanical Horse**, 1937–39, fresco, Hospicio Cabañas, Guadalajara, photograph by Bob Schalkwijk.

240

addressing the pre-Hispanic era close with Quetzalcoatl as a prophet surrounded by serpents of diverse forms, energies, and expressions. Orozco introduces us to the disorder and conflict of a past, oscillating between different illuminations, hours of the day, or moments in its history. There is the impression of a sunrise, but also of a dark and silent place. In contrast with the strident palette that complicates and distances our approach, the mythical aspects of this world are embodied in a mood, and one has the unavoidable sensation that something is hidden behind these images.

In contrast, the panel addressing the conquest (*Cortez and the Cross* [fig. 255]) draws one's attention because Orozco constructs an image of synthesis. Just as Quetzalcoatl, the god and the hero of culture, presides over the pre-Hispanic world, so Cortez and his gigantic figure, automata, and armor embody the conquest. Orozco, according to Mumford, had rightly established the relationship between militarism, the machine, and capitalism in portraying a Cortez of harsh and metallic deeds and a machine that feeds upon indigenous people. What triumphs in Mexico at the time of the conquest is an economic system imposed by a kind of mechanized totalitarianism whose principal characteristic is exploitation. The drive and development of the machine, according to Mumford, originate in the soldier, whose antecedent is the primitive hunter. Even though, at one point, the primordial impulse of the hunt was to provide nourishment, it progressively developed a repertoire of tools (arrowheads, spears, knives) and certain tactics (the surprise attack, fire) that would be utilized for war. "How far," asks this author, "shall one go back in demonstrating the fact that war has been perhaps the chief propagator of the machine?"[43]

Mumford's observations in relation to Cortez are also pertinent to the vision of the conquest that appears in the Hospicio Cabañas murals. Here the painter invents a new way of representing Cortez as

a great mechanical figure and extends similar characteristics to the horse, transforming its naturalness into an instrument of war (fig. 256). Likewise, at Dartmouth the panel *Anglo-America,* which occupies the center of the wall devoted to the modern world initiated by the mannerist image of Cortez, is paired with the soldier portrayed in the panel *Hispano-America* (figs. 181 and 182). The soldier's disproportionate size and automated aspect represent a version of the machine's destruction in another temporal and ethnic reality and within a particular civilizing process. The teacher in *Anglo-America* seems to be the incarnation of the relationship between industrialization and the loss of humanity, society as a bureaucratic machine dispossessed of individuality. Ultimately, this is also the vision of the Uruguayan writer José Enrique Rodó of an America that is spiritually lacking and materialistic, seen in light of Mumford's vision, and Orozco's, of Hispano-América: A Zapata who is surrounded by the caricatured alliance among capital, the military, and war technology, yet whose great vital instinct and integrity are highlighted by the chaos that surrounds him.

The Dartmouth mural is, among other things, the decomposition of an order. In the vision or revision of the past, there is a critical attitude toward the present that explains the sequence that begins with Cortez, who dominates through the brute force of war and technology, and ends with the panel that may well be understood as the death of culture (*Gods of the Modern World* [fig. 183]). Presented within a university setting, the cadaver surrounded by skeletal academics in togas, witnessing the birth of another of their kind, could well be interpreted as a critique of culture.

As I have suggested, there is certainly a tension in the absence of an order or linear sequence in the Dartmouth mural. Not only has it disrupted a sense of narrative in which one scene passes logically to another, but it also presents us with a group of

241

scenes that could be understood as a series of independent paintings or as scenes in a theatrical work.
However, it seems more likely that this particular
way of structuring the mural was conceived as an
alternation between allegory and direct reference to
the current times.

In the wake of the Dartmouth mural, Orozco's
critical perspective on ideologies over the course of
his work—from his views concerning the revolution, particularly in the mural *Catharsis* (1934) in the
Palace of Fine Arts to his *Political Circus* (1937–38)
in Guadalajara—reveals a growing regard for the
idea of the end of history. According to Perry
Anderson,[44] the first modern antecedent of the end
of history is a group of Franco-German thinkers,
including Benjamin, who in the years between the
Popular Front and the Marshall Plan suggested that
the end of history was imminent. This was an inversion of optimist theories of history in the eighteenth
and the first half of the nineteenth centuries that
foresaw universal peace, liberty, and fraternity as the
ultimate goals of human progress. Until World War
II, revolutionary ambitions remained strong among
these theorists of posthistory. Their subsequent loss
of faith in progress or collective change led to a
cultural pessimism that saw only petrification and
consumption in the Western democracies established after World War II. Posthistorians were the
products of a deep disappointment with modernity
and thus adopted the role of solitary prophets. One
cannot help recalling Orozco's self-portrait of 1943,
his enormous eyes gazing hypnotically from behind
his glasses, the idea of the artist as a privileged seer
bound to theosophy but also placed before history
as a prophet of catastrophe and critic of culture.
His final appraisals of the destruction of humankind
by technology and war are also coherent with the
vision of posthistory.

242

Conclusion

Orozco's statements and autobiography reveal his
profound interest in Pompeii and classical antiquity.
This theater of ruins influenced his vision of
modern warfare, which connects in various ways to
Benjamin's concept of allegory, in which history
is presented as a primordial and petrified landscape
with the ruin as its most distinctive iconography.
Orozco's gradual abandonment of academic classicism in the late 1920s and his transit to the baroque
and expressionism in the 1930s were interpreted
by the modernist mentality as residual expressions
of the nineteenth century. The story of the dispute
between the humanistic theory of painting and
Lessing's call for a painting free of allegory repeated
itself in the twentieth century in the guise of the
realism versus modernism conflict. However,
establishing connections between Orozco's work
and Benjamin's concept of baroque allegory casts
a different light on the definition of modernity.
Orozco's years in the United States were certainly
definitive in effecting this transition. It was there
that he developed the theme of the aesthetics of the
machine and its evil nature, deeply entwined with
war and capitalism. We can see, during his years in
New York and particularly in the Dartmouth mural,
the artist's encounter with a more complex and
dynamic possibility in the use of allegory as hermetic
and tragic, both key concepts in the aesthetic debate
of the first half of the twentieth century.

On the other hand, Orozco's turn from classicism has its roots in his discovery of expressionism
and his interest in Nietzsche and *The Birth of
Tragedy,* the text widely discussed in the gatherings
of the Delphic Circle. The tension between the
Apollonian and Dionysian seemed to re-create a
visual language capable of speaking eloquently
about the state of the world in the interwar period.
However, a more urgent issue involves possible

clues to the interpretation of pre-Hispanic culture and attempts to approach that world from its own aesthetic perspective. In this sense, the lure of *The Birth of Tragedy* among Mexican intellectuals becomes clear: The Dionysian, in contraposition to the Apollonian, seemed to legitimize the sense of estrangement vis-à-vis a past and its objects, which in theory were part of the configuration of the modern Mexican nation-state.

Orozco's images fluctuate between the remnants of his academic training and a sense of the modern, between the tragic and the ironic, between historical references and allegorical symbols. His mural painting, at Dartmouth in particular, becomes a space of ambiguous tension among scenes that momentarily evoke classicism as moments of truth and repose contrasted with convulsive or distorted forms related to the pathos of modernism and its alliance with technology. The extreme complexity and hidden qualities of his work are also a sign of a colonial condition that rebels against domination. There is much evidence of Orozco's rebellion against European influence or other models in painting during his years of academic training, as well as his desire to create a lasting artistic legacy. Together with Rivera and Siquieros, Orozco was determined to make mural-ism a contribution to Western painting, not only through a new public art but also through a modern paradigm of history painting.

Their primary questions were artistic language and the urgent need for valid models. His painting, polyvalent and excessive, explored the history of art in permanent tension between the construction of a national artistic identity and his attraction for Western myths and models. Perhaps explaining Orozco's painting from the perspective of German thought is part of a similar operation, the search for meaning by following the steps in his peculiar way of envisioning the national.

Orozco and Modern (Easel) Painting:
New York, 1927–34

Dawn Ades

In 1926, the year before he departed Mexico for a long sojourn in the United States, Orozco answered a questionnaire in the first issue of the arts review *Forma*. There were three questions: Why is the current movement in Mexican painting important? What are the principal influences of foreign art on the present development of Mexican painting? What should the sources of teaching be for Mexican art? Orozco's answers are characteristic in their mixture of confidence, dry humor, and irritation. Painting in Mexico has always been important, he writes, before as well as after the conquest, and it should recognize its own supremacy and compare its own production with "the abominable export painting sent us by Europe, with various labels, at so much the dozen…." The principal foreign influences are from Spain, Italy, and France, because these are the countries visited by Mexican artists; the day they go to India, Russia, and China, there will be Hindu, Russian, and Chinese influences. The only source for the plastic arts, he concludes, should be "Nature itself, as it is."[1]

There are few clues here to any interest Orozco might have in contemporary developments outside Mexico. There is no sense of a center of gravity for modern art outside Mexico, an "international" modernism with which he felt any affinity, or of a significant difference between mural and easel painting. His replies underline his absolute independence of thought, his strong commitment to Mexico, and his rejection of foreign "styles."

The last statement, in which he claims nature as the true model for artists, may seem too vague to offer any serious purchase on his thinking. However, it has certain negative implications that echo the sentiments of two texts of 1923, unpublished in his lifetime, which constituted a violent rejection not just of the picturesque and indigenist tendencies in Mexican painting but also of all art that placed subject matter, message, or propaganda above the pure fact of painting. To reclaim "nature" in this context may owe something to a belated nineteenth-century aesthetic piety, but it is also a reassertion of certain values outside style, free from propaganda and opening onto a modern search for a fundamental "nature of painting." Orozco's passionate assertion, in his 1923 texts, of the integrity and independence of painting as such is paradoxically expressed in terms that recall those of one of the founding texts of modernism, the highly influential tract by Albert Gleizes and Jean Metzinger, "Du cubisme," of 1912. I say "paradoxically" because Orozco also explicitly rejects cubism as "formula painting": "Painting that is not understood is pseudo-cubist painting [—] that is [,] painting done with so-called scientific formulas, imported from Paris. Such 'painting' is not understood by anyone, not even the one who does it."[2] Whether or not Orozco knew of this essay, his ideas share some of its basic assertions—for instance, that painting no longer imitates but creates its own reality. Gleizes and Metzinger believed not that they were advancing a new "style" for painting but that they were describing what modern painting now was, "the only possible conception of pictorial art," without excluding what it might also become. "A painting carries within itself its raison d'être…. Essentially independent, necessarily complete, it need not immediately satisfy the mind: on the contrary, it should lead it, little by little, toward the imaginative depths where burns the light of organization. It does not harmonize with this or that ensemble, it harmonizes with the totality of things, with the universe: it is an organism."[3] In his "Notes on the Early Frescoes…" Orozco writes: "A painting should not be a commentary but the fact itself; not a reflection but light itself; not an interpretation but the thing to be interpreted."[4] Arriving independently at this view, Orozco obviously differs from Gleizes and Metzinger in not envisaging a tension between the rejection of imitation and total abstraction. Gleizes and Metzinger foresaw the possibility, even the inevitability, of an abstract art: "[T]he reminiscence of natural forms cannot be absolutely banished; as yet at all events. An art cannot be raised all at once to the level of a pure effusion."[5] For Orozco, the fact of the painting, although it should no longer be reflection or imitation, was not seen primarily in terms of abstraction versus figuration. How he, with his interests fundamentally in mural painting and all that entails of a fixed site and purposive relation to the public, was to explore the—for him—lesser art of easel painting is one of the intriguing aspects of his sojourn in New York.

The easel paintings done in New York between 1927 and 1934 present a fascinating problem, partly because of their diversity and their ambiguous relationship with modernism. There are three broad groups of works in this period: those that respond to the place and the people of the city, those that treat Mexico and Mexican subjects, and those, less classifiable in terms of subject, that appear to engage with more imaginative, invented subjects. The latter have been described as surrealist,[6] but there is no evidence that Orozco had any interest in surrealism or that the genesis of these works is related in any way to that movement. If the subjects are diverse, there is nonetheless a much greater consistency than there might appear in terms of Orozco's approach to his painting and to the problem of form, which resolves itself in a very interesting way in relation to the modernist tensions between abstraction and figuration. Although this is not for Orozco the key problem, as it was for many European artists of the period, the manner in which he approaches the question of a "new art" leads him in practice to a highly individual as well as prophetic form of modernism.

There is no easy means of situating Orozco's work in relation to the dominant impulses in modern art during his stay in New York. His proclivities distance him from the "isms" of modernism. He never aligns himself with any specific tendency, and his enthusiasms and dislikes tend to center on individual artists rather than isms, while at the same time he is more interested in overarching aesthetic and plastic issues than in competing claims for any modern style. But his independence was not that of a recluse; on the contrary, he set out to inform himself as fully as possible about the painting of all ages. In New York, Orozco energetically visited museums and exhibitions, judging according to his own values. He liked Renoir and Matisse, was initially lukewarm about Picasso, and hated de Chirico, who, he writes, resorts to camouflage, tricks, is "extravagance, and farce, in short: very daring (?) but *nothing*."[7] The painter who most moved him was Seurat, whom he regarded as a man "pure of heart," his works so full of light that that they were almost religious in their effect. Coming again across Picasso, he found his drawings "like a glass of clear water" after so many tired and mediocre gallery shows. He loved a self-portrait by Rouault, was intrigued by the delicate paintings of Jacques Villon (Duchamp's "cubist" brother), and never wanted to see another Degas. But modern painting was of no special interest to him, and he did not seek to situate himself in relation to its trends. His judgments were just as freely and urgently expressed about earlier art: Ingres was admirable but of the "dead past," while Titian was the "living past."[8] An exhibition of Spanish art at the Metropolitan enthralled him, and Goya and El Greco were to remain of great importance for his work. On his one visit to Europe in 1932, his priorities were to see the great European works, such as Raphael's cartoons at the Victoria and Albert Museum.

Although Orozco joked to Charlot about the difference he felt between the "pure painting" of the Paris artists like Matisse and Derain, nourished in tea parties in the garden and society salons, and "us, revolutionaries, dying of hunger,"[9] the prominence of Mexican art on the modern art stage in the United States during the 1920s and 1930s should not be underestimated. The many mural projects by

245

Fig. 257 · **Mexican Pueblo**, 1932, oil on canvas, Detroit Institute of Arts, Founders Society Purchase, General Membership Fund; 42.103, photograph © 1999 Detroit Institute of Arts.

246

indigenous U.S. artists looked to Mexico for their models, and both Rivera and Orozco of course had their own commissions. Modern art in the United States was at this point embodied as much by Diego Rivera as it was by Picasso and Matisse.[10] But from Orozco's perspective, the situation was problematic because Rivera's ascendancy fostered a view of Mexican art that, as Orozco's letters to Charlot confirm, was governed by political, picturesque, and indigenous values of which he deeply disapproved. Everyone talks of Rivera, Orozco growls to Charlot; he would hope, on the contrary, that every Mexican artist would be valued in his own right and not for "*lo exotico-pintoresco-renacentista-mexicano-Riveriano.*"[11]

Orozco's position on this was abundantly clear but is worth stressing because his rejection of Rivera's "political-picturesque" Mexico did not entail a renunciation of Mexico as a key player in modern art. His 1929 manifesto "New World, New Races and New Art" called for an art dependent neither on the Old World nor on "the aboriginal traditions of

…our ancient indian peoples."[12] In fact, the architecture of Manhattan was the "new value" that should set the direction for the new art: "[P]ainting and sculpture must certainly follow." He was writing as a "New World" artist—in other words, for Mexico as much as for art in the United States. His "Mexican" subjects of this period could perhaps also be looked at in this light; they were dramatic, dynamic, and antipicturesque (figs. 257 and 258). Although the landscapes, people, and houses clearly signified "Mexico" and as such appealed to the U.S. market, they shared with his other paintings of the period the urge to find an expressive and constructive geometry independent of subject. His agaves, for instance, took on an almost architectural quality, which found an echo in later work by Ferdinand Léger.

Manhattan seems to have figured modernity for Orozco at this point, in both its positive and negative aspects. The crash of 1929 was inevitably to foreground the latter, but the natural formal parity between pictorial structure and modern architecture, in the form of bridges, subways, the elevated railway (el), and skyscrapers, was to be a significant factor in Orozco's thinking about his painting (figs. 15, 53, 54, and 58). His views of American painting are, however, characteristically dismissive. American painters are, he writes to Charlot, dreadful: "The true American artists are those who make the machines."[13] In preferring the machines themselves to art, he unconsciously echoes the views of Marcel Duchamp and Robert Coady of a decade earlier. In 1917 Duchamp had defended his "ready-made" *Fountain* with a little manifesto published in the proto-dada review *The Blind Man,* in which he asserts: "The only works of art America has given are her plumbing and her bridges."[14] Coady, in his review *The Soil,* had similarly drawn comparisons between "modern" sculpture and machines, to the benefit of the latter. Duchamp and Orozco of course drew different conclusions from this perception. Orozco's paintings of the Queensborough Bridge (figs. 259 and 53) and the El seek to translate his emotion in the face of the grandeur of the anonymous feats of engineering, compounded of both exhilaration and humanist dismay, into plastic terms rather than assert, like Duchamp, that the machine and the mass-produced object have superseded the work of art altogether.

Orozco was not interested in molding his art stylistically according to a machine aesthetic, by adopting a dry, engineering type of illusionist representation. With a few exceptions, such as the gouache *The Curb* (fig. 260), which uses stark, Sheelerlike contrasts and sharp geometrical lines, his paintings of the city of New York are somber, loosely painted, and almost impressionist in manner. This may in part be due to the speed with which he had to work to meet an exhibition deadline; he wrote to Charlot in February 1929 that his exhibition at the Downtown Gallery was to open on March 26, with paintings of New York *"que todavia no pinto."*

Orozco did nonetheless take some notice of the American machinist painters, and there are

interesting parallels between their choices of subject and treatment. He probably knew Louis Lozowick's essay "The Americanization of Art," written for the landmark *Machine-Age Exposition* of 1927, also published in the *Little Review* and "regarded as a manifesto for Precisionism as a machine aesthetic."[15] Without subscribing to its functionalist view of art, in which process, material, and structure are subordinated to an economic and objective order, he might have warmed to Lozowick's idea of the artist's active response to the "rigid geometry of the American

Fig. 258 · **Mexican Landscape**, 1932, oil on canvas, Nagoya City Art Museum, Nagoya, Japan.

Fig. 259 · **Queensborough Bridge, New York**, 1928, oil on canvas, Museo de Arte Carrillo Gil/INBA 17241.

247

city," upon whose "underlying mathematical pattern as a scaffolding may be built a solid plastic structure of great intricacy and subtlety. The artist who confronts his task with original vision and accomplished craftsmanship will note with exactitude the articulation, solidity and weight of advancing and receding masses...he will organize line, plane and volume into a well knit design.... The true artist will in sum objectify the dominant experience of our epoch in plastic terms that possess value for more than this epoch alone" (fig. 261).[16] Orozco might well have recognized an affinity with these general affirmations of belief in the importance of compositional structure; his own notes on the compositions for the National Preparatory School in 1923 express very similar concerns with *grandes mases dinamicas.*[17]

A group exhibition at the Daniel Gallery in autumn 1928 had included the work of Lozowick, Sheeler, and Elsie Driggs, whose *Queensborough Bridge* of 1927 (fig. 262) makes a fascinating contrast with Orozco's version of the subject. Whereas Driggs emphasizes the open network of the steel frame against the sky, Orozco takes a pedestrian's view, with the ground mass and heavy horizontal slabs echoing in the mass of the soaring bridge. In a way, he brings the subject down to earth rather than dwelling on dizzying and suprahuman scale and height. This is even more marked in *Eighth Avenue* (1928 [fig. 54]), in which a worker inhabits the industrial scene at eye level; few of the precisionist American pictures incorporate humans as other than tiny ciphers to enhance the scale and pure, clear geometry of the urban scene. One of Orozco's masterpieces from this series in *Subway Post* (fig. 263), which translates precisionist contrast into a dense chiaroscuro; the dramatically lit surface of the concrete post makes this vertical slab into a mysterious object, which invests the "solid plastic structure of great intricacy" with a metaphysical dimension.

The small group of paintings by Orozco, including *Vigil, That Night,* and *Embrace* (figs. 264–266), seems at first sight disconnected from his Manhattan and Mexican subjects. They have received relatively little attention and have been characterized as "mythological (Greek-inspired) or surreal subjects." Though "surreal" is probably not intended here in a precise sense, it is important to establish not only that there is no evidence that Orozco

Fig. 260 · **The Curb**, 1929–30, gouache on paper. Museo de Arte Carrillo Gil/INBA 17215.

had any interest in surrealism but also that these paintings could not be appropriated into surrealism in the way, for example, that Frida Kahlo's were. As I hope to show, the strange conjunctions of objects in these paintings do not derive from any automatist or "dream narrative" sources. He did not share the surrealists' concerns with the human unconscious, sexuality, and the problem of the self. If, on occasion, he adopts a kind of symbolism, it is not—consciously—Freudian. Any fantasy in these paintings has a different kind of origin, and any connection with surrealism is at several removes.

The very diversity of the different groups of oil paintings need not be seen as unusual in Orozco's career. The wide range of his subjects and his ability to adjust his manner accordingly are evident from the murals at the National Preparatory School. Here he created on each of the three floors a totally distinct atmosphere: revolutionary scenes on the first floor (fig. 48), powerful caricatures of "justice" and the "leaders of society" on the second floor (fig. 267), and quiet scenes of daily mourning and departure on the top floor (fig. 161). In each case, his treatment is adjusted: He varies his palette and chromatic range, from predominantly red and black with strong tonal contrasts on the first floor to paler pastel and earth colors in more gently graded and muted tones on the top floor. Orozco's "mythological" paintings are, in truth, too disparate to qualify as a group. They are unified neither in theme nor in treatment, and they are linked in a sense by their very individuality. It may be that he was flexing his muscles as an easel painter, trying out separate subjects that seemed appropriate for this smaller format and more private mode. The clearest links are between *Vigil* and *That Night,* both of which, as we shall see, treat ideas related to Mexico but in a manner distinct from his "Mexican" subjects of the period.

Woman with a mirror is a familiar subject (*The Mirror,* 1930 [fig. 268]), its roots lying in the traditional *vanitas* theme, which a number of

modern artists also treated: Picasso in his rose period and, more recently, the Italian artist Mario Sironi. *Broken Glass* (fig. 269) is a violent painting, which could be distantly related to the symbolic and sometimes partly abstract backgrounds of his murals, although there is no specific source for *Broken Glass* as there is with *Fallen Columns* (fig. 270), in which the collapsing architecture in the background of the National Preparatory School mural *Destruction of the Old Order* is now treated as a subject in its own right (fig. 219). In the mural, architectural and abstract forms are mingled. In *Broken Glass,* with its shattered fragments, Orozco has chosen a subject

249

Fig. 261 · Louis Lozowick, **Brooklyn Bridge**, 1930, lithograph, Philadelphia Museum of Art, given anonymously; 1942-56-6, reproduced by permission of Mary Ryan Gallery, New York, photograph by John Costello.

that is naturally consonant with the dynamic diagonals that he favored in paintings like that of the el,
where they take on independent, nonrepresentational form. The expressionist manner in these two
paintings is striking and distinct from the style of
Vigil and *That Night.*

That Night may be read on several levels. It is,
for one thing, a satire on Rivera's recent murals for
the Ministry of Education in Mexico. Among the
most recently completed of the murals on the top
floor, Rivera had painted a *Night of the Poor* and
Night of the Rich. The harp and the rose visible in
That Night figure prominently in Rivera's own
satires on bourgeois art; Salvador Nono and Jose
Juan Tablada both are depicted with harps, while a
rose lies beneath the chair of one of the capitalists
in *Wall Street Dinner* (fig. 271). Orozco disposes
these objects among the ruins of a Mexican landscape: The typical house is roofless and collapsing
on itself; the harp is balanced on a cross, while a
coffin opens to reveal a bottle and glass, which one
is tempted to read not only in an obviously sacri-
legious way but also as a reference to a by then
familiar trope of contemporary European painting.
Both Picasso and Braque's cubism and the purism
of Amédée Ozenfant and Le Corbusier had made of
these objects not just symbols of conviviality but
also sources of formal experiments. That this might
be a part of Orozco's idea is confirmed by the set
squares that lean against the ruined building. These
had become ambiguous symbols of a postcubist
modernism, just as the golden section had been
adopted as the signboard of prewar cubism. It is
also possible that they are references to the Masonic
imagery Orozco himself used in his Preparatory
School murals and again perhaps to the desired
architectural models for "New World" art.

In *Vigil,* Orozco depicts a devastated landscape
of collapsed hewn blocks of stone out of which two
specific icons emerge: a classical urn with draperies
and, on the distant horizon, a Mexican house that,

although far away, is of great emotive significance.
It recalls his classic image of the Mexican Revolution,
The White House (fig. 7). Is this the wreck of the Old
World, with the New signaled on the horizon? Or is
it an ironic conjunction of two disasters/promises?

While the classical Greek references may, as
has often been suggested, be related to Orozco's
close contacts with those around Alma Reed and
Mrs. Sikilianos and the Delphic Circle,[18] whose
name indicates their Hellenic affiliations, the tone
of these paintings recalls more particularly the work
of Orozco's friend the poet and essayist Alfonso
Reyes. Together with Vasconcelos and Alfonso Caso,
Reyes was one of the most influential of the postrev-
olution intellectuals in Mexico. He translated Homer
into Spanish, and his deep immersion in Greek
and Roman culture and literature went alongside
his passionate involvement in the development
of modern Mexico. Among his works are the verse
drama *Cruel Iphigenia* (1924), *Vision of Anáhuac*

Fig. 262 · Elsie Driggs,
Queensborough Bridge,
1927, oil on canvas, 40 ¼ x 30 ¼ in
(102.2 x 76.8 cm), Montclair Art Museum,
New Jersey, Museum Purchase,
Lang Acquisition Fund; 1969.4.

(1917), and, published in 1949, the year of Orozco's death, the poem cycle *Homer in Cuernavaca*. Intermingled in his writing are a sense of the heroic and tragic in both worlds and an ironic awareness of incongruity in the conjunction of modern and ancient. The following extract from a pair of sonnets by Reyes, "Face and Cross of the Cactus," contrasts the Mexican icon of the eagle clasping a serpent in its claws with the classical olive tree:

> Not Virgil's olive-tree of Rome.
> For forcing locks and filleting:
> a skyhook and a scaffolding
> the gardener's neck is dangled from.
>
> Why is it Mexico has spawned
> anger, the viper and the spike,
> the twisting reed that forms a pike,
> the talon on the gauntlet-hand?[19]

Orozco's mythological New York paintings also raise interesting points of comparison with the widespread return to figuration during the 1920s, the new realism or "new objectivity."[20] This was not of course a unified phenomenon, covering many different tendencies, including the neoclassical and metaphysical. One of the most important texts that attempted to account for this general shift in painting away from abstraction and back to the object was Franz Roh's *Nach-Expressionismus; magischer Realismus: Probleme der neuesten europäischen Malerei* ("Postexpressionism; Magical Realism: The Problem of Recent European Painting") of 1925.[21] One of the few clearly recorded instances of Orozco's engagement with a contemporary theoretical text on modern painting is his transcription of Roh's table of the respective characteristics of expressionism and postexpressionism (fig. 275).[22] Although Orozco's inclination in practice seems usually to be toward expressionism, his work is too various in this period to argue for an absolute commitment to one tendency rather than the other, and the mytho-

logical paintings in particular offer interesting parallels with postexpressionism.

Roh's book was translated into Spanish and published in a widely circulated version in *Revista de Occidente* in 1927, with the title reversed to *Realismo mágico: Post-expresionismo.* Roh had added "magical realism" because "postexpressionism" indicated only an ancestry and chronology, and he needed a more descriptive subtitle. The term "magical realism" as Roh used it was intended to qualify the terms "new objectivity" and "new realism," which lacked, in his opinion, the imaginative or spiritual dimension he perceived in the new

Fig. 263 · **Subway Post**, 1929, oil on canvas, Robert L. and Sharon W. Lynch Collection, photograph by Douglas M. Parker Studio.

251

painting; it is distinct from its later applications to literature and art in Latin America, where it has become almost interchangeable with *lo real maravilloso,* a term specifically coined by Alejo Carpentier to distance ideas from surrealism. Roh's magical realism has very slight links with surrealism, in the sense that he incorporated surrealist works by Max Ernst into his broad panorama, but his approach to the whole question of art is so different from that of the surrealists that it is awkward to fit them in the same theoretical frame. Roh's remit is so broad that he includes Ernst (reproducing *La Belle Jardinière* and a collage from *Les Malheurs des immortels*) as well as works by George Grosz, Georges de Chirico, Carlo Carrà, Alberto Savinio, Filippo de Pisis, and Andre Derain, among many others. Roh's interest in Ernst is not for the "disorienting" qualities of his collages or college-inspired paintings, but for examples of the complex realism he sets out to define. He sees the art of new realism or new objectivity as the reemergence of the real world after the excesses, fantasies, and "grandiose chromatic storms" of the expressionists, but a world transfigured—not in itself, that is, but in terms of its rediscovery in painting. Although he does not couch his ideas in terms of an opposition between abstraction and figuration (and indeed includes no wholly abstract or "nonobjective" examples in his plates), he nonetheless assumes a crisis in representation to have occurred.[23] His examples include nothing more radical than a Kandinsky of about 1911 (*Rider*) and a cubist still life (no Piet Mondrian, no Liubov Popova), but he is acutely aware of the fact that the new realism no longer takes the external world for granted. Objects are rediscovered, having in a sense been lost (in the abstract tendencies of expressionism). They have become a problem, and to make them "reappear," the artist starts from a point that is no longer simple imitation. The fact that they are re-presented, that their artificiality is now transparent, makes them, however domestic or banal in character, appear

252

"mildly transfigured." They are no longer part of a natural continuum but have been plucked from a void and for this reason "vibrate with energetic intensity." The "second objective world" (painting) resembles the first (external reality), but purified, a "mildly transfigured reality" endowed with the complexity of an object's appearance or presence, even a spiritual dimension.

Roh is not making a polemical case for a particular style; he argues that the new art is situated "between extremes" and bridges right and left, pragmatism and utopias. Some, he admits, dislike the "frigid, unanimated Realism," but that is because they do not recognize the magic of quietude in the midst of flux. Roh's term "postexpressionism" has never taken within art historical discourse in the way that "postimpressionism" did. But for someone without a vested interest in one or another of the modern movements like Orozco, it usefully defined two broad tendencies with which he found himself in sympathy and was already experimenting in New York. While the expressionist side of Roh's ledger

Fig. 264 · **Vigil**, 1929, oil on canvas, private collection, courtesy Mary-Anne Martin/Fine Art, New York, photograph by Peter Brenner Photography.

Fig. 265 · **That Night**, 1930, oil on
canvas, collection of Alfonso Dau,
photograph courtesy Sotheby's.

253

included qualities Orozco already favored—dynamism, rhythm, excitement, the monumental, the
diagonal—there are qualities on the other side that
share features of certain of the mythological paintings: depth, harmonious purification of objects,
the severe, static, and rectangular. The stillness and
quiet in *Cemetery* (fig. 272), for instance, are reinforced by the parallel blocks of the tombs; in *Vigil,*
there is tension between the moonlit stillness of the
scene and the cleft between the tumbled rocks and
the draped pedestal with the erect urn that reveals
the white house on a far horizon. There is nothing
systematic about Orozco's exploration of Roh's
ideas; it is rather a creative play with conflicting
pictorial forces.

The classical overtones already linked in
Orozco's subjects to the ideas of Reyes are also
abundant in Roh's examples of postexpressionism.
Neoclassicism was one of its signifiers, but although
this can appear in a straightforward manner, it is
more often, especially in the work of the Italian
artists whom Roh included, mingled with modern
or banal objects. The interplay between classical
statuary and the modern tailor's dummy is striking.
Savinio's caricatural classical figures, for instance,
are not unlike the female bust on a fluted pedestal

in *Mannikins,* her head averted haughtily from the
encounter between the headless dummies in
modern clothes (fig. 273). These belong to a widespread motif at the time, familiar from de Chirico
and Carra's "metaphysical interiors," Grosz's bitter
parodies, such as *Nude,* or Ernst's lithographs
Fiat Modes with their satire on fashion and taste.
In *Mannikins,* Orozco exaggerates the clash between
inanimate body and dummy, the clothes draped as
though on a real body but revealing an empty sleeve

Fig. 266 · **Embrace**, 1929, gouache
on paper, William H. and Shirley
Wilson Family Collection, photograph
by Scott McLaine.

Fig. 267 · **The Rich**, 1924, fresco,
National Preparatory School, Mexico
City, photograph by Bob Schalkwijk.

Fig. 268 · **The Mirror**, 1930, oil on
canvas, Museo de Arte Carrillo
Gil/INBA 5811.

Fig. 269 · **Broken Glass**, 1929,
oil on canvas, lent by Nikki R. Keddie,
photograph by Peter Brenner
Photography.

254

or leg. He seems to have intuited an emotional effect very similar to Freud's notion of the uncanny, which reverberates so strongly in both surrealism and Roh's magical realism, an effect in which anxiety renders strange and unearthly that which is homely and familiar.[24]

As with the works of de Pisis, such as *Onions of Socrates* (fig. 274), or Savinio, there is also in Orozco a strong ironic impulse. This irony comes, as a kind of objective humor, from the tension between a strongly held belief in the value of art and the need for a revision of its purposes and a perception of the failure and vacuity of so much of the art he was surrounded with, both Mexican and European.

Orozco painted two apocalyptic scenes that could almost be pendants representing past and present, modern and classical. *The Dead* (fig. 51) might have been prompted by the Wall Street crash of 1929, to which he refers in his autobiography as surreal economics. "A morning in 1929, something grave was happening in New York. People were

255

rushing more than usual.... You could hear the
sirens of the firemen and the Red Cross sounding
furiously.... Wall Street and its surrounding
area was [sic] an infernal sea. Many speculators
had thrown themselves from their windows onto
the street.... This was the crash, the disaster."[25]
A dizzying perspective of the Wall Street canyons
is violently disrupted, skyscrapers splitting and
cracking to reveal their innards or drawn out in
sweeping masses as if they were living, organic
beings distorted by speed, invested with the
experience of the living falling to their deaths.
In *Fallen Columns,* Orozco reinvents the trope of
ruins in a landscape, which typically in the eighteenth century would have offered a moral lesson,
inviting the viewer to meditate on past grandeur
and present decay. Classical columns are tumbling
in a weed-strewn landscape that might be broken
fragments of building or desiccated and cracked
ground. The whole scene might almost be
underwater, like the ruins of ancient Alexandria
under the Mediterranean.

Fig. 270 · **Fallen Columns**, 1930,
gouache, location unknown, from
Alma Reed, **José Clemente Orozco**
(New York: Delphic Studios, 1932), n.p.

Fig. 271 · Diego Rivera, **Wall Street
Banquet**, 1926, fresco, Secretariat
for Public Education, Mexico City,
photograph by Bob Schalkwijk.

Fig. 272 · **Cemetery**, 1931, oil on
canvas, private collection, photograph
courtesy Galería Arvil, Mexico City.

256

Fig. 273 · **Mannikins**, 1930,
oil on canvas, private collection,
photograph by Larry Sanders.

Fig. 274 · Filippo de Pisis,
The Onions of Socrates, 1927,
oil on canvas, private collection,
from **La Pittura metafisica**
(Venice/Istituto di Cultura di Palazzo
Grassi: Neri Pozza, 1979), pl. 8.

257

Orozco writes in his notebooks that "style is structure."[26] Structure is "composition, texture, color, form." In copying out Roh's lists of the chief characteristics of expressionism and postexpressionism respectively, Orozco registered his agreement with a form of pictorial analysis that laid the stress on form and emotional effect but at the same time was not a manifesto for abstract art (figs. 275, 276, and 277). Most of his sketches are of nonobjective shapes — solid bodies that are oblongs or cubes, lines at right angles or diagonals, exploring the effect of purely plastic composition, but not with the final aim of abstract composition. The sketches experiment with the effects of symmetry and asymmetry (the influence of Hambidge's notion of Dynamic Symmetry is discussed by Renato González Mello elsewhere in this catalog), of tension between bodies and objects variously disposed, lit, or angled within the composition. Working through these ideas in his own way, Orozco was to reach a highly individual point of synthesis between structure and subject.

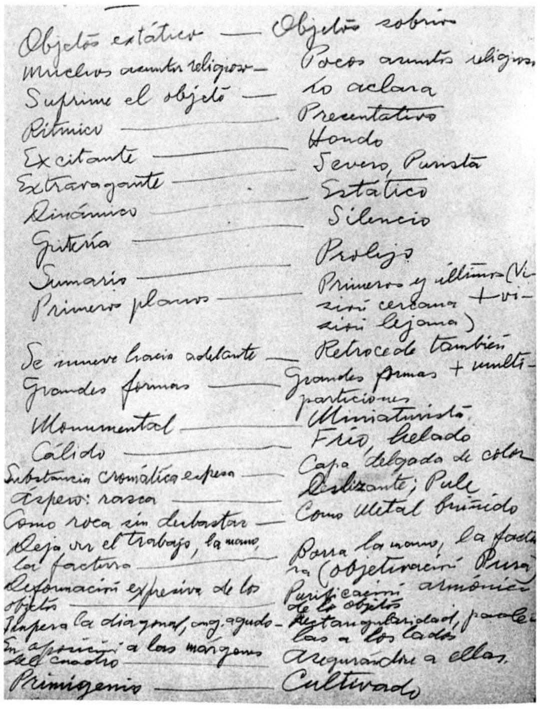

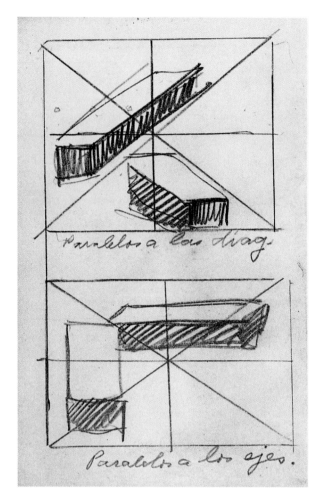

Fig. 275 · Lists of characteristics of expressionism (left) and postexpressionism (right) from Orozco's notebooks, early 1930s, from José Clemente Orozco, **Cuadernos** (Mexico City: Cultura SEP/CONAFE, 1983), 28.

Fig. 276 · Drawing from Orozco's notebooks, early 1930s, from José Clemente Orozco, **Cuadernos** (Mexico City: Cultura SEP/CONAFE, 1983), 99.

Although Orozco's late easel painting *Metaphysical Landscape* (1948 [fig. 278]) falls outside the time span of this exhibition, it depicts in an especially condensed form his highly individual response to and invention of a modern language of painting. *Metaphysical Landscape* presents two independent but interwoven pictorial dialogues with abstraction: first, through the trope of landscape; second, via the presence or absence of the object. Ever since the first experiments with abstraction, whether in Kandinsky's "expressionist" mode or in Mondrian's vertical/horizontal compositions, the power of the horizontal line within a picture to impose a "landscape" and, hence, space and depth on the most minimal of images has been both a strength and a problem. Miro, in *Composition* (1925), a lyrical blue field of color, evaded the abstraction that would have been unacceptable to his surrealist colleagues by drawing a thin horizontal line just above the center of the picture. On the other hand, postwar American painters sought to eliminate the disturbance to pure surface that the hint of a horizon line introduces. To anchor or allow to float freely oblongs and bands of color without thereby implying horizons was an important concern. Orozco, in *Metaphysical Landscape,* by contrast, emphasizes both the landscape and the pure compositional horizontality of his image: a strip of black (ground) versus a highly painterly, unmistakable sky. Within this sky, he flings an immense slab of black paint, an oblong, heavily textured, whose sides and therefore volume are dimly indicated. It is not simply a black geometrical form on the surface of the picture, but a mysterious object with an ambiguous solidity, suspended among clouds. But it is an unidentifiable object; it is essentially abstract. But unlike, for example, El Lissitsky's Prouns, which are abstract geometrical forms existing as volumes in their own space, Orozco does not impose an abstract construction on the entire canvas. He insists on the constructive tension between the different modes of representation: the nonfigurative (surface/shape) and the figure (landscape/object).

Fig. 277 · Drawing from Orozco's notebooks, early 1930s, from José Clemente Orozco, **Cuadernos** (Mexico City: Cultura SEP/CONAFE, 1983), 155.

Fig. 278 · **Metaphysical Landscape**, 1948, piroxiline on masonite, Instituto Cultural Cabañas/INBA, photograph by Rubén Orozco.

Maintaining his distance from the dominant discourses within modern painting, Orozco was free to experiment across false boundaries such as that between abstraction and figuration, or expressionism and magical realism, with a vigor that is perhaps only now being appreciated more widely.[27] His influence on the postwar New York abstract expressionists is a part of this story that still needs fully to be told. If his oil paintings of the New York period are but a footnote to his great achievements as a mural painter, they are nonetheless among the most living examples of modern (easel) painting.

259

Orozco and American Muralism: Re/viewing an Enduring Artistic Legacy

Víctor Alejandro Sorell

Public Art, "Communitas," Pageantry, Performance, Ritual, and Progressive Social Justice

This essay traces José Clemente Orozco's considerable influence on muralists in the United States from the late 1920s thorough the close of the twentieth century. Largely an art historical task, it is further complicated by the extensive breadth of Orozco's legacy, which propels the reader through periods of momentous and progressive social upheaval to the near present. That sweeping, almost eighty-year period, a seeming diachronic chasm in view of the tumultuous epoch in American history it brackets, renders in high relief the essence and enduring legacy of Orozco's mural art. Its American character, a patina or amalgam of elements issuing north and south of *la frontera* ("the border"), is deeply rooted in Aeschylean tragedy. The German philosopher Friedrich Nietzsche envisaged Aeschylean tragedy as marked by a profound yearning for justice[1] and pointed to its embodiment in the Promethean theme, one that Orozco, assisted by Jorge Juan

Crespo de la Serna, interpreted in Frary Hall at Pomona College near Los Angeles. Invoking his *Prometheus,* the artist stated that he "would much like this to be first fresco painted by a Mexican in this country and the beginning of many good things."[2] That prophetic start signaled an auspicious future for Orozco's own mural art. What, then, was in store for his contemporaries and successors? Against the backdrop of fresco painting's protracted history, we are made mindful of how murals during Orozco's lifetime persisted in transcending their physically commanding spatial presence—visual authority vested in sheer monumentality of scale— and retained their arguably ritualistic role, one that over the course of the century became ever more informed by intersecting Western and non-Western cultural and ethnic currents. Muralism evolved in a "democratic" sense, becoming less cloistered and emerging into the light of day. Murals became part of "the art show in the streets,"[3] that most democratic of venues, and thus were imbued with all of that public sphere's attendant "performative" and oftentimes "theatrical" propensities so appreciated by Orozco's fellow artist and friend Jean Charlot.

Fig. 279 · **Wall of Respect**, 1967–69, Chicago, photograph by Victor Sorell.

260

The spectacle of late-twentieth-century muralism was to unfold in the context of the progressive U.S. civil rights movement, borrowing from, and contributing back to, its verbal and nonverbal pageantry and ritual. The yearning and struggle to obtain social justice, the movement's hallmark objective, also became a powerful, persistent engine driving hosts of politically and socially engaged artists to display their indignant visions on conspicuous public walls throughout North America. That propagandistic, sociopolitical dimension of latter-day muralism is simply the resurgence of an earlier activist iconographic program associated with the mural renaissance in Mexico. In his splendid analysis of Diego Rivera's three-paneled fresco of 1929–35, *The History of Mexico,* painted in Mexico City's National Palace, the art historian Leonard Folgarait, attentive to the aesthetic principle that form follows function, argues persuasively that this mural embodies ritual in its content, form, and function.[4] The National Palace and public street sites of later murals are clearly well-trafficked loci, ideal settings for visual display. As such, they also lend themselves to the discursive nature of these murals. Folgarait explains how the conflation of verbal and nonverbal imagery in Rivera's fresco cycle invites the viewer to become "an initiate in [a] rite of passage."

Steeped in the rich Mexican tradition of ritual-istic muralism, contemporary Chican(a)o, African American, and related community murals in the United States and elsewhere have restored the cult value of the picture not merely because they bring people together through a communal process—what anthropologist Victor Turner calls *commu-nitas*—but also because they become ritual sites unto themselves by their very loci in their respec-tive barrios. Turner explains his preference for the Latin term *communitas* rather than "community" to "distinguish [the] modality of social relationship from an 'area of common living.'"[5] The kind of

calling Black People
calling all black People, maN woman c
wherever you are, calling you, urgent come iN
Black people,com iN wherever you are, urgent, calli
you; calling All black People,
lik all blackpeople, Come in, Black People, Com
ON IN   LeRoi Jones

"social relationship" one should educe from Turner's concept of *communitas* is posited as "one of the most important functions of ethnic rituals and celebra-tions"—namely "to restore, renew, and rejuvenate a personal sense of self tied to a larger community."[6] Murals mediate between the individual viewer and the larger community by engaging passersby in the speech acts of call and response. As I have written elsewhere, Amiri Baraka's exclamatory and exhorta-tive "SOS" poem, stridently "Calling all black people, man woman child…come in, wherever you are, urgent…," was inscribed on two landmark African American murals, Chicago's *Wall of Respect* (1967–69 [figs. 279 and 280]) and Detroit's *Wall of Dignity* (1968). Beseeching their respective audiences, these walls demanded a response. Call and response became the public mural's compass, particularly in communities mirroring a marked sense of ethnic consciousness stoked by the prevailing currents of civil discontent.[7] This dialogical aspect of muralism is itself an affirmation of Orozco's deeply held belief that mural art "is intended for the people…for all."[8] He called for a truly democratic, inclusive art, and his successors answered the call. However, he would remind us that illiterate passersby must also find nonverbal imagery to which they can relate. He expressed that point of view when he relocated to New York City in 1927, three years into the decline of the Mexican government's official promotion of public muralism. He found himself lamenting the demise of *biblias pintadas* ("painted Bibles"), com-pared with more "ordinary" painting: "[The good

Fig. 280 · **SOS** poem (Amiri Baraka), **Wall of Respect** (detail), 1967–69, Chicago, photograph by Victor Sorell.

261

murals] are actually painted Bibles, and people need them as much as 'spoken' Bibles. *There are many illiterate people: in Mexico there are legions of them: even in this country they exist and, undoubtedly, in any part of the world.* Obviously, to paint on public walls is a great responsibility for the artist. Because when a nation grants one its confidence, the painter will learn, will evolve and, in the end, will exact artistic dignity. Nothing yields more valuable experience or greater discipline than the opportunity to paint murals under such conditions."[9] These carefully considered words about public art, the function of the public artist in his *patria* ("homeland"), and the public's need of such art locate mural painting within the contours of ritual. That very inference can be drawn from the Mexicanist historians William H. Beezley, William E. French, and Cheryl English Martin. Recalling Turner's notion of *communitas* and Ramón Gutiérrez and Geneviève Fabre's understanding of the function of ethnic ritual, they argue that "ritual relates the individual to the collective by joining the emotional to the ideological."[10] Orozco's distinction between the depiction of words or images also invokes the domain of pageantry. Brilliantly conflating pageantry with allegorical mural painting, the art historian Trudy Baltz points out that "pageants and mural paintings conformed to the widely held educational theory that visual images could more successfully educate the public than written words." So understood, both pageants and murals conformed to Orozco's conception of the painted Bible. That allegory afforded pageantry and muralism common ground is explained by Baltz in historical and social terms. She first observes that the cumulative effect of racial and ethnic tension, coupled with class struggles, growing urbanization, and technological advances, led to the fragmentation of late-nineteenth-century America. "Allegory," she continues, "was one ritual form that recognized and expressed the disparate elements of American society" at that time.

Furthermore, "in turn-of-the-century (19th–20th) pageantry and mural painting, allegory made a profound participatory experience accessible to a broad cross section of people who could then feel one with a collective whole."[11] Processually, then, mural painting—and community muralism, in particular—pageantry, and ritual foster a sense of community. Ben Shahn, Orozco's contemporary and sometime collaborator with Rivera, eloquently conveys the important affinity *communitas* and public artistry hold for each other:

> The public function of art has always been one of creating a community. That is not necessarily its intention, but it is its result—the religious community created by one phase of art; the peasant community created by another; the Bohemian community that we enter into through the work of Degas and Toulouse-Lautrec and Manet; the aristocratic English community of Gainsborough and Reynolds, and the English low-life community of Hogarth. It is the images we hold in common, the characters of novels and plays, the great buildings, the complex pictorial images and their meanings, and the symbolized concepts, principles, and great ideas of philosophy and religion that have created the human community. The incidental items of reality remain without value or common recognition until they are symbolized, re-created, and imbued with value. The potato field and the auto repair shop remain without quality or awareness or the sense of community until they are turned into literature by a Faulkner or a Steinbeck or a Thomas Wolfe or into art by a Van Gogh.[12]

Henry Varnum Poor, another of Orozco's and Shahn's contemporaries, envisioned government sponsored painters, themselves, united under the sway of *communitas:* "If…a body of artists who were not necessarily the greatest, but who felt *real community* with each other, could work together for a year, encouraging and criticizing one another, gathering ideas from this *community of thought,* and carrying out a single, social, ordered, decorative theme—not each one blindly thinking of his own space—they might perhaps do something a little different from anything before."[13]

In the third section of this paper, we shall consider these New Deal muralists whom we maintain relate in substantive terms to Orozco.

Casting Orozco's "Tragic" Sensibility:[14]
His "Performance" in the Ritual Drama of the
Ashram and the Delphic Circle

Beyond Orozco's own memorable characterization of government-subsidized Mexican mural art as discursive, ritualistic gospel, the portrait of Orozco that emerges from the nineteen chapters of his biography written in 1956 by Alma Reed, his friend and patron, is one framed in ritual, including rites of passage, festivals, and ritual drama. The artist's letters to his wife, Margarita Valladares de Orozco, and to his kindred spirit Jean Charlot are likewise revealing. Two such missives, both written on September 10, 1928, anticipate Reed's later account of that ritualized "lived reality." I quote from the letter to Charlot:

> Incorporation of the Greek Indian into civilization. The same as in Mexico! The same damn thing: encouragement of Greek folk arts (the serapes are exactly alike!), dances with Greek flageolets. All this in Delphi. Olympic games and final performance of *Prometheus.* It all has to do with an elderly American millionaire, the wife of the poet Sikelianos, who is sponsoring some festivals and other things in Delphi, Greece. Miss Alma Reed…is involved in this affair. She is one of my admirers and bought one of my tragic drawings.[15] The other

night there was a gathering at her house and Mme. Sikelianos, in Greek costume and Greek sandals, danced a part of *Prometheus,* singing the words in Greek…. Also present were two dozen respectable old ladies, all theosophical[16] and Greek.[17]

In his letter to Margarita, Orozco adds that those gathered at Reed's home watched a film about the Delphic festivals. Designated that evening's guest of honor, Orozco found the goings-on "ridiculous but entertaining."[18] The Delphic imprint is encoded in these activities to such a degree that, as Orozco conveyed in another letter to his wife, "it has to do with a very vast and complicated cultural enterprise, they try to revive ancient Greek civilization and the movement has pretensions to operate on a universal level and, therefore, they invite intellectuals from *many countries,* they try to solicit the whole world's interest…."[19] Moreover, according to Reed, the Hindu term "ashram" had been conferred on her residence in honor of Mahatma Gandhi (Mohandas Karamchand), whom she and Mrs. Sikelianos had long admired.[20] Reed viewed her home in Manhattan as "the general headquarters of a cultural movement with a philosophical basis," like Gandhi's celebrated retreat, ashram in Wardha. One infers from Reed that among Ashram attendees, Emily Hamblen, a writer from New Jersey, probably best appreciated Orozco's real stature. She was also, Reed tells us, the first to interpret Nietzsche into English. Her book *Friedrich Nietzsche, and His New Gospel* was published in 1911, shortly after the philosopher's works had been edited in English translation. Reed recalls that, much to Orozco's liking, Hamblen gave a lecture at the Ashram titled "The Social Efficacy of Art," during which she illustrated certain of her themes with his paintings. One is left wondering to what extent Hamblen and Orozco exchanged ideas derived from Nietzschean philosophy and how these might have been translated into plastic forms

263

by the artist. That Orozco's "tragic" sensibility owes something to the philosopher is probable. After all, it was through his *Prometheus* that Reed herself saw Orozco anticipating, by more than a decade, the existentialist philosophy of Jean-Paul Sartre. Tellingly, "the Nietzschean antithesis between the 'Dionysian' and the 'Apollonian' is well suited to Sartre's '*esthétique d'opposition*' and his categories of 'being' and 'existence.'"[21] For years to come, from August 1928, when Anita Brenner first introduced Reed to the painter, until April 1940, when the studios closed for good,[22] Orozco's own existence and being—in short, his artistic destiny—were guided by the erratic and often fickle cultural compass of the Delphic Circle and Studios. A baptismal celebration held there crowned José Clemente with a laurel wreath, and, in homage, even conferred on him three new honorific names: Polyclitus (after a fifth-century Greek sculptor); Panselinos (after a Byzantine Greek painter); and Nike, "the Victorious."[23] When Charlot joined his friend in New York between September and November 1928, he found in Orozco's studio apartment a "tempera rendering of a naked Greek athlete" and the then-faded laurel wreath.[24] Apparently, what initially struck Orozco as "ridiculous" had come to assume something more than a trifling distraction in his life. His account of his experiences in the Mexican Revolution of 1910, as well as his eccentric characterization of that turbulent period, betrays the artist's flair for the dramatic. Or, perhaps, his retrospective look at earlier events acquires a veneer or residue endemic to the complex ambience peculiar to the Delphic Circle: "I played no part in the Revolution, I never suffered any harm, and I never ran any dangerous risk. For me *the Revolution was the most festive and entertaining of carnivals,* that is to say, as I understand carnivals to be, for I have never seen one *...Burlesque, drama, and barbarity.*"[25] In May 1929, undergoing a process of so-called social adjustment,

Orozco officiated as "costume master" in an evening's program held in the pulqueria[26] room of the Ashram. Not surprisingly, Orozco's own assessment of pulqueria painting—outdoor and indoor painted decoration adorning taverns[27]—is stated with tongue in cheek. His lament is at once his contempt: "The poor *pulqueria paintings have all disappeared without a trace....*"[28] One envisions the theatrical device of deus ex machina plucking unwanted tavern paintings from Orozco's stage!

Orozco and the First Wave of U.S. Muralists: From the Pre–New Deal Era to the Civil Rights Movement

In a letter of February 24, 1929, to his wife, Orozco wrote, "I imagined everything short of American painters asking for my help. I've begun to enjoy a kind of popularity here."[29] Alma Reed proudly declared: "Overnight, Delphic Studios have become a vigorous national center for contemporary mural art."[30] Of course it was anything but an "overnight" development. New York City itself had been the catalyst. Orozco's first visit there, in 1917 and 1918, came on the heels of what Arthur Frank Wertheim calls the New York Little Renaissance, a period of cultural efflorescence encapsulated within the years 1908 and 1917. "The Little Renaissance," Wertheim argues, "helped make New York the nation's leading art and literary capital.... Gallery 291 and the Armory Show were crucial events in New York's growth as the headquarters of avant-garde painting.... Because of the Little Renaissance, New York would always remain in the forefront of American culture."[31] Presumably, Reed's Delphic Studios trace their patrimony to the ambience of a Gallery 291. Founded by the highly influential photographer Alfred Stieglitz, that space was described by the painter-poet John Marin as "a place electric, a place alive," while another painter, Marsden Hartley, saw it function as "an indispensable force in bringing modern art to America."[32] Another locus of cultural activity at that time was Mabel Dodge Luhan's Greenwich Village salon. The likelihood that Reed looked to Stieglitz and Luhan as her models of cultural patronage suggests to us that Orozco himself probably looked back to the Ateneo de la Juventud ("Atheneum of Youth"), "a group of young Mexico City intellectuals formally constituted in 1909." The philosopher and muralist-advocate-mentor José Vasconcelos and Diego Rivera, Orozco's archrival, were among the group's founding members. In anticipation of the pervasive Grecian atmosphere of the Delphic Circle, the Ateneistas—throwbacks to the classical Atheneum, Greek Athena's Temple, and Hadrian's Roman Academy—looked to Nietzsche and applied themselves to learning Greek "dialogue" in Mexico's suburb of San Ángel. It was to this early intellectual and ideological crucible that Vasconcelos's 1920s crusade for national culture would be traced.[33]

There are at least twenty-one U.S. artists, active at different times from the New Deal era through the civil rights movement of the 1960s, who may be said to relate in varying degrees of significance to Orozco. Purposely limiting the scope of our essay for reasons of space, our argument will revolve largely around only half their number: Thomas Hart Benton (1889–1975), Jackson Pollock (1912–1956), Aaron Douglas (1899–1979), Hale Woodruff (1900–1980), Anton Refregier (1905–1979), Bernard Baruch Zakheim (1896–1985), Gilbert Wilson (1907–1991), Mitchell Siporin (1910–1976), Jacob Lawrence (1917–2000), and Charles White (1918–1979).[34]

A tongue-in-cheek attitude similar to Orozco's comes through in Thomas Hart Benton's writing. "The life I lived in New York," he wrote, "had no significance for my art." He saw himself and fellow artists as "Bohemians, adrift from the currents of our land and contemptuous of them" while drawn to Stieglitz's 291 shop, "New York's high temple of aesthetic pose and lunatic conviction."[35] He did

mention "a rival station up in the Bronx maintained by John Weichsel, a learned man with utopian urges about an abstraction called 'the people' which he believed would support art if given a chance…."[36] Where muralism was concerned, Benton did believe New York made a difference. Interested in rendering "a history of the United States in paint," the artist exhibited portions of that "project" at the Architectural League in New York. The critics began to think of him as a muralist, and in turn he "began to think of [himself] as such."[37] Impressed with the Latin American enthusiasm for public murals and admiring Orozco's work in particular, Benton was drawn to Alma Reed's circle. He exhibited at Delphic Studios in December 1928.[38] Enlisting the help of Lewis Mumford and the architect Joseph Urban, who had been commissioned to design the building for the New School for Social Research, Benton became a would-be muralist in search of a wall to paint.[39] As for Orozco, one mural was about to beget another. Writing Margarita from Pomona on April 13, 1930, Orozco mentions hearing from New York regarding someone's interest in his coming there in September or October "to paint a small wall in a school's new building…."[40] In a subsequent letter of April 29, Orozco tells Margarita of "the very nice letter" he received from the director of the New School for Social Research, conveying what a "great honor and privilege" it would be if he would come and paint there.[41] Benton, for his part, was championed by the well-known New York art critic Ralph Pierson, who admired the artist's Architectural League work. Pierson reminded Dr. Alvin Johnson, the New School's director, that Benton had worked long to develop his unique mural style for America and should have a hand in this important commission.[42] Johnson acceded. Given a chance to continue his "U.S. history project," Benton betrayed a boyish enthusiasm: "Itching to get a crack at a real mural, I set out. The subject on which Dr. Johnson and I agreed for the room allotted to me was contemporary America."[43] That space was the New School's third-floor boardroom. Orozco was assigned the dining room area, as he previously had in Pomona. Signifying the "battle cry of the young against the old," the New School's brand of modernism found in architect Urban a compatible visionary. He was to design the institution's new building as an "architectural affirmation" of the school's philosophy of democratic liberalism.[44] Reflective of this orientation, the auditorium's design, featuring a lowered stage and open seating, eliminated traditional barriers between performers and audience, a modernist architectural strategy of bridging the gap between art and life through theater. Period muralism and pageantry called forth similar populist strategies. Within this ultramodern setting, Orozco and Benton, according to Johnson, were to paint a contemporary subject "of such importance that no history written a hundred years from now could fail to devote a chapter to it." Johnson found their respective murals "essentially complementary."[45]

The art historian Erika Doss recognizes Orozco's empathy for those whom society disenfranchises. Arguably, he projects a class consciousness rivaling John Reed's earlier activist efforts on behalf of silk workers, whose salaries and working conditions in Paterson, New Jersey, had called his attention and inspired *The Paterson Strike Pageant*.[46] "Orozco's five frescoes, including *The Struggle in the Occident* and *The Struggle in the Orient*, are somber views of worker oppression relievable only through class revolution.... Orozco contrasted the good life of revolutionary activism in Russia and Mexico with grim scenes of imperialist brutality in India."[47] Conversely, Benton painted the aftermath of class-driven struggle. His Robinsonesque vision—lessons owed his teacher Boardman Robinson[48]—allows for compromise and redemption. Throughout *America Today*, Benton "hoped to see the resolution of labor conflict and the restoration of labor autonomy [by]

accommodating producerism in modern industry."[49] But in his depiction of black victims of chain gang labor in *Deep South*, he recognized "that for many the struggle for autonomy (was clouded by racism) and was by no means over."[50] The process of mural painting itself afforded Benton a kind of indulgent emotional catharsis approaching ritual: "A mural is for me a kind of emotional spree. The very thought of the large spaces puts me in an exalted state of mind, strings up my energies, and heightens the color of the world."[51] What he expressed resonates with the spirit of a rejuvenated personal sense of self, a signature objective of *communitas*.

Enter Jackson Pollock. "Intrigued by revolutionary aesthetics," Erika Doss explains, "Jackson visited Pomona College in June 1930 and viewed Orozco's recently completed mural.... The exuberant dynamism of Orozco's art, as well as its radical politics, so excited Pollock he visited Pomona several times that summer. When he learned that Orozco and Benton were beginning their murals at the New School...Pollock decided to join his (biological) brothers in New York."[52] In the fall of 1930 he enrolled in Benton's "Life Drawing, Painting, and Composition" class at the Art Students League. He came to be seen as a "sort of family intimate," and Benton eventually introduced him to Boardman Robinson.[53] Apprenticing with Benton at the New School and the Whitney Museum, Pollock "action posed" for certain scenes in the murals and, furthermore, had the invaluable opportunity to watch Orozco painting.[54] Pollock must have been awed to observe the author of *Prometheus*, the fresco he described to his sculptor friend and fellow alcoholic Tony Smith as "the greatest work of art in North America" (fig. 110). It so impressed Pollock that a photo reproduction of the mural was prominently displayed in his studio,[55] arguably assuming the proportions of a cult icon for him, and, in Pollock scholar Ellen G. Landau's opinion, might have suggested Pollock's *The Flame* (about 1934–38), an oil on canvas composition seemingly consumed by the very flames it depicts.[56] Understandably, Pollock came to be seduced by the infectious lure and power of muralism. Applying for a Guggenheim fellowship in 1947, he wrote: "I intend to paint large moveable pictures which will function between the easel and mural…. I believe the easel picture to be a dying form, and the tendency of modern feeling is towards the wall picture or mural…."[57] Years prior to this pronouncement, around 1933, Pollock had produced two mural studies, which were never realized, for a Greenwich Village settlement house. Rendered diminutively on heavy brown wrapping paper,[58] one of the studies clearly borrows the arched architectural setting of Orozco's in situ *Prometheus,* while the second study adds two wing panels to a central image, also consistent with the overall scheme for the *Prometheus* triptych. In 1934, on the walls of his Houston Street loft, Pollock executed what has been described as a "vast, lewd ('pornographic') mural in the style of Orozco," depicting what are presumed to be men "peeing."[59] In 1935 or 1936 Jackson, accompanied by his brother Sande Pollock and Philip Guston, among others, visited Dartmouth College to view Orozco's mural cycle *The Epic of American Civilization* (1932–34).[60] Landau thinks that these Baker Library frescoes are the source for "the loudest echoes of Orozco…[reverberating] strongly not only throughout Pollock's oils of 1938–1941, but [also] seen in his 'psychoanalytic' drawings…."[61] Of these fresco panels, *Modern Migration of the Spirit* and *Gods of the Modern World* (figs. 186 and 183) provided Pollock with rich grist for his mill. One Pollock painting, in particular, *Bald Woman with Skeleton* (about 1938–41) may pay tribute not only to Orozco's *Gods of the Modern World,* as Landau and scholars Francis V. O'Connor and Eugene V. Thaw suggest,[62] but, oddly enough, also to Orozco's artistic

progenitor José Guadalupe Posada and the latter's *Calavera Huertista.*[63] Also in 1936 Pollock worked briefly in David Alfaro Siqueiros's New York–based Experimental Workshop.[64] Around 1938 Pollock painted a striking porcelain bowl, titling it *The Story of My Life.* This ceramic piece, O'Connor and Thaw believe, "derives stylistically from Orozco's *Man of Fire* dome at Guadalajara."[65] While Pollock's adoption of the medium of ceramic may owe much to the experimentation promoted in Siqueiros's workshop, it also calls to mind another painter who found the two media of fresco and pottery perfectly compatible: "Even before the Mexican invasion of Rivera and Orozco, Poor had experimented extensively with fresco painting, and it was natural to turn to this ancient medium for his first government assignment. Fresco and pottery each demand the same degree of speed and finality, and Poor is happiest when working with materials that are pliable to the impatient urge of his will."[66]

Enter the New Deal and its attendant WPA labor enterprise. Orozco was at work on the mural program for Dartmouth when George Biddle wrote his old friend and schoolmate President Franklin D. Roosevelt, proposing "a revival of mural painting" in the United States modeled on the Mexican example:

> The Mexican artists have produced the greatest national school of mural painting since the Italian Renaissance. Diego Rivera tells me that it was only possible because Obregón allowed Mexican artists to work at plumbers' wages in order to *express on the walls of the government buildings the social ideals of the Mexican revolution.* The younger artists of America are conscious as they have never been of *the social revolution that our country and civilization are going through;* and they would be eager to *express these ideals in a permanent art form* if they were given the government's cooperation.

267

They would be contributing to and expressing in living monuments the social ideals that you are struggling to achieve. And I am convinced that our mural art with a little impetus can soon result, for the first time in our history, in *a vital national expression.*[67]

Echoing Orozco's sentiments of an accessible, readable "people's art," expressed a full decade earlier, and anticipating Philip Guston's congruent opinion—"that [painting] is a court where the artist is prosecutor, defendant, jury and judge…"[68] in the face of public opinion—Biddle reminded the reader that the yearning and struggle for social justice were persistent and powerful stimuli, enduring to that day and driving the ongoing spectacle of public muralism in the United States. More or less contemporaneous with Biddle's appeal for a mural renaissance was Diego Rivera's Rockefeller Center commission *Man at the Crossroads* (1932–33 [fig. 251]). Not despite the fresco's ultimate destruction, but probably because of it, the art historian Robert Linsley finds that "the affirmative utopianism" it symbolized continues to function today, into the twenty-first century, as "the prototype for an entire genre of contemporary mural painting …images of hope belonging to the dispossessed of capitalism."[69] Emulating the example of Mexico's

earlier president Álvaro Obregón (1920–24 and 1928), Roosevelt embraced wholeheartedly Biddle's "suggestion in regard to the expression of modern art through mural paintings." He urged the artist to talk with the assistant secretary of the treasury, after which, in an effort to assemble a self-selected group, Biddle recruited Henry Varnum Poor, Boardman Robinson, Tom Benton, Reginald Marsh, and John Steuart Curry.[70]

Invoked as the father of black American art, Aaron Douglas was at his creative peak during his New York residency, which coincided with Orozco's.[71] Key participants during the First American Artists' Congress against War and Fascism, held in 1936 and

Fig. 281 · Hale Woodruff, **Revolt Aboard the Amistad**, 1939, oil on canvas, Savery Library, Talledega College, Talledega, Alabama, photograph courtesy Savery Library Archives.

Fig. 282 · Hale Woodruff, **Settlement and Development** from **The Negro in California History, 1850–1949**, mural cycle executed in collaboration with Charles Alston, 1949, oil on canvas, Golden State Mutual Life Insurance Company, Los Angeles.

268

briefly cited below, the two artists surely knew each other and likely shared ideological interests. It is also logical that each knew something of the other's painting. Between 1925 and 1934 Douglas evolved stylistically, employing "a flat, sophisticated silhouette of the human form...."[72] Bodily gestures in the woodcuts *Forest Fear* and *Flight,* from *The Emperor Jones* series (about 1926),[73] prefigure Orozco's *Prometheus* with his extended arms, exaggeratedly reaching overhead.[74] That silhouetted vocabulary also typifies the murals Douglas undertook. While Orozco worked at Pomona, Douglas painted a series of allegorical murals at Fisk University in Nashville, Tennessee, and a commemorative mural titled *Harriet Tubman* (1931) at the Bennett College for Women in Greensboro, North Carolina. The latter tribute to the nineteenth-century antislavery activist depicts Tubman, Prometheuslike, atop a promontory, upraised arms breaking apart chains of bondage.[75] That Orozco might have seen a Douglas mural firsthand is likely. Douglas's first mural commission dates from 1927 at the Club Ebony in Harlem,[76] and Orozco, for his part, maintained an ongoing interest in and fascination with Harlem since his first visit to Manhattan in 1917.[77] We possess no similar evidence to suggest that Douglas experienced firsthand any of Orozco's murals outside New York City.

Hale Woodruff and Aaron Douglas were born and died but a year apart. Woodruff wanted "to get into the mural painting swing...[and] to paint great significant murals in fresco...," and therefore traveled to Mexico.[78] Aware of Charles White, the Federal Arts Project, and Orozco's New School murals, Woodruff chose to "learn [Rivera's] technique."[79] Yet one would have to agree with the art historian Elsa Honig Fine in her assessment of Orozco's influence on the remarkable three-panel *Amistad* murals Woodruff did in 1939 for the Slavery Library of Talladega College in Alabama (fig. 281). Commemorating the 1839 mutiny aboard the Spanish slaver, ironically translated as "Friendship," the mural narrative reflects on the true meaning of the judicial process on the centenary of the uprising.[80] In the first panel, *The Mutiny aboard the Amistad,* of Woodruff's larger mural cycle, Fine detects residues from Orozco's magisterial frescoes *Hidalgo* (fig. 253) and *Luchas por la libertad* ("Combats for Liberty") painted in the Governor's Palace, Guadalajara, in 1937 and 1938.[81] Beneath a monumental Father Hidalgo, a figure emblematic of Mexico's national independence, who harkens back to the earlier *Prometheus,* a bloodcurdling combat thick with bayonets and echoes of *The Trench* (fig. 239) "represents the rebellion of the masses against their exploiters."[82] Woodruff's slaves retaliate with the same vengeance. The friezelike arrangement and repetition of figures in the second *Amistad* panel, *The Amistad Slaves on Trial at New Haven,*

Fig. 283 · Bernard Baruch Zakheim, **English Explorers and Native California Herbs** from **The Art of Medicine**, 1936–38, fresco, Toland Hall amphitheater, University of California, San Francisco, photograph courtesy Anthony Lee.

Connecticut, 1840, recall the same visual device in Orozco's New School murals. No less distinguished an observer than W.E.B. Du Bois declared that *The Amistad Mutiny* cycle was "the most important work done by a black artist" when it was unveiled and dedicated on April 15, 1939.[83] Fine's detection of vestiges of *The Trench* in the *Amistad* cycle leads me to uncover the same visual roots in related oil on canvas sketches Woodruff painted in 1945 and 1946 in preparation for another mural cycle, *The Art of the Negro: Muses and Dissipation.* The dramatic use of fire in one scene points more directly to the Mexican genesis of the paintings. Another probable borrowing, although much muted in contrast with those already cited, occurs in a later two-panel mural, *The Negro in California History, 1850–1949* (1949 [fig. 282]), which Woodruff executed in collaboration with Charles Alston for the Golden State Mutual Life Insurance Company of Los Angeles. The heroic, "revolutionary" figures of *The Trench* (fig. 239), conjoined with builder and worker figures from the same National Preparatory School fresco cycles, have been transformed in the *Settlement* panel into a group of laborers, possibly bridge builders, hoisting what appears to be some heavy cable.

Initially, Bernard Baruch Zakheim's name brings Rivera to mind. Prior to the latter's arrival in San Francisco in late 1930, Zakheim visited Mexico.[84] Following Rivera's departure from the Bay Area in June 1931, this Eastern European immigrant became one of San Francisco's dominant mural painters. It was while he was engaged in his largest mural series, *The Story of California Medicine* (1936–38 [fig. 283]), painted in an amphitheater at Toland Hall on the University of California at San Francisco medical campus, that Zakheim came under Orozco's influence. He was "a more logical model than Rivera for a committed Stalinist." Zakheim met Orozco at the First American Artists' Congress and on the heels of the latter's completion of the Baker Library mural, what the art historian Anthony Lee considers the likely "formal model"[85] for the Toland Hall frescoes. It is precisely Orozco's spatial handling and figurative types that Lee finds stamped on Zakheim's evolving stylistic approach. However, he also finds that "in Zakheim's hands, the grating Orozcoesque style which he emulated was diluted and deflated."[86]

Anton Refregier, another Bay Area muralist, is noted for his twenty-seven-panel Rincon Annex Post Office fresco cycle. Painted between 1946 and 1948, the series was often criticized for what many saw as its "subversive pictorial strategies."[87] One panel in particular, *Maritime and General Strike* (fig. 284), strikes this writer for its indebtedness to Orozco. A labor union organizer who Lee suggests is Harry Bridges occupies the composition's focal center. This American Federation of Labor (AFL)[88] leader is

Fig. 284 · Anton Refregier, **Maritime and General Strike**, 1946–48, fresco, panel from a mural cycle at Rincon Annex Post Office, San Francisco, photograph courtesy Anthony Lee.

conspicuously derivative of the Baker Library's Quetzalcoatl as depicted in the panel *The Departure of Quetzalcoatl* (fig. 173). Orozco has chosen to portray that moment in the legendary account when the god is condemned to leave his beloved people and Tula, the capital of the Toltec dynasty. Afloat on a raft of serpents, an important attribute of this plumed serpent deity, Quetzalcoatl points eastward, his upraised and extended arm mimicking the thrusts of the many marine snakes. While Refregier's context is completely his own, he has Bridges pointing in parallel fashion at a clandestine bribery scene, a diminutive cameolike fragment painted in the middle ground. The waterfront boss shown accepting the bribe is confronted by a host of job seekers gathered in the panel's foreground area to the viewer's left. Uncannily, the outstretched arms and hands of the jobless call to mind the writhing serpents escorting Quetzalcoatl in the Dartmouth panel. No less likely an inspiration for the bribery cameo is another of Orozco's Preparatory School fresco fragments, *The Church* (1924), painted to complement a window area. Donations from the faithful are shown being put in the collection box, from which they ultimately fall into anonymous and greedy hands. Similar hand clusters also appear in the upper register of *Omniscience* (1925 [fig. 5]), a fresco Orozco painted in the famed Casa de Azulejos ("House of Tiles"). Although Lee does not ascribe Orozcoesque elements to Refregier's work, his description of certain visual elements evident in the Rincon Annex murals is evocative of Orozco's own formal vocabulary: "the blocky forms and careening perspectives, the caricatured faces and truncated bodies, the garish colors and abbreviated spaces...."[89]

In March 1936, following the meeting of the American Artists' Congress (convened in New York City's Town Hall and at the New School between February 14 and 16), during which Orozco read the "General Report of the Mexican Delegation," Ione

Robinson, who apprenticed briefly with Orozco, recalled being told by him "that he was not surprised that American painters were beginning to wake up to the world around them...art was a weapon more powerful than armed force."[90] Aaron Douglas and others shared the speakers' platform with Orozco.[91] Reporting on behalf of the twelve-member Mexican delegation attending the congress, Orozco discussed four principal points, the first of which was "the artists' position as far as the problems of imperialism, Fascism and war were concerned."[92] It is fitting given Orozco's own thirst for a more just world, one in which artists' struggles, to be sure, should also be taken into account, that his report would give voice to that very humanistic aspect: "The artists' means of struggle also include the open revealing of all crimes and criminal attempts practiced against intellectuals and artists in fascist countries, and the waging of an intense campaign against the forces which are leading humanity toward a new massacre."[93] It so happened that on the very day Orozco delivered his comments, fifteen thousand WPA workers were arrested in a demonstration in New York City. The session chairman, the artist Peter Blume, appropriately introduced a resolution

Fig. 285 · Gilbert Wilson, **Machinery Mural**, north wall, 1934, Woodrow Wilson Middle School, Terre Haute, Indiana, photograph by David Nearpass.

271

to the effect that "the Artists' Congress…declares its support of the WPA workers, and its condemnation of the arrests made of demonstrators, and demands their immediate release."[94]

During the congress's first closed session, devoted to the theme of "The Artist in Society," Gilbert Wilson, a muralist from Indiana, gave a talk titled "A Mural Painter's Conviction" in which he paid substantial tribute to Orozco. Recalling his 1934 visit to Mexico City, where he saw the artist's National Preparatory School murals firsthand, Wilson remarked that "Orozco's work stunned me."[95] "These frescoes," he continued, "gave me for the first time a sense of direction," and "…initial contact with those frescoes of Orozco made me see ever so clearly that I was interested in art as a social force." Anticipating by many years Guston's dramatic sense that a "canvas is a court," Wilson observes that "murals, today, can contain one of two things, either the cruelty of emptiness or the cruelty of truth… most murals will contain the cruelty of emptiness because the public taste finds emptiness more palatable than truth."[96] Orozco's own brand of artistic justice would of course bask in the revelations that Wilson's kind of "truth" implied. Wilson's newfound compulsion to do murals recalls Thomas Hart Benton's own emotional reliance on the medium: "From that trip to Mexico, I returned to my home in Indiana very much desiring to obtain some wall space for a mural…. I wanted a wall. I wanted it so badly that I put aside any thought of money for fear it might stand in my way of getting a wall." He was to find his space at Woodrow Wilson Junior High School in Terre Haute, Indiana. Naming his painting *Machinery Mural* (1934 [fig. 285]), he "depicted Science or Organized Knowledge liberating Youth from the menace of an abused machine age."[97] That wall echoes Rivera's unmistakable style, but upon closer inspection, Orozco's influence can be discerned as well through Wilson's "vocal" and sinister death mask, not unlike the ritual face

coverings Orozco depicted in the Dartmouth panel *Ancient Human Sacrifice* (fig. 169), and through a perspectival system incorporating massive machinery resembling in places that employed by Orozco in his fresco *Catharsis*,[98] also painted in 1934 inside the Palace of Fine Arts in Mexico City (fig. 252). The reader will recall that it was during the summer of 1934 that Wilson visited Mexico. "Out here," he wrote, "I have come to realize that a creative individual must accept the place where he comes into being and must seek to know that place. I have lived in Terre Haute and intend to remain there, feeling as I do that out of the Middle West, some day, will come something very wholesome and good of art. Here lies the richest possibilities [*sic*] for an indigenous culture…."[99] Mindful of the importance for Orozco of commissions from educational institutions and duly noting Wilson's admiration for Orozco, one might well quote further from the former's observations in Mexico: "My intentions as a mural painter are to identify my work closely with education. Therefore, I hope—and heartily—that the people of my state will see fit to go even as far, as here in Mexico, to build great chapels in connection with these schools and appropriate walls

Fig. 286 · Jacob Lawrence, **Events in the Life of Harold Washington**, 1991, fired ceramic tile, 126 x 183 x ¾ in (320 x 464.8 x 2 cm), Harold Washington Library Center, City of Chicago Public Art Collection, © Gwendolyn Knight Lawrence, courtesy of the Jacob and Gwendolyn Lawrence Foundation, photograph courtesy Chicago Department of Cultural Affairs/Michael Tropea.

for the murals I hope to create...."[100] Not surprisingly, maybe even predictably, Wilson, according to the writer Fred Ringel, left New York following the artists' congress to experience personally the Baker Library murals at Dartmouth.[101]

Taking stock of "American Resources in the Arts," Holger Cahill, the national director of the Works Progress Administration/Federal Arts Project (WPA/FAP) between 1935 and 1943, characterized Mitchell Siporin as "one of the most brilliant young muralists the project has developed."[102] Addressing "Mural Art and the Midwestern Myth," Siporin acknowledged "the amazing spectacle of the modern renaissance of mural painting in Mexico" and, echoing his fellow midwesterner Gilbert Wilson, said that his midwestern contemporaries were "at work on a native epic in fresco return[ing] to Giotto, Masaccio, [and] Orozco...."[103] To put it more precisely, the "profound artistry and meaning" endemic to Mexican muralism "deeply moved" midwestern artists, making them "aware of the scope and fullness of the 'soul' of [their] own environment, [and] aware of the application of modernism toward [creating] a socially moving epic art of [their] time and place."[104] Inspired by this vibrant current of *mexicanidad* ("Mexicanness"), Siporin, whose birth coincided with the advent of the Mexican Revolution, rejected a narrow-minded, jingoistic nationalism and, like Wilson, turned instead to a "human democratic art, deeply thoughtful and eloquent, an art out of the lives of the people."[105] The grand and heroic proportions of North America emerged for that region's muralists thanks to the sensibility of their brethren south of the border.

Charles Alston's renowned gathering place for artists, his studio 306 — recalling Gallery 291, Luhan's salon, and, of course, the Delphic milieu — beckoned Jacob Lawrence into its midst. There he installed himself, meeting fellow artist Aaron Douglas, writer Langston Hughes, and philosopher Alain Locke, among others. At 306, Alston directed the local mural activity for the Mural Division of the WPA Federal Arts Project.[106] Recalling his own desire to do murals in the early thirties, Lawrence remembered turning to "outside well-known artists." Orozco was the first of these he encountered.[107] In fact, Lawrence and Orozco had already met each other at New York's Museum of Modern Art in the summer of 1940. That occasion coincided with MoMA's exhibition *Twenty Centuries of Mexican Art*, Orozco's ongoing work on a six-panel fresco *Dive Bomber and Tank* (fig. 233), and Lawrence's in-progress *Migration* series. Their meeting had great significance for Lawrence,[108] motivating him to share his admiration for Orozco with his students: "I show this work [*The Trench*] to my beginning drawing classes because the composition is so strong. It's a very structured composition;...the diagonals. I relate Orozco to Giotto.... It's a very architectonic kind of structure."[109] Arguably, early in the forties, strong vestiges of *The Trench* (fig. 239) appear in Lawrence's diminutive canvases, such as *Number 6 — John Brown Formed an Organization among the Colored People of the Adirondack Woods to Resist the Capture of Any Fugitive Slave* (1946) — of the *John Brown* series (begun in 1941), and in *Beachhead, Number 8* from the *War* series (1946–47). During the 1950s, the residue from Orozco's same canonic work lingers in *Number 21, Tippecanoe — Westward Push* from another of Lawrence's series, *Struggle: From the History of the American People* (1955–56). Lawrence's caption for *Number 21* quotes the Shawnee chief Tecumseh, addressing the British at Tippecanoe, Indiana, in 1811: "Listen, Father! The Americans have not yet defeated us by land; neither are we sure they have done so by water — we therefore wish to remain here and fight our enemy...."[110] Another borrowing from Orozco's mural scale onto a mere twelve-by-sixteen-inch canvas occurs with *Number 10, Crossing the Delaware*, also from the *Struggle* series. Here,

273

possibly, Lawrence's source is *Luchas por la libertad* ("Combats for Liberty"), the same inspiration I claimed earlier for Woodruff's *Amistad* cycle. It is the serial sequence, rather than the individual work, that better conveys the range of emotion and ideas in the great stories Lawrence wants to tell.[111] Conceptually, then, Lawrence's small easel works bring to mind the narrative sequences fitting and typical in mural cycles.

Lawrence himself did not actually undertake mural commissions until the period 1978–87 and beyond. *Games* (1978–79), the first of these commissions, was realized in porcelain enamel on steel and involved the collaboration of David Berfield, a Seattle ceramic artist.[112] This choice of compatible but distinctly different materials recalls our earlier discussion of similar technical combinations employed by Pollock and Henry Varnum Poor. Turning now to what the Lawrence scholar Ellen Harkins Wheat refers to as the "boldly foreshortened massive athletes"[113] in the mural, I am reminded once again of the *Prometheus* template. Furthermore, the gesticulating and much smaller "overlooking crowd" is suggestive of the similarly diminutive figures in shallow space over which Prometheus towers. It is, then, largely through his spatial treatment that Lawrence most closely approaches Orozco. More recently, when Lawrence was already well into his seventies, he was commissioned to render *Events in the Life of Harold Washington* (1991 [fig. 286]) in ceramic tile mosaic for the first-floor lobby of Chicago's Harold Washington Library Center. The mosaic, according to the library's published guide to its public art collection, "recognizes the late Mayor's accomplishments as student, Civilian Conservation Corps worker, soldier, lawyer, U.S. congressman, and the city's highest elected official."[114] "These periods of his life," the guide continues, "are portrayed in the pages of books spread across the Mayor's desk, which collectively form a metaphoric mountain

culminating in Harold Washington's election as the first black Mayor of Chicago." Most of these details are read easily, although to limit our description of the dense, multilayered space to a desktop is a much too facile or even questionable analysis. Lawrence's use of insistent linear angularity together with his staggered placement of figures contributes, as Richard J. Powell writes, to the creation of "a rugged, mountainous form with a solitary, triumphant human figure at its apex."[115] That figure of Washington, in tandem with another figure, depicted, arms raised, striding just to the left of the composition's center, invokes *Prometheus* as well as the recycling of several elements from the Baker Library panel *The Arrival of Quetzalcoatl* (fig. 171). However, when Lawrence was asked, on my behalf, if the Pomona mural had been a source, he responded that he had been thinking only of the mayor and was unfamiliar with Orozco's *Prometheus*.[116]

That there is a special symbiosis between Orozco and Lawrence is so well appreciated by Wheat that her assessment in turn deserves our appreciation: "The unmistakable Orozco style includes diagonal lines and oblique slashes, angularly outstretched arms, strong but sensitive hands, bodies like the stylized designs of medieval wood

Fig. 287 · Charles White, **The Contribution of the Negro to Democracy in America**, 1943, egg tempera, Hampton University Museum, Hampton, Virginia.

carvings, heads often hairless with a spectral look, intensity of feeling yet stillness, and color patterns of black and white, grey, and brown. Lawrence's expressionism reveals the impact of Orozco in the manifestation of many of these features, especially the use of diagonal stresses and the rhythmic device of reiterated vertical forms with simplified contours...."[117]

Early in his career Charles White befriended two fellow Chicagoans, the muralists Siporin and Edward Millman. Both invited White to visit their studios and observe them painting. He considered them great painters and acknowledged that "they were a strong influence on his work."[118] Like Siporin, White traveled to Mexico City, having been invited by Siqueiros to the Taller de Gráfica Popular (TGP, "Popular Graphics Workshop"). Accompanied by his wife, the artist Elizabeth Catlett, he was made an honorary member of the workshop. The honor recalls the substantial tributes bestowed on Orozco by an appreciative New York City. At the TGP, White learned lithography and met two other celebrated Mexican muralists, Pablo O'Higgins and Diego Rivera.[119] According to White scholar Peter Clothier, White's return to New York following his Mexican experience "marked the period of his harshest satirical work as a cartoonist for such organs as the *Daily Worker* and *Congress Vue*."[120] In 1942, during World War II, the *Daily Worker* featured a story by Harry Raymond focusing on racist violence against black GIs in Freeport, New York. One of White's illustrations accompanied the article. Later, in 1946, in his drawing *Freeport,* "There is a reversal of roles...where [an] outraged Black [has] seized the initiative."[121] Resonating with much of the dramatic timbre of Orozco's fresco *Hidalgo* (fig. 253), White's *Freeport,* rendered in charcoal and ink heightened with the tint of white, "portrays the avenging spirit of the Black victim in tattered uniform, his face a mask of fearsome rage, still wearing the broken shackles of slavery and the

frayed ends of the lynching noose, now brandishing the torch of freedom in a gesture much like the Klansman in the earlier drawing [of 1942]." Clothier continues: "With it, the Black now threatens a group of white oppressors, which includes a crooked judge, chuckling over a 'Permit to Kill Negro Vets and Civilians.' Below the towering figure (recalling Orozco's torch-bearing Padre Hidalgo), protected by his massive frame, the dead and injured of both Freeport and Columbia (Tennessee) agonize in a devastated landscape (one similar to Orozco's)."[122]

Antedating both his 1942 and 1946 drawings, respectively, are White's own masterful murals: *Five Great American Negroes* (1941; renamed *Progress of the American Negro*) at Howard University in Washington, D.C., and *The Contribution of the Negro to Democracy in America* (1943 [fig. 287]) at Hampton University in Hampton, Virginia. Recollecting Wheat's earlier observation registered in her comparison of Lawrence and Orozco, we recognize that the latter's heavy reliance on "diagonal lines and oblique slashes, angularly outstretched arms, [and] strong but sensitive hands..." is no less relevant a comparative index between Orozco and White. Those visual elements are encoded in the first of the two murals through the painting's main protagonists: educator-reformer Booker T. Washington, statesman Frederick Douglass, agricultural chemist George Washington Carver, abolitionists John Brown, Nat Turner, and Denmark Vesey, and escaped slave and women's rights activist Sojourner Truth. They, among others, lead "a serpenting legion of the people out of a legacy of servitude towards knowledge, modern life, and a fuller participation in American society."[123] Discussing the importance of his own mural, White takes a position at one with the stances of Shahn, Siporin, and, of course, Orozco himself.[124] White may even be said to extend their ideological reach by regarding art as a "necessity": "My main concern is to get my work before common, ordinary

275

people.... A work of art was meant to belong to people.... Art should take its place as one of the necessities of life, like food, clothing, and shelter."[125] In its upper left quadrant, White's tempera mural *The Contribution of the Negro to Democracy in America* depicts a torch-bearing black man, the apparent and most immediate source for the avenging black victim later to appear in and dominate *Freeport.* This mural also celebrates the creativity, leadership, protection, and combat undertaken by the human hand, a highly evocative motif, enhanced in scale through monumental hands that envelop the Rivera-like machinery (resembling that depicted in the *Detroit Industry* fresco cycle [1932–33 (fig. 215)] at the Detroit Institute of Arts), surmounting the whole composition near its center. This painting, in particular, persuades us that Edmund Barry Gaither's argument that "White's work is infused with yesterday's anguish, today's strife, and tomorrow's victory"[126] is no less true for much of Orozco's oeuvre, and it revolves around the powerful arms and industrious hands that both artists are inclined to emphasize and heroicize.

Consideration of Ben Shahn's murals usually elicits his well-documented association with Diego Rivera. That his work has any affinity for Orozco is suggested by Matthew Baigell in a discussion of preliminary studies Shahn did for the never-realized Riker's Island Penitentiary murals he was to have executed with Lou Block in the early 1930s. That ill-fated commission was rescinded when New York's Municipal Art Commission rejected the proposed design as "psychologically unfit" and "antisocial."[127] "The compositional arrangements of the Riker's Island studies," Baigell writes, "are closer to Orozco's work than to Rivera's."[128] The rejection wounded Shahn deeply, given that his work, like Orozco's, centered on humanistic and social issues—epitomized in his series of works dedicated to the unjustly convicted and executed Italian immigrants

Nicola Sacco and Bartolomeo Vanzetti[129]—and that a poll taken of the prisoners at Riker's revealed their partiality to the aborted design.[130]

Although the art historian Jacinto Quirarte claims that Orozco "exerted a great influence"[131] on the youthful Edward Arcenio Chávez, a New Mexico–based Mexican American artist and contemporary of Jacob Lawrence's, Orozco's imprint is not readily apparent in Chávez's WPA output.

Clearly, the foregoing artists have all emulated or admired Orozco, *el maestro* ("the master-teacher"). A few, however, would resist either temptation. A fellow Chicano and contemporary of Chávez's, Arizonian Eugenio Quesada studied mural painting with Charlot and lived and worked in Guadalajara for almost six years during the 1960s. Despite his considerable exposure to Orozco's murals, Quesada judges Orozco, rather audaciously, as a "tremendous artist, but a very bad muralist …his watercolors are as good as anything that has ever been done…but he went mad with murals …he broke up spaces exactly the wrong way…" Commenting on the *Hidalgo* fresco that stimulated White, Quesada refers to the gargantuan priest unceremoniously as "this huge thing" that "is going to fall on top of you…distort[ing] the architectural spaces that are there." He concludes that "Orozco did not take care of these problems. He just painted as if he were dealing with an easel."[132] Philip Guston too was no Orozco sycophant. He disapproved of Orozco's "expressionist" tendencies, "dominated by emotion," but lauded the muralist's "plastic" sensibility.[133]

The question of how Archibald Motley, Marion Kay Greenwood, and Ione Robinson relate to Orozco invites further reflection and research beyond the reach of this essay.

276

Picturing Orozco's Legacy from the Vietnam Era through the Present: A Wall-to-Wall Pageant of Community Murals

Readers will remember Chicago muralist Mitchell Siporin's conception of "a socially moving epic art" endemic to the Midwest and Indiana muralist Gilbert Wilson's prediction that "out of the Middle West, some day, will come something very wholesome and good of art." That "something," which I choose to call a wall-to-wall pageant of community murals—predominantly streetside walls—arose in Chicago some thirty years later during the 1960s and, with the impetus of "a socially moving epic art," spread throughout the United States, Canada, and beyond, persisting unabated into the twenty-first century.[134] A manifesto, "The Artists' Statement," issued during February and March 1971 on the occasion of the *Murals for the People* exhibit at Chicago's Museum of Contemporary Art, cites 1967 as the year of inception for "the movement to create Peoples' Art on public walls in Chicago."[135] The muralist-authors were African Americans Eugene Eda (born 1939) and Bill Walker (born 1927) and white ethnics Mark Rogovin (born 1946) and John P. Weber (born 1942). Their invocation of a "people's art" suggests a widespread public investment in the creative product. Moreover, that same public is understood to be no less engaged and invested in the creative process. Otherwise, their collective "statement" would ring hollow with its claim that such walls have "been celebrated, loved, and protected by community residents because they had a part in it."[136] This notion of community is inextricably tied to Victor Turner's concept of *communitas*. Recall the "modality of social relationship" enlarging upon a mere locus or "area of common living." First and foremost, community murals must be understood as processual undertakings involving many individuals in their conception.

That same public tends to live in and care about the barrio for which the mural is intended. The process might rightly call to mind the "performative," ritualistic, and activist art of pageantry, championed by John Reed and Mabel Dodge Luhan and epitomized in their *Paterson Strike Pageant* of 1913.[137] More recently, community murals, beginning with Chicago's legendary *Wall of Respect* (1967–69 [fig. 279]),[138] have supplanted the communal pageantry of a bygone era.

Like many of Orozco's own mural executions requiring the assistance of others, most of whom have been rendered anonymous by exclusionary documentarians, community murals are not usually virtuoso, single-author, signature expressions. Rather, they are designed and conceived by many hands, often under the direction of one or more experienced mural veterans, for many others to experience. Collectively, these community muralists echo Ben Shahn's artistic and ideological disposition in their dedication "to becoming artists for the people, entering into a living relationship with this vast audience, [and] drawing on the people's boundless potential for creativity."[139] Calling for a response from their viewers, these walls solicit a dialogue of engagement with their public. Bill Walker's observation that such "art is…seen as a force designed to

Fig. 288 · Marcos Raya, **Homenaje a Diego Rivera (Homage to Diego Rivera)**, 1972, photograph by Victor Sorell.

277

dethrone ignorance from its pedestal of influence in the affairs of man…"[140] resonates with the brio of Orozco's remarks to Ione Robinson recognizing art's arsenal. If Orozco's frescoes were his "court," to repeat Guston's eloquent metaphor, where he negotiated for greater justice for humanity, then late-modern community muralists truly emulate his and Charles White's examples, ever mindful of "yesterday's anguish, today's strife, and tomorrow's victory": "Our murals will continue to speak of the liberation struggles of Black and Third-World peoples; they will record history, speak of today, and project toward the future. They will speak of an end to war, racism, and repression, of love, of beauty and of life.…"[141]

Contemporary muralists experienced momentous change. They lived through an epoch profoundly impacted by the fulminations of the war in Vietnam, the stridency of the women's movement, and, above all, the redemptive ethos of the civil rights movement, one fueled by the sheer magnitude of historical personalities/prophets from W. E. B. Dubois and Mahatma Gandhi through Dr. Martin Luther King and his Chicano contemporary the labor leader César Chávez. A need to affirm his black heritage led Eda, who studied with Jacob

Lawrence, to seek out "the most conspicuous buildings in deprived areas,"[142] where he would paint his "walls with tongues." Harvard-educated and white, Weber, who acknowledges Orozco's influence, learned that he too could "create an imagery which spoke directly to ordinary people, which was accepted as their own by people separated from [him] by culture and by a long history of prejudice and oppression."[143] Rogovin, who worked briefly as one of Siqueiros's assistants in Mexico, perceives the late-modern and contemporary mural movement in Marxist terms, eliciting the idea of cultural workers. "We need huge brigades of artists to 'take to the streets' and move along beside the people in their struggles."[144] A rhetoric of denunciatory words and images often communicates the people's yearnings. Such a denunciatory thrust is indeed consistent with the earliest impulses of Orozco's own muralism. Drawing here and there from that repository of remarkable images imbued by Orozco, a few Mexicano/Chican(a)o muralists have quoted him directly in their respective works. Arguably, the earliest of these borrowed denunciatory images dates from 1972, when Marcos Raya (born 1948), the Mexican-born and Chicago-based muralist, appropriated the "fallen" bejeweled prostitute from

Fig. 289 · Marcos Raya, **Cataclismo (Cataclysm)**, 1996, Pilsen neighborhood, Chicago, photograph courtesy Mexican Fine Arts Center/Chicago Historical Society.

the left foreground of *Catharsis* (fig. 252) for his painting *Homenaje a Diego Rivera* ("*Homage to Diego Rivera*") (fig. 288). Something of a parody on Rivera's celebrated mural *Man at the Crossroads* (fig. 251), acknowledged earlier in this paper as "the prototype for an entire genre of contemporary mural painting,"[145] Raya's work clearly paid tribute to Orozco as well with this unequivocal reflection on debauchery among society's rich and powerful.[146] Some four years later, during 1976, the same figure, admittedly reworked and now a casualty of crime and drugs, was again incorporated by Raya, directing the project in concert with Aurelio Díaz Tekpankalli, Juanita Jaramillo Lavadie (born 1949), and Salvador Vega, in a highly charged, dramatic untitled mural painted in Dvorak Park in the heart of Chicago's formerly Bohemian Pilsen community, then and now a Latino stronghold. That work, in Raya's words, "was the first (outdoor) community mural in Pilsen that dealt (explicitly) with community issues, particularly problems plaguing the neighborhood."[147] It was painted over an abandoned, in-progress work by Raymundo Patlán (born 1946). Most recently, during 1996, Raya executed an eight-by-twenty-foot portable mural, *Cataclismo* (*Cataclysm* [fig. 289]), commissioned by Chicago's Mexican Fine Arts Center/Museum and the Chicago Historical Society as part of their joint exhibition of that year, *Pilsen: Our Home, Our Struggle.* Raya's masterfully conceived and executed painting benefits from both Orozco's and Rivera's examples in the delicately drawn figures and complex mix of several perspectives. Orozco's supine prostitute from 1934 now occupies center stage and through her own "cataclysmic," convulsive movements has lost her necklace, replaced by the crown of the Statue of Liberty[148] appearing on "her" head, the only clearly discernible human vestige of what has metamorphosed into a highly abstracted, almost nonobjective being. Around "her" radiate details from others of Raya's works, those of his Mexican

Fig. 290 · Willie F. Herrón III, **La doliente de Hidalgo** (**Hidalgo's Anguish**), 1975–76, acrylic, East Los Angeles, California, photograph by Victor Sorell, © Herrón, 1976.

mentors, and unmistakable references to the Pilsen barrio itself. The composition is also about Chicago and the United States in general, caught in the throes of a global economy and its impact on the local. Raya denounces and laments the displacement of Mexicans and Mexican Americans from Pilsen, while simultaneously acknowledging the disproportionately high incarceration of blacks, two themes that unfold right and left of center, respectively. Below the "big house," military and police forces appear as sinister elements in collusion with politicians and bigots. Directly across from these collective menaces, police brutality is shown invading Pilsen itself. Oddly, or maybe predictably, between these portraits of angst appear symbols of technological progress, suggesting that what began as the promise of the machine age has resulted in humanistic setbacks. It is at this divide that Raya asks his viewers to understand that he, more like Orozco and progressively less like Rivera and Siqueiros, is pessimistic about where technology might, in a biblical sense, "deliver us." Raya's skepticism shares Orozco's "tragic" sensibility and his yearning for justice, tinged with Edward Kienholtz's dramatically infused satirical swipes at the American way of life. Raya's Kienholtzian tableaux extend the drama of

279

his murals into the performative space of multi-media installations.

"Parades," argue scholars Ramón Gutiérrez and Geneviève Fabre, "offer the best example of pageantry."[149] In the 1930s, muralist David Alfaro Siqueiros encouraged his New York–based Experimental Workshop collaborators and students to design political floats and posters for civic parades and rallies.[150] In 1973, some forty years later, Indiana-based artist José Gamaliel González (born 1933) designed a float for the East Chicago Mexican Independence Parade. Titled *Justicia* ("Justice") and mounted at the front of a thirty-five-foot trailer, the cutout Masonite sculpto-painting depicting Father Hidalgo was derived from Orozco's Guadalajara fresco. Surmounting a *casita* ("house-like") structure built with remnant wood from a community home deliberately set afire, the sculpted and painted image denounced in a not so subtle way the specter of imposed and unfair gentrification. Displayed at the rear of the float were photographs of the Mexican Revolution from the famed Archivo Casasola and the exclamatory textual inscription *"Viva la Revolución…*accept me for what I am: *CHICANO*!!!" Amerindian designs rendered on sackcloth skirted the trailer's sides.[151]

William F. Herrón III (born 1951) and Jesse Navarro, like González, draw on the same fresco. The former's mural *La doliente de Hidalgo* (Hidalgo's Anguish, 1975–76 [fig. 290]) and the latter's untitled mural of 1974, both painted in East Los Angeles, quote the elder Hidalgo, his mouth open in a cry and his right hand clutching a flaming torch. Navarro's composition is elegant but somewhat understated, while Herrón's gesticulating, highly agitated priest better retains the dramatic force and impact with which Orozco ignited his own triumphant masterpiece. Hidalgo's *grito* ("cry") was his impassioned "call" made on September 16, 1810, to his parishioners, imploring them to rise in revolt against the mother country Spain: "Long live

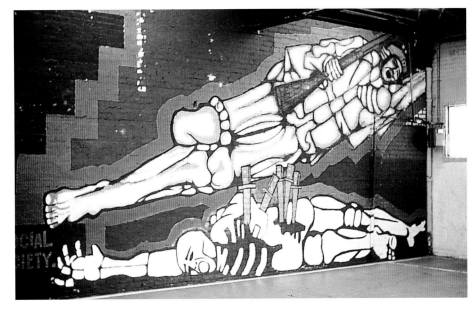

Our Lady of Guadalupe! Long live Mexico!" A militant "response" is attributed to his flock: "Death to the *Gachupines* ["Spaniards"]!" These murals are inscribed with the ongoing cry of Mexicans and Chican(a)os for independence and, ultimately, for justice, a road from denunciation to affirmation. That journey is also consistent with community muralism's inherent spirit of *communitas*, which affords murals the latitude to foster messages of celebration, commemoration, and lamentation, alongside denunciation and indignation. *The Rebirth of Our Nationality* (1972 [fig. 291]), a 260-foot mural directed by Leo Tanguma and painted with the assistance of 150 barrio youth on the side of a

Figs. 291 and 292 · Esteban Villa et al., **The Emergence of the Chicano: Social Struggle in a Bi-Cultural Society** (partial views), 1968, acrylic, Washington Neighborhood Center, Sacramento, California, photographs by Victor Sorell.

factory in Houston, Texas, is a monumental work fusing these disparate potential impulses. The commemorative UFW (United Farm Workers) banner with its distinctive red field and superimposed *huelga* ("strike") eagle-emblazoned white circle occupies a central and focal place. A melee of strident figures converges on that center from both the left and right wings of the mural's picture space. The viewer can discern an Orozcoesque passage at the composition's farthest reach to the right of center. Reflecting on the disproportionately large number of Chicano casualties during the Vietnam War, Tanguma and his collaborators depict a six-figure group denouncing and lamenting the war and its victims. A mother clutches a portrait of her son, probably one among the casualties, while three helmeted, skeletal soldiers in the company of a kneeling supplicant and a cross-carrying sixth figure denounce the war. The "soldiers" and cross-wielding figure recall similarly distorted or caricatured figures from the right-most fragment of *The Departure of Quetzalcoatl* (fig. 173) in Dartmouth's Baker Library. Its complementary panel, *The Coming of Quetzalcoatl* (fig. 171), depicts a supine figure in the foreground lying before two pyramids. Versions of that figure appear in four guises converging on a central giant *huelga* eagle in another mural, *Emergence of the Chicano: Social Struggle in a Bi-Cultural Society* (1968 [fig. 292]), painted by Esteban Villa (born 1930), with art students of Sacramento State College, inside the Washington Neighborhood Center in Sacramento, California. Not unlike the tension underlying the arrival versus the departure of Quetzalcoatl in Orozco's fresco cycle, motion and stasis establish the duality of the bicultural society that Villa et al.'s seminal Chicano mural asks viewers to "struggle" through or negotiate.

What, I wonder, would Orozco's reaction have been to the phenomenon of billboard "murals," or, predating those, what would his likely response have been to a "mural" rendered as a canvas banner,

one so realized by Mexican-born Carlos Almaraz (1941–1989) for the UFW on the occasion of its 1972 convention in Fresno, California (fig. 293). Encoded with Orozco's bold caricaturist impulse, Almaraz, assisted by M.T. Bryan, executed a sixteen-by-twenty-four-foot backdrop "mural" installed immediately behind the speakers' rostrum. Enclosed within a decorative border of repetitive, symbolic, and stylized *huelga* eagles (ubiquitous UFW icons), farm workers are depicted, as César Chávez wanted,

"being attacked by Teamster goons, growers and the Kern County Police."[152] The image of Our Lady of Guadalupe, patron saint of Mexicans and Chican(a)os alike, is held aloft, picket sign fashion, punctuating the confrontation with her talismanic aura. Conversely, a wholly secular indignation fills *No somos esclavos de la migra* ("We are not slaves of the Border Patrol [and the Immigration and Naturalization Service]"), Almaraz's textually inscribed mural of 1974, done with members of the Third Street Gang in the barrio of East Los Angeles (fig. 294). Another snippet of text, "With the worker we shall overcome" (*"Con el trabajador venceremos"*), painted on a facing wall, informs the viewer that the empowered immigrant workers will no longer tolerate their "enslavement"/exploitation by mercenary "bosses" who pay low wages and intimidate them with threats of exposing their "illegal" status to *la migra*. On a lintellike overhang above the doors to the building on which the mural is painted, workers' disembodied hands, conceived in the idiomatic visual vocabulary of both Orozco and Rivera, grasp the earth itself and the tools of their labor in an assertive, commanding way. Not unlike the banner's stylistic verve, this mural is also encoded with Orozco's noted brand of caricature. Recognizing that aspect, Alan W. Barnett, scholar of late-modern and contemporary muralism, observes with acuity that "Almaraz and a few others, following Orozco, have used the distortions of cartoons to create a monumental rhetoric of denunciation."[153] That denunciatory rhetoric's most contemporary guise takes its cue from corporate America. Bold conceptual painted and electronic billboard murals *advertise* their indignation. In 1989 New York Times Square's electronic display signboard, which had once captivated Orozco,[154] still remained but was now surmounted by the so-called twenty-by-forty-foot Spectacolor Board on which Chicana muralist Barbara Carrasco (born 1955) would display her computer-animated billboard

"mural" *Pesticides* (fig. 295). It unfolded in a series of sequential, filmlike frames "communicat[ing] to a vast audience [over the period of a month] a message [in behalf of the UFW] about the deadly effects of pesticides on agricultural workers."[155] Money and *la frontera* define the parameters of another, perhaps unintended intersection, between Orozco and the conceptual billboard art of the Chicano multimedia artist Daniel J. Martínez (born 1951). Mounted atop San Diego's Museum of Contemporary Art, Martínez's billboard, *Guerra de cultura* (Culture War, 1991), "marked the artist's initial visual research with the computer,"[156] featuring a U.S. dollar bill juxtaposed with a Mexican hundred-peso note. The writer and cross-media artist Susan Otto notes that "the currency is torn but merged to create a hybrid bill…underneath [which runs] an ominous quote from the Old Testament: the race is not to the swift nor the battle to the strong. The torn edges [of the bills] mimic the fragmented division that is the international border between the United States and Mexico."[157] Seemingly unknown to Otto is the fact that the Mexican bill bears the stamp of Orozco's *The Trench*! George Washington's serene portrait clashes with Mexico's combative revolutionaries, betraying the oftentimes irreconcilable differences, economic and otherwise, between unequal neighbors on both sides of a contested border. Notwithstanding these inequalities, the religious caption belies their unquestioned immutability through its allusion to a higher, God-given justice or a Promethean-like dispensation.

Conclusion

This study has examined a critical mass of prominent muralists and their monumental works executed during a socially momentous period nearly eight decades long. Our purpose has been to determine to what extent these artists and their respective murals have come under Orozco's far-reaching and pervasive influence in the United States. Ours has also been an examination of the evolution of American muralism from its earliest cloistered origins as commissioned paintings inside government and other public buildings to its current proliferation in outdoor, streetside settings in inner cities. The "theater" of those streets, whose charm captivated Jean Charlot long ago, has come to dominate and inform the mural process and murals themselves to such a degree that notions of public muralism, community identity, ritual observances, pageantry, and performance have become intimately intertwined. Such a revisionist vantage can also help explain more readily how the "tragic" sensibility of Orozco and his followers, a sensibility more easily accommodated in literary and theatrical venues, can express itself as well in the performative, ritualistic processes of community muralism. That significant evolution for murals also obliges art historians to look beyond their own cloistered discipline, even in its more enlightened and new guises, and transcend its often exclusive purview that overlooks the extra-artistic dimensions of the art they study. In Charlot's name, I extend an invitation to my colleagues to join me and imbibe the cultural feast awaiting them in the streets. Together, we shall thus arrive where late-modern and contemporary muralists have transported Orozco's grand legacy.

Fig. 295 · Barbara Carrasco, **Pesticides** electronic billboard mural, three sequential screens, 1989, Times Square, New York, photographs courtesy Public Art Fund, New York.

283

References

Exhibition Checklist

Unless otherwise noted, all works are by José Clemente Orozco.
Dimensions are unframed, height preceding width.

Portraits of the Artist

Self-Portrait (Autoretrato)
1928
Oil on canvas
24 ¼ x 20 in (61.5 x 51 cm)
Museo de Arte Carrillo Gil, Mexico City/INBA 50255
PROVENANCE:
Hudson D. Walker, New York
SELECTED EXHIBITIONS:
New York, Art Students' League, 1929, no. 13; New York, Hudson D. Walker Gallery, 1939, no. 1
Figure 43

EDWARD WESTON
(American, 1886–1958)
José Clemente Orozco
1930
Vintage gelatin silver print
9 ⅛ x 7 ⅜ in (23.2 x 18.7 cm)
Collection of David P. Mixer
Frontispiece/Figure 1

Mexico in Revolution

The exhibition cited as "New York, Art Students' League, 1929," represented the largest group display of drawings from this series in the United States; it featured forty drawings, although none specified by title.

Aristocratic Dance
(Baile aristocrático)
1926–28
Ink on paper
12 ⅝ x 17 ¾ in (32 x 45 cm)
Museo de Arte Carrillo Gil, Mexico City/INBA 16973
PROVENANCE:
Mrs. W. B. Force, New York; Weyhe Gallery, New York

SELECTED EXHIBITIONS:
New York, Art Students' League, 1929 (?)
Figure 39

La cucaracha 3
1926–28
Ink and graphite on paper
11 ¾ x 17 in (30 x 43 cm)
Museo de Arte Carrillo Gil, Mexico City/INBA 17018
PROVENANCE:
Delphic Studios, New York; Galería Central de Arte, Mexico City
SELECTED EXHIBITIONS:
New York, Art Students' League, 1929 (?); La Porte, 1934, no. 48
Figure 25

Dynamited Train (Landscape of Destruction)
1926–28
Ink over graphite on paper
12 3/16 x 18 15/16 in (30.9 x 48.1 cm)
Philadelphia Museum of Art; purchased with the Lola Downing Peck Fund from Carl and Laura Zigrosser Collection, 1976; 1976-97-31
PROVENANCE:
Carl and Laura Zigrosser, Philadelphia, until 1976
SELECTED EXHIBITIONS:
New York, Art Students' League, 1929 (?)
Figure 42

The Explosion (La explosión)
1926–28
Ink on paper
12 ¼ x 18 ⅞ in (31 x 48 cm)
Museo de Arte Carrillo Gil, Mexico City/INBA 16986
PROVENANCE:
Delphic Studios, New York; Galería Central de Arte, Mexico City
SELECTED EXHIBITIONS:
New York, Art Students' League, 1929 (?); La Porte, 1934, no. 46
Figure 296

The Hanged Man
(El ahorcado)
1926–28
Ink on paper
16 ½ x 12 ¼ in (42 x 31 cm)
Museo de Arte Carrillo Gil, Mexico City/INBA 16977
PROVENANCE:
Delphic Studios, New York; Serge Saxe, Fort Worth, Texas; Kleeman Galleries, New York
SELECTED EXHIBITIONS:
New York, Art Students' League, 1929 (?); New York, Hudson D. Walker Gallery, 1939, no. 21
Figure 11

The Rape
1926–28
Ink over graphite on paper
14 ⅛ x 18 15/16 in (35.8 x 48.1 cm)
Philadelphia Museum of Art; purchased with the Lola Downing Peck Fund from Carl and Laura Zigrosser Collection, 1976; 1976-97-32
PROVENANCE:
Carl and Laura Zigrosser, Philadelphia, until 1976
SELECTED EXHIBITIONS:
New York, Art Students' League, 1929 (?)
Figure 8

The Reactionary
(El reaccionario)
1926–28
Ink on paper
12 ⅝ x 19 ¼ in (32 x 49 cm)
Museo de Arte Carrillo Gil, Mexico City/INBA 16980
PROVENANCE:
Mrs. W. B. Force, New York, by 1932; Weyhe Gallery, New York
SELECTED EXHIBITIONS:
New York, Art Students' League, 1929 (?)
Figure 41

The Requiem (El réquiem)
1926–28
Ink on paper
13 x 17 ¾ in (33 x 45 cm)
Museo de Arte Carrillo Gil, Mexico City/INBA 16991
PROVENANCE:
James Vigeveno Galleries, Los Angeles
SELECTED EXHIBITIONS:
New York, Galleries of Marie Sterner, 1929, no. 12; New York, Art Students' League, 1929 (?)
Figure 10

Tears (Lagrimas)
1926–28
Ink and graphite on paper
12 ⅞ x 17 ⅜ in (32.8 x 44 cm)
Collection of Alfonso Dau

Fig. 296 · **The Explosion**.

Fig. 297 · **Under the Maguey**.

PROVENANCE:
Delphic Studios, New York; Fola La
Follette, by 1932; Mary B. Tarcher,
New York; by descent (sold Sotheby's,
New York, May 7, 1981, lot 21)

SELECTED EXHIBITIONS:
New York, Galleries of Marie Sterner,
1929, no. 14; New York, Art Students'
League, 1929 (?); La Porte, 1934, no. 41;
Chicago, 1934, no. 17

Figure 24

Under the Maguey
(Bajo el maguey)
1926–28
Ink and graphite on paper
13 x 17¾ in (33 x 45 cm)

Museo de Arte Carrillo Gil, Mexico
City/INBA 16894

PROVENANCE:
Delphic Studios, New York; Alma Reed,
New York; Weyhe Gallery, New York

SELECTED EXHIBITIONS:
New York, Art Students' League,
1929 (?); La Porte, 1934, no. 43; Chicago,
1934, no. 18

Figure 297

War *(Guerra)*
1926–28
Ink on cardboard
13¾ x 18⅞ in (35 x 48 cm)

Museo de Arte Carrillo Gil, Mexico
City/INBA 16983

PROVENANCE:
Alma Reed, New York; Genaro Estrada

SELECTED EXHIBITIONS:
New York, Galleries of Marie Sterner,
1928, no. 22; New York, Art Students'
League, 1929 (?); La Porte, 1934, no. 37;
Chicago, 1934, no. 15

Figure 162

Wounded *(Heridos)*
1926–28
Ink on paper
12¼ x 18⅞ in (31 x 48 cm)

Museo de Arte Carrillo Gil, Mexico
City/INBA 16993

PROVENANCE:
Alma Reed, New York; private collection, United States

SELECTED EXHIBITIONS:
New York, Art Students' League,
1929 (?); New York, Hudson D. Walker
Gallery, 1939, no. 24

Figure 9

Images of New York

The Strike *(La huelga)*
1926–28
Ink on paper
11¾ x 17⅛ in (30 x 43.5 cm)

The Hermes Trust Collection, courtesy
of Francesco Pellizzi

PROVENANCE:
Delphic Studios, New York; Sotheby's,
New York, June 15, 1979, lot 74; private
collection, Puerto Rico; Christie's,
New York, May 17, 1989, lot 21

SELECTED EXHIBITIONS:
La Porte, 1934, no. 45

Figure 16

Coney Island Side-Show
1928
Oil on canvas
20 x 16 in (50.8 x 40.6 cm)

Private collection, courtesy Galería
Arvil, Mexico City

PROVENANCE:
Delphic Studios, New York; Francis B.
Biddle, Philadelphia, 1929; Corcoran
Gallery of Art, Washington, D.C.
(sold Sotheby's, New York, May 20,
1986, lot 58)

SELECTED EXHIBITIONS:
Philadelphia, 1929; New York, Art
Students' League, 1929, no. 23; New
York, Downtown Gallery, 1931, no. 11;
La Porte, 1934, no. 17

Figure 13

Eighth Avenue
1928
Oil on canvas
19⅝ x 26 in (50 x 66 cm)

Private collection, courtesy Sotheby's

PROVENANCE:
Mrs. E. M. Allewelt, by 1932; sold
Sotheby's, New York, May 12, 1983,
lot 26

SELECTED EXHIBITIONS:
New York, Downtown Gallery, 1929;
New York, Art Students' League, 1929,
no. 27; New York, Downtown Gallery,
1931, no. 6

Figure 54

The Elevated *(El elevado)*
1928
Oil on canvas
20½ x 24½ in (52.1 x 62.3 cm)

Collection of Rosemary Rieser

PROVENANCE:
Delphic Studios, New York; Leonard M.
and Mrs. Margaret W. Rieser, Highland
Park, Ill.; Mrs. Margaret W. Rieser;
by descent to Leonard M. Rieser;
by descent to current owner

SELECTED EXHIBITIONS:
New York, Downtown Gallery, 1929 (?);
New York, Art Students' League, 1929,
no. 21 or 22 (?); New York, Downtown
Gallery, 1931, no. 3 or 4 (?); La Porte,
1934, no. 4 (?)

Citations reflect the fact that several
works of this title exist that are often
indistinguishable in exhibition records:
two nearly identical compositions of
1928 (the second in a private collection,
Mexico City), and a third of a different
composition, from 1929–30, collection
of the Museo Carrillo Gil, below.

Figure 64

New York Factory,
Williamsburg *(Fábrica)*
1928
Oil on canvas
28¼ x 19¾ in (71.5 x 50.3 cm)

Private collection, courtesy Galería
Arvil, Mexico City

PROVENANCE:
Collection of the artist; Inés Amor
(Galería de Arte Mexicano, Mexico City);
by descent; Galería Arvil, Mexico City

SELECTED EXHIBITIONS:
New York, Downtown Gallery, 1929;
New York, Art Students' League, 1929,
no. 17; New York, Downtown Gallery,
1931, no. 5

Figure 55

Queensboro Bridge, New York
(Puente de Queensboro)
1928
Oil on canvas
21⅝ x 27⅞ in (55 x 71 cm)

Museo de Arte Carrillo Gil, Mexico
City/INBA 17241

PROVENANCE:
Kleeman Galleries, New York

SELECTED EXHIBITIONS:
New York, Downtown Gallery, 1929;
New York, Art Students' League, 1929,
no. 16; New York, Downtown Gallery,
1931, no. 1

Figure 53

287

Fig. 299 · **Holiday**.

The Subway

1928

Oil on canvas

16 ⅛ x 22 ⅛ in (41 x 56.2 cm)

The Museum of Modern Art, New York, gift of Abby Aldrich Rockefeller, 1935; 203.35

PROVENANCE:
Abby Aldrich Rockefeller, New York, until 1935

SELECTED EXHIBITIONS:
New York, Downtown Gallery, 1929; New York, Art Students' League, 1929, no. 18 or 20; New York, Downtown Gallery, 1931, no. 7 or 8

Two works of this title and date exist (the other sold Sotheby's May 28/29, 1985, lot 30) but are indistinguishable in gallery records; the multiple citations reflect exhibitions where both were shown.

(Hanover venue only)

Figure 15

Fourteenth Street, Manhattan (Calle catorce, Manhattan)

1928–29

Oil on canvas

28 ¼ x 20 ¼ in (71.8 x 51.4 cm)

Private collection, courtesy Sotheby's

PROVENANCE:
Delphic Studios, New York; Jack D. Tarcher, New York, by 1959; sold Sotheby's, New York, May 7, 1981, lot 25

SELECTED EXHIBITIONS:
New York, Downtown Gallery, 1929; New York, Art Students' League, 1929, no. 28; New York, Downtown Gallery, 1931, no. 2; La Porte, 1934, no. 21

Figure 56

The World's Highest Structure (La estructura más alta del mundo)

1928–30

Oil on canvas

26 ¾ x 15 in (68 x 38 cm)

Orozco Farias Family Collection

PROVENANCE:
From artist by descent

SELECTED EXHIBITIONS:
New York, Delphic Studios, 1930, no. 2

(San Diego venue only)

Figure 57

Subway Post

1929

Oil on canvas

18 ³⁄₁₆ x 14 in (46.2 x 35.6 cm)

Robert L. and Sharon W. Lynch Collection

PROVENANCE:
Delphic Studios, New York; private collection; Mr. and Mrs. Serge Saxe, Fort Worth, Texas, to 1959

SELECTED EXHIBITIONS:
New York, Downtown Gallery, 1929

Figure 263

The Curb

1929–30

Gouache on paper

22 x 15 in (56 x 38 cm)

Museo de Arte Carrillo Gil, Mexico City/INBA 17215

PROVENANCE:
James B. Murphy

SELECTED EXHIBITIONS:
New York, Delphic Studios, 1930, no. 22

Figure 260

Elevated (Elevado)

1929–30

Oil on canvas

30 ⅜ x 23 ⅝ in (77 x 60 cm)

Museo de Arte Carrillo Gil, Mexico City/INBA 17238

PROVENANCE:
Delphic Studios, New York; Kleeman Galleries, New York

SELECTED EXHIBITIONS:
New York, Delphic Studios, 1930, no. 3; New York, Downtown Gallery, 1931, no. 3 or 4 (?); La Porte, 1934, no. 28; Chicago, 1934, no. 11

Citations reflect the fact that several works of this title exist that are often indistinguishable in exhibition records: two nearly identical compositions of 1928 (Rieser collection, above, and a private collection, Mexico City), and this third, different composition.

Figure 58

The Dead (Los muertos)

1931

Oil on canvas

43 ¾ x 36 ¼ in (111 x 92 cm)

Museo de Arte Carrillo Gil, Mexico City/INBA 17268

PROVENANCE:
Delphic Studios, New York; Kleeman Galleries, New York

SELECTED EXHIBITIONS:
La Porte, 1934, no. 3

Figure 51

Successful People (Gente afortunada)

1931

Oil on canvas

18 x 15 in (45.7 x 38 cm)

Private collection, courtesy Mary-Anne Martin/Fine Art, New York

PROVENANCE:
Delphic Studios, New York; Harry Schaeffer, Brooklyn, New York, by 1951; sold Sotheby's, New York, June 4, 1999, lot 131

Fig. 298 · **Three Heads**.

SELECTED EXHIBITIONS:
New York, Junior League, 1931, no. 34

Figure 61

The Committee on Art (*Comité de arte*)

1932

Black wash

14 x 21¼ in (35.6 x 54 cm)

Baltimore Museum of Art, gift of Blanche Adler; BMA 1933.61.2

PROVENANCE:
Delphic Studios, New York; Blanche Adler, by 1933

(U.S. venues only)

Figure 60

Three Heads (*Tres cabezas*)

1932

Oil on canvas

18⅞ x 15⅜ in (48 x 39 cm)

Museo de Arte Carrillo Gil, Mexico City/INBA 17279

PROVENANCE:
Delphic Studios, New York; Morton R. Goldsmith, Westchester, New York, by 1934; Kleeman Galleries, New York

SELECTED EXHIBITIONS:
La Porte, 1934, no. 6; New York, Hudson D. Walker Gallery, 1939, no. 10

Figure 298

Winter (*Invierno*)

1932

Oil on canvas

15 x 18⅛ in (38 x 46 cm)

Museo de Arte Carrillo Gil, Mexico City/INBA 17275

PROVENANCE:
Delphic Studios, New York; William Segall, by 1934; Kleeman Galleries, New York

SELECTED EXHIBITIONS:
La Porte, 1934, no. 7

Figure 230

Holiday (*The Unemployed*)

1933

Oil on canvas

25½ x 20¼ in (65 x 51.4 cm)

Private collection

PROVENANCE:
Aline Barnsdall, Los Angeles, 1933; Gertrude Finnerud; by descent (sold Christie's, New York, May 17, 1989, lot 22)

SELECTED EXHIBITIONS:
La Porte, 1934, no. 32

(Not presented)

Figure 299

Images of Mexico

Mexican House (*Casa mexicana; Adobe Walls*)

1929

Oil on canvas

16½ x 20½ in (41.9 x 52.1 cm)

Allen Memorial Art Museum, Oberlin College, Oberlin, Ohio, gift of Mrs. Malcolm McBride, 1943; 43.273

PROVENANCE:
Mrs. Malcolm L. McBride, Cleveland, Ohio, 1934 to 1943

SELECTED EXHIBITIONS:
New York, Art Students' League, 1929, no. 1 (as *Adobe Walls*); La Porte, 1934, no. 26

(U.S. venues only)

Figure 31

Mexican Hills (*Colinas mexicanas*)

1930

Oil on canvas

16⅞ x 24 in (43 x 61 cm)

Museo de Arte Carrillo Gil, Mexico City/INBA 17253

PROVENANCE:
Aline Barnsdall, Los Angeles; Kleeman Galleries, New York

Figure 30

Mexican Soldiers (*Soldados mexicanos*)

1930

Gouache on paper

33¼ x 25 in (84.5 x 63.5 cm)

Collection of Rodney and Gussie Medeiros

PROVENANCE:
Mrs. Malcolm L. McBride, Cleveland, Ohio, 1930 to about 1959

SELECTED EXHIBITIONS:
New York, Delphic Studios, 1930, no. 18; La Porte, 1934, no. 31

Figure 33

Fig. 301 · **Study for** *Zapata.*

Sleeping (*The Family*)

1930

Oil on canvas

23 3/16 x 31⅛ in (58.8 x 79.1 cm)

San Francisco Museum of Modern Art, Albert M. Bender Collection, bequest of Albert M. Bender; 41.2927

PROVENANCE:
Albert M. Bender, San Francisco, 1930 to 1941

SELECTED EXHIBITIONS:
New York, Delphic Studios, 1930, no. 10 (as *Family*); San Francisco, 1939, no. 927

Figure 300

Study for *Zapata*

1930

Oil on canvas

14½ x 9 in (37 x 23 cm)

Museo de Arte Carrillo Gil, Mexico City/INBA 17265

PROVENANCE:
Delphic Studios, New York; Dr. MacKinley Helm, Boston

SELECTED EXHIBITIONS:
La Porte, 1934, no. 23

Figure 34

289

Fig. 300 · **Sleeping.**

Study for *Zapata*

1930

Gouache on paper

22 ¾ x 14 ½ in (57.8 x 36.9 cm)

Private collection

PROVENANCE:
Sold Christie's, New York, November 16, 1994, lot 49

(Not presented)

Figure 301

Wounded Soldier (*Soldado herido*)

1930

Oil on canvas

44 ½ x 36 ½ in (113 x 93 cm)

Cleveland Museum of Art; gift of Mr. and Mrs. Michael Straight; 1954.864

PROVENANCE:
Delphic Studios, New York; private collection; Mr. and Mrs. Michael Straight, until 1954

SELECTED EXHIBITIONS:
American Federation of Arts, 1930–31, no. 413, as *The Soldier*; Chicago, 1934, no. 3

(U.S. venues only)

Figure 32

Fig. 302 · **Soldier's Wife**.

Pancho Villa

1931

Oil on canvas

27 ½ x 20 in (70 x 51 cm)

Museo de Arte Carrillo Gil, Mexico City/INBA 17271

PROVENANCE:
Delphic Studios, New York; Kleeman Galleries, New York

SELECTED EXHIBITIONS:
New York, Hudson D. Walker Gallery, 1939, no. 9

Figure 222

Zapatistas (*Desfile zapatista*)

1931

Oil on canvas

45 x 55 in (114.3 x 139.7 cm)

The Museum of Modern Art, New York, given anonymously, 1937; 470.37

PROVENANCE:
Stephen C. Clark, New York, 1931–37

SELECTED EXHIBITIONS:
Junior League, New York, 1931, no. 32; La Porte, 1934, no. 1; Chicago, 1934, no. 1; New York, 1940, no. 119

(Hanover venue only)

Figure 37

Mexican Pueblo (*Pueblo mexicano*)

1932

Oil on canvas

30 x 37 in (76.2 x 94 cm)

Detroit Institute of Arts, Founders Society Purchase, General Membership; 42.103

PROVENANCE:
Private collection, 1932 to 1942

Figure 257

The Delphic Circle

Portrait of Eva Sikelianos

1928

Oil on canvas

30 x 22 in (76 x 56 cm)

Museo de Arte Carrillo Gil, Mexico City/INBA 17244

PROVENANCE:
Delphic Studios, New York; Dr. Max Honigbaum and Else Honigbaum, San Francisco, by 1939; Kleeman Galleries, New York

SELECTED EXHIBITIONS:
New York, Art Students' League, 1929, no. 15; La Porte, 1934, no. 2; San Francisco, 1939, no. 928

Figure 59

Broken Glass (*Espejo roto*)

1929

Oil on canvas

About 12 x 20 in (30.5 x 50.8 cm)

Lent by Nikki R. Keddie

PROVENANCE:
Delphic Studios, New York; Mr. and Mrs. Harry Ragozin, New York, 1946–87; by descent to current owner

SELECTED EXHIBITIONS:
New York, Brooklyn Museum, 1931, no. 46; La Porte, 1934, no. 9

Figure 269

Embrace (*Abrazo*)

1929

Gouache on paper

14 ½ x 21 ½ in (36.9 x 54.6 cm)

William H. and Shirley Wilson Family Collection

PROVENANCE:
James B. Murphy, by 1930

SELECTED EXHIBITIONS:
New York, Delphic Studios, 1930, no. 19

Figure 266

Vigil (*Vigilia*)

1929

Oil on canvas

12 x 15 in (30.5 x 38.1 cm)

Private collection, courtesy Mary-Anne Martin/Fine Art, New York

PROVENANCE:
Fairfield Porter, by 1934; Estate of Fairfield Porter; sold Sotheby's, New York, May 11, 1979, lot 264 (as *Paisaje mitológico*)

SELECTED EXHIBITIONS:
New York, Delphic Studios, 1930, no. 5; Boston, 1930; La Porte, 1934, no. 10; Chicago, 1934, no. 4

Figure 264

Drama

1930

Oil on canvas

20 x 27 ⅞ in (50.6 x 70.8 cm)

Private collection, courtesy Galería Arvil, Mexico City

PROVENANCE:
Delphic Studios, New York; Victor Wolfson; sold Sotheby's, New York, November 20, 1990, lot 145

SELECTED EXHIBITIONS:
New York, Delphic Studios, 1930, no. 9; La Porte, 1934, no. 30; Chicago, 1934, no. 13

Figure 44

Have Another (*Échate la otra* [*Mexican Pulqueria*])

1930

Oil on canvas

20 x 26 in (50.7 x 66.3 cm)

Cleveland Museum of Art; gift of Mrs. Malcolm L. McBride; 1943.539

PROVENANCE:
Mrs. Malcolm L. McBride, Cleveland, Ohio, 1930–43

SELECTED EXHIBITIONS:
New York, Delphic Studios, 1930, no. 14; American Federation of Arts, 1930–31, no. 416, as *La Pulquería*; La Porte, 1934, no. 27

(U.S. venues only)

Figure 22

Fig. 303 · **Three Generations**.

Mannikins

1930

Oil on canvas

15 ⅛ x 21 in (38.4 x 53.3 cm)

Private collection, United States

PROVENANCE:
Delphic Studios, New York, 1930–32;
Charles Recht, by 1934

SELECTED EXHIBITIONS:
New York, Delphic Studios, 1930,
no. 12; American Federation of Arts,
1930–31, no. 417a; La Porte, 1934, no. 8

Figure 273

The Martyr (*El mártir*)

1930

Oil on canvas

24 ¼ x 16 in (61.6 x 40.6 cm)

Private collection

PROVENANCE:
Aline Barnsdall, Los Angeles, 1930; sold
Galería de Arte Mexicano. Mexico City
to Elizabeth and John Moors Cabot; by
1950s; by descent

(U.S. venues only)

Figure 26

That Night (*Aquella noche*)

1930

Oil on canvas

16 ⅞ x 12 in (43 x 30.5 cm)

Collection of Alfonso Dau

PROVENANCE:
Delphic Studios, New York; Clarence T.
Etter, Detroit, by 1932; sold Sotheby's,
New York, June 10, 1982, lot 38

SELECTED EXHIBITIONS:
New York, Delphic Studios, 1930, no. 11

Figure 265

Prints and Book Illustrations

PRINTS

(Note: Dimensions reflect image size;
arranged in order of execution)

Vaudeville in Harlem

1928

Lithograph on wove paper

11 ⅞ x 15 ⅞ in (30.1 x 40.4 cm)

San Francisco Museum of Modern Art;
Albert M. Bender Collection, gift of
Albert M. Bender; 35.3071

Museo de Arte Carrillo Gil/INBA 17112

Figure 12

The Flag (*La bandera*)

1928

Lithograph on wove paper

10 ⅛ x 16 in (25.7 x 41.9 cm)

Philadelphia Museum of Art; pur-
chased with the Lola Downing Peck
Fund from Carl and Laura Zigrosser
Collection, 1976; 1976-97-36

Museo de Arte Carrillo Gil/INBA 17109

Figure 67

The Requiem (*El réquiem*)

1928

Lithograph on wove paper

11 ¹³⁄₁₆ x 15 ⅞ in (30 x 40.3 cm)

Philadelphia Museum of Art; gift of
Henry P. McIlhenny, 1943; 1943-82-1

Museo de Arte Carrillo Gil/INBA 17106

Figure 68

Ruined House (*Casa arruinada*)

1929

Lithograph on wove paper

11 ¹³⁄₁₆ x 15 ⅞ in (32 x 45.2 cm)

Philadelphia Museum of Art; pur-
chased with the Lola Downing Peck
Fund from Carl and Laura Zigrosser
Collection, 1976; 1976-97-53

Museo de Arte Carrillo Gil/INBA 17119

Figure 69

Mexican Peasants Working (*Inditos*)

1929

Lithograph on wove paper

12 ⅛ x 17 ¹⁄₁₆ in (31 x 43.3 cm)

San Diego Museum of Art, gift of the
Latin American Arts Committee,
1972:182

Hood Museum of Art, Dartmouth
College, Hanover, New Hampshire; pur-
chased through the Julia L. Whittier
Fund; PR.930.15.1

Museo de Arte Carrillo Gil/INBA 17171

Figure 74

Mexican Landscape (*Paisaje mexicano*)

1930

Lithograph on wove paper

14 x 18 in (35.6 x 45.7 cm)

San Francisco Museum of Modern Art;
Albert M. Bender Collection, gift of
Albert M. Bender; 35.1644

Museo de Arte Carrillo Gil/INBA 17180

Figure 73

Mexican Pueblo (*Pueblo mexicano*)

1930

Lithograph on wove paper

10 ⅞ x 15 ¼ in (27.6 x 38.9 cm)

Philadelphia Museum of Art, gift of
Henry P. McIlhenny, 1943; 1943-82-9

Museo de Arte Carrillo Gil/INBA 17184

Figure 72

Grief (*Aflicción*)

1930

Lithograph on wove paper

11 ³¹⁄₃₂ x 9 ¹⁵⁄₁₆ in (30.4 x 25.2 cm)

Hood Museum of Art, Dartmouth
College, Hanover, New Hampshire;
purchased through the William S.
Rubin Fund, pr.985.40.2

Museo de Arte Carrillo Gil/INBA 17117

Figure 71

Soldier's Wife (*Embarazada*)

1930

Lithograph on wove paper

15 ⅞ x 10 in (40.4 x 25.4 cm)

Philadelphia Museum of Art; pur-
chased with the Lola Downing Peck
Fund from Carl and Laura Zigrosser
Collection, 1976; 1976-97-55

Museo de Arte Carrillo Gil/INBA 17161

Figure 302

Three Generations (*Tres generaciones*)

1930

Lithograph on wove paper

10 ⁷⁄₁₆ x 14 ¹³⁄₁₆ in (26.5 x 37.6 cm)

San Diego Museum of Art, gift of
University Women's Club, 1930:48

Hood Museum of Art, Dartmouth
College, Hanover, New Hampshire;
gift of Marc Efron, class of 1965, and
Barbara Bares; PR.2001.44.3

Museo de Arte Carrillo Gil/INBA 17165

Figure 303

291

Unemployed (*Desempleados*)
1932 (Paris)
Lithograph on wove paper
14⁹/₃₂ x 10¹⁵/₁₆ in (36.5 x 26.5 cm)

Philadelphia Museum of Art; purchased with the Lola Downing Peck Fund from Carl and Laura Zigrosser Collection, 1976; 1976-97-59

Figure 82

The Hanged Men
(*Negros ahorcados*)
About 1933
Lithograph on wove paper
12 ³/₄ x 8 ¹⁵/₁₆ in (32.3 x 22.7 cm)

Philadelphia Museum of Art; purchased with the Lola Downing Peck Fund from Carl and Laura Zigrosser Collection, 1976; 1975-36-10

Museo de Arte Carrillo Gil/INBA 17186

Figure 80

BOOK ILLUSTRATIONS

Mariano Azuela
The Underdogs (*Los de abajo*), first English edition

Illustrated by José Clemente Orozco
New York: Brentano's, 1929

Dartmouth College Library, Hanover, New Hampshire

Figures 76–79

The Hanged Man
(*El ahorcado*)
Illustration for *The Underdogs*
1929
Ink on paper
10 ¹/₂ x 7 in (26.7 x 17.8 cm)

Robert L. and Sharon W. Lynch Collection

PROVENANCE:
Mr. and Mrs. Serge Saxe, Fort Worth, Texas, to 1959

Figure 78

Soldier's Wives (*Soldaderas*)
Illustration for *The Underdogs*
1929
Ink on paper
10 ¹/₂ x 7 in (16.7 x 17.8 cm)

San Francisco Museum of Modern Art: Albert M. Bender Collection, gift of Albert M. Bender; 35.2999

PROVENANCE:
Albert M. Bender, San Francisco, until 1935

Figure 77

Susan Smith
*The Glories of Venus:
A Novel of Modern Mexico,*
first edition

Illustrated by José Clemente Orozco
New York/London: Harper & Brothers, 1931

Dartmouth College Library, Hanover, New Hampshire

Figure 304

Preparatory Drawings for Murals

Prometheus (1930), Pomona College, Claremont, California

The provenance and credit line for the preparatory drawings for *Prometheus* in the Pomona College collection are as follows: Collection of the artist; by descent to the Orozco family; Pomona College purchase, 2000; Museum purchase with funds provided by the estate of Walter and Elise Mosher.

Study for central panel
1930
Graphite on paper
17 ⁵/₈ x 23 ³/₈ in (44.7 x 59.4 cm)

Pomona College, Claremont, California; P2000.2.1 (1174)

Figure 115

Fig. 304 · Color drawings across from the title page and across from page 206 in Susan Smith, **The Glories of Venus**, Copyright 1931 by Susan Smith.
Drawings copyright 1931 by Harper and Brothers, renewed © 1959 by Harper and Brothers. Reprinted by permission of HarperCollins Publishers, Inc.

Study for ceiling panel
1930
Graphite on paper
6 ³/₈ x 28 in (16.2 x 71.1 cm)

Pomona College, Claremont, California; P2000.2.2 (1175)

Figure 119

Study for west panel (Zeus, Hera, and Io)
1930
Graphite on paper
13 ⁷/₈ x 6 ¹/₂ in (35.2 x 16.4 cm)

Pomona College, Claremont, California; P2000.2.3 (1176)

Figure 120

Study of centaur and baby for east panel
1930
Graphite on paper
8 ¹/₂ x 7 ³/₄ in (21.6 x 19.7 cm)

Pomona College, Claremont, California; P2000.2.5 (1178)

Figure 121

Study of right forearm and detail (central panel)
1930
Charcoal on paper
11 ³/₈ x 14 ⁵/₈ in (28.8 x 37.1 cm)

Pomona College, Claremont, California; P2000.2.9 (1182)

Figure 123

Study of torso from back (central panel)
1930
Charcoal on paper
16 ¹/₂ x 11 ³/₄ in (42 x 30 cm)

Pomona College, Claremont, California; P2000.2.11 (1184)

Figure 117

Study of raised left arm with outline of head (central panel)
1930
Charcoal on paper
11 ³/₄ x 7 ³/₈ in (29.8 x 18.6 cm)

Pomona College, Claremont, California; P2000.2.13 (1186)

Figure 125

Study of back of torso with
left arm raised over head
(central panel)
1930
Charcoal on paper
14⅝ x 11⅜ in (37 x 28.8 cm)

Pomona College, Claremont, California;
P2000.2.14 (1187)

Figure 118

Study of leaning figure
(central panel)
1930
Charcoal on paper
15¾ x 11¾ in (40 x 30 cm)

Pomona College, Claremont, California;
P2000.2.15 (1188)

Figure 116

**The New School for Social
Research (1930–1931),
New York, New York**

Study for *Struggle in the
Orient* (Gandhi)
1930–31
Graphite on paper
14⅜ x 17½ in (36.5 x 44.6 cm)

Instituto Cultural Cabañas,
Guadalajara/INBA 14657

PROVENANCE:
Collection of the artist; by descent to
the Orozco family

Figure 151

Study for *Struggle in the
Occident* (Lenin)
1930–31
Graphite on paper
14¼ x 19½ in (36.3 x 49.4 cm)

Instituto Cultural Cabañas,
Guadalajara/INBA 14858

PROVENANCE:
Collection of the artist; by descent to
the Orozco family.

Figure 150

Study for *Homecoming of
the Worker of the New Day*
1930–31
Graphite on paper
10 x 22½ in (25.4 x 57.4 cm)

New School University Art Collection,
New York; WP1133

Figure 149

Study for north wall
1930–31
Graphite on paper
13⅝ x 13⅞ in (34.5 x 35.4 cm)

Instituto Cultural Cabañas,
Guadalajara/INBA 12983

PROVENANCE:
Collection of the artist; by descent to
the Orozco family

Figure 153

Study of tools
1930–31
Graphite on paper
15⅛ x 12¼ in (38.4 x 31.2 cm)

Instituto Cultural Cabañas,
Guadalajara/INBA 13026

PROVENANCE:
Collection of the artist; by descent to
the Orozco family

Figure 154

Study for east wall
1930–31
Graphite on paper
14³⁄₁₆ x 16⅜ in (36 x 41.7 cm)

Hood Museum of Art, Dartmouth
College, Hanover, New Hampshire;
purchased through gifts from Mr. and
Mrs. Peter B. Bedford; Jane and Raphael
Bernstein; Walter Burke, class of 1944;
Mr. and Mrs. Richard D. Lombard;
Nathan Pearson, class of 1932; David V.
Picker, class of 1953; Rodman C.
Rockefeller, Class of 1954; Kenneth
Roman, Jr., class of 1952, and Adolph
Weil, Jr., class of 1935; D.988.52.244

PROVENANCE:
Collection of the artist; by descent to
the Orozco family; Hood Museum of
Art purchase 1988

Figure 152

Study for west wall
1930–31
Graphite on paper
14¼ x 17 in (36.2 x 43.2 cm)

Hood Museum of Art, Dartmouth
College, Hanover, New Hampshire;
purchased through gifts from Mr. and
Mrs. Peter B. Bedford; Jane and Raphael
Bernstein; Walter Burke, class of 1944;
Mr. and Mrs. Richard D. Lombard;
Nathan Pearson, class of 1932; David V.
Picker, class of 1953; Rodman C.
Rockefeller, class of 1954; Kenneth
Roman, Jr., class of 1952, and Adolph
Weil, Jr., class of 1935; D.988.52.206

PROVENANCE:
Collection of the artist; by descent to
the Orozco family; Hood Museum of
Art purchase 1988

Figure 84

Study of geometric patterns
1930–31
Graphite on paper
7¹¹⁄₁₆ x 17¹⁵⁄₁₆ in (19.5 x 45.6 cm)

Hood Museum of Art, Dartmouth
College, Hanover, New Hampshire;
purchased through gifts from Mr. and
Mrs. Peter B. Bedford; Jane and Raphael
Bernstein; Walter Burke, class of 1944;
Mr. and Mrs. Richard D. Lombard;
Nathan Pearson, class of 1932; David V.
Picker, class of 1953; Rodman C.
Rockefeller, Class of 1954; Kenneth
Roman, Jr., class of 1952, and Adolph
Weil, Jr., class of 1935; D.988.52.261

PROVENANCE:
Collection of the artist; by descent to
the Orozco family; Hood Museum of
Art purchase 1988

Figure 155

*The Epic of American
Civilization* (1932–34),
**Dartmouth College, Hanover,
New Hampshire**

Unless otherwise noted, the provenance and credit line for the preparato-
ry drawings for *The Epic of American
Civilization* in the Hood Museum of
Art collection are as follows: Collection
of the artist; by descent to the Orozco
family; Hood Museum of Art purchase
1988; purchased through gifts from
Mr. and Mrs. Peter B. Bedford; Jane and
Raphael Bernstein; Walter Burke, class
of 1944; Mr. and Mrs. Richard D.
Lombard; Nathan Pearson, class of
1932; David V. Picker, class of 1953;
Rodman C. Rockefeller, class of 1954;
Kenneth Roman, Jr., class of 1952, and
Adolph Weil, Jr., class of 1935.

Study for *Man Released
from the Mechanistic to the
Creative Life*
1932
Graphite on paper
20 x 15 in (50.8 x 38.1 cm)

Hood Museum of Art, Dartmouth
College, Hanover, New Hampshire;
D.988.52.262

Figure 195

Study of a hand (back) for
*Man Released from the Mech-
anistic to the Creative Life*
1932
Graphite and red chalk on
tracing paper mounted to
laid paper
16⅝ x 13⁵⁄₁₆ in (42.3 x 33.8 cm)

Hood Museum of Art, Dartmouth
College, Hanover, New Hampshire; gift
of Benjamin Weiss, D.992.20.1

PROVENANCE:
Benjamin Weiss

Figure 196

293

Study of Eleazar Wheelock
with Indians

1932–34

Graphite on cream paper

10 ½ x 26 ⅝ in (26.7 x 67.6 cm)

Hood Museum of Art, Dartmouth
College, Hanover, New Hampshire;
D.988.52.265

Figure 228

Study of turrets and guns

1932–34

Graphite on cream paper

18 ⅝ x 19 ⅛ in (47.3 x 48.6 cm)

Hood Museum of Art, Dartmouth
College, Hanover, New Hampshire;
D.988.52.264

Figure 305

Composition study for
Migration

1932–34

Ink on paper

19 ⅞ x 15 ⅜ in (50.5 x 39.1 cm)

Hood Museum of Art, Dartmouth
College, Hanover, New Hampshire;
W.988.52.14

Fig. 305 · Study of turrets and guns.

Figure 85

Figure study for *Migration*

1932–34

Graphite on cream paper

20 x 15 in (50.8 x 38.1 cm)

Hood Museum of Art, Dartmouth
College, Hanover, New Hampshire;
D.988.52.16

Figure 86

Anatomical studies

1932–34

Graphite on tracing paper

12 ³/₁₆ x 6 ⁹/₁₆ in (30.9 x 16.2 cm)

Hood Museum of Art, Dartmouth
College, Hanover, New Hampshire;
D.988.52.250

Figure 99

Study of head for *Migration*

1932–34

Ink on paper

14 x 18 ½ in (35.6 x 47 cm)

Hood Museum of Art, Dartmouth
College, Hanover, New Hampshire;
W.988.52.12

Figure 87

Fig. 306 · Study of arm for **Ancient Human Sacrifice**.

Composition study for
Ancient Human Sacrifice

1932–34

Graphite on cream paper

20 ⅞ x 15 ½ in (53 x 39.4 cm)

Hood Museum of Art, Dartmouth
College, Hanover, New Hampshire;
D.988.52.33

Figure 210

Study of arm for *Ancient
Human Sacrifice*

1932–34

Charcoal on cream paper

18 ¼ x 14 ½ in (46.4 x 36.8 cm)

Hood Museum of Art, Dartmouth
College, Hanover, New Hampshire;
D.988.52.32

Figure 306

Study of warriors' heads for
Ancient Human Sacrifice

1932–34

Tempera on paper

14 ⁷/₁₆ x 18 ⅞ in (36.7 x 47.8 cm)

Instituto Cultural Cabañas, Guadalajara
INBA 13797

PROVENANCE:
Collection of the artist; by descent to
the Orozco family

Figure 101

Study of head of
Quetzalcoatl for *The Coming
of Quetzalcoatl*

1932–34

Graphite on tracing paper

29 ¾ x 20 ½ in (75.6 x 52.1 cm)

Hood Museum of Art, Dartmouth
College, Hanover, New Hampshire;
D.988.52.36

Figure 307

Study for the
Pre-Columbian Golden Age

1932–34

Gouache on paper

17 ¼ x 24 ⅜ in (43.8 x 61.9 cm)

Orozco Farias Family Collection;
on extended loan to the Hood Museum
of Art, Dartmouth College, Hanover,
New Hampshire; EL.W.900.44.5

PROVENANCE:
Collection of the artist; by descent

Figure 201

Composition study for
left half of *The Departure
of Quetzalcoatl*

1932–34

Gouache on paper

19 ¼ x 9 ¾ in (48.9 x 24.8 cm)

Hood Museum of Art, Dartmouth
College, Hanover, New Hampshire;
W.988.52.80

Figure 102

Composition study for
left half of *The Departure
of Quetzalcoatl*

1932–34

Gouache on paper

19 ¾ x 14 ⅞ in (50.2 x 37.5 cm)

Hood Museum of Art, Dartmouth
College, Hanover, New Hampshire;
W.988.52.81

Figure 202

Fig. 307 · Study of head of Quetzalcoatl for **The Coming of Quetzalcoatl**.

Study of hand for
The Departure of Quetzalcoatl
1932–34
Graphite on paper
11 ⅞ x 22 ¼ in (30.2 x 56.5 cm)

Hood Museum of Art, Dartmouth
College, Hanover, New Hampshire; gift
of Adolph Weil, Jr., class of 1935, and
Robert S. Weil, class of 1940, in honor
of Churchill P. Lathrop; D.978.19

PROVENANCE:
William H. Duke; sold Sotheby's,
New York, April 5, 1978, lot 42a;
Adolph Weil, Jr., and Robert S. Weil,
Montgomery, Alabama

Figure 309

Composition study for
Cortez and the Cross
1932–34
Tempera on paper
17 ¾ x 17 ⅝ in (45 x 44.7 cm)

Instituto Cultural Cabañas, Guadalajara
INBA 14560

PROVENANCE:
Collection of the artist; by descent to
the Orozco family

Figure 212

Composition study for
The Machine
1932–34
Graphite on tracing paper
18 ⁹⁄₁₆ x 19 ⅝ in (47.1 x 49.8 cm)

Hood Museum of Art, Dartmouth
College, Hanover, New Hampshire;
D.988.52.117

Fig 310

Study of arms for
The Departure of Quetzalcoatl
1932–34
Graphite on tracing paper
7 x 11 ¼ in (17.8 x 28.6 cm)

Hood Museum of Art, Dartmouth
College, Hanover, New Hampshire;
D.988.52.104

Figure 308

Transfer drawing of head
with open jaw for
The Departure of Quetzalcoatl
1932–34
Graphite on tracing paper
13 ½ x 11 ½ in (34.3 x 29.2 cm)

Hood Museum of Art, Dartmouth
College, Hanover, New Hampshire;
D.988.52.77

Figure 88

Study of Quetzalcoatl for
The Departure of Quetzalcoatl
1932–34
Crayon on tracing paper
32 ¼ x 24 ⅛ in (81.9 x 61.3 cm)

The Museum of Modern Art, New
York; gift of Clemente Orozco
Valladares; 85.62

PROVENANCE:
Collection of the artist; by descent

(Hanover venue only)

Figure 203

Composition study for
right half of *The Departure
of Quetzalcoatl*
1932–34
Gouache on paper
17 ¾ x 17 ¾ in (45.1 x 45.1 cm)

Hood Museum of Art, Dartmouth
College, Hanover, New Hampshire;
W.988.52.82

Figure 103

Fig. 308 · Study of arms for **The Departure of Quetzalcoatl**.

295

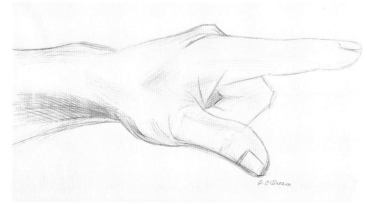

Fig. 309 · Study of hand for **The Departure of Quetzalcoatl**.

Composition study for
Anglo-America
1932–34
Graphite on paper
18¼ x 20¾ in (46.4 x 52.7 cm)

Hood Museum of Art, Dartmouth
College, Hanover, New Hampshire;
D.988.52.174

Figure 217

Composition study for
Anglo-America
1932–34
Graphite on paper
19½ x 16½ in (49.5 x 41.9 cm)

Hood Museum of Art, Dartmouth
College, Hanover, New Hampshire;
D.988.52.131

Figure 218

Composition study for
Hispano-America
1932–34
Graphite on paper
20 x 14 in (50.7 x 35.7 cm)

Instituto Cultural Cabañas,
Guadalajara/INBA 14705

PROVENANCE:
Collection of the artist; by descent to
the Orozco family

Figure 311

Study of head for
Hispano-America
1932–34
Graphite on cream paper
16¼ x 14¾ in (41.3 x 37.5 cm)

Hood Museum of Art, Dartmouth
College, Hanover, New Hampshire;
D.988.52.154

Figure 220

Composition study for
Gods of the Modern World
1932–34
Crayon and graphite on paper
18½ x 25⅛ in (46.9 x 63.6 cm)

The Museum of Modern Art, New York,
gift of Clemente Orozco Valladares;
86.62

PROVENANCE:
Collection of the artist; by descent

(Hanover venue only)

Figure 96

Composition study for
Gods of the Modern World
1932–34
Graphite on tracing paper
18¹¹⁄₁₆ x 23¹¹⁄₁₆ in (47.5 x 60.2 cm)

Hood Museum of Art, Dartmouth
College, Hanover, New Hampshire;
D.988.52.155

Figure 223

Fig. 310 · Composition study for **The Machine**.

Fig. 311 · Composition study for **Hispano-America**.

Fig. 312 · Composition study for **Modern Industrial Man**, right panel.

Anatomical studies for
Gods of the Modern World
1932–34
Graphite on tracing paper
6⁷⁄₁₆ x 9½ in. (16.4 x 24.1 cm)

Hood Museum of Art, Dartmouth
College, Hanover, New Hampshire;
D.988.52.167

Figure 98

Composition study for
Gods of the Modern World
1932–34
Gouache on paper
18⁹⁄₁₆ x 26 in (47.1 x 66 cm)

Hood Museum of Art, Dartmouth
College, Hanover, New Hampshire;
W.988.52.171

Figure 100

Composition study for
Modern Human Sacrifice
1932–34
Graphite on tracing paper
19¾ x 18¾ in (50.2 x 47.6 cm)

Hood Museum of Art, Dartmouth
College, Hanover, New Hampshire;
D.988.52.177

Figure 225

Composition study of Christ
chopping the cross for
*Modern Migration of the
Spirit*
1932–34
Graphite on tracing paper
19¾ x 17⁵⁄₈ in (50.2 x 44.7 cm)

Hood Museum of Art, Dartmouth
College, Hanover, New Hampshire;
D.988.52.207

Figure 90

Composition study for
*Modern Migration of the
Spirit*
1932–34
Graphite on tracing paper
18¾ x 23¾ in (47.6 x 60.3 cm)

Hood Museum of Art, Dartmouth
College, Hanover, New Hampshire;
D.988.52.196

Figure 91

Composition study for
*Modern Migration of the
Spirit*
1932–34
Graphite on tracing paper
21¼ x 18¾ in (54 x 47.6 cm)

Hood Museum of Art, Dartmouth
College, Hanover, New Hampshire;
D.988.52.197

Figure 95

Transfer drawing of head for
*Modern Migration of the
Spirit*
1932–34
Graphite on tracing paper
23⁵⁄₈ x 18¾ in (60 x 47.6 cm)

Hood Museum of Art, Dartmouth
College, Hanover, New Hampshire;
D.988.52.199

Figure 89

Composition study
for right panel of *Modern
Industrial Man*
1932–34
Graphite on paper
19 x 11¾ in (48.3 x 29.8 cm)

Hood Museum of Art, Dartmouth
College, Hanover, New Hampshire;
D.988.52.245

Figure 312

Figure study for central panel
of *Modern Industrial Man*
1932–34
Graphite on tracing paper
12½ x 18¾ in (31.8 x 47.6 cm)

Hood Museum of Art, Dartmouth
College, Hanover, New Hampshire;
D.988.52.228

Figure 231

Study for central panel of
Modern Industrial Man
1932–34
Graphite on paper
10½ x 28¾ in (26.7 x 73 cm)

Hood Museum of Art, Dartmouth
College, Hanover, New Hampshire;
D.988.52.237

Figure 232

297

Chronology

November 23, 1883

José Clemente Orozco is born in Zapotlán el Grande (now Ciudad Guzmán), Jalisco, Mexico.

1886–90

The Orozco family resides in Guadalajara.

1897–1905

As a student in Mexico City Orozco studies agronomy at an agricultural school while taking part-time classes in art and architecture at the San Carlos Academy. In 1905 an accident involving gunpowder leads to the amputation of Orozco's left hand.

1906

Orozco enrolls formally in the San Carlos Academy; he studies painting with Julio Ruelas and Geraldo Murillo, who was known as Doctor Atl.

November 20, 1910

The beginning of the Mexican Revolution: Francisco Madero designates this day as the start of the movement against the presidency of Porfirio Díaz. Political instability characterizes much of the next two decades of Mexican history.

1911

Death of Orozco's father; Orozco takes part in the student strike at the academy that leads to liberal reforms. He begins drawing political cartoons for leftist newspapers in Mexico City (*El Ahuizote, Multicolor, Ojo Parado*), often taking an anti-Madero stand. Diego Rivera travels to Europe and circulates in artistic circles in Paris during virtually all of the Mexican revolutionary period, returning to Mexico in 1920.

1912–13

Orozco establishes a studio in Mexico City and begins a watercolor series of brothel scenes titled *The House of Tears*; he continues political cartooning. Madero, now president, is arrested in February 1913, and his government is overthrown by General Victoriano Huerta. Further unrest follows, with factions led by Venustiano Carranza, Pancho Villa, and Emiliano Zapata.

1914–15

Constitutionalist government is established by Carranza in 1914; with the occupation of Mexico City by the forces of Villa and Zapata in 1915, Carranza supporters, including Orozco and Doctor Atl, flee to Orizaba, Veracruz. There Orozco contributes political cartoons to a local newspaper (*La Vanguardia*);

Fig. 314 · **La cucaracha 2**, 1926–28, ink on paper, private collection, courtesy Christie's, © Christie's Images NY.

David Alfaro Siqueiros, also in Orizaba, is a correspondent for the same publication.

September 1916

Orozco's first solo exhibition. He shows drawings and watercolors, mostly studies of women and brothel scenes, at the Librería Biblos in Mexico City, where they receive a mixed reception.

1917–19

Carranza is elected president in May 1917, and a new constitution is adopted. Zapata is murdered in April 1919. Meanwhile, in 1917 Orozco travels to the United States for the first time. Upon his arrival, many of his works from *The House of Tears* series are confiscated and destroyed by U.S. Customs. The artist visits San Francisco, where he paints signs and movie posters, and New York City.

1920

Orozco returns to Mexico City and establishes a studio in the suburb of Coyoacán. General Álvaro Obregón is elected president after the assassination of Carranza.

1922–23

Siqueiros and Rivera are among the artists invited by José Vasconcelos, minister of education, to paint murals in the National Preparatory School in Mexico City. With them, Orozco is among the founding members in 1923 of the Union of Revolutionary Painters, Sculptors, and Engravers of Mexico, which has links to the Mexican Communist Party. Orozco draws caricatures for the union's paper, *El Machete*. Orozco marries Margarita Valladares in 1923 in Mexico City; the couple will have three children: Clemente, Alfredo, and

Lucrecia. Uprisings against Obregón's government follow the murder of Pancho Villa.

1923–26

Orozco also executes murals in the National Preparatory School, eventually decorating three floors of the colonial structure. His first work period there ends amid student protests in July 1924; he returns and has finished the project by September 1926. In the interim, he paints the mural *Omniscience* (1925) at the House of Tiles in Mexico City and completes the mural *Social Revolution* (1926) at the Industrial School in Orizaba. He sends new work to Paris for an exhibition at the Galerie Bernheim-Jeune in December 1925. At the urging of the American art critic Anita Brenner, he begins in 1926 a series of ink drawings of Mexican revolutionary scenes, later titled *Horrors of the Revolution* (*Mexico in Revolution*). The Mexican government commissions Rivera to paint an extensive mural cycle at the Ministry of Public Education (1923–28); he also paints murals at the Agricultural University at Chapingo (1926–27). Siqueiros devotes himself to leftist political work during the late 1920s.

1927

Further political unrest, including the Cristero revolt against the anticlerical policies of the government of Plutarco Elías Calles. Pessimistic about prospects for future mural commissions, Orozco departs Mexico again. He arrives in New York City on December 16.

1928

Orozco begins a difficult transition to life in New York, which he makes his home base for most of his seven-year sojourn in the United States, by immersing himself in the city's culture and art. Brenner introduces him to Alma Reed, who becomes his friend, patron, and dealer. Through Reed, Orozco attends the Ashram, a salon in the home of Eva Sikelianos, wife of the Greek poet Angelos Sikelianos.

Inspired by the culture of ancient Greece, including the festival at Delphi, the group calls itself the Delphic Circle.

January–February 1928

Orozco participates in a Mexican art exhibition at the Art Center; he deems it "a total, absolute, and definite failure." He makes his first lithograph, *Vaudeville in Harlem,* in February. Most of his lithographs are printed in the studio of George Miller and sold at the Weyhe Gallery and later at Reed's gallery, Delphic Studios. Between 1928 and early 1930, while in New York, Orozco produces at least eighteen lithographic compositions.

September–October 1928

Orozco exhibits his drawings from the *Mexico in Revolution* series, first at the Ashram and then at the gallery of Marie

Sterner in New York City, bringing him his first critical attention in the city. He sets up a temporary studio at the Ashram and begins a portrait of Eva Sikelianos.

1929

In January, Orozco publishes a brief artistic manifesto, "New World, New Races and New Art," in the journal *Creative Art*. In April he displays his New York–themed paintings, Mexican scenes, lithographs, and preparatory studies for the Preparatory School murals at the Art Students' League, New York. Orozco illustrates the first English edition of Mariano Azuela's novel of the Mexican Revolution, *The Underdogs* (*Los de abajo*). Rivera works on major mural commissions at the National Palace, Mexico City, and in the Cortez Palace, Cuernavaca,

299

Fig. 315 · **Street Corner**, 1929, oil on canvas, location unknown, from Alma Reed, **José Clemente Orozco** (New York: Delphic Studios, 1932), n.p.

Fig. 316 · **New York Subway**, 1929, charcoal on paper, location unknown, from Reed, **José Clemente Orozco** (New York: Delphic Studios, 1932), n.p.

Fig. 317 · **Workers**, 1929,
oil on canvas, Nagoya City Art
Museum, Nagoya, Japan.

Fig. 318 · **Two Scholars
in Discussion**, 1930,
oil on canvas, private collection,
photograph courtesy Sotheby's.

the latter commissioned by U.S. Ambassador Dwight D. Morrow. At this time Rivera is expelled from the Mexican Communist Party and gravitates toward the politics of Leon Trotsky.

October 1929

The official inauguration of Alma Reed's New York gallery, Delphic Studios, with an exhibition of Orozco's works, coincides with the collapse of the New York stock market and the beginning of the Great Depression. The artist's works are on permanent display at the gallery, which also features works by other contemporary Mexican and American artists.

1930

Orozco receives his first U.S. mural commission (Pomona College, Claremont, California). During this year he also enjoys a burst of publicity, with works on view in exhibitions in Detroit, Boston, San Francisco, Denver, Los Angeles, and elsewhere in the United States. The year

begins with a solo exhibition at Delphic Studios of his recent work, strongly reflecting his synthesis of modern trends. On March 22, 1930, Orozco arrives in Claremont, California, to paint the *Prometheus* mural in Frary Hall at Pomona College with the assistance of Jorge Juan Crespo de la Serna. This will be the first Mexican mural painted in the United States. During the summer months Orozco resides in San Francisco, where he paints a number of canvases in preparation for a large touring exhibition, *Mexican Arts,* to open at the Metropolitan Museum of Art, New York. He returns to that city in September to begin his second U.S. mural commission, at the New School for Social Research, New York. In November 1930, Rivera arrives in California and begins work on his first three murals in the United States, all in the San Francisco area: the San Francisco Stock Exchange, the home of Mrs. Sigmund Stern, and the California School of Fine Arts (all 1931). On November 11, Orozco begins painting murals on the

theme of universal brotherhood for the New School of Social Research; the murals are dedicated on January 19, 1931.

October 1930 – September 1931

Seven paintings and four drawings by Orozco are on view in the *Mexican Arts* exhibition, seen at eight American institutions.

1931

Orozco has a solo show of New York scenes at the Downtown Gallery in New York City in March and April; he also participates in several group shows in New York and elsewhere during the year. Rivera is honored with a major retrospective at the new Museum of Modern Art, New York.

1932

In the spring, Orozco is invited to paint the reserve reading room of Baker Library at Dartmouth College in Hanover, New Hampshire. Soon after he begins the mural, he travels to

Europe for the first and only time, visiting cultural sites in England, France, Italy, and Spain during the summer and witnessing the troubled political climate. Upon his return, he resumes the Dartmouth commission, *The Epic of American Civilization* (1932–34), and makes frequent trips back to New York during the nearly two years he works on it; his family joins him in the United States for much of this period. Reed publishes her monograph on Orozco.

1932 – 33

This marks a particularly rich period for Mexican mural painting in the United States. Siqueiros leaves Mexico in 1932 for a short stay in Los Angeles, where he completes three murals: *Workers' Meeting, Tropical America,* and *Portrait of Present-Day Mexico* (1932). Rivera also executes his most important U.S. commission, the *Detroit Industry* frescoes (1932–33) at the Detroit Institute of Arts. He then goes to New York and begins a mural for the RCA Building at Rockefeller Center (*Man at the Crossroads*) but is dismissed before its completion. He subsequently paints portable murals at the New Workers' School and returns to Mexico in late 1933.

1934

On February 13, Orozco completes the Dartmouth mural, and he returns to New York shortly thereafter. Rivera's mural at Rockefeller Center was destroyed a few days earlier. Before departing for Mexico in the summer, Orozco exhibits in Chicago and La Porte, Indiana, the largest exhibition of his work to date. He returns to Mexico City to paint a Mexican government mural commission, *Catharsis,* at the Palace of Fine Arts and reestablishes permanent residence in his home country. Rivera also completes a mural commission at the palace,

Man, Controller of the Universe, based on his destroyed murals at Rockefeller Center. Meanwhile, Siqueiros is in New York for a short period, during which time he exhibits work at Reed's Delphic Studios.

1936–39

During a period of intense activity, Orozco moves to Guadalajara to paint important works at the Assembly Hall of the University (*Creative Man* and *The People and Its False Leaders,* 1936); the Government Palace, including a panel depicting Hidalgo (1937–38), and the Hospicio Cabañas (*Mexico before and after the Spanish Conquest,* 1937–39). In February 1936, Orozco returns to New York briefly to attend the American Artists' Congress as a part of the Mexican revolutionary writers' and artists' delegation. Siqueiros also attends as part of the delegation and spends much of 1936 in

New York, where he establishes a workshop for experimentation with artistic techniques and new materials; he spends most of the next two years in Spain supporting the Loyalists in the Spanish Civil War. In 1938 the Mexican collector Alvar Carrillo Gil purchases his first works by Orozco, forming the basis for an important collection of the artist's oeuvre.

1940

Orozco paints frescoes, including *Allegory of Mexico,* in the Gabino Ortíz Library in Jiquilipan, Michoacán. Siqueiros completes the mural *Portrait of the Bourgeoisie* (1939–40) at the Mexican Electricians' Union; he and other supporters of Stalin are involved in an aborted assassination attempt on Trotsky, now exiled in Mexico. In June, Orozco returns briefly to New York, where he paints the portable mural *Dive Bomber and Tank* for the Museum of Modern Art. He writes an ironic explanation of its meaning for the museum's *Bulletin.* Rivera also returns to the United States to paint the mural cycle *Pan-American Unity* at the City College of San Francisco.

1941

Orozco completes murals for the Supreme Court of Justice in Mexico City and paints several portraits. He directs renewed

attention during the last years of his life to easel paintings, drawings, and printmaking.

1942–44

Orozco works on murals at the church of the Jesús Hospital, Mexico City (unfinished). In 1943 he is named a founding member of the Colegio Nacional and exhibits his work there annually until his death.

September 1945–March 1946

Orozco leaves Mexico City in a final attempt to establish himself in New York City. Among the paintings he executes there is his *Self-Portrait* (1946; Museo de Arte Carrillo Gil).

1947

A retrospective exhibition of Orozco's works is held at the National Institute of Fine Arts in Mexico City.

1947–49

Orozco completes murals at the National Teachers' School and Chapultepec Castle, Mexico City, and at the Chamber of Deputies, Government Palace, Guadalajara; produces series of easel paintings *Los Teules* (*White Gods*).

September 7, 1949

Orozco dies in Mexico City.

Fig. 319 · The Mexican delegation to the American Artists' Congress, New York, February 1936 (left to right: Rufino and Olga Tamayo, David Alfaro Siqueiros, Orozco, Roberto Berdecio, Angélica Arenal de Siqueiros), photograph courtesy Library, Getty Research Institute, Los Angeles (960094).

"Orozco 'Explains'"

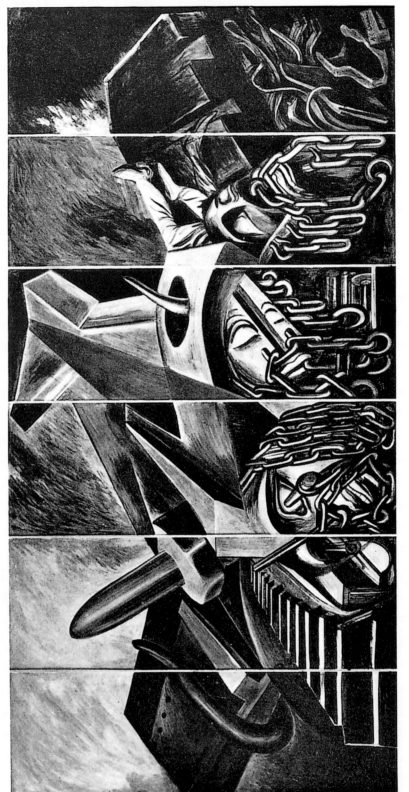

The Dive Bomber, by José Clemente Orozco

In conjunction with the summer exhibition of Twenty Centuries of Mexican Art, Mr. José Clemente Orozco was commissioned by the Museum of Modern Art to paint a fresco in six movable panels. He started work at the Museum on June 21 and did much of the painting before the public. The fresco was completed on June 30. Mr. Orozco was assisted by Mr. Lewis Rubenstein, who has supplied technical data for the ensuing captions. All photographs were taken by Eliot Elisofon.

Reprinted from **The Bulletin of the Museum of Modern Art**, vol. 7, no. 4, August 1940, pages 2–11. Offset, printed in black, page spread: 9 ¼ x 14 ⅜ in. (23 x 36.5 cm).
The Museum of Modern Art Library, New York. Photograph © 2001 The Museum of Modern Art.

"Movable panels (each 9 by 3 feet) are made with strong steel frames. The plaster is held by a wire mesh. Panels such as these are too heavy to be really movable without danger to the painting. That is a field where technology may be of great service to art by developing a process for the construction of special panels for fresco painting. They must be very light in weight and at the same time so absorbent as to slow the drying as much as possible. In addition, the plaster for these panels must be less brittle than the ordinary one, probably by adding some new material to the plaster or by any other way to turn it very hard and flexible and as absorbent as before."   J.C.O.

OROZCO "EXPLAINS"

This "explanation" was written by Mr. Orozco. The quotation marks in his title indicate his feeling that explanations are unnecessary.

The public wants explanations about a painting. What the artist had in mind when he did it. What he was thinking of. What is the exact name of the picture, and what the artist means by that. If he is glorifying or cursing. If he believes in Democracy.

Going to the Italian Opera you get a booklet with a full account of why Rigoletto kills Aïda at the end of a wild party with La Bohème, Lucia di Lammermoor and Madame Butterfly.

The Italian Renaissance is another marvelous opera full of killings and wild parties, and the public gets also thousands of booklets with complete and most detailed information about everything and everybody in Florence and Rome.

"Plaster is the same as for regular walls: lime and sand or lime and marble dust. A very small amount of Portland cement may be added if necessary to make a harder material, in certain cases. It is better to avoid it. For the intonaco or final coat upon which the painting is done no cement is used. Proportions: 2 parts sand to 1 lime or 2 to 1½. The number of coats of plaster must be as many as possible to hold a great deal of moisture. The number of coats depends upon the kind of material the wall is made of. The best material is the old hand-made brick because modern machine-made brick is as waterproof as concrete."   J.C.O.

Orozco made no full sized cartoon. The sketch was drawn in pencil to the scale of one inch to the foot. Salient lines were enlarged on the equalizing coat and fixed in light red pigment, ground in water.

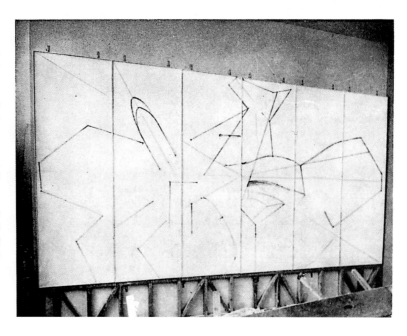

In the early stages Orozco continually repolished the surface with a small pointing trowel in the direction of the brush strokes. This seals the pigment firmly in the intonaco, burnishes and deepens the color. Sometimes when he wanted to make a change he scrubbed out a part with the brush and applied a small patch of fresh intonaco. In one part he applied flashes of lime white with the pointing trowel.

The mortar was smoothed with a finishing trowel at the joints. The joints were cut at night or the following day. They followed the main lines of the design and were sometimes quite intricate.

Pigments were diluted with water only. Orozco planned the final design and color directly on the wall, improvising as he worked. The main lines of the design were painted in Venetian red. The straight lines were brushed along a yardstick. In the first stage of painting, the under-painting was brushed in broadly in transparent red tones. Orozco enlarged the day's section from his sketch to join the lines with the previous painting and with the red lines on the equalizing coat. The points were found by vertical and horizontal coordinates and were painted in small red crosses.

And now the public insists on knowing the plot of modern painted opera, though not Italian, of course. They take for granted that every picture must be the illustration of a short story or of a thesis and want to be told the entertaining biography and bright sayings of the leaders in the stage-picture, the ups and downs of hero, villain, and chorus. Many pictures actually tell all that and more even including quotations from the Holy Scriptures and Shakespeare. Others deal with social conditions, evils of the world, revolution, history and the like. Bedroom pictures with *la femme à sa toilette* are still very frequent.

Suddenly, Madame Butterfly and her friend Rigoletto disappear from the stage-picture. Gone, too, are gloomy social conditions. To the amazement of the public the curtain goes up and nothing is on the stage but a few lines and cubes. The Abstract. The public protests and demands explanations, and explanations are given away freely and generously. Rigo-

The painting continued with washes or various low intensity colors, usually black or umber, to build up the local tones. Orozco paints with free sweeping strokes, holding the brush loosely on the end. Color washes were applied rapidly, sometimes to the point of allowing them to run down the walls.

letto and social conditions are still there but have become abstract, all dolled up in cubes and cones in a wild surrealist party with La Bohème, Lucia di Lammermoor and Madame Butterfly. Meanings? Names? Significance? Short stories? Well, let's invent them afterwards. The public refuses **TO SEE** painting. They want **TO HEAR** painting. They don't care for the show itself, they prefer **TO LISTEN** to the barker outside. Free lectures every hour for the blind, around the Museum. This way, please.

"The Artist must be sincere," they say. It is true. He must be sincere. The actor on the stage commits suicide to thrill or frighten the public to death. The actor feels exactly what a suicide feels, and acts the same way except that his gun is not loaded. He is sincere as an artist only. Next week he has to impersonate St. Francis, Lenin or an average business man, very sincerely!

The technique of painting is still in its infancy after ten thousand years of civilization, or whatever it is. Even college children know this fact, for abundant literature about the subject is on hand.

It seems incredible that science and industry have not yet provided the artist with better materials to work with. Not a single improvement through centuries. The range of colors available is still extremely limited. Pigments are not permanent at all in spite of manufacturers' claims. Canvas, wood, paper, walls are exposed to continuous destruction from moisture, changes in temperature, chemical reactions, insects and germs. Oils, varnishes, wax, gums and tempera media are dirty substances darkening, changing, cracking and disintegrating all the time.

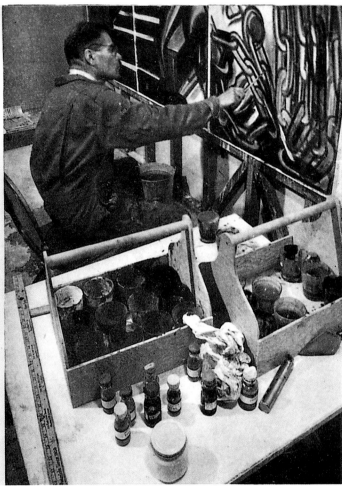

The mortar is ground thoroughly for a week before plastering and when applied is the consistency of ointment. The sand for the intonaco must contain no salt or organic impurities; the lime putty used was six years old. This mortar was smoothed with the finishing trowel as applied and was ready for painting immediately.

The colors were mixed in Old Fashioned glasses—one dozen glasses for the palette of pure color, one dozen for daily mixtures. *"Only lime-proof colors are used such as: earthen colors, Mars colors, cobalt, chromium oxide, non-animal blacks and lime white. Good cadmiums may be used also very thinly. The binding medium is the carbonate of lime produced during the drying process of the plaster. A fresco is never varnished."* J.C.O.

Fresco painting is free from the inconveniences of oils and varnishes, but the wall upon which the painting is done is subjected to many causes of destruction, such as the use of the wrong kind of building materials, poor planning, moisture from the ground or from the air, earthquakes, dive bombing, tanking or battleshipping, excess of magnesia in the lime or the marble dust, lack of care resulting in scratches or peeling off, et cetera. So, fresco must be done only on walls that are as free as possible from all these inconveniences.

There is no rule for painting al fresco. Every artist may do as he pleases provided he paints as thinly as possible and only while the plaster is wet, six to eight hours from the moment it is applied. No retouching of any kind afterwards. Every artist develops his own way of

Orozco painted about two square yards a day. He used flat, soft bristle brushes of the type used for oil painting.

planning his conception and transferring it onto the wet plaster. Every method is as good as the other. Or the artist may improvise without any previous sketches.

"The Dive Bomber," or Six Interchangeable Panels

A painting is a **Poem** and nothing else. A poem made of relationships between forms as other kinds of poems are made of relationships between words, sounds or ideas. Sculpture and architecture are also relationships between forms. This word **forms** includes color, tone, proportion, line, et cetera.

The forms in a poem are necessarily organized in such a way that the whole acts as an automatic machine, more or less efficient but apt to function in a certain way, to move in a certain direction. Such a machine-motor sets in motion our senses, first; our emotional capacity, second; and our intellect, last. An efficient and well-organized machine may work

308

In painting over the transparent red tones, Orozco often glazed the surface with a thin wash of semi-opaque grays mixed with lime white, with a resultant low intensity purplish tone. The outlining of the forms was done in Vine black. The basic tonal scheme used was red earth and Vine black combined with blue-blacks, opaque warm and cool grays. Accenting was done toward the end of the painting day in bold strokes of lime white, or in such arbitrary treatment as the strokes of pure cobalt on a black field, or the plastered strokes of lime white in the sky. Orozco often left an expanse of bare plaster in a light area. He used the fresco medium with great freedom.

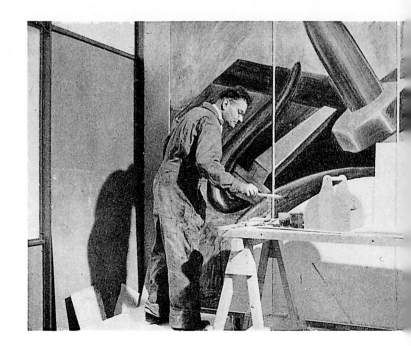

Orozco worked ten days. His working day was about six to eight hours.

in very different ways. It can be simplified to its last elementals or basic structure or may be developed into a vast and complicated organism working under the same basic principles.

Each part of a machine may be by itself a machine to function independently from the whole. The order of the inter-relations between its parts may be altered, but those relationships may stay the same in any other order, and unexpected or expected possibilities may appear. Suppose we change the actual order of the plastic elements of the vaults in the Sixtine Chapel . . .

A linotype is a work of art, but a linotype in motion is an extraordinary adventure affecting the lives of many human beings or the course of history. A few lines from a linotype in action may start a World War or may mean the birth of a new era.

JOSÉ CLEMENTE OROZCO

309

The following arrangements of the six panels are those preferred by Mr. Orozco.

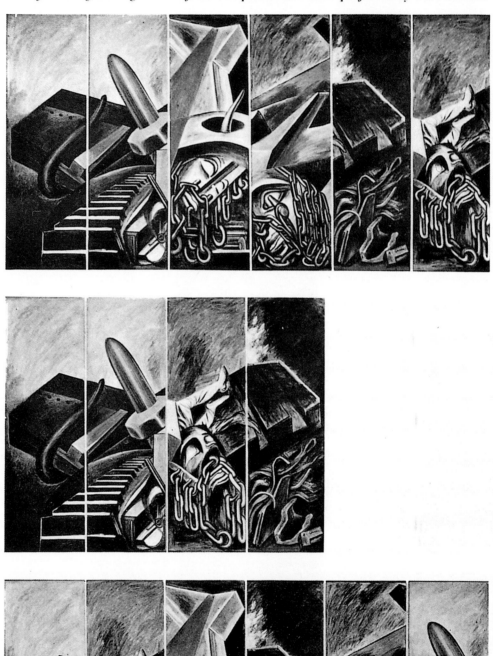

310

Anthology of Critical Reception

Alicia Azuela, Renato González Mello, and James Oles

Cartoons and Earthquakes

The *Art Digest* reluctantly presents the above reproduction [*Father God,* National Preparatory School]
to those of its readers who are likely to be shocked
or grieved by its sacrilege, but it feels that it would
not be fulfilling its function if it did not do so. It is
the outstanding work in an exhibition held at the
Art Center, sponsored by the Mexican Government
and paid for by Rockefeller money, and it is by an
artist signally honored by the Calles Administration.
It is significant and informative of what is going
on in Mexico in the clash between Christianity and
Atheism, and the part that art is playing in that
historical struggle by representing ideas pictorially
to people who cannot read.

> —"New York Sees Mexico's Revolutionary Art,"
> *Art Digest,* vol. 11, no. 8 (mid-January 1928).

Shortly thereafter, some minor tremors were felt
in Greenwich Village; a veritable *chair de poule* was
propagated, which horrified several standard-
plumed Plymouth cocks, and set other plume-
penned birds a-cackling wildly…. It seems Orozco
had ventured some social cartoons which left their
victims' flesh, bone, and blood daubed all over the
paper and pressed in as if by a steamroller: it
happened that Orozco had dramatized the ridiculous, but with such force that, compared to those
cartoons, the cruelest ones by Covarrubias—who is
here considered terrible—seem like alleluias or
New Year's greetings.

> —José Juan Tablada, "Nueva York de día y de noche:
> México en Nueva York," in Tablada, *La Babilonia de
> hierro,* interactive compact disc, ed. Esther Hernández
> Palacios (Mexico City: UNAM–Instituto de
> Investigaciones Filológicas, 1997 [originally published
> in *El Universal,* Mexico (October 21, 1928)]).[1]

With regard to the exhibition at the Art Center,
it was a total failure…the very few people who did
visit it said, "I am disappointed," because it had
been rumored that this was going to be a great exhibition of Mexican painting, representative of the
whole country and sponsored by the Mexican
government, and the only things that anyone could
see were the pictures by Pacheco, Ruiz and the
large number of *aficionados,* or amateurs, who are
regarded as "great artists." The comments that were
heard in the hall were enough to make one blush,
and the people laughed and howled. There were
also many of Hidalgo's little wax monkeys and
dressed fleas.

> —Letter from Orozco to the mother of Jean Charlot,
> February 22, 1928, in *José Clemente Orozco: The
> Artist in New York,* transl. Ruth L.C. Simms, foreword
> and notes by Jean Charlot (Austin: University of
> Texas Press, 1974), 33–34.[2]

He liked reading *The New Yorker* very much, because
it always had interesting articles…. He really enjoyed
its cartoons, generally socially critical, pointed, and
sarcastic as well as funny. He was also amused by
some newspaper comic strips, saying that the North
Americans were very good at that kind of work.

> —Testimony of Margarita Valladares, included in
> José Clemente Orozco, *Cartas a Margarita* (Mexico:
> Era, 1987), 45.[3]

I trust that it will not seem irrelevant to discuss
Covarrubias in close proximity with Orozco. Both
have been called caricaturists, and both, in a degree,
merit the cognomen. Orozco is a caricaturist in
the same sense that Goya and Daumier were caricaturists: he reports the human document with
merciless precision.

> —José Juan Tablada, "Recent Activities in Mexican Art,"
> *Parnassus,* vol. 11, no. 4 (April 1930), 17.

The most effective user of caricature in paint has undoubtedly been José Clemente Orozco. There is no pity in his representations. They are brutal, almost fantastically brutal, in their annihilation of local types, be they priests, elegantly gowned women, politicians, or generals.

…There is a desperate, glaring sort of laughter in his portrayals; the *vacilada* is lifted to frightful Promethean hilarity, not quite sane, and therefore as illuminating as Dostoievskian pathological insight into human depravity. A tormented soul! Orozco's satires have a passion and hate utterly devoid of the geniality lurking in the *caprichos* of Goya, a painter to whom he is in many ways comparable. Orozco's laughter, his cruelty, is [*sic*] harsher than any European satire. It is Hogarthian and Swiftian, plus the Mexican irresponsible maliciousness; and it is far more dramatic than the work of Goya or Daumier. Even Orozco's rare moments of compassion possess a brutal torment. He will rip the universe open with both satire and compassion; until even his compassion becomes mocking satire.

—Carleton Beals, *Mexican Maze* (New York: Book League of America, 1931), 245.

We may be so bold as to say that this artist is also in decline. The North American environment has infected him and, although his conceptions are still dramatic, the weakening trend is evident. The fresco at the Palacio de Bellas Artes lacks the magnificent hand of his first frescoes; it reminds one of a *Saturday Evening Post* illustration, done rapidly like a large-scale sketch, which diminishes its seriousness. If one observes his Dartmouth College paintings, one can see that the technique is even more theatrical there; his "Christ Destroying the Cross" cannot impress us, despite his raw flesh; and Hernando Cortez, even if interesting because it reminds us of Don Quijote, is an unreal and stiff figure who seems never to have moved in his entire

life. Would that we were wrong, and that we should be able to see at least one more work by this artist that was worthy of his earlier production.…

—Justino Fernández, *El arte moderno en México: breve historia—Siglos XIX y XX* (Mexico: Antigua Librería Robredo, José Porrúa e Hijos, 1937), 233.[4]

I challenge you to define exactly at what point caricature begins and at what point it ends. In other words: Why a given figure is caricature and why some other is not. If you step out of Art then everything is not. If you step out of Art then everything is caricature, one hundred per cent caricature!

"ART IS NOT CARICATURE
CARICATURE IS NOT ART"

—Letter from Orozco to Laurence E. Schmeckebier, in Luis Cardoza y Aragón, *Orozco* (Mexico City: UNAM-IIE, 1959), 296.

Rivera and Orozco

As time goes by, I find myself liking Orozco's [work] more and more, I feel the genius. His things overflow with an inner potentiality which one never feels in Diego's things. Diego comments too much, lately he paints details with an irritating precision, he leaves nothing to one's imagination. With Orozco's things, you feel that you can begin where he leaves off and that is very satisfying.

—Letter from Tina Modotti to Edward Weston, September 18, 1928, in Amy Stark, "The Letters from Tina Modotti to Edward Weston," *Archive* (Arizona) no. 22 (January 1986), 56.

[Rivera] is already known and admired in the United States; when we know more of Orozco it seems certain that we shall add his name to the roll of the great men of our time.

—Walter Pach, *Ananias, or the False Artist* (New York: Harper & Brothers, 1928), 205.

A comparison between the work of Orozco and that of his countryman, Diego Rivera, who happens to be so much better known abroad, would doubtless be very revealing. Both are tremendous personalities and have helped make contemporary art in Mexico function as a social necessity. But in the very nature of their medium each remains, in the end, unclassifiable. However, it is very interesting to note that where Rivera has breadth and a certain well-organized power that is philosophic, Orozco retains a greater intensity of emotion through his very violence.

—William Spratling, "Orozco," *Mexican Life,* vol. 5, no. 10 (October 1929).

Diego is a good, old friend.… But I have never met the man about whom I am now writing—OROZCO.

Our paths crossed three times—in Los Angeles, New York, and Mexico City—and three times we missed the opportunity for the handshake that we have hoped for for so long. Even though geography has not helped us, we managed to find a meeting point. Somewhere in the Elysian fields of ecstasy, we met. There is an old, convenient method for classifying personalities, especially when two are to be compared: either the Apollonian or the Dionysian. This is so old and convenient that it has gone out of style. Nevertheless, let us adopt it for our pair, Orozco/Diego—Diego/Orozco.

[…]

But next to a Falstaffian Martin Luther shrieks a fiery Savanarola. As the men—so their work. Their intensity is distinct. Quantitative in Diego. Qualitative in Orozco. Square kilometers in area for the one, and so much explosive energy for the other.

[…]

Squeezed. Narrowed. Pressed. Concentrated in an outburst of one tremendous, unnatural, clenched, crashing fist—appears Orozco in the Preparatoria walls.

—Sergei Eisenstein, "The Prometheus of Mexican Painting" (date unknown, after 1930), from "Film Essays and Lecture," reprinted in Inga Karetnikova, *Mexico According to Eisenstein* (Albuquerque: University of New Mexico Press, 1991), 159–60.

Slightly younger than Diego Rivera; in career, character, outlook, and style his antithesis. The Opposition in the Syndicate and always. Training chiefly in revolutionary army papers, cartooning, lampooning, winning plenty of real victories and making hundreds of enemies. Most violent, most passionate of the mural decorators, smashes the walls with his planes and welds them together again by sheer emotional force. At his best sublime; at his worst, bitter.

—Anita Brenner, *Your Mexican Holiday* (New York: G. P. Putnam's Sons, 1935), 257.

I propose that in Diego Rivera, it is not his pugnacity that is characteristic; it is not when he brandishes the sword, when he goes on the offensive, when he is aggressive, that Diego is great, but when he puts up a shield. Clemente Orozco is the opposite: he truly is the category of absolute aggression. It is not a matter of which of the two is better, has greater merit: there can be no comparison between one and the other, save when one assumes the attitude that is characteristic of the other. Diego is Homeric; his work is Achilles' shield. Orozco is all sword, all cutting, all crushing hand, welt-raising whip. When Diego tries to be sword, he is inferior to Orozco; when Orozco wants to be shield, he is inferior to Diego; when each is true to himself, each is unsurpassable.

—Roberto de la Selva, "El arte en México: agresividad, defensa y fuga," *El Nacional, Diario Popular,* Mexico (January 23, 1936).[5]

And while Clemente Orozco, silently, religiously glorifies the proletarian family, Diego Rivera blazes his trail with brushstrokes and oratory.

—Rafael López, "Entre Lenín y Rockefeller," *El Nacional, Diario Popular,* Mexico (May 18, 1933), 3.[6]

But there is no occasion which presents itself that I do not take advantage of. In February or March, an article is to be published on Clemente Orozco, as long as or longer than the one on Diego Rivera that I attach herewith, which will be illustrated, which is exceptional, with three or four full-color plates and many more illustrations in black and white....

—José Juan Tablada, "From José Juan Tablada to Genaro Estrada," December 4, 1923, *Archive of the Secretariat of Foreign Relations, Personal file of Genaro Estrada,* Book III, f. 46.[7]

A woman friend from San Francisco sends me an engraving from the *Examiner* with a note concerning the coward [Diego Rivera], and believe me, I don't know whether to laugh out loud or send the poor coward my most heartfelt condolences, in an obituary with a cross and crown over a cold grave. The engraving shows a huge belly atop a ladder, charcoal in hand and on the wall...manila paper! He is making a preparatory drawing, full-size! The subject: FORTYNINERS! The aesthetic, or rather, the anti-supercounter-dis-aesthetic: English pre-Raphaelism, of the weakest, sweetest, most effeminate sort! Or, in other words, the poor belly has been inflated overnight. Of the worst American academicism, the kind that fills banks, State Capitols, and other skyscrapers by the square mile, and which by now is only done by girl painters!...The note says he's going to paint California's prosperity or fecundity as a lady with Grecó-Roman clothing, with a Greek nose, high bosoms, hips and everything, with fruits and other attributes...not even in the Academia!

—Letter from Orozco to Jorge Juan Crespo de la Serna, January 31, 1931, reproduced in Cardoza y Aragón, *Orozco,* 284–85.[8]

The academics keep attacking us Mexican mural painters; the other day on the radio, they trashed Rivera and myself and blasted Dartmouth. Packard wrote me telling me that they were also preparing a defense.

—Letter from Orozco to his wife, March 30, 1934, in Orozco, *Cartas a Margarita,* 273.[9]

Famed Fresco-Painters Rivera, Orozco, and Siqueiros, whose work is well known in the U.S., had little new to show. Strongest, technically most interesting contemporary items were a group of bronzed, sculptural-looking paintings done in Duco automobile paint by deep-dyed Revolutionist Siqueiros, a couple of scenes of violence by rugged Peasant-Painter Orozco. Biggest disappointment was a series of smart, sugary, sometimes pornographic paintings by Diego Rivera, onetime high priest of Mexican muralism.

—"Mexican Show," *Time* (May 27, 1940), 57. Review of *Twenty Centuries of Mexican Art.*

Rivera railed against the art dealers who fabricated stories for their own benefit and sensationalism: "The merchants, or exploiters of artists' art, take advantage of or create differences between them, to draw the public's attention and increase sales. That is why they have so often imagined and even published the newspaper stories about rivalries which never existed between us."

Orozco nodded in agreement, and added: "Naturally, we have many differences of opinion about our profession, but in our private life, the harmony of our friendship can be traced back many years."

—Interview published by the *Mexico City Herald*,
April 24, 1946, quoted by Clemente Orozco
Valladares in *Orozco, verdad cronológica*
(Guadalajara: EDUG/Universidad de Guadalajara,
1983), 437.[10]

You can print in your book whatever nonsense
I've written [but] don't put anything against my
fellow painters.

—Letter from Orozco to Jean Charlot, April 18, 1943, in
Orozco Valladares, *Orozco, verdad cronológica*, 437.[11]

Recognition

Friday night was the gathering at Alma Reed's
house…there was a gentleman reciting some very
long verses and afterwards he called me, seated me
in the middle of the room and recited some verses
he had written just for me, praising me to high
heaven. Very ridiculous, but these people take it
very seriously.

—Letter from Orozco to Margarita Valladares,
October 1, 1928, in Orozco, *Cartas a Margarita*, 133.[12]

Mrs. Reed was very clever to get Orozco.

—Comment at the Reinhart Gallery in New York,
quoted by Orozco to his wife in a latter dated
February 8, 1930, in Orozco, *Cartas a Margarita*, 189.

"Delphic Studios," the picture gallery off Fifth
Avenue is, in spite of its Greek name, a Mexican art
emporium. Let us be the good omen! It is because
Alma Reed, the muse who presides therein, was
Mayan before Attic and still believes that this
evolution, from marbled Hellas to tropical Mayab,
continues to be harmonious.…

—José Juan Tablada, "Nueva York de día y de noche,"
El Universal, Mexico (April 13, 1930), supplement 3.[13]

An avalanche of newspapers, magazines, pamphlets,
letters, all pulsating with sanctifying enthusiasm,
overflows my working table, and from this mighty
stream a name emerges and culminates like an
eminent promontory: "Mexico," and upon this rock,
as a budding laurel, another name: "José Clemente
Orozco."…"Mexico, Mexico, Mexico!" thunders this
roaring river, the clamorous, unanimous press;
"Mexico," repeats the deep and sonorous echo of the
specialized magazines and university journals, and
the cordial murmuring of the private letters…in
sum, in its broadest regard, Orozco's triumph is
Mexico's triumph.

—José Juan Tablada, "Nueva York de día y de noche:
México en triunfo," in Tablada, *La Babilonia de
hierro* (originally published in *El Universal*, Mexico
[August 10, 1930]).[14]

There is an extraordinary woman by the name of
Alma Reed, who has a gallery called the "Delphic
Studios!" She is going to sponsor Orozco. Mrs. Reed
originally came from California, and I'm afraid she
carried with her some of the mystic ailments that
sometimes befall the people out there. Mrs. Reed
is a very fat woman, and wears long black dresses,
but she has the face and hands of a Madonna! She
belongs to a secret Greek order called the Delphic
Society. (I only hope that she concentrates on
selling Orozco's work.)

The other night she invited me to one of the
meetings of the Delphic Society. A Mrs. Hambidge,
the wife of the man who is supposed to have
discovered Dynamic Symmetry (a system of drawing in mathematical forms) was there, dressed
in white veils, and she wore Greek sandals. The rest
of the people (all women) wore long chains with
Greek crosses. The lights were dimmed and the
discussion of "Art on a Higher Plane" commenced.
I was really frightened.

…But in spite of her foolishness, Mrs. Reed has a rare quality. No matter what cause she is devoted to, she makes the most of every moment in order to arrive at some climax. She is determined that Orozco will paint a fresco in New York, that his genius will be recognized, and that with his recognition Diego Rivera will fall into oblivion.

—Ione Robinson, *A Wall to Paint On* (New York: E.P. Dutton and Co., 1946), 150. The recollection is from November 1930.

The Orozco cult is rapidly growing in the United States, judging by the sales made during Summer and Fall by Mrs. Alma Reed of the Delphic Studios.

—Note from *Art Digest,* vol. 5, no. 4 (November 15, 1930).

As you can see, nothing can be expected from Alma.…

—Orozco, letter to Margarita Valladares, October 20, 1935, in Orozco, *Cartas a Margarita,* 286.[15]

"When did you begin to make yourself known?"

"Well, here in Mexico one never makes oneself known. Nobody knows you."

—Rafael Heliodoro Valle, "José Clemente Orozco, pintor impar," in *La Prensa,* San Antonio, Texas (September 5, 1935), in Orozco Valladares, *Orozco: verdad cronológica,* 305.[16]

In Mexico…we learn to work under all conditions—sometimes behind the barricades or dodging missiles on the walls.

—Statement by Orozco in a conversation with Alma Reed and Eva Sikelianos, recalled by Alma Reed in *Orozco,* 44.[17]

Orozco, after taking part in many military adventures and losing his left arm in one of the battles, returned to Mexico City in about 1917 and worked on newspapers, drawing cartoons of great satirical strength.

—Morris Topchesky, "Clemente Orozco I," *El Nacional Revolucionario,* Mexico (July 26, 1930), 4.

In the many drawings of Orozco shown in the Art Institute, one could see the tragedy of the peasant turned brigand and soldier, living in trenches, riding in box cars or marching in the desert heat, fighting and dying on the battlefield. Then there was a series of pictures of victims. Mutilated, some alive, some dead. Not only men and beasts are victims of the tragic events, but trees with all their branches destroyed resemble the mutilated human beings. Another symbol Orozco uses is the maguey plant.

—Morris Topchesky, "Clemente Orozco II," *El Nacional Revolucionario,* Mexico (July 28, 1930), 4.

They strove to destroy. They were proud to belong to the Mexican Revolution.… Orozco told me as a great joke that he and other like-minded men and youths in the village would raid the Church and make a bonfire in the Plaza in front of the Church with the wooden saints, the antique vestments, church furniture, dressers, and books.

—Carlos Sánchez, Orozco's assistant at Dartmouth College, unpublished article, about 1984.

[S]haped right here, as if unrelated to the present time, to be simply in Time, by being so present, for in Orozco resides not only the Mexican Revolution, but the Mexican tragedy. He knew what he ignored, but he seemed to ignore nothing without ever having known it.

—Luis Cardoza y Aragón, "José Clemente Orozco," *Futuro,* Mexico (January 1, 1934), 20.[18]

I played no part in the Revolution, I came to no harm, and I ran no danger at all.... It was consequently very funny to read the many articles that American papers published about my wartime adventures.... Other stories had me carrying the banner of the Indian Cause, and these were accompanied by a picture of my person in which I could recognize a Tarahumara. I have never espoused the Cause of the Indians, or thrown a bomb, or even, though another paper reported it, been shot on three separate occasions.

—Orozco, *José Clemente Orozco: An Autobiography* (Austin: University of Texas Press, 1962), 40–41.[19]

The privilege of horror belongs, for a century now, to popular printmaking.

—Gaston Poulain, "Un pintor del México en revolución," *Bandera de provincias* (facsimile; September 15, 1929), supplement. This is a reproduction of a French article, surely published with reference to Orozco's exhibit that same year at the Parisian gallery Fermé la Nuit.[20]

These drawings by the great Mexican are the most terrific indictment of humanity against humanity since Goya's "Horrors of War," with the possible exception of the work of the German, George Grosz. The famous murals of Orozco's great countryman, Diego Rivera, seem mellow and mild in comparison. But why compare? Here is an artist who, in his own intensely personal way, tells his story. It is sufficient to state that the way in which he tells it is more moving, more monumental, more humanly exciting than anything that has been told through the plastic arts for several generations.

Orozco proves to those who would ban all story telling from the plastic arts that, even today, it can be done without loss of artistic significance. In fact, he describes, glorifies, indicts, and moralizes through purely artistic means.

—Arnold Ronnebeck, review of show at Denver Museum circulated by Delphic Studios, in *Rocky Mountain News*, cited in "An Orozco Tribute," *Art Digest*, vol. 4, no. 20 (September 1930), 13.

The same energy that made his caricatures fairly bite into their victims yields the magnificent blacks and grays, the long vital lines in such a print as "Ruined House." Who can escape the sweep of the squad of soldiers marching away in another print or miss the power of his architectural conception in which the houses and the land remain while the people march toward an abyss? The appreciation of Orozco in this country is only beginning.

—Arthur Millier, "Art Season Is Under Way," *Los Angeles Times*, October 12, 1930, section 3, 16.

[Orozco's prints] are so forbiddingly stark and dry that at first they cause the spectator physical pain. It is seen that they are the productions of a man who has been horribly hurt by the injustices of life and who strives to put the bald facts of the case to you without any of the seductions of art, and though this aridity is impressive it does not win quick converts. In the end the artist's implacable honesty converts.... The feelings let loose by the revolutionary constructors of the new Mexico are [in the murals] permanently imprisoned in an acceptable art form, and it is not necessary to share the author's politics in order to sympathize with the exaltation he got from them.

—Carlyle Burrows, review of Reed's *José Clemente Orozco*, in the *New York Herald Tribune*, cited in "The Orozco Book," *Art Digest*, vol. 7, no. 7 (January 1, 1933), 22.

Rivera and Orozco have emerged as two outstanding figures. The one-armed Orozco is R's nearest competitor. His interpretation of the revolution is explosive, terrifying, grotesquely powerful. His work has a Hogarthian, a Swiftian satire, cruel

318

and derisive. He has something in common with that remarkable Mexican caricaturist of the last century, Posada; something decidedly in common with the Caprichos of Goya. There is a Grecco-like [*sic*] abnormality to his painting, a constant straining at the leash, as of a desire to leap over and beyond the possibilities of all artistic expression. Hence his work is more erratic. It is as erratic as the revolutionary hosts he depicts on the march, whirling over the harsh deserts with gun and Juana, battling, looting, burning, fornicating, boozing, shouting freedom.

— Beals, *Mexican Maze,* 279.

The Painter's Personality

José C. Orozco in.... Says he sees nobody except to insult them, and talks more through his teeth than ever.

— Anita Brenner, *Diaries* (February 3, 1926).

Orozco is one of the few Mexican painters who have not studied in Europe. Eager to be an architect, he didn't get around to his art until 1909, when he was 26. Intolerant even then of the pretty, sun-lit school of painting, Orozco expressed his contempt by painting prostitutes, night life, used dark, lurid colors. To this day he has never painted a landscape.
[…]
As the result of encountering some Mexican dynamite when he was 17, Orozco has no left hand, is partly deaf, and wears thick glasses. Peering through them, he says: "I paint the today feeling. Anything made with passion, interest will last."

— Elizabeth Sacartoff, "Modern Art Museum Gets Fresco Mural," *PM* (June 19, 1940), 21.

Orozco is fifty-seven, has no left hand, no hearing in his left ear, and very poor eyesight. His disabilities

are the result of an explosion that injured him when he was in his teens. We had read that this accident occurred during an experiment in a chemical laboratory, but he told us this was nonsense. "I was just playing in the street with some powder," he said. "It was just an ordinary explosion."
[…]
We asked him how he amused himself in town, and he grinned evasively. "The whole life is very amusing," he said. We stopped by Mr. Abbott's office on our way out and besought him for an extra-curricular note on the muralist. "Orozco has a great grasp of night life from Harlem to the Battery," Mr. Abbott stated flatly. "He talks knowingly of floor shows all over town."

— "Interchangeable Dive Bomber," *New Yorker,* vol. 16, no. 21 (July 6, 1940), 13.

Mexicanness

The archaeological style of seven years ago was replaced by another similar one, which is the prevailing style at present. It consists in attributing to the pure indigene, now in a state of complete degeneration in the process of disappearing, or pretending to attribute to him, the beautiful objects of the minor folk arts that are the natural product of the creole and the mestizo of the cities, an aesthetics that he neither feels nor can falsify by suppressing and ignoring his own aesthetic faculties.

— Unpublished document by Orozco, about 1923, in Orozco, *The Artist in New York,* 89.[21]

The "democractic" idea had emerged, a sort of artistic Christianity and the beginning of Nationalism. Students themselves were very different. Instead of the student of art all sorts of people appeared, from schoolboys and truants to clerks, young ladies, workers, and peasants, the young as well as the old. They quite lacked previous training. Without more

319

ado they were handed colors, canvas, and pencils and told to paint as they pleased whatever they had before them…. Blessed are the ignorant and the imbecile, for theirs is the supreme glory of art!

—Orozco, *An Autobiography*, 76–77.[22]

I am absolutely certain that no Mexican painter, ancient or modern, has respected the Indian in his works as I have. Many of my mural paintings and canvases have been a real glorification of the Indian race, a noble reference to its virtues, its sufferings, its heroism. Never have I painted them as grotesque figures, or dressed them as fancy riders or China Poblana, or represented them as personages of theatrical, pornographic or political magazines. Never have I mocked the folk customs and always when there was an opportunity I have attacked those who exploit, deceive and weaken the race, as anyone can see in the very patio of the National Preparatory School. I have never flattered nor falsified the true nature of the Indian.

—José Clemente Orozco, "A Correction," *Mexican Folkways*, vol. 5, no. 1 (January–March 1929), 9. There is also a Spanish version of this text. Orozco is responding to Frances Toor, editor of *Mexican Folkways*, who had titled a fresco panel by Orozco at the National Preparatory School "Cortes and Malintzi: The Indian Race under Their Feet." She commented; "I am perfectly willing to be called an 'imbecile' by such a great artist and to publish his explanation. The Editor of *Mexican Folkways* is just as sincere in her respect for the Indian Race as José Clemente Orozco."

Tell me something: Was Rouault acquainted with things Mexican, such as, for example, the saints of the churches, the scourged Christ of Holy Week, illustrated pennysheets, or pulque-shop painting?

—Letter from Orozco to Jean Charlot, September 25, 1928, in Orozco, *The Artist in New York*, 73.[23]

I feel like leaving no puppet un-beheaded, and propagating as far as possible our already-famous *pulquería* painting, the best in the world.

—Letter to Jorge Juan Crespo de la Serna, February 19, 1930, in Luis Cardoza y Aragón *Orozco*, 280.[24]

Our little Mexican children, unhampered by conventional knowledge in art, make apparent what is their true, natural inheritance, by inventing their own art forms.

—José Clemente Orozco, "The Heritage of the Mexican Child," *Everyday Art*, vol. 12, no. 3, (February–March 1934), 9.

There are no better craftsmen in the world today doing mural paintings than the Mexican Indians Orozco and Rivera. Yet both of them are failures, so far as the United States are concerned. Why? Because in the first place they are propagandists. In the second, they have failed to clarify their thought. In the third, they have violated propriety by work totally unsuited to its setting. Finally, they have painted the thing of the moment as they see it instead of giving the mighty surge of irresistible currents of thought leading to profound modifications of the social structure. Both these men can draw, both know their pigments, both see on a large scale; in both is the same boiling vitality, demanding expression. But race has poisoned them both against the white man, and they are not intellectually, artistically honest.

…When our people recover their vision, when they once more see art as standing alone and beautiful, helpful to all without regard to politics or religion, profession or trade, we shall see these tumbled, ugly, violently conceived murals in their true light.

—Arthur Stanley Riggs, "Murals, Mexican and Otherwise," *Art and Archaeology*, vol. 35, no. 2 (March–April 1934), 90.

What more do you want? …Well, now I'm going to Mexico to see if I can distract myself and learn from you, especially from you, dear friend, and my very Mexican, Mexicanizing, and Mexicanating great friend Orozco, whom I also love so much.

— José Pijoán, "From José Pijoán to Genaro Estrada," April 28, 1937, *Archive of the Secretariat of Foreign Relations, Personal Archive of Genaro Estrada,* Book II, 149.[25]

América, America

Imagine a sickle and a hammer painted…over the door of the Columbia University Library.

— John Dos Passos, "Paint the Revolution," *New Masses* (March 1927), 15.

Democracy, you see, has provided no mythology adaptable to the symbolical apparatus of painting; its ideals have been continually shifting, have accommodated themselves to the rapid changes in the mechanics of production and distribution. Democratic society has created no background of vital belief, no general conviction that behind the shifting dance of expedients there exists a spiritual reality, absolute and unchangeable.

Democracy has drained the substance from the old illusions to which art was faithfully united: the illusion that eternal life actually lay beyond the horizon of fact; that the King was divine and his antics inspired. Today the King is not even a figure-head—he is an obsolete dunce, and the Church, like the old aristocracy with its ideals of power, grandeur and gentility, survives as a clearing house for social indulgences.

Rivera's declaration [that "art is propaganda or it is not art" and that all the "distinctions and subtleties" of modernism "were but the outcome of a bourgeois psychology"], therefore, cannot be disposed of with a sneer. As already noted, it goes

deeper than party affiliations; it enters into the profound restlessness of the human spirit confronted with inevitable change. By implication at least, it voices the old undying truth that art cannot subsist on itself. And inasmuch as that is exactly what art has been trying to do, it will be worth while to consider a system which, whatever its claims, would relieve art from the ignominy of self-consumption.

— Thomas Craven, *Modern Art: the Men, the Movements, the Meaning,* 2d ed. (1st, 1934; New York: Simon and Schuster, 1940), 361, 357.

Orozco has come to visit and study New York. He says: "I am interested in painting the spirit of American achievements, not in portraying skyscrapers as such but using their monumental quality as symbolical. My pictures expressing the Revolution in Mexico have completed my reaction to it, and now I expect to paint other subjects."

— "New York Sees Mexico's Revolutionary Art," *Art Digest,* 2.

The secret of the Sphinx is no secret to any Mexican who has seen his country's old sculptures, and every peasant, every worker has [sic] done so; it is a secret said by men who present things not as they seem, but as they are. Because of this, Juanita and Miguelito do not understand the falsification of art when it is imported from Europe or the United States. Woe to us when it is sometimes called "*gringo* art."…And a Mexican would never say "*gringo* art" before some of our products, perhaps because we have neglected to label them. "Look what I have bought today," says don D., pulling out a .45 caliber revolver, and offering it for his young wife to inspect. "Oh, how pretty!" was the delighted response. And it did not come so spontaneously from that charming lady because of the barbaric instrument's usefulness for "business"; it was because of its clean and logical surfaces, the strong and elegant lines,

321

the truly architectural quality of the thing. If the man in Connecticut who made it had placed upon it some aesthetic decoration, as his neighbor places pseudo-Greek drawings of acanthus with gold paint on his sewing machine, the logic of the thing would have been lost, and the revolver would have disgusted the lady. In its natural beauty, it appeared to her mind as an appropriate attribute for a man, just as a piece of lace was appropriate for herself.

> —Walter Pach, "El arte en México," *Forma* 1926–28, facsimile of the seven issues of the journal *Forma,* originally published in no. 7 (1928), 19 (Mexico: Fondo de Cultura Económica, 1982), 335. (It may be that the "don D." in the anecdote is Diego Rivera, who liked to strut about with a revolver; however, defenders of this hypothesis would have to demonstrate that the "piece of lace" reference was appropriate for his wife, Lupe Marín.)[26]

He is the American painter par excellence.

> —Nadia Larovna, *San Francisco Examiner* critic, quoted by José Juan Tablada, "Nueva York de día y de noche: México en triunfo," in *La Babilonia de hierro* (original in *El Universal,* Mexico [August 10, 1930]).[27]

Orozco has energized that wall [in Pomona College] with his sublime conception of Prometheus bearing fire to cold, longing humanity, until it lives as probably no wall in the United States today.... Actually it brings to us a bit of the most significant art outburst of our time. The esthetic experiments of modern Paris are trifling matters compared to the Mexican wall paintings of the last nine years.

> —Arthur Millier in the *Los Angeles Times,* cited in "Orozco and Pijóan Dream of Giants," *Art Digest,* vol. 4, no. 19 (August 1930), 5.

The murals in the New School are American; one can not conceive of their being painted anywhere else. Which seems to me a hopeful sign that American painting, after some centuries of heavy leaning on Europe, and of being distinguishable

from European work chiefly by the inferiority of its technique and the slow maturity of its practitioners, is becoming infused with a spirit which marks it off from European art as a thing different rather than inferior.

> —Suzzane La Follette, "America in Murals," *New Freeman,* New York (February 18, 1931), 54.

It would be ridiculous certainly, for us to claim kinship with this Mexican painter in a parochial sense, but to the larger plane of American life Orozco is as autochthonous as New Hampshire granite, or the Mississippi River, or Samson Occom himself. To the latter worthy the art of José Clemente Orozco would have been far more intelligible than any of the works that have come out of Concord.

> —Stacy May, professor of economics, Dartmouth College, in the *Dartmouth,* cited in "A Vast Fresco," *Art Digest,* vol. 6, no. 17 (June 1, 1932), 5.

Its order and its rationality: the neat country barn, the town meeting, the village school, the fundamentally cooperative group life, made possible by a tamping down of wanton impulse. Dominating the whole scene stands the schoolmistress, a gaunt unlovely female, a pioneer possessed of the more masculine virtues. Here are the fundamental institutions of our older America together with the more mechanized animus of the new: here, too, one senses the danger of such discipline. The children grouped around the teacher are too much of one mold, and that mold a stupid one. One can hear the high parrot chatter of I-pledge-allegiance-to-my-flag-and-to-the-republic-for-which-it-stands. In opposition to this Northern conception of civilization is Hispano-America's instinct for life at its more primitive organic levels: better a simple peasant, thriving on a few tortillas and a little pulque, than a machine worker starving as the result of the abundance of goods he has produced.

322

—Lewis Mumford, "Orozco in New England," *New Republic* (October 10, 1934), 232. He refers to the panels *Anglo-America* and *Hispano-America,* part of the mural cycle at Dartmouth College, *The Epic of American Civilization.*

Still, this last panel that he painted has Christ hacking his cross to pieces, using a mycenean mask for the face and all painted in strident colors—brilliant reds and other colors, *pure* colors. Ironically, in the dechristianized New England at the time this theme of Christ meant practically nothing. As they say today, "they couldn't have cared less."

The painting does show how profound was the revulsion of the Mexican Revolutionaries to Christ and his Church. For them, Christ was still alive and they had to destroy him. The cross was a burning symbol to die for, but not so at Dartmouth where the cross did not exist.

—Carlos Sánchez, unpublished article, about 1984.

I must admit that I relish the sweet irony of events which made it possible for a college, originally founded for the purpose of converting the heathen Indian, to be converted, in turn, by one! But this, I think, is a healthy state of affairs and the students of Dartmouth College are the lucky beneficiaries.

—E. M. Benson, "Mr. Watts' Attack on Orozco's Murals Stirs a Hornet's Nest," *Art Digest,* vol. 9, no. 1 (October 1, 1934), 6.

In its more imaginative sons, this New England has always been at home on a world stage, just as its merchants were at home in Hongkong [*sic*], Singapore and Rio.

—Mumford, "Orozco in New England," 232.

Excited youngsters and serious-minded people who formerly would have gone to Paris for all their sweetness and light now come to Mexico, and collectors and critics have begun to take the Mexican School very seriously indeed. Furthermore two of its leaders—Diego Rivera and José Clemente Orozco—have decorated important buildings in American cities, and many American painters have studied under them and are spreading the style, so it will be forced upon your attention sooner or later, if it has not been so far.

—Anita Brenner, *Your Mexican Holiday,* 257.

Social protest is one thing that American artists did not "crib" from the French (to a Frenchman art is an escape not a reminder of the defects in his national life). It came up from the south below the Rio Grande via such Mexican artists as Rivera and Orozco. And while social protest is merely a minor segment of contemporary art in the United States, it provides the underlying theme of most of Mexico's art production.

—"The Art of Mexico—Land of Social Protest," *Art Digest,* vol. 12, no. 12 (March 15, 1939), 45.

Modernity and *Modernism*

"This is worth a thousand times more than all the work of your famous Rodin (whom he liked very much)." At this, the train arrived, and we had to board quickly, but once we were seated, José Clemente Orozco went back on the offensive: "Provincial idiot. Provincial idiot...." To which I replied, with the same rhythm: "It's worth a thousand times, a million times more than your stinking Rodin." The North Americans, passengers like ourselves on the same train car, without understanding what we were saying, watched amazed at our shouting match.

—A conversation on the New York subway between Siqueiros and Orozco, around 1919; in David Alfaro Siqueiros, *Me llamaban El Coronelazo (memorias)* (Mexico: Grijalbo [Biografías GANDESA], 1977), 134.[28]

323

Art in San Francisco was one hundred percent academic. Even New York was as yet untouched by the Modern Art of the Paris School, with which as yet only a select minority was acquainted.

—Orozco, *An Autobiography,* 66.[29]

There is no denying the fact that Orozco is a force; and as such he moves forward with unconquerable enthusiasm…. "Embrace" (fig. 266), also a gouache, reverts, in the formalized postures, to an earlier mood. And, while arresting, it prompts the uneasy fear that in Orozco's art there may prowl a largely latent tendency to become mannered. What has so often in past performances created an impression of simple, passionate majesty here comes perilously close to reminding one of "go-stop" signals. Also one is made a little bit uneasy by the present penchant for cerebral abstractions, that sometimes savor of the French. "Still Life" and "Aquella Noche" (fig. 265) are beautiful abstractions. But are they Mexican?

—Edward Alden Jewell, "Orozco Exhibits," *New York Times* (February 9, 1930), section 8, 13. Review of show at Delphic Studios.

The owners of a gallery in Berlin visited the Gallery and were amazed that I was unknown in Germany.

—Letter from Orozco to Margarita Valladares, February 13, 1930, in Orozco, *Cartas a Margarita,* 191.[30]

Orozco uses paraphernalia of the surrealists but in an original mode. *Aquella Noche,* in which a wine glass, a donkey's skull, a lyre, a rose, and wierd [*sic*] undersea plant forms float before a ruined wall, while two cloud-streaked crescents face each other across a ghostly sky, is a perfect phantasmagoria.

—An article in *Parnassus,* vol. 2, no. 2 (February 1930), 7.

The new paintings show a decided leaning toward the abstract, a field in which Orozco is not yet entirely impressive. His cast of mind is more sombre than ever and this even extends to the color schemes, which are concerned largely with blacks and browns. Although the sincerity and passion of these pictures can be readily felt, they nevertheless do not match the power of the famous murals, nor even the early drawing for the "House of Tears," which is included in this exhibition. But Mr. Orozco is among the artists to be watched.

—Review of Delphic Studios show, in the *New York Sun,* cited in "Orozco," *Art Digest,* vol. 4, no. 10 (mid-February 1930), 19.

Without the exaggerations which made of radical cubism a mere display of decorative pattern, Orozco demonstrated the disciplinary values of cubism, the elimination of the non-essential and the final attainment of the universal. There is a cosmic quality in Orozco's work, an end achieved through a profound tragedy.

—Tablada, "Recent Activities in Mexican Art," 16.

It has been said of Orozco that he is a modern without being a modernist. His representations are often painful and violent, but saved from being brutal by a great pity and a great love. Nor is Orozco uninfluenced by the dynamic force present in the Colossus of the North. The sources of his inspiration lie deep in America's history and tradition. He is an American painter par excellence.

—Nadia Lavrova, review of show at Courvoisier Gallery, San Francisco, in the *San Francisco Examiner,* cited in "Orozco's Art," *Art Digest,* vol. 4, no. 18 (July 1930), 19.

[Orozco] regretted the fact that modern science had not contributed at all to painting. He pointed out that painters still use the same traditional materials and methods and, what is worse, in a manner more backward than forward-looking.

> —Alma Reed, *Orozco*, 213. The recollection refers to roughly 1930.[31]

Just what did José Clemente Orozco eat or drink—that night? In the painting which he calls "Aquella Noche," which has just been bought from the Delphic Studios, New York, by C. T. Etter of Detroit, there appears a coffin with a bottle and glass standing on it, a harp, the jaws of some terrifying animal, a ghostly ruin with one moon (turned one way) seen through a spectral window, and another moon (turned the other way) over the roof. "That night," even though a bit disorganized, must have been memorable.

> —"That Night," *Art Digest*, vol. 5, no. 4 (November 15, 1930), 5.

It is important, too, that Orozco's painting is sufficiently abstract and sufficiently universal in theme to give the promise of wearing well over the years to come. It is no doubt true that no one can predict with certainty what our great grandchildren will judge to be fine. But if the people in colleges have not the courage to stake their judgments upon the matter, who in contemporary life will? The work of José Clemente Orozco has as good a chance of weathering the judgment of time as that of any living mural painter.

> —Stacy May, cited in "A Vast Fresco," 5.

The return to fresco is a sign of revolution in artistic methods—the methods of the sculptor, the writer, the architect, as well as of the painter. The sculptor, for instance, must give up soft, tricky and misleading materials such as clay, plaster and plastiline, and take instead chisel and hammer to carve directly in the stone. Only when artists go back to—or go forth to—the natural and classical methods will art recover its normal function and be ready to do its duty at the right moment in the development of culture.

> —José Clemente Orozco, unpublished text prepared for the preface to Gardner Hale's *Fresco Painting*, cited in Justino Fernández, *Textos de Orozco*, 2d ed. (Mexico City: UNAM-IIE, 1983), 46.

Interpreting the Work

The critics have been unanimous in acknowledging the significance of [Orozco's] painting with its uncompromising statements and paradoxical abstractions. The cruelty of the subject matter, the pathos of many of the canvases was [*sic*] understood in the light of narrative and admitted as a necessary document in setting forth the tragic pathos of a suffering country: the intrinsic qualities of the artist have never for a moment been lost, his power and his masterful technique ever present.

> —Tablada, "Recent Activities in Mexican Art," 16.

Neither in the representation of legends nor in the current themes that he includes in his murals is there a commitment to any formal tradition. Rather, he tries to capture, through forms, deeply lived and felt themes, which have impact because of the immediate situation....

> —Hans Tietze, *Deutsche Kunst und Dekoration* (February 1933), in Clemente Orozco Valladares, *Orozco; verdad cronológica*, 272.[32]

To find Orozco's meaning the reader must go again and again to the pictures themselves; even the painter cannot tell him what they mean, except by the means he has already used.

> —Lewis Mumford, "Orozco in New England," 232.

325

But a wild bird like Orozco was not so easy to tame. He gave them the school they wanted and the Democratic group discussion at a New England meeting but he got back at them; or perhaps he just had to explode from such foreign constraint by painting President Woodrow Wilson, Winston Churchill and the other important characters of the First World War as capitalists and church dignitaries grabbing bags of gold. From the open bags, gold is pouring down the wall. These were all the old, tired themes of the Mexican Revolutionary murals.

— Carlos Sánchez, unpublished article, about 1984.

I had very bad luck. The pamphlet you know of, which the Colegio people published, was done any which way, putting down the names they made up "so as not to compromise themselves" and even what is there with my name was a trick, because it was just an "explanation" for stupid students who wanted "explanations" for a little paper they publish, but not for the pamphlet. All in all, an attempt which only served to exploit me, selling that so-called pamphlet by the thousands and misrepresenting me.

— Letter from Orozco, March 14, 1937, reproduced in Cardoza y Aragón, *Orozco,* 310. Despite his claims, the pamphlet about which he complains was preceded by Orozco's own explanatory text.[33]

"Painting is not to be explained. I abhor the easy road of complications. Commentators like Pater, Ruskin, Fromentin pose a problem and provide an enjoyment similar to that of the work of art."

— Luis Cardoza y Aragón quoting Orozco, *Orozco,* 41.[34]

Orozco conserves his energy, makes each detail count for a great deal: money is yellow, and we can hear the clink of the coin: there are chains which clink, metallically, too. A wreath of flowers, a flag, a badge, a mask, a serpent, a screw, each becomes

something magnified as it contributes in meaning and intensity to the cumulative theme.

— Dorothy Adlow, "Decoration at Dartmouth Takes On New Significance," *New York Times* (August 28, 1941), 10.

As you have already seen, painting is something essentially objective; that is, it is not spoken, but really made directly with objects or materials.

— Letter from Orozco to his daughter Lucrecia, October 13, 1945, in Orozco, *Cartas a Margarita,* 359.[35]

Color

Orozco is best in his element with brilliant colors. There is nothing restful about his painting, either in the subjects or in the color combinations. His decorations—cubical, triangular, and vivid—would serve as an excellent tonic for those whose reactions to color have become jaded.

— Review of Delphic Studios show, in the *New York Herald Tribune,* cited in "Orozco," *Art Digest,* vol. 4, no. 10 (mid-February 1930), 19.

In the blacks and whites Orozco resorts to all the possibilities that shades can give him, from the darkest dark to the lightest white. It is as worthy of note that Orozco alone is not swept by any isms, not even the Indianismo which Diego Rivera and his followers are exploiting.

— Topchesky, "Clemente Orozco II," 4.

The suggestive force of red is, however, surpassed by the dramatic potential of black and white. For the last quarter-century, this potential has found in cinema all its meaning and has been brought by it to its paroxysm, allying pathetic silence in this sort of mathematical fatality born of the regulation of mechanical rhythm.

On the one hand, red implies for us fire and blood; on the other, black and white are the transcription of mourning.

The poignant work extracted by Orozco from the Mexican revolution is parallel in its procedure to that of the illuminators whose object is to deliver a blow to the simplistic imagination of the naive and rouse the propensity toward sadism in collectivities, reconstituting anguish and terror with a prodigious intensity.

No red. No blood. Nothing but black and a little gray on the white paper, and at the same time, terror in its primordial reality; terror made more sinister thanks to the funereal use of that gray, that black, that white.

— Gaston Poulain, "Un pintor del México en revolución," *Bandera de provincias* (September 15, 1929,) facsimile, supplement. It reproduces a French article, surely published with reference to Orozco's exhibit that same year, in the Paris gallery Fermé la Nuit.[36]

Note the way that color itself is used to create movement and progression. The opening notes are somber: but the final chords of yellow and red are already struck in the totem-pole panels that frame the opening in the western side of the room. Even at a distance one is prepared for that final clang of the cymbals: the flag-draped victim and the resurrected Christ.

— Mumford, "Orozco in New England," 232. He refers to the Dartmouth College murals.

Style

The forms—physical and psychological—that the painter has registered have the precision of the primitive, that is, of art in a state of such intensity that when it divides and recombines its elements, it constantly gains richness. This aspect of Mr. Orozco's art is more evident in the almost-geometrical definition of his drawing than in his color.

— Walter Pach, "Impresiones sobre el arte actual de México" *México moderno* (October 22, 1922), 131–38.[37]

The trouble would seem to be that the walls are so lacking in rhythm, in sustained emotion as communicated in terms of pattern. If this were a piece of music instead of fresco, one would probably say that it contained no trace of melodic line. And for a room whose walls are expected to hold together, as an encompassing stream of pictorial representation, this is indeed a serious defect.... Those who have seen his frescoes in Mexico know what summits of mural expression Orozco can attain. In this case, however, he seems to have followed, from the beginning, a mistaken conception of the room's resources, of its defects; also, perhaps, the job was unduly rushed to completion. It was finished, one learns, in forty-six and a half days.

— Edward Alden Jewell, "The Frescoes by Orozco," *New York Times* (January 25, 1931), 12.

Artistically, the most convincing portions of these murals are those that are most realistic. The portraits, such as those of [Carrillo] Puerto, Lenin, Gandhi, and the figures around the council table, are uniformly fine, painted with a precise grasp of character combined with a large, sculptural feeling for form.... In matters of style, as in other respects, Orozco has always been a law unto himself, saying what he wanted to say in his own way. His work is uneven, at times marked by great intensity, at others not adequately representing his gifts. These traits characterize the present murals. Parts of them are so fine that one can only wish that as a whole they had been carried to the same high point.

— Lloyd Goodrich, "The Murals of the New School," *Creative Art* (March 4, 1931), 399.

327

On the other hand, Michelangelo's frescoes would seem entirely out of place in a modern setting. He felt that much of Michelangelo's painting lacked solidity. With his characteristic flair for graphic and often exaggerated analogy, he remarked that there were many places in the Sistine ceiling that would "explode" if one were to stick a pin into their "billowy, pillowy volumes."

— Letter from Orozco to Alma Reed, 1932, glossed in Reed, *Orozco*, 252.[38]

I prefer the majestic creation, in which he shaped passions with a wisely governed impulse, to the unbridled baroque expressionism of some murals or mural fragments. Dominating the passions, and not allowing them to drag him along. The contrast of these two tones is often to be found in a single mural: severe fragments that stand out amid the storm he could not or would not subdue. The frequency of this tension, hammering on the anvil, forges his most austere forms.

— Cardoza y Aragón, *Orozco*, 46.[39]

Still being on trial, he had to paint another tentative panel in the Baker Library basement next to the space in the middle of the hall, where they dispensed books and received returned books from students.…If I remember correctly, it represented riding medieval knights in armor. These were painted not in Orozco's fast strokes, but in what he himself of others would derogatorily call "estilo lamidito." Mexicans use a lot of diminutives. *Lamido* is what a dog does when he licks his wounds. "Lamidito," applied to painting, means that the artist goes over the same area over and over again, like an artisan, not like an artist painting with "bravura," because his demon impels him to express himself and he chisels away at the marble like Michelangelo in fury, or paints like Franz [*sic*] Hals, in few strokes conveying the image on the canvas. Lamidito is something like a school exercise. The works suffers because of this.

— Carlos Sánchez, unpublished article, about 1984.

Orozco has two tendencies in his career. A destructive one, in which, turning himself into a god of vengeance, trying to purify the world around him, it is he himself who is purified, understanding that Art exists to serve the greatest yearnings and is not to be taken as a whip or a machine gun. And the other, contrary tendency, in which, synthesizing the values of history, which are still axes around which present activity revolves, he finds higher forms of expression and speaks his new word through them.

— Agustín Aragón Leyva, "El Prometeo de José Clemente Orozco," *El Nacional, Diario Popular* (June 7, 1933), 3.[40]

I think that, if one were to look for the place and era whose expression could be most aptly considered, one would have to look to the Italy of the Quattrocento; the pride of his granite would live there with less artificiality together with other irreducible and solitary pitfalls of time.

— Jorge Cuesta, "La pintura de José Clemente Orozco," in Jorge Cuesta, *Obras*, ed. Miguel Capistrán, Jesús R. Martínez Malo, Victor Peláez Cuesta, and L.M. Schneider (Mexico: El Equilibrista, 1994), vol. 1, 272 (originally published in El Universal [February 15, 1934]).[41]

José Clemente Orozco, about 1930, photograph courtesy Dartmouth College Library, photograph by Doris Ullman.

Notes

Abbreviation

UNAM-IIE: UNAM—Instituto de Investigaciones Estéticas

Introduction

(Timothy Rub)

1. José Clemente Orozco, *An Autobiography,* transl. Robert C. Stephenson (Austin: University of Texas Press, 1962), 123.

2. José Clemente Orozco, *The Artist in New York: Letters to Jean Charlot and Unpublished Writings, 1925–1929* (Austin: University of Texas Press, 57).

3. Ibid., 13.

4. Ibid., 14.

5. Orozco, *An Autobiography,* 88.

Orozco in the United States: An Essay on the History of Ideas

(Renato González Mello)

1. David Brading, *Los orígenes del nacionalismo mexicano* (Mexico: Era, 1973), 15–94.

2. David Brading, *Mito y profecía en la historia de México,* transl. Tomás Segovia (Mexico: Vuelta, 1988), 199, analyzes the contradictions in Vasconcelos's thought and compares him with Coleridge. Regarding Vasconcelos's book *La raza cósmica,* Brading asserts that "in truth, to an English ear accustomed to Mexican rhetoric, there is in his work a hemispheric optimism which sounds more like Eagle Pass than Piedras Negras."

3. Since this biographical essay is not exhaustive, I also refer the reader to the general chronology in this volume. Anyone wishing to follow Orozco's life step by step must consult Clemente Orozco Valladares, *Orozco, verdad cronológica* (Guadalajara: Universidad de Guadalajara, 1983). Concerning Orozco's stay in New York, Alma Reed's memoir *Orozco* (Mexico City: Fondo de Cultura Económica, 1955) is particularly helpful. A recent account of Orozco's stay in New York, focusing on the New School for Social Research murals and his easel painting, can be found in Alejandro Anreus, *Orozco in Gringoland: The Years in New York* (Albuquerque: University of New Mexico Press, 2001).

4. On "high and low" in modern art, see Kirk Varnedoe and Adam Gopnik, *High and Low: Modern Art, Popular Culture* (New York: Museum of Modern Art–Harry N. Abrams, Inc., 1990).

5. José Clemente Orozco, *An Autobiography,* transl. Robert C. Stephenson (Austin: University of Texas Press, 1962), 8.

6. Orozco's memory is not reliable in this regard; it is difficult to imagine that he would remember such specific technical details from his earliest childhood. This story, moreover, is similar to Diego Rivera's recollection; twelve years earlier Rivera also had referred to Posada's shop. Finally, far from being the kind of ingenuous act that could be attributed to a child, the comparison of academic art with Posada's work is a highly sophisticated operation that belies intellectual refinement. I make this argument in "Orozco y Posada: un parricidio," *El Alcaraván,* Mexico, vol. 2, no. 5 (1991), 6–9, and "Posada y sus coleccionistas extranjeros," in *México en el mundo de las colec-*ciones de arte: *México moderno* (Mexico City: Azabache, 1994), 313–78.

7. Fausto Ramírez, "Tradición y modernidad en la Escuela Nacional de Bellas Artes, 1903–1912," in *Las academias de arte,* VII Coloquio Internacional en Guanajuato (Mexico City: UNAM-IIE, 1985), 209–59. See also Jean Charlot, *Mexican Art and the Academy of San Carlos: 1785–1915* (Austin: University of Texas Press, 1962).

8. See Renato González Mello, "Posada y sus coleccionistas extranjeros," 313–78; see also the catalog *Posada y la prensa ilustrada: signos de modernización y resistencias* (Mexico City: Museo Nacional de Arte–INBA, 1996), 103–19, especially the essay by Thomas Gretton, which addresses the technical problems in Posada's work and demonstrates that this was no precapitalist craftsman, as had been believed since the 1920s.

9. On the *Escuelas al aire libre,* see Karen Cordero, "Alfredo Ramos Martínez: 'un pintor de mujeres y flores' ante el ámbito estético posrevolucionario," included in the catalog *Alfredo Ramos Martínez (1861–1867): una visión retrospectiva* (Mexico City: Consejo Nacional para la Cultura y las Artes, 1992), 66–75. See also Raquel Tibol, "Las escuelas al aire libre en el desarrollo cultural de México," in *Homenaje al movimiento de escuelas de pintura al aire libre,* Coord. Sylvia Pandolfi (Mexico City: Instituto Nacional de Bellas Artes, 1981), 16–49.

10. Orozco, *An Autobiography,* 61.

11. It is always risky to extrapolate upon terms that are so specific to a particular culture and time that they have become almost theoretical categories, as is the case with the French flaneur. Orozco was not one in the strict sense, lacking as he did one of the primary characteristics of that peculiar Parisian Orpheus, aristocratic consciousness. The painter, who appears in his self-portraits as well groomed and at times almost affected, was not a dandy. He saw himself less as an aristocrat than as a bourgeois going about the city streets. On the other hand, although he set up his studio in the red-light district, it would be imprecise to call him a bohemian. Unlike Orozco, nineteenth-century bohemians were generally declassed. See Robert L. Herbert, *El impresionismo: arte, ocio y sociedad,* Spanish version by Gian Castelli, Pablo Valero, and Federico Zaragoza (Madrid: Alianza Editorial, 1989), 33–36.

12. Quoted in Teresa del Conde, *José Clemente Orozco: antología crítica* (Mexico City: UNAM-IIE, 1982), 15–19.

13. Alan Knight, *The Mexican Revolution* (Cambridge: Cambridge University Press, 1986), vol. I, pp. 68–69, and vol. II, pp. 173–74; Arnaldo Córdova, *La ideología de la Revolución Mexicana: la formación del nuevo régimen,* 18th ed. (Mexico City: Era, 1995), 44–59 and 87. Both authors argue that the Maderist revolution's ideology was fed by an "intense nostalgia" among the elites for classical Mexican liberalism and that the revolution was, in this sense, a reclaiming of the past against the positivism that had been used to justify Porfirio Díaz's regime in the early twentieth century.

14. Orozco, *An Autobiography,* 30.

15. I am referring above all to a note by Rafael Pérez Taylor, under

the pseudonym Juan Amberes, that is quoted in Del Conde, *José Clemente Orozco*, 23–24. Orozco's reply is in Justino Fernández, *Textos de Orozco*, 2d ed., addenda by Teresa del Conde (Mexico City: UNAM-IIE, 1983), 39–40.

16. Orozco, *An Autobiography*, 59–67. Orozco must have left for the United States in mid-1917, since in May of that year he submitted his resignation as a professor of drawing at the National Preparatory School. See José Clemente Orozco's letter of resignation, May 15, 1917, in the Archivo de la Secretaria de Educación Pública (hereafter called SEP Historical Archive), *Expediente personal, Orozco, José Clemente*. Although he probably returned to Mexico in 1919, it is certain that he had done so by July 1920, since at that time he began publishing political cartoons in *El Heraldo*. See *Sainete, drama y barbarie: centenario [de] J.C. Orozco, 1883–1983, caricaturas, grotescos*, catalog of the exhibition at the Museo Nacional de Arte (Mexico City: Instituto Nacional de Bellas Artes, 1983), 91.

17. Orozco, *An Autobiography*, 29. See also *1910: el arte en un año decisivo: la exposición de artistas mexicanos*, catalog of the exhibition at the Museo Nacional de Arte, May–June 1991, texts by Álvaro Matute, Fausto Ramírez, and Pilar García (Mexico City: INBA–CNCA–Museo Nacional de Arte, 1991).

18. Claude Fell, *José Vasconcelos, los años del águila (1920–1925): educación, cultura e iberoamericanismo en el México postrevolucionario*, 1st ed. (Mexico City: UNAM–Instituto de Investigaciones Históricas), 1989.

19. See Orozco's appointments as illustrator for SEP's Editorial Board between 1922 and 1924 in the SEP Historical Archive, *Expediente personal: Orozco, José Clemente*.

20. Nicola Coleby, "La construcción de una estética: el ateneo de la juventud, Vasconcelos y la primera etapa de la pintura mural posrevolucionaria, 1921–1924," master's thesis in history of art (Mexico City: UNAM–Facultad de Filosofía y Letras, 1985), especially 13–60; for an overview of the period, see Enrique Krauze, *Caudillos culturales en la Revolución Mexicana* (Mexico City: SEP-Cultura-Siglo XXI, 1985), and Víctor Díaz Arciniega, *Querella por la cultura "revolucionaria"* (Mexico City: Fondo de Cultura Económica, 1989).

21. Pedro Henríquez Ureña, *Obra crítica* (Mexico City: Fondo de Cultura Económica, 1981), 617.

22. J.C. Orozco, "Casa de los azulejos," unpublished, undated manuscript. I owe my copy of this document to Clara Bargellini's timely alert and Carlos Pellicer López's generosity. The document is in the archives of the poet Carlos Pellicer Cámara. It surely dates from 1925, but immediately after the execution of the only panels that were painted. The exactness with which they are described makes it unlikely that this document was written prior to the panels' completion. Orozco's manuscript speaks of the sides of the stairway that were still to be painted but does this in much less precise terms.

23. Walter Leslie Wilmshurst, *The Meaning of Masonry* (New Jersey: Random House, 1995), 109.

24. Xavier Moyssén, *Diego Rivera, textos de arte*, 1st ed. (Mexico City: UNAM-IIE, 1986), 89.

25. In the remaining panels, the body of Emiliano Zapata, wrapped in a red shroud, is a sacralization of this revolutionary hero but also alludes to the neophyte's symbolic death upon his being initiated into a secret society.

26. I refer especially to Charles A. Hale's *La transición del liberalismo mexicano a fines del siglo XIX* (Mexico City: Vuelta, 1991); Francois Xavier Guerra, *México: del Antiguo régimen a la revolución* (Mexico City: Fondo de Cultura Económica, 1988); Daniel Cosío Villegas, *Historia moderna de México* (Mexico City: Hermes, 1974); and Knight, *The Mexican Revolution*.

27. See Fausto Ramírez, "Artistas e iniciados en la obra mural de Orozco," in *Orozco, una relectura* (Mexico City: UNAM-IIE, 1983), 61–102.

28. The incident is described in Jean Charlot, *El renacimiento del muralismo mexicano, 1920–1925* (Mexico City: Domés, 1985), 322–23; see also Coleby, *La reconstrucción de una estética*, 179, and Raquel Tibol, *José Clemente Orozco: una vida para el arte. Breve historia documental* (Mexico City: Secretaría de Educación Pública-Cultura, 1984), 71.

29. See the catalog of publications in which Orozco participated in *Sainete, drama y barbarie*, 88–93.

30. Anita Brenner, diaries, January 2 and 8, and February 3, 1926. Susannah Glusker allowed me to consult Brenner's unpublished diaries and furnished me with valuable biographical information.

31. José Clemente Orozco, *The Artist in New York: Letters to Jean Charlot and Unpublished Writings, 1925–1929*, foreword and notes by Jean Charlot, letters and writings transl. Ruth L.C. Simms (Austin and London: University of Texas Press, 1974), 72.

32. Quoted by Orozco Valladares, *Orozco, verdad cronológica*, 164.

33. Brenner, diaries, December 17, 1925.

34. Ibid., December 26, 1925. *Idols behind Altars* includes other anecdotes, which culminate in the description of a hospital. Anita Brenner, *Idols behind Altars*, 1st ed. (New York: Payson-Clarke, 1929), 208–11.

35. Brenner, diaries, January 14, 1926.

36. Orozco, *An Autobiography*, 54.

37. Quoted by Orozco Valladares, *Orozco: verdad cronológica*, 164.

38. Ibid.

39. Ibid.

40. Ibid.

41. Ibid.

42. For biographical information, I draw upon conversations with her daughter, Susannah Glusker. For both biographical information and an interpretation of *Idols behind Altars*, see Susannah Glusker, *Anita Brenner: A Mind of Her Own* (Austin: University of Texas Press, 1998).

43. Brenner, *Idols behind Altars*.

44. Brenner, diaries, November 25, 1925. At least some chapters had already been written by 1927; ibid., December 27, 1925.

45. Brenner, *Idols behind Altars*, 40.

46. Ibid., 253, 270.

47. Ibid., 155.

48. Gershom Sholem, *La cábala y su simbolismo* (Madrid: Siglo XXI, 1978); Esther Cohen, *La palabra*

331

inconclusa (ensayos sobre Cábala), 2d ed. (Mexico City: UNAM-Taurus, 1994).

49. Morris Adler, *El mundo del Talmud* (Buenos Aires: Paidós, 1964), 1–74.

50. During the first half of the twentieth century, interpretations of cabalism that saw in its episodes a social and revolutionary messianism became widely accepted. As Gershom Sholem states, "What concerns us here is the manner in which the mystical experience becomes condensed in a symbol—through men's contact with the original source of life—which contains within itself the nihilistic destruction of authority. Messianic freedom in salvation, and in the content of the enlightenment concerning the essence of that freedom, crystallize around the symbol of life." Sholem, *La cábala y su simbolismo,* 31–32. More recently, Moshé Idel has criticized this point of view, showing that messianism, mysticism, and revolution are extremes that only occasionally touch one another. He has described, moreover, how that interpretation was used to support the ideology of the nascent State of Israel. Moshé Idel, *Mesianismo y misticismo,* transl. Miriam Eisenfeld (Barcelona: Riopiedras, 1994). See also Cohen, *La palabra inconclusa,* 29–31. This is a plausible criticism, since in Mexico we have seen similar ideas; suffice it to recall the generalized reading that John Leddy Phelan made of Jerónimo de Mendieta, picking up from Norma Cohn in *The Millenial Kingdom of the Franciscans in the New World* (Berkeley: University of California Press, 1970), and the exorbitant meanings that have been attributed to Guadalupan apparitionism and Fray Servando's

exegetic sermons, to say nothing of more recent and less academic happenings.

51. Brenner, diaries, December 16, 1925.

52. Ibid., August 12, 1927.

53. Ibid., August 25, 1925.

54. Orozco, *The Artist in New York,* 26–27.

55. Ibid., 34–35. Orozco wrote to Charlot's mother to see if her son could convince Brenner to give up the project. He wrote to Charlot himself, trying to convince him to do this (35). Orozco always feared that Brenner's book would be merely an instrument of Diego Rivera's propaganda.

56. José Clemente Orozco, *Cartas a Margarita* (Mexico: Era, 1987), 113.

57. Orozco Valladares, *Orozco: verdad cronológica,* 201.

58. José Juan Tablada, "Nueva York de día y de noche: México, rival del Rusia," *El Universal,* Mexico (June 19, 1927). The preceding paragraph is a summary of Tablada's articles during the 1920s, which can be consulted in José Juan Tablada, *La Babilonia de hierro,* 1st ed., compact disc, ed. Esther Hernández Palacios (Mexico City: UNAM–Instituto de Investigaciones Filosóficas, 1997). See also José Juan Tablada's correspondence with Genaro Estada in Archivo de la Secretaría de Relaciones Exteriores, Archivo Particular de Genaro Estrada, Libro III, especially folio 130; José Juan Tablada, "De José Juan Tablada a Genaro Estrada," folio 26 (November 1929): "It is already being considered a serious and 'businesslike' thing here to absorb systematically all our artistic production; it is already accepted that Mexico is the great artistic center of the continent and this

nation, this market is ready to come to us with all their cultural and aesthetic needs in visual arts, and perhaps in music...."

Tablada's article on Orozco, "Orozco, the Mexican Goya," published originally in *International Studio* (March 1924), is reproduced in Del Conde's *J.C. Orozco: antología crítica,* 31–44.

59. Orozco, *An Autobiography,* 62.

60 Julio Scherer García, *Siqueiros, la piel y la entraña,* 2d ed. (Mexico City: Consejo Nacional para la Cultura y las Artes, 1996), 113.

61. Alma Reed, *Orozco* (New York: Oxford University Press, 1956), 197.

62. Orozco, *An Autobiography,* 65.

63. I take the idea of the "spectator" from José Ortega y Gasset, *El espectador de José Ortega y Gasset* (Madrid: Biblioteca Nueva, 1943), 13–27: "To accentuate this difference between contemplation and life—life, with its political articulation of interests, desires and conveniences... was necessary. Because the spectator has a second intention: he speculates, looks... but what he wants to see is life as it flows before him."

64. Undated letter from José Clemente Orozco, David Alfaro Siqueiros, and Juan Olaguíbel to Luis G. Serrano, in the Museo Nacional de Arte, Archivo de Luis G. Serrano, box 7.

65. Orozco, *An Autobiography,* 72.

66. Ibid., 136–38.

67. Bertoldt Brecht, "Effetti di straniamento nell'arte scenica cinese," in *Scritti teatrali* (Milan: Einaudi, 1979), 82–83.

68. Orozco, *An Autobiography,* 60.

69. Reed, *Orozco,* 49–50.

70. Attributed to José Clemente Orozco, "En New York," *L'ABC* (November 22, 1925), 8: "Y ahora, pichoncito mío, es necesario que no te pintes la fachada y que salgas a la calle lo más desnuda que puedas para que estos yanquis no vayan a acusarme por 'trata de blancas.'" Although the drawing is not signed, other caricatures in this magazine were identified as Orozco's in the catalog *Sainete, drama y barbarie,* published in 1983. The bolder, looser drawing style of Orozco's caricatures is easy to distinguish from the much more refined art deco style of other cartoonists in the same magazine. In addition, there is another drawing of a New York subject in the same magazine that Siqueiros attributed to Orozco when he was asked about it by Alvar Carrillo Gil, who published it in *Obras de José Clemente Orozco en la colección Carrillo Gil* (Mexico: Alvar Carrillo Gil, 1953), n.p.

71. Letter to J.B. Neumann, July 16, 1935, Archives of American Art, roll NJBN 2/64–65.

72. On the correspondences between the two systems, see Lizzetta LeFalle-Collins, *In the Spirit of Resistance: African-American Modernists and the Mexican Muralist School,* prologue by Raquel Tibol, essay by Shifra M. Goldman, exhibition catalog, Studio Museum in Harlem (New York: American Federation of Arts, 1996.)

73. As advocated by Manuel Gamio, *La población del Valle de Teotihuacán: el medio en que se ha desarrollado. Su evolución étnica y social. Iniciativas para procurar su mejoramiento* (Mexico City: Secretaría de Agricultura y Fomento, 1922), lvi.

74. Vol. 4, no. 1 (January 1929). Fernández also reproduces this manifesto in *Textos de Orozco*, 41–42.

75. Ibid.

76. Ibid.

77. Ibid.

78. Ibid.

79. Ibid.

80. See, for example, John Dos Passos, *Manhattan Transfer* (Harper & Brothers: New York and London, 1925 [1st ed.]), 12: "There were Babylon and Nineveh; they were built of brick. Athens was gold marble columns. Rome was held up on broad arches of rubble. In Constantinople the minarets flame like great candles round the Golden Horn….Steel, glass, tile, concrete will be the materials of the skyscrapers. Crammed in the narrow island the millionwindowed buildings will jut glittering, pyramid on pyramid like the white cloudhead above a thunderstorm."

81. Luis Mario Schneider, *El estridentismo [en] México, 1921–1927* (Mexico City: UNAM–Difusión Cultural, 1985), 45.

82. Serge Guilbaut, *How New York Stole the Idea of Modern Art* (Chicago: University of Chicago Press, 1985), describes the ideological problems related to the hegemony of abstract expressionism during the Cold War. Although Guilbaut places more emphasis on the painters' abandonment of critical commitment, his text seems to indicate that the rise of abstract expressionism had much to do with "American" claims with respect to the "Old World."

83. Orozco, *Cartas a Margarita*, 104.

84. Ibid., 170. See also José Juan Tablada, "Nueva York de día y de noche: México en Nueva York," *El Universal*, Mexico (October 21, 1928):

Pale, infected by the tragic force of one of those drawings, a lady asked me anxiously:

"But…why do Mexicans do this?"

And I had to reply, to Alma Reed's sad smile, who already guessed the answer: "It is not Mexicans who do this, dear lady, but all men!…Have you forgotten the catastrophe of the War?"

85. Orozco, *Cartas a Margarita*, 170, 186.

86. Orozco, *The Artist in New York*, 82.

87. On the Delphic Circle, it is worth consulting Jacqueline Barnitz's essay "Los años délficos de Orozco," in *Orozco, una relectura* (Mexico City: UNAM-IIE, 1983), 103–28.

88. Reed, *Orozco*, 3. An analysis of the relationship between Orozco and Reed can be found in Anreus, *Orozco in Gringoland*, 26–46.

89. Eva Palmer, *Upward Panic: The Autobiography of Eva Palmer-Sikelianos*, edited with an introduction and notes by John Anton (Philadelphia: Harwood Academic Press, 1993), xvi, 7.

90. Ibid.

91. Ibid., 105. Decades later the Works Progress Administration blocked one attempt to present Aeschylus's *The Persians* and another to present Aristophanes. Ibid., 148–50.

92. Ibid., xvi: "Behind the prevailing cultural movements she suspected the long shadow of the great figure of Emerson, whose oration before the Phi Beta Kappa Society of Harvard on August 31, 1837, declared the intellectual independence of the American scholars. The idealistic optimism of Emerson's idyllic pragmatism filled the souls of the young men with dreams of new and endless conquest. The wind of innovation began to blow, powerful and uncontrolled, but for that matter also fraught with dangers."

93. Although, as his biographer says, these were simpler than the Parnassians. Renée Jacquin, *L'Esprit de Delphes: Angelos Sikelianos* (Aix-en-Provence, France: Université de Provence, 1988), 17–18, 55–56, 93–107, and 118–41.

94. Spanish translation in Miguel Castillo Didier, *Poetas griegos del siglo XX*, 2d ed. (Caracas: Monte Avila Editores, 1991), 68.

95. Jacquin, *L'Esprit de Delphes*, note 3.

96. What follows is a summary of Angelos Sikelianos, *Plan général du mouvement delphique: L'Université de Delphes* (Paris: Les Belles Lettres, 1929).

97. Ibid., 5.

98. Ibid., 7.

99. Ibid., 8.

100. Ibid., 15.

101. Auguste Comte, *Systems de politique positive ou traité de sociologie, instituant la Religion de l'humanité* (Paris: Carilian-Goeury et Vor Dalmont, 1854). Sikelianos was specifically inspired by Fabre d'Olivet's synarchism (Jacquin, *L'Esprit de Delphes*, 94).

102. Orozco, *The Artist in New York*, 22.

103. Jacquin, *L'Esprit de Delphes*, 18.

104. Ibid., 35–36.

105. Palmer, *Upward Panic*, 94–104 and 130–50.

106. Ibid., 121–27.

107. José Juan Tablada, "Nueva York de día y de noche: México en Nueva York," *El Universal*, Mexico (October 21, 1928).

108. Laurance P. Hurlburt, *The Mexican Muralists in the United States* (Albuquerque: University of New Mexico Press, 1989), 26.

109. Years later, in 1926, Jean Charlot, one of Orozco's closest friends, also joined the Carnegie excavations in Chichén Itzá as an illustrator, an experience that had a determining influence on his later works and ideas. Brenner, diaries, December 1925–January 1926.

110. Alma Reed, "Poetas de la moderna Hélade, II y último," *México en la Cultura*, supplement to *Novedades*, Mexico (August 16, 1964).

111. Orozco, *An Autobiography*, 129.

112. Reed, "Poetas de la moderna Hélade."

113. Jacquin, *L'Esprit de Delphes*, 19–27; Palmer, *Upward Panic*, 54–85.

114. Orozco, *An Autobiography*, 128.

115. Reed, *Orozco*, 121–22. This information is confirmed by Orozco in *Cartas a Margarita*, 158; it is also mentioned by Helen Delpar, *The Enormous Vogue of Things Mexican: Cultural Relations between the United States and Mexico, 1920–1935* (Tuscaloosa: University of Alabama Press, 1992), vii.

116. Reed, *Orozco*, 43.

117. Orozco, *The Artist in New York*, 66, translation altered.

118. Orozco, *An Autobiography*, 133. See also José Juan Tablada, "Nueva York de día y de noche: México en Nueva York." "In that kindly studio, there are two prestiges, one of which the Greek represented by the worthy wife of the poet Angelo Sikelianos, who is like a caryatid in the work that the lyrical creator builds for the world in the revived Delphic festivals that include the continuation of the Orphic tradi-

tion and precede the creation of a Spiritual University....She treasures this studio, as well as the Greek blankets that cover the walls and are reminiscent of our sarapes from Texcoco, the marvelous collection of dresses worn by the Oceanids in the *Prometheus Bound* of these festivals."

119. Orozco, *The Artist in New York,* 73. Pulquería painting was one of the reference points for Mexican aesthetics in the 1920s. Pulquerías are bars that serve pulque, a mildly alcoholic beverage made from the maguey plant that had been fiercely combated by a variety of hygienist projects since the eighteenth century. At the turn of the century the pulquerías were decorated with murals. Mexican painters saw in this an antecedent for the mural paintings of the 1920s, although Orozco generally had little sympathy for these claims. See, for example, what he says in his autobiography: "As for retablos, there are some very interesting ones, some magnificent ones, even works of genius, but the rest are like pulque-shop painting, like the tiny figures that amateurs make the world over." Orozco, *An Autobiography,* 120. Thus his tolerance of Sikelianos's, Reed's, and Naidu's populism should be seen as a concession necessary to his adaptation to this new nationalist-universalist context.

120. Angelo Sikelianos, *The Delphic Word: The Dedication,* transl. Alma Reed (New York: Harold Vinal, Ltd., 1928), 16.

121. Sarojini Naidu, *The Sceptred Flute: Songs of India* (New York: Dodd, Mead and Co., 1928), vii–viii.

122. Ibid., 80.

123. Reed, *Orozco,* 104; in the Spanish translation published in 1955, see page 112. She states that Orozco especially liked a parable from *The Forerunner* (Mineola, N.Y.: Dover Publications, 2000, p. 44, reprint of Alfred A. Knopf edition, 1920) that clearly refers to the cave myth, as it appears in *Phaedon:* "A fish said to another fish, 'Above this sea of ours there is another sea, with creatures swimming in it—and they live there even as we live here.' The fish replied, 'Pure fancy! Pure fancy! When you know that everything that leaves our sea by only an inch, and stays out of it, dies. What proof have you of other lives in other seas?'"

124. Kahlil Gibran, *The Prophet* (New York: Alfred A. Knopf, 1996).

125. Reed, *Orozco,* 106. "Come Ye Living" was published in Leonard Van Noppen's *The Challenge: War Chants of the Allies—Wise and Otherwise* (London: Elkin Mathews, Cork Street, 1919), 8.

126. Barnitz, "Los años délficos de Orozco," 110–11. For further discussion of Orozco's use of Nietzschean categories, see Rita Eder's essay in this catalog.

127. Reed, *Orozco,* 57.

128. Emily Hamblen, *Interpretation of William Blake's Job* (New York: Occult Research Press, undated). See Jacquelynn Baas's essay in this catalog.

129. The New Jersey scholar arrived at those conclusions using a theory of language and a philological method inspired by Neoplatonism. Emily Hamblen, *On the Minor Prophecies of William Blake* (New York: Haskell House Publishers, 1968), xiii.

130. Emily Hamblen, *Walt Whitman, Bard of the West* (Philadelphia: R. West, 1978).

131. Ibid., 6.

132. Artemas Packard, *Excerpts from Our Artistic World* (Chicago: Delphian Society, 1942). I have not found any other publications or traces of this later "Delphian Society," but it is worth recalling that by 1942 Eva Sikelianos was back in New York, so it would not be inconceivable that this should be a revival of the original Delphic Circle. In any case, Packard's association with Reed and Orozco makes some form of continuity a reasonable conjecture.

133. Ibid., 62.

134. Lewis Mumford, "Orozco in New England," *New Republic,* (October 10, 1934), 232. "Its order and its rationality: the neat country barn, the town meeting, the village School, the fundamentally cooperative group life, made possible by a tamping down of wanton impulse. Dominating the whole scene stands the schoolmistress, a gaunt unlovely female, a pioneer possessed of the more masculine virtues. Here are the fundamental institutions of our older America together with the more mechanized animus of the new: here, too, one senses the danger of such discipline. The children grouped around the teacher are too much of one mold, and that mold a stupid one. One can hear the high parrot chatter of I-pledge-allegiance-to-the-flag-and-to-the-republic-for-which-it-stands. In opposition to this Northern conception of civilization is Hispano-America's instinct for life at its more primitive organic levels: better a simple peasant, thriving on a few tortillas and a little pulque, than a machine worker starving as the

result of the abundance of goods he has produced."

135. Packard, *Excerpts from Our Artistic World,* 70.

136. Ibid., 100. "When the philosopher of Art seeks to analyze this mass of evidence for us and tries to abstract from it the basic 'laws of beauty,' what does he find? He finds that men seem always to have derived their deepest sense of beauty from the perception of order, rhythm, balance and symmetry, repetition and variation, harmony of the part with the whole, economy of means to end, and inevitability in the sequence of cause and effect—precisely the things that science reveals to us in the operation of the 'laws of nature'!"

137. Ibid., 164.

138. John Dos Passos, "Zapata's Ghost Walks," *New Masses* (September 1927), 11–12. I am indebted to Alicia Azuela for providing copies of the art criticism that I quote in this essay.

139. John Dos Passos, "Paint the Revolution!" *New Masses* (March 1927), 15.

140. Ibid.

141. On the image of Mexico in the United States, Delpar's *The Enormous Vogue of Things Mexican* may be consulted, as well as James D. Oles's *South of the Border: Mexico in the American Imagination, 1917–1947* (Washington, D.C.: Smithsonian Institution, 1993). Oles's text reviews the history of North American artists traveling to Mexico during the first half of the twentieth century, many of them precisely to search for lost nature.

142. Walt Whitman, *Saludo al mundo y otros poemas,* selection, translation, and prologue by

334

Carlos Montemayor (Mexico: Aldus, 1997), 113.

143. Although not for their political leadership (*cacicazgo*). Stuart Chase, *Mexico: A Study of Two Americas,* in collaboration with Marian Tyler and illustrated by Diego Rivera (New York: Literary Guild, 1931), 128–29.

144. Packard, *Excerpts from Our Artistic World,* 197–98, 214.

145. Ibid., 214.

146. Its rules were consistent enough for Edsel Ford to simulate a protest against Diego Rivera's murals at the Detroit Arts Institute, thus provoking a strong reaction in favor of the murals. See Terry Smith, *Making the Modern: Industry, Art and Design in America* (Chicago: University of Chicago Press, 1993), 237–45.

147. Hurlburt, *Mexican Muralists,* 85–86.

148. On this problem, see Juan Antonio Ortega y Medina, *Destino manifiesto: sus razones históricas y su raíz teológica* (Mexico City: Sepsetentas, 1972).

149. *The Orozco Frescoes at Dartmouth,* text by José Clemente Orozco (Hanover, N.H.: Albert I. Dickerson, 1934), [12].

150. Ibid.

151. José Enrique Rodó, *Cinco ensayos* (Madrid: América, 1915). For a brief but forceful critique of Rodó's ideas, see Edmundo O'Gorman, "Latinoamérica: así no," *Nexos,* *México* (March 1988), 13–14.

152. Rubén Darío, *Antología poética,* selection by Pedro Henríquez Ureña (Mexico City: UNAM, 1971), 74.

153. *Twenty Centuries of Mexican Art,* exhibition catalog (New York: Museum of Modern Art, 1940), 11. Although the catalog's introductory text is not signed by Barr, Stanton Loomis Catlin, who participated in its publication, assured me that Barr was the author. See Renato González Mello, "Una manifestación maravillosa de variedad ordenada humanamente en la naturaleza; entrevista con Stanton Loomis Catlin," *Curare,* vol. 12 (January 1997), 80–105.

154. Barnitz, "Los años 'délficos' de Orozco," 121.

155. Sikelianos, *Plan général du mouvement delphique,* 31–32: "rattacher…le peuple même à la tradition de la Terre et à ses propres traditions, en lui inculquant encore une fois le dogma profond…que la Terre elle-même est plus que le peuple car elle est la mè de tous ses descendants."

156. For an analysis of this theme in Orozco's iconography, see Ramírez's essay "Artistas e iniciados en la obra mural de Orozco."

157. Chase, *Mexico.*

158. Agustín Aragón Leyva, "La tecnocracia," in *El Nacional, Diario Popular,* Mexico (January 27, 1933), 3. Despite the not inconsiderable number of goals that the technocrats took from communism, they always made important efforts to differentiate themselves. Technocracy was a reformist project. "Whereas communism announces the dictatorship of the proletariat, the death of a social class, violent destruction of the old order and in order to come about it is estimated that this would cost TWO MILLION DOLLARS—in destruction of property, machinery, works of art, missiles, bombs, gunpowder, gas, electronic propaganda and deaths—TECHNOCRACY hopes to create a classless society peacefully, just by intelligent application of technology and the establishment of a social system which will correspond to this technology."

159. Smith, *Making the Modern,* 35–55, 69. "And the Ford company mass-production network became a natural order, the new Nature, a man-made machine for controlling both Nature and Man."

160. Orozco himself uses the term "negro" in Orozco, *An Autobiography,* 144–45, to refer to these African characters or characters of African ancestry.

161. On the politicization of African American art during the 1930s, see David C. Driskell, *Two Centuries of Black American Art,* exhibition catalog at the Los Angeles County Museum of Art, catalog notes by Leonard Simon (New York: LACMA–Alfred A. Knopf, 1976), 59–79.

162. Miguel Covarrubias also searched for a universal scope, beginning in the 1930s. Recall his trips to Pacific islands, his maps for the Golden Gate Exposition, and his participation in the *Twenty Centuries of Mexican Art* exhibition. In all three cases, as in his *Negro Drawings,* there was a reflection on race and exoticism, avoiding the context of U.S. national and racial discourse, which had become dangerous.

163. *The Orozco Frescoes at Dartmouth,* [10].

164. *José Clemente Orozco,* introduction by Alma Reed (New York: Delphic Studios, 1932), 3.

165. Ramón López Velarde, "El edén subvertido," in *Obras,* ed. José Luis Martínez (Mexico City: Fondo de Cultura Económica, 1986).

And gunshots engraved in the lime
of all the walls
of the spectral village,

black and foreboding maps,
for the prodigal son to read in them
returning to his threshold
one evil nightfall
by the oily light of a wick
his hope dismembered.

166. Reed, *Orozco,* 189–95.

167. Reed (*Orozco,* 194) affirms that Orozco bought the largest stretchers on the market to paint this series.

168. Reed (*Orozco,* 195) mentions the preparation of this study. *Exposición nacional José Clemente Orozco; catálogo que el Instituto Nacional de Bellas Artes publica con motivo de la exposición nacional retrospectiva de José Clemente Orozco* (Mexico City: Secretaría de Educación Pública, 1947), oil painting no. 5. A catalog that Orozco must have personally treasured, it reproduces the oil study with the legend "study" for a painting."

169. A third version, which belonged to Moisés Sáenz, essentially copies the Chicago painting. Justino Fernández reproduces it in *Obras de Orozco en la collección Carrillo-Gil* (Mexico: Alvar Carrillo Gil, 1949), painting no. 40.

170. Orozco, *An Autobiography,* 110.

171. Del Conde, *J.C. Orozco,* 15.

172. José Juan Tablada, "Nueva York de día y de noche: La exposición se clausura," *El Universal,* Mexico (November 23, 1930). Orozco sweetened Zapata but did not moderate his own prejudices. In 1931 he painted a canvas, *Pancho Villa,* in which Villa appears in the midst of a thundering, bloody battle, dressed in indigenous garb (Villa was not an Indian). Around him, dozens of

335

suffering bodies, like those that surround Prometheus at Pomona College, wail without hope of redemption. In the background, Victoriano Huerta and other characters take flight. The painting, small and very thinly painted, could be a study for another, larger piece. Like the Zapata study, it has the loose lines and ungainly figures that we have already seen in Orozco's less charitable works. Villa is not an initiate, but a sort of destroying angel; he anticipates Orozco's apocalyptic fantasies of the 1940s, such as *La Victoria* (1944).

173. Brenner, *Idols behind Altars*, 287.

174. Knight, *The Mexican Revolution*, vol. 1, pp. 311–13, discusses the different versions proposed by historians of Zapatism and its ideology.

175. Jean Clair, "Red October, Black October," in his *The 1920s: Age of the Metropolis*, exhibition catalog, (Montreal: Montreal Museum of Fine Arts, 1991), 37–40. In this same catalog, see also Helen Adkins, "George Grosz and the American Dream," 284–99.

176. Reed, *Orozco*, 124.

177. Federico García Lorca, *Poeta en Nueva York*, ed. María Clementa Millán (Mexico: Rei-Mexico, 1994).

178. Olivier Debroise, *Figuras en el trópico*, 2d ed. (Barcelona: Océano, 1983), 97, reviews several of the galleries that attempted to establish themselves; nearly all were very informal.

179. The list of publications for which Orozco drew cartoons can be found in *Sainete, drama y barbarie*, 87–93. In the 1920s Orozco drew cartoons for *El Heraldo* (1920) and for *El Machete* and *L'ABC* (1924 to 1926).

180. In SEP's Historical Archive, *Expediente personal: Orozco, José Clemente*, which is currently being inventoried and cataloged, there exists documentation that refers to Orozco's being hired and fired from different posts.

181. See *Acuerdo del presidente que nombra a José Clemente Orozco ayudante de dibujante del Departamento Editorial*, January 24, 1924, and following documents, in the SEP Historical Archive.

182. See note 28 above.

183. Alicia Azuela, *Diego Rivera en Detroit* (Mexico City: UNAM-IIE, 1985); also Delpar, *The Enormous Vogue of Things Mexican*, 55–58.

184. Orozco, *Cartas a Margarita*, 225, assures his wife that Morrow was one of the principal patrons of the New School for Social Research and that it was he who would pay his salary. In October 1932 he planned to paint a portrait of Mrs. Morrow. Ibid., 259.

185. Orozco Valladares, *Orozco, verdad cronológica*, 183.

186. Hurlburt, *Mexican Muralists*, 162. See also Robert Linsley, "Utopia Will Not Be Televised: Rivera at the Rockefeller Center," *Oxford Art Journal*, vol. 17, no. 2 (1994), 48–62.

187. Avis Berman, *Rebels on Eighth Street: Juliana Force and the Whitney Museum of American Art* (New York: Atheneum, 1990), 250. I am indebted to David Kiehl for this reference.

188. Orozco, *The Artist in New York*, 50.

189. Ibid. Orozco was aware that this was the gallery that exhibited the German avant-garde; he was also interested in it because it handled Rouault's work.

190. Orozco Valladares, *Orozco, verdad cronológica*, 201. Orozco, *The Artist in New York*, 118–19.

191. Ibid., 210.

192. Ibid., 215.

193. Reed, *Orozco*, 90–97. For a complete list of exhibitions in which Orozco participated, see Orozco Valladares, *Orozco, verdad cronológica*, 182–295. This source includes all the exhibitions for which there are traces in the painter's archive, lists of his work, and some reproductions of gallery invitations.

194. Orozco, *Cartas a Margarita*, 136; Orozco, *The Artist in New York*, 127.

195. Orozco Valladares, *Orozco, verdad cronológica*, 209.

196. Reproduced in Gaston Poulain, "Un pintor del México en revolución," *Bandera de Provincias*, Guadalajara (September 15, 1929), supplement.

197. Orozco Valladares, *Orozco, verdad cronológica*, 205. Iturbe's gossip is plausible; at that time, Eva Sikelianos was beginning to agonize over the lack of resources for the next Delphic festival.

198. Orozco, *Cartas a Margarita*, 153.

199. Orozco Valladares, *Orozco, verdad cronológica*, 210.

200. Reproduced in Luis Cardoza y Aragón, *Orozco* (Mexico: UNAM-IIE, 1959), 275.

201. Orozco, *Cartas a Margarita*, 184.

202. Orozco Valladares, *Orozco, verdad cronológica*, 218–19; Orozco, *Cartas a Margarita*, 167.

203. Ibid.

204. According to Reed (*Orozco*, 224), Orozco turned down Frank Lloyd Wright's offer to paint murals in his buildings. She also states that

a mural project in La Porte, Indiana, could not be carried out (267).

205. For example, Carlos Mérida (José Juan Tablada, "Nueva York de día y de noche," *El Universal*, Mexico [April 13, 1930]), and Roberto Cueva del Río (José Juan Tablada, "Nueva York de día y de noche: Cueva del Río," *El Universal*, Mexico [May 28, 1931]).

206. *José Clemente Orozco*, 1932.

207. Orozco, *Cartas a Margarita*, 59, 60.

208. Reed, *Orozco*, 191.

209. Orozco, *Cartas a Margarita*, 170–71, 177, 198.

210. Ibid., 177.

211. On the Galería de Arte Mexicano, see Jorge Alberto Manrique and Teresa del Conde, *Una mujer en el arte mexicano: memorias de Inés Amor* (Mexico City: UNAM-IIE, 1987); also Delmari Romero Keith, *Historia y testimonios: Galería de Arte Mexicano* (Mexico City: Galerí de Arte Mexicano, 1985).

212. With the exceptions of *Primavera*, which he painted at the home of José Moreno, and the series of panels he made to decorate the Mexico City Turf Club, both in 1945.

213. Relations between Mexico and the United States had deteriorated considerably as a result of the expropriation of oil company properties by decree of President Lázaro Cárdenas in March 1938. On the 1940 exhibition, see Charity Mewburn, "Oil, Art and Politics: The Feminization of Mexico," *Anales del Instituto de Investigaciones Estéticas*, vol. 72 (1998), 73–186.

214. Orozco Valladares, *Orozco, verdad cronológica*, 438.

215. *Exposición nacional José Clemente Orozco*.

216. The letters to Lucrecia Orozco are in Orozco, *Cartas a Margarita,* 358–62.

217. Octavio Paz, "Ocultación y descubrimiento en Orozco," in Octavio Paz, *México en la obra de Octavio Paz. III: Los privilegios de la vista* (Mexico: Fondo de Cultura Económica, 1987), 318.

218. Reed, *Orozco,* 13–14.

219. Orozco, *Cartas a Margarita,* 104.

220. Ibid., 102, 117, 123; Orozco, *The Artist in New York,* 34, letter to Jean Charlot's mother: "I don't see Anita anymore—I have broken off all relations with her—and as to 'Friends,' they do not exist for me. Here in New York there is only self-interest and deception and bad faith."

221. Reed, *Orozco,* 14, 214. Conde, *Una mujer en el arte mexicano,* 26. Inés Amor states that the letters, whose headings Carrillo Gil did not reproduce, were addressed to her.

222. Orozco, *Cartas a Margarita,* 243, 266.

223. Orozco, *The Artist in New York,* 71. Teresa del Conde found this reference, in researching the self-portrait's authenticity. See also Reed (*Orozco,* 119–20), who affirms that Orozco refused to admit having painted the portrait when it was displayed at an exhibition at Hudson A. Walker's gallery. *J.C. Orozco: Paintings and Drawings, Hudson A. Walker, 38 East 57th Street, New York, October 2–21, 1939.*

224. Reed, *Orozco,* 150.

225. Orozco, *An Autobiography,* 156.

226. Ibid., 153–54.

227. The mural painting project in the Soviet Union was Jay Leyda's

idea; Orozco Valladares, *Orozco: verdad cronológica,* 311–12. On the idea to paint in Rome shortly after the end of World War II, see the same source, 490 and 536, as well as Fernández, *Textos de Orozco,* 106.

228. Orozco, *An Autobiography,* 157–60.

229. Orozco Valladares, *Orozco: verdad cronológica,* 334.

230. Edmundo O'Gorman, "José Clemente Orozco y la gran tradición de Nuestra América," unpublished manuscript (1944–45), unclassified, Archive of El Colegio Nacional.

231. From Alma Reed to A. Washington Pezet, July 19, 1935, Archives of American Art, NAG/107.

232. However, Alma Reed continued to serve as his agent for a while longer. Orozco, *Cartas a Margarita,* 287. In 1935 he continued to report to Margarita that Alma was the one selling his new lithographs in New York.

233. Orozco, *Cartas a Margarita,* 300–306.

234. The letters were reproduced in Alvar Carrillo Gil, *Obras de José Clemente Orozco en la colección Carrillo Gil* (Mexico: Alvar Carrillo Gil, 1953), n.p. In Manrique and Del Conde, *Una mujer en el arte mexicano,* 26, Inés Amor states that the letters, whose headings Carrillo Gil did not reproduce, were addressed to her.

235. Orozco, *Cartas a Margarita,* 300.

236. Fernández, *Textos de Orozco,* 17.

237. Orozco, *Cartas a Margarita,* 311.

238. Manrique and del Conde, *Una mujer en el arte mexicano,* 58. Amor refers to Gloria Campobello as his *noviecita* ("sweetheart") and

affirms that she was the painter's "only object of affection," although apparently she officially maintained another relationship.

239. Fernandez, *Textos de Orozco,* 103, 108.

Public Painting and Private Painting: Easel Painting, Drawings, Graphic Arts, and Mural Studies

(Renato González Mello)

1. Raquel Tibol, *David Alfaro Siqueiros* (Mexico: Empresas Editoriales, 1969), 90. A partial translation can be found in Anita Brenner, *Idols behind Altars* (New York: Payson & Clarke, 1929), 255.

2. Justino Fernández, *Textos de Orozco,* 2d ed. (Mexico City: UNAM-IIE, 1983), 42 (from *Creative Art* [New York], vol. 4, no. 1). For an in-depth discussion of this manifesto, see this catalog's biographical essay.

3. Ibid., 44.

4. The notion of avant-garde (*vanguardia*) is frequently used in Mexican art criticism to name the exact opposite of muralism: an art with no political constrictions and with pure abstraction as a goal. This is a consequence of Clement Greenberg's influence on some Mexican critics. See, for example, Juan García Ponce, *La aparición de lo invisible* (Mexico City: Siglo XXI, 1968).

5. Octavio Paz, "Re/visiones: la pintura mural," in *México en la obra de Octavio Paz: III: Los privilegios de la vista* (Mexico City: Fondo de Cultura Económica, 1986), 236.

6. As seen in the biographical essay in this catalog.

7. See "Public Art, Meyer Shapiro and Mexican Muralism," *Oxford Art Journal,* vol. 17, no. 1 (1994), 56; Helga Prignitz, *El Taller de Gráfica Popular en México, 1937–1977* (Mexico City: INBA, 1992); and Orozco's utterly sarcastic opinion on his own caricatures in this catalog's biographical essay.

8. In this respect, it would be interesting to compare the muralists' points of view with what Mark Arthur Cheetham says about Mondrian and Kandinsky in *The Rhetoric of Purity: Essentialist Theory and the Advent of Abstract Painting* (Cambridge: Cambridge University Press, 1991), 120.

9. On changes at the Academia de San Carlos, see Fausto Ramírez, "Tradición y modernidad en la Escuela Nacional de Bellas Artes, 1903–1912," in *Las academias de arte (VII Coloquio Internacional en Guanajuato)* (Mexico City: UNAM-IIE, 1985), 209–59.

10. David Alfaro Siqueiros, *Me llamaban El Coronelazo (memorias)* (Mexico: Grijalbo [Biografías GANDESA], 1977); José Clemente Orozco, *Autobiografía,* 3d ed. (Mexico: Secretaría de Educación Pública-Cultura-Era, 1983).

11. Regarding the academic teaching of drawing, see Jean Charlot, *Mexican Art and the Academy of San Carlos: 1785–1915* (Austin: Austin University Press, 1962), and Clara Bargellini and Elizabeth Fuentes, *Guía que permite captar lo bello: Yesos y dibujos de la Academia de San Carlos, 1778–1916* (Mexico City: UNAM-IIE, 1989), 49–50, on surviving plaster copies, and 33–34.

12. Ramírez, "Tradición y modernidad," 217. This article is the

most complete account of the peda-gogical crisis at the academy in the early years of the twentieth century.

13. José Clemente Orozco, *An Autobiography,* transl. Robert C. Stephenson (Austin: University of Texas Press, 1962), 19. My italics.

14. Included in Teresa del Conde, *J.C. Orozco: antología crítica* (Mexico City: UNAM-IIE, 1982), 16.

15. Ramírez, "Tradición y modernidad," note 43.

16. MacKinley Helm, *Modern Mexican Painters* (New York: Harper, 1941), 11.

17. Reed mentions this in *Orozco* (New York: Oxford University Press, 1956), 91. At this writing, this notebook has not yet been located.

18. Included in Luis Cardoza y Aragón, *Orozco* (Mexico City: UNAM-IIE, 1959), 292.

19. Ibid.

20. Siqueiros, *Me llamaban el Coronelazo,* 83, remembers this period of extraordinary creative freedom: "We thought we would transform the nude from life class by using several figures at once, since the custom had been only one.... Another way of pedagogical subver-sion was to make the models, men, women or children, adopt daring poses, naturally opposed to those of our classical plaster models. I remember that some of us, including myself and José Guadalupe Escobedo (Lupito), passionately proclaimed the virtues of poses which were strained to the utmost...."

21. See, for example, Loló de la Torriente, *Memoria y razón de Diego Rivera* (Mexico: Renacimiento, 1959), vol. 1, pp. 192–220.

22. Xavier Moyssén, *Diego Rivera, textos de arte* (Mexico City: UNAM-IIE, 1986), 99.

23. See Jean Charlot, *Mexican Art;* Justino Fernández, *El arte moderno y contemporáneo de México,* 2d ed. (Mexico City: UNAM-IIE, 1993), vol. 1. It is also illuminating to read Ida Rodríguez Prampolini's introduction in *La crítica de arte en México en el siglo XIX* (Mexico City: UNAM-IIE, 1964).

24. See Ramírez, "Tradición y modernidad."

25. Orozco, *An Autobiog-raphy,* 40.

26. The biographical essay in this catalog reproduces the "program" for a fresco by Orozco.

27. Manuel Rodríguez Lozano, *Pensamiento y pintura* (Mexico City: UNAM–Imprenta Universitaria, 1960), 61.

28. Fernández, *Textos de Orozco,* 78.

29. David Alfaro Siqueiros, *Cómo se pinta un mural* (Mexico: Ediciones Taller Siqueiros, 1979), 47–51.

30. Ibid., 95 ff.

31. Jean Charlot, "José Clemente Orozco, su obra monumental," *Forma,* Mexico, vol. 6 (1928), 37, facsimile in *Forma, 1926–28* (Mexico City: Fondo de Cultura Económica [Revistas Literarias Mexicanas Modernas], 1982), 293.

32. Tezontle is the name for red volcanic rock, frequently used for the finishing of Mexican colonial buildings.

33. De la Torriente, *Memoria y razón de Diego Rivera,* vol. 2, p. 212: "planeó pintar, en el entresuelo y en *grisaille,* como si fuesen piedras esculpidas en bajo relieve, con objeto de no debilitar la arquitectura dando la sensación de agujerear el entre-suelo muy bajo del techo y, al mismo tiempo, armonizar con el estilo del edificio, sin sacrificar el de las pinturas."

34. José Clemente Orozco, *The Artist in New York: Letters to Jean Charlot and Unpublished Writings, 1925–1929,* foreword and notes by Jean Charlot, letters and writings transl. Ruth L.C. Simms (Austin: University of Texas Press, 1974), 27–28.

35. Ibid., 39.

36. Ibid., 39.

37. Ibid., 43.

38. Ibid., 38.

39. Ibid., 43.

40. Ibid., 47.

41. Ibid., 43.

42. Ibid., 43.

43. Ibid., 48.

44. Ibid., 48.

45. Ibid., 27, 32, and 43.

46. Ibid., 40.

47. Ibid., 48.

48. Ibid., 32.

49. Reed (*Orozco,* 136) refers to the trip that the painter made to Mexico in 1929: "In his letters written during August, Orozco enthu-siastically described Mexico's first extensive show of modern art, a summer exhibition at the San Carlos Academy. He writes that the event was a 'fortunate break' for Mexico's younger artists who, at long last, were able to enjoy *a privilege that had been denied him and his fellow students.*" My emphasis.

50. In this regard, see Ramírez, "Tradición y modernidad."

51. Orozco, *The Artist in New York,* 48.

52. Franz Roh, *Realismo mágico: Post expresionismo: Problemas de la pintura europea más reciente,* transl. Fernando Vela (Madrid: Revista de Occidente, 1927).

53. Jean Clair, "Sobre el realismo mágico," in Marga Paz, curator, *Realismo mágico: Franz Roh y la pintura europea, 1917–1936,* exhibition catalog (Valencia: Institut Valencia d' Art Modern, 1997), 28–29.

54. Roh, *Realismo mágico,* 16: "It seems that the history of all human manifestations and forms of life never consists...of a pure succes-sion...nor of simultaneity.... It is always a combination of both possi-bilities."

55. Lionel Richard, *Del expre-sionismo al nazismo: arte y cultura desde Guillermo II hasta la República de Weimar* (Barcelona: Gustavo Gili, 1979), 11.

56. Roh, *Realismo mágico,* 79.

57. Ibid.

58. Ibid., 83.

59. Ibid., 79.

60. Ibid.

61. Nonetheless, as a cautious historian, he constantly pointed to the different rhythms of history and the numerous processes that continued in spite of the ruptures. The path he proposed from impres-sionism to postexpressionism goes from uncommitted observation of reality, to immersion in the world and in life, and finally to a committed dominion over the material world. This, and his conception of different rhythms in history, lead one to suspect the presence, between the lines, of the Bergson of *Creative Evolution.*

62. José Clemente Orozco, *Cuadernos,* organized and with prologue by Raquel Tibol (Mexico: Secretaría de Educación Pública-Cultura, 1983), 28. I am indebted to

Luis Martín Lozano for having pointed out this relationship to me and to Dafne Cruz Villegas for having insisted on its importance.

63. Roh, *Realismo mágico*. 79.

64. Ibid., 57.

65. Which, in addition to the painting of Lyonel Feininger and Ludwig Meidner, had great relevance for German cinema (remember *Metropolis*). My inspiration for the foregoing considerations came from a paper that Dietrich Neumann presented on the subject of "World Cities" at the colloquium "*Megalopolis — La modernización de la Ciudad de México en el siglo XX*," Mexico, March 31 – April 2, 1998, organized by the Goethe-Institut Mexiko and Curare-Espacio Crítico para las Artes.

66. Henry Bergson, *La evolución creadora*, transl. María Luisa Pérez Torres (Madrid: Espasa-Calpe, 1973), 261 – 75: "El devenir y la forma."

67. José Vasconcelos, "Bergson en México," in *Homenaje a Bergson* (Mexico City: UNAM – Imprenta Universitaria, 1941), 133 – 35. In spite of its title, the article talks only about the importance of Bergson for Vasconcelos himself.

68. See the biographical essay in this catalog.

69. Fernández, *Textos de Orozco*, 44.

70. Orozco, *The Artist in New York*, 72.

71. Renato González Mello, *Orozco, ¿pintor revolucionario?* (Mexico City: UNAM-IIE, 1995), 80 – 81.

72. Claude Bragdon, *Architecture and Democracy*, 2d ed. (New York: Alfred A. Knopf, 1926), 14 – 15.

73. Lewis Mumford, *The Brown Decades: A Study of the Arts in America, 1865 – 1895* (New York: Harcourt, Brace and Co., 1931), 153.

74. Bragdon, *Architecture and Democracy*, 39.

75. Ibid., 164.

76. Mumford, *The Brown Decades*, 13.

77. Ibid., 242.

78. This was the New York Zoning Resolution of 1916. See Thomas A. P. Van Leeuwen, "The Skyscraper Says City," in Jean Clair, curator, *1920's: Age of the Metropolis*, exhibition catalog (Montreal: Montreal Museum of Fine Arts, 1991), 436 – 37, 441, 443.

79. Mumford, *The Brown Decades*, 152.

80. González Mello, *Orozco, ¿pintor revolucionario?*, 80 – 81.

81. See the biographical essay and the essay by Jacquelynn Baas on the murals at Dartmouth College, in this catalog.

82. See the biographical essay in this catalog.

83. Roh, *Realismo mágico*, 37 – 40, 79 ff.

84. Ibid., 108.

85. Ibid., 43.

86. Orozco, *The Artist in New York*, 76.

87. Ibid., 59.

88. This was that evil would befall whoever wore it without being its owner, as happened to Sikelianos's sister-in-law Isadora Duncan, who lost her children when she borrowed the necklace. Reed, *Orozco*, 35.

89. Ibid.

90. Ibid., 92. The description of the cartoon is on page 49: "The caricature was a caustic pen-and-ink impression of the bumptious individ-uals who frequently assume the civic responsibilities of awarding cash prizes and blue ribbons at art competitions; whose momentous decisions make or break the painter, determine his long-range financial status, often his very survival as a professional artist."

91. See what Orozco says of Gedovius in *An Autobiography*, 26; Ramírez, "Tradición y modernidad…," 231; and, above all, Siqueiros, *Me llamaban El Coronelazo*, 88 – 89: "One of his most habitual expressions, cutting short his syllables like people from Yucatán, was *lakefranka*, and by this he meant to say, 'frankness, spontaneity,' and this teacher's *lakefranka*, pictorially speaking, consisted in using a very Germanic impressionist style, using great quantities of pigment, which in fact got to be a real problem for the school, because we stopped painting with brushes, instead squeezing the tubes out directly onto the canvas."

92. Unpublished letter from Carlos Sánchez to Jacquelynn Baas, to whom I am indebted for having provided me with a photocopy. Sánchez was Orozco's assistant at Dartmouth College, and the foregoing paragraph refers to the first panel that Orozco decorated, as a trial, in a hallway and that contrasts with the Baker Library frescoes, as we shall see. Sánchez, a Guatemalan who had become a priest, does not stress the possible sexualization of the expression *lamidito*, which would be noticeable to an average Mexican male and would permit us to think of the categories *lamidito/bravura* in terms of an opposition between feminine and masculine.

93. Cennino Cennini, *El libro del arte [el arte y los artistas]* (Buenos Aires: Argos, about 1947); Jean Charlot, *El renacimiento del muralismo mexicano: 1920 – 1925* (Mexico: Domés, 1985), 188, 203, 296.

94. Cennini, *El libro del arte*, 112 – 18.

95. See Diane Miliotes's essay on the technique of the New School murals in this catalog for more details.

96. For the Chevreul theory's influence on modern art, see Georges Roque, *Art et science de la couleur: Chevreul et les peintres de Delacroix à l'abstraction* (France: J. Chambon, 1997). I have no evidence that Orozco knew Chevreul's theory directly. However, by the turn of the century it was universally widespread, so it is possible that he knew it secondhand.

97. Orozco, *Cuadernos*, 52 – 54.

98. Lewis Mumford, "Orozco in New England," *New Republic* (October 10, 1934), 232.

99. "Des lors, on le voit, la nature même de l'oeuvre subit une profonde transformation, même si, à nouveau, il faudra du temps pour que toutes ces conséquences voient le jour. À partir de la loi du contraste, en effet, et tel est peut-être sur ce point l'apport capital de la science a l'art, le tableau n'est plus tant considéré comme une surface d'inscription illusionniste, mais comme un champ, de forces et de tensions, champ autonome dont les éléments constituants — les couleurs pour ce qui nous concerne ici — forment un tout organique en interaction." Roque, *Art et science de la couleur*, 108 – 109, 114.

100. Orozco, *The Artist in New York*, 39. Regarding Miller, see Clinton Adams, *American Lithographers, 1900 – 1960: The Artists and Their*

Printers (Albuquerque: University of New Mexico Press, 1983), 32–34.

101. Orozco, *The Artist in New York,* 82.

102. Reed, *Orozco,* 244–45.

103. Delphic Studios opened on October 14, 1929 (Alejandro Anreus, *Orozco in Gringoland: The Years in New York* [Albuquerque: University of New Mexico Press, 2001], 37). The break happened in early November 1929 (José Clemente Orozco, *Cartas a Margarita* [Mexico City: Era, 1987], 171). In April of that year, he had said that he "had only made three lithographs" in his life (ibid., 157); in May, he said that before traveling to Mexico he had to do some more lithos (158); in October, on his return from Mexico, he said he had just finished three more lithos, still with Weyhe, and was about to make two more "with old material, from the Preparatory School frescoes" (169–70). On November 12, he said he was about to receive two more lithographs from the printer (173). The total number of lithographs, after his return from Mexico, was seven, which is also the number of lithographs that copy his frescoes from the Preparatory School. As a result of his break with Weyhe, he said on November 2: "Now I'm going to start doing some different lithos so I can have something to sell to interested buyers." These were probably the ones from the new printing press. Sometimes they used the reamer; only one of them (*Revolution*) is a copy of an earlier work; they tend generally more toward lines and less toward shades of gray. This may have been because, as Charlot said, some of them, such as *Maguey,* had serious printing-related defects.

104. See Reba Williams, "First Impressions: Tamayo, Orozco and Siqueiros," in *Mexican Prints from the Collection of Reba and Dave Williams,* exhibition catalog (Brooklyn, N.Y.: Brooklyn Museum of Art, 1998), 33.

105. See Víctor Díaz Arciniega, *Querella por la cultura "revolucionaria" (1925)* (Mexico City: Fondo de Cultura Económica, 1989), 14–15, for a historical treatment of this issue. Also see Stanley L. Robe, *Azuela and the Mexican Underdogs* (Berkeley: University of California Press, 1979), 73–74.

106. Enrique Munguía, "Correspondencia," Archivo de la Secretaría de Relaciones Exteriores, Archivo particular de Genaro Estrada, Libro II (1929), 68–69. However, Anreus points out, the cover of the book reproduced a painting by Rivera (*Orozco in Gringoland,* 80).

107. In Spanish, there is a difference between *línea* ("line") and *raya* or *rayón.* The latter is equivalent to the English "scratch," but *raya* can refer to a drawn line, not just to a scratched one. The difference is between order and disorder, such as the difference between "sound" and "noise."

108. Orozco again took up this style of drawing fifteen years later, in his drawings in *Serie de la verdad* that, in fact, were also reproduced in offset, although he did not like the results. Fernández, *Textos de Orozco,* 100. The drawings are reproduced in *Veinte dibujos de José Clemente Orozco de la exposición de agosto de 1945, en el Colegio Nacional* (Mexico: Talleres Gráficos de la Nación, 1945).

109. Janet A. Flint, *Art for All: American Print Publishing between the Wars* (Washington, D.C.: Smithsonian Institution Press, 1981),

catalog number 32. There is a great deal of confusion about the making of this lithograph. See Jon H. Hopkins, *Orozco: A Catalogue of His Graphic Work* (Flagstaff: Northern Arizona University Publications, 1967), 23, and Luigi Marrozzini, *Catálogo completo de la obra gráfica de Orozco* (Puerto Rico: Instituto de Cultura Puertorriqueña-Universidad de Puerto Rico, 1970), 19. Both affirm that it was elaborated by the "American Civil Rights Congress." This is denied by Anreus, *Orozco in Gringoland,* 88. The American Civil Rights Congress was founded in 1946. However, the lithograph was included in two antilynching exhibitions, both organized in 1935 by the National Association for the Advancement of Colored People and the John Reed Club. See also Marlene Park, "Lynching and Antilynching: Art and Politics in the 1930s," *Prospects: An Annual of American Cultural Studies* (Cambridge: Cambridge University Press, 1993), vol. 18, pp. 311–65, and Helen Langa, "Two Antilynching Exhibitions: Politicized Viewpoints, Racial Perspectives, Gendered Constraints," *American Art,* vol. 13, no. 1 (Spring 1999), 10–39.

110. Other works from this period seem to confirm this impression. John Steuart Curry's *The Fugitive* (1935) shows a slave hiding from his pursuers behind a tree, his shape blending into that of his hiding place. Langa, "Two Antilynching Exhibitions," 23 ff., discusses the way in which castration was represented in antilynching works, as well as some important gender issues related to that topic.

111. The work was created in 1930 in George C. Miller's printshop

(Luigi Marrozzini, ed., *Catálogo completo, de la obra gráfiez de Orozco,* [Rio Piedras, Puerto Rico: Instituto de Cultura Puertorriqueña, Universidad de Puerto Rico, 1970], note 19). Alvar Carrillo Gil bought a print in the Weyhe Gallery (Alvar Carrillo Gil, *Obras de José Clemente Orozco en la colección Carrillo Gil* [Mexico: Alvar Carrillo Gil, 1953]).

112. See the works mentioned by Park, "Lynching and Antilynching," and Langa, "Two Antilynching Exhibitions."

113. See the biographical essay in this catalog.

114. Orozco, *Cartas a Margarita,* 57; Reed, *Orozco,* 250, says that Orozco came from Paris with two lithographs: *Desempleados* and one more, a copy of a fragment of the Pomona mural that she calls "The Lovers." Clemente Orozco Valladares, *Orozco: verdad cronológica* (Guadalajara, Jalisco: Universidad de Guadalajara, 1983), 267, says he saw a copy of the latter lithograph, "very retouched…I think he never finished it."

115. Philippe Ariès, "Para una historia de la vida privada" in *Historia de la vida privada,* ed. Philippe Ariès and Georges Duby, transl. Ma. Concepción Martín Moreno (Madrid: Taurus, 1987), vol. 3, p. 19.

116. See, for example, the drawings for several frescoes in *Exposición nacional José Clemente Orozco: catálogo que el Instituto Nacional de Bellas Artes publica con motivo de la exposición nacional retrospectiva de José Clemente Orozco* (Mexico City: Secretaría de Educación Pública, 1947).

117. Laurance P. Hurlburt, *The Mexican Muralists in the United*

States (Albuquerque: University of New Mexico Press, 1989), 39.

118. Reproduced in Orozco, *The Artist in New York,* 91.

119. Orozco, *An Autobiography,* 146, also includes a concise and effective description of the system: "Dynamic Symmetry is Hambidge's interpretation of the Greek phrase 'commensurate when raised in degree,' the notion applied by Hellenic philosophers to the relations between the areas of 'square root' rectangles, that is, of those figures having unity for the shorter sides and square root of two, three, four, or five for the longer ones." For a complete explanation, see Jay Hambidge, *Practical Applications of Dynamic Symmetry,* edited and arranged by Mary C. Hambidge (New Haven: Yale University Press, 1932).

120. Piersol's book is mentioned in one of the anatomical studies of the newborn that belong to the Hood Museum of Art (D.988.52.167), and Orozco was able to consult it in Baker Library, where the following edition is to be found: George Arthur Piersol, *Human Anatomy: Including Structure and Development and Practical Considerations,* 9th ed. (Philadelphia: J.B. Lippincott Co., about 1930).

121. Rensselaer Wright Lee, *Ut pictura poesis: la teoría humanística de la pintura* (Madrid: Cátedra, 1982).

122. Justino Fernández, *Orozco, Forma e idea* (Mexico: Porrúa, 1942), 24.

123. See the biographical essay in this catalog.

124. Olivier Debroise, *Figuras en el trópico,* 2d ed. (Barcelona: Océano, 1983), 56: "In the time when the students of the Open Air Schools, and those working under Adolfo Best

Maugard's method, practice a pure painting, the muralists under Vasconcelos don't recover academic formalism, but they do recover nineteenth-century historicist painting's typical theatralization." Luis Cardoza y Aragón, *La nube y el reloj: pintura mexicana contemporánea* (Mexico: UNAM, 1940), 6: "We are facing artists who are modern in their means of expression, although uncommitted respecting social and political ideas. And the opposite: artists who have progressive social and political ideas, while uncommitted to respecting esthetical ideas."

125. See Vasconcelos, "Bergson en México."

Prometheus Unraveled: Readings of and from the Body: Orozco's Pomona College Mural

(Karen Cordero Reiman)

1. Harold Davis, member of the English faculty of Pomona College, in a letter to the editor of the Claremont College's student newspaper, *Student Life* (May 15, 1930), 2.

2. L. Kent Wolgamott, "Mexican Muralist Had Influence on Pollock's Painting," *Lincoln* [Nebraska] *Journal Star* (February 2, 1999), A4, cited in *http://sheldon.unl.edu* (February 22, 2000). In his article, Wolgamott relies heavily on Ellen Landau's research on Pollock's reception of Mexican muralism in her *Jackson Pollock* (New York: Harry N. Abrams, 1989).

3. Jorge Juan Crespo de la Serna, "Sentido y gestación del Prometeo de Orozco," in *José Clemente Orozco: Homenaje en ocasión del 1er aniversario de la Fundación del Museo Taller dedicado

a su memoria* (Guadalajara: INBA, 1952).

4. Alma Reed, *Orozco* (Mexico: Fondo de Cultura Económica, 1955).

5. Luis Cardoza y Aragón, *Orozco* (Mexico City: UNAM, 1959).

6. David W. Scott, "Orozco's *Prometheus*: Summation, Transition, Innovation," *College Art Journal,* vol. 17, no. 1 (Fall 1957), 1–18.

7. Ibid., 18.

8. Jacqueline Barnitz, "Los años délficos de Orozco," in *Orozco: una relectura* (Mexico City: UNAM, 1983), 103–28.

9. Fausto Ramírez, "Artistas e iniciados en la obra de José Clemente Orozco," in *Orozco: una relectura,* 61–102; Renato González Mello, "La máquina de pintar: Rivera, Orozco y la invención de un lenguaje," doctoral thesis in art history, Universidad Nacional Autónoma de México, Facultad de Filosofía y Letras, 1998.

10. Laurance P. Hurlburt, *The Mexican Muralists in the United States* (Albuquerque: University of New Mexico Press, 1989).

11. Justino Fernández, *Orozco: forma e idea* (Mexico: Porrúa, 1942), 53–56; MacKinley Helm, *Man of Fire. J.C. Orozco: An Interpretive Memoir* (Westport, Conn.: Greenwood Publishers, 1953), 47–51; Antonio Rodríguez, *A History of Mexican Mural Painting* (London: Thames Hudson, 1969), 312.

12. González Mello, "La máquina de pintar," 193. The translation is my own, exclusively for the purposes of this essay.

13. Hurlburt, *Mexican Muralists,* 39.

14. Hurlburt, ibid., discusses this aspect in great detail, integrating the information offered by previous

sources and expanding on it on the basis of his own research.

15. Ramírez, "Artistas e iniciados"; González Mello, "La máquina de pintar"; and Marina Vázquez, "Zuno, un secreto a voces," thesis in progress in art studies at the Universidad Iberoamericana, Mexico City.

16. José Clemente Orozco, *Portrait of José Pijoán, Art Historian,* about 1930. Oil on linen on board, 23 x 20 inches. Image in the archive of the 1991 exhibition of drawings for *Prometheus* at the Montgomery Art Gallery, Pomona College.

17. González Mello, "La máquina de pintar."

18. Carl Kerényi, *Prometheus: Archetypal Image of Human Existence* (Princeton: Princeton University Press, 1963); Hesiod, *Teogonía* (Mexico: Porrúa, 1990).

19. Kerényi, *Prometheus,* 88–89; Carlos García Gual, *Prometeo: mito y tragedia* (Madrid: Ediciones Hiperión, 1995); Aeschylus, *Prometheus Bound and Other Plays* (London: Penguin Books, 1961). Fernández, *Orozco,* and Barnitz, "Los años délficos," emphasize the importance of this source.

20. Scott, "Orozco's Prometheus"; Ramírez, "Artistas e iniciados"; Barnitz, "Los años délficos."

21. Barnitz, "Los años délficos," 108, indicates Orozco's authorship of this unsigned illustration but does not cite her source for this information. The drawing style evidenced in the vignette, however, lends cogency to the attribution.

22. Ibid., 111–12. The book mentioned is Giuseppe Consoli Fiego, *Cumae and the Phlegraean Fields,*

transl. Alma Reed (Naples: American and British Club, 1927), 230.

23. Ramírez, "Artistas e iniciados," 63–64.

24. Fernández, Orozco, 53–54.

25. Scott, "Orozco's Prometheus," 6–8.

26. Helm, Man of Fire, 49–51; Kerényi, Prometheus, xxiv–xv.

27. Barnitz, "Los años délficos," 110; Friedrich Nietzsche, The Birth of Tragedy, transl. Douglas Smith (New York: Oxford University Press, 2000).

28. José Clemente Orozco, in the pamphlet The Orozco Frescoes at Dartmouth (Hanover, N.H.: Dartmouth College Publications, 1934), n.p.

29. Esquilo, Tragedias, transl. D. Fernando Segundo Brieva from the Greek (Salvatierra: UNAM, 1921), 9.

30. José Clemente Orozco, El artista en Nueva York, prologue by Luis Cardoza y Aragón, appendixes by Jean Charlot (Mexico: Siglo XXI, 1971), 56 and 73. See also the essay "From Art History to Avant-Garde: Orozco's Easel Paintings, Drawings, Prints, and Preparatory Studies" by Renato González Mello in this catalog.

31. Dynamic Symmetry is a theory developed by Jay Hambidge, a Canadian mathematician and artist, that derives formulas for calculating ideal proportions, based on Greek art and the mathematical relationship between art and nature. Orozco became familiar with this theory through his Delphic Circle friendship with Hambidge's widow and experimented with the application of his theories at Pomona College and, more rigorously, in his New School mural (Barnitz, 115). Orozco discusses this theory in his Autobiografía (Mexico: Ediciones Era, 1970), 99–104.

32. Hurlburt, Mexican Muralists, 264, notes: "Twenty-three studies for the Prometheus are extant, sixteen (the general study, three sketches for the side panels, and twelve figure drawings) in the collection of the Orozco family, two (both for the Prometheus figure) in the collection of Crespo de la Serna, four (one Prometheus, three general figure studies) in the collection of John Goheen, and one (figure study) in the collection of Murray Fowler, a young Pomona faculty member and Orozco's roommate in 1930. Two studies in the Merritts' possession were lost when their house burnt down and five to eight, strangely enough, apparently were lost within the Claremont Colleges' Honnold Library during the mid-1950s." Recently the drawings that were owned by the Orozco family were acquired by the Montgomery Art Gallery.

33. See Julio Scherer García, Siqueiros, la piel y la entraña (Mexico City: Consejo Nacional para la Cultura y las Artes, 1996), 115–16, cited by González Mello in his essay "From Art History to Avant-Garde" in this catalog.

34. On the compositional strategies of Rodin, see Leo Steinberg, "Rodin," in Other Criteria: Confrontations with Twentieth Century Art (New York: Oxford University Press, 1979), 322–403.

35. Jorge Juan Crespo de la Serna, in a letter to David Scott written between October 21 and December 4, 1951, and cited by Hurlburt, Mexican Muralists, 1989, 28–29.

36. Zeus was the lover of Io, who, when confronted with the jealous wrath of Hera, his wife, turned her into a white heifer. In Aeschylus's Prometheus Bound, Io encounters Prometheus in her wanderings and tells him her story. Readers interested in additional information on these myths may consult, in addition to the historical and literary sources mentioned above, Robert Graves, The Greek Myths (Harmondsworth, England: Penguin Books, 1955), vol. 1, pp. 143–49, 190–93.

37. José Clemente Orozco, "New World, New Races and New Art," in Creative Art, Magazine of Fine and Applied Art, New York, vol. 4, no. 1 (January 1929), reproduced in the exhibition catalog by David Elliott et al., ¡Orozco! 1883–1949 (Oxford, England: Museum of Modern Art, 1980), 46.

38. Crespo de la Serna, "Sentido y gestación del Prometeo," 21.

39. Julia Kristeva, "Giotto's Joy," in Desire and Language: A Semiotic Approach to Literature and Art (New York: Columbia University Press, 1980), 212–36.

40. Dante, La divina comedia (Mexico City: UNAM, 1921). In Orozco: verdad cronológica (Guadalajara: Universidad de Guadalajara, 1983), 122, Clemente Orozco Valladares indicates that Orozco was the author of these illustrations. I thank Pablo Miranda and Mercurio López for bringing this volume and the attribution of its vignettes to Orozco to my attention. Like the drawings for Aeschylus's Prometheus Bound, these illustrations are unsigned, but the conception and style here are clearly those of Orozco.

41. Frida Gorbach Rudoy, "El monstruo, objeto imposible: un estudio sobre la teratología mexicana (1860–1900)," doctoral thesis in art history, Universidad Nacional Autónoma de México, Facultad de Filosofía y Letras, 2000, 62. The portrait in question, illustrated in the 1896 Catalogue of the Anomalies Collected in the National Museum, was painted by a professor at the Academy of San Carlos, Dr. Joséph María Guerrero, in 1796.

42. Testimonies recorded in typescript in the Montgomery Art Gallery archive, Pomona College. I thank Marjorie J. Harth, director of the gallery, for making this archival material available to me.

43. Sally Stein, "Peculiar Grace: Dorothea Lange and the Testimony of the Body," in Dorothea Lange, a Visual Life, ed. Elizabeth Partridge (Washington, D.C., and London: Smithsonian Institution Press, 1994), 57–89.

44. Ruth Behar, "The Girl in the Cast," in The Vulnerable Observer: Anthropology That Breaks Your Heart (Boston: Beacon Press, 1996), 104–35.

45. "Prometheus Painted on Frary Wall," Student Life, Claremont, California (April 17, 1930), 2.

46. Orozco, Autobiografía, 25.

47. As Fausto Ramírez has noted, the current combination of the Lucifer and Prometheus panels with a Fuster painting of St. Sebastian in the Casa de Cultura de Tlacotalpán does not correspond to the original conception of the triptych, which is documented in a newspaper article and photograph of 1917; Fausto Ramírez, Crónica de las artes plásticas en los años de Lopez Velarde, 1914–1921 (Mexico City: UNAM, 1990), 69.

48. Alfonso Toro, "El año artístico," Revista de Revistas, vol. 8, no. 400 (December 30, 1917), 14, cited in Ramírez, López Velarde, 68.

342

The translation is my own, exclusively for the purposes of this article. Currently the Lucifer panel is registered by the National Institute of Fine Arts of Mexico as "Luzbel."

49. Rodríguez, *History of Mexican Mural Painting*, 312.

50. Gaston Bachelard in *Fragments of a Poetics of Fire* comments as well on the duality present in the very symbol of fire. He finds the confirmation of this archetypal symbolism in the two versions of the Prometheus myth: that of the hero who stole fire from the gods and that of the Prometheus who modeled a human form in clay and breathed life into it, which he associates with the complementary impulses of the human psyche. See Gaston Bachelard, *Fragmentos de una poética del fuego* (Buenos Aires: Paidos, 1992), 120–23.

51. Nietzsche, *Birth of Tragedy*, 56–57.

52. Ibid., 57–58.

53. Orozco, *Autobiografía*, 94–95.

54. Helm, *Man of Fire*, 49–51, associates this latter scene with Orozco's memories of the stock market crash and its human impact.

55. Chad Frick, "Exhibit Exposes Prometheus," *Student Life* (September 20, 1991).

56. Hurlburt, *Mexican Muralism*, 40–42.

57. Testimony of Earl Merritt, recorded by Gerald M. Ackerman, Art Department, December 8, 1972. Typescript in Montgomery Art Gallery archive.

58. Typescript in Montgomery Art Gallery archive by Gerald M. Ackerman, January 2, 1976.

59. Memorandum to President Alexander from G. Ackerman, Art Department, December 14, 1972. Montgomery Art Gallery archive.

60. Caricature and article "Prometheus Unbound, Myth Revealed," *Student Life* (November 7, 1972); Chad Frick, "Exhibit Exposes Prometheus"; Mike Boyle, "And on the Sixth Day God Created Man: The Time Has Come for Prometheus to Be Delivered from Genderless Shame" (article and caricature), *Student Life* (April 21, 1995).

61. "Prometheus Revealed, Fresco Comes Clean," *Student Life* (January 16, 1973), 6; Roberta Demesko, "Vandalism Reveals Students' Indifference," article without indicated source, Montgomery Art Gallery archive.

The Murals at the New School for Social Research (1930–31)

(Diane Miliotes)

1. Rita Susswein, "The New School for Social Research," *Parnassus*, vol. 3 (January 1931), 12.

2. This mural is the subject of an essay in this catalog by James Oles. The most infamous example of the destruction of the muralists' legacy was the demolition in 1934 of Rivera's unfinished mural *Man at the Crossroads* (1933) in the RCA Building at Rockefeller Center, ostensibly for his inclusion of a portrait of Lenin. Rivera's portable fresco panels on various themes, painted for his one-person exhibition at the Museum of Modern Art (1931–32), were also dispersed to various collections, and his portable panels for the New Workers School (1933) in New York were dismantled and moved to Pennsylvania, where the majority were eventually destroyed by fire in 1969. Siqueiros never succeeded in securing a mural commission in New York. See Laurance P. Hurlburt, *The Mexican Muralists in the United States* (Albuquerque: University of New Mexico Press, 1989), for an overview of the issues facing these artists while in this country and a discussion of Rivera's and Siqueiros's surviving major mural cycles in Detroit and California, as well as Orozco's other commissions; *Diego Rivera: A Retrospective* (New York: Detroit Institute of Arts and W. W. Norton), 1986; and Linda Downs, *Detroit Industry* (Detroit Institute of Arts and W. W. Norton, 1999).

3. In *Orozco in Gringoland: The Years in New York* (Albuquerque: University of New Mexico Press, 2001), 105, Alejandro Anreus cites Hugo Gellert's 1928 murals at Worker's Cooperative in Union Square as the first to portray Lenin. Major contemporary reviews include Ralph Flint, "Modernity Rules New School of Social Research," *Art News*, vol. 29 (January 17, 1931), 3–4; E. A. J. [Edwin Alden Jewell], "The Frescoes by Orozco," *New York Times* (January 25, 1931), section 8, p. 12; Malcolm Vaughan, "Orozco's Murals Are Out of Scale," *New York American* (January 25, 1931), M5; Susswein, "The New School," defenses of the murals by Herron, Wilcox, and Quenneville, *New York Times* (February 1, 1931), section 8, p. 13; Anonymous, "Orozco Completes New York Frescoes and the Critics Criticize," *Art Digest* (February 15, 1931), 9; Suzanne La Follette, "America in Murals," *New Freeman* (February 18, 1931), 540–44; Lloyd Goodrich, "The Murals of the New School," *Arts*, vol. 17, no. 6 (March 1931), 399–403, 422, 424; Laurance Schmeckebier, "The Frescoes of Orozco in the New School for Social Research," *Trend*, vol. 1, no. 2 (June–August 1932), 35–40.

4. New School administrators succumbed to pressure during the height of McCarthyism when they covered the entire west wall of the murals, including the Yucatán and Soviet panels, with a yellow curtain: Peter M. Rutkoff and William B. Scott, *New School: A History of the New School for Social Research* (New York: Free Press, 1986), 227; "New School Keeps Red Mural Hidden," *New York Times* (May 22, 1953).

5. The murals were restored in 1988 and 1996 by the Williamstown (Massachusetts) Art Conservation Center. The room no longer serves its original function as a dining hall and was fully renovated in 1995–96 as a conference room; it had been converted to a classroom during the 1960s. According to the head restorer Thomas Branchick, the extensive deterioration suffered by the murals was primarily due to moisture penetration of the plaster support. Contributing to this were such environmental factors as high room humidity, seeping moisture from the roof garden on the floor above, and air pollutants, as well as physical and technical factors, including inconsistencies in the artist's technique (mixing true fresco technique with passages of overpainting on dry plaster), inadequate time allowed for the new building construction to settle, and the moisture-attracting properties of a wax varnish applied as a protectant by Thomas Hart Benton during the 1950s (personal communication, January 21, 1998). In her biography of the artist, Alma Reed recounts Orozco's outrage at

the accusations of New York critic Malcolm Vaughan that his murals were not true fresco: Alma Reed, *Orozco* (New York: Oxford University Press, 1956), 219–22.

6. See, for example, MacKinley Helm, *José Clemente Orozco: An Interpretive Memoir* (New York: Harcourt, Brace, 1953), 51–53; or Hurlburt, *Mexican Muralists*, 42–55. Anreus, *Orozco in Gringoland*, 91–111, represents the most recent English-language scholarship on the mural and takes a more balanced approach.

7. José Clemente Orozco, *Cartas a Margarita* (Mexico: Ediciones Era, 1987), 230. November 16, 1930: "Esta trabajo va a tener muchas buenas consecuencias, pues estando precisamente aquí en N. York y en tan magnífico lugar, que no puede ser mejor, ya te imaginarás que todo mundo lo va a ver a diario." Translations are the author's unless otherwise noted.

8. Reed, *Orozco*, 215.

9. It is now designated as the seventh floor in the current building configuration.

10. Fausto Ramírez, "Artistas e iniciados en la obra mural de Orozco," *Orozco: una relectura* (Mexico City: UNAM, 1983), 61–102, provides an important exploration of the occult and Masonic resonances of this piece and others in Orozco's oeuvre.

11. Reed, *Orozco*, 207, 209; Hurlburt, *Mexican Muralists*, 47; "Frescoes by Orozco" (typescript, Rauner Special Collections, Dartmouth College).

12. Reed, *Orozco*, 207, 209. In racially segregated interwar North America, the representation of a meeting of equals among all races, along with the Soviet panel, would

certainly have been seen as a provocation by some.

13. Jewell, "Frescoes," 12. Another reviewer, betraying his own biases as well as his perception of caricature, criticized some "funny generalized figures" in the portrayal of "the Aristocratic Oriental who looks like an Italian puppet of same, and an African, as distinguished from American, Negro who resembles the Ape-Man currently on view at the 42nd Street Flea Circus": unidentified clipping, Orozco files, Rauner Special Collections, Dartmouth College.

14. New School director Alvin Johnson made this observation in *Pioneer's Progress: An Autobiography* (New York: Viking Press, 1952), 328.

15. Hurlburt, *Mexican Muralists*, 48–49; Ernest Gruening, "A Maya Idyll," *Century Magazine* (April 1924), 832–36.

16. Reed, *Orozco*, 208.

17. Alvin Johnson, *Notes on the New School Murals* (New York: New School for Social Research, 1943), 9, 11; Anreus, *Orozco in Gringoland*, 106. I am grateful to New School staff for providing research and visual materials for this essay, especially Audrey Barnes, Stefano Basilico, Kathleen Goncharov, Margaret Hedrich, Alberta Lonergan, Donna-Marie Peters, and Karen Zebulon.

18. In her biography of the artist, Reed relates Orozco's admiration for Gandhi, Mrs. Naidu, and the Indian nationalist movement. He followed with interest the Indian leader's 1930 march to the sea in defiance of the imperial monopoly on salt collection: Reed, *Orozco*, 60–65.

19. The identification of this form as a tank is confirmed by Orozco's assistant Lois Wilcox in her

published defense of the mural: *New York Times* (February 1, 1931), section 8, p. 13.

20. *Cartas a Margarita*, 122, August 15, 1928. Reed also purchased a drawing from the *Mexico in Revolution* series at this time. There is a recent journalistic biography of Reed by Antoinette May, *Passionate Pilgrim: The Extraordinary Life of Alma Reed* (New York: Marlowe & Co., 1994).

21. Reed's biography of Orozco details the development of their friendship and working relationship, as well his involvement with the Delphic Circle; see also *Cartas a Margarita*, 127–48, especially the period September 1928–January 1929, and José Clemente Orozco, *The Artist in New York*, foreword J. Charlot; transl. Ruth L.C. Simms (Austin: University of Texas Press, 1974), 72, September 9, 1928. Orozco's letters throughout his U.S. period, especially those to his wife, make clear his precarious financial situation.

22. Reed makes clear that Orozco was not enamored of this plan. *Cartas a Margarita*, 165–66, September 27, 1929; Reed, *Orozco*, 162–65. In 1929 Orozco signed a formal agreement with Reed to represent him.

23. Reed, *Orozco*, 163–65; Rutkoff and Scott, *New School*, 50; *Cartas a Margarita*, 201–205, April 13, 18, and 29, 1930; Johnson, *Pioneer's Progress*, 327–28.

24. Thomas Hart Benton, whom Reed also represented, received the commission for the third-floor boardroom, where he contributed a portable mural in egg tempera, *America Today*, now in the collection of the Equitable Life Assurance Society, New York. Johnson, *Pioneer's*

Progress, 328–29, and Rutkoff and Scott, *New School*, 50–51, outline Benton's and colleagues' efforts to ensure that this second commission went to an American artist.

25. Johnson, *Pioneer's Progress*, 327–28.

26. April 18 and 29, 1930. Letters of September 23, 1930, and January 22, 1931, suggest that besides materials, he was paid a stipend of $150 per month while he worked on the mural. This may be "the amount so kindly contributed by you [Johnson] towards his [Orozco's] studio during the progress of his work" referred to in Reed's letter to Johnson cited in note 8.

27. Reed to Johnson, April 28, 1931, and Johnson to Reed, May 11, 1931, Johnson Papers, Deyrup Collection, cited in Rutkoff and Scott, *New School*, note 50, and excerpted in Laurance Hurlburt, "Notes on Orozco's North American Murals: 1930–34," in *¡Orozco! 1883–1949* (Oxford: Museum of Modern Art, Oxford, 1980), 52. These letters also suggest how deeply Orozco depended on Reed's financial support for basic living expenses during this period, when she claims to have paid "for his personal and family needs during the progress of the work at the New School"; this seems to be the basis upon which she designates herself in the letters as donor of the murals. Orozco's extreme financial straits are evident in his letters to Margarita from the period and had been ongoing for some time. In her Orozco biography (213), Reed claims that the "artist never received a dollar for his work."

28. *Cartas a Margarita*, 221, September 23, 1930; 225, October 18, 1930; 235–36, January 22, 1931.

Also see Helen Delpar, *The Enormous Vogue of Things Mexican: Cultural Relations between the United States and Mexico, 1920–1935* (Tuscaloosa: University of Alabama Press, 1992), 55–90, regarding Morrow's cultural initiatives and their repercussions. Reed, *Orozco*, 212, recounts the cool reception the murals received at their inauguration from wealthy supporters of the New School, from among whom Johnson hoped a benefactor would emerge.

29. Johnson, *Pioneer's Progress,* 328.

30. Johnson, "Notes," 3.

31. Johnson, *Pioneer's Progress,* 328.

32. This also mirrored emerging U.S. attitudes toward the value of public art that were basic to the government's New Deal art programs of the 1930s and 1940s, as well as the assumptions grounding the general proliferation in interwar Europe and the Americas of programs of monumental didactic art designed to buttress national and political projects of the greatest variety. The example of Mexican muralism associated with that country's revolutionary project was key in this regard.

33. Reed, *Orozco*, 189–98. *Cartas a Margarita,* 217, August 7, 1930; 222, September 30, 1930.

34. Reed, *Orozco*, 198.

35. Ibid., 198–99.

36. *Cartas a Margarita,* 205, April 29, 1930; 221, September 23, 1930; 223, October 14, 1930; 224, October 18, 1930. It is not clear if the artist's time estimates for completion of the project were intended to allay Margarita's nervousness about an extended period without significant income or if he had indeed miscalcu-

lated the extent of the project and the time required.

37. *Cartas a Margarita,* 227, October 26, 1930. In Alvin Johnson's unabridged manuscript to *Notes on the New School Murals* (about 1943, New School archives), the director confirms Orozco's practice of showing him preparatory studies and relates Johnson's difficulty in deciphering the drawings, as well as Orozco's English. Reed (207) seems to have acted as intermediary on such occasions as discussions about the impact and appropriateness of the Soviet panel. In his published writings, Johnson always expressed confidence in Orozco's talent and held firmly to his position in favor of artistic freedom, at the same time that he acknowledged the potential for opposition to Orozco's subject matter from some quarters: Johnson, *Notes on the New School Murals,* 328–31.

38. *Cartas a Margarita,* 229–30, November 16, 1930.

39. Reed, *Orozco*, 204; the first two concerns probably contributed to the later deterioration of the murals.

40. Reed, *Orozco*, 203–204, 208; *Cartas a Margarita,* 226 October 19, 1930; 227–28, November 2, 1930; 228–29, November 9, 1930, Jewell. Lois Wilcox was only one among many students and artists who approached Orozco and Reed in fall 1930 in the hope of assisting with the murals. Trained in fresco technique in Europe and an interior designer by profession, she worked with Orozco on a volunteer basis.

41. *Cartas a Margarita,* November 16, 1930: "I believe it is going to be something not only good but sensational" ("[C]reo va ser algo no sólo bueno, sino sensacional");

December 13, 1930: "It is continuing to develop splendidly and it appears it is going to be a great success in New York" ("[E]stá quedando magnífico y que parece va a ser un gran éxito en N. York"). January 3, 1931: "The frescoes really look very good and have already received very favorable commentaries. It is something completely new in New York" ("Realmente se ven muy bonitos los frescos y han provocado ya comentarios muy favorables. Es algo completamente nuevo en Nueva York"). Orozco's confidence in the quality of the murals and their groundbreaking significance was in sharp contrast with their initial published reviews, which Reed describes as the greatest disappointment of his New York career: Reed, 215–24.

42. Letter of December 14, 1930, to Jorge Juan Crespo de la Serna: "Parece que esta quedando bien y ademas es algo completamente diferente de/cuanto he hecho hasta ahora. Este si que no es hijo del de Pomona": Luis Cardoza y Aragón, *Orozco* (Mexico City: UNAM, 1959), 284.

43. "Architect Hails Orozco Frescoes," April 1, 1931, unidentified clipping, Orozco files, Rauner Special Collections, Dartmouth College.

44. *The New School for Social Research* (New York: Murbull Press, 1930), n.p.

45. The open floor plan was eventually changed by removing the stairway and separating the two floors in order to create a quiet study environment for graduate students affiliated with the University in Exile: Johnson, *Pioneer's Progress,* 322.

46. Rutkoff and Scott, *New School,* xi–18. Unlike conventional academic institutions, the New School also sought to integrate

professors and students into the school's governance and maintain an informal class structure with no prerequisites or grades and nominal course fees. The school's core commitments were later extended with the foundation in 1933 of the University in Exile, a safe haven for European intellectuals fleeing Nazi repression that was unique in American academia.

47. Quote from Alvin Johnson, *Autobiographical Note* (New York: Alfred A. Knopf, about 1936), 7. Rutkoff and Scott, 32–34.

48. Rutkoff and Scott, *New School,* 35–38.

49. Ibid., 43–48; Johnson, *Pioneer's Progress,* 316–20. These sources include accounts of Johnson's extraordinary financial arrangements to ensure the construction of the building during the economic crisis.

50. Rutkoff and Scott, *New School,* 47–48; Johnson, *Pioneer's Progress,* 319–20; *The New School for Social Research,* 1930; Flint, "Modernity," 3; Johnson, *Autobiographical Note,* 12 (quote). Johnson's desire to create a modern art center was well understood and hailed as a breakthrough by many contemporary commentators (Flint, for example). The young Philip Johnson's critique of the New School building as an example of the international style gives a particularly clear, if purist, articulation of the style's precepts at this time: Philip Johnson, "The Architecture of the New School," *Arts,* vol. 17, no. 6 (March 1931), 393–98.

51. Quote from *The New School for Social Research,* 1930.

52. Johnson, *Autobiographical Note,* 12–13. Urban and Johnson

345

worked particularly closely in the early design stages to plan the function of each part of the building.

53. Johnson, *Pioneer's Progress*, 321.

54. Randolph Carter and Robert Reed Cole, *Joseph Urban: Architecture, Theatre, Opera, and Film* (New York: Abbeville Press, 1992), 203. I rely on this source and on Timothy Rub's useful overview "Joseph Urban," *ID*, vol. 35 (January–February 1988), 60–63, in the foregoing discussion of Urban's career.

55. Shepard Vogelgesang, "The New School for Social Research," *Architectural Record*, vol. 67, no. 4 (April 1930), 305–309, and *The New School for Social Research, Architectural Record*, vol. 69, no. 2 (February 1931), 139–50 (both these sources include floor plans); Susswein, "The New School," 11–12; Philip Johnson; and Flint, "Modernity."

56. *The New School for Social Research*, 1930.

57. Carter and Cole, *Joseph Urban*, 204; Rub, "Joseph Urban," 63; Susswein, "The New School," 11; Vogelgesang, "The New School," 138, 143.

58. Flint, "Modernity," 3. These spaces included the large oval auditorium designed for both intimacy and audibility, the basement dance studio with its sunken floor, the penthouse and basement studios and workshops, Benton's murals in the third-floor seminar room, and the fifth-floor exhibition gallery, which was adjacent to the lounge and dining room where Orozco's murals were located. In its opening weeks alone, there were no fewer than four exhibitions or workshop displays on view throughout the building, including contemporary English prints, an exhibition of

"masters of the modernist school" organized by the Société Anonyme, and furniture and industrial design.

59. Vogelgesang, "The New School," 144.

60. *Cartas a Margarita*, 230, November 16, 1930, my translation; "El salón va a ser algo extraordinario como decoración, el 'guardapolvo' y el piso van a ser de un solo material, pizarra, la misma que sirve para las pizarras de las escuelas, sólo que en grandes bloques y el techo es liso con cavidades semiesféricas para las lámparas. Todo es sugerido por mí y me preguntan cómo quiero todos los detalles." It is not entirely clear where the lamps Orozco mentions might have appeared in the dining room. It is possible that these plans were changed as the murals progressed; see the following discussion of the lighting scheme.

61. Reed, *Orozco*, 213–14; Jewell, "Frescoes"; Vaughan; "Orozco Completes New York Frescoes and the Critics Criticize."

62. The function of the wainscoting is noted in a defense of the murals by Stella Wynne Herron, published in the *New York Times* (February 1, 1931), section 8, p. 13, as a response to E. A. Jewell's critique of the murals. Defenses by Lois Wilcox, Orozco's assistant, and the French artist Chantal Quenneville are also featured. There are no period photographs of the room's original seating arrangement. Judged from architectural renderings, furnishings were to include small round tables arranged in a grid pattern.

63. Johnson, *Notes on the New School Murals*, 2.

64. Vogelgesang, "The New School," 143. This illumination may have been provided by ceiling boxes that were used for diffuse lighting in

other parts of the building. The lighting scheme for Orozco's murals was in contrast with that for Benton's, which "throws all of the light on the murals, leaving the center portion of the room to be illuminated only by light reflected from the walls."

65. Johnson, *Pioneer's Progress*, 327.

66. Johnson, *Notes on the New School Murals*, 2.

67. Quote from Lloyd Goodrich, "New School for Social Research" (exhibitions section), *Arts*, vol. 17, no. 4 (January 1931), 274; Reed, *Orozco*, 218–19; Jewell, "Frescoes"; Vaughan. The contemporary criticism of the mural, at least in published reports, curiously seems to focus on the compositional aspects of the mural rather than its themes. Accusations of propaganda with regard to the Soviet panel appear to have surfaced as informal protests shortly after its inauguration, but New School authorities remained firm in the face of this. Johnson (*Notes*, 12) reports conservative criticism of the Soviet panel, as well as of the interracial *Table of Universal Brotherhood*. In his autobiography, Orozco claims that both these panels were to blame for the loss of benefactors, something consistently denied by Johnson and other New School authorities. See letter from Orozco to Crespo de la Serna (January 21, 1931) in Cardoza y Aragón, *Orozco*, 285; *Art Digest* (February 15, 1931); and Reed, *Orozco*, 212–13; José Clemente Orozco, *An Autobiography*, transl. Robert C. Stephenson (Austin: University of Texas Press, 1962), 144. See note 4 regarding censorship of the murals.

68. Quote from Jewell, "Frescoes"; Reed, *Orozco*, 218.

69. Orozco's letters to Charlot dated August 10, October 8, October 13, 1928, in *Artist in New York*, 60–61, 75–79, are particularly interesting in this regard.

70. Jacqueline Barnitz, "Los Años 'Délficos' de Orozco," *Orozco: una relectura*, 121–22, discusses something similar in terms of Orozco's elaboration of "equivalent themes."

71. Orozco speaking to Alma Reed, as recounted in Reed, *Orozco*, 208.

72. Renato González Mello's biographical essay in this catalog addresses at length the Delphic Circle and its impact on Orozco. Barnitz, "Los Años," 103–28, was the first to explore Orozco's "Delphic Years" in depth.

73. The term "ashram," as in "a commune of spiritual aspirants organized around a guru" (Bhikhu Parekh, *Gandhi*, Oxford: Oxford University Press, 1997, 105) and the "dwelling and teaching center" of Gandhi at Wardha, was somewhat humorously applied to the home base of the Delphic Circle in admiration for the Indian leader and his nationalist followers who attended meetings: Reed, *Orozco*, 33.

74. Reed, *Orozco*, 36–37.

75. See Angelos Sikelianos, *Plan général du mouvement delphique. Université de Delphes* (Paris: Société d'Édition "Les Belles Lettres" [about 1929]), for the following summary.

76. Reed, *Orozco*, 29–37; Orozco, *An Autobiography*, 127–30, 133–35.

77. See, for example, his early letters to Charlot in *Artist in New York*, in which he braces against the circle's admiration for traditional handicrafts and things folkloric. His long-held position is rooted in his rivalry with Rivera, who strove to

incorporate just these elements into his work.

78. See González Mello's biographical essay in this catalog.

79. Orozco, *An Autobiography*, 144.

80. Besides Hambidge's publications, see Hurlburt, *Mexican Muralists*, 51–52, 157–59; and Elizabeth Mitchell Walter, "Jay Hambidge and the Development of the Theory of Dynamic Symmetry, 1902–1920," University of Georgia, Ph.D. thesis, 1978, esp. 4–8.

81. Orozco, *An Autobiography*, 149.

82. The only hint of other drawings is what appears to be a crayon or ink study of the *Slaves* panel illustrating a review of the murals by Orozco patron Suzanne La Follette: "America in Murals," *New Freeman* (February 18, 1931), 540–44.

83. Reed, *Orozco*, 208; Hurlburt, *Notes*, 127, based on an interview with Goodrich. Margaret Hedrich, reference librarian at the New School's Fogelman Library, confirms that according to Johnson family members, Orozco offered to include Johnson's portrait in the mural, but he declined for fear of political fallout and out of concern for his place in history (personal communication, December 1997).

84. Orozco, *An Autobiography*, 150. Orozco's extensive explanation of the theory here suggests its continued importance to him.

85. "Orozco Has Begun New York Murals," press release.

86. Barnitz, "Los Años," 117, also notes this.

87. First published in *Creative Art*, vol. 4, no. 1 (January 1929).

88. Reed, *Orozco*, 210–11.

89. There does not appear to be any similarity between how Orozco

seems to have envisioned the room to function and the conceptual experiments with "painted environments" and spectator's viewpoint that Siqueiros was making from 1933 onward. I find no evidence in Orozco's notebooks of the period of "plastic exercises" of the sort in which Siqueiros engaged. José Clemente Orozco, *Cuadernos*, ed. Rachel Tibol (Mexico: Cultura SEP, 1983); Hurlburt, *Mexican Muralists*, 217–20.

90. Renato González Mello, "La máquina de pintar: Rivera, Orozco y la invención de un lenguaje," doctoral thesis in art history, Universidad Nacional Autónoma de México, Facultad de Filosofía y Letras, 1998, 187–88.

91. Reed, *Orozco*, 206; Barnitz, "Los Años," 119.

92. Roberta Smith, "New School Unveils Its Restored Orozco Murals," *New York Times* (October 11, 1988).

93. *The New School for Social Research* (1930). In *Pioneer's Progress* (273–74), Johnson makes a clear distinction between the kind of advanced adult education training he envisioned at the New School and the training of militants for such activities as trade union organizing, something that he thought the school could not successfully undertake.

The Epic of American Civilization: *The Mural at Dartmouth College*

(Jacquelynn Baas)

Quotations without citations are from correspondence and documents preserved in Special Collections, Dartmouth College Library.

1. I should like to thank the National Endowment for the Arts for a 1987–88 fellowship that enabled

me to travel to Mexico and conduct much of the research for this essay, a first version of which was written in 1989. (An even earlier version was published in the *Dartmouth Alumni Magazine* [January–February 1984], 45–49.) Clemente, Alfredo, and Lucrecia Orozco, along with Renato González Mello, each deserve special thanks for their helpfulness and generosity. Thanks are due too to the staff of the Dartmouth College Library, particularly Special Collections, as well as the good staff of the Hood Museum of Art, particularly Diane Miliotes.

2. David McClure and Elijah Parish, *Memoirs of the Rev. Eleazar Wheelock* (Newburyport, Mass.: Edward Little and Co., 1811), 97.

3. "Orozco in New England," *New Republic* (October 10, 1934), 231–35. See the bibliography for other citations. The most extensive recent scholarship on the Dartmouth mural in English has been published by Dartmouth alumnus Laurance P. Hurlburt in *The Mexican Muralists in the United States* (Albuquerque: University of New Mexico Press, 1989).

4. Quoted by Peter B. Flint in Buñuel's *New York Times* obituary, July 31, 1983.

5. See González Mello, "Orozco in the United States: An Essay on the History of Ideas," in this catalog. In his autobiography, Orozco gives this date as 1929 (José Clemente Orozco, *An Autobiography* [Austin: University of Texas Press, 1962], 127).

6. The dominant theme of *Prometheus Bound* is resistance to tyranny. Zeus knew that like his father, Kronos, and his grandfather Uranos, he was in danger from his own offspring. What he didn't know was who the mother would be. For a

god with Zeus's amorous ambitions, this was a problem. Prometheus knew: Thetis was the problem paramour. But certain that this information would eventually win him his freedom, Prometheus wouldn't tell.

7. "Orozco: Mexican Conscience," *Art in America* (September 1979), 78.

8. Orozco, *An Autobiography*, 40.

9. From the Foreword to José Clemente Orozco, *The Artist in New York: Letters to Jean Charlot and Unpublished Writings, 1925–1929* (Austin: University of Texas Press, 1974), 10–11.

10. Orozco, *An Autobiography*, 54.

11. See, on this subject, Joséfina Zoriada Vázquez, "An Historian Views Orozco's Works," in Montgomery Endowment Symposium, *The Orozco Murals at Dartmouth College*, Dartmouth College, 1980, esp. 25–26.

12. "New World, New Races and New Art," *Creative Art* (January 1929), xiv. See Alma Reed, *Orozco* (New York: Oxford University Press, 1956), 84–85, for an account of the writing of this article.

13. The late Professor Churchill Lathrop told me that Orozco was highly recommended by Thomas Hart Benton, who visited the college on February 10, 1931, to "conduct groups in drawing practice," according to an article in the *Dartmouth* of that date (4).

14. See Henry Adams, *Thomas Hart Benton: An American Original* (New York: Alfred Knopf 1989), 127–30 (but not for Adams's inaccurate account of Alma Reed and the New School commission, 156–57).

15. Ibid., 129.

16. In the introduction by John Hubert Cornyn, *The Song of Quetzalcoatl*, 2d ed., transl. and ed.

347

John Hubert Cornyn (Yellow Springs, Ohio: Antioch Press, 1931) which Orozco probably consulted (see note 51), there is a description of Quetzalcoatl as "the Nahua Prometheus who descends into the Subterrestrial Regions in search of the Fire" (41).

17. Bernardino de Sahagún, *Fragment C.* See Enrique Florescano, *The Myth of Quetzalcoatl,* transl. Lysa Hochroth (Baltimore: Johns Hopkins University Press, 1999), 248, note 8, in which Florescano cites what he considers the most reliable sources of facts and analysis regarding Ce Acatl Topiltzin Quetzalcoatl.

18. Churchill Lathrop, "How the Murals Were Commissioned," in Montgomery Endowment Symposium, *Orozco Murals,* 2. Here Lathrop cites Orozco's dedication to "universal values" and his craft. In personal conversation with me, Lathrop stressed the high regard in which Orozco was held as an artist by Packard and him. That the president and trustees finally agreed with the art department in the choice of Orozco over Rivera is implied in a letter of June 29, 1933, from President Hopkins to Roy F. Bergengren:

> I have gone pretty carefully into the comparative merits of Orozco and Rivera. Mr. Thayer, of our Board of Trustees, got interested enough to go down to Mexico and go back to the original sources. The Mexicans can't understand, according to Mr. Thayer, where the vogue of Rivera came in this country, or why he is considered in the same class with Orozco.... [M]y belief is that Rivera is one of the kings of the racketeers. He hates

humanity in general and most of its representatives in particular.... He is a sensationalist, and actually makes big money by the controversies which he arouses. Orozco, on the other hand, is sweet, gentle, and unacquisitive; convinced that the world needs betterment, but entirely unwilling to ascribe individual responsibility or collective responsibility to any group for the fact that we do not improve faster than we have done.

In the letter of March 8, 1934, to a Mrs. F.C. Lewis, President Hopkins wrote: "[T]hough we know the skill of Rivera's technique we considered Orozco as his superior even here, and a much more normal-minded citizen in addition."

19. In a letter to Mrs. Rockefeller of August 8, 1931, Packard uses her suggestion of Rivera as a pretext for proposing an even more ambitious plan:

> I am more than a little excited by your suggestion of Rivera, who, without any doubt, is a greater all-round painter than Orozco.... I am writing directly to him to find out whether he could consider doing a mural for us if we should find it possible to have him. I am now wondering whether, if this sort of thing is as well worth working for as we think, it is not worth undertaking as part of a more ambitious program. Would it not be eminently worth while to think of a continuous series of mural paintings being executed at Dartmouth at intervals of three to five years during the next fifty or a hundred years by the most competent artists available so that in the course of time we should have in this one

place a sequence of original works such as no institution of our day possesses? ...I am of the opinion that it would not require a very large endowment to guarantee such a program.... But I am not as competent to judge of this or of the wisest method of raising the funds necessary to make a start as you and President Hopkins are.

No response has been preserved.

20. The source for this "small lecture budget" was Rockefeller tutorial money, a fund for special educational initiatives.

21. Lathrop, "How the Murals Were Commissioned," 8.

22. In this memorandum, Hopkins conflates Orozco's politics with those of the communist Diego Rivera. It is difficult to believe that Hopkins did not understand this distinction, for according to Churchill Lathrop, both Packard and Lathrop spoke with him frequently on this topic, and in other letters, he wrote of the research that he and the trustees had carried out on Orozco versus Rivera (see note 18, above). Lathrop recalls that Hopkins and his politically conservative treasurer enjoyed teasing each other. The last sentence of the memorandum suggests that this was Hopkins's intent here.

23. Diego Rivera was paid about $21,000 to paint the 4,030-square-foot walls of the central court of the Detroit Institute of Arts that same spring, a project that may have removed him from consideration for the Dartmouth mural. The following year Rivera was paid $21,000 to paint the mural at Rockefeller Center, a project that was considerably smaller than the Dartmouth

mural, about 1,000 square feet versus about 3,000 square feet at Dartmouth.

24. A stack wing was later added to Baker Library, lowering the ceiling in this passageway and blocking a window that was a key factor in Orozco's composition. *Release* shows a young man reaching toward the light, which at one time streamed into the space from the directly adjacent window (fig. 28).

25. Raquel Tibol, *José Clemente Orozco: Cuadernos* (Mexico City: Secretaría de Educación Pública, Subsecretaría de Cultura, 1983), 13.

26. Reed published this book (it bears the Delphic Studios imprint) in order to publicize Orozco's work. It is possible that the drawing was dashed off to satisfy the promise made in the *Dartmouth* of May 2 that Orozco's sketches for the Daedalus mural would be "available for publication."

27. Leo Katz claimed that he was the model for the head of Quetzalcoatl in *Departure,* "but for the hand that points to the Spaniards, he did not use the sketch he had made of my hand but wanted it to be his own" (quoted in Reed, *Orozco,* 246).

28. The charter for Dartmouth College was signed by the royal governor of New Hampshire in 1769. The quoted statement was written during Orozco's second visit to Dartmouth in early May 1932, presumably for publication in a press release issued on May 25, 1932.

29. In a letter to his wife of May 15, 1932, Orozco says he has been given a budget of $6,200 for the Dartmouth frescoes, including preparation of the walls, travel, and his fee. The extra $1,000 was prob-

348

ably what the college had budgeted for the preparation of the walls. (José Clemente Orozco, *Cartas a Margarita* [Mexico City: Ediciones Era, 1987], 248.)

30. Hopkins had Artemas Packard prepare for him comparative figures for other mural projects. According to Packard, Puvis de Chavannes was paid $60,000 for the Boston Public Library stairway mural ("less than half the size of ours"), and the library paid John Singer Sargent $20,000 for the murals he did on the top floor. Edwin Howland Blashfield's "regular price" was $450 per square foot, José María Sert was being paid $60,000 to $300,000 for the Waldorf-Astoria mural ("according to early and late statements to the press"), and Rivera was being paid $21,000 on the Rockefeller Center contract ("presumably an especially low figure"). Orozco's fee "under ordinary circumstances" would be $50,000 for the Dartmouth project. Packard figured that the college was actually paying him $2 per square foot on his original contract, $3 per square foot on the six-month extension.

31. In a letter of August 28, 1934, to Edward Bruce, Hopkins wrote: "I have not given publicity to the exact details of the arrangement in general because of the deep professional jealousy that prevails between Orozco and Rivera, and the inclination which Rivera apparently has to boast of the larger income which he secures for his work as compared with anything which Orozco gets. Orozco's whole attitude toward us has been one of generous consideration, and I do not want to give support to his greatest living rival by the publication of data

which might be misunderstood by the public.... I should prefer that the exact figure of approximately $10,000 should not be quoted."

32. Reed, *Orozco,* asserted that Orozco did not allow assistants such as Katz, Carlos Sánchez, and Gobin Stair to work on the mural itself, and this is reinforced by a statement in a letter from President Hopkins to Matt B. Jones on June 8, 1932: "Leo Katz, the Austrian painter, has suspended all operations on his own and is up here seeking the privilege simply of holding Orozco's brushes and sitting beside him on the staging to see how he works."

33. *Dartmouth* (June 18, 1932), 4–5.

34. In fact, problems had already begun to arise, even before the contract was signed. On May 26, Matt B. Jones, president of the New England Telephone and Telegraph Company, had written Hopkins with "a plea that no further progress be attempted in connection with the murals for the Baker Library that were advertised in the article in last evening's *Transcript.*... It may be that it will be the 'largest' mural, but I do not believe that is a word that connotes appropriateness or quality in art." There followed a lengthy exchange of correspondence, in the course of which Hopkins argued on pragmatic grounds, "I know nothing whatever about art...my original interest in Orozco arose from the suggestion of one of the wealthy patrons of the College [he is probably referring to Mrs. Rockefeller] that in our teaching of the various eras of art...it seemed that the College ought to give something in the way of instruction about Mexican art and about mural painting, both of which

could be combined in the person of Orozco" (letter of May 31, 1932). He also reveals, "[W]e are having a more violent division of opinion in regard to the Orozco venture than in regard to anything that has happened for a long time, and there is no neutral ground. We are receiving encomiums as the most enlightened and the most culturally inclined institution operating on the face of the earth, and at the same time we are receiving comments which make your kindly inquiry seem like an approving benison" (letter of June 8, 1932).

35. Other positive articles appeared in the library *Bulletin* (March 1933), 6–8, the *Alumni Magazine* (November 1933), 7–12; (January 1934), 17–18; (February 1934), 21; (April 1934), 11–12, numerous issues of the *Dartmouth,* and a 1933 issue of the occasional publication *Arts Chapbooks* (No. 4, *Orozco at Dartmouth: A Symposium,* ed. Kimball Flaccus [Hanover: Arts Press, 1933], with articles by Churchill Lathrop, Stacy May, Artemas Packard, Kimball Flaccus, William Gaston Raoul, and Gobin Stair).

36. Reed, *Orozco,* 247.

37. The *New York Times,* June 10, 1933. Articles also appeared on this date in the *New York American, New York Herald Tribune,* and *Bridgeport* [Connecticut] *Telegram.* The *New York Times* story pointed out that "the newly organized national Commission to Advance American Art is composed of a group of conservative artists. The membership of its governing board is recruited heavily from the National Academy of Design.... The commission was organized several weeks ago when Diego Rivera was dismissed from Rockefeller Center.

At the National Arts Club yesterday, ...it was said that few of the members had seen either Señor Orozco's work in Mexico or his half-finished fresco at Dartmouth, on which he has been engaged for a year."

38. In a letter of June 29, 1932, to Roy F. Bergengren, President Hopkins wrote: "The last regret list published by our 'Sell American' artists has apparently proved a boomerang, for we are now getting more proffers of support and substantiation than at any other time during the whole discussion." For more on this topic, see Churchill Lathrop in the *Dartmouth Alumni Magazine* (January–February 1983).

39. Quoted by Lathrop, *Dartmouth Alumni Magazine* (November 1983).

40. Quoted in the *Dartmouth* (March 14, 1951), 2.

41. From a letter of March 8, 1934, to Mrs. Franklin C. Lewis, 2.

42. Ironically, Nelson Rockefeller was one of the Dartmouth mural's supporters. In a letter of March 4, 1934, from President Hopkins to Fred A. Howland of Montpelier, Vermont, Hopkins wrote: "I was talking with Nelson Rockefeller...a week ago when he was expressing his conviction that in the Orozco murals we had the greatest murals in the United States." Regarding the Rockefeller Center mural, see the article by Lucienne Bloch in *Art in America:* "On Location with Diego Rivera," vol. 74, no. 2 (February 1986), 102–23; and Irene Herner de Larrea et al., *Diego Rivera: Paradise Lost at Rockefeller Center* (Mexico City: Edicupes, 1987).

43. See Jean Charlot, *The Mexican Mural Renaissance 1920–*

349

1925 (New Haven and London: Yale University Press, 1963), ch. 9.

44. Orozco was not paid for the New School project, and at Pomona he barely recouped his expenses.

45. Orozco, *An Autobiography*, 158. Those tempted to believe that Orozco is here simply being flattering should compare the statements in *An Autobiography* about Pomona College (139). President Hopkins did ask Artemas Packard to suggest to Orozco that he "review" his racial stereotyping in the *Anglo-America* panel (note 83). Whether Packard did so or not is unknown. Leo Katz recounted that "it was amusing to see how the different members of the faculty tried to impress their own ideas or pet theories on Orozco.... He would listen politely, never argue, never contradict, just let them talk. Once in a while he would say, 'Yes?' and then he would go ahead and paint exactly what he had in mind in the first place" (Reed, *Orozco*, 246).

46. Charlot, *Mexican Mural Renaissance*, 229.

47. Ibid., 235.

48. Important for understanding *The Epic of American Civilization* are a pair of articles by Orozco and Packard published in the *Dartmouth Alumni Magazine* of November 1933, 7–12. The interpretations of the various panels provided here are valuable for two reasons. First, their source seems to have been Orozco himself; an original document in Orozco's hand with a few minor editorial changes by Packard is preserved in the Dartmouth College archives. These comments thus can be used as evidence of the artist's own intentions. Second, a comparison between the descriptions and the finished

panels indicates that the artist had completed only about half the east wing panels at the time of the article and none of the central panels across from the reserve desk. The marked discrepancies between Orozco's plan, even at this late date, and the final solutions testify to the artist's faith in his own creative logic.

49. "The Bulletin," Hanover, N.H., no. 11 (February 20, 1934), 1–2 (Dartmouth College archives).

50. Florescano, *Myth of Quetzalcoatl*, 172–73.

51. One source was almost certainly *The Song of Quetzalcoatl*, sent to Dartmouth by Cornyn on May 25, 1932, after Cornyn had read in the papers that "the library of your college is to make the myth of Quetzalcoatl the motive for the mural decorations that are soon to be placed in it and that the Mexican artist José Clemente Orozco has been entrusted with the work" (letter to President Hopkins of May 25, 1932). In his letter of thanks (June 13, 1932), Hopkins stated that "at the present moment Orozco has this [book], having expressed his great interest in reading it." The book did not enter the collection of the Dartmouth College library until October 9, 1933, after the west wing had been completed. In Cornyn's book, Quetzalcoatl is referred to as "the prophet" (see Orozco's title, *The Prophecy*, for the scene showing the departure of Quetzalcoatl), and many aspects of Quetzalcoatl mythology are related in detail.

52. "...there is no literary or other record of the exact implications of this ancient myth of Quetzalcoatl ...this interpretation grows out of the inspired idealism and creative imagination of Orozco." From Artemas

Packard's handwritten notes made during his May 1932 discussion with Orozco (Dartmouth College archives).

53. From an unpublished manuscript written in 1983 (5–6) and submitted to the *Dartmouth Alumni Magazine*, now in the Dartmouth College archives. One of the "others" whose fresco technique Orozco derided was almost certainly Diego Rivera.

54. In a letter of October 15, 1932, the college information officer Albert Dickerson wrote to Albert Franz Cochrane, art editor of the *Boston Evening Transcript:* "Orozco returned to Hanover a little over a week ago after spending the summer abroad. He had begun work on the first panel of this large library project last June and half finished a figure of Quetzalcoatl. He is now working on his drawings for the complete series and will probably not resume painting on the walls until sometime in November."

55. Described by Orozco in his 1933 manuscript for the *Alumni Magazine* as "Teotihuacán—The Gods" (see note 48).

56. One such account was given by Orozco's erstwhile friend Anita Brenner in her book *Idols behind Altars* (New York: Payson & Clarke, 1929), 49.

57. *Dartmouth Alumni Magazine* (November 1933), 11 (see note 48).

58. Ibid.

59. Ibid.

60. Ibid.

61. Orozco, *An Autobiography*, 158.

62. From a letter in the Philadelphia Museum of Art, available on microfilm through the Archives of American Art, P17 680–87.

63. Earl H. Morris, Jean Charlot, and Ann Axtell Morris, *The Temple of the Warriors at Chichén Itzá, Yucatán* (Washington, D.C.: Carnegie Institution, 1931).

64. Reed, *Orozco*, 241.

65. Orozco, *An Autobiography*, 127.

66. Hamblen published three books on Blake: *Interpretation of William Blake's Job (Its Ancient Wisdom and Mystic Ways)* (New York: Occult Research Press, n.d.); *On the Minor Prophecies of William Blake* (New York: Dutton, 1930); and *The Book of Job Interpreted* (New York: Delphic Studios [Alma Reed's imprint], 1939).

67. My thanks to Renato González Mello for pointing this out to me.

68. The identification of the migrating men in this panel specifically with the Aztecs is based on early proposals. A diagram that probably dates to early 1933 (see note 103) describes the subject of this panel as "Migration of the Aztecs from the North: symbol of the origin of American civilization." Anecdotal accounts have it that members of the Dartmouth football team were models for this composition.

69. This panel was described by Orozco in his fall 1933 manuscript for the *Dartmouth Alumni Magazine* as "Human Sacrifice to Huitzilopochtli." Orozco portrayed Huitzilopochtli in his blue-and-yellow-striped guise in the panel showing *The Coming of Quetzalcoatl*. The model for the disembodied head that presides over *Ancient Human Sacrifice* can be identified, on the basis of its closed eyes, strongly defined brow, flat nose, and slack, downturned mouth, with the head of

the goddess Coyolxauhqui. Associated with darkness and with sorcery, Coyolxauhqui was decapitated and dismembered by her half brother Huitzilopochtli when she led an attack on their mother, the earth fertility goddess Coatlicue. Stone heads or masks of Coyolxauhqui are preserved in a number of collections, including a famous one discovered in Mexico City in 1830. In 1928 the Peabody Museum in Boston acquired a example that is strikingly similar to Orozco's representation. (See H. B. Nicholson with Eloise Quiñones Keber, *Art of Aztec Mexico: Treasures of Tenochtitlán* [Washington, D.C.: National Gallery of Art, 1983], 51.)

70. Verbal communication from Churchill Lathrop.

71. In a letter of May 31, 1932, to Matt B. Jones, for example, President Hopkins makes the argument that the subject of the murals is appropriate to Dartmouth because of the college's early connection with the American Indians. In the process he misattributes to Orozco a statement actually written by John Hubert Cornyn: "The resolution of your college is in line with its traditions which connect it with the Indian races of America" (letter to the president of May 25, 1932). This assertion was questioned by Jones, who, in a letter of June 3, 1932, replied to Hopkins: "…it is rather a far cry from the Aztec civilization of Mexico to the rude savages of the Algonquin strain with which Eleazer [*sic*] Wheelock worked, between which, as I understand it, the archaeologists have been unable as yet to show a common ancestry."

72. The artist's original scheme for this section, published as late as November 1933 in the *Dartmouth*

Alumni Magazine (see note 50), laid out the following subjects: "The Missionaries—Dartmouth College; Missionaries and Explorers; Settlers (the Puritans in New England); 19th Century Immigrants."

73. Alma Reed recounts that "my file of carbon duplicates reveals that on 17 June 1933, Orozco dictated to me a letter to Professor Packard in which he presented the ideas he wished to incorporate into his future painting at Dartmouth" (*Orozco,* 260–61). The revised subjects for the east wing that she cites—for example, "next to the Cortez panel there will be one dealing with our legendary wealth, which from the earliest days was the lure of the settler…"—have a slightly more negative cast than the original concept but are still far from the caustic critique of modern society that we see in the final version. It is unfortunate that Orozco's correspondence with Packard, which apparently included some drawings, has disappeared. The last trace of it is contained in a copy of a note in the archives of the Museum of Modern Art from Packard's son to Alfred H. Barr, Jr., written after the elder Packard's death: "[W]e've uncovered a wealth of original sketches, correspondence, etc. concerning the Orozco murals, and are a bit at loose ends as to what to do with them.…" In his reply, Barr suggested that the family get in touch with Dartmouth. In 1989 I visited the younger son and his wife and was in touch with the older son, who was unable to locate this material.

74. Orozco, *An Autobiography,* 156.

75. *Dartmouth Alumni Magazine* (November 1933), 12.

76. Orozco's enthusiasm for El Greco and Velázquez is conveyed in a 1928 letter to Jean Charlot (Orozco, *The Artist in New York,* 38; see also Reed, *Orozco,* 250).

77. *Christ Destroying His Cross* of 1923, painted over in 1926, has already been mentioned (fig. 35). In addition, compare *The Destruction of the Old Order* at the Preparatory School with *Hispano-America* at Dartmouth; *Ancient Races* with corresponding panels in the east wing of the reserve room; *Social and Political Junkheap* with *Symbols of Nationalism;* and the very beautiful sleeping man derived from Giotto in *The Grave Digger* with the sleeping figure in *The Coming of Quetzalcoatl.*

78. Orozco, *An Autobiography,* 156.

79. The *Little Review,* vol. 9, no. 2 (Winter 1927), 63. On January 4, 1928, Orozco wrote Jean Charlot: "The real American artists are the ones who make the machines: you have to take off your hat to them" (Orozco, *The Artist in New York,* 32).

80. Lewis Mumford, *Technics and Civilization* (New York: Harcourt, Brace, 1934), 6.

81. See Linda Bank Downs, *Diego Rivera: The Detroit Industry Murals* (New York and London: Detroit Institute of Arts in association with W. W. Norton, 1999). Downs convincingly argues that on the north wall of this cycle Rivera emphasized visual resemblances between modern machines and pre-Cortesian sculpture: "Just as the Aztecs were human fodder for the sun, Rivera drew the analogy to the factory workers who sacrifice their energy for the technological universe" (166).

82. The letter is from Paul Allen, reference librarian, the College Library. A reply was sent on July 10 from H. H. Brinker, Department of Promotion, A Century of Progress International Exposition: "…we are sending you under separate cover two or three photographs which may be of some assistance to Mr. José Clemente [*sic*], in connection with the fresco he is painting in the Dartmouth College Library. We would suggest, however, that you write to some of the manufacturers of machinery who, we are sure, would be glad to send you photographs." The photographs to which Brinker refers are not in the Dartmouth files.

83. This is the only panel to which President Hopkins seems to have recorded his objections. In a letter of November 23, 1933, to Artemas Packard, Hopkins informs Packard of his instructions to the bursar to continue Orozco's payments past January 1, adding:

> In regard to the murals in general, I should like to have Mr. Orozco feel that he has the enthusiastic support of the College in the principles for which he stands and the ideas which he wishes to represent. …I wish, however, that he would, before he gets done, review the panel "Anglo-America, Town Meeting and School Teacher." … Perhaps racial characteristics do not mean so very much in an artist's life, but there never was a group of children in New England, either in Puritan times or since, that looked anything like this group of Scandinavian square-heads.… That is the only panel so far that I have taken any exception

351

to, and I genuinely believe that the criticism is justified that whatever inspiration there may have been in the idea, the panel as a whole and the representation of the figures given are completely out of keeping with the library building or the locale.... I do feel very strongly...that in the one spot where he touches upon the school children, provision for whose education was first made in New England and where the public school first developed, he ought to give us New England characters and the sense of New England atmosphere.

84. Reed, *Orozco,* 49.

85. *Dartmouth* (February 17, 1934), 3.

86. Orozco, *An Autobiography,* 158.

87. From a press release in the files of the Museum of Modern Art. I should like to thank Eloise Ricciardelli for kindly making these files available to me.

88. This figure is usually identified with Zapata, but he more closely resembles Villa. According to Friedrich Katz ("Pancho Villa and the Attack on Columbus, New Mexico," *American Historical Review,* vol. 83, no. 1 [February 1978], 101–30), Villa's "primary motivation was his firm belief that Woodrow Wilson had concluded an agreement with Carranza that would virtually convert Mexico into a U.S. protectorate. Although such an agreement never existed, Villa had reasonable grounds for supposing that it did" (102). Wilson sent a punitive expedition led by General John Pershing into Mexico to subdue Villa. The expedition failed, and Villa "is still celebrated

[in Mexico] as the man who attacked the United States—and got away with it" (130). Villa was assassinated in 1923 by political enemies in Mexico.

89. See Ramón Eduardo Ruíz, *The Great Rebellion: Mexico, 1905–1924* (New York: W.W. Norton, 1980), 103.

90. *Dartmouth Alumni Magazine* (November 1933), 12.

91. Reed, *Orozco,* 245.

92. Ibid.

93. From an unpublished paper given at the Dartmouth College symposium "In Celebration of José Clemente Orozco," October 12–13, 1984 (11).

94. Leonard Folgarait, *Mural Painting and Social Revolution in Mexico, 1920–1940: Art of the New Order* (New York: Cambridge University Press, 1998), 203.

95. *Dartmouth Alumni Magazine* (November 1933), 12.

96. Orozco, *An Autobiography,* 8. Renato González Mello believes that Orozco was convinced of Posada's worth by Jean Charlot; the fact that skeleton imagery does not appear in Orozco's caricatures before 1925 would appear to support his position.

97. Reed, *Orozco,* 262.

98. Gobin Stair, "The Making of a Mural: A Handyman's Memoir of José Clemente Orozco," *Dartmouth Alumni Magazine* (February 1973), 23.

99. Letter to Mrs. Franklin C. Lewis, March 8, 1934, 2.

100. Brenner, *Idols behind Altars,* 17–18.

101. See Anna D. Kartsonis, *Anastasis: The Making of an Image* (Princeton: Princeton University Press, 1986).

102. Orozco, *An Autobiography,* 134–35. In addition, as David Scott

has pointed out, "just before he left for California [in 1930], Alma Reed had held an exhibit showing the paintings of Mistra at her Delphic Studios" (Scott, "Orozco's Prometheus," *College Art Journal,* vol. 17, no. 1 [Fall 1957], 16).

103. From a plan for the mural probably produced around March 1933 in connection with the article "Orozco," published in the Dartmouth *Library Bulletin* of this month, 6–8, Dartmouth College archives.

104. Orozco, *An Autobiography,* 158.

105. Claude Bragdon, *The Arch Lectures* (New York: Creative Age Press, 1942), 102.

106. See note 13.

107. For more information on Benton's mural projects, which must have been of tremendous interest to Orozco, see Adam, cited above, and Emily Braun and Thomas Branchick, *Thomas Hart Benton: The America Today Murals* (New York: Equitable Life Assurance Society, 1985).

108. "New World, New Races and New Art," *Creative Art* (January 1929), xlvi.

109. Reed, *Orozco,* 185.

110. Orozco, *An Autobiography,* 159.

111. "Social Realism in Mexico: The Murals of Rivera, Orozco and Siqueiros," *artscanada* (December–January 1979–80), 60.

112. *Boletín de la Secretaría de Educación Pública,* 2, 1923, 17, cited and quoted in Charlot, *Mexican Mural Renaissance,* 92–93.

113. Reed, *Orozco,* 59, 95.

Orozco at War: Context and Fragment in Dive Bomber and Tank *(1940)*

(James Oles)

1. "Mexico's Art through Twenty Centuries Installed in Modern Museum," *Art Digest,* vol. 14, no. 17 (June 1, 1940), 15.

2. "Interchangeable Dive Bomber," *New Yorker,* vol. 16, no. 21 (July 6, 1940), 13; Clemente Orozco, *Orozco, Verdad Cronológica* (Guadalajara: EDUG/Universidad de Guadalajara, 1983), 390.

3. With the $7,500 fee, he planned to bring his wife, Margarita, up to visit the New York World's Fair and Niagara Falls. See José Clemente Orozco, *Cartas a Margarita* (Mexico City: Ediciones Era, 1987), 300–310. For further details on the commission, including information based on unpublished letters, see Alejandro Anreus, *Orozco in Gringoland* (Albuquerque: University of New Mexico Press, 2001), 118–22.

4. The panels were constructed of galvanized wire lath attached to a welded steel frame. Three coats of plaster (scratch, brown, and equalizing) were applied to the lath; the fourth, or intonaco coat, was added just before he began painting. José Clemente Orozco, *Dive Bomber and Tank* collection file (notes on the preparation of panels and the fresco technique used in painting *Dive Bomber and Tank*), Museum of Modern Art, Department of Painting and Sculpture.

5. MacKinley Helm, *Man of Fire, J.C. Orozco: An Interpretive Memoir* (Westport, Conn.: Greenwood Publishers, 1953), 87.

352

6. Author's interview with Lewis Rubenstein, Poughkeepsie, New York (1992). Rubenstein (born 1908) painted murals for Harvard's Busch-Reisinger Museum and the U.S. Post Office in Wareham, Massachusetts, in the 1930s and later taught fresco painting at Vassar. He recalled that unlike Rivera and many of the French and American painters, Orozco used a less absorbent "recipe" for the intonaco coat, which allowed him to paint more freely, something Rubenstein admired: "He was lawless, he'd take a trowel of pure lime putty and smear it on the painting." See Lewis W. Rubenstein, "Fresco Painting Today," *American Scholar,* vol. 4, no. 4 (Autumn 1935), 418–37, and Ruth Middleton, *Lewis Rubenstein: A Hudson Valley Painter* (Woodstock, N.Y.: Overlook Press, 1993).

7. José Clemente Orozco, *Orozco "Explains"* (New York: Museum of Modern Art, 1940).

8. Orozco, *Cartas a Margarita,* 302. All translations from Spanish by the author. Orozco noted that the portable panels Rivera had painted for MoMA in 1931–32 (and that measured five by eight feet each) had not survived well, yet Orozco's individual panels are hardly smaller or more easily transportable. As far as I know, *Dive Bomber and Tank* has never left the museum, precisely because of conservation concerns.

9. "Interchangeable Dive Bomber," 13; Orozco, *Cartas a Margarita,* 305. An early abstract "Study" and two more detailed sketches (current whereabouts unknown) are illustrated in *José Clemente Orozco: exposición nacional* (Mexico City: INBA, 1947), n.p.

10. "Interchangeable Dive Bomber," 13. For mixed reviews, see

"Orozco's Dive Bomber Crashes into Tank at the Museum of Modern Art," *Art Digest,* vol. 14, no. 19 (August 1, 1940), 7.

11. "Muralist Gives Explanation of 'Dive Bomber,'" *New York Herald Tribune* (July 4, 1940).

12. The mural was featured in MoMA's *Art of the Forties* (1991) and *Latin American Artists of the Twentieth Century* (1992) and is discussed in Anreus, *Orozco in Gringoland,* 113–33.

13. The catalog included a biographical essay by Paine and shorter texts by Jere Abbott on Rivera's style and fresco technique, the latter foreshadowing the technical notes in "Orozco 'Explains.'" See *Diego Rivera* (New York: Museum of Modern Art, 1931).

14. Bertram Wolfe was among the first to hint at the linkage between the commercial and cultural interests of the Rockefellers in *Diego Rivera: His Life and Times* (New York: Alfred A. Knopf, 1939), 335. For Alma Reed's more partisan view, see Reed, *Orozco* (New York: Oxford University Press, 1956), 234–35.

15. Sabine Mabardi has carefully analyzed this retrospective in "The Politics of the Primitive and the Modern: Diego Rivera at MoMA in 1931," *Curare,* Mexico City, no. 9 (Fall 1996); see also Laurance P. Hurlburt, *The Mexican Muralists in the United States* (Albuquerque: University of New Mexico Press, 1989), 123–27.

16. After the exhibition, these panels were purchased by the Weyhe Gallery in New York. The four based on his Mexican cycles, not surprisingly, entered U.S. collections relatively quickly: *Sugar Cane* and *Liberation of the Peon* went to the Philadelphia Museum of Art, *Agrarian*

Leader Zapata was acquired by MoMA, and *Knight of the Tiger* went to the Smith College Museum of Art. The others remained in storage and were sold at auction by Sotheby Parke Bernet in May 1977.

17. Rivera used portable panels in his mural cycles for the New Workers School, New York (1933), the Communist League of America, New York (1933), and the Hotel Reforma, Mexico City (1935). Orozco's *Catharsis* (1934, Palace of Fine Arts) is not permanently affixed to the wall, nor is it "portable" in the proper sense of the term.

18. Elizabeth McCausland, writing for the *Springfield* [Massachusetts] *Republican,* was explicit in her comparison, praising Orozco's expressionist brushwork and partial abstraction by contrasting them with Rivera's "shallow" images that "lie on the top of the plaster like decalcomania transfers." Cited in "Orozco's Dive Bomber Crashes into Tank at the Museum of Modern Art," 7.

19. See Frederick Kelly, "A Passion for Landscape: The Paintings of Frederic Edwin Church," in *Frederic Edwin Church* (Washington, D.C.: National Gallery of Art, 1989), 57.

20. Wolfe, *Diego Rivera,* 337.

21. See Barbara Kirshenblatt-Gimblett, *Destination Culture: Tourism, Museums, and Heritage* (Berkeley: University of California Press, 1998), 17–78.

22. I have no information that the public was able to watch Rivera paint in 1931–32, although he was visited by critics and fellow artists. He was certainly on prominent "display" while he painted at the RCA Building and the New Workers

School in 1933, and he was a willing participant in the *Art in Action* exhibit at the Golden Gate International Exposition in San Francisco in 1940, which also entailed a live performance.

23. In 1930 Paine and Rockefeller, among others, had founded the Mexican Arts Association, a short-lived organization designed to promote all aspects of Mexican art in the United States. See Wolfe, *Diego Rivera,* 333–35.

24. Jorge Alberto Manrique and Teresa del Conde, *Una mujer en el arte mexicano: memorias de Inés Amor* (Mexico City: UNAM, 1987), 57–58.

25. A remark of 1935, cited in Cary Reich, *The Life of Nelson A. Rockefeller: Worlds to Conquer, 1908–1958* (New York: Doubleday, 1996), 145.

26. From a letter dated February 23, 1928, in Orozco, *The Artist in New York,* 37. In the original Spanish, the "(?)" specifically challenges the use of the word "art" to describe the creations of the Mexican folk.

27. Three early events were particularly important in setting up this canon: the Art Center exhibition of 1928; the publication of Anita Brenner's *Idols behind Altars* in 1929; and the *Mexican Arts* show curated by René d'Harnoncourt and circulated by the American Federation of the Arts in the early 1930s.

28. For details, see James Oles, *South of the Border: Mexico in the American Imagination, 1914–1947* (Washington, D.C.: Smithsonian Institution Press, 1993), and Helen Delpar, *The Enormous Vogue of Things Mexican: Cultural Relations between the U.S. and Mexico, 1920–*

353

1935 (Tuscaloosa: University of Alabama Press, 1992).

29. Manuel Toussaint, "Veinte siglos de arte Mexicano," *Anales del Instituto de Investigaciones Estéticas,* vol. 2, no. 5 (1940), 5–10, remains an excellent overview of the genesis and installation of the show. For a checklist, see *Bulletin of the Museum of Modern Art,* vol. 7, no. 2–3 (May 1940), 10–13. The exhibition also included Orozco's *Brothel Dance* (n.d.); *The Attack* (1924); *Zapata* (1930); *Zapatistas* (1931); *The Cemetery* (1931); and *Self-Portrait* (1940).

30. The political and commercial interests that influenced the exhibition have been discussed in some detail. See Oles, *South of the Border,* 141. See also Eva Cockcroft, "The United States and Socially Concerned Latin American Art: 1920–1970," *The Latin American Spirit: Art and Artists in the United States, 1920–1970* (New York: Bronx Museum in association with Abrams, 1988), 192, and Waldo Rasmussen, "Introduction to an Exhibition," *Latin American Art of the Twentieth Century* (New York: Museum of Modern Art, 1992), 11–13.

31. "Foreword of the Museum of Modern Art," *Twenty Centuries of Mexican Art* (New York: Museum of Modern Art, 1940), 12.

32. "Mexico's Art through Twenty Centuries," 15. Another critic referred to the "new Aztec empire [that] has risen on the banks of the Rhine." Paul Rosenfeld, "The Genius of Mexico," *Nation,* vol. 150, no. 21 (May 25, 1940), 661.

33. Jean Charlot, "Twenty Centuries of Mexican Art," in *Art-Making from Mexico to China* (New York: Sheed and Ward, 1950), 40 (originally published in *Magazine*

of Art [July 1940]). Charlot's review echoes Orozco's angry letters of the late 1920s.

34. Of course, not every work in *Twenty Centuries* was folkloric or escapist. Antonio Ruiz's *Street Meeting* (oil on canvas, 1935) and Leopoldo Méndez's *Parade* (woodcut, 1933), for example, are commentaries on contemporary politics. Although both appear in the catalog, it is revealing that they were never included in illustrated reviews of the show.

35. Alfred H. Barr, Jr., *What Is Modern Painting?* (New York: Museum of Modern Art, 1946), 10, cited in Riva Castleman, *Art of the Forties* (New York: Museum of Modern Art, 1991), 140. Stanton L. Catlin confirmed the fact that most people at the time read the mural as a specific allegory of the war, despite Orozco's hesitation to do so in his own "explanations." Renato González Mello, "La máquina de pintar? Rivera, Orozco y la invención de un lenguaje," doctoral thesis in art history, Universidad Nacional Autónoma de México, Facultad de Filosofía y Letras, 1998, p. 367.

36. Cited in "Orozco's Dive Bomber Crashes into Tank," 7. See also Helm, *Man of Fire,* 84.

37. "Interchangeable Dive Bomber," 13.

38. Ibid.

39. Ibid.

40. For more on Mexico's involvement in World War II, see Blanca Torres, *México en la segunda guerra mundial* (Mexico City: El Colegio de México, 1979); María Emilia Paz, *Strategy, Security and Spies: Mexico and the U.S. as Allies in World War II* (University Park: Pennsylvania State University Press, 1997); Stephen R. Niblo, *Mexico in the 1940s: Modernity, Politics, and*

Corruption (Wilmington, Del.: Scholarly Resources, 1999).

41. "Interchangeable Dive Bomber," 13.

42. "Orozco Blitzpaints Modern Museum Mural," *PM* (July 9, 1940), 20. The short article goes on to describe how Orozco "broke up" the panels and "pummeled" his theme.

43. "Mexicans and Friends," *Time,* vol. 30, no. 21 (November 22, 1937), 27.

44. Torres, *México,* 14. Mexico ended this trade after the invasion of Poland in September 1939. See also Friedrich E. Schuler, *Mexico between Hitler and Roosevelt: Mexican Foreign Relations in the Age of Lázaro Cárdenas* (Albuquerque: University of New Mexico Press, 1998), esp. ch. 5.

45. The major point "won" by the Mexicans was that the oil companies would be compensated only for uninsured capital investments and not for the value of underground oil fields, which the Mexicans had declared national patrimony. See Torres, *México,* 36–37.

46. See Reich, *Life of Nelson Rockefeller,* 170.

47. Joe Alex Morris, *Nelson Rockefeller: A Biography* (New York: Harper & Brothers, 1960), 123. Later in 1940 Rockefeller was named coordinator of the Office of Inter-American Affairs, a branch of the Roosevelt administration established during the tense period preceding the outbreak of war and charged with promoting the Good Neighbor policy through textual and visual propaganda.

48. See Ida Rodríguez Prampolini, *Juan O'Gorman: arquitecto y pintor* (Mexico City: UNAM, 1982), 54–55.

49. Carlos Monsiváis, "Sociedad y cultura," in *Entre la guerra y la estabilidad política: El México de los 40,* ed. Rafael Loyola (Mexico City: Grijalbo/Conaculta, 1990), 278.

50. José Clemente Orozco, *Dive Bomber and Tank* collection file, Museum of Modern Art, Department of Painting and Sculpture. Press release: "Noted Mexican Artist Paints Fresco 'The Dive Bomber' on Walls of the Museum of Modern Art."

51. José Clemente Orozco, *Autobiografía* (Mexico City: Era, 1981), 34.

52. Luis Cardoza y Aragón, *Pintura mexicana contemporánea* (Mexico City: Imprenta Universitaria, 1953), 297. Emphasis added.

53. Octavio Paz, "The Concealment and Discovery of Orozco," *Essays on Mexican Art* (New York: Harcourt, Brace, Jovanovich, 1983), 179.

54. Antonio Rodríguez, *La pintura mural en la obra de Orozco* (Mexico City: Secretaría de Educación Pública, 1986), 105.

55. González Mello discusses this theme in detail in "La máquina de pintar."

56. Antonio Rodríguez, *A History of Mexican Mural Painting* (New York: G. P. Putnam's Sons, 1969), 348. Here the panel is referred to as "The Contemporary Circus."

57. As if to emphasize this point, the artist Carlos Mérida titled this panel *Manifestation Presided over by Cannibals. Orozco Frescoes in Guadalajara* (Mexico City: Frances Toor Studios, 1940), n.p.

58. For an important reading of this mural as a visual statement that interfered with RCA's self-image as benevolent broadcaster, see Robert Linsley, "Utopia Will Not Be Televised: Rivera at Rockefeller

Center," *Oxford Art Journal,* vol. 17, no. 2 (1994), 48–62.

59. Justino Fernández finds more exaggerated Christian symbolism in the mural in his *José Clemente Orozco: forma e idea* (Mexico City: Librería de Porrúa Hermanos, 1942), 95–98. One early sketch shows more of these snaking forms, less overtly reptilian than the creatures in many of Orozco's previous murals.

60. *Orozco "Explains,"* n.p.; González Mello, "La máquina de pintar," 367.

61. See Rivera's own description of his project, cited in Wolfe, *Diego Rivera,* 358–59. In the 1934 version in Mexico City's Palace of Fine Arts Rivera placed a fasces and swastika in the lap of Caesar.

62. See the text fragments, which Charlot dates to around 1923, included in José Clemente Orozco, *The Artist in New York* (Austin: University of Texas Press, 1974), 92–93.

63. *Orozco "Explains,"* n.p. Emphasis in the original.

64. Helm, *Man of Fire,* 84–85.

65. Rodríguez, *History of Mexican Mural Painting,* 351.

66. "Muralist Gives Explanation of 'Dive Bomber.'"

67. Press release (see note 50).

68. *Orozco "Explains,"* n.p.

69. "Pintura cubista y críticos" was first published in *El Heraldo,* Mexico City (July 14, 1920). In this cartoon, the reader is in on the joke from the beginning, since the painting is numbered, as are the two "descriptions." See also González Mello, "La máquina de pintar," 148–49.

70. Around 1923 he further clarified this position: "Painting *that is not understood* is pseudo-cubist painting, that is, painting done with so-called scientific *formulas,* imported from Paris. Such 'painting' is not understood by anyone, not even the one who does it." Orozco, *Artist in New York,* 92. Emphasis in original.

71. Though I hesitate to venture into psychoanalytic terrain, could Orozco's fascination with bodies fragmented by machines (in *Dive Bomber and Tank,* as elsewhere) have anything to do with the fact that he lost his left hand in a machine accident before embarking on his career as an artist?

72. As will be clear, I fully disagree with the idea that Orozco's proposed reconfigurations were a pure "farce" or that his use of formalism was merely sarcastic. See Anreus, *Orozco in Gringoland,* 126–127. Such interpretations efface the most compelling aspects of this radical mural.

73. According to Diana Linden, this is the only Nazi in any New Deal mural: "Zion in the Garden State: Ben Shahn's Murals for the Jersey Homesteads," paper presented at the Reunión Internacional Re-visión del Muralismo del Siglo XX, Mexico City, August 2000.

74. See Anthony Lee, *Painting on the Left: Diego Rivera, Radical Politics, and San Francisco's Public Murals* (Berkeley: University of California Press, 1999), 212–13. This mural was later moved to the theater at the City College of San Francisco.

75. See Barbara Haskell, *Ralston Crawford* (New York: Whitney Museum of American Art, 1985), 62–66. For further information on U.S. artists' representations of World War II, see Cécile Whiting, *Antifascism and American Art* (New Haven: Yale University Press, 1989); Stephen Polcari, *From Omaha to Abstract Expressionism: American Artists Respond to World War II* (New York: Baruch College, 1995); and Frederick S. Voss, *Reporting the War: The Journalistic Coverage of World War II* (Washington, D.C.: Smithsonian Institution Press for the National Portrait Gallery, 1994).

76. See Whiting, *Antifascism,* 111–23; Erika Doss, *Benton, Pollock, and the Politics of Modernism: From Regionalism to Abstract Expressionism* (Chicago: University of Chicago Press, 1991), 282–304.

77. Emily Genauer, cited in "Orozco's Dive Bomber Crashes into Tank at Museum of Modern Art," 7.

78. Reed, *Orozco,* 289.

79. Ibid., 161. Reed probably refers to a Latin American exhibit postponed from the anniversary year of 1954 to November 1955.

80. See, especially, Serge Guilbaut, *How New York Stole the Idea of Modern Art: Abstract Expressionism, Freedom and the Cold War* (Chicago: University of Chicago Press, 1983).

81. Octavio Paz, "Tamayo en la pintura mexicana," reprinted in *Rufino Tamayo: 70 años de creación* (Mexico City: Museo Rufino Tamayo, 1987), 98.

The Making and Reception of the Imaginary of Artistic and Revolutionary Mexico

(Alicia Azuela)

1. Carleton Beals was persecuted for refusing to serve in World War I, and Frank Tannenbaum spent a year in jail for his antiwar activism during the conflict. Bertram Wolfe and Robert Habermas were convicted under the Espionage Act. These men, together with many other radicals, took refuge in Mexico, and some of them played significant roles within Mexican workers', peasants', and cultural organizations.

2. Frank Tannenbaum, "Mexico, a Promise," *Survey Graphic* (May 5, 1924), 132.

3. "Populism" here refers to the political movement, its political organization known as the People's party (1890–1896), and the ideology that has outlived it.

4. Mauricio Tenorio, "Viejos gringos radicales norteamericanos en los años treinta y su visión de Mexico," unpublished manuscript, 104.

5. See Alan Trachtenberg, *The Incorporation of America* (New York: Hill and Wang, 1987), 158–61.

6. See Tenorio, "Viejos gringos," 106.

7. Both Tenorio and John Briton did important work on U.S. authors interested in Mexico. For further references, see the bibliography.

8. See John Briton, "In Defense of Revolution: American Interest in Mexico, 1920–1929," *Journalism History,* vol. 5, no. 4 (Winter 1978–79), 124.

9. The abundant material published in the 1924 Mexico issue of the radical New York magazine *Survey Graphic,* which Tannenbaum edited as its in-country correspondent, was paradigmatic of the image that artists and intellectuals from both countries constructed in their attempt to explain to U.S. audiences the complex and foreign Mexican situation. This issue featured contributions by Ramón Denegri on agrarian reform, the governor of the Yucatán, Felipe Carrillo Puerto, on his experience heading that state's socialist government, and General Calles himself on the meaning and legitimacy of the revolution of 1910.

355

In the cultural arena, it included contributions by Pedro Henríquez Ureña, Doctor Atl, Katherine Anne Porter, and Diego Rivera.

10. According to Fuentes Mares, nineteenth-century indigenist nationalism was originally promoted by U.S. Ambassador Joel Roberts Poinsett and his "York" Masonic lodge, with the aim of extending U.S. power in Latin America during the period of local revolt and weakening of the Spanish Empire. Ideologically it played up republican Hispanophobia, counterposing the greatness of the pre-Hispanic past, which the continent as a whole shared, to the Spanish fanaticism and violence that allegedly destroyed the pre-Columbian world in its full bloom. That greatness was about to blossom once again, however, thanks to the independence and support of the new United States of America. See José Fuentes Mares, *Poinsett, historia de una intriga* (Mexico: Editorial Jus, 1951).

11. Tannenbaum, "Mexico, a Promise," 129–32.

12. Manuel Gamio, *Programa de la dirección de antropología para el estudio y mejoramiento de las poblaciones regionales de la República Mexicana*, 2d ed. (Mexico: Poder Federal, Departamento de Aprovisionamientos Generales, Talleres Gráficos de la Nación, 1919), 166.

13. Franz Boas's theory of cultural relativism was crucial for the definitive disqualification of racist and Eurocentric views regarding "primitive" peoples and their artistic and cultural manifestations. Boas proposed that every human culture be valued in a singular manner and in relationship to the particular geographical, historical, and psychological circumstances that determined it. In *Primitive Art*

(Cambridge: Harvard University Press, 1927), he showed that artistic production responds to an innate artistic necessity among human beings. In consequence, primitive art is not just utilitarian, anonymous, or collective. It could also be related to an individual aesthetic need or to the creative results of a singular personality who had the gifts and specialized knowledge to produce a particular artistic object, which could be appreciated as such.

14. Katherine Anne Porter, "Corridos," *Survey Graphic* (1924), 157.

15. Doctor Atl, "Popular Arts of Mexico," *Survey Graphic* (1924), 161.

16. Tannenbaum, "Mexico, a Promise," 132.

17. Carleton Beals, *Mexican Maze* (New York: Book League of America, 1931), 279.

18. Gonzalo Aguirre Beltrán, "Panorama de la Antropología social y aplicada," *Manuel Gamio: arqueología e indigenismo*, ed. Eduardo Matos Moctezuma (Mexico City: SepSetentas, 1972), 200–201. This author's characterization of Gamio's anthropological thought could be equally applied to *Idols behind Altars* (New York: Payson & Clarke, 1929) not only because he directly guided Brenner in determining her book's structure and methodology but also because both he and Brenner shared this type of mythical reasoning, which is typical of modern cosmogony.

19. See Elvira Burgos Díaz, *Dionisio en la filosofía del joven Nietzsche* (Zaragoza: Universidad de Zaragoza, 1993).

20. Brenner, *Idols behind Altars*, 138.

21. Susannah Joel Glusker, *Anita Brenner: A Mind of Her Own* (Austin: University of Texas Press, 1998), 99–110.

22. Katherine Anne Porter, "Old Goods and New Messiahs," *New York Herald Tribune* (September 29, 1929).

23. Ernest Gruening, "The Mexican," *Portland* [Oregon] *News*, (October 1, 1929).

24. "Big Mexican Exhibition," *Art Digest,* vol. 2, no. 7 (January 1, 1928), 4.

25. Ibid.

26. *The Art Center Announces an Exhibition of Mexican Art,* catalog, introductory note by Frank Crowninshild, 1928, 2. Anita Brenner's Archive, Box 9.

27. Certificate of Incorporation of Mexican Arts Association, Inc.: Pursuit to Membership Corporations Law (copy), Rockefeller Center archives.

28. See Warren I. Susman, *Culture as History* (New York: Pantheon Books, 1984), xxvi. Also see Richard Pells, *Radical Vision and American Dreams* (New York: Harper and Row, 1973), 410–21.

29. See "New York Sees Mexico's Revolutionary Art," *Art Digest*, vol. 11, no. 8 (mid-January, 1928), 1.

30. For more information on the image of Mexico presented in the landowners' newspapers, see Briton, "In Defense of Revolution."

31. The museum distributed a copy of the exhibition catalog's text, written by curator René d'Harnoncourt, to several art journals, which simply reproduced it. This text originally appeared in the October *Bulletin of the Metropolitan Museum of Art*. Also see "Mexican Arts," in *American Magazine of Art* (October 1930), 5, 8, 9, and 10.

32. Ibid., 10.

33. Ibid., 5.

34. Visitors' enthusiasm for this exhibit was mainly due to the predominance of popular art objects

above the rest of the pieces on display. This issue is addressed in "Notes," *American Magazine of Art* (October 1930), 589, and "The Mexican Exhibition," *American Magazine of Art* (January 1931), 3.

35. "Mexico in New York," *Arts* (October 1930), 16–19.

36. Ibid., 17.

37. Ibid.

38. Ibid., 18.

39. Ibid. See also Helen Delpar, *The Enormous Vogue of Things Mexican: Cultural Relations between the United States and Mexico, 1920–1935* (Tuscaloosa: University of Alabama Press, 1992), 145–46, and note 62.

40. Richard H. Pells, *Radical Visions and American Dreams: Culture and Social Thought during the Depression Years* (New York: Harper Row, 1973), 96.

41. Lewis Mumford, "Orozco in New England," *New Republic* (October 10, 1934), 231–35.

42. This was the most lucid contemporary analysis of the elements necessary to artistic and technological production and thought, so that through the combination of art and technology, modernity could become the best of the worlds.

43. Lewis Mumford, *Art and Technics* (New York: Columbia University Press, 1952). Spanish transl. Luis Fafricant, *Arte y Técnica* (Buenos Aires: Editorial Nueva Visión, 1957), 103.

44. Mumford, "Orozco in New England," 233.

45. Harvey M. Watts, director of the Philadelphia's Moore Institute of Art, Sciences, and Industry, was a critic and art historian.

46. Harvey M. Watts, "Orozco's 'American Epic' at Dartmouth Starts

a Controversy," *Art Digest,* vol. 8, no. 20 (September 1, 1934), 6.

47. "The American Artists Professional League," *Art Digest,* vol. 7, no. 4 (November 15, 1932), 31.

48. Ibid.

49. See "Dartmouth Indicted," *Art Digest,* vol. 7, no. 18 (July 1, 1933), 12.

50. *Art Digest,* vol. 7, no. 17 (June 1, 1933), 11.

51. See Pells, *Radical Visions,* 1973.

Mural Devices

(Francisco Reyes Palma)

1. This story appears in "Museo," a chapter of Borges's *El hacedor,* under the heading "Del rigor en la ciencia": Jorge Borges, *Obrás completas* (Buenos Aires: Emere Editores, 1964), vol. 2, p. 225.

2. In my approach to mural painting, I incorporate the intersection of two fertile analytic notions: on the one hand, that of devices of power, or machines of vision and sense, developed by Michel Foucault, Gilles Delleuze, and Félix Guattari; on the other, that of the imaginary as symbolic machine, capable of organizing the totality of social life, a term coined by Cornelius Castoriadis and reworked by such authors as Benedict Anderson and Bronislaw Baczko. Please refer to the end of this essay for a list of works consulted.

3. In Mexico, as in most Catholic countries, "Jacobin" is an adjective used for radical liberal rationalists who, following the French revolutionary model, have an anti-Catholic partisanship.

4. The Partido Nacional Revolucionario, the National Revolutionary party, was instituted

in 1929, an alliance between a number of different, and frequently opposing, revolutionary factions. It changed names in 1938, to Partido de la Revolución Mexicana, Mexican Revolution's party, and 1946, to Partido Revolucionario Institucional, Institutional Revolutionary party. Under that name, the PRI successfully retained power throughout the twentieth century.

5. Around that time another group of avant-garde painters, known as rupture artists, displaced the muralists and printmakers. Rupture artists identified with the New York school following the alignments of cold war discourse and distanced themselves from realism and political pedagogy. Although the real cause of this displacement was the development of mass media communication, the newcomers inhabited only the fine arts portion of the territory, as the social space of their predecessors shifted to the realm of the mass media.

6. Jean Charlot, another early creator of frescoes in Mexico, documented this clearly in José Clemente Orozco, *El artista en Nueva York: Cartas a Jean Charlot y textos inéditos,* 1925–1929 (Mexico: Siglo XXI, 1971).

Against the Laocoon: Orozco and History Painting

(Rita Eder)

1. These works include Fausto Ramírez, "Artistas e iniciados en la obra mural de Orozco," in *Orozco: una relectura* (Mexico City: UNAM-IIE, 1983), 61–112; Renato González Mello, "La máquina de pintar: Rivera, Orozco y la invención de un lenguaje," doctoral thesis in art history,

Universidad Nacional Autónoma de México, Facultad de Filosofía y Letras, 1998. *Orozco: una relectura* contains essays that have contributed to new interpretations of the works of the painter from Ciudad Guzmán. In addition to the important work of Fausto Ramírez in that collection, I must mention the works of Jacqueline Barnitz, "Los años délficos de Orozco," 103–128, and Alicia Azuela, "Presencia de Orozco en la sociedad y el arte anglosajones," 177–204, which put forward ideas and facts concerning this significant period in the life and work of the painter. There have been substantial advances in the study of Siqueiros as well; see *Otras rutas hacia Siqueiros* (Mexico City: INBA, CONACULTA, 1998), coordinated by Olivier Debroise. As far as Rivera is concerned, of particular note is the thesis by González Mello already mentioned and the group work to realize the CD-ROM developed at the Instituto de Investigaciones Estéticas on the theme "Los murales de Diego Rivera en la Secretaría de Educación Pública."

2. Octavio Paz, "Ocultación y descubrimiento de Orozco," *México en la obra de Octavio Paz,* vol. 111, *Los privilegios de la vista* (Mexico City: Fondo de Cultura Económica, 1987), 286.

3. Luis Cardoza y Aragón, *Orozco* (Mexico City: UNAM, 1959); Octavio Paz, "Revisiones: Orozco, Rivera, Siqueiros," *Sabado,* supplement to *Uno más uno* (September 9, 1978), 43, 6.

4. Luis Cardoza y Aragón, "Dos apuntes para un retrato," in *Orozco: una relectura,* 10–11.

5. Jorge Alberto Manrique, "Orozco y la crítica," in *Orozco: una relectura,* 171.

6. Clement Greenberg, "Review of Exhibitions of the Jane Street Group and Rufino Tamayo," in *Clement Greenberg: The Collected Essays,* ed. John O'Brian (Chicago: University of Chicago Press, 1986), vol. 2, p. 133.

7. Kirk Varnedoe, "Abstract Expressionism," *Primitivism in XXth Century Art* (New York: Museum of Modern Art, 1984), vol. 111, p. 615.

8. José Clemente Orozco, *An Autobiography,* transl. Robert S. Stephenson (Austin: University of Texas Press, 1962), 30.

9. Mark Thistlethwite, "Revival, Reflection and Parody: History of Painting in the Postmodern Era," in *Redefining American History Painting,* ed. Patricia M. Burnham and Lucretia Hoover Giese (Cambridge: Cambridge University Press, 1995), 208.

10. Marie-Areti Hers, "Manuel Gamio y el arte prehispánico: contradicciones nacionalistas," in *El arte en México: autores, temas y problemas,* coord. Rita Eder (forthcoming).

11. Rensselaer W. Lee, *Ut Pictura Poesis; The Humanistic Theory of Painting* (New York: W.W Norton, 1967).

12. Ibid., 43.

13. Gotthold Ephraim Lessing, *Laocoon: An Essay on the Limits of Painting and Poetry,* transl., with introduction and notes, Edward Allen McCormick (Baltimore: Johns Hopkins University Press, 1984); Clement Greenberg, "Towards a Newer Laocoon," *Clement Greenberg: The Collected Essays and Criticism,* vol. 1, pp. 23–37.

14. Greenberg, "Towards a New Laocoon," 28.

15. José Clemente Orozco, "Notas; pintura en el teatro al aire

357

libre. Escuela nacional de maestros," in *Textos de Orozco,* ed. Teresa del Conde (Mexico City: UNAM-IIE, 1983), 86.

16. José Clemente Orozco, foreword, *The Orozco Frescoes at Dartmouth* (Hanover, N.H.: Albert I. Dickerson, 1934).

17. Walter Benjamin, *The Origins of German Tragic Drama* (London: NLB, 1977).

18. Ibid.

19. Ibid., 24.

20. Justino Fernández, *Arte moderno y contemporáneo de México* (Mexico City: UNAM-IIE, 1994), 49.

21. Justino Fernández, *Prometeo* (Mexico: Editorial Porrúa, 1945), 215.

22. Heinrich Wölfflin, *Principles of Art History,* transl. M.D. Hottinger ([New York]: Dover Publications, 1932), 15.

23. Ibid.

24. Omar Calabrese, *La era neobarroca* (Madrid: Cátedra, 1987).

25. Paz, "Ocultación," 289–91.

26. Joan Weinstein, *The End of Expressionism: Art and the November Revolution in Germany, 1918–19* (London and Chicago: University of Chicago Press, 1990).

27. González Mello, "La máquina de pintar," 287. This author also addresses the affinities among Otto Dix, Max Beckmann, and Orozco, who came into contact with the works of these artists through the New Arts Circle galleries.

28. José Gorostiza, "Importancia de la nueva pintura en nuestro país," *El Nacional, Diario Popular,* Mexico (January 31, 1938), cited in González Mello, "La máquina de pintar," 360.

29. See note 1.

30. *The Orozco Frescoes at Dartmouth.*

31. González Mello, "La máquina de pintar," 242–52.

32. Benjamin, *Origins,* 22.

33. Gianni Vattimo, *Introducción a Nietzsche* (Barcelona: Editorial Península, 1985), 10.

34. Emily S. Hamblin, *Fredrich Nietzsche, and His New Gospel* (Boston: Gorham Press, 1911), 155.

35. Ibid., 163.

36. Vattimo, *Introducción a Nietzsche,* 23–32.

37. Ibid., 14–39.

38. Edmundo O'Gorman, "El arte o de la monstruosidad," in *Estudios sobre arte: 60 años del Instituto de Investigaciones Estéticas,* ed. Marta Fernandez and Louise Noelle Grass (Mexico City: UNAM, 1998), 471–76.

39. Ibid., 474.

40. Ibid., 476.

41. Orozco, *An Autobiography,* 157.

42. Rita Eder, "De héroes y maquinas. Reflexiones para la reinterpretación del estilo y las ideas en la obra de José Clemente Orozco," in *Orozco: una relectura,* 147–67.

43. Lewis Mumford, *Técnica y civilización* (Madrid: Alianza Universitaria), 100–105; quote from Lewis Mumford, *Technics and Civilization* (New York: Harcourt, Brace and Co., 1934), 86.

44. Perry Anderson, *Los fines de la historia* (Barcelona: Anagrama, 1996).

Orozco and Modern (Easel) Painting: New York 1927–34

(Dawn Ades)

1. "Encuesta," *Forma, revista de artes plasticas* (October 1, 1926). *Forma,* like the contemporary review *Los contemporaneos,* was a pluralist, open review of modern art covering developments inside as well as outside Mexico.

2. "Unpublished Notes" (1923), probably written for *La falange,* Orozco (Oxford: Museum of Modern Art, Oxford, 1980), 35; previously published in English in José Clemente Orozco, *The Artist in New York* (Austin: University of Texas Press, 1974); orig. ed., Orozco, *El artista en Nueva York (Cartas a Jean Charlot y textos ineditos 1925–29)* (Mexico City: Siglo XXI, 1971).

3. Albert Gleizes and Jean Metzinger, "Cubism" (1912), *Modern Artists on Art,* ed. Robert Herbert, (Englewood Cliffs, N.J.: Prentice-Hall, Inc., 1964), 5.

4. "Notes on the Early Frescoes at the National Preparatory School," Orozco, *Artist in New York,* 35.

5. Gleizes and Metzinger, "Cubism," 7.

6. See, for example, Alejandro Anreus, *Orozco in Gringoland* (Albuquerque: University of New Mexico Press, 2001), 48: "mythological (Greek-inspired) or surreal subjects."

7. Letter to Jean Charlot, February 23, 1928, in Orozco, *Artist in New York,* 48.

8. Ibid., letter to Charlot, March 1928.

9. Ibid., letter to Charlot, 38.

10. See David Craven, *Diego Rivera as Epic Modernist* (New York: G.K. Hall, 1997), Anreus, *Orozco in Gringoland,* and see also Helen Delpar, *The Enormous Vogue of Things Mexican: Cultural Relations between the United States and Mexico, 1920–1935* (Tuscaloosa: University of Alabama Press, 1992).

11. Letter to Charlot, January 1928, in Orozco, *Artist in New York,* 64.

12. José Clemente Orozco, "New World, New Races and New Art," *Creative Art,* vol. 4, no. 1 (January 1929), in Orozco, *Artist in New York,* 46.

13. Ibid., letter to Charlot, 41.

14. "The Richard Mutt case," *The Blind Man,* no. 2 (1917). Although anonymous, this first statement about the "readymades" was probably written or at least overseen by Duchamp.

15. Louis Lozowick, "The Americanization of Art," *Precisionism in America, 1915–1941: Re-ordering Reality* (New York: Harry Abrams, 1994), 155.

16. Ibid., 153.

17. "Notes on ENP Frescoes" (1923), in Orozco, *Artist in New York,* 133–34.

18. See Alma Reed, *Orozco* (New York: Oxford University Press, 1956).

19. Alfonso Reyes, "Cara y cruz del cacto," *Obras completas* (Mexico City: Fondo de Cultura Económica, 1959), vol. 10, p. 288; "Face and Cross of the Cactus," transl. Tim Ades, *Outposts* (Somerset, England: Hippopotamus Press, 1993), 63.

20. In 1931 Alfred Barr, Jr., the influential director of the Museum of Modern Art, was to link the American precisionist painters with European "New Objectivity."

21. Franz Roh, *Nach-Expressionismus: magischer realismus: Probleme der neuesten europaischen Malerei* (Leipzig: Klinkhardt and Biermann, 1925). The English translation of Roh's Spanish text is in *Magical Realism: Theory, History, Community,* ed. L.P. Zamora and W.B. Faris, (Durham, N.C.: Duke University, 1995); it unfortunately does not include Roh's table. The

impulse to take stock of the contemporary situation in painting was widespread in Europe in the mid-1920s. Hans Arp and El Lissitsky published *The Isms of Art* in 1925, and Wieland Herzfelde and George Grosz published *Die Kunst ist in Gefahr* ("Art Is in Danger") the same year. The latter, unlike Roh, saw the new "realism" as reactionary and regretted the insight of dada, which, in retrospect, had forged through collage a unique form of visual critique of the contemporary political situation.

22. José Clemente Orozco, *Cuadernos*, ed. Raquel Tibol (Mexico City: SEP, 1983), 28–30. Unfortunately, this edition does not indicate the pagination and order of the original.

23. Although Roh does not foreground his argument on an opposition between pure abstraction and figuration, it is an underlying assumption. It would not, however, have been perceived with the same polemical force in the 1920s and early 1930s in the United States and in Mexico as in Europe. It was not until the mid-1930s that Alfred Barr put on at the Museum of Modern Art the two exhibitions that defined for America the two main trends in modern art as he saw it: the first, cubism and abstract art in 1934, the second, "fantastic art," dada, and surrealism in 1935–36.

24. Sigmund Freud, "The Uncanny," *Art and Literature: Jensen's Gradiva, Leonardo da Vinci and Other Works* (Harmondsworth, England: Pelican Freud Library, 1985), vol. 14, pp. 335–76.

25. José Clemente Orozco, *Autobiografía* (Mexico City: Secretaría de Educación Pública-Cultura-Era, 1984), 94–95.

26. Orozco, *Cuadernos*, 31.

27. For discussion of an "alternative modernism," see Oriana Baddeley and Valerie Fraser, *Drawing the Line: Art and Cultural Identity in Contemporary Latin America* (London: Verso, 1989).

Orozco and American Muralism: Re/viewing an Enduring Artistic Legacy

Víctor Alejandro Sorell

1. Friedrich Nietzsche, *The Birth of Tragedy or Hellenism and Pessimism*, transl. William A. Haussmann, *The Complete Works of Friedrich Nietzsche*, ed. Oscar Levy (New York: Russell & Russell, 1909–11/1964), vol. 1, p. 76. With respect to Aeschylus's tragic play *Prometheus Bound*, the classical scholar David Grene writes: "Prometheus is, politically, the symbol of the rebel against the tyrant who has overthrown the traditional rule of Justice and Law." He adds that "everybody in [ancient] Greece knew the legend of the Titan who stole fire from heaven to give it to man." As for contemporary readers, Grene foregrounds "the directness and universality of the theme drawn from the community of man's experience." David Grene and Richard Lattimore, eds., *The Complete Greek Tragedies* (Chicago: University of Chicago Press, 1959), vol. 1, pp. 305–306.

2. From a letter courtesy of the artist's daughter, Lucrecia, quoted in Laurance P. Hurlburt, *The Mexican Muralists in the United States* (Albuquerque: University of New Mexico Press, 1989), 32, 264. That letter from Orozco was written in New York on Saturday, June 18,

1930, and sent to his wife, Margarita: Orozco, *Cartas a Margarita* (Mexico City: Ediciones Era, 1987), 185. The letter asserts that his mural is "the first fresco by a Mexican painted in this country" ("por ser el primer fresco pintado por un mexicano en este país"). It is important to note that Orozco had "turned muralist" scarcely seven years before, in June 1923. Orozco, *The Artist in New York: Letters to Jean Charlot and Unpublished Writings, 1925–1929* (Austin: University of Texas Press, 1974), 11. From our dual thematic vantage, weighing Orozco's influence on Chicana(o)s, among others, while also investigating the possible relationship among mural painting, performance, and ritual, we must underscore two observations: (1) While Orozco's Pomona College mural dates from 1930, arguably, Siqueiros's own L.A. mural, *América tropical* ("Tropical America," 1932), has been a greater conspicuous influence on Chicanos. The art historian Shifra M. Goldman thinks this is due to the mural's documentation in the 1971 nationally televised film *América Tropical*, by the Chicano filmmaker Jesús Salvador Treviño. In her opinion, Orozco and Rivera were secondary influences on Chicano muralists. S. M. Goldman, *Dimensions of the Americas: Art and Social Change in Latin America and the United States* (Chicago: University of Chicago Press, 1994), 9. This writer would add that the outdoor location of Siqueiros's L.A. mural supports Goldman's argument, given that so many contemporary Chican(a)o murals are not only streetside paintings but landmarks in their respective barrios. (2) The subject of Prometheus appears depicted

pageantlike among *The Greek Heroes* cycle of early-twentieth-century murals painted by Walter McEwen for the Library of Congress. *The Library of Congress Mural Paintings (in the Colors of the Originals with the Library Quotations, the Poems of the Poetry Series, and the Greek Hero Myths)* (New York and Washington, D.C.: Foster & Reynolds, 1902), n.p. A final art historical point bears mention: that of Orozco's own inspiration for the figure of *Prometheus*. It is my opinion that probably one very important source is *The Prodigal Son* (1880–82), a fifty-four-inch-high bronze sculpture by the French artist François-Auguste-René Rodin (1840–1917). Consider the fact that according to the art historian Albert Elsen, Rodin was so highly regarded that "when he gave a sculpture to Mexico, the art students carried it triumphantly through the streets of Mexico City." A. Elsen, "Introduction," *Rodin* (New York: Museum of Modern Art, 1963–67), 9 and 56–59.

3. Jean Charlot, *An Artist on Art: Collected Essays of Jean Charlot* (Honolulu: University Press of Hawaii, 1972), 122. "Pulquería Painting" was originally published in Spanish in *Forma*, no. 1 (October 1926). In 1932, the year he painted *América tropical* in fresco on the exterior of the Plaza Art Center on Olvera Street in Los Angeles, Siqueiros wrote a letter to his friend William Spratling acknowledging the importance of outdoor muralism: "I believe I have done something of interest, because I believe I have initiated a drive to paint murals in the open, exposed to the sun and the rain…you will realize its importance, because it is something totally new in the world, and establishes the

359

basis of future art, which must be public to the highest degree." D. A. Siqueiros, *Art and Revolution,* transl. Sylvia Calles (London: Lawrence and Wishart, 1975), 191–92.

4. "There are ultimate rituals here: the mural becoming a flag, the history on the central wall changing from narrative incoherence to coherence…Mexican politics going from figurative to discursive, and Revolutionary Mexico becoming a post-Revolutionary, capitalist state. The mural viewer becomes an initiate in this rite of passage…. The ritual produced by the mural served the purpose of the capitalist state under a government partly invoking the laws of the land in order to claim legitimacy and continuity in the face of induced and profound change." Leonard Folgarait, "Revolution as Ritual: Rivera's National Palace Mural," *Oxford Art Journal,* vol. 14, no. 1 (1991), 31.

5. V. W. Turner, *The Ritual Process: Structure and Anti-Structure* (Chicago: Aldine Publishing Co., 1969), 96.

6. Ramón A. Gutiérrez and Geneviève Fabre, eds., *Feasts and Celebrations in North American Ethnic Communities* (Albuquerque: University of New Mexico Press, 1995), xi.

7. V. A. Sorell, *"Call and Response:* John Pitman Weber's Persistence in the *Public Sphere,"* in the exhibition catalog for the show *John Pitman Weber,* Gahlberg Gallery, Arts Center, College of Du Page, Glen Ellyn, Illinois, March 1994, 2.

8. José Clemente Orozco, "New World, New Races and New Art," *Creative Art,* vol. 4, no. 1 (January 1929), supplement 46.

9. Alma Reed, *Orozco* (New York: Oxford University Press, 1956), 13. (All translations are this writer's unless otherwise noted.) Implicit in Orozco's juxtaposition of "painted" versus "spoken" Bibles is the role Mexican society assigned to visual images vis-à-vis words (textual and verbal images) for didactic ends. Particularly with respect to religious education, this argument, which revolves around choosing the best means, images or words, to use for edification or instruction, has its roots in the iconoclastic controversy that began under the Byzantine emperor Leo III (717–741) and continued under his successor, Constantine V (741–775). St. John of Damascus, *On the Divine Images: Three Apologies against Those Who Attack the Divine Images,* transl., with an introduction, by David Anderson (Crestwood, N.Y.: St. Vladimir's Seminary Press, 1980), 7. Subsumed as the seventeenth point within his First Apology, St. John of Damascus wrote: "We use all our senses to produce worthy images of Him, and we sanctify the noblest of the senses, which is that of sight. For just as words edify the ear, so also the image stimulates the eye. *What the book is to the literate, the image is to the illiterate.* Just as words speak to the ear, so the image speaks to the sight; it brings us understanding" (25); emphasis is this writer's. To complicate matters, a medieval picture book, *Biblia Pauperum,* pairs Old and New Testament scenes, conflating both text and pictures printed from woodblocks. This artifact can be considered, at one and the same time, a painted and spoken Bible. Avril Henry, *Biblia Pauperum* (Ithaca, N.Y.: Cornell University Press, 1987).

For an extended analysis and discussion of this complex relationship or reciprocity between words and images in the context of Chican(a)o art and culture, refer to V. A. Sorell, "Articulate Signs of Resistance and Affirmation in Chicano Public Art," in *Chicano Art: Resistance and Affirmation,* ed. Richard Griswold del Castillo et al. (Los Angeles: UCLA Wight Art Gallery, 1991), 141–54.

10. W. H. Beezley et al., eds., *Rituals of Rule, Rituals of Resistance: Public Celebrations and Popular Culture in Mexico* (Wilmington, Del.: A Scholarly Resources Inc. Imprint, 1994), xv. Thanks to my friend historian Mary Kay Vaughan for referring me to this source.

11. Trudy Baltz, "Pageantry and Mural Painting: Community Rituals in Allegorical Form," *Winterthur Portfolio: A Journal of American Material Culture,* vol. 15, no. 3 (Autumn 1980), 211, 214, 220, 228.

12. Ben Shahn, *The Shape of Content* (Cambridge: Harvard University Press, 1957–72), 130–31.

13. George Biddle, *An American Artist's Story* (Boston: Little, Brown and Co., 1939), 269–70; emphasis is mine.

14. Alma Reed interpreted the artist's vision as one informed by an appreciation for the dramatic and tragic: Reed, *Orozco,* 34. She admits that at this time she could not yet accept or share Orozco's conception of New York, including his happy encounters with Coney Island, as "pure tragedy." No less distinguished a critic than the Guatemalan poet Luis Cardoza y Aragón would recognize the persistence of that same visual ethos some three years later. Echoing Reed, he situates Orozco's tragic vision in the capacious Mexican arena: "Through Orozco, one plumbs Mexico's deep reality in plastic terms. Tragedy dominates his work. The never-quelled real tragedy of the human spirit." Luis Cardoza y Aragón, *Orozco* (Mexico City: UNAM, 1959), 291. Anticipating the poet, the social historian of art Felipe Cossío del Pomar places Orozco's tragic sense on a continental and virtual universal plane: "[Orozco] is the only tragic poet America has produced." Felipe Cossío del Pomar, *La rebelión de los pintores: Ensayo para una sociología del arte* (Mexico City: Editorial Leyenda, S.A., 1945), 165.

15. A likely reference to one of the pieces from the *Revolutionary* series. Given the artist's own invocation of the "tragic" label, together with the importance we and others have already ascribed to his sense of the tragic, it is revealing to refer to another letter he wrote, this one quite testy, to L. E. Schmeckebier. As "point VI," Orozco writes: "The most misleading and treacherous words in Art Criticism are: Morals, Ideals, Social Significance, Revolution, More Revolution, *Tragic* Phatos, Histeria, Fanaticism and the like"; emphasis is mine. Cardoza y Aragón, *Orozco,* "Apéndice," letter from Guadalajara, dated May 1939; year is corroborated by the artist's wife, 329–32.

16. A reference to a modern religious sect, the Theosophical Society, which incorporated aspects of Buddhism and Brahmanism.

17. Orozco, *Artist in New York,* 66.

18. Orozco, *Cartas a Margarita,* 127–28. Orozco's sense of irony is not lost on the reader; recall his own use of a term he denies another (see note 15).

19. Ibid., 141.

20. Reed, *Orozco,* 40. Reed also acknowledges the presence at the Ashram of Sarojini Naidu, a Gandhi collaborator and head of a committee supporting the Indian cause against British domination (66). Reed adds that Naidu contributed to Orozco's sensitivity to human suffering on a global scale (71). In his autobiography, Orozco characterizes the Sikelianoses' efforts as the "Greek nationalist movement pretending nothing short of the resurgence of ancient Hellenic culture." Orozco, *An Autobiography* (Austin: University of Texas Press, 1962), 100. He also cites Naidu (101).

21. George Howard Bauer, *Sartre and the Artist* (Chicago: University of Chicago Press, 1969), 167. Through the duplexity of the Apollonian and the Dionysian — "two interwoven artistic impulses" — Nietzsche recognizes the origin and essence of Greek tragedy. These impulses are attributable to two antithetical ancient Greek deities, Apollo and Dionysus. The former is associated with the "art of the shaper," while the latter is tied to "the nonplastic art of music." Nietzsche, *Birth of Tragedy,* 21, 94.

22. Orozco, *Cartas a Margarita,* 300.

23. Ibid., 138.

24. Orozco, Foreword, *Artist in New York,* 20–21.

25. Orozco, *An Autobiography,* 33, 46; emphasis is mine. The closing verbal qualifiers in Orozco's autobiographical testimony remind one, parenthetically, of his fresco *The Carnival of the Ideologies,* painted in 1937 and 1938 in the Governor's Palace, Guadalajara.

26. In a letter of October 20, 1929, to his wife, Orozco mentions this same pulquería room: Orozco, *Cartas a Margarita,* 169.

27. Charlot's praise for pulquería painting is unambiguous; "Pulquería Painting," *An Artist on Art,* 118–22.

28. Orozco, *An Autobiography,* 95.

29. Orozco, *Cartas a Margarita,* 151. I wonder if Orozco's surprise is somewhat feigned in light of his derisive remarks, written to Charlot just slightly more than a year earlier, concerning unnamed American painters whose work he viewed in the Metropolitan Museum: "I assure you that the [American painters] are a real tragedy." Orozco, *Artist in New York,* 31–32, January 4, 1928.

30. Reed, *Orozco,* 178.

31. A. F. Wertheim, *The New York Little Renaissance: Iconoclasm, Modernism, and Nationalism in American Culture, 1908–1917* (New York: New York University Press, 1976). The legendary Randolph Bourne, highly respected member of the Seven Arts group, explained that "the celebration of the senses, artistic creativity, and *ancient Greek civilization* became a dominant motif in the Little Renaissance," not to mention the profound impact Friedrich Nietzsche's philosophy had on the era: 6, 10, 245; emphasis is mine.

32. Ibid., 121.

33. Mary Kay Vaughan, *The State, Education, and Social Class in Mexico, 1880–1928* (De Kalb: Northern Illinois University Press, 1982), 239, 241, 249.

34. Passing reference will be made to John Steuart Curry (1897–1946), Boardman Robinson (1876–1952), Henry Varnum Poor (1888–1970), Philip Guston (1913–1980), George Biddle (1885–1973), Ben Shahn (1898–1969), Charles Alston (1907–1977), Marion K. Greenwood (1909–1970), Archibald Motley, Jr. (1891–1981), Edward Arcenio Chávez (1917–1985), Eugenio Quesada (born 1927), and Ione Robinson (1910–?). Robinson's birth and death dates are problematic. She herself acknowledges that "although I have always been told that I was born on October 3, 1910, in Portland, Oregon, I have no birth certificate." Ione Robinson, *A Wall to Paint On* (New York: Dutton, 1946), 3. This writer cannot ascertain if the artist is still living.

35. T. H. Benton, *An Artist in America* (New York: Robert M. McBride & Co., 1937), 41.

36. Ibid. It is interesting to note that John Weichsel goes unacknowledged in Wertheim's study *The New York Little Renaissance.* The invocation of "the people" remains but an "abstraction" to this day, although it's probably used more often than any other expression in the cant of public art. Over the years this writer has been researching the more concrete idea of vox populi in relation to mural art. Of course, Orozco himself speaks of art "intended for the people" (see note 8).

37. Ibid., 247.

38. Wilma Yeo and Helen K. Cook, *Maverick with a Paintbrush: Thomas Hart Benton* (New York: Doubleday and Co., 1977), 64.

39. Orozco, *An Artist in America,* 247.

40. Orozco, *Cartas a Margarita,* 201–202.

41. Ibid., 205.

42. Yeo and Cook, *Maverick with a Paintbrush,* 66.

43. Benton, *An Artist in America,* 247.

44. Erika Doss, *Benton, Pollock, and the Politics of Modernism: From Regionalism to Abstract Expressionism* (Chicago: University of Chicago Press, 1991), 78–79.

45. Ibid., 79.

46. Coorganized with Mabel Dodge Luhan, this pageant was mounted as the strident cultural demonstration in support of the striking Paterson silk workers. "Low salaries, a wage cut, and an increase in the number of looms operated per worker had caused approximately 25,000 textile mill laborers to leave their jobs" in 1913, under the banner of the Industrial Workers of the World. Wertheim, *The New York Little Renaissance,* 52. Reed selected nearly a thousand striking workers and their families "in order to realistically recreate the most dramatic strike episodes." The spectacle attracted almost fifteen thousand spectators to the old Madison Square Garden. The observer-participant Randolph Bourne commented on the emergent social art of pageantry: "Who that saw the Paterson Strike Pageant in 1913 can ever forget that thrilling evening when an entire labor community dramatized its wrongs in one supreme outburst of group-emotion? Crude and rather terrifying, it stamped into one's mind the idea that a new social art was in the American world, something genuinely and excitingly new," ibid., 56; an unpublished manuscript by Bourne, "Pageantry and Social Art," is quoted.

47. Doss, *Benton, Pollock, and the Politics of Modernism,* 79.

48. "As a mentor to Thomas Hart Benton, [Robinson] played a major role in the development of the American mural movement in the

1920s and 1930s." *Boardman Robinson: American Muralist and Illustrator, 1876–1952* (Colorado Springs: Colorado Springs Fine Arts Center, September 21, 1996–January 12, 1997), 3. Robinson's social conscience had been finely honed early in his career when he accompanied John Reed in 1915 through war-torn regions of Eastern Europe. "To Robinson's contemporaries his drawings revealed in a new way the true horrors of war" (7). An article of 1915 appearing in *Vanity Fair* praised the level to which Robinson raised the cartoon. It was said of Robinson, recognized for his Orozcoesque command of the cartoonist's medium, that "a few of his swift lines and a little of his grim, sardonic humor are more deadly than columns of editorials" (5). With respect to his own murals, it proved providential that Robinson had teamed up with Reed. Consider what Alfredo Varela writes in an Argentine edition of *Insurgent Mexico*, Reed's 1914 book about the Mexican Revolution of 1910: "In the end [Reed] is a *mural painter*. The *great fresco* is his specialty, the panoramic picture which reveals history in a thousand details." Renato Leduc, "Preface to the New Edition," John Reed, *Insurgent Mexico* (New York: International Publishers, 1914/1969/1982), 19.

49. Doss, *Benton, Pollock, and the Politics of Modernism*, 81.

50. Ibid., 79.

51. Benton, *Artist in America*, 255.

52. Doss, *Benton, Pollock, and the Politics of Modernism*, 319.

53. Ibid., 321. Painstakingly thorough Pollock biographers Naifeh and Smith acknowledge that there were "ambiguities" in the relation-

ship between Benton and Pollock. Steven Naifeh and Gregory White Smith, *Jackson Pollock: An American Saga* (New York: Clarkson N. Potter, 1989), 342.

54. Ibid., 348. Ellen Landau believes Pollock joined Orozco at dinners hosted by Benton. E.G. Landau, *Jackson Pollock* (New York: Harry N. Abrams, 1989), 48. She also suggests that Pollock's oil on masonite painting *Composition with Ritual Scene* (about 1938–41) might trace its genesis to Orozco's New School frescoes (47–48, 271).

55. Naifeh and Smith, *An American Saga*, 298, 664.

56. Landau, *Jackson Pollock*, 39, 47, 271.

57. Francis Valentine O'Connor and Eugene Victor Thaw, eds., *Jackson Pollock: A Catalogue Raisonné of Paintings, Drawings, and Other Works* (New Haven: Yale University Press, 1978), vol. 4, p. 238.

58. Ibid., vol. 1, p. 8, color plate 1.

59. Francis Valentine O'Connor, ed., "A Note about Murals," *Jackson Pollock: A Catalogue Raisonné of Paintings, Drawings and Other Works* (New York: Pollock-Krasner Foundation, 1995), supplement 1, p. 52. Also, *An American Saga*, 263, 280. Apparently, no photographs exist of the no longer extant mural.

60. That this visit occurred is based on evidence that emerged during the 1980s. Naifeh and Smith, *An American Saga*, 298; Landau, *Jackson Pollock*, 48.

61. Landau, *Jackson Pollock*, 48.

62. Ibid., 48, 52, 272, and O'Connor and Thaw, *Jackson Pollock*, vol. I, pp. 43, 46 (fig. 59).

63. In the 1944 Posada exhibition held at the Art Institute of Chicago,

the catalog attributes *Calavera of Huerta* to this artist. Fernando Gamboa et al., *Posada: Printmaker to the Mexican People* (Chicago: Art Institute of Chicago, 1944), 44, fig. 302, plate XLI, n.p. Thirty-five years later Alan Fern, Ron Tyler, et al. argue that this engraving, known also by the title *La hambrienta calavera* ("The Hungry Skeleton"), is not by the hand of Posada but is "probably the work of another of the artists in the employ of [Antonio] Vanegas Arroyo." The argument is that the print seems to be a caricature of General Victoriano Huerta, who didn't ascend to power ("and therefore become a subject of caricature") until after Posada's death. The art historian Antonio Rodríguez, who published an article about Posada as early as 1943, still maintained in the late 1970s that this print was the work of Posada or an assistant. Ron Tyler, ed., *Posada's Mexico* (Washington, D.C., and Fort Worth, Texas: Library of Congress in cooperation with the Amon Carter Museum of Western Art, 1979), 293.

64. O'Connor and Thaw, *Jackson Pollock*, vol. 4, p. 219.

65. Ibid., vol. 3, pp. 14–15. They date the Hospicio Cabañas project between 1936 and 1940 and explain that Pollock would have seen reproductions of the cycle at Delphic Studios or in the art press. Renato González Mello dates *Man of Fire* in 1938 and 1939: *José Clemente Orozco: La pintura mural mexicana* (Mexico City: Edición en Círculo de Arte, 1997), n.p.

66. Peyton Boswell, Jr., *Varnum Poor* (New York: Hyperion Press/Harper and Brothers, 1941), 61.

67. George Biddle, *An American Artist's Story* (Boston: Little, Brown

and Co. 1939), 268; emphasis is mine. The "living monuments [expressing] the social ideals that [President Roosevelt] struggl[ed] to achieve," alluded to by Biddle, recall what Mexicanist historian Barbara Tenenbaum refers to as murals of stone. These latter sculpted public monuments were sponsored in the late nineteenth through the early twentieth centuries in Mexico City by Vicente Riva Palacio, leader of the so-called nationalist mythologizers. B.A. Tenenbaum, "Streetwise History: The Paseo de la Reforma and the Porfirian State, 1876–1910," in Beezley et al., *Rituals of Rule*, 127–50.

68. Mark Rosenthal, ed., *Philip Guston: retrospectiva de pintura* (Madrid: Julio Soto Impresor, S.A., 1989), 166. Guston's comments are drawn from an article, "Faith, Hope and Impossibility," published in *Artnews Annual*, vol. 31 (1966), and quoted by Carrie Rickey in his essay "Twilight's Last Dreaming: Philip Guston 1969–1980," contributed to this catalog published on the occasion of Guston's 1989 exhibition held at two Spanish venues.

69. R. Linsley, "Utopia Will Not Be Televised: Rivera at Rockefeller Center," in *Oxford Art Journal*, vol. 17, no. 2 (1994), 60. Thanks to Renato González Mello for referring me to this important article.

70. Biddle, *An American Artist's Story*, 269.

71. Amy Helene Kirschke, *Aaron Douglas: Art, Race, and the Harlem Renaissance* (Jackson: University Press of Mississippi, 1995), 125.

72. Ibid.

73. This series was based on Eugene O'Neill's controversial play *The Emperor Jones*, which opened in

1924 in London with Paul Robeson in the title role of Brutus Jones. Mary Schmidt Campbell et al., *Harlem Renaissance Art of Black America* (New York: Studio Museum in Harlem and Abradale Press/Harry N. Abrams, 1987–94), 57, 59, 170, 192.

74. Of course, Auguste Rodin's *Prodigal Son* and Michelangelo's heroic painted and sculpted struggling figures are other likely influences.

75. The allegorical subjects depicted included Apollo, Diana, Philosophy, Drama, Music, Poetry, and Science. Kirschke, *Aaron Douglas,* 109.

76. Ibid., 36–37.

77. Orozco, *An Autobiography,* 58. Orozco and Rivera also visited Harlem on different occasions to discuss their artistic ideas and to win support for black artists. Romare Beardon, *A History of African-American Artists: From 1792 to the Present* (New York: Pantheon, 1993), 236.

78. "Albert Murray: An Interview with Hale Woodruff," *Hale Woodruff: 50 Years of His Art* (New York: Studio Museum in Harlem, 1979), 80. Woodruff's penchant for Mexican travel was shared by many of his compatriots. The art historian Lizzetta LeFalle-Collins explains that "as African-American artists shaped their own group identification, they recognized a shared outlook in the work of the Mexican muralists. What was most engaging was the way the Mexican muralists successfully combined a reverence for the traditional folk cultures of Mexico and *a persistent demand for social and political justice for the oppressed.*" "Redefining the African-American Self," in Lizzetta LeFalle-Collins and Shifra M. Goldman, *In the Spirit of Resistance: African-American Modernists and the Mexican Muralist School* (New York: American Federation of the Arts, 1996), 26; emphasis is mine.

79. Ibid., 81.

80. The mutiny was led by the tribal chief Cinqué, whose intent it was to have the ship return to Mendi, the West African homeland of the captives. In retaliation, the two seamen spared during the mutiny steered *Amistad* toward Long Island, New York, where it was captured by an American ship, the *Washington.* The mutinous slaves were imprisoned and charged with piracy, and simultaneously, the Spanish government requested their return. The slaves' plight was widely publicized and attracted the support, financial and otherwise, of abolitionists, black church groups, and self-improvement societies. The Mendians were freed by the Supreme Court pursuant to an eighteen-month period of litigation. John Quincy Adams, who became senior counsel toward the end of the case, is largely credited with the acquittal. During the late 1990s the nineteenth-century events surrounding *Amistad* once again came before the public eye, this time popularized through the medium of film.

81. Elsa Honig Fine, *The Afro-American Artist: A Search for Identity* (New York: Holt, Rinehart and Winston, 1973), 103, 124–26.

82. David Elliott, ed., *¡Orozco! 1883–1949* (Oxford: Museum of Modern Art, Oxford, 1980), 76. Elliott and contributor Desmond Rochfort refer to *Luchas por la libertad,* which title this writer takes from *Orozco: forma e idea,* fig. 51, as *The Masses.*

83. Edmund Barry Gaither, citing Winifred Stoelting, Mary Schmidt Campbell, and Gylbert Coker, *Hale Woodruff: 50 Years of His Art,* in his essay "The Mural Tradition," in *A Shared Heritage: Art by Four African Americans,* ed. William E. Taylor and Harriet G. Warkel (Indianapolis: Indianapolis Museum of Art in cooperation with Indiana University Press, 1996).

84. Anthony W. Lee, *Painting on the Left: Diego Rivera, Radical Politics, and San Francisco's Public Murals* (Berkeley: University of California Press, 1999), 95.

85. Ibid., 175–77.

86. Ibid., 181.

87. Ibid., 222.

88. Ibid., 136, 220.

89. Ibid., 222.

90. Robinson, *A Wall to Paint On,* 252–53.

91. Lincoln Rothschild, "The American Artists' Congress," in *Art for the Millions: Essays from the 1930s by Artists and Administrators of the WPA Federal Art Project,* edited and with an introduction by Francis V. O'Connor (Greenwich, Conn.: New York Graphic Society Ltd., 1973), 251. Rothschild was very active in the American Artists' Congress. A rendering by the artist Peppino Mangravite emphasizing the stage area on the occasion of the congress identifies nine other dignitaries, most of them artists, in Orozco and Douglas's Company: Heywood Broun, George Biddle, Stuart Davis, Julia Codesido of Peru, Lewis Mumford, Margaret Bourke-White, Rockwell Kent, Paul Manship, and Peter Blume. *Artists against War and Fascism: Papers of the First American Artists' Congress,* intro. Matthew Baigell and Julia Williams (New Brunswick, N.J.: Rutgers University Press, 1986), 222–23.

92. J.C. Orozco, "General Report of the Mexican Delegation to the American Artists' Congress," one of the "Reports and Resolutions of Delegates and [the] Permanent Organization" (fourth closed session, New School for Social Research, Peter Blume, chairman), *Artists against War,* 54, 203.

93. Ibid., 204.

94. Ibid., 207.

95. Ibid., 129.

96. Ibid., 129–30.

97. Ibid.

98. The intriguing possibility that Wilson's work in turn might have influenced Orozco suggests itself in the latter's 1940 commission for New York's Museum of Modern Art. MoMA's *Dive Bomber and Tank* shares a number of Wilson's icons, particularly the prominent and decoratively rendered chain links and masks.

99. Fred J. Ringel, "Gilbert Wilson: Mural Painter," *Scribner's Magazine* (May 1937), 47.

100. Ibid.

101. Ibid., 50.

102. H. Cahill, Foreword, in O'Connor, *Art for the Millions,* 41.

103. M. Siporin, "Mural Art and the Midwestern Myth," in *Art for the Millions,* 64. Whether the notion of a *"native* epic in fresco" is Siporin's own idea or one he borrowed from Wilson may be largely moot, but in art historical terms, we are obliged to attribute to each his own. Although two drafts of Siporin's manuscript "Mural Art and the Midwestern Myth" are documented by Francis V. O'Connor, he found no evidence that Siporin dated the pieces. We do, however, know that a version of the six-page paper was included in the dummy of *Art for the Millions*

363

prepared about 1939. Since Wilson's Mexican observations date from the summer of 1934, there's a chance his perceptions predate Siporin's. "Appendix B," *Art for the Millions,* 296, 301.

104. Ibid.

105. Judith Hansen O'Toole, director of the Sordoni Art Gallery (Wilkes University, Wilkes Barre, Penn.), citing Dorothy C. Miller, ed., *American 1942: Artists from Nine States* (New York: Museum of Modern Art, 1942) in *Mitchell Siporin: The Early Years, 1930–1950* (New York: Babcock Galleries, 1990), n.p.; text accompanying fig. 6.

106. Ellen Harkins Wheat, *Jacob Lawrence: The "Frederick Douglass" and "Harriet Tubman" Series of 1938–40* (Hampton, Va., and Seattle: Hampton University Museum in association with the University of Washington Press, 1991), 15–16.

107. E. McCausland, "Jacob Lawrence," *Magazine of Art,* vol. 38 (November 1945), 254.

108. Wheat, *Jacob Lawrence: American Painter,* with a contribution by Patricia Hills (Seattle: University of Washington Press in association with the Seattle Art Museum, 1986), 61.

109. Ibid., 105.

110. Aline B. Saarinen, *Jacob Lawrence* (New York: American Federation of Arts, 1960), 19.

111. Wheat, *Jacob Lawrence: The "Frederick Douglass,"* 16.

112. Wheat, *Jacob Lawrence: American Painter,* 151.

113. Ibid.

114. "A Guide to the Public Art Collection of the Harold Washington Library Center" (Chicago: Chicago Public Library, May 1995), n.p.

Sincere thanks to Elizabeth Kelley, public art curator with the Public Art Program of Chicago's Department of Cultural Affairs, for her gracious help in obtaining photographs of the mural and background information about it.

115. R. J. Powell, *Jacob Lawrence* (New York: Rizzoli International Publications, 1992), fig. 4, unpaginated.

116. On January 12, 2000, I wrote Francine Seders, Lawrence's dealer, posing a question she was to ask the artist: "Was Jacob Lawrence thinking about Orozco's celebrated fresco, *Prometheus* (painted in 1930 at Pomona College, not far from Los Angeles), when he created his mosaic tribute, *Events in the Life of Harold Washington,* in 1991 in Chicago's Harold Washington Library Center?" The letter continued: "I ask this question based not only on the documented fact of 'influence,' but, more significantly, because Lawrence's mosaic mural resonates with some of the same formal/compositional elements I perceive present in the *Prometheus.* Symbolically, one might easily argue that Harold Washington—whom I had the pleasure and privilege of knowing—was himself a Titan whose keen sense of justice for his fellow beings played a Promethean-like role in his life and progressive politics." A week later, January 19, I received an e-mail from Alison Stamey, an associate of Ms. Seders's: "Thank you for your fax dated January 12. Yesterday we had the chance to ask Mr. Lawrence your question. He answered 'no.' He was only thinking of Harold Washington. He also said he was not familiar with Orozco's *Prometheus.*

While I'm incredulous concerning Lawrence's unfamiliarity with such a celebrated work by the muralist he so admired, I attribute the unexpected response either to the artist's failing memory, his unwillingness to reveal direct sources, his deliberate subterfuge—something not uncommon among visual artists—or, quite possibly, although I'm dubious, his unabashed candor in admitting what he simply didn't know."

117. Wheat, *Jacob Lawrence: American Painter,* 41.

118. Benjamin Horowitz, "Images of Dignity: The Drawings of Charles White," *Charles White Drawings* (Nashville: Art Gallery, Ballentine Hall, Fisk University [a collaborative project of the art departments of Howard University, Morgan State College, and Fisk University], about 1967), unpaginated. Horowitz was White's dealer at the Heritage Gallery, Los Angeles.

119. Ibid.

120. Peter Clothier, "Charles White: A Critical Perspective," in the exhibition catalog *Images of Dignity: A Retrospective of the Works of Charles White* (New York: Studio Museum in Harlem, 1982), 18.

121. Ibid.

122. Ibid.

123. Richard J. Powell and Jock Reynolds, *To Conserve a Legacy: American Art from Historically Black Colleges and Universities,* intro. Kinshasha Holman (Conwill, Mass., and New York: Addison Gallery of American Art, a department of Phillips Academy, and the Studio Museum in Harlem, 1999), 45.

124. Orozco's comments in this vein appeared originally in English in the context of his brief essay "New World, New Races and New Art": "The highest, the most logical, the purest and strongest form of painting is the mural. It is, too, the most disinterested form, for it cannot be made a matter of private gain; it cannot be hidden away for the benefit of a certain privileged few. It is for the people. It is for all." Reproduced in *Textos de Orozco,* with a study and appendix by Justino Fernández (Mexico City: Imprenta Universitaria, 1955), 42–43.

125. *To Conserve a Legacy,* 235. Scott Allan's entry on the mural cites Lizetta LeFalle-Collins, "Contribution of the American Negro to Democracy: A History Painting by Charles White," *International Review of African-American Art,* vol. 12, no. 4 (1995), 51.

126. E. B. Gaither, "Introduction," *The Work of Charles White: An American Experience,* catalog for the exhibition organized by the High Museum of Art, Atlanta, Georgia, 1976, p. 7.

127. Mary Takach, "The Shape of Humanistic Content," *The Mural Art of Ben Shahn: Original Cartoons, Drawings, Prints and Dated Paintings* (Syracuse: Joe and Emily Lowe Art Gallery, College of Visual and Performing Arts, Syracuse University, 1977), n.p.

128. Matthew Baigell, *The American Scene: American Painting of the 1930's* (New York: Prager, 1974), 176.

129. Refer to this author's essay "Telling Images Bracket the 'Broken-Promise(d) Land': The Culture of Immigration and the Immigration of Culture across Borders," in *Culture across Borders: Mexican Immigration and Popular Culture,* ed. David R.

364

Maciel and María Herrera-Sobek (Tucson: University of Arizona Press, 1998), 103–105. Foregrounding the activist perspective of Chicana(o) artists on the multivalent issue of immigration across the Mexico-U.S. border, I also address the larger background topic of U.S. immigration history itself. Against that expansive context, Shahn emerges as one among a relatively small number of visual artists whose work addresses xenophobia explicitly and, in Orozcoesque fashion, underscores the need for justice to prevail. Like Orozco, Shahn affords Chicana(o) artists a remarkably rich source of inspiration for their own indignation against social injustice. Interestingly, as a footnote to a footnote, Alma Reed recalls a memorable occasion when she and Orozco watched a public parade commemorating the unjust executions of Sacco and Vanzetti. Noting his sadness, she points out how sympathetic Orozco remained, believing fervently in the anarchists' innocence. *Orozco,* 151.

130. *The Mural Art of Ben Shahn,* n.p. The prisoners' favorable reaction underlines the vitally important issue of viewer response to murals, including even potential viewers who are incarcerated. How different passersby appreciated his efforts as a mural painter, something Shahn enjoyed precisely because "more people see them [murals] than they do easel pictures," is engagingly conveyed in an interview the artist did for the April 1944 issue of the *Magazine of Art,* excerpted in *Ben Shahn,* ed. John D. Morse (New York: Praeger, 1972), 62–63. Without relying explicitly on what have become public art's tired, oftentimes vacuous

catchphrases, Shahn does address the concept of "art for the people," or "people's art." Implicit in his comments is a "democratic" sense of public art, its raison d'être, after all.

131. Jacinto Quirarte, *Mexican American Artists* (Austin: University of Texas Press, 1973), 59.

132. Ibid., 75 and 78.

133. Dore Ashton, *A Critical Study of Philip Guston* (Berkeley: University of California Press, 1990), 31.

134. Since the 1970s the extensive geographic reach of the contemporary mural movement has been well documented in several sources. Among these, I refer readers to the following: Eva and James Cockcroft, with John Weber, *Toward a People's Art: The Contemporary Mural Movement,* foreword by Jean Charlot (New York: Dutton, 1977); A.W. Barnett, *Community Murals: The People's Art* (Philadelphia and New York: Art Alliance Press and Cornwall Books [Associated University Presses], 1984); Melba Levick and Stanley Young, *The Big Picture: Murals of Los Angeles* (Boston: Little, Brown and Co. [New York Graphic Society Book], 1988); Robin J. Dunitz, *Street Gallery: Guide to over 1000 Los Angeles Murals* (Los Angeles: Mural Conservancy of Los Angeles, rev. 2d ed., 1998); and R.J. Dunitz and James Prigoff, *Walls of Heritage, Walls of Pride: African American Murals,* foreword Edmund Barry Gaither, essays by Floyd Coleman and Michael Harris (Los Angeles: Pomegranate Communications, 2000).

135. "The Artists' Statement," typescript, 1971, 1. The museum exhibition/demonstration of in-

progress portable murals recalls that occasion, some thirty years earlier, when Orozco's six-panel fresco *Dive Bomber and Tank* was executed and shown at New York City's MoMA.

136. Ibid.

137. See note 46.

138. V.A. Sorell, ed., *Guide to Chicago Murals: Yesterday and Today* (Chicago: Chicago Council on Fine Arts, 1979), 40–41.

139. "The Artists' Statement," 2.

140. Ibid., 9.

141. Ibid., 3.

142. Ibid., 5.

143. Ibid., 11 and 12.

144. Ibid., 15.

145. See note 69.

146. It is interesting from a comparative standpoint to acknowledge the fact that both Orozco's *Catharsis* composition and Rivera's *Man at the Crossroads,* a smaller version of 1934, appear side by side in the National Palace of Fine Arts in Mexico City.

147. The author has known Marcos Raya some twenty-five years, during which time we have engaged many times in informal and formal interview exchanges.

148. The multivalent and highly evocative nature of the Statue of Liberty motif in the works of Mexicano and Chicana(o) artists is addressed at some length in my essay "Telling Images Bracket the Broken-Promise(d) Land."

149. Gutiérrez and Fabre, *Feasts and Celebrations,* 3.

150. Desmond Rochfort, *Mexican Muralists: Orozco, Rivera, Siqueiros* (San Francisco: Chronicle Books, 1993), 150–51.

151. Interview with the artist, August 7, 2000.

152. Carlos Almaraz, "The Artist as a Revolutionary," *Chismearte* (Fall 1976), 47.

153. Barnett, *Community Murals: The People's Art,* 181.

154. In Charlot's company, Orozco encountered and "remained fascinated by the electric sign that belted Manhattan's Times Square building with a running review of the news" (Foreword, *The Artist in New York,* 21). In this context, it is revealing to quote from the preface Orozco contributed to Gardner Hale's 1933 book *Fresco Painting:* "Because the crowd demands it, art has again come out to the crowd. Again, fresco assumes its historic role in this contact. And what medium more appropriate than fresco to speak to the crowd? In modern times, *the printed picture of the newspaper and of the book has served efficiently, but the large public fresco is equally efficient.*" Orozco's original text, written in English, is reproduced in his *Textos de Orozco,* 47; emphasis is mine.

155. Paul Von Blum, *Other Visions, Other Voices: Women Political Artists in Greater Los Angeles* (Lanham, Md.: University Press of America, 1994), 89–90. When Carrasco unveiled her work, UFW leader César Chávez was also in New York to promote his campaign against the use of pesticides in the fields. A press conference featured the Chicano labor leader accompanied by Mayor David Dinkins and the UFW flag raised over City Hall: Max Benavides, "Chávez's Legacy: He Nurtured Seeds of Art," *The Fight in the Fields: César Chávez and the Farmworkers' Movement,* compiled by Susan Ferriss and Ricardo Sandoval and edited by Diana Hembree, with

365

a foreword by Gary Soto, the companion to the PBS documentary by the same title by Rick-Tejada Florés and Ray Telles (New York: Harcourt, Brace and Co., 1997), 259. This writer was one of seven project advisers to the documentary.

156. D. J. Martínez, *The Things You See When You Don't Have a Grenade! Writings by David Levi Strauss et al.* (Santa Monica: Smart Art Press, 1996), 101.

157. Ibid. Of related interest is the work of "money artist" J. S. G. Boggs, whose drawings of actual currency beg the issues of "value" and "real money" and often put him at odds with treasury police around the globe. Refer to Lawrence Weschler, *Boggs: A Comedy of Values* (Chicago: University of Chicago Press, 1999).

Anthology of Critical Reception

(Alicia Azuela, Renato González Mello, and James Oles)

1. "[Mid-January 1928]: Poco después, en Greenwich Village, se produjeron mínimos terremotos; propagose una verdadera chair de poule que hizo esponjarse de horror a varios gallos Plymouth de plumaje standard y cacarear despavoridas a otras aves de pluma-fuente.... Era que Orozco había intentado algunas caricaturas sociales que dejaban a las víctimas, en carne, hueso y sangre, untadas sobre el papel y como laminadas por una aplanadora: era que Orozco había dramatizado lo ridículo, pero con impactos tales que junto a esas caricaturas las más crueles de Covarrubias—que aquí pasa por terrible—semejaban

aleluyas o felicitaciones de Año Nuevo...."

2. "En cuanto a la exposición del 'Art Center' ha sido un completo fracaso.... La gente, muy poca, que visitó la exhibición, sólo decía: 'I am disappointed,' porque se dijo que esto iba a ser una gran exhibición de pintura mexicana, representativa del país y patrocinada por el Gobierno Mexicano y lo único que se veía eran los cuadros de Pacheco, de Ruiz, y de toda la gran cantidad de aficionados o amateurs que figuran como 'grandes artistas.' Los comentarios que se oían en el salón eran para sonrojar y la gente se reía y soltaba la carcajada. Además había muchos monitos de cera de Hidalgo y Pulgas vestidas."

3. "Le gustaba mucho leer la revista The New Yorker porque siempre encontraba artículos interesantes.... Gozaba verdaderamente con sus caricaturas, generalmente de crítica social, eran agudas, sarcásticas además de graciosas. También le divertían algunas tiras cómicas de los periódicos, decía que los norteamericanos eran muy buenos para este trabajo."

4. "Podemos aventurarnos a decir que este artista también se encuentra en camino descendente. El medio ambiente norteamericano lo ha contagiado, y, aunque sus concepciones siguen siendo dramáticas, la tendencia a debilitarse es evidente. El fresco del Palacio de Bellas Artes carece de la magnífica factura que caracteriza sus primeros frescos; tiene algo de ilustración del 'Saturday Evening Post,' hecha rápidamente como un croquis a gran escala, que le resta seriedad. Si se observan sus pinturas de Dartmouth College, se

verá que allí la técnica es aún más teatral; su 'Cristo destruye la Cruz' no consigue impresionarnos, a pesar de estar en carne viva; y Hernán Cortés, si bien tiene el interés de recordar a Don Quijote, es una figura irreal y acartonada, que no parece haber podido moverse alguna vez en la vida. Ojalá que nos equivoquemos y que podamos ver siquiera una obra más de este artista, que se encuentre a la altura de sus primeras producciones...."

5. "Yo propongo que en Diego Rivera no es la pugnacidad lo característico; no es cuando blande espada, cuando quiere arremeter, cuando agrede, que Diego es grande, sino cuando hace obra de escudo. Al contrario es Clemente Orozco: éste sí que es la categoría de agresión absoluta. No es cuestión de cuál de los dos sea mejor, tenga mayores méritos: No cabe comparación entre yno y otro sino cuando cualquiera de ellos asume actitud que al otro le es característica. Diego es homérico; su obra es escudo de Aquiles. Orozco es todo espada, todo cosa cortante, todo mano que aplasta, látigo que levanta verdugones. Cuando diego quiere ser espada, es inferior a Orozco; cuando Orozco quiere ser escudo, es inferior a Diego; cuando cada uno es fiel a sí mismo, cada uno resulta insuperable."

6. "Y mientras Clemente Orozco, silenciosa, religiosamente hace la glorificación de la familia proletaria, Diego Rivera se abre paso a golpes de pincel y de oratoria."

7. "Pero no hay ocasión que se presente que no aproveche yo. En febrero o marzo se publica un artículo sobre Clemente Orozco, tan extenso o más que el de Diego Rivera que hoy le acompaño, irá ilustrado,

cosa excepcional, con tres o cuatro tricromías y muchas mas ilustraciones a blanco y negro...."

8. "Una amiga de San Francisco me envía un grabado del Examiner con una nota referente al rajón [Diego Rivera] y créame que no sé si soltar la carcajada o mandarle al pobre Rajón mi más sentido pésame en esquela de luto y cruz con corona sobre una tumba fría. En el grabado se ve una enorme barriga trepada en una escalera, en la mano un carboncillo y en la pared...¡papel manila! Está haciendo ¡al tamaño! Un boceto. El asunto: ¡FORTYNINERS! La estética, o mejor dicho anti-recontrarestética: Prerrafaelismo inglés, del más débil, sweet y afeminado! O en otras palabras, la pobre panza se ha influenciado overnight! Del peor academismo americano, del que llena por millas cuadradas los State Capitols, bancos y demás rascacielos y que a la fecha lo hacen ya solamente las girls pintoras!...La nota dice que va a pintar a la prosperidad o fecundidad de California como una señora con paños greco-romanos, nariz griega, altos pechos, caderas y demás, con frutos y demás atributos ¡ni en la Academia!"

9. "Los académicos siguen atacándonos a los pintores murales mexicanos, el otro día, por radio, nos pusieron verdes a Rivera y a mí y hablaron horrores de Dartmouth. Packard me escribió diciéndome que también ellos se preparan para la defensa."

10. "Rivera estalló contra los comerciantes de arte que fabrican historias para su provecho y sensacionismo: 'Los mercaderes, o explotadores del arte de los artistas se aprovechan o inventan diferencias

366

entre ellos, para atraer la atención del público y para ganar ventas. Eso es por lo que muchas veces se han imaginado y aún publicado en los periódicos cuentos acerca de…rivalidades que nunca existieron entre nosotros.'

"Orozco aprobó con un movimiento de cabeza y agregó:

"'Naturalmente tenemos muchas diferencias de opinión acerca de nuestra profesión, pero en nuestra vida privada, la armonía de nuestra amistad se puede rastrear muchos años atrás.'"

11. "Puedes reproducir en tu libro cualquier tontería que haya yo escrito…no pongas nada que sea contra los compañeros del oficio."

12. "El viernes en la noche fue la reunión en casa de Alma Reed…. Se trataba de que un señor recitó unos versos muy largos y después me llamó, me sentó en la mitado de la sala y me recitó unos versos que escribió expresamente para mí poniéndome por las nubes. Cosa muy ridícula pero que esta gente toma muy en serio."

13. "Los 'Delphic Studios,' la galería pictórica a la vera de la Quinta Avenida, es, a pesar de su nombre griego, un emporio de arte mexicano. ¡Seamos el agüero propicio! Y es que Alma Reed, la musa que allí preside, fue maya antes de ser ática, y aún pretende que tal evolución, de la Hélade Marmórea al Mayab tropical, no ha dejado de ser armoniosa…."

14. "Un aludo de periódicos, magazines, panfletos, cartas, todo vibrante de consagrador entusiasmo, se desborda sobre mi mesa de trabajo y en medio de ese río

caudaloso, emerge y culmina como una egregia roca un nombre: 'México,' y sobre esa peña, como un brote de laureles, otro nombre: José Clemente Orozco….(1) '¡México, México, México!,' clama el sonoro río, la prensa vocinglera y unánime; 'México,' repite el eco grave y profundo de los magazines especialistas y los órganos universitarios y el cordial murmullo de las cartas íntimas…en fin, en su más vasto aspecto el triunfo de Orozco es el triunfo de México."

15. "Ya ves que de Alma no se puede esperar nada…."

16. "—¿Cuándo comenzó dándose a conocer?

"—Bueno, aquí en México nunca se hace uno conocer. Nadie lo conoce a uno."

17. "En México…aprendemos a trabajar bajo todas las condiciones: a veces detrás de las barricadas o sobre muros, evadiendo los proyectiles."

18. "Formado aquí mismo, como sin relación con el tiempo presente, para estar simplemente en el Tiempo, por serlo tan presente, porque en Orozco no sólo está la Revolución mexicana, sino la tragedia mexicana. Sabía lo que ignoraba, parecía nada ignorar sin haberlo sabido nunca."

19. "Yo no tomé parte alguna en la revolución, nunca me pasó nada malo y no corrí peligro de ninguna especie….Por esto me resultaban muy cómicos los numerosos artículos que aparecieron en los periódicos americanos acerca de mis hazañas guerreras…. Hubo varios que me hicieron aparecer como uno de los abanderados de la causa indígena y hacían un retrato de mi persona en el cual podía reconocerse a un tarahumara. Yo jamás me preocupé

por la causa indígena, ni arrojé bombas, ni me fusilaron tres veces, como aseguraba otro diario."

20. "El privilegio del horror pertenece, a partir de un siglo, a la estampería popular."

21. "La moda arqueológica de hace siete años fue sustituida por otra semejante y que es la que impera en la actualidad. Consiste en atribuirle o hacer creer que se le atribuye al indígena puro, hoy en plena degeneración y en vías de desaparecer, las preciosidades de las artes menores populares que son producto natural del criollo y del mestizo del campo e imponerle al criollo y al mestizo de las ciudades una estética que no siente ni puede suplantar ahogando e ignorando sus propias facultades estéticas."

22. "Apareció la idea 'democrática,' una especie de cristianismo artístico bastante raro y un principio de nacionalismo. También los discípulos eran muy diferentes. En vez del estudiante de arte llegaron toda clase de gentes, desde escolares y boleros hasta empleados, señoritas, obreros y campesinos, lo mismo chicos que grandes. No había preparación ninguna. De buenas a primeras se les ponían en las manos colores, telas y pinceles y se les pedía que pintaran como quisieran lo que tenían enfrente….¡Bienaventurados los ignorantes y los imbéciles, pues de ellos es la gloria suprema del arte! ¡Bienaventurados los idiotas y los cretinos, porque de su mano saldrán las obras maestras de la pintura!"

23. "Dime una cosa: ¿Conoció Rouault cosas mexicanas, como por ejemplo los santos de los templos, el Cristo azotado de semana santa,

estampería popular o pintura de pulquería?"

24. "Me siento con ganas de no dejar títere con cabeza y de propagar lo más posible nuestra ya famosa pintura de pulquería, la mejor del mundo."

25. "Qué más quiere Ud?… Pues que ahora voy a México a ver si me distraigo y aprendo entre Uds., sobre todo de Ud. ¡querido amigo! y mi mexicanísimo, mexicanizante y mexicanizador gran amigo Orozco a quien también quiero tanto."

26. "El secreto de la Esfinge no es un secreto para cualquier mexicano que ha mirado las viejas esculturas de su país, y cada campesino, cada obrero lo ha hecho; es un secreto dicho por hombres que presentan las cosas no como parecen, sino como son. Por eso, Juanita y Miguelito no comprenden la falsificación del arte cuando se importa de Europa o de Estados Unidos. ¡Ay de nosotros cuando a veces es llamado 'arte gringo'!…Y un mexicano no dirá nunca 'arte gringo' delante de ciertos de nuestros productos, quizás porque hemos olvidado ponerles una etiqueta. 'Mira lo que he comprado hoy,' dice don D. sacando un revólver de 45, y ofreciéndolo para la inspección de su joven esposa. '¡Oh, qué bonito!' fue la respuesta llena de deleite. Y no salió tan espontáneamente de aquella encantadora señora a causa de la habilidad para 'negocios' del bárbaro instrumento; era a causa de las superficies limpias y lógicas, de las líneas fuertes y elegantes, de la calidad verdaderamente arquitectónica de la cosa. Si el hombre en Connecticut quye lo hizo hubiera puesto alguna decoración estética, como su vecino pone dibujos pseudo-

griegos de acantus en pintura dorada sobre la rueda de su máquina de coser, la lógica de la cosa se hubiera echado a perder, y el revólver hubiera disgustado a la señora. En su belleza natural, parecía a su mente un atributo apropiado para un hombre; cabal como un pedacito de encaje convenía para ella misma."

27. "Es el pintor americano por excelencia."

28. "'Esto vale mil veces más que toda la obra junta de tus famosos Rodin (que a él le gustaba mucho). En esto llegó el tren, tuvimos que treparnos rápidamente, pero ya sentados, José Clemente Orozco volvió a la carga: 'Provinciano idiota. Provinciano idiota....' A lo cual yo contestaba con el mismo ritmo: vale mil veces, millones de veces más que tu cochino Rodin.' Los norteamericanos, pasajeros como nosotros en el mismo carro, sin comprender lo que decíamos, observaban asombrados nuestra pelea a gritos."

29. "El arte de San Francisco era ciento por ciento académico. Ni a Nueva York llegaba todavía el arte moderno de la Escuela de París, conocido únicamente por una pequeña minoría selecta."

30. "Fueron a la Galería los dueños de una galería en Berlín y se admiraron de que yo no fuera conocido en Alemania."

31. "[Orozco] lamentó el hecho de que la ciencia moderna no hubiera contribuido en nada a la pintura. Señaló que el pintor usa todavía los mismos métodos y materiales tradicionales y, lo que es peor, en una forma más bien atrasada que mejorada."

32. "Ni en la representación de leyendas ni en los temas de actualidad que incluye en sus murales, existe una tradición formal como compromiso. Más bien se trata de captar mediante las formas, temas muy profundamente vividos y sentidos, que impactan por la situación inmediata...."

33. "Tuve muy mala suerte. El folleto que usted conoce, que publicaron los del Colegio, lo hicieron como les dio la gana, poniendo los nombres que inventaron ellos 'para no comprometerse' y hasta lo que hay ahí con mi nombre fue una mala jugada, pues era sólo una 'explicación' para estudiantes necios que querían 'explicaciones' para un periodiquito que publican ellos, pero no para el folleto. Total, una tanteada que sólo sirvió para explotarme, vendiendo el tal folleto a millares y mal representándome."

34. "La pintura no se explica. Aborrezco las facilidades de la complicación. comentaristas como Pater, Ruskin, Fromentin, plantean un problema y proporcionan un gozo similar al de la obra de arte."

35. "Ya has visto que la pintura es cosa esencialmente objetiva, es decir, que no es hablada, sino hecha realmente con los objetos o materiales directamente."

36. "La fuerza sugestiva del rojo es, sin embargo, sobrepasada por la potencia dramática del negro y del blanco. Desde el último cuarto de siglo esta potencia ha tomado en el cinema toda su significación y ha sido llevada por él a su paroxismo, aliando el patético silencio en esta suerte de fatalidad matemática, nacida de la regulación del ritmo mecánico.

"Por una parte, el rojo implica para nosotros el fuego y la sangre; y de la otra, el blanco y el negro forman la transcripción del duelo.

"La obra punzante extraída por Orozco de la revolución mexicana, es paralela en su procedimiento a la de los iluminadores que tienen por fin golpear la imaginación simplista de los elementales y de conmover la propensión al sadismo en las colectividades, reconstituyendo la angustia y el espanto con una prodigiosa intensidad.

"Nada de rojo. Nada de sangre. Nada más que negro y un poco de gris sobre el papel blanco y al mismo tiempo el terror en su realidad primera; el terror vuelto más siniestro a causa del empleo fúnebre de ese gris, de ese blanco, de ese negro."

37. "Las formas —físicas y psicológicas— que el pintor ha registrado tienen la precisió de lo primitivo, es decir, del arte en tal estado de intensidad que cuando divide y recombina sus elementos, va ganando siempre en riqueza. Este aspecto del arte del Sr. Orozco es más evidente en la definición casi geométrica de su dibujo que en su color."

38. "Por otro lado, los frescos de Miguel ángel, declaraba, parecerían enteramente fuera de lugar en un marco moderno. Creía que muchas pinturas de Miguel Àngel carecían de solidez. Con su característico olfato para la analogía gráfica y frecuentemente exagerada, recalcaba que había muchos lugares en el cielo de la Sixtina que estallarían si se introdujera un alfiler en sus volúmenes inflados, inflados."

39. "Prefiero la creación mayestática en que concretó pasiones con impulso sabiamente gobernado, al desenfreno de expresionismo barroco de algunos murales o fragmentos de murales. Dominando las pasiones y no éstas arrastrándolo a él. El contraste de estas dos tónicas suele hallarse en el mismo mural: fragmentos severos que se destacan entre la tormenta que no quiso o no pudo domeñar. La frecuencia de tal tensión, martilleo sobre el yunque, forja sus más austeras formas."

40. "Orozco tiene en su carrera dos tendencias. Una destructiva, en la que convertido en un dios de las venganzas, tratando de purificar el mundo que le rodea es él mismo quien se purifica, comprendiendo que el Arte está para servir a los anhelos más grandiosos y no para tomarse como un látigo o una ametralladora. La otra, opuesta, en la que, sintetizando los valores de la historia, que son todavía, ejes en los que gira la actividad presente, encuentra las formas superiores de expresión y dice en ellas su nueva palabra."

41. "Pienso que, si se buscaran el lugar y la época cuya expresión podría considerarse más justamente, habría que señalar la Italia del Cuatrocientos; allí viviría con menos artificialidad el orgullo de su granito, junto a otros irreductibles y solitarios escollos del tiempo."

Opposite: see caption for fig. 133, p. 118.

368

Selected Exhibitions of Orozco's Work in the United States, 1926–40

NEW YORK, WHITNEY STUDIO CLUB, 1926. *Exhibition: Paintings, Drawings & Caricatures,* from March 13, 1926

NEW YORK, ART CENTER, 1928. *Mexican Art,* January 19–February 14, 1928

NEW YORK, ASHRAM, 1928. September 1928

NEW YORK, GALLERY OF MARIE STERNER, 1928. *Ink and Pencil Drawings from a Series "Mexico in Revolution" by José Clemente Orozco,* October 10–22, 1928

PHILADELPHIA, 1929. New Students' League, Little Gallery, February 13–27, 1929

NEW YORK, DOWNTOWN GALLERY, 1929. *New York by José Clemente Orozco,* March 26–April 14, 1929

NEW YORK, ART STUDENTS' LEAGUE, 1929. *Paintings & Drawings by José Clemente Orozco,* April 15–30, 1929

CHICAGO, 1929. Chicago Arts Club, *Drawings and Paintings by José Clemente Orozco,* June 15–29, 1929

CHICAGO, 1929–30. Art Institute of Chicago, December 1929–January 1930

NEW YORK, DELPHIC STUDIOS, 1930. *Exhibition of Recent Paintings by José Clemente Orozco,* February 3–25, 1930

DETROIT, 1930. Detroit Institute of Arts, March, 1930

BOSTON, 1930. Grace Horne Galleries, April 20–May 8, 1930

SAN FRANCISCO, 1930. Courvoisier Galleries, June 1930

DENVER, 1930. Denver Art Museum, September 1930

LOS ANGELES, 1930. Los Angeles Museum, Exposition Park, *Lithographs by José Clemente Orozco,* October 1930

NEW YORK, TOWN HALL CLUB, 1930. November 1930

AMERICAN FEDERATION OF ARTS, 1930–31. *Mexican Arts,* Metropolitan Museum of Art, New York, October 13–November 9, 1930; Museum of Fine Arts, Boston, November 25–December 16, 1930; Carnegie Institute, Pittsburgh, January 7–February 4, 1931; Cleveland Museum of Art, February 18–March 11, 1931; Corcoran Gallery, Washington, D.C., April 1–22, 1931; Milwaukee Art Museum, May 13–June 3, 1931; J.B. Speed Memorial Museum, Louisville, June 24–July 15, 1931; Pan-American Round Table, San Antonio, August 12–September 2, 1931

NEW YORK, DELPHIC STUDIOS, 1930–31. *Exhibition of Works of Mexican Artists and Artists of the Mexican School,* December 1, 1930–January 4, 1931

NEW YORK, DOWNTOWN GALLERY, 1931. *Exhibition of Works of José Clemente Orozco,* March–April 1931

NEW YORK, BROOKLYN MUSEUM, 1931. *The International Group,* October 1931

NEW YORK, JUNIOR LEAGUE, 1931. *Exhibit by Contemporary Mexican Artists, and Artists of the Mexican School Presented by Delphic Studios, New York City,* November 16–30, 1931

COLLEGE ART ASSOCIATION OF AMERICA, 1933–35. *Mexican Art: A College Art Association Exhibition,* 1933–35

LA PORTE, INDIANA, 1934. Civic Auditorium, *Exhibition of Lithographs, Mural Studies, Photographs of Frescoes, Paintings,*

Drawings by José Clemente Orozco, April 6–29, 1934

CHICAGO, 1934. Art Club of Chicago, *Jose Clemente Orozco: [Exhibition] Catalog, Paintings, Drawings, Lithographs,* May–June 1934

NEW YORK, A.C.A. GALLERY, 1936. *Two Papers Presented at the American Artists' Congress, February 15, 1936, for the Mexican Delegates by Orozco and Siqueiros, and the Catalog of the Exhibition at the A.C.A. Gallery, 52 W. 8th St., New York City,* February 24–March 7, 1936

SAN FRANCISCO, 1939. Palace of Fine Arts, *Golden Gate International Exposition,* May 25–September 29, 1939

NEW YORK, HUDSON D. WALKER GALLERY, 1939. *J.C. Orozco: Paintings and Drawings,* October 2–21, 1939

NEW YORK, MUSEUM OF MODERN ART, 1940. *Twenty Centuries of Mexican Art,* May–September 1940

Selected Bibliography

A corner of Orozco's studio in Guadalajara, late 1940s, photograph courtesy Dartmouth College Library.

Note: UNAM–Instituto de Investigaciones Estéticas is abbreviated UNAM-IIE. Additional bibliographic references can be found in "Selected Exhibitions of Orozco's Work in the United States, 1926–40" and "Anthology of Critical Reception."

Archives

Archives of American Art, Washington, D.C.

Archivo General de la Nación, Mexico City: Ramo Presidentes

Archivo de la Museo Nacional de Arte, Mexico City

Archivo de la Secretaría de Educación Pública, Mexico City: Personal files on various painters

Archivo de la Secretaría de Relaciones Exteriores, Mexico City

Dartmouth College, Hanover, New Hampshire: Rauner Special Collections Library; Hood Museum of Art

Museum of Modern Art, New York: Curatorial records; museum archives.

New School for Social Research, New York: President's Office archives; curatorial records; Fogelman Library

Pomona College, Claremont, California: Honnold Library; Pomona College Museum of Art

Writings by Orozco

Orozco, José Clemente. *The Artist in New York: Letters to Jean Charlot and Unpublished Writings, 1925–1929.* Foreword and notes by Jean Charlot. Translated by Ruth L. C. Simms. Austin: University of Texas Press, 1974.

———. *El artista en Nueva York (cartas a Jean Charlot, 1925–1929, y tres textos inéditos).* Mexico City: Siglo XXI, 1971.

———. *Autobiografía.* Mexico City: Ediciones Occidente, 1945.

———. *Autobiografía.* 3d ed. Mexico City: Secretaría de Educación Pública-Cultura-Era, 1983.

———. *An Autobiography.* Translated by Robert C. Stephenson. Austin: University of Texas Press, 1962.

———. *Cartas a Margarita.* "Memorias/Testimonios" by Margarita Valladares de Orozco. Selected and edited by Tatiana Herrero Orozco. Mexico City: Ediciones Era, 1987.

———. "Correction." *Mexican Folkways,* Mexico, vol. 5, no. 1 (1929).

———. Correspondence, in *Obras de José Clemente Orozco en la colección Carrillo Gil,* 1953.

———. Correspondence, in Luis Cardoza y Aragón, *Orozco,* 1959.

———. "The Dartmouth Frescoes: Their Significance." With Artemas Packard. "History of the Project," *Dartmouth Alumni Magazine,* vol. 26, no. 2 (November 1933), 7–12.

———. "The Heritage of the Mexican Child." *Everyday Art,* vol. 12, no. 3 (February–March 1934), 9–10.

———. *José Clemente Orozco: Cuadernos.* Edited by Raquel Tibol. Mexico City: Secretaría de Educación Pública-Cultura, 1983.

———. "New World, New Races and New Art." *Creative Art,* vol. 4 (January 1929), 44–46.

———. "Orozco 'Explains.'" *Bulletin of the Museum of Modern Art,* vol. 7, no. 4 (August 1940).

———. Preface to Gardner Hale, *Fresco Painting, a Technical Manual.* New York: William Edwin Rudge, 1933.

———. Preface to *The Orozco Frescoes at Dartmouth.* Edited by Albert I. Dickerson. Hanover, N.H.: Dartmouth College Publications, 1934.

———. *Textos de Orozco.* With an essay and appendix by Justino Fernández. Mexico City: Imprenta Universitaria, 1955.

Orozco and the United States

Anreus, Alejandro. *Orozco in Gringoland: The Years in New York.* Albuquerque: University of New Mexico Press, 2001.

Azuela, Alicia. "Presencia de Orozco en la sociedad y el arte anglosajones; apéndice documental." In *Orozco: una relectura.*

Azuela, Mariano. *The Underdogs.* Illustrated by José Clemente Orozco. New York: Brentano's, 1929.

Barnitz, Jacqueline. "Los años délficos de Orozco." In *Orozco: una relectura.*

Benson, E. M. "Orozco in New England: Dartmouth College Murals." *American Magazine of Art,* vol. 26 (October 1933), 443–49.

Berman, Avis. *Rebels on Eighth Street: Juliana Force and the Whitney Museum of American Art.* New York: Atheneum, 1990.

Bragdon, Claude. *Architecture and Democracy,* 2d ed. New York: Alfred A. Knopf, 1926.

Braun, Emily, and Thomas Branchick. *Thomas Hart Benton: The America Today Murals.* Williamstown, Mass.: Williams College Museum of Art, 1985.

Brenner, Anita. *Idols behind Altars.* New York: Payson & Clarke, 1929.

———. "Orozco: Murals with Meaning." *Creative Art,* vol. 12 (February 1933), 134–36.

———. *The Wind That Swept Mexico.* New York: Harper & Brothers, 1943.

Brundage, Burr Cartwright. *The Phoenix of the Western World: Quetzalcoatl and the Sky Religion.* Norman: University of Oklahoma Press, 1982.

Charlot, Jean. "Orozco in New York." *College Art Journal,* vol. 19, no. 1 (Fall 1959), 40–53.

Cornyn, John Hubert, transl. and ed. *The Song of Quetzalcoatl.* 2d ed. Yellow Springs, Ohio: Antioch Press, 1931.

Crespo de la Serna, Jorge Juan. "La obra de José Clemente Orozco." *El Nacional* (March 10, 1933).

———. "Sentido y gestación del Prometeo de Orozco." In *José Clemente Orozco: Homenaje en ocasión del 1er aniversario de la Fundación del Museo Taller dedicado a su memoria.* Guadalajara: Instituto Nacional de Bellas Artas, 1952.

Delpar, Helen. *The Enormous Vogue of Things Mexican: Cultural Relations between the United States and Mexico, 1920–1935.* Tuscaloosa: University of Alabama Press, 1992.

Doss, Erika. *Benton, Pollock, and the Politics of Modernism: From Regionalism to Abstract Expressionism.* Chicago: University of Chicago Press, 1991.

E. A. J. [Edwin Alden Jewell]. "The Frescoes by Orozco." *New York Times* (January 25, 1931), section 8, p. 12.

Eder, Rita. "De héroes y de máquinas: reflexiones para una interpretación del estilo y las ideas en la obra de José Clemente Orozco." In *Orozco: una relectura.*

Flaccus, Kimball, ed. *Orozco at Dartmouth: A Symposium.* Hanover, N.H.: Arts Press, 1933. With essays by Churchill Lathrop, Stacy May, Artemas Packard, Kimball Flaccus, William Gaston Raoul, and Gobin Stair.

Flint, Ralph. "Modernity Rules New School of Social Research." *Art News,* vol. 29 (January 17, 1931), 3–4.

Florescano, Enrique. *The Myth of Quetzalcoatl.* Translated by Lysa Hochroth. Baltimore: Johns Hopkins University Press, 1999.

Glusker, Susannah. *Anita Brenner: A Mind of Her Own.* Austin: University of Texas Press, 1998.

Goodrich, Lloyd. "The Murals at the New School." *Arts,* vol. 17, no. 6 (March 1931), 399–403, 422, 424.

Hambidge, Jay. *Practical Applications of Dynamic Symmetry.* Edited by Mary C. Hambidge. New Haven: Yale University Press, 1932.

Hamblen, Emily. *Interpretation of William Blake's Job.* New York: Occult Research Press, undated.

———. "Notes on Orozco's Murals." *Creative Art,* vol. 4, no. 1 (January 1929), xlvi.

Henderson, Linda Dalrymple. *The Fourth Dimension and Non-Euclidean Geometry in Modern Art.* Princeton, N.J.: Princeton University Press, 1983.

Hurlburt, Laurance P. *The Mexican Muralists in the United States.* Albuquerque: University of New Mexico Press, 1989.

———. "Notes on Orozco's North American Murals: 1930–34." In *¡Orozco! 1883–1949.*

Hutton, John. "'If I Am to Die Tomorrow'—Roots and Meanings of Orozco's *Zapata Entering a Peasant's Hut.*" *Art Institute of Chicago Museum Studies,* vol. 11, no. 1 (Fall 1984), 38–51.

Jacquin, Renée. *L'Esprit de Delphes: Angelos Sikelianos.* Aix-en-Provence: Université de Provence, 1988.

Johnson, Alvin. "Notes on the New School Murals." New York: New School for Social Research, about 1943.

The Latin American Spirit: Art and Artists in the United States, 1920–1970. New York: Bronx Museum of the Arts/Abrams, 1988.

LeFalle-Collins, Lizzetta, and Shifra M. Goldman. *In the Spirit of Resistance: African-American Modernists and the Mexican Muralist School.* New York: American Federation of Arts, 1996.

May, Antoinette. *Passionate Pilgrim: The Extraordinary Life of Alma Reed.* New York: Paragon House, 1993.

Mead, Dorothy. "Rolling Back Twenty Centuries: The Delphic Festival and the Reproduction of Classical Drama." *Mentor* (May 1927), 23–32.

Mumford, Lewis. "Orozco in New England." *New Republic* 80 (October 10, 1934), 231–35.

———. *Technics and Civilization.* New York: Harcourt, Brace, 1934.

O'Connor, Francis V. "The Influence of José Clemente Orozco on Jackson Pollock." Unpublished symposium paper given at Dartmouth College, October 13, 1994.

Oles, James, ed. *South of the Border: Mexico in the American Imagination, 1914–1947.* Washington, D.C.: Smithsonian Institution Press, 1993.

The Orozco Frescoes at Dartmouth. Edited by Albert I. Dickerson, with a text by José Clemente Orozco. Hanover, N.H.: Dartmouth College Publications, 1934.

The Orozco Murals at Dartmouth College, Montgomery Endowment Symposium, Hanover, N.H., 1980. With essays by Churchill P. Lathrop, Clemente Orozco, Louis Wolf Goodman, and Josefina Zoraida Vázquez.

Pach, Walter. *Queer Thing, Painting: Forty Years in the World of Art.* New York: Harper, 1938.

Palmer, Eva. *Upward Panic: The Autobiography of Eva Palmer-Sikelianos.* Edited with an introduction and notes by John P. Anton. Philadelphia: Harwood Academic Press, 1993.

Pells, Richard H. *Radical Visions and American Dreams: Culture and Social Thought during the Depression Years.* New York: Harper & Row, 1973.

Platt, Susan. *Art and Politics in the 1930s: Modernism, Marxism, Americanism. A History of Cultural Activism during the Depression Years.* New York: Midmarch Arts Press, 1999.

372

Pollock, Orozco, Siqueiros. New York: Washburn Gallery, about 1998.

Ramírez, Fausto. "Artistas e iniciados en la obra mural de Orozco." In *Orozco: una relectura.*

Reed, Alma. *José Clemente Orozco.* New York: Delphic Studios, 1932.

———. *Orozco.* Translated by J. A. Topete. Mexico City: Fondo de Cultura Económica, 1955.

———. *Orozco.* New York: Oxford University Press, 1956.

———. "Orozco and Mexican Paintings." *Creative Art,* vol. 9 (September 1931), 198–207.

Rutkoff, Peter M., and William B. Scott. *New School: A History of the New School for Social Research.* New York: Free Press, 1986.

Scott, David. "Orozco's Pomona College and New School Murals and Their Kinship to Dartmouth." Unpublished symposium paper given at Dartmouth College, October 13, 1994.

———. "Orozco's *Prometheus:* Summation, Transition, Innovation." *College Art Journal,* vol. 17, no. 1 (Fall 1957), 2–18.

Sikelianos, Angelos. *The Delphic Word: The Dedication.* Translated by Alma Reed. New York: Harold Vinal, Ltd., 1928.

———. *Plan général du mouvement delphique: L'Université de Delphes,* Paris: Les Belles Lettres, 1929.

Smith, Susan. *Glories of Venus.* Illustrated by José Clemente Orozco. New York: Harper, 1931.

Stair, Gobin. "The Making of a Mural: A Handyman's Memoir of José Clemente Orozco." *Dartmouth Alumni Magazine* (February 1973), 22–23.

Orozco: General Scholarship and Reception

Abreu Gómez, Ermilo. "José Clemente Orozco." *El Nacional* (May 11, 1946).

Aragón Leyva, Agustín. "El Prometeo de José Clemente Orozco." *El Nacional* (June 7, 1933).

———. "José Clemente Orozco. España y Mexico." *El Nacional* (January 22, 1933).

Bailey, Joyce Waddell. "José Clemente Orozco (1883–1949): Formative Years in the Narrative Graphic Tradition." *Latin American Research Review,* vol. 15, no. 3 (1980), 45–93.

"La bóveda del Palacio Legislativo la decorará el pintor Clem. Orozco." *El Informador, Diario Independiente* (October 27, 1935).

Brenson, Michael. "Orozco: Mexican Conscience." *Art in America* (September 1979), 77–79.

Camarena, Leopoldo E. "Los frescos de Clemente Orozco." *Las Noticias: diario libre de la mañana* (December 23, 1936).

Cardoza y Aragón, Luis. "José Clemente Orozco." *Futuro* (January 1, 1934).

———. *José Clemente Orozco: pinturas murales en la Universidad de Guadalajara.* Mexico City: Imprenta Mundial, 1937.

———. *Orozco.* Mexico City: UNAM-IIE, 1959.

———. *Tierra de belleza convulsiva.* Mexico City: El Nacional, 1991.

Carrillo Gil, Alvar. *Obras de José Clemente Orozco en la colección Carrillo Gil.* Mexico City: Alvar Carrillo Gil, 1953.

Charlot, Jean. "José Clemente Orozco, su obra monumental." *Forma,* Mexico, no. 6 (1928). Also reproduced in *Forma, 1926–1928*

(facsimile). Mexico City: Fondo de Cultural Económica, 1982.

De la Selva, Roberto. "El arte en Mexico; valoración del arte de Diego Rivera y del de Clemente Orozco." *El Nacional* (January 25, 1936).

Del Conde, Teresa. *J.C. Orozco: antología crítica.* Mexico City: UNAM-IIE, 1982.

Exposición nacional José Clemente Orozco: catálogo que el Instituto Nacional de Bellas Artes publica con motivo de la exposición nacional retrospectiva. Mexico City: Secretaría de Educación Pública, 1947.

"Exposición pictórica de J.C. Orozco." *Las noticias, diario libre de la mañana* (March 14, 1936).

Exposición nacional de homenaje a José Clemente Orozco, con motivo del XXX aniversario de su fallecimiento. Sala Nacional and Palacio de Bellas Artes, September–December 1979. Mexico City: Instituto Nacional de Bellas Artes, [1979].

Fernández, Justino. *José Clemente Orozco: 10 Reproductions of His Mural Paintings.* Mexico City: Eugenio Fisherground Modern Art Editions, 1944.

———. *José Clemente Orozco, forma e idea,* 2d ed. (1st ed., 1942). Mexico City: Editorial Porrúa, 1956.

———. *José Clemente Orozco: obra gráfica.* Mexico City: Instituto Nacional de Bellas Artes, 1977.

———. *Obras de Orozco en la colección Carrillo-Gil.* Mexico City: Alvar Carrillo Gil, 1949.

———. *Prometeo, ensayo sobre pintura contemporánea.* Mexico City: Porrúa, 1945.

———. *Textos de Orozco.* 2d ed. Mexico City: UNAM-IIE, 1983.

Gardulno, Ana. *Orozco en la colección del Museo Carrillo Gil.* Mexico City: Instituto Nacional de Bellas Artes, Museo de Arte Alvar y Carmen T. de Carrillo Gil, 1999.

Godoy, Bernabé. "José Clemente Orozco." *Et Caetera,* vol. 1, no. 3 (July–September 1950).

González Mello, Renato. "Del caudillo al hombre fuerte: Orozco y el patrocinio del Estado." In *XX Coloquio internacional de historia del arte: patrocionio, colección y circulación de las artes.* Mexico City: UNAM-IIE, 1997.

———. *José Clemente Orozco.* Guadalajara: Secretaría de Cultura de Jalisco, 1995.

———. "La máquina de pintar: Rivera, Orozco y la invención de un lenguaje." Doctoral thesis in art history, Universidad Nacional Autónoma de México, Facultad de Filosofía y Letras, 1998.

———. *Orozco, ¿pintor revolucionario?* Mexico City: UNAM-IIE, 1995.

———. "Orozco y Posada: un parricidio." *El alcaraván,* vol. 2., no. 5 (April 1991).

Graphic Works of José Clemente Orozco. Washington, D.C.: Pan American Union, 1952.

Helm, MacKinley. *Man of Fire: J.C. Orozco. An Interpretive Memoir.* Boston: Institute of Contemporary Art and New York: Harcourt, Brace, 1953.

Holms, Jack D. L. "A Selected Bibliography on José Clemente Orozco." *Inter-American Review of Bibliography,* no. 9 (January 1960), 26–36.

373

"Homenaje al pintor C. Orozco." *Las noticias, diario libre de la mañana,* July 9, 1936.

Hopkins, Jon H. *Orozco: A Catalogue of His Graphic Work.* Flagstaff: Northern Arizona University Publications, 1967.

Hutton, John. "Dies Irae: The Easel Paintings of José Clemente Orozco." Unpublished symposium paper given at Dartmouth College, October 13, 1994.

Icaza, Xavier. "La magna obra de Orozco." *Futuro* (March 1, 1934).

J.C. Orozco en el Instituto Cultural Cabañas. Guadalajara: Instituto Cultural Cabañas, 1983.

J.C. Orozco Memorial Exhibition. Boston: Institute of Contemporary Art, 1952.

José Clemente Orozco. Paris: Musée d'Art Moderne de la Ville de Paris, 1979.

José Clemente Orozco, 1883–1949. Berlin: Leibniz-Gesellschaft für kulturellen Austausch, 1981.

José Clemente Orozco, 1883–1949. Chicago: University of Chicago/Committee on Social Thought and the Renaissance Society, 1951.

José Clemente Orozco, 1883–1949. San Antonio, Texas: Marion Koogler McNay Art Institute, 1959.

"José Clemente Orozco decorará el Palacio legislativo de Guadalajara." *El Jalisciense* (October 27, 1935).

José Clemente Orozco: Exposición Nacional. Mexico City: Instituto Nacional de Bellas Artes, 1947.

"José Clemente Orozco va a pintar aquí." *Las noticias, diario libre de la mañana* (October 27, 1935).

Lazo, Agustín. "Nuevos frescos de José Clemente Orozco." In *Forma, 1926–1928.* Mexico City: Fondo

de Cultura Económica (RLMM), 1982.

López, Rafael. "Los frescos de Clemente Orozco." *El Nacional* (March 11, 1933).

Lynch, James B. "José Clemente Orozco: The Easel Paintings and the Graphic Art." Ph.D. thesis, Harvard University, 1960.

Manrique, Jorge Alberto. *Orozco, pintura mural.* Mexico City: Fondo Editorial de la Plástica Mexicana, 1989.

Marrozzini, Luigi, ed. *Catálogo completo de la obra gráfica de Orozco.* [Rio Piedras], Puerto Rico: Instituto de Cultura Puertorriqueña, Universidad de Puerto Rico, [1970].

Martínez Ulloa, Enrique. "La revolución mexicana y los cuadros de la revolución de José Clemente Orozco." *Bandera de Provincias, quincenal de cultura* (August 15, 1929, and September 1, 1929).

Mata Torres, Ramón. *Los murales de Orozco en el Instituto Cultural Cabañas.* Guadalajara: n.p., 1988.

Mérida, Carlos. "José Clemente Orozco." *El Nacional* (March 17, 1940).

———. *Orozco's Frescoes in Guadalajara.* Mexico City: Frances Toor Studios, 1940.

"Mexicanos universales; José Clemente Orozco, frescos en el Hospicio de Guadalajara. Jal." *El Nacional* (May 20, 1939).

"Número especial, reportaje fotográfico sobre los murales de José Clemente Orozco." *Artes de Mexico* (February 25, 1959).

¡Orozco! 1883–1949. Oxford: Museum of Modern Art, Oxford, 1980.

Orozco: A Small Tribute. With an essay by Hayden Herrera. New

York: Mary-Anne Martin/Fine Arts, New York, 1996.

"Orozco, cumbre entre montañas." *Guadalajara, revista gráfica de Occidente* (April 1, 1949).

Orozco, Rivera, Siqueiros, cuatro obras del Museo Nacional de Bellas Artes de La Habana, Cuba. Mexico City: Museo de Arte Carrillo Gil-INBA, 1991.

Orozco: una relectura. Mexico City: UNAM-IIE, 1983.

Orozco, Clemente Valladares. *Orozco, verdad cronológica.* Guadalajara: EDUG/Universidad de Guadalajara, 1983.

Paz, Octavio. "Social Realism in Mexico: The Murals of Rivera, Orozco and Siqueiros." *artscanada* (December–January 1979–80), 56–65.

———. "Ocultación y descubrimiento de Orozco." *Vuelta,* vol. 10, no. 119 (October 1986), 16–28.

"Protesta por la destrucción de pinturas de Orozco." *El universal, el gran diario de Mexico* (July 3, 1924).

Ramírez, Javier. "León Muñiz: recuerdos del Centro Bohemio y de José Clemente Orozco." *Siglo 21* (September 4, 1994).

Rodríguez, Antonio. *La pintura mural en la obra de Orozco.* Mexico City: Cultura-SEP, 1983.

Sainete, drama y barbarie: centenario [de] J.C. Orozco, 1883–1983, caricaturas, grotescos. Mexico City: Instituto Nacional de Bellas Artes, 1983.

Sánchez Flores, Francisco. "José Clemente Orozco." *Nosotros, revista de cultura popular,* nos. 3–4 (March–April 1938).

———. "José Clemente Orozco: obrero pintor." *Nosotros, revista de cultura popular,* no. 6 (May 1, 1939).

Tablada, José Juan. "Orozco, the Mexican Goya." *International Studio* (March 1924).

Tibol, Raquel, ed. *José Clemente Orozco: una vida para el arte: breve historia documental.* Mexico City: Fondo de Cultura Económica, 1996.

Topchesky, Morris. "Clemente Orozco I." *El Nacional* (July 26, 1930).

———. "Clemente Orozco II." *El Nacional* (July 28, 1930).

Veinte dibujos de José Clemente Orozco de la exposición de agosto de 1945, en el Colegio Nacional. Mexico City: Talleres Gráficos de la Nación, 1945.

Vidrio Beltrán, Lola. "Mi confesión a Clemente Orozco." *Guadalajara, revista gráfica de Occidente* (April 1, 1948).

———. "Orozco a través de nuestros intelectuales." *Guadalajara, revista gráfica de Occidente* (December 25, 1947).

Zuno, José Guadalupe. *José Clemente Orozco, el pintor ironista.* Guadalajara: Impr. Talleres Linot. de la Universidad de Guadalajara, 1962.

———. *Orozco y la ironía plástica.* Mexico City: Cuadernos Americanos, 1953.

Mexican Muralism and Cultural History

1910: el arte en un año decisivo: la exposición de artistas mexicanos. Mexico City: Museo Nacional de Arte-INBA-CNCA, 1991.

Las academias de arte (VII Coloquio Internacional en Guanajuato). Mexico City: UNAM-IIE, 1985.

Acevedo, Esther. "Las decoraciones que pasaron a ser revolucionarias." In *El nacionalismo y el arte mexi-*

cano (IX Coloquio de Historia del Arte). Commentary by Mari Carmen Ramírez. Mexico City: UNAM-IIE, 1986, pp. 171–216.

Acha, Juan. *Arte y sociedad en Latinoamérica.* Mexico City: Fondo de Cultura Económica, 1979–81.

Ades, Dawn. *Art in Latin America.* New Haven: Yale University Press, 1989.

Alfredo Ramos Martínez (1971–1946), una visión retrospectiva. Mexico City: INBA–Museo Nacional de Arte, 1992.

Art for the Millions: Essays from the 1930s by Artists and Administrators of the WPA Federal Art Project. Edited and with an introduction by Francis V. O'Connor. Greenwich, Conn.: New York Graphic Society, 1973.

Artists against War and Fascism: Papers of the First American Artists' Congress. Introduction by Matthew Baigell and Julia Williams. New Brunswick, N.J.: Rutgers University Press, 1986.

Azuela, Alicia. *Diego Rivera en Detroit.* Mexico City: UNAM-IIE, 1985.

———. "Public Art, Meyer Schapiro, and Mexico Muralism." *Oxford Art Journal,* vol. 17, no. 1 (1994), 55–59.

Baldwin, Neil, *Legends of the Plumed Serpent: Biography of a Mexican God.* New York: Public Affairs/BBS, 1998.

Barnitz, Jacqueline. *Twentieth Century Art of Latin America.* Austin: University of Texas Press, 2001.

Beals, Carleton. *Mexican Maze.* New York: Book League of America, 1931.

Bloch, Lucienne. "On Location with Diego Rivera." *Art in America,* vol. 74, no. 2 (February 1986), 102–23.

Cardoza y Aragón, Luis. *La nube y el reloj: pintura mexicana contemporánea.* Mexico City: Imprenta Universitaria, 1940.

———. *Mexico: pintura activa.* Mexico City: Era, 1961.

Casado Navarro, Arturo. *Gerardo Murillo, El Doctor Atl.* Mexico City: UNAM-IIE, 1984.

Charlot, Jean. *An Artist on Art: Collected Essays of Jean Charlot.* Honolulu: University Press of Hawaii, 1972.

———. *Mexican Art and the Academy of San Carlos, 1785–1915.* Austin: University of Texas Press, 1962.

———. *The Mexican Mural Renaissance, 1920–1925.* New Haven: Yale University Press, 1963.

———. *El renacimiento del muralismo mexicano: 1920–1925.* Mexico City: Domés, 1985.

Craven, David. *Diego Rivera as Epic Modernist.* New York: G. K. Hall, 1997.

Los cuadernos de Vlady. Mexico City: UNAM-DIF, 1985.

De la Torriente, Loló. *Memoria y razón de Diego Rivera.* Mexico City: Renacimiento, 1959.

Debroise, Olivier. *Figuras en el trópico: plástica mexicana, 1920–1940.* 2d ed. Barcelona: Océano, 1983.

———. *Modernidad y modernización en el arte mexicano.* Mexico City: Instituto Nacional de Bellas Artes, 1991.

Del Conde, Teresa. *Un pintor mexicano y su tiempo: Enrique Echeverría (1923–1972).* Mexico City: UNAM-IIE, 1979.

Del Moral, Enrique. *El estilo: la integración plástica.* Mexico City: Seminario de Cultura Mexicana, 1966.

Diego Rivera: A Retrospective. Detroit: Detroit Institute of Arts, 1986.

Downs, Linda Bank. *Diego Rivera: The Detroit Industry Murals.* Detroit: Detroit Institute of Arts and New York: W. W. Norton, 1999.

Dulles, John W. F. *Yesterday in Mexico: A Chronicle of the Revolution, 1919–1936.* Austin: University of Texas Press, 1961.

El grupo del "Olimpo House"; aproximación a un capítulo en la historia de Jalisco. Guadalajara: Universidad de Guadalajara, 1992.

Farías, Ixca. *Casos y cosas de mis tiempos.* Guadalajara: Colegio Internacional, 1963.

Favela, Ramón. *Diego Rivera: The Cubist Years.* Phoenix: Phoenix Art Museum, 1984.

Fell, Claude. *José Vasconselos, los años del águila (1920–1925): educación, cultura e iberoamericanismo en el Mexico postrevolucionario.* Mexico City: UNAM–Instituto de Investigaciones Históricas, 1989.

Fernández, Justino. *El arte moderno en Mexico; breve historia; siglos XIX y XX.* Mexico City: Porrúa, 1937.

———. *El arte moderno y contemporáneo de Mexico.* 2d ed. Mexico City: UNAM-IIE, 1993.

———. *Estética del arte mexicano: Coatlicue, el retablo de los reyes, el hombre.* Mexico City: UNAM-IIE, 1972.

Flores Guerrero, Raúl. *Cinco pintores mexicanos: Frida Kahlo, Guillermo Meza, Juan O'Gorman, Julio Castellanos, Jesús Reyes Ferreira.* Mexico City: UNAM-DGP, 1957.

Folgarait, Leonard. *Mural Painting and Social Revolution in Mexico, 1920–1940: Art of the New Order.*

Cambridge: Cambridge University Press, 1998.

Forma, 1926–1928. Mexico City: Fondo de Cultura Económica (RLMM), 1982.

Franco Fernández, Roberto. *La pintura en Jalisco.* Guadalajara: Gobierno del Estado de Jalisco–UNED, 1989.

Gamio, Manuel. *Forjando patria.* 4th ed. Mexico City: Porrúa, 1992.

———. *La población del valle de Teotihuacán.* 2 vols. Mexico City: Talleres Graficos, Secretaria de Education Pública, 1922.

González Mello, Renato. *José Clemente Orozco: La pintura mural méxicana.* Mexico City: Consejo Nacional para la Cultura y las Artes, 1997.

García Barragán, Elisa, and Luis Mario Schneider. *Diego Rivera y los escritores mexicanos: antología tributaria.* Mexico City: UNAM–Instituto de Investigaciones Bibliográfi, 1986.

García Oropeza, Guillermo. *Murales de Jalisco.* 2d ed. Guadalajara: Gobierno del Estado, 1976.

García Ponce, Juan. *La aparición de lo invisible.* Mexico City: Siglo XXI, 1968.

Goldman, Shifra M. *Contemporary Mexican Painting in a Time of Change.* Austin: University of Texas Press, 1981.

Guilbaut, Serge. *How New York Stole the Idea of Modern Art: Abstract Expressionism, Freedom, and the Cold War.* Translated by Arthur Goldhammer. Chicago: University of Chicago Press, 1983.

Helm, MacKinley. *Modern Mexican Painters.* New York: Harper, 1941.

Herrera, Hayden. *Frida, a Biography of Frida Kahlo.* New York: Harper & Row, 1983.

375

Herner de Larrea, Irene, et al. *Diego Rivera's Mural at the Rockefeller Center*. Mexico City: Edicupes, 1990.

————. *Diego Rivera: Paradise Lost at Rockefeller Center*. Mexico City: Edicupes, 1986.

Historia de la caricatura en Mexico. Guadalajara: Talleres Linotip. de la Universidad de Guadalajara, 1961.

Historia del arte mexicano. Mexico City: Secretaría de Educación Pública-Salvat., 1982.

Homenaje al movimiento de escuelas e pintura al aire libre. Mexico City: Instituto Nacional de Bellas Artes, 1981.

Horna, José. *Murales en la Ciudad Universitaria. interpretaciones a pluma de José Horna*. Mexico City: UNAM–Departamento de Difusión de la Gerencia de Relaciones de Ciudad Universitaria, 1954.

Los intelectuales y el poder en Mexico. Memorias de la VI Conferencia de Historiadores Mexicanos y Estadounidenses. Mexico City: Colmex–UCLA Latin American Center Publication, 1991.

Jamis, Rauda. *Frida Kahlo: autorretrato de una mujer*. Mexico City: Best Seller Edivisión, 1987.

Joaquín Clausell y los ecos del impresionismo en Mexico. Mexico City: Museo Nacional de Arte–Instituto Nacional de Bellas Artes, 1995.

José Chávez Morado: para todos internacional. Mexico City: Banco Internacional, 1989.

Katz, Friedrich. *The Life and Times of Pancho Villa*. Palo Alto, Calif.: Stanford University Press, 1998.

Knight, Alan. *The Mexican Revolution*. 2 vols. Cambridge: Cambridge University Press, 1986.

Krauze, Enrique. *Caudillos culturales en la revolución mexicana*. Mexico City: SEP-Cultura-Siglo XXI, 1985.

Latin American Art of the Twentieth Century. New York: Museum of Modern Art, 1992.

Latin American Art of the Twentieth Century. Edited by Edward Sullivan. London: Phaidon, 1996.

Lee, Anthony. *Painting on the Left: Diego Rivera, Radical Politics, and San Francisco's Public Murals*. Berkeley: University of California Press, 1999.

Leopoldo Méndez: dibujos, grabados, pinturas. Mexico City: Fondo Editorial de la Plástica Mexicana, 1984.

Linsley, Robert. "Utopia Will Not Be Televised: Rivera at Rockefeller Center." *Oxford Art Journal*, vol. 17, no. 12 (1994), 48–62.

López Rangel, Rafael. *Diego Rivera y la arquitectura mexicana*. Mexico City: SEP–Dir. Gral. de Publicaciones y Medios, 1986.

Lozano, Luis-Martín. *Mexican Modern Art, 1900–1950*. Mayo Graham, general editor. Ottawa: National Gallery of Canada, 1999.

Luis Nishizawa: realismo, expresionismo, abstracción. Mexico City: Difusión Cultural–UNAM, 1984.

Mabardi, Sabine. "The Politics of the Primitive and Modern: Diego Rivera at MoMA in 1931." *Curare*, Mexico City, no. 9 (Fall 1996).

Manrique, Jorge Alberto, and Teresa del Conde. *Una mujer en el arte mexicano, memorias de Inés Amor*. Mexico City: UNAM-IIE, 1987.

Mariscal, Federico E. *La patria y la arquitectura nacional: resúmenes de las conferencias dadas en la casa de la Universidad Popular Mexicana. del 21 de octubre de 1913 al (29 de julio de 1914)*.

Mexico City: Stephan y Torres, 1915.

Martínez, Ignacio. *Pintura mural: siglo XX*. Guadalajara: Planeación y Promición, 1960.

Mewburn, Charity. "Oil, Art and Politics: The Feminization of Mexico." *Anales del Instituto de Investigaciones Estéticas*, no. 72 (1998).

Mexico en el mundo de las colecciones de arte. Mexico City: Azabache, 1994.

Mexico: Splendors of Thirty Centuries. New York: Metropolitan Museum of Art and Boston: Little, Brown, 1990.

Monografía de las escuelas de pintura al aire libre. Mexico City: Cultura, 1926.

Monsiváis, Carlos. "Notas sobre la cultura mexicana en el siglo XX." In *Historia general de Mexico*. Mexico City: El Colegio de Mexico, 1976.

Moreno, Salvador. *El pintor Antonio Fabrés*. Mexico City: UNAM-IIE, 1981.

Morris, Earl H.; Jean Charlot; and Ann Axtell Morris. *The Temple of the Warriors at Chichén Itzá, Yucatán*. Washington, D.C.: Carnegie Institution, 1931.

Moyssén, Xavier. *Diego Rivera: textos de arte*. Mexico City: UNAM-IIE, 1986.

————. *Joaquín Clausell*. Mexico City: Coordinación de Humanidades–UNAM, 1992.

Murillo, Gerardo. *Las artes populares en Mèxico*. Mexico City: Cultura, 1921.

Myers, Bernard. *Mexican Painting in Our Time*. New York: Oxford University Press, 1956.

Navarrete, Sylvia. *Miguel Covarrubias: artista y explorador*.

Mexico City: CNCA–Ediciones Era, 1993.

O'Gorman. Juan. *La palabra de Juan O'Gorman*. Mexico City: UNAM-IIE, 1983.

Otras rutas hacia Siqueiros. Coordinated by Olivier Debroise. Mexico City: INBA-Conaculta, 1998.

Paz, Octavio. *Essays on Mexican Art*. Translated by Helen Lane. New York: Harcourt, Brace, 1993.

————. *Mexico en la obra de Octavio Paz: III: los privilegios de la vista*. Mexico City: Fondo de Cultura Económica, 1986.

————. *Tamayo en la pintura mexicana*. Trilingual edition, English and French translations by Sita Garst. Mexico City: UNAM–Dirección General de Publicaciones. 1959.

La pintura mural de la revolución mexicana. Mexico City: Fondo Editorial de la Plástica Mexicana, 1960.

Posada y la prensa ilustrada; signos de modernización y resistencias. Mexico City: Museo Nacional de Arte–Instituto Nacional de Bellas Artes, 1996.

Prignitz, Helga. *El Taller de Gráfica Popular en Mexico: 1937–1977*. Mexico City: Instituto Nacional de Bellas Artes, 1992.

Ramírez, Fausto. *La obra de Germán Gedovius: una reconsideración*. Mexico City: Instituto Nacional de Bellas Artes, 1984.

————. *Saturnino Herrán*. Mexico City: UNAM–Dirección General de Publicaciones, 1976.

————. "Tradición y modernidad en la Escuela Nacional de Bellas Artes: 1903–1912." In *Las academias de arte (VII Coloquio Internacional en Guanajuato)*. Mexico City: UNAM-IIE, 1985.

Reed, Alma. *The Mexican Muralists.* New York: Crown Publishers, 1960.

Releer a Siqueiros: ensayos en su centenario. Mexico City: Cenidiap-tai/Conaculta, 2000.

Reyes Palma, Francisco. *Leopoldo Méndez.* Mexico City: CNCA–Ediciones Era, 1994.

Reyes, Alfonso. "Pasado inmediato." In *Obras completas* ("Complete Works of Alfonso Reyes"). Mexico City: Fondo de Cultura Económica, 1955–79.

Rivera, Diego. *Pintura de caballete y dibujos.* Mexico City: Fondo Editorial de la Plástica Mexicana, 1979.

Robinson, Ione. *A Wall to Paint On.* New York: Dutton, 1946.

Rochfort, Desmond. *Mexican Muralists: Orozco, Rivera, Siquieros.* New York: Universe, 1993.

Rodríguez, Antonio. *A History of Mexican Mural Painting.* London: Thames and Hudson, 1969.

———. *Siqueiros.* Mexico City: Fondo de Cultura Económica, 1974.

Rodríguez Lozano, Manuel. *Pensamiento y pintura.* Mexico City: UNAM–Imprenta Universitaria, 1960.

Rodríguez Prampolini, Ida. *El surrealismo y el arte fantástico en Mexico.* Mexico City: UNAM-IIE, 1983.

———. *La crítica de arte en Mexico en el siglo XIX.* 2d ed. Mexico City: UNAM-IIE, 1997.

Romero Keith, Delmari. *Historia y testimonios: Galería de Arte Mexicano.* Mexico City: Galería de Arte Mexicano, 1985.

The Rouge: the Image of Industry in the Art of Charles Sheeler and Diego Rivera. Detroit: Detroit Institute of Arts, 1978.

Rufino Tamayo: 70 años de creación. Mexico City: Instituto Nacional de Bellas Artes, 1987.

Rufino Tamayo: pinturas. Madrid: Ministerio de Cultura–Centro Nat. de Expos., 1988.

Ruíz, Ramón Eduardo. *The Great Rebellion: Mexico, 1905–1924.* New York: W. W. Norton, 1980.

Ruptura: 1952–1965. Mexico City: Museo Carrillo Gil–INBA, 1988.

Schmeckebier, Laurence E. *Modern Mexican Art.* Minneapolis: University of Minnesota Press, 1939.

Schneider, Luis Mario. *El estridentismo [en] Mexico: 1921–1927.* Mexico City: UNAM–Difusión Cultural, 1985.

Serrano, Luis G. *Una nueva perspectiva, la perspectiva curvilínea.* Mexico City: Cultura, 1934.

Setenta obras recientes de David Alfaro Siqueiros. Mexico City: Instituto Nacional de Bellas Artes, 1947.

Sheridan, Guillermo. *Los contemporáneos ayer.* Mexico City: Fondo de Cultura Económica, 1985.

Siqueiros, David Alfaro. *Art and Revolution.* Translated by Sylvia Calles. London: Lawrence and Wishart, 1975.

———. *Cómo se pinta un mural.* Mexico City: Ediciones Taller Siqueiros, 1979.

———. *Me llamaban El Coronelazo (memorias).* Mexico City: Grijalbo (Biografías Gandesa), 1977.

———. *No hay más ruta que la nuestra.* 2d ed. Mexico City: Sala de Arte Público Siqueiros, 1978.

———. *Por la vía de una pintura neorrealista o realista social moderna en Mexico.* Mexico City: Instituto Nacional de Bellas Artes, 1951.

Smith, Terry. *Making the Modern: Industry, Art, and Design in America.* Chicago: University of Chicago Press, 1993.

Solís, Ruth. *Vida y obra de David Alfaro Siqueiros: juicios críticos.* Mexico City: Fondo de Cultura Económica–Archivo del Fondo, 1975.

Suárez, Luis. *Confesiones de Diego Rivera.* Mexico City: Grijalbo, 1975.

El surrealismo entre viejo y nuevo mundo. Madrid: Fundación Cultural Mapfre Vida-Turner, 1989.

Taibo II, Paco Ignacio. *Los Bolshevikis: historia narrativa de los orígenes del comunismo en Mexico (1919–1925).* Mexico City: Joaquín Mortiz, 1986.

Taracena, Berta. *Vlady.* Mexico City: UNAM–Dirección General de Publicaciones, 1974.

Tenorio Trillo, Mauricio. *Artilugio de la nación moderna: Mexico en las exposiciones universales, 1880–1930.* Mexico City: Fondo de Cultura Económica, 1998.

Tibol, Raquel. *David Alfaro Siqueiros.* Mexico City: Empresas Editoriales (Un mexicano y su obra), 1969.

———. *Gráficas y neográficas en Mexico.* Mexico City: UNAM–Secretaría de Educación Pública, 1987.

———. *Siqueiros, vida y obra.* Mexico City: Departamento del Distrito Federal, 1973.

Tibol, Raquel, ed. *Diego Rivera: arte y política.* Mexico City: Grijalbo, 1979.

Rodríguez, Antonio. *Siqueiros.* Mexico City: Fondo de Cultura Económica, 1974.

———. *Textos de David Alfaro Siqueiros.* Mexico City: Fondo de Cultura Económica (Arch Fondo 22–23), 1974.

Toussaint, Manuel. *Saturnino Herrán y su obra.* Mexico City: Mexico Moderno, 1920.

Tyler, Ron. *Posada's Mexico.* Washington, D.C.: Library of Congress, 1979.

Twenty Centuries of Mexican Art. New York: Museum of Modern Art, in collaboration with the Mexican Government, [1940].

Vasconcelos, José. *The Cosmic Race.* Baltimore: Johns Hopkins University Press, 1997.

Vaughan, Mary Kay. *The State, Education, and Social Class in Mexico, 1880–1928.* De Kalb: Northern Illinois University Press, 1982.

Velázquez Chávez, Agustín. *Contemporary Mexican Artists.* New York: Covici-Riede, 1937.

———. *Indice de la pintura mexicana contemporánea.* Mexico City: Arte Mexicano, 1935.

———. *La pintura mexicana: boceto retrospectivo.* Mexico City: Arte Mexicano, 1937.

Wolfe, Bertram. *Diego Rivera: His Life and Times.* New York: Alfred A. Knopf, 1931.

Zabludovski, Jacobo. *Siqueiros me dijo…* Mexico City: Novaro, 1974.

377

Index

378

Page numbers in **boldface** indicate illustration.

Hood Museum of Art Staff

Gary Alafat | *security/buildings manager*

Kristin Bergquist | *school programs coordinator*

Juliette Bianco | *exhibitions manager*

Mary Brower | *security guard*

Derrick R. Cartwright | *director*

Theresa Delemarre | *administrative assistant for development*

Rebecca Fawcett | *registrarial assistant*

Cynthia Gilliland | *assistant registrar*

Elisabeth Gordon | *teacher and family programs coordinator*

Kellen Haak | *collections manager/registrar*

Mary Ann Hankel | *exhibitions assistant*

Katherine Hart | *curator of academic programming*

Deborah Haynes | *data manager*

Linda Ide | *tour coordinator*

Alfredo Jurado | *security guard*

Amelia Kahl | *curatorial/programming assistant*

Barbara MacAdam | *curator of American art*

Evelyn Marcus | *curator of exhibitions*

Mary McKenna | *administrative assistant to the director*

Nancy McLain | *business manager*

Diane Miliotes | *research curator*

Nils Nadeau | *editor and publications coordinator*

Nicolas Nobili | *chief preparator*

Jack O'Leary | *security guard*

Kathleen O'Malley | *associate registrar*

Sharon Reed | *public relations coordinator*

Mary Ellen Rigby | *gift shop manager*

Roberta Shin | *business assistant*

Margaret Spicer | *adjunct curator, costume collection*

T. Barton Thurber | *curator of European art*

Lesley Wellman | *curator of education*

Kathryn Whittaker | *security guard*

Janet Whyte | *security guard*

Board of Overseers of Hopkins Center and Hood Museum of Art

Maxwell L. Anderson	Robert A. Levinson
Andrew E. Asnes	David V. Picker
Ambassador Stephen W. Bosworth	Jan Seidler Ramirez
	Frederick A. Roesch
Judith Carson	Thomas C. Ruegger
Jonathan Cohen	George T. M. Shackelford
Robert A. Dance	Barbara Dau Southwell
Marc F. Efron	Constance Spahn
David F. Frankel	Norman L. Steinberg
Andrew J. Greenebaum	Deborah Hope Wedgeworth
Alan S. Grubner	Robert S. Weil
Charles H. Hood	Robert O. Wetzel

The Friends of Hopkins Center and Hood Museum of Art Board of Directors

James Adler	Bruce Macdonald
David Allen	Betsy Magill
Ginia Allison	Nancy Mitchell
Patricia Baxter	Sylvia Nelson
Charlotte Bimba	Fran Sherley
Pam Booma	Anne Silberfarb
Helen Bridge	Lynne Stahler
Nancy Cole	Gordon Thomas
Marguerite Collier	Susan Valence
Robert Coyle	Vin Vieten
Linda Dooley	Betsy Wakeman
Joan Frankenstein-Mitchell	Doug Wise
Joan Hartwell	
Yvonne Herz	Trudi Brock	*Office Manager*
Henry Nachman, Jr.	Judy Ybarra	*Office Assistant*

383